Ius Comparatum - Global Studies in Comparative Law

Volume 9

More information about this series at http://www.springer.com/series/11943

Académie Internationale de Droit Comparé
International Academy of Comparative Law

Ewa Bagińska
Editor

Damages for Violations of Human Rights

A Comparative Study of Domestic Legal Systems

Springer

Editor
Ewa Bagińska
Department of Civil Law
Gdańsk University
Gdańsk, Poland

This book was supported by a grant awarded to the Editor and financed by the Polish National Science Centre - the decision no DEC-2013/9/B/HS5/01416.

ISSN 2214-6881 ISSN 2214-689X (electronic)
Ius Comparatum - Global Studies in Comparative Law
ISBN 978-3-319-18949-9 ISBN 978-3-319-18950-5 (eBook)
DOI 10.1007/978-3-319-18950-5

Library of Congress Control Number: 2015953214

Springer Cham Heidelberg New York Dordrecht London

Printed on acid-free paper

Springer International Publishing AG Switzerland is part of Springer Science+Business Media (www.springer.com)

Preface

This collection is composed of national reports and the general report presented to the 19th International Congress of Comparative Law, organised by the International Academy of Comparative Law in Vienna in 2014. The topic 'damages for the infringements of human rights' was assigned to the section on public international law. The list of all initial reports included twenty reports that came from thirteen European civil law jurisdictions, including six from post-socialist countries, three reports from common law countries (the UK, Ireland, the USA), two reports from mixed jurisdictions (Canada and Israel) and two reports from South America (Argentina, Brazil). A few of these reports were not revised for publication and hence do not appear in this volume. Two additional contributions were solicited solely for this volume: the Dutch law report (written by Jessy Emaus) and the contribution on EU law (authored by Nina Półtorak). Since the study has been inadvertently dominated by legal developments in Europe, the law of the EU could not go unnoticed.

The national experts were requested to write their reports on the basis of a questionnaire (attached in the *Appendix*), prepared by the editor. The topic relates to the legal grounds, premises and extent of pecuniary compensation (damages, *réparation*) for the violations of human rights in domestic legal systems; hence, it transcends the divides, on the one hand, between private and public law and, on the other hand, between national and international normative systems. The inherent intricacy of the topic has made this comparative study an exceptionally challenging task, even more so as the experts nominated by the respective national committees are scholars who specialise in different fields: public international law, human rights law, constitutional law and in private law. This book concludes with a comparative report which is based on the findings contained in all the reports prepared for the Congress and the two additional reports solicited by the editor.

The editor is immensely grateful to all the colleagues for their excellent work and inspiring collaboration. Special thanks go to Jessy Emaus and Nina Półtorak for the preparation of their illuminating chapters in a short period of time.

The making of this volume would not have been possible without the help of Paulina Ślufińska, assistant professor in the Department of Civil Law, Gdańsk University. Her tireless work during the process of completing the book deserves highest praise.

Gdańsk, Poland Ewa Bagińska

Contents

Contributors

Merris Amos is a reader in human rights law in the Department of Law, Queen Mary University of London, where she teaches UK human rights law and European human rights law. She is the author of *Human Rights Law Second Edition* (Hart: Oxford, 2014) and of a number of books and articles concerning the Human Rights Act 1998 and the relationship between national courts and the European Court of Human Rights. Her recent articles include 'The dialogue between United Kingdom courts and the European Court of Human Rights', *International and Comparative Law Quarterly* (2012), 557–584, and 'The principle of comity and the relationship between British courts and the European Court of Human Rights' in *Yearbook of European Law* (Oxford: Clarendon, 2009 P. Eeckhout and T. Tridimas (Eds.)). Her research has been cited and influential in a variety of reports, most recently *The UK and the European Court of Human Rights* (London: EHRC, 2012) and *A UK Bill of Rights? The Choice Before Us* in the Commission on a Bill of Rights (London: Ministry of Justice, 2012). From 2006–2013 she was the general editor of the *Human Rights Law Reports UK Cases.*

Ene Andresen is a lecturer of administrative law at the Faculty of Law, University of Tartu. Previously she worked as an assistant to the chief justice of the Estonian Supreme Court and as consultant to the Administrative Law Chamber of the same court. She was a member of the working group of the Estonian State Liability Act and member of the expert group on corruption formed by the Government of the Republic of Estonia.

Ewa Bagińska is professor of civil law and chair of civil law at the School of Law and Administration, University of Gdańsk, Poland. She was a Fulbright Visiting Scholar (1998/1999) and NATO Science Fellowship grantee (2000/2001) at the CUA Columbus School of Law, Washington, DC. She has authored a few books on products liability, public liability and medical law, as well as over 140 other contributions in the field of civil law and comparative law. Her recent book is entitled *Tort Liability Under Uncertainty and Complexity of Causation. A Comparative Law Study* [in Polish] (Toruń 2013). She is a member of the European Group on

Tort Law, the International Academy of Comparative Law and the European Law Institute. She is also a member of the advisory board of the European Review of Private Law.

Michał Balcerzak, Ph.D., Dr. habil. is associate professor at Human Rights Department, Faculty of Law and Administration, Nicolaus Copernicus University in Toruń, Poland. He teaches in the areas of international human rights law, protection of national minorities, international judiciary and litigation. His research interests include law of state responsibility and international disaster response law. He serves as deputy member of the Management Board of the EU Agency for Fundamental Rights as well as member of the UN Working Group of experts on people of African descent.

Samo Bardutzky is currently postdoctoral research associate ('The Role and Future of National Constitutions in European and Global Governance') at the University of Kent in Canterbury. He studied law in Ljubljana and Greifswald and obtained his doctorate from the University of Ljubljana in 2013. After passing his state examination, he served as legal adviser to the Slovenian Ministry of Justice. In 2012/2013, he was Fulbright Research Scholar at the University of Michigan Law School.

Veronika Bílková, Doc. JUDr. Ph.Dr. Ph.D., E.M.A. is associate professor in international law at the Faculty of Law of the Charles University in Prague and a researcher at the Institute of International Relations in Prague. She is the holder of the Diploma in International Law from the University of Cambridge. Since 2010, she has been a member of the Venice Commission of the Council of Europe on behalf of the Czech Republic. She has authored three books and more than 50 articles in Czech, English and French on international law and international relations.

Iris Canor is professor of European law, public international law and private international law at the Haim Striks School of Law, Colman, Israel, and an adjunct professor at Europa-Institut, Saarbruecken, Germany. She is a visiting researcher at the Max Planck Institute for Comparative Public Law and International Law, Heidelberg, Germany, and currently is a Fernand Braudel Senior Fellow, at the European University Institute, Florence, Italy.

Maria José Reis Rangel de Mesquita is associate professor of the Faculty of Law of the University of Lisbon (EU law, international law and public law); coordinator of the Jean Monnet Teaching Module 'European Union's External Action Role in a Global World' (2012–2015); judge at the Constitutional Court (since 2012); participating member of the Jean Monnet Centre of Excellence of the University of Lisbon, Faculty of Law (2011–2014); and member of *Project on Principles of European Tort Law – Public Liability* (Institute for European Tort Law, 2010–2015) and the Direction Board of the AIDA-Portugal.

Jacques deLisle is the Stephen A. Cozen Professor of Law, professor of political science, deputy director of the Center for the Study of Contemporary China, and codirector of the Center for Asian Law at the University of Pennsylvania. He is the coeditor of *The Internet, Social Media and a Changing China* (forthcoming 2015),

China's Challenges (2014) and *Political Changes in Taiwan under Ma Ying-jeou* (2014). He also has written on comparative tort law, the use of US legal mechanisms to address human rights abuses abroad and China's engagement with human rights and other international legal norms.

Jessy M. Emaus (1985) is assistant professor in private law at Utrecht University, the Utrecht Centre for Accountability and Liability Law (Ucall) and the Utrecht Centre for Regulation and Enforcement in Europe (Renforce), with a special interest in the interaction between noncontractual liability law and European fundamental rights law. She has recently obtained her doctorate with a dissertation on the enforcement of ECHR by means of liability law and introduced in academic literature a new legal basis to enforce fundamental rights more directly and more specifically geared towards ECHR: the concept of the breach of a fundamental right. At this moment she studies and publishes on the responsibility of powerful non-state actors. Emaus is curious to know why and how these actors are made more responsible in law than others.

Tamar Gidron is professor of tort law, human rights and comparative law. She was the dean of the Haim Striks Law School, College of Management, for 8 years and is now the head of the Zefat Academic College, Law School, Israel.

Noelle Higgins, Dr. is a senior lecturer in law at Maynooth University in Ireland. She undertook her Ph.D. studies at the Irish Centre for Human Rights in Galway, Ireland. She specialises in international law, particularly international human rights law, international humanitarian law and international criminal law. In addition her research also focuses on Irish domestic human rights.

Zeynep Oya Usal Kanzler is an assistant professor in human rights law at Koç University Law School in Istanbul, Turkey. Before joining Koç University in 2011, Dr. Usal Kanzler worked as a lawyer at the European Court of Human Rights (ECHR) in Strasbourg. Besides her work at Koç, she works in expert capacity for a variety of intergovernmental and non-governmental organisations, including the United Nations (UN) Women and the Council of Europe.

Saša Nikšić He graduated law at the Faculty of Law, University of Zagreb, Croatia (1998), and studied at the T.M.C. Asser Institute in The Hague, the Netherlands, and finished his postgraduate study at the Faculty of Law, University of Zagreb, Croatia. He earned his Ph.D. degree at the Faculty of Law, University of Zagreb, Croatia (2007), and is currently employed as associate professor at the Civil Law Department at the Faculty of Law, University of Zagreb, Croatia.

Xavier Philippe Professeur de droit public à la faculté de droit et de science politique de l'Université d'Aix-Marseille, est aujourd'hui directeur de l'Institut Louis Favoreu – GERJC (*Groupe d'études et de recherches sur la justice constitutionnelles comparée*) (*Unité Mixte de Recherche du CNRS 7318*). Il est également Professeur extraordinaire auprès de l'Université de Western Cape en Afrique du sud. Il est également expert international dans les processus constituants.

Nina Półtorak is professor of the Jagiellonian University in Krakow (Chair of European Law), judge and head of the European Law Department of the Supreme Administrative Court of Poland.

Graziella Romeo is assistant professor of constitutional law at Bocconi University. She was visiting scholar and guest lecturer at Fordham Law School, NY. She has authored a monographic work (*La cittadinanza sociale nell'era del cosmopolitismo: uno studio comparato*, Padova, CEDAM, 2011) and a number of essays on constitutional law and human rights issues, including 'Measuring cosmopolitanism in Europe: standards of judicial review over non citizens' rights', in 3(3) *Cambridge J. Int'l Comp. L.*, 2014; 'The recognition of same-sex couples' rights in the US between counter-majoritarian principle and ideological approaches', in Gallo et al. (Eds.); and 'Same-Sex Couples before National, Supranational and International Jurisdictions', Berlin, Springer, 2013.

Ioannis Stribis is an associate professor of the University of the Aegean, Faculty of Social Sciences. He holds a Ph.D. from the University of Paris 1 (Pantheon-Sorbonne) and has been a research fellow at the Academy of Athens. He has been the legal adviser of the organisation of the Black Sea Economic Cooperation (BSEC) and legal officer of the Organization for Security and Co-operation in Europe (OSCE). He is the author of several books and articles in the fields of international law, human rights law, European law and international organisations.

Pavel Šturma is professor and head of the International Law Department, Charles University in Prague, Faculty of Law. He has been senior research fellow at the Institute of Law, Czech Academy of Sciences, Prague; editor in chief of the Czech Yearbook of Public & Private International Law; lecturer and visiting professor at various universities in Austria, France, Slovakia, etc; member of the UN International Law Commission; and author and/or co-author of 16 books and more than 140 articles and studies in international and European law.

Bjarte Thorson is a postdoctoral fellow at the University of Oslo. Besides obtaining his doctorate, on the basis of a dissertation on pure economic loss and a trial lecture on the liability system suggested in the Draft Common Frame of Reference, he has had a diverse practise as a civil and criminal court deputy judge, private attorney specialised in tort and insurance law and senior adviser to the Parliamentary Ombudsman. As a university teacher and researcher, he has focused on constitutional European Union law alongside comparative and national patrimonial law.

Andreas von Arnauld is professor of public law, public international and European law at the Faculty of Law, University of Kiel, and codirector of the Walther Schücking Institute for International Law. Previously he held professorships at the University of Münster (Westphalia) and at Helmut Schmidt University/University of the Federal Armed Forces in Hamburg.

Haya Zandberg is head of the Civil Litigation Department at the Israel Attorney General Office and a lecturer of criminal procedure and evidence at the Faculty of Law, Hebrew University of Jerusalem

Chapter 1
Introduction

Ewa Bagińska

1.1 The Scope of the Comparative Project

The subject matter of this book relates to the legal grounds, premises and extent of pecuniary compensation for the violations of human rights in domestic legal systems.

'Human rights' is used an umbrella term which encompasses human rights, constitutional rights and any other right considered as fundamental in the given legal system. This working definition does not assume that all rights are equally protected by monetary damages. The content of the rights is not examined here, but rather taken for granted. The following national chapters will show the differences in the degree of protection awarded to civil and political rights and to other human rights (so called second and third generation rights), as well as a possible distinction between internationally and nationally embedded rights.

Compensation is understood broadly and includes any form of monetary damages, reparation or just satisfaction. The inquiry does not cover all possible remedies that are available in national jurisdictions in cases of infringement of human rights, such as restitution (e.g. return of property), injunctions, declaratory judgments, guarantees of non-repetition, rehabilitation, satisfaction, annulment of decisions, revocation of judgments, etc. It concentrates on financial reparation (compensation) which can be provided by judicial awards or by other public law mechanisms, such as special (alternative) compensation systems.

The particular features of human rights as 'rights for humans' or 'rights for individuals' and their international dimension implicate several questions and controversies as to the availability, foundations and scope of a claim for pecuniary compensation. The main focus of this inquiry is whether compensatory claims for

E. Bagińska (✉)
Department of Civil Law, Gdańsk University, Gdańsk, Poland
e-mail: baginska@prawo.ug.edu.pl

E. Bagińska (ed.), *Damages for Violations of Human Rights*,
Ius Comparatum - Global Studies in Comparative Law 9,
DOI 10.1007/978-3-319-18950-5_1

compensation in their broad sense, arising from infringements of human rights (or constitutional rights), have been made available through a special, independent cause of action, or rather through existing liability rules. These rules may be part of public authority law or a general law of torts (law of civil liability). Compensation for historical injustices and gross and systemic violations are also discussed. Although the reasons and ramifications of existing national solutions are explored, the analysis is not meant to assess the efficiency of pecuniary remedies aiming to protect human rights.

This topic has rarely been undertaken as a subject of a comprehensive and thorough comparative research, although it has been emerging as a subject of academic interest in recent years in Europe.[1] Neither of the two European tort law harmonisation projects (the Principles of European Tort Law[2] and Book VI of the Draft Common Frame of Reference[3]) addresses the specific case of liability for human rights violations.

1.2 The General Background

A few general issues should be considered as a background for the subsequent jurisdiction-based chapters.

On the one hand, the topic of financial compensation for human rights violations clearly belongs to public international law (international human rights law). This law governs the entitlements (claims for just satisfaction) that are enforced before international tribunals. On the other hand, the compensatory nature of individual claims available under domestic rules directs the analysis to private (tort) law, which is by definition national law. Hence, *prima facie* different tools should be used to illuminate the construct of those entitlements.

The international dimension of either harmful conduct (a violation) or the origin of the human right the protection of which is sought invokes the problem of the relationship between international law and domestic legal systems. The traditional approach, based on the divide between so-called monist and dualist systems, has been losing its usefulness in this context as the delineating line has become significantly blurred. In practice, the differences between the monist and the dualist legal

[1] The most comprehensive and influential scholarly work to date is Shelton, Dinah. 2005. *Remediesin international human rights law*, 2nd edn. Oxford: Oxford University Press. See also Tortell, Lisa. 2006. Monetary Remedies for Breach of Human Rights. A Comparative Study. Oxford and Portland: Hart Publishing (the comparative analysis encompasses four common law jurisdictions: the United States, the United Kingdom, India and New Zealand).

[2] Principles of European Tort Law, Text and Commentary. 2005. Vienna: Springer Verlag.

[3] von Bar et al. (2009). Principles, definitions, and model rules in European private law: Draft Common Frame of Reference (DCFR), Book VI. Non-contractual liability arising out of damage caused by another. Munich: Sellier European Law Publishers.

systems are subtle and the names of the two categories do not fully explain the methods and techniques employed by legislators and courts in order to give effect to international norms in the given jurisdiction.[4] According to the latest comparative research the distinction is rather between those States which give international law sources a constitutional rank and those which position it below the constitution. Among the latter, some give international law supremacy over statutory law and the others do not.[5] Many systems take a hybrid approach.

This book will not dwell on the subject of horizontal or vertical, direct or indirect, effect of human rights, although it can be anticipated that national methods of the incorporation of international law into a domestic legal system may predetermine the solutions employed in respect of damages remedies for human rights abuses.[6]

In national legal systems violations of human rights may trigger protection on different normative levels, and hence different methods of regulation are used. On the one hand, the protection may be guaranteed on the constitutional and on the statutory level, and on the other hand, in substantive law and procedural regulations. The array of available remedies in the cases of infringements is to be found traditionally and primarily in administrative law, criminal law and tort law. However, the contributions collected in this volume reflect a growing role of special statutory mechanisms that escape easy classification and thus belong to the grey area between public and private law.

In a few jurisdictions based in common law (the U.K., Ireland, Canada) legislators have enacted special acts on human rights protection, which are to a lesser or greater degree comprehensive, and which created a separate regime of liability for human rights violations. Those acts aim at fulfilling the international obligations of governments under the relevant international or supranational agreements and in some instances they also provide protective instruments for internal constitutional norms (as in Ireland). The majority of investigated legal systems, however, lack either a special human rights legislative enactment, which would grant a direct claim for compensation on the statutory level, or explicit constitutional safeguards of the right to have the damage redressed.

---

[4] See Gerards et al. 2014. Comparative analysis. In *Implementation of theEuropean Convention on Human Rightsand of the judgments of the ECtHR in national case-law. A comparative analysis*. ed. Gerards, Janneke and Fleuren, Joseph, 335–337. Cambridge-Antwerp-Portland: Intersentia.

[5] See Shelton, Dinah. 2011. International Law in Domestic Systems. In *General Reports of the XVIIIth Congress of the International Academy of Comparative Law/ Rapports Généraux du XVIIIème Congrès de l'Académie Internationale de Droit Comparé*, ed. Karen Brown, David Snyder, no. 21.8. Dordercht et al.: Springer.

[6] The recommended literature includes: Brüggemeier et al. (2010). Fundamental Rights and Private Law in the European Union. Vol. 1 and vol 2. Cambridge: Cambridge University Press. Oliver and Fedtke (2007) Human Rights and the Private Sphere – A Comparative Analysis, 3, 499 ff. London: Routledge Cavendish; Fairgrieve et al. (2002). Tort liability of public authorities in comparative perspective. London: BICL.

1.3 Comparative Approach: Selected Issues

When a claim for damages is made available under a domestic rule, the questions which arise are manifold. They concern the nature of the claim (public or private), the rules upon which it should be decided (special rules, the general rules of civil liability, public liability rules) and its prerequisites. Most of these issues will be determined by private law (tort law, the law of civil liability) or by administrative law (in particular, when public authority liability is in the realm of public law in a given jurisdiction).

First, the language of 'rights' demands an explanation of the relationship between human 'rights' and other 'private law' rights, as well as the relation of the former to the values and interests (not necessarily depicted as 'rights') that have always been protected by tort law (the scope of protection by tort law is of course dynamic). 'Rights' imply that when a conflict of rights arises, the court will be obliged to determine whose right (interest) must prevail. This balancing takes place in the concrete factual circumstances.

Second, the prerequisite of 'damage' can also prove problematic. The notion of 'damage' lies in the heart of tort law, but it does not enjoy a uniform definition in the legal systems. What is the damage that is required in human rights abuses cases? Is 'pure' violation considered as harm which entitles to compensation without the proof of any harmful consequences?

Third, the role of fault and unlawfulness should be explained; whether fault (and/or unlawfulness) is relevant and what is its interpretation in the context of human rights abuses. This question necessitates a more general inquiry into the principle (basis) of liability for infringement of human rights (fault liability, no-fault/strict liability, equity or other).

The next issue relates to the legal standing. International human rights law is primarily concerned with obligations that the State owes to its own citizens (or others in its territory), principally to protect them from abuses by the State's organs, officials and other citizens. This is often conceptualised as the 'vertical effect of human rights'. In several jurisdictions this approach was the earliest starting point as regards effectiveness of constitutional rights. That has changed over time and the constitutional norms regarding fundamental rights are by and large directly applicable (albeit there may be distinctive treatment of some categories of so-called second- and third-generation human rights).

Accordingly, the traditional focus of the protection of human rights has been on public law and State obligations and, as will be shown, it has remained so until today in a number of surveyed jurisdictions. Although tort law rules protect most basic and most valued human rights, the law of torts has not been at the centre of attention of the international human rights and constitutional scholarship. Liability consequences of actions or inactions of public authority organs involving infringements of fundamental rights have been considered as subsidiary in many countries (the approach taken e.g. in Germany, the U.K. and the Czech Republic).

Legal standing in domestic lawsuits is a particularly interesting problem in cases of non-state actors who violate human rights globally. A growing number of codes of conduct (OECD guidelines of 1970, sector specific codes of conduct) define the conduct of global traders in relation to particular commercial practices or business sectors. However, such codes of conduct speak of responsibility, and not of a legal obligation (to protect human rights standards).[7] A code of conduct may eventually trigger liability based on unfair commercial practices regulations, but the liability grounded in the regional human rights law is contested both in practice and in doctrine. So far, global corporations have successfully defended lawsuits based on human rights violations (involving e.g. child labour, labour conditions, lack of safety), so the damages remedy does not seem to be the best solution in this field.

Furthermore, an important question concerns the interplay between national liability rules and the supranational human rights law. In particular, the correlation between monetary remedies (financial compensation, just satisfaction) available to victims of violations of human rights under international law and claims made under domestic law must be examined.

Finally, the inquiry also concerns historical and systematic violations. The problem of gross and/or systematic violations in international human rights law relates to violations that are both qualitatively and quantitatively serious in nature ('gross') and are an element of an official, widespread pattern or practice ('systematic').[8] The violations often stem from armed conflicts, not necessarily of international dimension, but often authored by a political terror regime. These kinds of violations are especially unsuitable to be embraced by a compensatory tort action. The category of mass violations of human rights overlaps with the category of 'historical injustices' that are linked to big international conflicts. Moreover, a mass number of victims means that the whole society has in fact suffered, thus remedies other than compensation granted to individual victims are regarded as more appropriate to reach the aim of reparation.[9] This notwithstanding, victims of gross and systemic human rights violations have an internationally recognised individual right to reparation.[10]

1.4 Main Research Questions

The comparative study has a number of research objectives.

The main objective is to analyse the theoretical and practical conditions for domestic monetary remedies for breach of human rights.

[7] See van Dam, Cees. 2011. Tort law and human rights: brothers in arms. On the role of tort law in the area of business and human rights. In *Journal of European Tort Law* (vol. 2) 3: 221–254.

[8] See Shelton (2005, 389).

[9] See Shelton (2005, 389–390).

[10] The UN "Basic Principles and Guidelines on the Right to a Remedy and Reparation for Victims of Gross Violations of International Human Rights Law and Serious Violations of International Humanitarian Law" adopted in December 2005, U.N. GA Res. 60/147 of 16 December 2005.

It should also be considered whether the value of protection of human rights as expressed in international treaties, *ius cogens* and in national constitutional laws justifies the conclusion that the interests at stake should enjoy protection under the existing civil liability rules, or rather calls for another general system (a new set of rules) to be developed alongside the existing traditional systems of liability. To put a bit differently, whether human rights protection requires a new cause of action to be created in a given system, or modification of existing causes of action will generally suffice to meet the standard of effective protection.

Further aim is to consider whether an individual claim for compensation (typically sought before a court) is the best means of effecting the protection of individuals whose rights were violated. Hence, special indemnity mechanism will be investigated as they generally provide alternatives to causes of action based on tort law.

The research also inquires into policy considerations that have exerted the greatest influence on the development of particular solutions in domestic legal systems.

1.5 A Note on European Law

As the selection of contributions shows, it is heavily weighted towards Europe. Therefore, further preliminary observations regarding European reports should be made.

First, on a general note, the process of European integration has increased the complexity of fundamental rights enforcement in the European countries. European human rights law is currently shaped by two centres: the Council of Europe and the European Union.

The European Convention on Human Rights of 1950 (ECHR) is binding on the Council of Europe Member States as international law. The ECHR is regarded both as a constitutional instrument of the European public order for the protection of individuals and as a multi-lateral treaty operating in the legal space of the Contracting States. The focus of the Convention is first of all on special categories of rights (art. 5 and art. 6 are of our particular interest). Secondly, it provides the right to effective remedy (art. 13) and a general competence for the Strasbourg Court (European Court of Human Rights, ECtHR) to award just satisfaction to a claimant (art. 41). The competence of the ECtHR has been interpreted in such a way that the Court's declaration that a violation has occurred may be considered *ad casum* as sufficient satisfaction for the applicant.

It should be noted that the topic of the implementation of the ECHR system of protection in domestic case-law has been thoroughly and comparatively examined by Gerards and Fleuren in their recent book.[11] They have concluded that the impact of the ECHR on national court practice is significant, regardless of the countries'

[11] See Gerards and Fleuren (2014). The scope of comparison encompasses six countries only: Belgium, France, Germany, the Netherlands, Sweden and the United Kingdom.

constitutional systems and of the competences of the courts. Although the national courts are strongly inclined to follow the ECtHR interpretation of the Convention, they do it critically and with respect to their own legal systems. The minimum standards of protection required by the ECtHR are not easily raised by the national courts (Gerards and Fleuren, 364–374). The question asked in this book centres on the influence of a damages award adjudicated under international human rights law (such as e.g. under the European Convention system) on a subsequent claim for further compensation brought by the unsatisfied victim under her domestic law.

Second, except for Turkey and Norway, the other European jurisdictions are also European Union (EU) Member States. The EU is a growing source of human rights law, which can be enforceable not only against public bodies, including the Union itself, but also between private parties, mainly through primary/treaty law, laws implementing directives and the case law of the Court of Justice of the EU. European human rights law can thus also be considered as general principles of EU law, subject to the jurisdiction of the Court of Justice. It must be borne in mind that despite the on-going accession procedure to the ECHR by the European Union, currently the Charter of Fundamental Rights of the European Union (2000/2009), which has the status of the EU primary law, must also be respected in the EU Member States, in addition to the ECHR.[12] The Charter stipulates the right to effective remedy (art. 47) in cases of breach of the rights contained therein. Hence, EU law not only accepts the liability for the infringements of human rights, but the right to compensation for damage caused by the EU is recognised as a fundamental right.

1.6 The Outline of the Book

Apart from two single chapters coming from North America (the United States) and Israel, the book encompasses 15 European legal systems. All are democratic states. The main types of legal systems and approaches are represented: civil law, common law, Nordic law, Roman Dutch law and the mixed jurisdiction. Within the civil law countries, special attention should be paid to Central and Eastern European legal systems.

The national experts were asked to prepare their chapters on the basis of a detailed questionnaire. The 17 national chapters have been structured in the way that is most appropriate to a given jurisdiction, while providing a plethora of materials for the purpose of comparative analysis.

In the chapter on EU law the evolution of the basis and the conditions for an action for damages against the EU based on a breach of fundamental rights is analysed. The author also recapitulates the principles on the EU liability and examines the change brought by the EU Charter of Fundamental Rights in this respect. The report on the liability of the EU also addresses the main issues under discussion.

[12] See art. 2 of the Protocol no 30 on the Application of the Charter of Fundamental Rights of the European Union to Poland and to the United Kingdom.

In general, the countries under review and EU law demonstrate a combination of approaches to a claim for damages in cases of human rights abuses: the approach of civil law, the approach of administrative law (depending on the jurisdiction under survey) and the approach of public international law.

The book is concluded with a comparative analysis (Chap. 20), where comparative methodology is to be applied to the findings contained in the jurisdiction-based chapters. The conclusions are heavily dependent on the type of a legal system, the method of incorporation of international law, the socio-cultural circumstances and the historical underpinnings as well as other influential intervening factors.

References

Brüggemeier, Gert, Aurelia Colombi Ciacchi, and Giovanni Comandé. (eds.). 2010. *Fundamental Rights and Private Law in the European Union*, vol. 1 and vol. 2. Cambridge: Cambridge University Press.

European Group on Tort Law. 2005. *Principles of European tort law, text and commentary*. Vienna: Springer.

Fairgrieve, Duncan, Mads Andenas, and John Bell (eds.). 2002. *Tort liability of public authorities in comparative perspective*. London: BIICL.

Gerards, Janneke and Joseph Fleuren. 2014. *Implementation of the European Convention on Human Rights and of the judgments of the ECtHR in national case-law. A comparative analysis*. Cambridge-Antwerp-Portland: Intersentia.

Oliver, Dawn, and Jőrg Fedtke (eds.). 2007. *Human rights and the private sphere – A comparative analysis*. London: Routledge Cavendish.

Shelton, Dinah. 2005. *Remedies in international human rights law*, 2nd ed. Oxford: Oxford University Press.

Shelton, Dinah. 2011. International law in domestic systems. In *General reports of the XVIIIth Congress of the International Academy of Comparative Law/Rapports Généraux du XVIIIème Congrès de l'Académie Internationale de Droit Comparé*, ed. Karen Brown, David Snyder, no. 21.8. Dordrecht: Springer.

Tortell, Lisa. 2006. *Monetary remedies for breach of human rights. A comparative study*. Oxford/Portland: Hart Publishing.

van Dam, Cees. 2011. Tort law and human rights: Brothers in arms. On the role of tort law in the area of business and human rights. *Journal of European Tort Law* 2(3): 221–254.

von Bar, Christian, Eric Clive, and Hans Schulte-Nölke. 2009. Principles, definitions, and model rules in European private law: Draft common frame of reference (DCFR). In *Book VI. Non-contractual liability arising out of damage caused by another*. Munich: Sellier European Law Publishers.

Chapter 2
Damages for Violation of Human Rights in Croatia

Saša Nikšić

2.1 General Introduction

Liability of public authorities in Croatia is mainly governed by private law. Croatian private law is not codified in a single civil code.[1] Instead, private law is regulated by separate legislation on property law, law of obligations, inheritance law, family law, company law etc. The law of obligations, and liability for damages as a part of it, are regulated by the Obligations Act (hereinafter OA).[2] In order to understand the system of compensation for damages in case of human rights infringement a few remarks on Croatia's law of civil liability are necessary. The first version of the OA was drafted under the strong influence of French and Swiss law and enacted in 1978, despite the fact that Croatia, like the rest of former Yugoslavia, was a socialist country. The new OA, which was enacted in 2005 and came into force on 1 January 2006, retained much of its original comparative law origin. French law was particu-

[1] The absence of a civil code is mainly caused due to historical reasons. During the period between 1918 and 1991, when Croatia was part of former Yugoslavia, civil codification was not enacted because the drafting process was not finished before the beginning of World War II. After the end of World War II, when former Yugoslavia was transformed into a socialist and federal state, preparatory work on the civil code was initiated, but after 1974, when a new Constitution came into force, the division of legislative jurisdiction between federal state and federal units was so complex that it hindered adoption of a civil code. Former Yugoslavia failed to enact a civil code also because of the fact that the federal state after 1974 did not have exclusive constitutional competence to regulate entire civil law. After 1991, when Croatia (re)gained its independence, legislative changes affected almost all areas of civil law, but after such a long period without a codification, the idea of a single legislative act (civil code) was somehow lost.

[2] Official Gazette 35/05, 41/08, 23/13.

S. Nikšić (✉)
Civil Law Department, Faculty of Law, University of Zagreb,
Trg m. Tita 3, Zagreb, 10 000, Croatia
e-mail: sniksic@pravo.hr

E. Bagińska (ed.), *Damages for Violations of Human Rights*,
Ius Comparatum - Global Studies in Comparative Law 9,
DOI 10.1007/978-3-319-18950-5_2

larly influential in the field of civil law liability, and can be clearly recognised in the *neminem laedere* principle and the absence of the so-called objective wrongfulness as a separate condition for civil law liability (Gliha et al. 2007).[3] However, regardless of the significant French influence on the OA, legal tradition, or more precisely Austrian law, which was in force in Croatia for a long time after the collapse of the Austro-Hungarian Empire, also played an important role.[4] Both legal theory and case law are strongly influenced by Austrian and German law.

In the respect of public authority liability, Croatian law, unlike French law, deals with this issue within civil law, and does not consider public authority liability as a separate system of compensation, like the French *le droit de la responsabilité administrative*. It is also important to note that civil law liability in Croatia will arise regardless of whether the damage occurred as a consequence of acts or omissions of public authorities in its public law role, or in a situation when it acts in a private law capacity. Consequently, the private law rules will apply if public authorities infringe human rights of individuals.

Although public authorities can generally be liable on the basis of private law, certain provisions of public law are also relevant. However, these provisions are not general provisions on liability of public authorities, but are limited to monetary compensation in cases of the infringement of human rights in specific cases. The right to monetary compensation in certain cases of human rights infringement is also regulated by the Constitutional Act on the Constitutional Court of the Republic of Croatia.[5] Public law regime is also applicable to compensation that is granted to victims of violent crime. Liability for damages is not the only remedy for violation of human rights. Croatian tort law also recognises other instruments, for example *restitution in integrum*, preventive action and action to remove the violation.[6] Injunctions are available on the basis of the Enforcement Act.[7] Victims of human rights violations are in any case entitled to compensation on the basis of general private law regime. Apart from the general private law, special legislation on civil law liability is applicable in cases of discrimination, human rights violations by terrorist activities etc.

---

[3] See Gliha et al. (2007, 256).

[4] One should also bear in mind that other parts of civil law (property law and inheritance law) were developed in accordance with Swiss, Austrian and German law (strangely enough, even during the period of socialism).

[5] Official Gazette 99/99, 29/02, 49/02 – consolidated version.

[6] Arts. 1048 and 1085 OA.

[7] Official Gazette 112/12, 93/14.

2.2 Private Law and Public Law Remedies for Violation of Human Rights

In the respect of monetary compensation for violations of human rights, particular cases are dealt with by both private and public law. This is true not only in the respect of substantive law, but also regarding the procedural framework. Victims of human rights infringement are entitled to claim damages in civil litigation before an ordinary civil law court. This is the main instrument for the compensation of damages in cases of human rights infringement. Apart from the civil law remedy, one could argue that the compensation is also available under criminal law, while criminal procedural law allows compensation claims to be filed within criminal procedure. However, this is not the exclusive feature of the criminal offences violating human rights, but a possibility that can be exploited in any case when damage was inflicted by committing a crime. Even these cases, which are dealt with in the course of criminal proceedings,[8] are resolved on the basis of substantive private law, i.e. provisions of the OA.

The claim for damages can also be submitted within administrative proceedings. However, this claim cannot be submitted as a main claim, but can only be filed along with the other claims in administrative proceedings (e.g. claim to set aside the administrative act).[9] More importantly, even if the claim for damages is filed within administrative proceedings, only the procedure is governed by public-administrative law. In the absence of substantive law that regulates administrative liability, private law is again a legal source relevant for damages for the infringement of human rights.

The most important public law instrument in compensating damage to a victim of human rights violation is the so-called appropriate compensation, which can be awarded by the Constitutional Court of the Republic of Croatia (hereinafter: Constitutional Court). According to Article 63/3 of the Constitutional Act on the Constitutional Court of the Republic of Croatia, the Constitutional Court is entitled to determine the appropriate compensation for the applicant in case of a violation of his/her constitutional right committed by the (ordinary) court by not deciding within a reasonable time about his/her rights and obligations, or about the suspicions or accusations of a criminal offence. The compensation shall be paid from the state budget within the term of 3 months from the date when the applicant lodged a request for its payment. Even in this example that belongs, beyond any doubt, to public law regime, there is a connection to private law. According to certain sources, 85 % of case law of the Constitutional Court originates from civil litigations over private law issues (Radolović 2012, 67).

If damage was caused by a violent criminal offence, a victim can claim monetary compensation on the basis of specific public law legislation. This system of mone-

[8] Article 158 of the Criminal Procedure Act, Official Gazette 152/08, 76/09, 80/11, 91/12, 143/12, 56/13, 145/13.

[9] Article 22/4 of the Act on Administrative Disputes, Official Gazette 20/10, 143/12.

tary compensation belongs to public law, regarding both the proceedings and the substance. This instrument is not specifically designed to compensate victims of human rights infringements, but is available to victims of violent crime regardless of who committed the crime.[10]

2.3 Legal Basis for Damages

2.3.1 Human Rights Granted by the Constitution

The awarding of monetary compensation for damage inflicted by human rights infringement covers a broad category of different rights. Human rights and freedoms guaranteed by the Croatian Constitution[11] are as follows: right to life[12] (the death penalty was abolished in 1990), right to freedom,[13] presumption of innocence,[14] right to due process,[15] legal consequences of criminal conviction,[16] conditions for criminal conviction (it is forbidden to convict a person if certain behaviour was not a crime at the time when it was committed),[17] freedom of movement and residence,[18] right to asylum,[19] protection of home,[20] right to private and family life, dignity, reputation and honour,[21] freedom and confidentiality of correspondence,[22] data protection,[23] freedom of thought and freedom of expression,[24] right to tolerance (expressed as proscription of invoking or encouraging war or violence, national, racial, religious or any other form of intolerance),[25] freedom of consciousness and freedom of religion,[26] right to public assembly and peaceful protest,[27] right to

[10] On the basis of Act on Monetary Compensation for Victims of Criminal Offences, Official Gazette 80/08, 27/11.

[11] Official Gazette 56/90, 135/97, 113/00, 28/01, 76/10.

[12] Article 21 of the Constitution.

[13] Article 22 of the Constitution.

[14] Article 28 of the Constitution.

[15] Article 29 of the Constitution.

[16] Article 30 of the Constitution.

[17] Article 31 of the Constitution.

[18] Article 32 of the Constitution.

[19] Article 33 of the Constitution.

[20] Article 34 of the Constitution.

[21] Article 35 of the Constitution.

[22] Article 36 of the Constitution.

[23] Article 37 of the Constitution.

[24] Article 38 of the Constitution.

[25] Article 39 of the Constitution.

[26] Article 40 of the Constitution.

[27] Article 42 of the Constitution.

association,[28] right of citizens to be admitted in and to perform duties of public office,[29] right of citizens to vote and to be elected to/for the Croatian Parliament, the President of the Republic of Croatia and the European Parliament,[30] right to lodge complaints or submit proposals to public authorities and right to obtain an answer,[31] right to conscientious objection in the respect of military duties,[32] right of ownership (special regime when foreigners are acquiring ownership is permitted) and right to inherit,[33] entrepreneurial and market freedoms and rights of investors (foreign investors are free to withdraw invested capital and profit from Croatia),[34] right to work and freedom of work,[35] right to income,[36] right to social security and social insurance,[37] right to social benefits to certain categories of people,[38] right to health protection,[39] right to establish unions of workers and right to establish and to be a member of an employers association,[40] right to strike,[41] right and freedom of parents to decide independently on bringing up their children,[42] equal access to education, freedom to establish schools, autonomy of university, guarantee of scientific, cultural and artistic activities,[43] and the right to healthy life and environment.[44]

2.3.2 Right to Damages

The Croatian Constitution explicitly grants the right to compensation in case of unlawful apprehension or conviction (Article 25/4). This right is furthermore regulated by criminal procedural law regarding damages for wrongful conviction or unjustified arrest or detention (Krapac and Bagić 2012, 1237–1281). Explicit legal basis for claiming damages can be also found in the Constitutional Act on the

[28] Article 43 of the Constitution.
[29] Article 44 of the Constitution.
[30] Article 45 of the Constitution.
[31] Article 46 of the Constitution.
[32] Article 47 of the Constitution.
[33] Article 48 of the Constitution.
[34] Article 49 of the Constitution.
[35] Article 55 of the Constitution.
[36] Article 56 of the Constitution.
[37] Article 57 of the Constitution.
[38] Article 58 of the Constitution.
[39] Article 59 of the Constitution.
[40] Article 60 of the Constitution.
[41] Article 61 of the Constitution.
[42] Article 64 of the Constitution.
[43] Article 69 of the Constitution.
[44] Article 70 of the Constitution.

Constitutional Court of the Republic of Croatia (Article 63/3).[45] The Constitutional Act on the Constitutional Court grants the right to appropriate compensation in case of violation of a person's constitutional right committed by the (ordinary) court by not deciding within a reasonable time about the rights and obligations, or about the suspicions or accusations of a criminal offence.

The explicit legal basis for claiming damages in case of human rights infringements can be found in other legal sources as well. The Republic of Croatia is a member of the Council of Europe and a contracting party of the European Convention on Human Rights (hereinafter: ECHR). Croatian law belongs to the so-called monistic legal systems in the respect of the application of international treaties,[46] and therefore Croatian courts and other public authorities are obliged to apply the provisions of the ECHR, especially when the national legislation is not in accordance with the ECHR (Smerdel 2013, 111). In the past, courts were generally reluctant to directly apply provisions of international treaties, but this attitude is gradually changing.

The general civil liability system also recognises one further legal category that is closely connected to human rights. The main legal source of civil law liability, the OA, regulates and protects so-called personality rights. The infringement of personality rights is by legal definition non-patrimonial damage (Art. 1046. OA) and, if other conditions of civil liability are met, a person who infringed personality rights will be held liable. Personality rights are recognised in the respect of both natural and legal persons[47] in a similar way as human rights, in the framework of the ECHR, belong to both categories of legal subjects (Emberland 2006, 2–4). Broadening of the scope of the application of human rights protection legislation can be observed in areas that are typically occupied by legal persons, such as the public procurements (Arrowsmith 2005, 85–97). Naturally, one should not consider personality rights as just another name for human rights. Human rights exist in the respect of both patrimonial rights (e.g. right to property) and non-patrimonial rights (e.g. right to life, right to privacy). Personality rights are, on the other hand, exclusively of non-patrimonial nature. Therefore, a legal basis for damages because of violation of human rights can also be found in general provisions on compensation of both patrimonial and non-patrimonial damage.

---

[45] The Constitutional Act on Constitutional Court of the Republic of Croatia, Official Gazette 49/02 – consolidated version (English translation is available at: http://www.usud.hr/default.aspx?Show=ustavni_zakon_o_ustavnom_sudu&m1=27&m2=49&Lang=en. Accessed 12 Oct 2013.

[46] According to Article 134 of the Croatian Constitution, international treaties that are concluded and ratified in accordance with the Constitution and that are in force are part of Croatian legal system, and are in hierarchy or legal sources above acts of parliament.

[47] According to Article 19/2 OA, personality rights are: right to life, physical and psychical health, reputation, honour, dignity, name, privacy of personal and family life, freedom, etc. Legal person has the same personality rights with the exception of the rights that are connected to the biological character of a natural person. Legal person in particular has the right to reputation, honour, name or firm name, business confidentiality, freedom to conduct business, and other (Article 19/3 OA).

2.4 Liability Regime in Detail

2.4.1 General Conditions of Liability

2.4.1.1 General Remarks

A victim of human rights infringement is entitled to compensation according to the general civil law liability regime only if the conditions for civil law liability are met. In order to receive compensation a victim has to suffer a damage that was caused by the other person, which, as a matter of principle acted with a fault (Klarić and Vedriš 2014).[48] This means that 'pure violation' of human rights is not enough. However, in real life situations, it is difficult to imagine that a human rights infringement could be pure violation without fulfilling the conditions for civil law liability. In most cases the human rights infringements will cause emotional distress of a victim, which means that he or she suffered non-patrimonial damage.

2.4.1.2 Victim and Tortfeasor

Civil law liability is a relation between a victim and a tortfeasor. The State cannot invoke immunity in human rights violation, which is a consequence of the fact that in general civil law liability the state simply does not have immunity. Certain public officials do have immunity, but it should be emphasised that the state is liable in the first place, and individual liability comes second (reimbursement if the state paid damages). Therefore, the state will be liable even if a public official successfully relies on the immunity. A victim can claim damages directly from the individual tortfeasor only in exceptional cases when additional conditions are met. In this case the immunity would be an obstacle, but the victim would not be deprived of compensation because of the liability of the state.

Liability is incurred by the state in the case of the violation of human rights by natural persons employed by the state. The state will also be liable if the damage is a consequence of the illegal or irregular activities of governmental bodies, bodies of local or regional self-governance, or legal persons who possess public authority in public administration affairs that have been conferred to them.[49] The state is also liable for the damage caused by judges.[50] As a matter of principle, the state is not liable for private companies.

Individuals who have committed human rights violation can also be personally liable. Different rules prescribe different conditions regarding the individuals who act on behalf of legal persons. If an individual is an employee of public authority, a victim can file the claim directly against the individual only if he or she acted

[48] Klarić and Vedriš (2014, 583–584).

[49] Article 14 Act on System of State Administration.

[50] Article 105 of the Act on Courts.

intentionally (*dolus*).[51] If a legal person has paid damages to a victim, the amount paid can be claimed from the individual who has actually inflicted the damage, but only if the individual acted with gross negligence or intent.[52] The legal person is entitled to file the claim during the period of 6 months after the damages were paid to the victim.[53]

Individuals who are members of the bodies of legal persons are also liable for damages that the legal persons paid to a victim. Similarly to a relation between an employer and an employee, a legal person is entitled to claim the reimbursement during the period of 6 months after damages were paid to a victim if an individual acted with gross negligence or intent.[54]

Specific legislation regulates the liability of judges in a similar way, which can also be relevant for damages in case of human rights violations. The Act on Courts prescribes that the state is liable for damage suffered by a party in the proceedings because of illegal or irregular work of a judge.[55] The state is entitled to claim the reimbursement of the amount paid to the person who suffered damage if a judge acted with gross negligence or intent.[56] The Act on Courts explicitly regulates the liability in case of trials not finished in a reasonable time.[57]

Foreign nationals are, as a matter of principle, entitled to compensation under the general regime of private law, but also if monetary compensation is awarded on the basis of public law. In some cases the public law regime excludes foreign nationals from its protective scope, but these are very rare occasions. For example, according to Article 7 of the Act on Monetary Compensation for the Victims of Criminal Offences, in order to claim the compensation, a victim must be a national of the Republic of Croatia or have habitual residence in the Republic of Croatia. The same right is recognised in respect of nationals of EU member states and victims who have residence in the territory of the EU member states. Foreign nationals who do not fulfil these conditions are not entitled to claim the damage on the basis of specific legislation.

If a victim contributed to the damage, he or she is entitled to a reduced amount of damages.[58] If it is impossible to establish the extent of the victim's contribution, the judge will award damages by taking the circumstances of the case into account.[59] These rules, explicitly mentioned in the chapter of the OA that regulates the compensation of patrimonial damage, are also applicable *mutatis mutandis* in the cases of non-patrimonial damage.[60]

---

[51] Article 1061/2 OA.

[52] Article 1061/3 OA.

[53] Article 1061/4 OA.

[54] Article 1062 OA.

[55] Article 105/1 of the Act on Courts.

[56] Article 105/2 of the Act on Courts.

[57] Article 105/3-4 of the Act on Courts.

[58] Article 1092/1 OA.

[59] Article 1092/2 OA.

[60] Article 1106 OA.

2.4.1.3 Damage

The existence and degree of damage must be proven by the claimant. It should be emphasised that the court can award damages even if the exact degree of damage was not proven. In this respect, the rules of civil procedure prescribe that the judge awards damages in the amount determined by free assessment.[61] Free assessment does not mean arbitrary judgments, but must be elaborated by the judge. The infringement of human rights can have different consequences of both patrimonial and non-patrimonial nature. According to Article 1046 OA, a damage is defined as diminishing of someone's patrimony (*damnum emergens*) and preventing its increase (*lucrum cessans*), as well as the infringement of one's personality rights (non-patrimonial damage, non-pecuniary damage). The notion of patrimonial damage also covers various costs and expenses incurred by the victim (e.g. legal expenses, medical expenses). The general principle of civil law liability is that a victim is not entitled to 'double' compensation. The amount that was awarded will be taken into account if the victim has been awarded the compensation in one type of the proceedings and if the claimant is entitled to initiate another type of proceedings.

2.4.1.4 Causal Connection

The tortfeasor shall be liable for damages only if his or her act or omission has caused the damage. If, in a particular case, there was more than one cause of a damage and if all of the causes are of human origin, the so-called theory of adequate causation is applicable (Klarić and Vedriš 2014, 594–595). According to the theory of adequate causation, the damage is considered to be a consequence of someone's act or omission if it is a typical consequence of that act or omission (Klarić and Vedriš 2014, 595).

2.4.1.5 Wrongfulness and Fault

As a matter of principle, Croatian civil law liability is a fault-based liability system.[62] In order to obtain monetary compensation for a human rights infringement, a victim that relies on private law liability within civil litigation proceedings before ordinary courts has to prove the conditions of civil law liability. All typical conditions of liability have to be proven: damage and a causal link between damage and activity/omission of a wrongdoer, but not the fault (Klarić and Vedriš 2014, 584). The existence of a fault is a rebuttable presumption.[63] The fact that certain violations

[61] Article 223 of the Civil Procedure Act, Official Gazette of ex-Yugoslavia 4/77, 36/77, 36/80, 6/80, 69/82, 43/82, 58/84, 74/87, 57/89, 20/90, 27/90, 35/91, Official Gazette of the Republic of Croatia 53/91, 91/92, 112/99, 129/00, 88/01, 117/03, 88/05, 2/07, 96/08, 84/08, 123/08, 57/11, 25/13.

[62] Article 1045/1 OA.

[63] Article 1045/1 OA.

were gross and/or systematic can be taken into account in order to establish whether a victim is entitled to monetary compensation and also when assessing the amount of damages in cases of non-patrimonial damage. The monetary compensation for non-patrimonial damage can be awarded only if the seriousness of the personality right infringement and other relevant circumstances of cases justify it.[64] Gross violation, as well as systematic violation, of human rights can qualify as justification for monetary compensation. At the same time, it can serve to determine the amount of damages. Both systematic and gross violation of human rights could lead to increasing the amount of damages that the court would award to a victim.

Croatian legislation also recognises strict liability as an exception, and case law confirms the application of the strict liability rules in cases of human rights violations. It is interesting to note that according to case law developed by the Constitutional Court the liability regulated by the Act on the State Administration System is an example of strict liability.[65] The Constitutional Court was of the opinion that strict liability of the state in this context is justified by the rule of law. Because of the fact that the human rights infringement can originate from acts or omissions of the state administration, this is a clear case of strict liability. If a victim of the human rights infringement claims compensation on the basis of public law, specific conditions prescribed by public law have to be met in order to receive the compensation.

2.4.2 *Special Legislation*

Civil law liability in Croatia is not only regulated by the general provisions of the OA, but also by numerous different legislative acts. The same is true of liability for damages in cases of human rights infringement. The right to damages in such cases is afforded, for example, on the basis of the Act on the Repression of Discrimination.[66] Because of the fact that human rights infringements are connected to the activities of public authorities, relevant legal sources also include the Act on the State Administration System[67] and the Act on Courts.[68] The right to damages for wrongful conviction or unjustified arrest or detention is recognised by the Constitution and the Criminal Procedures Act. Unlike the compensation for crime victims mentioned earlier, which considerably deviates from the general private law liability system, the aforementioned specific legislation corresponds to the general liability system to a large extent. This means that cases of discrimination and damages inflicted by the courts or public administration are dealt with before ordinary courts in civil litigation proceedings, and that general civil law is applicable as a substantive law. In the

[64] Article 1100/1 OA.

[65] Case number U-III /2314/2006 (Constitutional Court).

[66] Official Gazette 85/08, 112/12.

[67] Official Gazette 150/11, 12/13.

[68] Official Gazette 28/13.

respect of damages for wrongful conviction or unjustified arrest or detention, the combination of general rules on civil law liability and special rules of criminal procedural law are applied.

There are examples when special legislation explicitly regulates cases of gross or systematic infringements of specific human rights. For example, the Act on the Repression of Discrimination contains provisions on multiple discrimination, repeated discrimination, discrimination committed during a prolonged period of time and discrimination when the consequences of discrimination are particularly burdensome for a victim.[69] In such cases the court that deals with the claim for non-patrimonial damages shall take into account these circumstances.[70] It is important to note that victims of discrimination are entitled to claim compensation for both patrimonial and non-patrimonial damage, in accordance with the general provisions of civil law liability.[71] Therefore, cases of monetary compensation for discrimination fall into the scope of private law.

Pecuniary damages generally cover diminishment of existing patrimony (*damnum emergens*) and lost profit (*lucrum cessans*) (Klarić and Vedriš 2014, 593). The OA explicitly prescribes the right to damages in case of personal injury. In this case, the damages cover medical expenses and compensation for the loss of working ability.[72] If a victim of the human rights infringement loses his or her life, family members or other persons who were dependent on the victim's income are entitled to damages for the loss of maintenance.[73]

2.4.3 Damages

When one deals with the issue of damages in cases of infringement of human rights, the purpose of damages is in essence the same as in any other case of civil law liability. In respect of the purpose of damages, one should differentiate between the so-called patrimonial and non-patrimonial damage. The main purpose of damages in the case of patrimonial damage is compensation, meaning that the victim who suffered the damage should be compensated in a manner that would bring him/her to the condition that existed before the damage was inflicted. Patrimonial damage can be more or less easily calculated in the form of a monetary equivalent, and damages are paid in the amount that equals the amount of damage. In the case of non-patrimonial damage, this goal cannot be achieved, and therefore damages do not serve as the monetary equivalent of inflicted damage, but serve the purpose of giving satisfaction to the victim. Unlike compensation for patrimonial damage, damages for non-patrimonial damage cannot be the monetary equivalent of damage, and

[69] Article 6/1 Act on Repression of Discrimination.

[70] Article 6/2 Act on Repression of Discrimination.

[71] Article 11 Act on Repression of Discrimination.

[72] Article 1095/1 OA.

[73] Article 1094 OA.

therefore are not compensation in the standard meaning of the word. Instead of that, the amount of damages is individualised and largely depends on the characteristics of the person who suffered the damage (age, profession, emotional state after suffering the damage). The standard explanation regarding damages paid for inflicted non-patrimonial damage is that the damage provides just satisfaction to the victim. Because of the fact that non-patrimonial damage cannot be expressed as the monetary equivalent of damage, the monetary satisfaction is an award determined by a subjective criterion. The expression 'just satisfaction' should not be confused with the same expression that can be found in the European Convention of Human Rights and which also covers compensation for the infringement of patrimonial rights (e.g. the right to property). In Croatian law the satisfaction is awarded only for the infringement of non-patrimonial rights.

Legal theory recently also offers an additional explanation for the purpose of damages, especially in the case of non-patrimonial damage. That is to influence the behaviour of individuals who committed wrongful acts, but also the behaviour of the general public to refrain from actions/omissions that can cause damage to others (Baretić 2006, 175–176). Damages do not have a penal purpose under Croatian law, since punitive damages do not exist within the legal system.

Since compensation for human rights infringement falls under the scope of the general private law liability regime, cases of monetary compensation for human rights do not have any specific doctrinal fundament different than general liability law. The monetary compensation for infringements of human rights is not a uniform category and consequently cannot be explained by a single theory. From the perspective of general civil law liability, the compensation for damage is justified as a means to protect the subjective (private) rights of individuals (Klarić and Vedriš 2014, 583). In this respect, the nature of the infringed right is irrelevant. As a matter of principle, civil law protects various subjective rights. Only in the respect of the compensation for wrongful conviction, unjustified arrest or detention is justified on the basis of subjective public right theory (Krapac and Bagić 2012, 1247).

2.4.4 The Relation Between Damages and Other Remedies

Civil law liability is an autonomous instrument in the case of violations of human rights, independent from the other remedies. However, in some cases, the application of one remedy could exclude the application of another. In the respect of damages in the form of monetary compensation, one has to bear in mind that, according to Article 1100/1 OA, the monetary compensation for non-patrimonial damage shall be awarded only if the seriousness of the personality right infringement and other relevant circumstances of a case justify it. Therefore, if the aforementioned conditions are not met, only non-monetary remedies can be claimed (e.g. an apology, publishing of the judgement of a court). Because of the seriousness of human rights infringement cases, generally speaking, the conditions to award monetary damages are usually fulfilled.

Infringements of human rights can also lead to patrimonial damage (e.g. destruction of property, medical expenses for the treatment of bodily injuries). Croatian civil law liability for patrimonial damage recognises two instruments for the compensation of patrimonial damage. One is the so-called *restitutio in integrum*, and the other is monetary compensation. At least at the level of legislation, *restitutio in integrum* is the principle instrument for the compensation of patrimonial damage. Monetary compensation comes second, only if *restitutio in integrum* is not possible.[74] However, case law traditionally favours monetary compensation.

2.4.5 Assessing the Amount of Damages

Damages for patrimonial damage are the monetary equivalent of the inflicted damage. In this case, damages are established by an objective criterion, which means the market value of the destroyed object or, for example, the expenses that were necessary to repair the damaged object. In extraordinary circumstances, damages for patrimonial damage are awarded on the basis of a subjective criterion – the value that the destroyed object had for its owner. In order to award damages according to this criterion, the victim has to prove that the damage was inflicted in the course of committing a criminal offence with intent.[75]

Damages for non-patrimonial damage are awarded on the basis of subjective criteria, and one could argue that they are awarded discretionarily. The legal term for damages in this case is equitable monetary compensation. However, because of various reasons, the Supreme Court of the Republic of Croatia published *the Orientation criteria and the amounts for determining the value of equitable monetary compensation of non-patrimonial damage*, which serves as a means to make the awards more uniform. *The Orientation criteria* contain the values for typical awards for non-patrimonial damage. Because of the fact that they were published in 2002, when the old OA (1978) was in force, they are to some extent obsolete, but they still serve their purpose when they are compatible with the new OA. This does not exclude the possibility for the courts to award higher damages, because *the Orientation criteria* should not be applied without taking all relevant circumstances of a particular case into account. The fact that non-patrimonial damage was inflicted because of the human rights infringement could lead to the increase of the award, in comparison to the values that can be found in *the Orientation criteria,* because of the extraordinary circumstances in which the damage was inflicted. The values determined by *the Orientation criteria* can be increased even without extraordinary circumstances. However, even without extraordinary circumstances this amount can be multiplied, for example, in the case of death or serious disability of the next of kin, since every family member mentioned in the relevant provision of the OA is entitled to full compensation. According to *the Orientation criteria*, the highest

---

[74] Article 1085/3 OA.

[75] Article 1089/4 OA.

amount of damages that can be awarded is 30,000 Euros. *The Orientation criteria* should not be misunderstood as the limitation of liability (cap). The courts are free to award higher amounts of damages, but must bear in mind that the Supreme Court can set aside the decision of a lower court. Therefore, lower courts that consider awarding damages in excess to *the Orientation criteria* should elaborate the reasons why they award a certain amount in the specific case.

The law does not explicitly mention punitive damages, and case law does not recognise this type of damages. On the other hand, legal theory takes into account the fact that fault, which is closely connected to the idea of punishment, is one of the conditions of liability. Nevertheless, at this stage, punitive damages are still not a reality, and they are probably not going to be in the near future.

There are examples of special rules that apply to the amount of damages. For instance, Articles 10–13 of the Act on Monetary Compensation for Victims of Criminal Offences limit the compensation for medical expenses, lost profit (limited to approximately 4,650 Euros), loss of the maintenance of indirect victims (limited to approximately 9,300 Euros) and funeral expenses (limited to approximately 670 Euros).

Interest rates that are generally applicable are also applicable, to damages paid for the human rights infringement, and to damages in general. The only difference regarding interest that is paid for damages that are due is that, in the respect of non-pecuniary harm damages, the interest starts to accumulate from the day when the victim claims damages in written form.[76] This applies to every written claim, regardless of whether it was submitted to a court or only to a liable person. The interest on the damages for pecuniary loss start to accumulate on the day after the responsibility has arisen.

Multiple violations can lead to the increase of damages. Firstly, multiple violations can lead to the increase of patrimonial damage, and consequently this will have an influence on the amount of damages, because damages for patrimonial damage are the monetary equivalent of the damage that has been inflicted. Secondly, multiple violations could also have an influence on the increase of damages for non-patrimonial damages. The explanation for that is that, according to the provision of Article 1100/2 OA, the court will take into account the purpose of damages when determining the amount of damages for non-patrimonial damage. As mentioned earlier, one of the purposes of damages is to discourage potential tortfeasors from inflicting damage in the future. Because of the fact that multiple violations should be discouraged even more, one of the ways to do this is to increase the damages.

2.5 Death and Personal Injury

Pecuniary claims can be made after the death of a direct victim if certain conditions are met. In the respect of patrimonial damage (e.g. damage to a property, lost profit, medical expenses), the claim will be inherited by persons who are entitled to inherit.

---

[76] Articles 29 and 1103 OA.

In this case, the general conditions of inheritance law that regulate the transfer of rights and obligations, in the event of death, to the heirs are relevant. The situation is different in the respect of non-patrimonial damage. Damages can be inherited in this case if the direct victim has filed a written claim, regardless of whether the claim was filed to a court or submitted to a person who is obliged to pay the compensation.[77] It is also necessary that the general conditions of inheritance law be fulfilled.

Family members are entitled to claim damages for both patrimonial and non-patrimonial damage. Patrimonial damage will consist of the loss of maintenance because a direct victim losing his or her life. Non-patrimonial damage will take the shape of pain and suffering because of the loss of life or serious disability of a family member. According to Article 1101 OA, only immediate family is entitled to damages for non-patrimonial damage (spouse, children and parents); other family members are entitled to damages only if they lived with the direct victim permanently. In the latter case, the law grants the right to damages only to specific family members (brothers and sisters, grandchildren and grandparents, unmarried partners).

2.6 Procedural Law Issues and Time Limits

As a matter of principle, no special procedure is available for awarding damages in cases of human rights violations. In a case of liability of the state, the only difference, in comparison to the liability of a private person, is that the claimant is obliged, to submit his or her claim to the public prosecutor before submitting it to the court, in order to try to reach a settlement.[78]

General rules on time limits are also applicable to human rights violations cases.[79] Therefore, any claim for damages must be submitted not later than 3 years from the moment when a victim realises that he or she has suffered damage, and the identity of the tortfeasor, and at the latest 5 years from the moment when the damage was inflicted to the victim.[80] The time limit is prolonged if the damage was caused by a criminal offence.[81] However, if a victim of violent crime claims compensation from the state on the basis of special legislation, he or she must submit a claim within 6 months from the day when the crime was committed.[82] If a victim is not able to file a claim for health reasons, the claim has to be filed no later than 3 months after this reason ceased to hinder the victim from filing the claim. The

[77] Article 1105/1 OA.

[78] Article 186a of the Act on Civil Litigation.

[79] The subject matter of time limits is regulated by substantive law of obligations, not civil procedural law.

[80] Article 230/1-2 OA.

[81] Article 231 OA.

[82] Article 25/1 of the Act on Monetary Compensation for Victims of Criminal Offences.

definitive time limit is 3 years from the time when the crime was committed.[83] A special time limit is prescribed for victims younger than 18 years of age and persons who lack the capacity to act if their legal guardian did not file a claim. It starts to run after the person attains the age of 18, after the commencement of criminal proceedings or after the person regains the capacity to act. The time limit in these cases is 6 months.[84] Group claims are available, according to the general provisions of civil procedural law.

Bibliography

Arrowsmith, Sue. 2005. *The law of public and utilities procurement*. London: Sweet & Maxwell.

Baretić, Marko. 2006. Povreda prava na slobodu. In *Odgovornost za neimovinsku štetu zbog povrede prava osobnosti*, ed. Petar Klarić, 175–176. Zagreb: Narodne novine.

Emberland, Marius. 2006. *The human rights of companies, exploring the structure of ECHR protection*. New York: Oxford University Press.

Gliha, Igor, Marko Baretić, and Saša Nikšić. 2007. Pure economic loss in Croatian law. In *European tort law, Eastern and Western perspectives*, ed. Mauro Bussani, 249–293. Berne: Stämpfli Publishers Ltd.

Klarić, Petar, and Martin Vedriš. 2014. *Građansko pravo*. Zagreb: Narodne novine.

Krapac, Davor, and Snježana Bagić. 2012. Pravo na naknadu štete zbog neopravdane osude ili zbog neutemeljenog uhićenja ili pritvaranja te njegova suvremena ustavnopravna i kaznenopravna regulacija. *Zbornik Pravni fakultet u Zagrebu* 62(5–6): 1237–1281.

Radolović, Aldo. 2012. Građansko pravo u ustavnom sudovanju. *Zbornik Pravnog fakulteta Sveučilišta u Rijeci* 33(1): 67–83.

Smerdel, Branko. 2013. *Ustavno uređenje europske Hrvatske*. Zagreb: Narodne novine.

[83] Article 25/2 of the Act on Monetary Compensation for Victims of Criminal Offences.

[84] Article 25/3 of the Act on Monetary Compensation for Victims of Criminal Offences.

Chapter 3
Damages for the Infringement of Human Rights – The Czech Republic

Pavel Šturma and Veronika Bílková

3.1 Introduction

3.1.1 What Kind of Liability Regime?

The discourse on the protection of human rights both on the international and national level includes the issue of compensation or, broadly speaking, of liability for damage. In spite of the growing unification of the international catalogues of human rights, the regimes of compensation have not yet been fully developed in international law. The regulation under national law is therefore of great importance.

At the outset, it should be pointed out that the national legal order of the Czech Republic does not have a special concept of liability for the violations of human rights. Violations of human rights are expressly referred to in relation to the constitutional complaint to the Constitutional Court. However, the protection of fundamental human rights and freedoms of individuals by the Constitutional Court does not include financial compensation. The Constitutional Court has the power to quash any unconstitutional decision, including judgments of ordinary courts, and, under certain conditions, even relevant parts of legislation that are at odds with the constitutionally guaranteed rights. Nevertheless, damages do not count as measures that the Constitutional Court may decide upon.

Otherwise, cursory references to the violations of human rights can be found in special acts (lex specialis) dealing with certain losses and injuries caused in the past, especially during the communist regime (1948–1989), see *infra* (historical injustices). However, most of this legislation is no longer in force.

P. Šturma (✉) • V. Bílková
Faculty of Law, Charles University in Prague,
nám. Curieových 7, CZ-11640 Praha, Czech Republic
e-mail: sturma@prf.cuni.cz; bilkova@prf.cuni.cz

E. Bagińska (ed.), *Damages for Violations of Human Rights*,
Ius Comparatum - Global Studies in Comparative Law 9,
DOI 10.1007/978-3-319-18950-5_3

In fact, the main legal basis for financial compensation for certain infringements of human rights is the Act on Liability for Damage Caused in the Exercise of Public Power by Decision or Incorrect Official Conduct.[1] This act forms the general law of public authority liability. It includes both the State responsibility and the responsibility of the territorial self-governing entities. This is an objective (no fault) civil liability.

The present report focuses on this form of liability, as the classical concept of human rights conceptualises these rights as the rights of individuals and entailing obligations of the States. Therefore the main interest lies in the area of the liability of State for the infringements of human rights. Although the theory of human rights admits that certain violations may also occur between private persons, this approach implies the State responsibility for its failure to protect or to ensure the respective human rights to individuals in its territory or under its jurisdiction. Therefore such claims to compensation are to be directed against the State.

3.1.2 Dichotomy of Public Law and Private Law

The public authority liability under Act No. 82/1998 falls under private law. This act has replaced Act No. 58/1969, on Liability for Damage Caused by the Decisions of State Authority. Both acts are considered as special laws in relation to the Civil Code.[2] The case law of the Supreme Court clearly confirms that claims to compensation under the Act on Liability for Damage Caused by a Decision or incorrect official conduct are of civil claims by nature.[3]

It is worth noting that Section 26 of Act No. 82/1998 clearly provides that legal relations under this act are governed by the Civil Code, unless there are special provisions in this Act. It seems to confirm the subsidiary application of the Civil Code.

On January 1st, 2014, a new Civil Code came into effect.[4] This new Code brought a fundamental change to private law in the Czech Republic. Stemming from the natural law inspiration, Roman law and continental (civil) law traditions, the Civil Code includes subchapters dealing with the reparation for injury to the natural rights of human beings. According to Sec. 2956 of the Civil Code, "If a wrongdoer incurs liability, to make good someone's injury of his/her natural right, which are protected by the First part of this Code, he/she shall make reparation for the damage and moral injury caused thereby; as a moral injury he/she shall make good also mental suffering." However, the Civil Code governs private law relations, i.e. private rights and obligations of a personal and pecuniary nature to the extent that they are not regulated by other legal acts (Sec. 9). As it was the case under the old Civil Code,

[1] See Act No. 82/1998 Coll., of 17 March 1998, as amended by later laws.

[2] Cf. Jehlička et al (1999, 1188–1189).

[3] Decision of the Supreme Court, R 35/1977, pp. 175–176.

[4] Občanský zákoník (Civil Code), Act No. 89/2012 Coll.

liability for damage to the rights of a human being under this Code should cover damage arising in private relationships. In view of the subsidiary application of the new Civil Code to individual claims related to violations of human rights by State or other public authorities, it is still unclear what impact (if any) the new, more generous rules may have on civil liability damages payable by State under the special legislation, namely Act No. 82/1998.

Act No. 82/1998 Coll. does not prevent victims of human rights violations from seeking, when appropriate, compensation under criminal law. Criminal courts may award damages in the framework of criminal proceedings but this compensation has a different nature because the defendant is the perpetrator of the crime, not the State.

3.1.3 What Is the Legal Basis for Claiming Damages for the Violations of Human Rights?

There is no explicit legal basis for claiming damages for the violations of human rights. However, the most general legal basis is set forth in Article 36, para. 3 of the Charter of Fundamental Rights and Freedoms,[5] which forms part of the constitutional order of the Czech Republic.[6] Under this provision of constitutional value, "Everyone has the right to compensation of damage caused to him/her by unlawful decision of the court, other state authority or an organ of public administration or by an incorrect official conduct."

This provision, which follows and extends the respective obligations under the major Human Rights treaties (such as Article 2 para. 3 and Article 9 para. 5 of the International Covenant on Civil and Political Rights and Article 5 para. 5, Article 6 and Article 13 of the European Convention on Human Rights), puts the issue of compensation in the context of constitutional protection of human rights.

According to Article 36 para 4 of the Charter, the conditions and details of the right to compensation shall be set forth by a law (i.e. an act of Parliament).

More specifically, a claim for financial compensation may be submitted under Act No. 82/1998, as this act provides for the liability of the State and of territorial self-governing entities. The purpose of this legislation is broader than just providing a remedy for infringement of human rights, as it provides compensation for all unlawful decisions issued in civil, administrative and criminal proceedings, as well as for damage caused by incorrect official conduct (in the absence of a formal deci-

[5] Listina základních práv a svobod, vyhlášená pod č. 2/1993 Sb. (promulgated under No. 2/1993 Coll.).

[6] According to Article 112 of the Constitution (Constitutional Act No. 1/1993 Coll., as amended by later acts), "the constitutional order of the Czech Republic consists of the Constitution, the Charter of Fundamental Rights and Freedoms, constitutional acts adopted under the present Constitution, constitutional acts of the National Assembly of Czechoslovak Republic, the Federal Assembly of the Czechoslovak Socialist Republic and the Czech National Council regulating state borders of the Czech Republic, and constitutional acts of the Czech National Council adopted after 6 June 1992."

sion). The relatively broad scope of the application seems to address all (or most of) the violations of human rights, but also some cases that do not involve human rights as defined by the constitutional and international catalogues of human rights.

It is possible to conclude that clear violations of human rights (for example the right to personal freedom, cases of detention, penalties, constraints, etc.) are included in the scope of application of the Act. Nevertheless, these violations are not subject to any special rules but remain under the general provisions of the Act.

3.1.4 What Is the Purpose (Idea) of the Damages in Cases of Infringement of Human Rights?

The general purpose of the analysed legislation is to address the injurious consequences of various unlawful decisions and misconducts of public authorities. The cases of infringement of human rights are not singled out. They are included into the regime of compensation on an implicit basis. However, two express references in the footnotes included in Act No. 82/1998 point to human rights: first, in relation to the right to liberty (Article 5 of the European Convention on Human Rights, ECHR), second, in relation to the incorrect conduct which consists of the failure to act or to issue a decision in the due delay under law (e.g. Art. 5 and Art. 6 of the ECHR).

Moreover, the amendment to the Act of 2006 recognized the right to compensation for non-pecuniary injury (Sec. 31a).[7] This amendment was clearly aimed at resolving numerous cases where the Czech Republic was found, by the European Court of Human Rights, in violation of Article 6(1) of the ECHR (right to decision in reasonable delays).[8]

3.1.5 What Is the Correlation Between the Different Remedies for the Violations of Human Rights in Your Jurisdiction? Does One Remedy Exclude the Other?

With the exception of the constitutional complaint to the Constitutional Court, the Czech legal order does not know remedies specifically designed for the violations of human rights. Moreover, the Constitutional Court is only competent to declare violation of human rights guaranteed under constitutional and/or the international human rights treaties, and to quash individual decisions, including judgments of other courts, or even a law or a single provision of law. The Constitutional Court does not have the power to award damages for violations of human rights. Therefore,

[7] Act No. 160/2006 Coll.

[8] See e.g. *Hartman c. République tchèque*, arrêt du 10 juillet 2003, p. 12, § 66.

a claim for compensation under Act No. 82/1998 does not exclude a constitutional complaint and vice versa.

The main general principle is that a claim to compensation may be made only when an unlawful decision has been quashed or altered by a competent authority. The decision of the competent authority is thus binding upon the court deciding upon compensation (Sec. 8(1)). If the damage is caused by an unlawful decision enforceable (liable to execution) regardless of whether it is final and binding the claim for compensation may be made/submitted even if the decision in question has been quashed or altered by way of application of the ordinary legal remedy (Sec. 8(2)).

To be eligible for compensation, the applicant (a person who has suffered damage or injury) must exhaust all the legal remedies available under the Czech legal order, in procedural terms set by law. This condition may be waived by the court in exceptional cases (Sec. 8(3)). The exhaustion of all the legal remedies, including judicial remedies, is also a precondition for constitutional complaints. In some cases, violations of human rights may entail criminal law sanctions. However, criminal proceedings are not considered as remedies able to exclude or precede compensation which is of a civil law nature.

3.1.6 Doctrines Used to Support a Claim for Financial Compensation

It is not clear what doctrines can best support a claim for financial compensation. Mostly, claims under Act No. 82/1998 are considered as civil rights and obligations, i.e. individuals assert their civil rights before the civil courts.

It is worth mentioning, however, that the Czech Constitutional Court concluded that a civil court had to apply directly the provision of Article 36, para. 3, of the Charter of Fundamental Rights and Freedoms and not to limit the applicable law only to (then in force) Act No. 58/1969, on the liability for damage caused by the decisions of State authority. The competent court was obliged to do so, given the fact that the right to compensation had been guaranteed by the Charter but it could not be adjudicated under the Act.[9] This makes a plausible argument that the right to compensation is a right of constitutional nature, arising from constitutional and international catalogues of human rights.

[9] Decision of the Constitutional Court No. 128/1999, Collection of decisions of CC, vol. 15.

3.2 Scope of Liability Regime

3.2.1 What Types of Infringed Rights Are Covered by the Liability Rules?

Since Act No. 82/1998 provides rather general rules on liability for damage caused in the exercise of public power, there is no limitative list of rights, the violation of which gives rise to the liability of the Czech Republic. The key concept under this Act is unlawful decision (issued in civil, administrative or criminal procedure) or incorrect official conduct. It appears that the liability mostly covers the rights to judicial remedy and to a fair trial, and as the condition of the claim, the issue could be quashed or altered as unlawful. The general liability scheme also protects, indirectly, other individual rights (whether qualified as human rights or not), affected by judicial or administrative decisions which were eventually found unlawful. This makes the scope of application of the Act relatively broad.

The exercise of public power under the Act is interpreted broadly. It also includes public documents and legal deeds of a notary[10] and deeds of a notary as "judicial commissioner",[11] as well as deeds and acts of a judicial bailiff acting under the authorization of a court according to a special law.[12]

Moreover, certain violations of human rights are expressly included in Act No. 82/1998, namely violations of the right to liberty (Sec. 6a) and cases of detention, penalties or other protective measures (Sec. 9). Interestingly, Section 31a (introduced by an amendment, Act No. 160/2006) provides for compensation for non-pecuniary injury, aiming thus mostly at incorrect official conduct in a form of undue delays in proceedings (Sec. 13).

3.2.2 Compensation for Historical Injustices

In view of the statutory limitations set forth in Sections 32 to 35, Act No. 82/1998 does not provide adequate legal rules on the compensation for historical injustices. Instead, several special acts have been adopted relating to restitution and/or compensation for certain losses and injuries suffered by Czechoslovak and Czech citizens during the periods of the Nazi occupation (1938–1945)[13] and the communist regime (1948–1989).[14] The most important *lex specialis* was Act No. 87/1991 on

[10] See Sec. 2 and 62 ff., Act No. 358/1992 Coll., on Notaries and their acts.

[11] See Sec. 38 of the Civil Procedure Code.

[12] Act No. 120/2001 Coll., on Judicial bailiffs and enforcement acts.

[13] Act No. 212/2000 Coll., on Mitigation of Certain Property Injuries caused by Holocaust and on Amendment of other acts.

[14] Cf. Act No. 403/1990 Coll., Act No. 87/1991 Coll., Act No. 229/1991 Coll.

Extra-judicial Rehabilitations which addressed the largest scope of historical injustices. However, no new claims may be submitted under these special acts.

The only new piece of legislation in force is the Act on Settlement of Claims of Churches and Religious Associations.[15] This act aims at mitigating certain injuries from the period of 1948–1989 and at reaching settlements of property relations between the State and churches and religious associations. The Act envisages both restitution in kind and financial compensation. The financial compensation is separate from restitution. The Act sets forth the precise amount for each of the 17 recognised churches and religious societies in the Czech Republic to be paid in 30 annual instalments.

3.2.3 Other Issues of Compensation

Although there is no special rule on gross and systematic violations, they are not expressly excluded from the general compensation legislation. One can assume that such gross and systematic violations would also give rise to compensation. However, due to the lack of specially tailored rules, victims of such violations have to follow the same rules and procedures which are set for cases of individual violations.

In addition to special laws designed to remedy, at least partially, certain historical injustices, the Czech legal order also includes a few special compensation rules. The first example is in the Act on Crisis Management; its Section 36 deals with damage occurred to natural and juridical people in a causal nexus to the crisis measures and training exercised under this act.[16] Another special rule provides for the liability of the State for damage caused to a soldier under the Act on Professional Soldiers.[17]

3.3 State Liability Regime in Detail

3.3.1 The Foundation of Claims for Damages (Grounds and Premises of Liability)

Act No. 82/1998 Coll. establishes a regime of objective responsibility (strict liability) which is not based on fault. It however presupposes a certain wrong committed by the State or a territorial self-governing entity, consisting either in issuing an unlawful decision, or in adopting an incorrect official conduct; or a certain deficiency implied in the decision on detention, punishment or protective measures. The regime of the civil compensation for harm done to the natural rights of individuals

[15] Act No. 428/2012 Coll. (o majetkovém vyrovnání s církvemi a náboženskými společnostmi).

[16] Act No. 240/2000 Coll., on Crisis management and amendment to some laws (Crisis Act).

[17] Act No. 221/1999 Coll., on Professional soldiers.

established under the (New) Civil Code, is, on the contrary, based on the concept of delictual responsibility, i.e. responsibility for the violation of the legal rules or of good manners.

Act No. 82/1998 Coll. solely foresees compensatory remedies for violations of human rights or, more specifically, for damage caused in the exercise of public power by decision or by incorrect official conduct. Non-compensatory remedies have not so far been used in the Czech Republic. The adoption of Section 2957 of the (New) Civil Code, dealing with the compensation for harms done to natural rights of individuals, might be the first step towards introducing such remedies into the Czech legal order. This Section might also have some impact on the interpretation and application of Act No. 82/1998 Coll., yet due to the recent entry into force of the (New) Civil Code, its extent is difficult to predict.

Compensation provided under Act No. 82/1998 Coll. is a compensation for "damages", the occurrence of damage is therefore a prerequisite for an individual to be able to make claims under the Act. The regime of the civil compensation for harm done to the natural rights of individuals established under the (New) Civil Code also presupposes the existence of harm.

Act No. 82/1998 Coll. requires causality (causal nexus) between the unlawful decision or the incorrect official conduct on one hand and the damage on the other hand. The decision or the conduct need to be a substantial, albeit not necessarily the only, cause of the damage. In other words, it is necessary to prove that the damage would not have been brought about without the decision or the conduct; causality may not be conflated with temporal correlation.[18] Proving the causal link is often difficult in practice, especially in complex cases which have both a private and public law component.[19] The burden of proof is, in principle, on the plaintiff. An exception to this rule exists with respect to non-material (non-pecuniary) damage consisting in the state of uncertainty, which results from excessive length of judicial proceedings. In this case, there is a presumption in favour of the existence of the damage and it is up to the wrongdoer to rebut this presumption. If, however, the plaintiff invoked other damages in addition to the non-material state of uncertainty, standard rules on the burden of proof would apply.

3.3.2 The Nature of Damage

Originally, Act No. 82/1998 Coll. applied only to material (pecuniary) damage caused in the exercise of public power by decision or incorrect official conduct. By an amendment of 2006,[20] a new provision was added to Section 1 of the Act stating

[18] The Decision of the Supreme Court of Czechoslovakia, No. 1 Cz 86/90, 30 November 1990.

[19] See the decisions of the Supreme Court of the Czech Republic No. 25 Cdo 1802/2002, 23 October 2003; No. 25 Cdo 1421/2004, 24 November 2004; No. 25 Cdo 1395/2004, 25 November; and the decision of the District Court in Svitavy, No. 9 C 583/98, 9 November 1998.

[20] Act No. 160/2006 Coll., *amending the Act No. 82/1998 Coll., and several other acts.*

that the State and territorial self-governing entities shall under the conditions stated in the Act compensate also non-material (non-pecuniary) damage (para. 3). Compensation for non-material (non-pecuniary) damages is further specified in Section 31a of the Act, which was also added by the amendment of 2006.

This provision stipulates that adequate compensation for non-material (non-pecuniary) damages for unlawful decision or incorrect official conduct shall be provided regardless of whether the decision or the conduct had also resulted in material (pecuniary) damage. This is important in cases relating to the excessive length of judicial proceedings which haunt the Czech Republic.[21] In such cases, no material damage usually arises but the failure to decide in an appropriate term may in itself be qualified, and has repeatedly been qualified, by the European Court of Human Rights, as a violation of the right to free trial protected under Article 6 of the European Convention on Human Rights.[22] The drafting report of Act No. 160/2006 Coll. confirms that the inclusion of the provisions on non-material (non-pecuniary) damage into Act No. 82/1998 Coll. was primarily motivated by the need to react to the judgments of the European Court in this area.[23]

Act No. 82/1998 Coll. fails to define the concept of non-material (non-pecuniary) damage. This concept, however, was known to the Czech legal order even before the adoption of Act No. 160/2006 Coll. Section 43 of the Code of Criminal Procedure (Act No. 141/1961 Coll.), setting forth rights and claims of people injured by criminal offences, granted injured people the right to claim compensation for "moral and other damage" (para. 1) resulting from criminal offences. It is considered that such damage may result, for instance, from criminal offences against human dignity or against civic cohabitation. Moral or other damage may also be made part of other damages, for instance damages to health implying pain and the decrease of the social use[24]; or it may follow from violations of human rights, typically the right to a fair trial (see above). The concept of non-material (non-pecuniary) damage is also present in the (New) Civil Code[25] where it applies to instances of delictual responsibility (Section 2894 para. 2). These instances include the obligation to provide civil compensation for harms done to natural rights of individuals under Section 2956 of the (New) Civil Code. Such compensation shall cover both material damage and non-material harm, the latter including mental hardship.[26] In practice, most cases involving compensation for non-material (non-pecuniary) damage relate to the excessive length of judicial proceedings and to the unlawful deprivation of liberty.

Material (pecuniary) damage is not defined in Act No. 82/1998 Coll. either. The doctrine defines it as "Harm which has occurred in the material sphere of the injured

[21] See Kmec (2006, 12 ff).

[22] See e.g. *Hartman v. the Czech Republic*, judgment, 10 July 2003, p. 12, § 66.

[23] Parlament České republiky, *Vládní návrh 1117 – Důvodová zpráva*, 2005.

[24] In the Decision No. 30 Cdo 1436/2013, of 4 September 2013, the Supreme Court of the Czech Republic stipulated that anxious depressive mental states resulting from excessive length of judicial proceedings could be qualified either as a damage to health (mental illness) or as a non-material damage (intensive mental troubles).

[25] Act No. 89/2012 Coll., *Civil Code*.

[26] See Švestka et al. (2014, 1100–1102).

person and which can be expressed by a general equivalent (money)."[27] The Civil Code, which is applicable to the relations stemming from Act No. 82/1998 Coll. as a subsidiary source, specifies that "Compensation shall cover both real damage and what the injured person has lost (lost profit/*lucrum cessans*)."[28] This provision applies both to the compensation provided under Act No. 82/1998 Coll. and to the civil compensation for harm done to the natural rights of individuals. Act No. 82/1998 Coll. adds that the compensation provided in its framework may also cover the subsistence of individuals dependent on a person who has died as a result of an exercise of public power by the State or territorial self-governing entities, as well as the expenses related to the medical treatment and the funeral or such a person (Section 27); and the judicial costs effectively used in the case (Section 31).

3.3.3 Scope of Damages (Compensation)

The content and extent of the compensation under Act No. 82/1998 Coll. are partly regulated by the Act itself and partly by the (New) Civil Code. The Code also applies to the compensation for harms done to the natural rights of individuals. Compensation for material (pecuniary) damages under Act No. 82/1998 Coll. shall include real damage, as well as lost profit, expenses related to the death of a breadwinner (subsistence of dependent people, costs of the medial treatment, costs of the funeral) and, if appropriate, judicial costs including the costs of the representation. Non-pecuniary damage shall be compensated "Taking into account the gravity of the harm and the circumstances in which it occurred." (Section 31a(2) of the Act). In case of non-pecuniary damage caused by the excessive length of judicial proceedings, the following factors shall be taken into account: the overall length of the proceeding, the complexity of the proceeding, the behaviour of the plaintiff (including his/her contribution to the delays and the use of adequate means of dealing with such delays), the conduct of the public organ during the proceedings, and the importance of the object of the proceedings for the plaintiff (Section 31a(3) of the Act).

With respect to material damage, Act No. 82/1998 Coll. expressly foresees only financial compensation. The (New) Civil Code, applicable in a subsidiary way, stipulates however that "damage shall be compensated by restitution," (Section 2951) and only when restitution is not possible and when the injured requires it, damage shall be compensated financially. This provision could be of some relevance for the compensation provided under Act No. 82/1998 Coll., although in most cases, restitution will be difficult to imagine.

Section 2956 also applies to the civil compensation for harm done to the natural rights of individuals. Non-material damage shall – both under the Act and under the (New) Civil Code – be compensated financially, unless there is another means of redressing the damage, including the mere recognition of the violation of law. There

[27] See Jehlička et al. (2004, 580).

[28] Section 442 para. 1 of the *(Old) Civil Code* and Section 2952 of the *(New) Civil Code.*

is no limitation on damages foreseen by the Act; nor is there any limitation imposed on the number of claims. Claims under Act No. 82/1998 Coll. may pass on legal successors, unless they are of a personal nature. This is, for instance, the case of damages to health or of non-pecuniary damage caused by excessive length of judicial proceedings, which do not survive the death of the victim.[29]

3.3.4 Are Punitive or Exemplary Damages Allowed?

The concept of punitive/exemplary damages has not traditionally been part of the Czech legal order. Nonetheless, over the past years, voices in support of introducing this institution into the Czech law have grown in strength, especially in the legal doctrine.[30] The original draft of the (New) Civil Code, presented in 2007, aimed at introducing certain institutions similar to the punitive/exemplary damages. Section 2644 of the Draft stipulated that, "In addition to the compensation that the wrongdoer is otherwise obliged to provide, the damage gives rise to adequate increase of this compensation, if the harm has been caused intentionally (…)." A similar provision was included in Section 2657 of the Draft dealing with the compensation for material damage. This regulation would have applied to classical civil liability arising among private actors, not in the relationship between individuals and State organs covered by Act No. 82/1998 Coll. Yet, since the Civil Code is applicable to the relationships stemming from the Act in a subsidiary way, its wording could have some impact upon the interpretation and application of the Act.

In the course of the drafting of the Civil Code, the text of the two draft provisions was altered quite substantively doing away with references to increased compensation. A similar reference was nonetheless included in Section 2957 of the (New) Civil Code dealing with the compensation for harm done to the natural rights of individuals. This Section stipulates: "The means and extent of the adequate compensation shall be determined in the manner to redress circumstances deserving special consideration. Such circumstances include the intention in causing harm (…)."[31]

Due to the subsidiary application of the Civil Code, this provision could be of relevance not only for compensation awarded in civil proceedings but also to that awarded for violations of human rights under Act No. 82/1998 Coll. Since, however, the (New) Civil Code entered into force only very recently, on 1st January 2014, it is difficult to predict whether and to what extent the latter possibility will materialize.

[29] See Decision of the Supreme Court of the Czech Republic, No. 30 Cdo 3394/2010, 26 January 2011.

[30] See, for instance, Kuhn (2007), http://jinepravo.blogspot.com, 23 October 2007. Accessed 3 Dec 2013; Vlasák (2010), https://www.law.muni.cz/sborniky/cofola2010/files/sankce/Vlasak_Michal.pdf. Accessed 1 March 2015; Janeček (2013, 989–1012).

[31] See Švestka et al. (2014, 1103–1104).

3.3.5 Defences

Contributory conduct can be taken into account in the application of Law No. 82/1998 Coll. One instance is explicitly foreseen under Section 12 of the Act, which relates to the damages for the decision about detention, punishment or protective measures. Individuals having brought about detention, punishment or protective measures on themselves lose the right to claim damage (the Act speaks about individuals being "at fault" with regard to detention, punishment or protective measure – (Section 12 par. 1(a)). Moreover, general rules of the Civil Code, which finds subsidiary application in this context, stipulate that contributory conduct, unless it is of inconsiderable importance, shall be taken into account by the organ determining compensation, resulting in the proportional decrease of this compensation.[32] This regulation of the Civil Code also applies to the civil compensation for harm done to the natural rights of individuals.

Under Law No. 82/1998 Coll., all claimants are required to "Exhaust all the legal remedies available under the Czech legal order, in procedural terms set by law" (Section 8 para. 3). The relevant legal remedies include regular remedies, extraordinary remedies with the exception of renewal of proceedings, and other procedural remedies foreseen by law. The requirement of the exhaustion of legal remedies may be waved in exceptional cases, which are not further specified in the Act.

The rationale for the inclusion of the requirement of the exhaustion of local remedies is twofold. First, compensation for damages caused by a decision issued in the exercise of public power may be claimed only, if the relevant decision is first found unlawful and quashed or altered by a competent organ. This is usually the result of a proceedings initiated by the claimant him/herself. Secondly, the proceedings under Act No. 82/1998 Coll. are considered as subsidiary to those available under other, more general legal acts, such as the Civil Code. Courts have repeatedly confirmed that an unlawful decision gives rise to the right to compensation for damage under Act No. 82/1998 Coll., only on the condition that the damage cannot be remedied otherwise. No exhaustion of legal remedies is, on the contrary, required in the regime of the civil compensation for harm done to the natural rights of individuals established under the (New) Civil Code.

There are no exclusions of liability under either Law No. 82/1998 Coll. or the (New) Civil Code and no immunities applicable in this respect.

3.3.6 Who to Sue and Who May Sue

Under Act 82/1998 Coll., the State (the Czech Republic) and territorial self-governing entities may incur liability for the infringement of human rights. In addition, it is possible to claim compensation from legal entities which are entrusted

[32] See Section 441 of the *(Old) Civil Code* and Section 2918 of the *(New) Civil Code.*

with the exercise of some elements of the public power.[33] Other entities, including non-state actors and individual public officials/agents, cannot be sued under the Act. It is nonetheless possible for individuals or legal entities to claim compensation for damage from such actors either in civil law proceedings (tort law) or as a part of criminal law proceeding (so called adhesive procedure). Although damages awarded in such proceedings would not strictly speaking qualify as "damages for infringement of human rights" due to the prevailing vertical conception of human rights as rights owed by the State, they might contribute to the elimination of the negative consequences caused by violations of human rights committed by the State.

At the same time, the State or territorial self-governing entities having provided compensation under Act No. 82/1998 Coll. may subsequently claim this compensation from public organs or individual officials which/who caused the damage (regressive compensation, Sections 16–18 and 23–25 of the Act). The right to claim damages under Act 82/1998 Coll., falls on all individuals regardless of their nationality. Thus, Czech citizens and non-citizens (aliens, stateless persons etc.) have the same legal status in this respect.

The regime of the civil compensation for harm done to the natural rights of individuals established under the (New) Civil Code is a classical civil law mechanism. As such, it is open to all individuals, regardless of their nationality, who may sue other individuals responsible for the violation of their natural rights.

3.3.7 Courts and Other Competent Bodies and Procedures

Claims for compensation for damage under Act No. 82/1998 Coll. are considered by the ministries and by other central executive organs (Section 6). The competent organ is determined by the type of the decision or conduct having caused the damage. For instance, claims relating to civil law and criminal law proceedings fall within the competence of the Ministry of Justice. This Ministry is also competent for claims against decisions and conduct of territorial self-governing units. The organ shall decide upon the claim within 6 month after its submission. If it awards compensation, this compensation shall also be paid in full within this 6-month period. If on the contrary no decision is made, or full compensation is not provided within 6 months, the plaintiff may claim compensation in a court.[34]

Only the individuals directly concerned may submit the claim. The Czech legal order does not know the institution of group actions, ie. "actions submitted in the interest of a larger group of persons with identical or similar claims who however are not participants to the proceedings although they may benefit from them."[35] Neither does the Czech law know *actio popularis*.

---

[33] Decision by the Municipal Court in Prague, No. 51 Co 304/2003, 7 November 2003 (relating to the liability of the Czech Pharmaceutic Chamber).

[34] See Section 244 of the *Code of Civil Procedure* (Act No. 99/1963 Coll.).

[35] See Winterová (2008, 22).

Claims for compensation under Act No. 82/1998 Coll. are subject to statutory limitations of 3 years from the day on which the injured person becomes aware of the damage and the identity of the responsible actor or from the day of the annulation of the unlawful decision (subjective term) and of 10 years from the day on which the unlawful decision was delivered to the injured person (objective term). Damages to health are excluded from the objective term of the statutes of limitations. Claims for non-pecuniary damages are subject to statutory limitations of 6 months (subjective term) and 10 years (objective term). Claims for compensation for damages caused by the decision on detention, punishment or protective measures are subject to statutory limitations of 2 years since the entry into force of the new decision (objective term). Claims for regressive compensation are subject to statutory limitations of 1 year since the provision of the compensation.

3.4 The Interplay Between Principles of National and International Human Rights Law (Concerning Compensation)

The Czech Republic is party to most of the international and European conventions on human rights. For the purpose of this concise report, we will focus on the major human rights instruments binding on the Czech Republic, i.e. the European Convention on Human Rights (1950),[36] as amended by Protocols, and the International Covenant on Civil and Political Rights (1966).[37]

According to Article 10 of the Constitution, as amended in 2001, "The promulgated international treaties, which ratification was approved by the Parliament, and binding on the Czech Republic shall be part of the legal order; if an international treaty lays down otherwise than a law, the international treaty shall be applied." This is the most important constitutional change since the adoption of the Constitution of the Czech Republic. It means a shift from the predominantly dualistic system to the predominantly monistic system. The meaning of the rule is the incorporation of international treaties included also the treaties ratified in the past, with approval expressed by any past Czech or Czechoslovak parliament. Therefore all major human rights treaties, including those ratified before 2001, have been incorporated into the Czech legal order.

Both the European Convention and the Covenant include some provisions dealing with financial compensation. It is important to distinguish between two kinds of provisions on compensation.

On the one hand, both international instruments include compensation (or another effective remedy) as a matter of substantive human rights obligations, such as Article 5, para. 5, and Article 13 of the European Convention, and Article 2, para. 3,

[36] Promulgated under No. 209 /1992 Coll.

[37] Promlugated under No. 120/1976 Coll.

and Article 9, para. 5, of the Covenant. Financial compensation under Act No. 82/1998 is an internal legal remedy, able to ensure compliance with the respective obligations under human rights treaties.

On the other hand, certain provisions of human rights treaties provide for financial compensation as a possible consequence of the violation of one or more rights under the respective treaty catalogue. The only express rule to this effect is in Article 41 (Just satisfaction) of the European Convention: "If the Court finds that there has been a violation of the Convention or the protocols thereto, and if the internal law of the High Contracting Party concerned allows only partial reparation to be made, the Court shall, if necessary, afford just satisfaction to the injured party."

The International Covenant does not include the same rule. Instead, its Article 2, para. 3, only requires that in addition to effective protection of Covenant rights, States Parties must ensure that individuals also have accessible and effective remedies to vindicate these rights. However, the UN Human Rights Committee (HRC) adopted the General Comment No. 31 (2004) with the authoritative interpretation of the nature of the general legal obligation under the Covenant. According to this interpretation, Article 2, para. 3, requires that State parties make reparation to individuals whose Covenant rights have been violated. "In addition to the explicit reparation required by articles 9, paragraph 5, and 14, paragraph 6, the Committee considers that the Covenant generally entails appropriate compensation."[38]

In spite of the different legal force of the judgment of the ECtHR and the conclusions of the HRC, such compensation has certain typical features. It is contingent on the declaratory decision on violation of human rights by the competent international body. Therefore, it is independent and different from a possible compensation under Czech law.

However, there is an interesting interplay between the compensation under Act No. 82/1998 and the compensation awarded by the ECtHR in case of moral (non-pecuniary) harm. Section 31a of the Act, introduced by the 2006 amendment,[39] was adopted in reaction to frequent cases of violation of Article 6 para. 1, namely the requirement "Fair and equitable hearing within a reasonable time." The ECtHR found the Czech Republic in violation of Article 6, as courts failed to comply with reasonable delays, and declared the lack of an effective national remedy.[40]

This situation has changed thanks to the new Sec. 31a, in particular para. 3, providing criteria on adequate satisfaction. The court has to take into account particular circumstances of the case, such as the entire length of the procedure, the complex nature of the procedure, contribution of the victim to the delays, conduct of public authorities and the importance of an object of procedure for the victim. The criteria included in Act 82/1998 mirror the criteria applied by the ECtHR. Therefore the ECtHR reviewed its case-law and declared that the new Czech national remedy was effective.[41]

[38] General Comment No. 31 [80]: The Nature of the General Legal Obligation Imposed on States Parties to the Covenant. CCPR/C/21/Rev.1/Add.13 (2004), para. 16.

[39] Act No. 160/2006 Coll.

[40] See e.g. *Hartman c. République tchèque*, arrêt du 10 juillet 2003, p. 12, § 66.

[41] See Vokurka v. Czech Republic, decision of 16 October 2007.

This turnover has two important implications. First, as an effective remedy the claim under Act No. 82/1998 has become one of domestic remedies that must be exhausted according to conditions of admissibility (Article 35 para. 1 of the European Convention). Secondly, in practice, the ECtHR ceased awarding just satisfaction for the excessive length of procedure before Czech courts. Although sums awarded by competent Czech authorities (Ministry of Justice or civil courts) need not amount to the same sums as the just satisfaction by the ECtHR, the payment at the national level excludes, in principle, a success of such applications to the Court. The ECtHR also noted that national authorities paid compensation faster than it would be done by the Court under Article 41.[42]

The ECtHR takes into account compensation awarded by national court or other competent body (e.g. Ministry of Justice) and *vice versa*. The compensation may be reduced or excluded if the sum already awarded was considered as sufficient. However, the conditions for "just satisfaction" under Article 41 of the ECHR differ from those for compensation under Act No. 82/1998, therefore the claimant may seek compensation in the domestic system if the domestic decision is ultimately declared unlawful. The greatest influence on the development of the compensation system under Act No. 82/1998 was provided by the case law of the European Court of Human Rights. This led to the 2006 amendment to Act No. 82/1998. The underlying policy considerations sought to minimize the number of violation judgments and awards of just satisfaction under Article 41 of the ECHR.

3.5 Conclusions

The regime of liability for the violations of human rights is an important additional means of strengthening the protection of human rights. Despite the incorporation of human rights treaties into the internal legal order and the acceptance of jurisdiction of international control bodies, in particular the European Court of Human Rights, Czech law did not establish a special regime of liability focused on compensation of human rights violations. Nevertheless, Czech law allows for compensation of both material and non-material harm caused by the infringement of human rights. The legal regulation stems from the domestic legal tradition but it also responds to challenges arising from international law of human rights. The regime of compensation is based on civil liability. Its sources include mainly the Act on Liability for Damage Caused in the Exercise of Public Power by Decision or Incorrect Official Conduct (Act No. 82/1998), as a *lex specialis*, and the (new) Civil Code (Act No. 89/2012), as a *lex generalis*.

[42] See Bako v. Slovak Republic, judgment of 15 March 2005.

References

Janeček, Václav. 2013. Sankční náhrada škody. *Právník* 152(10): 989–1012.

Jehlička, Oldřich, Jiří Švestka, and Marta Škárová. 1999. *Občanský zákoník komentář* [Civil code commentary], 5th ed. Praha: C.H. Beck.

Jehlička, Oldřich, Jiří Švestka, Marta Škárová, et al. 2004. *Občanský zákoník, komentář*. Praha: C. H. Beck.

Kmec, Jiří. 2006. K výši zadostiučinění za nemajetkovou újmu způsobenou nepřiměřenou délkou řízení. *Právní zpravodaj* 8: 12–16.

Kühn, Zdeněk. 2007. Má mít náhrada škody v soukromém právu sankční funkci? http://www.jinepravo.blogspot.com/2007/10/m-mt-nhrada-kody-v-soukromm-prvu-sankn.html. Accessed 3 Dec 2013.

Švestka, Jiří, Jan Dvořák, and Josef Fiala. 2014. *Občanský zákoník. Komentář* [new Civil Code. Commentary], vol. VI. Praha: Wolters Kluwer.

Vlasák, Michal. 2010. Vybrané otázky sankční náhrady škody. In *COFOLA 2010: The conference proceedings*, 1st ed. Brno: Masaryk University. https://www.law.muni.cz/sborniky/cofola2010/files/sankce/Vlasak_Michal.pdf. Accessed 1 Mar 2015.

Winterová,Alena. 2008. Hromadné žaloby (procesualistický pohled) [Group Actions. A view of procedural law]. *Bulletin advokacie* 10: 21–27.

Chapter 4
Compensation for Human Rights Violations in Estonia

Ene Andresen

4.1 Introduction

The right to compensation for damage is one of the mechanisms to ensure the effective protection of human rights. In Estonia, the human rights protection system has been laid down in the Constitution. Upon implementation of the constitution and laws the public authorities are bound to the generally recognised principles and rules of international law as well the international agreements ratified by Estonia, these being an inseparable part of the Estonian legal system. If the Estonian legislation proves to be in conflict with an international treaty ratified by the *Riigikogu*, provisions of the international treaty apply.[1] Accordingly, Estonian laws are interpreted in conformity with the provisions of international law that are binding for Estonia.

To achieve the objectives of the constitution and to fulfill the international obligations in human rights protection, inter alia, a body of laws for guaranteeing effective remedies to human rights abuses has been enacted in Estonia. The judicial protection against violations of human right relies first and foremost on the administrative courts.

[1] See § 3 (1) and § 123 of the Constitution. The English version of the Estonian Constitution is available at www.riigiteataja.ee/en/eli/530102013003. Accessed 1 Nov 2014.

E. Andresen (✉)
Faculty of Law, University of Tartu, Näituse 20, Tartu 50409, Estonia
e-mail: ene.andresen@ut.ee

E. Bagińska (ed.), *Damages for Violations of Human Rights*,
Ius Comparatum - Global Studies in Comparative Law 9,
DOI 10.1007/978-3-319-18950-5_4

4.2 Legal Framework

4.2.1 *Fundamental Right to Compensation for Damage Under Estonian Constitution*

The foundations of the Estonian state liability law have been laid down in the Constitution of the Republic of Estonia. In contrast to the pre-World War II Constitutions, the 1992 Constitution sets forth a fundamental right to the compensation for damage caused by an unlawful action. Pursuant to § 25 of the Constitution, everyone has a right for "moral" (non-pecuniary) and "material" (pecuniary) damage caused by the unlawful action of any person. This fundamental right is a specific fundamental right in several respects. Firstly, it guarantees a right to compensation for damage not only against a public authority but also against a private person. Secondly, although the right to compensation for damage is a substantive, not procedural right, it is subsidiary in nature, i.e., another fundamental right or other individual right must have been violated first in order to claim for compensation for damage. In the cases where there is no law governing the compensation for damage, or if the regulation has been declared unconstitutional, a person whose rights have been violated may claim for compensation for damage directly under the provisions of the Constitution. Paragraph 25 of the Constitution was directly applied for the first time by the Civil Law Chamber of the Supreme Court, which in a 1996 decision found that although the then existing laws did not provide for the compensation for non-pecuniary damage caused by bodily injury, it was to be compensated directly under § 25 of the Constitution.[2] Later, the direct applicability of § 25 of the Constitution has been confirmed by the Administrative Law Chamber of the Supreme Court,[3] as well by the Supreme Court *en banc*.[4] Upon the compensation for damage directly under § 25 of the Constitution, the Supreme Court has furthermore taken into account the general principles of compensation for damage, especially the gravity of violation and the part the injured person had in causing the damage.[5]

As the wording of § 25 of the Constitution implies, only a damage caused by an unlawful action is covered by this fundamental right. No general provision for the compensation for damage caused by a lawful action has been stipulated in the Estonian Constitution. However, pursuant to § 32 (1) of the Constitution, every

[2] Supreme Court [Supr.Ct.] Civil Law [Civ.] Chamber judgment of 12.12.1996, 3-2-1-111-96, www.nc.ee/?id=11&tekst=RK/3-2-1-111-96 (judgments are available in the Estonian language). Accessed 1 Nov 2014.

[3] Supr.Ct, Administrative Law [Adm.] Chamber judgment of 6.6.2002, 3-3-1-27-02, paras. 13–16, www.nc.ee/?id=11&tekst=RK/3-3-1-27-02. Accessed 1 Nov 2014.

[4] Supr.Ct, *en banc* judgment of 22.3.2011, 3-3-1-85-09, para. 105 – in English at www.riigikohus.ee/?id=1257. Accessed 1 Nov 2014. See also Supr.Ct. *en banc* judgment of 31.8.2011, 3-3-1-35-10, para. 62 – in English at www.riigikohus.ee/?id=1356. Accessed 1 Nov 2014.

[5] Supr.Ct. *en banc* judgment of 22.3.2011, 3-3-1-85-09, para. 131 (Note 4); Supr.Ct *en banc* judgment of 31.8.2011, 3-3-1-35-10, para. 62 (Note 4).

person is entitled to obtain a just and immediate compensation for the expropriation. The Estonian Supreme Court *en banc* has found that in order to guarantee the proportionate interference with the right of ownership (§ 32 of the Constitution) and equal treatment (§ 12 of the Constitution), the state is also obliged to pay just compensation in other cases, where the right of ownership has been restricted more than is justified by the duty to tolerate the interference with one's rights in public interests.[6] Though the Supreme Court has not yet taken a position regarding other fundamental rights, it can be assumed that besides an interference with the right of ownership a person has a constitutional right to claim for just compensation upon unequal interference with other fundamental rights.

4.2.2 State Liability Act as a General Public Law Source

In Estonia, damages for violations of human rights are governed by the general provisions of state liability law on compensation for damage. The liability for violations of person's rights caused by a public authority in a public law relationship is governed mainly by public law. As a general law, the compensation for damage caused by public authority is regulated by the State Liability Act (SLA).[7] The private law provisions are applied only complementarily, on condition that such an application is in conformity with the nature of public law relationship (§ 7 (4) of the SLA). The main source of private law provisions is the Law of Obligations Act (LOA).[8] Should a public authority or any other person cause damage to a person in a private law relationship, only the provisions of private law apply.[9]

A public authority against whom a claim can be filed under the State Liability Act includes the state, a local government, another legal person in public law or any other person performing public duties on a public law basis outside of relationships of subordination (§ 2 (1) of the SLA). The State Liability Act covers not only the

[6] The need to ensure the proportionality of the restriction of a fundamental right caused by a lawful act of a public authority through paying a fair compensation has arisen in court practice in connection with lawful arrest of a person (Supr.Ct. *en banc* judgment of 31.3.2011, 3-3-1-69-09 – in English at www.riigikohus.ee/?id=1261. Accessed 1 Nov 2014), exclusion from office in pre-trial criminal proceedings (Supr.Ct *en banc* judgment of 30.8.2011, 3-3-1-15-10 – in English at www.riigikohus.ee/?id=1357. Accessed 1 Nov 2014.), and in connection with the obligation to tolerate utility networks or utility works required in public interests (Supr.Ct. Constitutional Review Chamber judgment of 17.4.2012, 3-4-1-25-11 – in English at www.riigikohus.ee/?id=1353. Accessed 1 Nov 2014.).

[7] The State Liability Act entered into force on 1.1.2002. The English version of this Act is available at www.riigiteataja.ee/en/eli/515112013007. Accessed 1 Nov 2014.

[8] The English version of this Act is available at www.riigiteataja.ee/en/eli/516092014001. Accessed 1 Nov 2014.

[9] This has been emphasised also in § 1 (2) of the SLA: 'This Act does not regulate the restoration of rights or compensation for damage in private law relationships.' An illustrative list of circumstances of causing damage by a public authority which fall under the private law, is given in § 1 (3) of the SLA.

liability of the executive authority, but also provides for the bases for compensation for damage caused by the legislation of general application (§ 14 of the SLA) and for compensation for damage caused upon administration of justice (§ 15 of the SLA). However, compared to general provisions on compensation for damage (§§ 7–13 of the SLA), the liability of public authority caused by performing the legislative or judicial functions is much more limited.

The claim for compensation for damage is central but not the only state liability claim in the Estonian state liability law. Most of the other claims provided for in the State Liability Act are concerned with the liability of the administrative authority for unlawful acts and measures: the claim for repeal of administrative act (§ 3 SLA); the claim for termination of administrative measure (§ 4 SLA); the claim for refrainment from administrative act or measure (§ 5 SLA); the claim for issue of administrative act or taking of administrative measure (§ 6 SLA). The claim for compensation for damage, by contrast, with different prerequisites and to a different extent, can be filed both in cases of unlawful and lawful actions of an administrative authority (§§ 7–13 SLA and § 16 SLA respectively) as well in cases of unlawful activities of legislative and judicial authorities (§ 14 SLA and § 15 SLA respectively). A claim arising from unjust enrichment in public law relationships can be filed against any public authority, regardless of the character of its activities (§§ 22–24 SLA). Finally, the claim for elimination of unlawful consequences of the action of an administrative authority has been recognised, though in a contradictory manner, in practice. According to § 11 (1) SLA, the elimination of unlawful consequences serves as simply a variation of the claim for compensation for damage. Also the Administrative Law Chamber of the Supreme Court has argued in most of the cases that upon claiming for the elimination of unlawful consequences a person must have suffered damage.[10] However, since 2012, the Code of Administrative Court Procedure (CACP) recognises the elimination of unlawful consequences as an independent claim.[11]

Although the State Liability Act was supposed to be a general law regulating the compensation for damage caused by public authority in any public law relationship insofar as not otherwise regulated by specific law,[12] the Supreme Court has narrowed the scope of this Act. The Supreme Court *en banc* has come to somewhat surprising conclusion that the general provisions on compensation for damage in the State Liability Act (§§ 7–13 of the SLA) are applicable only if the damage was caused by an administrative authority.[13] More precisely, since the

[10] See, e.g. Administrative Law Chamber of the Supr.Ct. decision of 23.11.2010, 3-3-1-43-10, para. 33 – available in Estonian at www.nc.ee/?id=11&tekst=RK/3-3-1-43-10. Accessed 1 Nov 2014.

[11] See § 5 (1) 5) and § 37 (2) 5) of the Code of Administrative Court Procedure. The English version of this Act is available at www.riigiteataja.ee/en/eli/508072014005. Accessed 1 Nov 2014. About theoretical arguments and Estonian case law until 2005 see Andresen (2005) 168–179.

[12] See § 1 and § 2 (2) of the SLA.

[13] See Supr.Ct. *en banc* judgment of 31.8.2011, 3-3-1-35-10, para. 50 (Note 4). By contrast, some months earlier the Supreme Court *en banc* had held that, in principle, the general provisions on compensation for damage in the State Liability Act were applicable in cases where the damage was caused in pre-trial criminal proceedings. See the Supr.Ct. *en banc* judgment of 31.3.2011, 3-3-1-69-09, paras. 75 and 76 (Note 6) and Supr.Ct. *en banc* judgment of 22.3.2011, 3-3-1-85-09, paras. 110–118 (Note 4).

special law did not regulate the compensation for damage caused in pre-trial criminal proceedings exhaustively, the Supreme Court declared in a constitutional review proceedings that the lack of regulatory framework regarding the compensation for non-pecuniary damage caused in pre-trial criminal proceedings by exceeding reasonable time of proceedings[14] and regarding the compensation for pecuniary damage caused by lawful[15] or unlawful[16] exclusion from office in pre-trial criminal proceedings is in conflict with the Constitution. Although the interpretation given by the Supreme Court *en banc* did not follow the aim of the State Liability Act, the court sought to urge the legislator to enact detailed regulation in these areas of law. Currently, the new provisions are being prepared by the *Riigikogu* and presumably a new specific Act for the compensation for damage caused by the body conducting the misdemeanour or pre-trial criminal proceedings will be adopted.[17]

4.2.3 Specific Laws on State Liability

In addition to the State Liability Act, some specific law norms regulate the compensation for damage caused by public authority. So the compensation for damage caused by unjust deprivation of liberty is regulated by the Compensation for Damage Caused by State to Person by Unjust Deprivation of Liberty Act (CUDLA).[18] The cases for which compensation is prescribed under the CUDLA have been listed exhaustively in this Act.[19] For example, a person may request compensation under the CUDLA for being detained on suspicion of a criminal offence but released when the suspicion ceased to exist. However, the scope of application of this Act is not limited to criminal law but also comprises the cases where liberty has been deprived under the private or administrative law provisions. Compensation for damage under the CUDLA does not require the establishment of lawfulness or unlawfulness of the deprivation of liberty.[20] Pursuant to this Act, all people who have been unjustly deprived of liberty shall be paid an equal amount for compensation which is deemed to cover the non-pecuniary damage and the loss of profit. Yet, the amount of compensation for direct pecuniary damage shall be determined in accordance with

---

[14] Supr.Ct. *en banc* judgment of 22.3.2011, 3-3-1-85-09, para. 124 (Note 4).

[15] Supr.Ct. *en banc* judgment of 30.8.2011, 3-3-1-15-10, para. 64 (Note 6).

[16] Supr.Ct. *en banc* judgment of 31.8.2011, 3-3-1-35-10, para. 61 (Note 4).

[17] See about the legislative procedure of the draft Act on Compensation for Damage Caused in the Proceedings of Offences (Draft Act No. 635), www.riigikogu.ee/?op=ems&page=eelnou&eid=f4eb3b6d-fc0b-4cc7-9452-98dc0db0e448& (in Estonian). Accessed 1 Nov 2014.

[18] The English version of this Act is available at www.riigiteataja.ee/en/eli/530102013021. Accessed 1 Nov 2014.

[19] See § 1 (1) of the CUDLA (Note 18).

[20] Supr.Ct *en banc* judgment of 31.3.2011, 3-3-1-69-09, para. 70 (Note 6).

the provisions of the State Liability Act.[21] In order to receive compensation under the CUDLA, the actual damage or its extent need not to be proven. However, the question to which extent the compensation for damage would be just is not assessed either upon determination of compensation under the CUDLA. The Supreme Court *en banc* has noted that the regulation of the CUDLA which precludes compensation for loss of profit to the extent exceeding that prescribed in the CUDLA and therefore precludes compensation for loss of profit in a specific case to a fair extent may be in conflict with §§ 32, 12 and 11 of the Constitution.[22]

Further, a specific regulation on compensation for damage is provided for in the Civil Service Act (CSA).[23] Under this Act, an official who is unlawfully released from service may, inter alia, claim for compensation in the amount of 3 months' average salary of the official, as a rule.[24] The court may, however, amend the amount of compensation taking account of the circumstances of the termination of the service relationship and considering mutual interests.

As to the compensation for lawfully caused damage, the Immovables Expropriation Act provides for the compensation for damage caused upon the lawful expropriation.[25]

4.2.4 Compensation for Historical Injustices

In order to compensate for the injustice committed in Estonia in the 1940s and the 1950s, a law was adopted in 1988 which instructed the executive power to establish a procedure for the compensation for damage caused to the victims of extrajudicial mass repressions.[26] Based on this law, the regulation on "returning the property of and compensating damages to the victims of mass repressions" was adopted in

[21] See § 5 of the CUDLA (Note 18).

[22] Supr.Ct *en banc* judgment of 31.3.2011, 3-3-1-69-09, para. 87 (Note 6). The Supreme Court left this question open since it was not clear at that stage of the proceedings whether the compensation already payed to the person was just. Whereas the courts later found that the claimant had received a just compensation for damage, the claim was dismissed (Supr.Ct. Adm. Chamber judgment of 25.3.2013, 3-3-1-55-12, para. 21 – available in Estonian at www.nc.ee/?id=11&tekst =RK/3-3-1-55-12. Accessed 1 Nov 2014.

[23] The English version of this Act is available at www.riigiteataja.ee/en/eli/509072014003. Accessed 1 Nov 2014.

[24] See § 105 (1) of the CSA (Note 23). The exceptions from this rule, according to which an official may claim for compensation in the amount of 3 months' salary or without any limitations, are provided for in § 105 (2) and (3) of the CSA.

[25] The English version of this Act is available at www.riigiteataja.ee/en/eli/504112013002. Accessed 1 Nov 2014.

[26] The Supreme Soviet of the Estonian Soviet Socialist Republic (ESSR) Act On Extrajudicial Mass Repressions in Soviet Estonia in 1940s and 1950s of 7.12.1988, article 4.1. – ESSR Gazette 1988, 52, 754.

1989.[27] The regulation required that all people or heirs thereof who were unjustly repressed in Soviet Estonia in the 1940s and 1950s and later rehabilitated must have their previously owned property returned or, if returning it is not possible, receive a compensation of the value equal to the property.

In 1991, more extensive Principles of Ownership Reform Act entered into force, providing that all former owners of property which was unlawfully seized during the Soviet occupation have their property returned to them or be compensated for.[28] Property that was in the use of collective farms and other agricultural state organisations was returned or compensated for on the basis of the Agricultural Reform Act.[29]

The said legal acts provided for different principles of compensating for property that was unlawfully seized in the Soviet period. The execution of the ownership reform gave rise to many legal disputes. Many people against whom unlawful rulings had been made during the ownership reform filed claims for damages against the state and local governments. These claims were solved on the basis of general rules of state liability law.

4.2.5 *Compensation for Human Rights Violations Under Other Branches of Law*

Apart from the state liability law, a human rights violation can be compensated in money in other disciplines of law.

So a person to whom "physical, pecuniary or moral damage" has been directly caused by a criminal offence or by an unlawful act committed by a person not capable of guilt, may file a civil action whether, in the criminal proceedings pursuant to the Code of Criminal Procedure[30] or in an independent civil court procedure. In these cases, the claim for compensation for damage is based on private law provisions.

Another important specific law concerning the compensation for damage resulting from crimes is the Victim Support Act.[31] According to this Act, victims of crimes of

[27] ESSR Council of Ministers Regulation No 81 of 20.2.1989. – ESSR Supreme Council and Government Gazette 1989, 10, 118.

[28] Republic of Estonia Principles of Ownership Reform Act, adopted by the *Riigikogu* (parliament of Estonia) on 13.6.1991 – *Riigi Teataja* (State Gazette) 1991, 21, 257. The English version of this Act is available at www.riigiteataja.ee/en/eli/527012014004. Accessed 1 Nov 2014. The grounds for determining the value of the property being the object of the ownership reform and the extent and manner of compensation thereof were set forth in the Unlawfully Expropriated Property Valuation and Compensation Act of 19.5.1993. – *Riigi Teataja*, 1993, 30, 509. The English version of this Act is available at www.riigiteataja.ee/en/eli/522012014004. Accessed 1 Nov 2014.

[29] Agricultural Reform Act of 11.3.1992 – *Riigi Teataja*, 1992, 10, 143.

[30] See §§ 37–41 and § 274 (4) of the Code of Criminal Procedure. The English version of this Act is available at www.riigiteataja.ee/en/eli/522082014002. Accessed 1 Nov 2014.

[31] The English version of this Act is available at www.riigiteataja.ee/en/eli/517062014014. Accessed 1 Nov 2014.

violence and their dependants are entitled to a state compensation for the pecuniary damage suffered, including damage resulting from the inability to work, medical bills, damages to clothes and glasses, etc., damage to the dependants in case of the death of the victim, and the victim's funeral expenses. Further, the payment conditions of the compensation, its amount and limits of the compensation are specified by law. If necessary, persons entitled to victim support may also receive compensation for psychological therapy costs on the basis of the same Act.

4.3 Compensation for Damage Under the State Liability Act

4.3.1 Claims for Compensation for Damage in the State Liability Act

According to the State Liability Act, the composition of liability depends on three circumstances: firstly, which branch of the state power was exercised by the public authority which caused the damage; secondly, whether the damage was caused to an individual by an unlawful or lawful act or measure of the public authority; and thirdly, what type of damage the person is claiming for.

General provisions on compensation for damage in the State Liability Act include the liability for unlawful administrative activities. As to the claim for compensation of pecuniary damage caused unlawully by an administrative authority, the following prerequisites have to be fulfilled pursuant to § 7 (1) of the SLA:

1. unlawful administrative act or measure of the public authority in the public law relationship;
2. violation of a right of injured person;
3. occurrence of pecuniary damage on the side of individual;
4. causal link between the violation of a right and the damage sustained by injured person;
5. the exhaustion of obligatory primary legal remedies.[32]

As can be seen, the compensation for pecuniary damage is not based on fault in the Estonian state liability law.

As to the compensation for non-pecuniary damage caused unlawfully by an administrative authority, the same prerequisites apply. However, an additional prerequisite has been imposed in § 9 (1) of the SLA. The compensation for non-pecuniary damage is generally made conditional upon the existence of fault on the side of public authority. Thereby, the burden of proof rests on a public authority. As an exception, fault is not taken into consideration if the compensation for non-pecuniary damage is applied for on the basis of a decision of the European Court of Human Rights (ECtHR) establishing a violation of the European Convention on

[32] See, in detail, Chapter II, section 3.4.

Human Rights (ECHR) or any of its protocols by a public authority (§ 9 (3) of the SLA). Finally, according to § 9 (1) of the SLA, only the violation of certain rights gives rise to a claim for compensation of non-pecuniary damage.[33]

In comparison, grounds for compensation for damage lawfully caused by an administrative authority are much more limited. Pursuant to § 16 of the SLA, only a "fair compensation" for pecuniary damage can be claimed provided that an administrative act or measure extraordinarily restricts the fundamental rights or freedoms of the person.

A similar limited approach applies to the liability for damage caused by legislation of general application and for damage caused upon administration of justice. The compensation for damage caused by legislation of general application or by failure to issue legislation of general application may be claimed only if the damage was caused by a significant violation of the obligations of a public authority, the legal provision forming the basis for the violated obligation is directly applicable, and the person belongs to a group of people who have been specially injured due to the legislation of general application or by failure to issue legislation of general application (§ 16 (1) of the SLA). Damage caused upon administration of justice can be claimed only if a judge committed a criminal offence in the course of judicial proceedings (§ 15 (1) of the SLA).

Since the Supreme Court *en banc* has ruled that §§ 7 and 9 of the SLA are applicable only to claims for compensation for damage caused upon the exercise of administrative power, all other cases that are not covered by §§ 14–16 of the SLA or specific law, e.g., the damage caused in pre-trial criminal proceedings, need to be solved under § 25 of the Constitution. According to court practice, for granting the damages under § 25 of the Constitution, the following prerequisites must be met: the unlawful act of public authority in a public law relationship; violation of subjective (individual) right of a person; occurrence of pecuniary or non-pecuniary damage; causation.[34]

Since the claim for compensation of damage caused unlawully by an administrative authority has been most common in practice and many of its elements coincide with the ones of other compensatory claims, the main features of the compensation for human rights violations in Estonia will be outlined by this example.

4.3.2 *Aim of the Compensation for Damage*

The general purpose of the compensation for damage in case of violation of human rights or any other individual right of a person is the reparation of damage caused to this person.[35]

---

[33] See, in detail, Chapter II, section 3.1.

[34] Supr.Ct. *en banc* judgment of 22.3.2011, 3-3-1-85-09, para. 76 (Note 4).

[35] See, e.g. Supr.Ct. Adm. judgment of 15.3.2010, 3-3-1-93-09, para. 14 – in Estonian at www.nc.ee/?id=11&tekst=222523451. Accessed 1 Nov 2014.

In regard to the pecuniary damage caused unlawfully by a public authority, the State Liability Act provides for the principle of full compensation for damage. Pursuant to § 8 (1) of the SLA, with a compensation the financial situation must be created in which the injured party would be if his or her rights were not violated. The Administrative Law Chamber of the Supreme Court has emphasised in a recent judgment that such a purpose serves as one of the general principles of the compensation for damage caused unlawfully in a public law relationship.[36] Although § 8 (1) of the SLA is part of a paragraph which regulates the compensation of pecuniary damage, it does not appear from the case-law that the courts would follow upon awarding the non-pecuniary damages any other goal than that by the pecuniary damage. However, the fact that the extent of non-pecuniary damage can only be estimated but not objectively calculated, complicates the fulfillment of the full compensation principle.

On the other hand, it follows from the principle of full compensation for damage that damages may not lead to an unfounded enrichment, *i.e.*, to the situation where the injured person would be economically better off after compensation than without suffering the damage. Based on that principle, § 127 (5) of the LOA stipulates that any gain received by the injured person as a result of the damage caused has to be deducted from the compensation for the damage unless deduction is contrary to the purpose of the compensation. This private law provision is applied also in the state liability law.[37] So, for example, if the injured person suffers bodily injury or health damage, the pecuniary damage has to be compensated in full (§ 8 (2) of the SLA). At the same time, the compensation for loss of income due to incapacity for work cannot be claimed to the extent to which the injured party is entitled to pension for incapacity for work due to the damage caused (§ 8 (3) of the SLA).

The Administrative Law Chamber of the Supreme Court has not yet specified whether the principle of full compensation for damage is a sole purpose of the damages. For instance, the Civil Law Chamber of the Supreme Court has stated that the award for non-pecuniary damage serves a preventive function. This court has noted that an award for any non-pecuniary damage embodies a deterrent purpose while it reflects in addition to the compensatory purpose to a certain extent the condemnation of the society in regard to the unlawful act of the offender, and it furthermore offers to the injured party a relief for the injustice caused with the violation of his or her personality rights.[38] The Administrative Law Chamber of the

[36] Supr.Ct. Adm. judgment of 25.3.2013, 3-3-1-55-12, para. 21 (Note 22). However, in some cases the Administrative Law Chamber of the Supreme Court has mistakenly followed from § 127 (1) LOA. See, e.g. the Supr.Ct Adm. judgment of 8.3.2012, 3-3-1-85-11, para. 15 – in Estonian at www.nc.ee/?id=11&tekst=222543664. Accessed 1 Nov 2014.

[37] See, e.g. Supr.Ct. Adm. judgment of 8.3.2012, 3-3-1-85-11, para. 15 (Note 36) and Supr.Ct. Adm. judgment of 24.5.2010, 3-3-1-23-10, para. 16 –in Estonian at www.nc.ee/?id=11&tekst=RK/3-3-1-23-10. Accessed 1 Nov 2014.

[38] Supr.Ct. Civ. judgment of 26.6.2013, 3-2-1-18-13, para. 29 –in Estonian at www.nc.ee/?id=11&tekst=222561999. Accessed 1 Nov 2014. Since 31.12.2010, the preventive function of the award for non-pecuniary damage upon violations of personality rights is provided for also in the LOA (see § 134 (6) of this Act).

Supreme Court has not taken a clear position whether this opinion is to be also followed in the state liability law. Still, the Administrative Law Chamber of the Supreme Court has emphasised that, as a rule, the purpose of damages is not to punish the offender.[39] Therefore, in circumstances where the exact extent of the damage cannot be established, the court may not upon determination of the award take into account whether the public authority was acting in bad faith nor may the court give a fair assessment to the act of the public authority through maximising the amount of the award.[40]

4.3.3 The Characteristics of the Claim for Compensation for Damage

4.3.3.1 Protected Rights

One of the prerequisites of the claim for compensation for damage caused unlawfully by a public authority is that a public authority has violated peron's subjective (individual) right (§ 7 (1) of the SLA).

The Estonian legal order does not distinguish the treatment of claims stemming from violations of international norms and violations of domestic norms. Likewise, § 25 of the Estonian Constitution stipulating the fundamental right for damages does not limit the compensation for damage only to certain individual rights violations. Hence, a person is entitled to claim for compensation for damage upon violation of any individual right under the Estonian constitution, regardless of whether a public authority has violated the national law or has infringed a norm of international law incorporated into the Estonian legal system.

In contrast, the State Liability Act provides for differences depending on whether a person claims for pecuniary or non-pecuniary damage. As to the claim for the compensation of pecuniary damages, it is irrelevant what individual right has been violated. The compensation of non-pecuniary damage requires, however, the violation of one of the fundamental rights enumerated in § 9 (1) of the SLA. Into that exhaustive list belong the degradation of dignity, damage to health, deprivation of liberty, violation of the inviolability of home or private life or the confidentiality of messages or defamation of the honour or good name of the person.[41] This kind of closed list is not justified because it may result in unconstitutional interference with the fundamental right to damages. For example, § 9 (1) of the SLA does not allow compensation for non-pecuniary damage caused by unreasonably extended

[39] Supr.Ct. Adm. judgment of 8.3.2012, 3-3-1-85-11, para. 15 (Note 36).

[40] Supr.Ct. Adm judgment of 4.4.2006, 3-3-1-13-06, para. 23 – available in Estonian at www.nc.ee/?id=11&tekst=RK/3-3-1-13-06. Accessed 1 Nov 2014.

[41] Besides, only a natural person is entitled to claim for compensation of non-pecuniary damage under § 9 (1) of the SLA.

administrative proceedings.[42] Therefore, the decisive factor should be the intensity of the individual right's violation but not the individual right itself.

The claim for compensation of damage may include a number of legal offences as a set. It has been emphasised in court practice that the circumstances of each individual violation need to be taken into account along with the cumulative effects of legal offences upon the compensation for damage. The Supreme Court has pointed out, particularly with regard to the non-pecuniary damage, that it may occur in conjunction of multiple violations.[43]

4.3.3.2 Damage

The State Liability Act does not specify the nature of the damage but stipulates that both the direct pecuniary damage and the loss of profit, as well as non-pecuniary damage need to be reimbursed to the injured person. The definitions of different types of damages are provided for in § 128 of the LOA.

According to § 128 (3) of the LOA, the direct pecuniary damage includes, primarily, the value of the lost or destroyed property or the decrease in the value of property due to deterioration even if such decrease occurs in the future, and reasonable expenses which have been incurred or will be incurred in the future due to the damage, including reasonable expenses relating to the prevention or reduction of damage and receipt of compensation, including expenses relating to establishment of the damage and submission of claims relating to compensation for the damage.

The loss of profit is loss of the gain which a person would have been likely to receive in the circumstances, in particular as a result of the preparations made by the person, if the circumstances on which compensation for damage is based would not have occurred. Loss of profit may also include the loss of an opportunity to receive gain (§ 128 (4) of the LOA).

The non-pecuniary damage involves primarily the physical and emotional distress and suffering caused to the injured person (§ 128 (5) of the LOA). Psychological damages, for example, can include humiliation, insult, fear, indignation, worry, grief, stress, or anxiety.[44] Any physical or emotional distress that was brought upon the person needs to be related to the fault-based violation of person's subjective (individual) right provided for in § 9 (1) of the SLA.

---

[42] The Supreme Court *en banc* has declared the State Liability Act to be in conflict with the Constitution in the part which does not prescribe compensation for non-pecuniary damage caused by unreasonably extended pre-trial criminal proceedings. See the Supreme Court *en banc* judgment of 22.3.2011, 3-3-1-85-09 (Note 4). In that case, § 9 (1) of the SLA was declared to be not applicable because the damage was not caused by an unlawful administrative act or administrative measure.

[43] Supr.Ct. Adm. judgment of 10.10.2013, 3-3-1-38-13, paras. 22–23 – in Estonian at www.nc.ee/?id=11&tekst=RK/3-3-1-38-13. Accessed 1 Nov 2014.

[44] See Supr.Ct. Adm. judgment of 6.6.2002, 3-3-1-27-02, para. 14 (Note 2); Supr.Ct. Adm. judgment of 14.12.2006, 3-3-1-56-06, para. 7 – in Estonian at www.nc.ee/?id=11&tekst=RK/3-3-1-56-06. Accessed 1 Nov 2014.

In general, the person who has filed the claim for compensation of damage must prove the occurrence of damage.[45] The requirements for proving the damage depend on both the type of the damage as well as circumstances of the violation of law. As for the type of the damage, in cases of pecuniary damage, the injured person usually needs to prove both the occurrence of the damage as well as its extent, then in cases of non-pecuniary damage there is no way for the injured person to prove the extent of the damage.[46] Still, when filing a claim for non-pecuniary damage the injured person must prove which one of the rights provided in § 9 (1) of the SLA has been violated and to substantiate the non-pecuniary damage he/ she sustained as a result of the violation.[47] For instance, when someone's honour is defamed the person must, in addition to proving the fact that a public authority has wrongfully defamed his or her honour, also substantiate the non-pecuniary damage resulting from the violation of his or her rights.

For certain violations of law, the injured person does not need to prove that the damage occurred but it is presumed. For example, in order to receive compensation for unlawfully caused non-pecuniary damage, the injured person does not need to prove having suffered non-pecuniary damage in case of unjust deprivation of liberty[48] or the use of force.[49] Also a person who has been unjustly deprived from his or her liberty in the meaning of the CUDLA does not need to prove neither the occurrence of the damage nor the extent of the damage. The CUDLA regulation draws on the assumption that the restriction of the fundamental right of liberty causes non-pecuniary damage and results in a loss of profit in any case.[50]

4.3.3.3 Causation

One of the prerequisites of any compensation claim is a causation between an unlawful act and the damage. As the State Liability Act does not regulate the conception of causation, it needs to be substantiated on the basis of § 127 (4) of the LOA, stating that the damage is to be compensated for only if the circumstances on which the liability of the person is based and the damage caused are related in such a manner that the damage is a consequence of the circumstances. In the state liability law, the liability is based on an unlawful act committed by a public authority in

[45] As an exception, damage which the court deems generally known does not need to be proved. This exception has been stipulated in § 60 (1) of the Code of Administrative Court Procedure. About the court practice, see the Administrative Law Chamber of the Supreme Court judgment of 14.12.2006, 3-3-1-56-06, para. 8 (Note 44).

[46] See, e.g., the Administrative Law Chamber of the Supreme Court judgment of 30.01.2012, 3-3-1-78-11, para. 15 – available in Estonian at www.nc.ee/?id=11&tekst=RK/3-3-1-78-11.

[47] *Ibid.*

[48] Supr.Ct *en banc* judgment of 1.2.2008, 3-3-1-15-07, para. 27 – English version is available at www.nc.ee/?id=890. Accessed 1 Nov 2014.

[49] Supr.Ct. *en banc* judgment of 11.12.2012, 3-3-1-75-11, para. 22 – available in Estonian at www.nc.ee/?id=11&tekst=222554106. Accessed 1 Nov 2014.

[50] Supr.Ct. *en banc* judgment of 31.3.2011, 3-3-1-69-09, para. 86 (Note 6).

the extent which violates the person's subjective (individual) right. Whether the damage was caused by the unlawful act is established on the basis of the rule *conditio sine qua non*.

Even when an indispensable causal link is established between the unlawful act of public authority and the damage, it does not necessarily render the public authority responsible. The conception of an indispensable causal link alone does not make it possible to consider unusual or unpredictable circumstances that could result in an unfair distribution of liability. This is why the proceedings of establishing a causal link is complemented by additional elements and principles usually limiting the liability. Both the principle of the foreseeability of damage and the theory of the purpose of a rule have been implemented in court practice.

According to the principle of foreseeability of damage, liability is also not incurred when the damage was, an unavoidable result of an unlawful act and compensation for the damage is not contrary to the purpose of the norm but the damage was a result of extremely unlikely or unforeseeable circumstances or occurrences. The principle of the foreseeability of the damage has been formulated in § 13 (3) of the SLA. According to this rule, public authority shall be relieved of liability for damage caused in the course of performance of public duties if the damage could not have been prevented even if diligence necessary for the performance of public duties had been fully observed.

In some cases, the Administrative Law Chamber of the Supreme Court has additionally proceeded from the protective purpose of the rule doctrine provided for in § 127 (2) of the LOA.[51] According to this theory, not all negative consequences of an unlawful act are to be compensated for, but only the damage, the preventing of which was the purpose of the rule. So, e.g., the court has found that the provisions of procedural rights can, as a rule, be directed only to the avoidance of the reliance damage and therefore, a person whose procedural rights have been violated in the tendering procedure may claim only the reimbursement of expenses incurred upon the participation in the procedure but not the loss of profit due to the non-conclusion of the contract.[52]

4.3.3.4 The Obligation to Use Primary Legal Remedies

As a rule, the non-application of a certain state liability claim does not exclude filing another state liability claim. This, however, does not apply to the claim for compensation for damage caused in an administrative law relationship. A person who wishes to file a claim for compensation for damage caused by an unlawful action of

[51] Supr.Ct. Adm. judgment of 4.4.2006, 3-3-1-13-06, para. 16 (Note 40); Supr.Ct. Adm. judgment of 22.10.2009, 3-3-1-66-09, paras. 19–21 – in Estonian at www.nc.ee/?id=11&tekst=222519815. Accessed 1 Nov 2014.

[52] Supr.Ct. Adm. judgment of 22.10.2009, 3-3-1-66-09, para 20 (Note 51).

an administrative authority must have tried to prevent such damage or to eliminate the damage already caused through the timely contesting of the action of public authority. This so-called obligation to use primary legal remedies is provided in § 7 (1) of the SLA: "A person whose rights were violated by the unlawful action of a public authority in a public law relationship [...] may claim for damages caused to this person if the damage could not be prevented and cannot be eliminated by the protection or restoration of rights in the manner provided for in §§ 3, 4 and 6 of this Act." Under the obligatory primary legal remedies belong the claim for repeal of administrative act (§ 3 of the SLA), the claim for termination of administrative measure (§ 4 of the SLA) and the claim for issue of administrative act or taking of administrative measure (§ 6 of the SLA). The Administrative Law Chamber of the Supreme Court initially took the view that the obligation to use primary legal remedies applies also to the claim for compensation for damage caused in pre-trial criminal proceedings.[53] The Supreme Court *en banc* has altered that position later by establishing that the legal remedies enumerated in § 7 (1) of the SLA do not enable to apply this provision beyond the administrative law.[54] Notwithstanding the explicitness and acceptability of § 7 (1) of the SLA, the implementation of this provision has proved to be problematic in several respects.[55] To put it in a nutshell, firstly, it is relevant to notice that the obligation to use primary legal remedies is not an absolute one while it is subject to a number of exceptions[56]; secondly, the obligation to use primary legal remedies has a function of precluding liability, not only restricting it.[57]

4.3.3.5 Forms of Compensation

If the claim for compensation of damage is to be granted, the damage may be compensated in money as well through the restitution in kind. In this case, the prerequisites of the claim are basically the same. The only exception concerns the administrative act, the restitution in kind is allowed only when the administrative act has been repealed.

The restitution in kind is provided in § 11 of the SLA: "Instead of financial compensation, an injured party may request a public authority to eliminate the unlawful consequences of a repealed administrative act or partially amended administrative act or measure."[58]

---

[53] See Supr.Ct. Adm. judgment of 20.11.2008, 3-3-1-47-08, para. 22 –in Estonian at www.nc.ee/?id=11&tekst=222512691. Accessed 1 Nov 2014.

[54] See the Supr.Ct. *en banc* judgment of 22.3.2011, 3-3-1-85-09, para. 115 (Note 4).

[55] See, in detail, Andresen (2010) 116–127.

[56] See, in detail Andresen (2010) 124–126.

[57] See, in detail, Andresen (2010) 119–120.

[58] See Chapter I, section 2.

4.3.3.6 Determination of the Amount of the Award

When all prerequisites of the claim for compensation for damage are fulfilled, there are no grounds for limiting the liability, and the damage have been proven, then pecuniary damage needs to be compensated for in full.

In the case that the claim for compensation for damage is to be granted but the injured person is not able to prove the precise extent of the damage (for example, in case of loss of profit) or it is not possible to establish the amount of damage (for example, in case of non-pecuniary damage), then the amount of award shall be determined by the discretion of the court (§ 127 (6) of the LOA).[59] When compensating non-pecuniary damage, § 9 (2) of the SLA must be considered, stating that non-pecuniary damage is to be compensated for in proportion to the gravity of the offence and taking into consideration the form and gravity of fault.

Since it is not possible to measure the extent of non-pecuniary damage and the damages are estimated, the amount of the award for non-pecuniary damage is decided by the court. When bringing an action in the court, the injured person does not necessarily have to state the amount of damages he or she wants to claim. The applicant may forgo indicating the amount of damages in the action and request a just compensation at the discretion of the court pursuant to § 38 (2) of the Code of Administrative Court Procedure (CACP). The court has the right of discretion not only regarding to the amount of the award, but according to the court practice, the court may, instead of ordering payment of compensation, confine itself to ascertaining the unlawfulness of the act or omission of an administrative authority which caused the damage.[60]

The court has, furthermore, a wide discretion at ordering the payment of compensation for lawfully caused damage. According to the court practice, in cases when fundamental rights are restricted to such a degree that it exceeds the person's obligation of toleration in the public interests, then the person is entitled to claim for a fair compensation. A fair compensation is the difference between the actual pecuniary loss and the toleration obligation. To give an assessment on the fairness of the compensation, the interests of individuals must be considered with regard to public interests.[61]

The State Liability Act does not provide any limits on damages. There are limits, however, on the compensation for a loss of profit and non-pecuniary damage provided

---

[59] Supr.Ct. Adm. judgment of 10.10.2013, 3-3-1-38-13, para. 21 (Note 43); Supr.Ct. Adm. judgment of 30.01.2012, 3-3-1-78-11, para. 15 (Note 46).

[60] Supr.Ct. Adm. judgment of 11.12.2009, 3-3-1-80-09, para. 12 –in Estonian at www.nc.ee/?id=11&tekst=RK/3-3-1-80-09. Accessed 1 Nov 2014. This court practice is problematic since there is no respective legal basis in material law (§ 9 (2) of the SLA does not provide such basis). However, the Code of Administrative Court Procedure from 2012 provides a procedural provision: 'If the preconditions established in the law for a claim of compensation for non-pecuniary damage are met, and the court refuses to order payment of the compensation pursuant to the conditions provided in the law, the court may, instead of ordering payment of the compensation, ascertain the unlawfulness of the administrative act or measure which caused the damage.'

[61] Supr.Ct. *en banc* judgment of 31.3.2011, 3-3-1-69-09, paras. 63–67 (Note 6).

in § 5 (4) of the CUDLA and this regulation rules out the possibility of receiving additional compensation for loss of profit or non-pecuniary damage caused by unlawful deprivation of liberty on the basis of any other legislation.[62] The Supreme Court *en banc* has noted that this regulation may not be in accordance with §§ 32, 12 and 11 of the Constitution in conjunction, as in case of exceptional circumstances the person must have the chance to claim for compensation to a fair extent.[63] Paragraph 5 (4) of the CUDLA has not yet been declared unconstitutional.

4.3.3.7 Reduction of Damages

None of the branches of the state authority are entirely exempt from the liability. However, as noted above, the prerequisites for the compensation of damage resulting from court action, misdemeanour procedure or a legislative act are significantly more strict than the general liability provisions.

As mentioned before, the obligation to use primary legal remedies only applies to the claim for compensation for damage caused by unlawful administrative proceedings and even then the bulk of obligatory legal remedies has been exhaustively established by the law. In all other cases, the person does not need to file any other claims before claiming compensation. However, the failure to file a claim that was available to the person can be a basis for reducing the damages. If the injured person has in any other way failed to avoid the damage or omitted doing anything that could have mitigated the damage or the damage was in any other way in part caused by circumstances that were under the injured person's control, monetary damages may be reduced or eliminated entirely as provided in § 13 (1) 4) of the SLA.[64]

4.3.3.8 Taxation of Damages and Interest

Taxation of damages has not been specified in a precise and conclusive manner in Estonian legislation. According to § 12 (1) of the Income Tax Act (ITA), income tax is charged from income derived by a resident natural person during a period of taxation from all sources of income in Estonia and outside Estonia.[65] The same provision includes a list of examples of different types of income, but the Act does not include the definition of income. It is specified in the Act that the compensation for direct pecuniary damage shall not be deemed to be income of a natural person, except for compensation paid in connection with business activities (§ 12 (3) of the

---

[62] *Ibid.*, para. 73.

[63] *Ibid.*, para. 87.

[64] In this question also § 139 of the LOA is applied. As to the non-granting of damages as a result of reduction of damages, see, e.g., Supr.Ct. Adm. judgment of 15.4.2008, 3-3-1-6-08, para. 14 – available in Estonian at www.nc.ee/?id=11&tekst=RK/3-3-1-6-08. Accessed 1 Nov 2014.

[65] The English version of the Income Tax Act is available at www.riigiteataja.ee/en/eli/528082014008.

ITA). There are no provisions addressing the taxation of loss of profit and non-pecuniary damage.

Court practice does not regard irregular income that was not created through a person's everyday business activities as taxable income.[66] In order to assess whether the damages is covered under the definition of income, a comparison needs to be made with the income the injured person would have received if the damage had not been inflicted upon him/her.[67] Based on the above, in court practice compensation for a loss of profit has been subject to income tax. Compensation for non-pecuniary damage, however, is regarded as a type of irregular income not taxable with income tax.[68]

Compensation paid upon expropriation and compensation paid under the Victim Support Act are not taxable with income tax (§ 15 (4) 3) and § 19 (3) 8) of the ITA).

Upon a delay in paying compensation to the injured person, the injured person may require a public authority to pay interest on the delay until the compensation is paid.[69] This late interest is not taxable with income tax (§ 17 (1) of the ITA).

4.3.4 *Involved Parties*

4.3.4.1 Person Obligated to Compensate for Damage

The liability in damages for infrigement of human rights incurs, as a rule, the public authority. The notion "public authority" includes the state, a local government, another legal person in public law or another person performing public duties on a public law basis outside of relationships of subordination (§ 2 (1) of the SLA). As a rule, a public official is not responsible for damage caused to a person (§ 12 (1) of the SLA).

Also when the damage is caused by a person in private law acting in the name of a public authority, then usually it is the public authority that is liable for the damage before the injured person (§ 12 (3) of the SLA). Exceptions can be made by specific laws. However, the public authority who has compensated for damage may later file a recourse claim against the public official or private person whose unlawful activities resulted in the occurrence of damage (§§ 80–81 of the CSA and § 19 of the SLA).

[66] Supr.Ct. Adm. judgment of 17.12.2009, 3-3-1-72-08, para. 12 –in Estonian at www.nc.ee/?id=11&tekst=222521270. Accessed 1 Nov 2014.

[67] *Ibid.*, para. 13.

[68] *Ibid.*

[69] The State Liability Act does not contain a corresponding provision, but § 113 of the LOA is applied pursuant to court practice. See Supr.Ct. Adm. judgment of 16.12.2010, 3-3-1-83-10, para. 22 – available in Estonian at www.nc.ee/?id=11&tekst=RK/3-3-1-83-10. Accessed 1 Nov 2014. According to §§ 113 and 94 (1) of the LOA, the rate of penalty for late payment is equal to the last interest rate applicable to the main refinancing operations of the European Central Bank before 1 January or 1 July of each year plus eight per cent per year.

An official or a person in private law acting in the name of a public authority or a person holding a public position is only liable before the injured person when it is provided by a specific law.[70] A public authority may, however, later file a recourse claim against an official.[71]

4.3.4.2 Injured Person

As to the compensation for pecuniary damage, both natural and legal people may claim for damages under the State Liability Act. According to § 9 (1) of the SLA, the non-pecuniary damage, however, will be compensated only to a natural person.

No distinction has been made in the Estonian law whether the injured person is an Estonian citizen or a foreigner. According to § 9 (1) of the Estonian Constitution, the rights, freedoms and duties of each and every person, as set out in the Constitution, apply equally to Estonian citizens and to citizens of foreign states and stateless people in Estonia. As the fundamental right to compensation for damage as provided in § 25 of the Constitution is a fundamental right of 'each and every person', it also applies to foreigners. For this reason, the Estonian state liability law does not include specific rules for foreigners and they are subject to the same rules as the citizens of Estonia.

4.3.4.3 Assignment of Right to Reparation

Pursuant to § 29 (1) of the CACP, in the case of the death of a participant of the proceedings, the court will permit the universal successor of the participant to enter the proceeding, unless the law provides otherwise.[72] However, as stipulated in § 6 (1) of the General Part of the Civil Code Act, civil rights may transfer from one person to another only if the rights are not inseparably bound to the person pursuant to law.[73]

It is currently not clear whether and under which conditions the successor of the deceased person is entitled to enter the proceedings in case of the claim for compensation of damage in the administrative court because this question has not yet arisen in the administrative court practice.[74]

---

[70] In Estonia, the notaries and bailiffs are independent public authorities who are individually liable for any damage occurring due to their fault when performing their official duties. See Andresen (2006) 146–157.

[71] See §§ 80–81 of the CSA (Note 23).

[72] If the universal succession is allowed, it is possible at any stage of the proceedings (§ 29 (1) of the CACP) and all procedural acts performed before the universal successor entered the proceedings apply in respect of the universal successor in the same manner as they would apply in respect of the legal predecessor of the universal successor (§ 29 (2) of the CACP) (Note 11).

[73] The English version of this Act is available at www.riigiteataja.ee/en/eli/528032014002. Accessed 1 Nov 2014.

[74] Besides, the Supr.Ct. Administrative Law Chamber has not yet taken a position whether the assignment of claims is allowed in administrative court procedure. There are no public law norms but pursuant to 166 (1) of the LOA, the claims for compensation for damage arising from a bodily injury, health damage or the death of a person shall not be assigned. Such claims may be, however, assigned if counter-performance of equal economic value is received in exchange for the assignment.

Besides, upon the causing of death, a third person has a separate claim under the State Liability Act. Pursuant to § 10 of the SLA, a third person is entitled to claim compensation for expenses incurred due to the causing of death to another person, for loss of support and non-pecuniary damage on the bases provided by private law.[75] Compensation for loss of support cannot be claimed to the extent to which the third person is entitled to survivor's pension due to the death caused (§ 10 (2) of the SLA).

4.3.5 *Procedural Law*

4.3.5.1 Competent Bodies

The person who claims for the compensation of damage may decide at his or her own discretion whether to submit an application for the compensation of damage to an administrative body which caused the damage or to file an action with an administrative court.[76] Applications for compensation for damage caused by courts shall be submitted to the Ministry of Justice (§ 17 (1) of the SLA). The submission of an application for the compensation of damage to an administrative authority is free of charge. However, when filing an action for the compensation of damage with an administrative court, a state fee usually needs to be paid.[77] No state fee is charged when claiming the pecuniary damage caused by unjust deprivation of liberty or by unlawful imposition of punishment for a misdemeanour, or claiming the restitution of property expropriated or abandoned in the course of unlawful repression and concerning compensation for the corresponding damage, or claiming for compensation for damage caused by bodily injury, another health disorder or the death of a provider.[78]

---

[75] See § 129 and § 134 (3) of the LOA.

[76] As an exception, mandatory pre-trial proceedings are laid down for claims of compensation for damage submitted by imprisoned persons. Pursuant to § 1^1 (8) of the Imprisonment Act, a prisoner or person in custody has the right of recourse to an administrative court for compensation for damage caused by a prison provided that the prisoner or the person in custody has previously submitted an application to the prison for compensation for damage pursuant to the procedure provided for in the State Liability Act and the prison has rejected the application or refused to satisfy the application or review the application during the term. The English version of this Act is available at www.riigiteataja.ee/en/eli/517062014015. Accessed 1 Nov 2014.

[77] The state fee for claims of compensation for damage is 3 % of the amount of the payment of which is applied for or of the value of the property the return of which is applied for, but not less than 15 euros and not more than 750 euros. If a person applies for a fair compensation at the discretion of the court the state fee is 250 euros. See § 57^1 (2) and (3) of the State Fees Act. The English version of this Act is available at www.riigiteataja.ee/en/eli/509092014003. Accessed 1 Nov 2014. The grounds for exemption in part or in full from the payment of the state fee are regulated in Chap. 12 of the CACP (Note 11).

[78] See § 22 (1) 3) 6) and 11) of the State Fees Act (Note 77).

Upon submitting an application for the compensation of damage to an administrative body, the administrative body is required to adjudicate an application within 2 months as of the submission of the application (§ 18 (1) of the SLA).

When a person wishes to contest the negative decision of an administrative body or when an administrative body fails to adjudicate an application for the compensation of damage on time, the person must file an action with an administrative court within thirty days for an order of payment of compensation (§ 18 (2) of the SLA).

4.3.5.2 Time Limits

An application or action is to be filed within three years of the date on which the injured party became aware or should have become aware of the damage and of the person who caused it, but not later than ten years as of the causing of damage or the event which caused the damage regardless of whether the injured party became aware of the damage and of the person who caused it (§ 17 (3) of the SLA).

4.3.5.3 Group Claims

Estonian law recognises the individual as well the group claims. Several applicants may bring a joint action, if the dispute relates to a right that these people hold jointly, or several people contest the same administrative act or measure, or the administrative acts or administrative acts or measures, which constitute the subject matter of the claim, are of the same type and were issued or taken on the same legal basis and in relation to the same of similar facts (§ 19 (1) of the CACP). In relation to the other party, each applicant participates in the proceedings independently. Unless the law provides otherwise, an act of one applicant does not entail any legal consequences for other applicants (§ 19 (2) of the CACP).

4.4 Implementation of the European Convention on Human Rights

4.4.1 Practical Effectiveness of the Convention

The ECHR is the most common relevant international agreement in guaranteeing the enjoyment of human rights in Estonia.[79] Upon compensation for damage, courts draw on the provisions of the convention and practices of the ECtHR both in the stages of identifying a violation and ordering the payment of compensation. The Supreme Court, for example, has considered the practices of the ECtHR in matters

---

[79] See about the application of the ECHR in the Estonian Supreme Court: Rohtmets, Eve. 2012.

concerning exceeding a reasonable time limit for the proceeding,[80] violation of human dignity[81] and establishing the lawfulness of the means of restraint,[82] as well as the division of the burden of proof,[83] the choice of the manner of reparation[84] and the amount of damages.[85]

4.4.2 The Influence of Compensation Granted by the European Court of Human Rights

Without prejudice to the judgment of the ECtHR having granted a person compensation for damage sustained, the person may still file a claim for compensation for damage to his or her national extrajudicial body or court. However, it is likely that the 3-year time limit for filing a claim for compensation has passed by then.

In order to ensure an effective legal protection to the person, legislation on court proceedings provides the possibility of reviewing court decisions that have already entered into force, provided new facts have come to light. One of the grounds for this reviewing is that ECtHR has found that there has been a violation of ECHR or

---

[80] See e.g. Supr.Ct. *en banc* judgment of 22.3.2011, 3-3-1-85-09, paras. 83 and 84 (Note 4).

[81] Previously, the Supr.Ct. – Administrative Chamber held the position that detaining a person in a punishment cell without any legal basis constitutes a violation of dignity in the meaning of § 9 (1) of the SLA. Based on the practices of ECtHR, in later rulings, the Administrative Chamber of the Supreme Court has moved to the position that detaining a person in a punishment cell without any legal basis is not a violation of human dignity in itself, but detaining a person in a punishment cell without any legal basis can be a violation of human dignity when it includes additional limitations and distress to the person that are not necessary for the detention regime. See the Administrative Law Chamber of the Supreme Court judgment of 15.3.2010, 3-3-1-93-09, para. 11 (Note 35). However, detaining a person in a punishment cell without any legal basis does constitute unlawful deprivation of liberty, in case of which the non-pecuniary damage is to be reimbursed with a monetary compensation. *Ibid*., para. 12.

[82] See Supr.Ct. Adm. judgment of 3.10.2013, 3-3-1-47-13, para. 25 – available in Estonian at www.nc.ee/?id=11&tekst=RK/3-3-1-47-13.

[83] Based on the ECtHR ruling in the matter of *Scordino v. Italy* (judgment of 29.3.2006, application no. 36813/97), the Supreme Court has held that if an unreasonably extended time of proceedings has been established, causing of non-pecuniary damage to the accused shall be generally presumed, unless proven otherwise. See Supr.Ct. *en banc* judgment of 22.3.2011, 3-3-1-85-09, para. 93 (Note 4).

[84] Having regard to the practices of ECtHR (*Ommer v. Germany*, judgment of 13.11.2008, application no. 10597/03), the Supreme Court holds the position that in cases where proceedings have been terminated or the person has been acquitted only after the end of reasonable time of proceedings and on other considerations than due to expiry of the reasonable time of proceedings (e.g. due to inability to provide evidence), the only fair measure upon compensation for non-pecuniary damage caused to a person is fair monetary compensation. – See Supr.Ct. *en banc* judgment of 22.3.2011, 3-3-1-85-09, para. 130 (Note 4).

[85] The Supreme Court has noted, for example, that the compensation imposed may not be unjustly low when compared to compensations imposed by ECtHR in similar cases. See Supr.Ct. Adm. judgment of 10.10.2013, 3-3-1-38-13, para. 21 (Note 43).

its protocol concerning the case to be reviewed, provided the infringement have affected the determination of the matter and cannot reasonably be cured, and the damage that it caused cannot be compensated otherwise than by means of review.[86]

In administrative and criminal proceedings a petition for reviewing the case can be filed also by the person who has lodged an application with the ECtHR in a similar matter and on the same legal basis or who is entitled to lodge such an application in a similar matter and on the same legal basis regarding the time-limit established in Article 35 (1) of the ECHR.[87] The petition for reviewing the case must be lodged with the Supreme Court within 6 months from the day on which the corresponding judgment of the ECHR became final.[88] If the Supreme Court finds that a petition for review is well founded, it enters a judgment or a ruling by which it annuls the corresponding decision which is under review and returns the matter for a new hearing to the lower court which made the decision. In the case that the facts of the case under review are clear, the Supreme Court varies the decision of the lower court, or annuls that decision and enters a new judgment or ruling in the matter.[89]

The Administrative Law Chamber of the Supreme Court, for example, recently granted a petition for review based on the judgment of the ECtHR.[90] In the previous administrative matter, the person had brought an action in the administrative court for the compensation for non-pecuniary damage caused upon the strip-search in prison. Based on the multiple applications lodged by the person, the ECtHR established that the state had breached Articles 3 and 6 (1) of the ECHR, yet dismissed the claim for compensation regarding the strip-search in prison.[91] As a result of the breach of Article 6 (1) of the ECHR, the Administrative Law Chamber of the Supreme Court satisfied the petition for review and sent the administrative matter to the administrative court to open the proceedings, as previously national courts had refused to open the proceedings concerning the non-pecuniary damage caused upon the strip-search in prison as the required mandatory pre-trial proceedings had not been completed. In its judgment, the Supreme Court stated that, though the ECtHR imposed a compensatory obligation on the Republic of Estonia for the benefit of the appellant, the damages did not concern the alleged damage of this administrative

[86] See § 240 (2) 8) of the CACP (Note 11); § 366 7) of the Code of Criminal Procedure (CCP) (Note 30) and § 702 (2) 8) of the Code of Civil Procedure. The English version of the Code of Civil Procedure is available at www.riigiteataja.ee/en/eli/504092014001. Accessed 1 Nov 2014.

[87] See § 240 (3) of the CACP and § 367 (2) of the CCP.

[88] See § 241 (2) of the CACP; § 368 of the CCP and § 704 (2) of the Code of Civil Procedure. Pursuant to § 704 (3) of the Code of Civil Procedure, the petition for review must be filed not later than within 10 years from the day on which the corresponding judgment of the ECHR became final.

[89] See § 245 (2) and (3) of the CACP; § 373 (2) and (3) of the CCP and § 710 (1) of the Code of Civil Procedure.

[90] See Supr.Ct. Adm. judgment of 18.3.2013, 3-3-2-2-12 – in Estonian at www.nc.ee/?id=11&tekst=RK/3-3-2-2-12. Accessed 1 Nov 2014.

[91] ECtHR judgment of 29.5.1012 in case *Julin v. Estonia* (applications nos. 16563/08, 40841/08, 8192/10 and 18656/10).

case.[92] With this judgment the Supreme Court remedied the violation of Article 6 (1) of the ECHR and granted the person the right to bring an action of compensation for non-pecuniary damage caused upon the strip-search.

In addition to the review proceedings in the codes of court procedures, the State Liability Act provides the right to file a claim for compensation for damage on the basis of national law also when the ECtHR has established a violation of the ECHR, given that the person's rights were violated to a significant extent and the person has no other means to restore the his or her rights.[93] In general, this right extends both to the person whose personal complaint was satisfied by the ECtHR as well as to the person who has filed a personal complaint to the ECtHR in a similar matter and on the same legal basis or who has the right to do so and the time-limit for filing such complaint has not yet passed.[94] The purpose of these rules was to create an opportunity for granting damages on national level, eliminating the need for the ECtHR to impose the damages on the basis of Article 41 of the ECHR. So far, these rules have been rarely applied in practice. The main reason is the fact that regardless of the existence of the said rules on national level, the ECtHR has deemed it necessary to afford a just satification itself.[95] If the ECtHR has already awarded damages, the national court has to, in order to avoid unfounded enrichment of the injured person, take into account the damages already awarded in the same case.

4.5 Conclusion

The most important goal of the Estonian state liability law is to guarantee the effective protection of individual rights in public law relationships. This goal includes the full application of the fundamental right to compensation for damage provided in § 25 of the Estonian Constitution. At the same time, the provisions of the State Liability Act must consider the public interest. That is why the objective of the draft legislation of the State Liability Act was to provide a basis for compensation for damage caused to a person by a public authority in a manner which would restore the person's rights but which would not be too burdensome to public resources.

The State Liability Act has been functioning well in the area of administrative law. Problems have surfaced due to the fact that the legislator has not laid down all necessary specific rules concerning the compensation for damage caused upon the

[92] See Supr.Ct. Adm. judgment of 18.3.2013, 3-3-2-2-12, para. 11.3. (Note 90).

[93] See § 7 (2^1), § 9 (3) and § 15 (3^1) of the SLA.

[94] As an exception, it is provided in § 15 (3^1) of the SLA that in matters concerning damages that occurred during the administration of justice, only the person whose application has been satisfied by the ECtHR has such right.

[95] For example, in ECtHR judgment of 29.5.1012 in case *Julin v. Estonia* (Note 103) the ECtHR has expressed an opinion that 'an applicant who has already exhausted domestic remedies to no avail before complaining to this Court of a violation of his or her rights is not obliged to do so a second time in order to be able to obtain just satisfaction from the Court' (para. 199).

pre-trial criminal proceedings. Thereby, the Supreme Court has not regarded the wider interpretation of the provisions of the State Liability Act as justified. This is why new provisions are necessary to regulate the compensation for damage caused upon the pre-trial criminal proceedings. Draft legislation is currently being devised.

The grounds for the compensation of damage, caused upon the administration of justice or with a legislative act also, need to be analysed thoroughly. Another aspect which needs an analysis is whether the current limitations, according to which the compensation for damage is possible only if a judge committed a criminal offence in the course of judicial proceedings, is in conformity with the Constitution.

References

Andresen, Ene. 2005. The claim for elimination of unlawful consequences and the claim for compensation for damage under Estonian state liability law. *Juridica International* 10: 168–179.

Andresen, Ene. 2006. State liability without the liability of state: Constitutional problems related to individual professional liability of Estonian Notaries, Bailiffs and Sworn Translators. *Juridica International* 11: 146–157.

Andresen, Ene. 2010. The law aids the vigilant, not the negligent: The obligation to use primary legal remedies under Estonian state liability law. *Juridica International* 17: 116–127.

Rohtmets, Eve. 2012. Case-law of the European Court of Human Rights in decisions of the Supreme Court of Estonia. The English version of this case-law analysis is available at www.riigikohus.ee/vfs/1364/Article%20by%20Estonian%20Supreme%20Court.pdf. Accessed 1 Nov 2014.

Chapter 5
Les dommages-intérêts pour violation des droits de l'homme en France

Xavier Philippe

5.1 Introduction[1]

Le droit public français, pourtant reconnu pour ses règles et principes protecteurs des droits fondamentaux de la personne humaine depuis la Révolution de 1789, ne connaît pas ou très peu de règles spécifiques en termes d'octroi de dommages-intérêts pour la méconnaissance de tels droits. Plus exactement, la violation des droits fondamentaux ne connaît pas d'un régime spécifique d'indemnisation : elle obéit simplement aux règles de la responsabilité civile ou administrative suivant la juridiction compétente pour traiter de la demande portée en justice. Le préjudice né de la violation d'un droit – fondamental ou non - donne naissance à un droit à indemnisation. La France, à l'opposé de certains autres Etats, ne consacre pas de régime spécifique de responsabilité pour violation des droits de l'Homme,[2] comme celui de *Constitutional Damage*,[3] reconnu dans certains pays de *Common Law* ou de droit mixte.

---

[1] Ce chapitre est la reproduction d'une étude réalisée par l'auteur dans le cadre des contributions françaises au Congrès mondial de droit comparé qui s'est tenu à Vienne en juillet 2014. Ces études ont été rassemblées dans un numéro spécial de la *Revue internationale de droit comparé* publiée sous l'égide de l'Association française de droit comparé. Il est paru dans le volume 2, 2014 pp.527–560. L'auteur remercie la revue pour son aimable autorisation.

[2] V. en ce sens l'intéressante contribution prospective de M. Disant (2011) 1181.

[3] V. en ce sens, par exemple, S. Nahmod (1990) 997.

X. Philippe (✉)
Institut Louis Favoreu – GERJC, Aix Marseille Université, CNRS, Université de Pau, Université de Toulon (Droit international, comparé et européens), DICE UMR 7318, 13628 Aix-en-Provence, France

Université de Western Cape, Cape Town, South Africa
e-mail: xphilippe@gmail.com

E. Bagińska (ed.), *Damages for Violations of Human Rights*,
Ius Comparatum - Global Studies in Comparative Law 9,
DOI 10.1007/978-3-319-18950-5_5

Toutefois, au-delà des apparences, cette situation initiale est plus complexe qu'il n'y paraît. Si le régime général de responsabilité est considéré comme la source principale de toute demande d'indemnisation, il est complété par d'autres régimes spéciaux, législatifs ou jurisprudentiels, qui confèrent aux dommages-intérêts un autre visage que celui dans lequel il est traditionnellement cantonné. Ces questions ont notamment pris une acuité particulière avec le traitement de violations graves possédant un connotation historique marquée, telles que l'attitude de l'Etat français sous l'occupation pendant la Deuxième Guerre mondiale ou encore les activités des autorités publiques françaises ayant été à l'origine de violations des droits de l'Homme à l'étranger, comme dans l'affaire du *Rainbow Warrior*.[4]

Cette contribution cherche donc avant toute chose à présenter un état des lieux des dommages-intérêts pour violation des droits de l'homme, mais également à tenter d'envisager les perspectives d'évolution sur cette question qui semble, à certains égards, en pleine mutation. Elle évoquera également de façon incidente les répercussions des jurisprudences des juridictions internationales ou européennes qui pourraient avoir des répercussions sur le système de réparation tel qu'il existe dans le cadre national. Si la question des dommages-intérêts concentrera l'essentiel de cette réflexion, elle évoquera également, lorsque cela apparaîtra indispensable, les liens qui peuvent exister avec les autres formes de réparation non-monétaires.

5.2 Le régime général français de responsabilité pour violation des droits et libertés fondamentaux

1. Le système français de responsabilité est principalement et historiquement fondé sur l'existence d'une faute, d'un dommage et d'un lien de causalité entre les deux, qu'il s'agisse de la responsabilité civile ou de la responsabilité administrative de la puissance publique.

Cette responsabilité pour faute, commune aux deux ordres de juridiction,[5] repose cependant sur des fondements différents et est appréciée de façon autonome suivant les ordres de juridiction devant lesquels la demande de dommages-intérêts est portée. On peut donc estimer que la France a originairement adopté un régime de responsabilité commun à double visage qui ne peut normalement déboucher sur l'octroi de dommages-intérêts que s'il existe un préjudice rattachable à un fait fautif identifiable. Toutefois, sur ce régime de responsabilité pour faute, est venu se greffer en droit public un régime de responsabilité sans faute de la puissance publique, destiné à permettre une indemnisation des victimes, soit sur le fondement du risque, soit sur le fondement de la rupture de l'égalité des citoyens devant les charges publiques. On remarquera immédiatement que ces régimes de responsabilité ne sont

---

[4] V. Charpentier (1986) 873–885 ; égal. Charpentier (1990) 395–407.

[5] La distinction remonte à la décision du Tribunal de Conflits du 8 février 1873, *Blanco* Rec. 1er sup. 61, GAJA n°1, Dalloz, 19ème éd., 2013 et crée un double régime de responsabilité civile et administrative.

pas spécifiques aux violations des droits de l'Homme[6] mais s'appliquent à de telles violations et constituent même parfois un pan important de celle-ci. Ces régimes sont cependant limités par l'exigence de caractères spécifiques du dommage.[7]

La violation des droits fondamentaux ressortit normalement de la responsabilité de la puissance publique : en effet, la violation de ces droits est généralement associée à l'idée de méconnaissance du respect ou de la protection de ces droits par la puissance publique à laquelle elle incombe. En conséquence, une méconnaissance de ces droits, que ce soit par action ou par omission, fait naître un possible recours en responsabilité de la puissance publique. La violation d'une liberté ou d'un droit fondamental peut-être imputable soit à une faute de l'agent public qui était supposé faire respecter un tel droit ou une telle liberté et qui a manqué à ses obligations, soit à un défaut de fonctionnement normal du service, qui n'a pas été en mesure d'assurer le respect du droit ou de la liberté qui a été méconnu. Ce type de responsabilité correspond souvent dans la réalité à un mélange des deux causes susmentionnées, et un régime de subrogation et d'action récursoire[8] permet de mettre en cause ou d'appeler en garantie l'autorité administrative ou l'agent à l'origine du dommage. Ce régime de responsabilité pour faute de la puissance publique a été développé depuis près d'un siècle et demi par la voie prétorienne. Il s'est forgé et développé progressivement à travers la jurisprudence des juridictions administratives et du Conseil d'Etat. Très protecteur de l'Etat et des autorités publiques (ainsi que des deniers publics) à l'origine, ce régime s'est progressivement développé et aligné sur celui de la responsabilité civile considéré comme plus généreux que le régime d'indemnisation public.

Le régime de responsabilité administrative pour faute, bien que largement privilégié dans la réparation des violations des droits fondamentaux ne possède toutefois pas l'exclusivité de la reconnaissance de ce type de responsabilité, ni de celui de son indemnisation. Le juge judiciaire peut également prononcer des dommages-intérêts pour violation des droits fondamentaux dès lors que la question relève de sa compétence. La responsabilité est ici fondée sur le fondement des articles 1382 et suivants du code civil qui organise le régime de responsabilité quasi-délictuelle : « *tout fait de l'homme qui cause à autrui un dommage, oblige celui par la faute duquel il est arrivé à le réparer* ». Tout est dit dans ce court texte. Si le fait fautif est constitutif de la violation d'une liberté ou d'un droit fondamental, le juge judiciaire appliquera le régime de responsabilité civile pour faute.[9] Evidemment, les

---

[6] Pour la commodité de la présentation, et sans méconnaître les distinctions qui peuvent exister entre droits et libertés fondamentaux et droits de l'Homme, on utilisera indifféremment ces expressions pour désigner la violation d'un droit constitutionnellement (et conventionnellement) protégé. Dans la perspective du sujet traité – l'octroi de dommages-intérêts – la présente contribution considérera ces termes comme similaires.

[7] V. infra. Ces critères sont cependant appréciés de plus souplement par le juge administratif.

[8] CE, Ass. 28 juillet 1951 *Laruelle et Delville*, Rec. 464 et GAJA n°65, op.cit.

[9] Nous exclurons ici pour des raisons de place la responsabilité civile contractuelle. Outre qu'elle est peu concernée par la violation des droits de l'Homme, elle présente un caractère spécifique dans la mesure où elle naît d'une convention entre les parties. Toutefois, il est possible dans certains cas, d'y voir une forme de responsabilité pour violation d'un droit fondamental si la convention se

risques de mise en cause de la responsabilité pour violation d'une telle liberté ou d'un tel droit sont plus réduits que dans le cadre de la responsabilité administrative. En effet, cette dernière est par essence confrontée à l'action des personnes publiques chargées de mettre en œuvre les droits fondamentaux ou de les protéger alors que le juge judiciaire est par définition davantage concerné par la sphère des relations privées. Toutefois, cette perception schématique doit être nuancée : d'une part, certaines activités de la puissance publique relèvent exclusivement du juge judiciaire comme le service public de la justice, par exemple ; d'autre part, certains droits et libertés peuvent être méconnus dans les rapports entre personnes privées. Alors que pendant longtemps les menaces à l'égard des droits de l'Homme ne pouvaient venir que de l'action de la puissance publique, les relations entre personnes privées ont également pu donner naissance à la méconnaissance de certains droits fondamentaux. Ceci s'explique d'une part, par la diversification et la multiplication des droits reconnus depuis plus d'un demi-siècle, comme les droits économiques et sociaux ou les droits environnementaux, et d'autre part, par la mise en œuvre d'une responsabilité pour violation horizontale (c'est à dire entre personnes privées) de ces droits fondamentaux : le droit du travail ou le contentieux des droits de propriété en fournissent de multiples exemples. Alors que la violation des libertés et droits fondamentaux était perçue dans une relation exclusivement verticale entre la puissance publique et l'individu, s'y est ajouté aujourd'hui une relation horizontale entre les personnes de droit privé. Il est vrai, dans ce dernier cas, que la relation entre personnes privées s'observe souvent dans un cadre hiérarchique ou entre personne morale et personne physique, ce qui peut contribuer à expliquer cette invasion de la protection des droits fondamentaux dans la relation entre les personnes privées. Cette extension de la perception de la violation des droits fondamentaux devant les personnes publiques, issue de la doctrine allemande de la *Drittwirkung*,[10] n'est pas officiellement qualifiée comme telle mais a connu certaines répercussions dans le domaine de la responsabilité en cas de méconnaissance de ces droits.

Les dommages-intérêts issus de la responsabilité pour violation des droits de l'Homme trouvent donc leur fondement originaire dans un comportement fautif de l'auteur de la méconnaissance de ces droits, qu'il s'agisse de la puissance publique ou de personnes privées, que ce comportement consiste en une action ou une omission. Il n'existe pas de régime de responsabilité général propre à la violation de ces droits et en conséquence, le partage de compétence juridictionnelle suit la clef générale de répartition entre le juge judiciaire et le juge administratif.

2. On relèvera une exception – mais de taille – à cette clef de répartition qui concerne le juge pénal français. Le système pénal français, suivant en cela le modèle continental de droit romano-germanique, reconnaît la possibilité pour les victimes de se porter partie civile lors d'un procès pénal. L'action civile se greffe sur l'action

---

réfère à la protection de certains droits fondamentaux ou même si la liberté contractuelle et son régime sont considérés comme érigés au rang de liberté fondamentale (liberté économique).

[10]V. Beaud (2013).

pénale et le juge pénal peut donc octroyer des dommages-intérêts aux victimes.[11] Si le droit pénal est traditionnellement rangé en France sous la bannière du droit privé, les raisonnements qu'il emprunte font largement appel au droit public. De surcroît, les infractions pénales dont il s'agit constituent la violation des droits fondamentaux les plus élémentaires et ceux qui sont considérés comme le noyau dur de ces droits : le meurtre ou l'assassinat ne sont jamais que des atteintes au droit à la vie, la torture un acte inhumain et dégradant, et la liste comparative pourrait facilement s'allonger. Le juge pénal se trouve donc au cœur de la violation des droits fondamentaux et doit y répondre en prononçant une peine pénale mais également en apportant une satisfaction aux victimes dont les dommages-intérêts peuvent être une expression. Toutefois, cette conséquence découle, là encore, davantage du système pénal que d'une volonté délibérée de soumettre la violation des droits fondamentaux à un régime spécifique de dommages-intérêts. Le juge pénal possède l'avantage de bien connaître le contexte de la violation et se trouve dans une position favorable pour répondre aux demandes des victimes. Ceci n'en fait toutefois pas un juge privilégié et exclusif des dommages-intérêts en matière de violations de droits de l'Homme.

A côté de ce régime général de responsabilité pour faute, il existe en droit français de la responsabilité un droit spécifique de la responsabilité sans faute de la puissance publique. Ce régime était traditionnellement fondé sur deux notions assez différentes l'une de l'autre, auxquelles s'en est ajouté apparemment une troisième[12] qui ne concerne qu'indirectement la violation des droits fondamentaux : le risque et la rupture de l'égalité devant les charges publiques. Le premier fondement – le risque – ne concerne pas directement la violation des droits fondamentaux : il se fonde sur l'idée que la puissance publique à travers les activités qu'elle mène, peut faire naître un risque susceptible de créer des dommages graves, anormaux et spéciaux. Si un tel risque se réalise, la puissance publique est responsable et doit indemniser les victimes de tels dommages : les activités militaires, les activités de police, le recours à certaines méthodes d'exécution des peines en milieu ouvert peuvent ainsi donner lieu à des recours en responsabilité pour risque. Cependant, à moins de déceler dans l'exercice de ces activités un manquement à l'obligation de protection des droits et libertés de l'individu, il semble difficile de rattacher un tel fondement à une forme de responsabilité pour violation des droits fondamentaux. En revanche, le deuxième fondement pour rupture de l'égalité devant les charges publiques fait

[11] V. Agostini (2000). La victime d'une infraction, qui a personnellement souffert du dommage causé directement par l'infraction, a, conformément aux articles 1, alinéa 2, 2 et 3 du Code de procédure pénale, droit à agir devant la juridiction répressive. En se constituant, elle devient partie civile au procès pénal. Par l'action qu'elle porte devant les juridictions répressives, la partie civile tout à la fois participe à l'action publique et s'ouvre la possibilité d'obtenir réparation de tous les chefs de dommages, aussi bien matériels que corporels ou moraux, qui découlent des faits objets de la poursuite.

[12] Un troisième fondement pourrait également reposer sur la responsabilité d'une loi contraire à une convention internationale (Cons. Etat 8 février 2007 *Gardedieu*, RFDA 2007, 361, concl. L. Derepas) mais il ne nous concerne pas directement dans le cadre de cette étude dans la mesure où il s'agit d'octroyer des dommages-intérêts à un requérant victime d'une contradiction entre une convention internationale et une loi.

plus directement appel à la garantie des droits fondamentaux et se rattache à l'idée de garantie par la puissance publique d'indemnisation en cas de violation d'un droit. L'idée régissant cette forme de responsabilité repose sur l'existence d'une discrimination entre les individus au sein de la collectivité qui ferait reposer sur les épaules de quelques uns, une décision qui devrait incomber à tous et prise dans l'intérêt général de la collectivité. Il peut bien entendu s'agir d'une décision juridique (loi, règlement, décision juridictionnelle) mais il peut également s'agir d'une action ou d'une inaction de la collectivité publique. Cette forme de responsabilité est souvent la conséquence d'une violation d'un droit pour la personne ou le groupe de personnes qui en est victime. Son fondement – la rupture de l'égalité – mais également les raisons qui poussent la puissance publique à intervenir sont souvent liées à la méconnaissance ou l'atteinte à certains droits fondamentaux. Sans chercher à identifier un responsable particulier, cette forme de responsabilité conduit à faire admettre que la collectivité toute entière est responsable et qu'elle doit indemniser celles et ceux qui ont fait l'objet de discriminations et de violations de leurs droits fondamentaux. Il faut cependant souligner que dans les deux hypothèses citées – le risque et la rupture de l'égalité devant les charges publiques, cette responsabilité est exceptionnelle, qu'elle ne peut être mise en œuvre que s'il existe un dommage présentant simultanément trois caractères d'anormalité, de gravité et de spécialité. Elle recèle néanmoins des potentialités importantes qui pourraient donner naissance à un régime spécifique de dommages-intérêts pour violation d'un droit constitutionnel.[13] Certains autres Etats, sans emprunter les mêmes mots s'inspirent de cette démarche.

3. La situation française du droit de la responsabilité sans faute à l'égard des dommages-intérêts pour violation d'un droit fondamental ou violation des droits de l'Homme est donc tout aussi claire que celle de la responsabilité pour faute. Il n'existe pas de régime spécifique officiel dédié à la violation des droits de l'Homme. Toute demande de dommages-intérêts doit donc passer par le régime général de responsabilité, qu'il s'agisse des règles de la responsabilité civile ou des règles de la responsabilité de la puissance publique.

On relèvera toutefois dans ce panorama de la responsabilité pour violation des droits fondamentaux l'évolution marquée des régimes législatifs de responsabilité de la puissance publique. Fondés davantage sur un ensemble de fonctions sociales que sur la seule réparation du préjudice, ces régimes de responsabilité d'origine législative se sont multipliés dans différents secteurs[14] et notamment, pour certains d'entre eux, pour traiter de violations revêtant une certaine ampleur. Tel a été par exemple le cas de plusieurs textes législatifs ou réglementaires qui ont reconnu la responsabilité de l'Etat à la suite de la spoliation des biens de personne de confession

[13] V. Disant (2011) 1181. Nul doute que cette question reste un sujet en devenir en droit français. Néanmoins, la reconnaissance d'une telle responsabilité n'est pas destinée à se substituer à celles existantes et qui se concentrent sur la réparation des dommages. La nature de cette responsabilité se traduirait plutôt par des mesures de réparations non-financières.

[14] V. Lochak (1993).

juive durant la Deuxième Guerre mondiale[15] ou encore de l'indemnisation des rapatriés d'Algérie[16] ayant perdu leurs biens à la suite de la guerre civile et de l'indépendance de cet Etat. Ces régimes de responsabilité ne sont pas véritablement qualifiés par le législateur et il s'agit la plupart du temps davantage de régimes d'indemnisation que de textes reconnaissant un fondement spécifique à la responsabilité qui y préside. Toutefois, si l'on analyse la *ratio legis* de ces textes, il ressort qu'il s'agit davantage d'un régime de responsabilité sans faute assez proche éthiquement de la responsabilité pour rupture de l'égalité devant les charges publiques.

4. L'octroi de dommages-intérêts pour violation des droits de l'Homme ou des droits fondamentaux repose sur une alchimie complexe liée à l'ambiguïté de la demande des requérants lorsque l'un de leurs droits a été violé. Bien qu'il n'existe pas de règle en la matière et que le droit de la responsabilité en France soit largement tourné vers la demande de dommages-intérêts, il semble que celles relatives à la violation de droits fondamentaux puissent reposer sur des motivations profondément différentes en fonction des droits qui ont été méconnus. Si la perspective d'une indemnisation financière n'est jamais complètement écartée par une victime, elle peut ne pas constituer le fondement principal de sa demande en réparation. Telle est d'ailleurs la raison de certaines demandes d'indemnisation à l'Euro symbolique, démontrant que l'indemnisation financière n'est pas nécessairement systématiquement la raison première de toute action en responsabilité pour violation des droits fondamentaux. Ce sont davantage les conséquences de la violation d'un droit qui justifient la demande de dommages-intérêts : si celles-ci sont durables, affectent la vie quotidienne des victimes ou laissent des séquelles difficilement compensables dans leur intégralité, le recherche d'une indemnisation constituera probablement l'un des éléments clef de la demande. En revanche, si ces conséquences sont sans effet sur l'existence ultérieure du demandeur, la demande de compensation n'aura guère de sens.

5. D'une façon générale, le droit français analyse la demande de dommages-intérêts en matière de violation des droits fondamentaux comme une façon de compenser financièrement les dommages subis plus que comme une évaluation mathématique d'un préjudice parfois difficile à apprécier. L'évaluation du préjudice s'opère en principe dans toutes ses dimensions, mais sur de nombreux points, elle peut laisser place à une appréciation subjective du juge qui ne pourra l'évaluer que par approximation ou par comparaison. Dans le cas où la demande de réparation

[15] V. not. Décret no 2000-657 du 13 juillet 2000 instituant une mesure de réparation pour les orphelins dont les parents ont été victimes de persécutions antisémites ; Décret n° 2004-751 du 27 juillet 2004 instituant une aide financière en reconnaissance des souffrances endurées par les orphelins dont les parents ont été victimes d'actes de barbarie durant la Deuxième Guerre mondiale.

[16] V. not. : Loi n° 70-632 du 15 juillet 1970 relative à une contribution nationale à l'indemnisation des Français dépossédés de biens situés dans un territoire antérieurement placé sous la souveraineté, le protectorat ou la tutelle de la France ; loi n° 78-1 du 2 janvier 1978 relative à l'indemnisation des Français rapatriés d'outre-mer dépossédés de leurs biens ; loi n° 82-4 du 6 janvier 1982 portant diverses dispositions relatives à la réinstallation des rapatriés ; loi n° 87-549 du 16 juillet 1987 relative au règlement de l'indemnisation des rapatriés.

d'un droit violé porte sur une évaluation matérielle aisée (un bien fongible disparu, par exemple) la réparation pourra s'opérer sur le fondement de la *restitutio in integrum*. En revanche, dès lors que la violation porte sur un droit dont les conséquences sont difficilement évaluables, il devient extrêmement difficile de calculer avec précision la compensation adéquate. L'aspect le plus étonnant de la violation des droits fondamentaux repose sur le caractère inversé de la facilité d'évaluation du dommage : plus le droit méconnu fait partie du cœur des droits fondamentaux, plus il est difficile à évaluer. A combien peut-on évaluer le prix d'une vie ou celui de la douleur d'une torture ? Il est plus facile de verser des dommages-intérêts compensatoires adéquats pour la confiscation d'un bien immobilier que pour la violation des droits fondamentaux considérés comme non-dérogeables. Cependant, il faut rappeler une fois encore que le droit français – public et privé – ne reconnaît pas de régime d'indemnisation spécifique à la violation des droits fondamentaux. Dès lors, ce sont les règles générales de la responsabilité qui s'appliquent à ce type de violations lorsqu'elles sont reconnues. Si le principe de la restitution intégrale reste le principe cardinal, son appréciation peut être délicate suivant les contextes.

6. Les doctrines qui viennent au soutien de la demande de réparation financière ont évolué au cours du temps et continuent d'évoluer encore aujourd'hui. Le droit privé et le droit public ont cheminé séparément, même si les fondements initiaux étaient centrés – et le restent dans une large mesure – sur la faute ou le fait fautif. L'idée d'une responsabilité « garantie » ou d'une responsabilité fondée sur « l'équité » a cependant fait son chemin tant en droit privé qu'en droit public. Elle a progressivement transposé la responsabilité en un mécanisme de garantie d'indemnisation. Le législateur a souvent été à l'origine de ces mécanismes de responsabilité garantie à travers lesquels il cherchait à indemniser un dommage pour lequel la faute ne devait plus être prouvée. Si, à l'origine, la responsabilité constituait une forme de sanction à l'égard de l'auteur du dommage à côté de la réparation imposée,[17] l'idée d'une responsabilité constituant une forme d'assurance a progressivement fait son chemin.[18] Ici encore, les justifications doctrinales de l'indemnisation ne sont pas centrées ou concentrées sur la violation des droits fondamentaux. En d'autres termes, il n'y a pas de justification de la responsabilité ou de l'indemnisation qui repose sur une analyse de la protection des droits fondamentaux ou des droits de l'Homme. La France ne connaît pas, à la différence de l'Allemagne par exemple, de doctrine des droits fondamentaux objectifs qui permettraient de justifier une responsabilité – et par là même une indemnisation particulière fondée sur la seule violation d'un droit. A titre d'exemple, la méconnaissance du droit de vote en raison d'un oubli d'inscription ou d'une erreur, ne peut donner naissance à une réparation financière ni à un double droit de vote à l'élection suivante. En revanche, la violation d'un droit fondamental qui porte atteinte aux droits subjectifs de la victime pourra ouvrir un droit à réparation pourvu que le dommage soit évaluable. L'absence de droit à indemnisation spécifiquement fondé

[17]V. en ce sens Flour (1987) 36.

[18]V. Ewald (1992) 12.

sur la violation des droits fondamentaux explique cette situation. Il est cependant possible de déceler dans les initiatives législatives qui se sont développées depuis la fin du 19ème siècle, l'idée d'une garantie de protection de l'individu contre les dommages anormaux que la vie sociale lui fait courir.[19] L'évolution du droit de la responsabilité législative s'est ainsi concentrée sur l'idée d'indemnisation d'un dommage qui pourrait éventuellement toucher les droits reconnus à chaque individu. Ainsi par exemple, la loi de 1898 sur l'indemnisation des accidents du travail se fonde sur l'idée que les conséquences d'un accident du travail ne peuvent être laissées à la charge du salarié. Même en respectant les obligations de prudence, de tels accidents peuvent survenir et quelles que soient les circonstances et les auteurs impliqués, il serait anormal de laisser à la charge de l'individu qui en est victime l'aléa de la mise en jeu d'une responsabilité juridique hypothétique. On peut ainsi considérer que les fondements de ces régimes ont souvent été inspirés par la protection des droits (subjectifs) des victimes.[20] Ceci n'est toutefois qu'une interprétation générale des textes et ne peut être considéré comme un fondement juridique ou doctrinal de ce type de responsabilité.

5.3 L'etendue du regime français de responsabililté pour violation des droits de l'Homme ou des droits fondamentaux

1. L'absence, précédemment mentionnée, d'un régime de responsabilité spécifique à la violation des droits fondamentaux rend la question de l'étendue de sa mise en œuvre tributaire de l'analyse portée par le juge sur cette violation. En d'autres termes, le juge appréciera la violation à l'aune du régime général de responsabilité. La conséquence directe de cette situation conduit toutefois à une protection effective de tous les droits fondamentaux, qu'il s'agisse des droits civils et politiques ou des droits économiques et sociaux ou encore les droits de solidarité incluant ceux relatifs à la protection de l'environnement. L'absence de mise en œuvre d'un droit fondamental peut donc potentiellement donner lieu à responsabilité et à indemnisation pour peu que cette violation donne lieu à un préjudice indemnisable. La responsabilité peut être engagée pour la violation combinée de plusieurs droits

[19] Lois sur l'indemnisation des accidents du travail (1898); – des dommages subis du fait de l'évolution des aéronefs ou des objets qui s'en détachent(1924) ; – des dommages occasionnés par l'exploitation de téléphériques (1941) ; – des accidents nucléaires (1965 et 1968) ; – des actes de chasse lorsque l'auteur est inconnu ou non assuré (1966) ; – des dommages causés par les aliénés (1968) ; – des dommages causés par les grands gibiers (1968) ; – des victimes d'infractions pénales dont les auteurs sont inconnus ou insolvables (loi de 1977, modifiée en 1983 et 1990) ; – de la pollution maritime par les hydrocarbures (1977) ; – des victimes d'accidents de la circulation (1985) ; – des actes de terrorisme (1986) ; – des personnes qui se prêtent à des recherches biomédicales sans finalité thérapeutique directe (1988) ; – des personnes contaminées par le virus du SIDA (loi du 31 décembre 1991)

[20] V. en ce sens Lochak (1993).

fondamentaux. Ainsi, par exemple, le droit à la scolarisation des enfants handicapés découle de l'exigence constitutionnelle d'égal accès à l'instruction et mais également de protection des personnes handicapées.[21] Il faut cependant relever ici que la responsabilité ne mentionne pas directement, ou très rarement, la violation du droit fondamental comme source de responsabilité[22]: le juge se réfère à la substance du droit sans pour autant fonder sa démarche sur la violation du droit. Le résultat final sera le même mais l'invocation directe de la violation du droit fondamental ne sera qu'implicite. Ceci tient probablement à la position du juge français qui est davantage confronté aux textes de mise en œuvre des droits fondamentaux qu'à ceux qui les reconnaissent, au premier rang desquels le texte constitutionnel.

On soulignera néanmoins, qu'à l'instar d'autres Etats européens, le juge français s'est trouvé confronté à la multiplication des catalogues de protection des droits de l'Homme. Entre les textes constitutionnels nationaux (texte constitutionnel, Déclaration des droits de l'Homme et du citoyen de 1789, Préambule de la Constitution de 1946, Charte de l'environnement), les textes européens et les textes internationaux à portée universelle, les droits et libertés fondamentaux sont fréquemment protégés par plusieurs fondements directement invocables devant les juges nationaux. En termes de responsabilité et de dommages-intérêts, cette protection multiple n'a cependant que peu d'incidence sur le résultat final dans la mesure où le juge se fonde davantage sur la substance de la violation plus que sur son fondement. Le choix de la source de la violation est souvent le résultat d'un calcul stratégique des autorités de défense qui évaluent leurs chances de succès par anticipation et compte tenu de la jurisprudence existante. La hiérarchie traditionnelle des normes n'est pas nécessairement celle qui s'imposera car si les sources constitutionnelles apparaissent traditionnellement en droit interne comme les plus sûres et les plus effectives, elles sont concurrencées par celles que le juge ordinaire peut appliquer directement sans avoir à soulever une question préjudicielle (question prioritaire de constitutionnalité en France). Cependant, ces choix stratégiques influent davantage sur la constatation de la violation que sur son indemnisation. On peut donc retenir que le fondement de la violation – international ou interne – n'a que peu d'incidence sur l'octroi d'éventuels dommages-intérêts.

On remarquera néanmoins que la jurisprudence du Conseil d'Etat dans sa décision précitée de 2007 *Gardedieu*[23] a consacré une forme de responsabilité d'un type original qui reconnaît la responsabilité de l'Etat en cas de contrariété d'une loi à une convention internationale. Ce type de responsabilité, dont le fondement reste discuté, reconnaît néanmoins un droit à réparation pour violation d'une règle conventionnelle. Nul doute qu'une liberté ou un droit consacré par un traité et qui

---

[21] CE, réf., 15 décembre 2010 *Ministre de l'éducation nationale c. M.et Mme B.*, req. n°344729, Rec.; CE 8 avril 2009 *M. et Mme L.*, AJDA 2008. 668.

[22] V. cependant *a contrario* CE 17 décembre 2008 *Section française de l'Observatoire international des prisons*, AJDA 2008, 2364 dans lequel le Conseil d'Etat semble admettre que la responsabilité de l'Etat pourrait être engagé si le droit à la vie des détenus n'était pas suffisamment protégé. V. égal. TA Rouen 27 mars 2008 *Donat* AJDA 2008. 668.

[23] CE, Ass 8 février 2007 *Gardedieu*, op.cit. RFDA 2007, 361.

serait en contradiction avec une disposition législative nationale entrerait dans ce cas de figure. Toutefois, une telle hypothèse sans être impossible reste limitée en raison de la protection multiple des droits et libertés et notamment de l'effet miroir provoqué par la protection constitutionnelle et conventionnelle. Si la disposition est inconventionnelle, il y a de fortes chances pour qu'elle soit aussi inconstitutionnelle. En termes d'indemnisation, cela ne changerait d'ailleurs pas grand chose car il serait nécessaire de démontrer un préjudice et un lien de causalité entre l'inconventionnalité et le dommage. Cette forme de responsabilité permet d'ailleurs de s'interroger sur les conséquences à tirer de la mise en œuvre de la nouvelle procédure de question prioritaire de constitutionnalité devant le Conseil constitutionnel. Certes, cette procédure ne consacre pas à ce jour un droit à indemnisation pour violation d'un droit fondamental mais si le juge constitutionnel relève l'inconstitutionnalité d'une disposition législative et la censure, cette dernière peut faire naître un droit à indemnisation en fonction de la situation subjective du requérant. Cette situation ne s'est encore jamais produite mais rien ne s'oppose à ce qu'elle le soit marginalement. Formellement cependant, il n'existe pas de responsabilité spécifique de l'Etat pour violation d'un droit fondamental.

2. La compensation des « préjudices historiques » n'a pas reçu de consécration jurisprudentielle spécifique et, officiellement, il n'existe pas de responsabilité de l'Etat pour les préjudices historiques. Le régime juridique français de responsabilité ne consacre pas de régime spécifique pour de tels préjudices et il incombe aux demandeurs de prouver l'existence d'une faute personnelle ou d'une faute des autorités publiques pour qu'un préjudice de cette nature puisse être reconnu.[24] Toutefois, la situation est plus complexe qu'il n'y paraît. Sous cette apparente indifférence, le législateur et les juridictions françaises ont fait évoluer notablement la réparation de tels préjudices tout en restant cantonnés – au moins pour le juge – aux catégories traditionnelles de la responsabilité.[25] En premier lieu, le législateur a – sans en qualifier le fondement – reconnu un droit à indemnisation pour certains préjudices « historiques »: ces processus d'indemnisation, aux dénominations variables, ont permis de compenser des victimes de dommages subis directement ou indirectement à la suite des spoliations de la Deuxième Guerre mondiale ou encore de la perte des biens des français d'Algérie. Ces régimes textuels *ad hoc* traduisent une double préoccupation : d'une part, ils constatent l'existence d'une créance des victimes sur l'Etat en raison des dommages subis ; d'autre part, ils évitent la qualification de la responsabilité en termes de faute ou d'absence de faute. En se concentrant sur le résultat, le législateur a ainsi pu éviter le débat sur le caractère historique de la responsabilité. Il faut toutefois reconnaître que pendant les décennies qui suivirent la Deuxième Guerre mondiale, le débat ne se posait pas dans les mêmes

---

[24] CE 12 avr. 2002, *Papon*, Rec. Leb. 139.

[25] V. Sur ce point l'important avis contentieux d'assemblée du CE, 16 février 2009 *Hoffman Glemane*, Req n° 315499, concl. F. Lénica, RFDA 2009, p.316. Les conclusions de F. Lénica sont particulièrement éclairantes sur l'évolution du raisonnement du juge.

termes qu'aujourd'hui. L'idée d'une responsabilité collective historique[26] était assez peu présente dans les esprits et l'indemnisation était davantage perçue comme un régime d'aide et d'assistance que comme la rétribution d'une attitude fautive.

La reconnaissance en 1995 par le Président de la République d'alors, Jacques Chirac, d'une responsabilité politique de l'Etat français a constitué un tournant dans l'appréhension des préjudices «historiques». Si cette reconnaissance n'avait pas en soi de lien direct avec la consécration d'une responsabilité juridique spécifique, elle a néanmoins donné lieu à une réflexion sur la nature du lien entre l'origine de la responsabilité et l'existence d'un droit à indemnisation. Lorsque le Président de la République reconnaît qu'en livrant ses propres citoyens ou des personnes placées sous sa protection, *«la France commettait l'irréparable»*, il reconnaît d'une part que l'Etat a failli à sa mission de garant des droits et libertés publics qui étaient reconnus et d'autre part, que les autorités publiques de l'époque ont adopté un comportement fautif en méconnaissant les règles qu'elles étaient supposées faire respecter. La déconstruction du discours présidentiel n'a cependant pas eu pour effet de créer un mécanisme de garantie spécifique. Elle a en revanche engendré plusieurs régimes législatifs d'indemnisation et donné lieu en 2009 à la délivrance d'un avis contentieux du Conseil d'Etat qui générera une analyse renouvelée de la responsabilité de l'Etat pour des actes fautifs commis à l'occasion d'évènements historiques.[27] La position de la haute juridiction administrative a permis de reconnaître que les fautes commises par les fonctionnaires et les administrations de l'Etat avaient généré un dommage d'une ampleur telle qu'elle constituait une source de responsabilité de l'Etat. L'avis contentieux examine en revanche, du point de vue de l'indemnisation, l'ensemble des dispositifs textuels et jurisprudentiels qui ont permis d'apporter aux victimes ainsi qu'à leurs ayant-droits une indemnisation adéquate. Cette analyse conduit le Conseil d'Etat à considérer que, malgré le caractère éclaté de la réparation, cette dernière couvrait l'ensemble des préjudices subis. Ainsi, s'il n'est guère possible de considérer qu'il existe un régime spécifique de réparation des préjudices historiques, ces derniers ont cependant fait l'objet d'un examen spécifique renouvelé ces dernières années. La raison induite repose indéniablement sur le caractère massif et graves des violations représentées par ce préjudice historique. Ce sont des violations dans lesquelles les droits les plus fondamentaux de l'individu sont méconnus et comme tels, ils ont provoqué une réponse, certes tardive, du législateur, des autorités politiques et du juge.

3. Les violations graves et systématiques des droits fondamentaux n'ont pas reçu de réponse spécifique mais sont – comme cela vient d'être mentionné – prises en considération compte tenu de leur nature et de leur gravité. La France n'a – heureusement - toutefois pas connu de violations de ce type depuis nombre d'années et les hypothèses de telles violations ne pourraient intervenir que par ricochet,

[26]V. le discours du Président de la République, J. Chirac du 16 juillet 1995 : *«La France, patrie des lumières et des droits de l'homme, terre d'accueil et d'asile, la France ce jour là, accomplissait l'irréparable. Manquant à sa parole, elle livrait ses protégés à leurs bourreaux. Elle commettait une faute collective»*

[27]V. supra CE Avis, ass. 16 février 2009, op.cit.

comme par exemple la conséquence de certains actes d'une telle gravité commis à l'étranger et pour lesquels l'Etat n'aurait pas assuré la protection qu'il devait. On peut signaler, à titre anecdotique, un cas particulier qui n'a pas été fondé sur la responsabilité de l'Etat mais sur une violation du principe d'égalité. Il s'agissait en l'espèce d'une discrimination entre les anciens combattants de nationalité française et ceux qui avaient combattu pour la France durant la Deuxième Guerre mondiale mais relevant d'Etats devenus indépendants à la suite du processus de décolonisation. Ces derniers touchaient une pension fortement dévalorisée compte tenu de leur lieu de résidence. Les juridictions ont considéré – sous l'impulsion du Conseil constitutionnel[28] – qu'une telle discrimination était injustifiée et ont exigé une indemnisation qui corresponde au rattrapage des pensions de leurs homologues habitant sur le territoire français. Si ce cas de figure est tout à fait particulier, il correspond à la même logique que celles des préjudices graves ou des préjudices nés de situations historiques.

4. Les régimes législatifs d'indemnisation ont été en France régulièrement utilisés pour traiter de situations particulières et spéciales qui étaient considérées comme devant nécessiter une réponse politique à une question qui n'était pas strictement juridique. En réalité, cette technique d'indemnisation permettait de satisfaire des revendications auquel le seul droit de la responsabilité ne pouvait pas répondre. Cependant, le revers de cette situation repose sur l'absence de qualification de la responsabilité. En utilisant la loi comme réponse à une demande de réparation, le législateur évite de se prononcer sur l'imputabilité d'une éventuelle faute. La responsabilité est diluée dans une attitude générale dont l'Etat endosse la responsabilité : si faute il y a, elle est assumée par l'ensemble de la collectivité.

5.4 Le régime Français détaillé de responsabilité pour violation des droits fondamentaux

5.4.1 Les fondements des demandes de réparation (sources et principes)

Les fondements de la responsabilité en droit français restent largement emprunts par leur origine fondée sur la faute. Ils ont cependant évolué et ce tant en droit privé qu'en droit public. Si la faute reste largement présente, d'autres fondements ont progressivement vu le jour : la garantie de l'indemnisation s'est progressivement imposée en s'appuyant sur le risque social encouru par les individus qui pouvaient être victimes d'activités tant de la puissance publique que des personnes privées,[29] notamment dans le domaine économique. Rapportée à la question de la violation

[28] Cons. Constit. Décision n° 2010-1 QPC du 28 mai 2010 Consorts L. [Cristallisation des pensions], Rec. 91.

[29] V. Lochak (1993).

des droits de l'Homme ou des droits fondamentaux, cette responsabilité s'est diversifiée dans les mêmes proportions que le régime de responsabilité générale.

Dans le cadre de la responsabilité des autorités publiques chargées de la protection et de la mise en œuvre des droits fondamentaux, le droit administratif a fait progressivement évoluer sa jurisprudence en développant les théories du cumul des fautes puis de cumul de responsabilités par lesquelles il a cherché à rattacher la faute personnelle d'un agent à celle commise à l'occasion du service.[30] Cette idée a progressivement transformé la responsabilité pour faute exclusivement personnelle de l'agent public – qui relevait du juge judiciaire et pouvait faire douter de l'indemnisation en cas –fréquent- d'insolvabilité – en une responsabilité partagée pour faute de service. La théorie du cumul des fautes a fait entrer indirectement la notion de garantie dans le droit de la responsabilité pour faute dans la mesure où la part représentée par la faute de service a pu devenir de plus en plus faible pour permettre à la victime d'être indemnisée. Les mécanismes de subrogation et d'action récursoire permettaient ensuite à l'administration de se retourner contre son agent si elle estimait que sa faute devait engendrer un remboursement en raison d'un comportement fautif qu'elle sanctionnait de cette façon. Parallèlement, les formes de responsabilité sans faute se développaient également en se fondant sur le risque ou la rupture de l'égalité devant les charges publiques. Toutefois, ces formes de responsabilité sans faute restaient exceptionnelles en raison des exigences liées à la spécificité, la gravité ou l'anormalité du dommage. L'idée d'une responsabilité administrative de la puissance publique garantissant l'indemnisation ne s'est cependant imposée que progressivement. Pendant longtemps, les victimes d'activités de la puissance publique étaient moins bien traitées que ne l'étaient celles d'activités relevant du juge judiciaire, qui se montrait plus généreux dans l'indemnisation accordée. Cette tendance s'est inversée dans le dernier tiers du vingtième siècle à travers le recours à des mécanismes de présomption favorisant l'indemnisation des victimes. La violation des droits fondamentaux n'a cependant pas donné lieu à l'application d'un régime plutôt qu'un autre en raison de l'absence de considération spécifique liée à l'origine du fondement de la responsabilité. Il n'est donc pas possible pratiquement de rattacher la responsabilité pour violation d'un droit fondamental à l'un plutôt qu'à l'autre de ces fondements.

Dans le cadre de la responsabilité civile, le fondement de la faute, toujours présent, a été concurrencé par les régimes de responsabilité spécifiques issus de transformations sociales et notamment de l'obligation de garanties des dommages. Les mécanismes d'assurance obligatoire[31] ont également renforcé cette situation qui visait à couvrir la réalisation d'un risque dont les potentialités de réalisation se sont accrues. La même remarque que celle relative au droit de la responsabilité de la puissance publique prévaut. Le régime de responsabilité civile pour violation d'un droit fondamental ne présente pas de spécificité particulière : il s'insère dans le cadre de la responsabilité générale et s'identifie davantage par la nature du préjudice

[30] CE 26 juillet 1918 *Lemonnier*, Rec. p. 761.

[31] V. par exemple, la loi du 27 février 1958 sur l'assurance automobile obligatoire reprise à l'article L 211-1 du code des assurances.

plus que par le fondement qui lui donne naissance. On remarquera cependant que les formes de responsabilité issues de mécanismes de garanties et d'assurances, recherchés par des régimes de responsabilité spécifiques issus de réformes législatives, se rattachent d'une certaine façon à la protection de droits individuels qui seraient méconnus ou traités de façon inégalitaire si ces mécanismes n'existaient pas. Si cette raison n'est jamais mise en avant officiellement, la protection des libertés fondamentales est souvent l'une des causes profondes de ces mécanismes sociaux de responsabilité.

Le régime français de responsabilité repose ainsi sur à peu près tous les fondements potentiels : la faute a certes perdu le terrain prédominant qu'elle occupait mais elle s'est adjointe d'autres fondements incluant le risque, la rupture d'égalité et l'équité. La doctrine a cherché une forme de cohérence explicative à ces mutations progressives du fondement de la responsabilité. La théorie de l'équité est ainsi apparue comme un élément fédérateur qui permettait d'expliquer cette mutation et correspondrait à une prise en compte des conséquences de la vie sociale sur l'individu.[32] Sans que ce fondement apparaisse exclusif et puisse également reposer sur l'idée de responsabilité collective, on voit poindre une logique reconstructive ou restauratrice des droits fondamentaux derrière ces interventions législatives instaurant ces régimes de responsabilité sans faute.

La particularité de la responsabilité pour violation d'un droit fondamental en France repose non pas sur l'analyse du fondement de la responsabilité mais sur l'existence d'un dommage réparable. S'il faut toujours un fait générateur de la responsabilité – fautif ou non – cela ne suffit pas. Il est nécessaire que ce fait générateur ait donné naissance à un dommage ou un préjudice et qu'existe un lien de causalité direct entre ce fait et le dommage. La situation française implique donc que le dommage soit réel, direct et certain et puisse être réparable. Il s'agit d'ailleurs là d'un élément fondamental de distinction entre les systèmes qui reconnaissent que la seule violation d'un droit fondamental constitue un source suffisante d'engagement de la responsabilité et ceux – tel celui de la France – qui exigent que la violation soit source d'un préjudice ou d'un dommage évaluable pour permettre cet engagement. Les deux systèmes reposent sur des logiques différentes car si le premier constitue un fondement objectif de la responsabilité, le second est subjectif et n'accorde à la violation du droit qu'une importance secondaire par rapport à l'indemnisation du dommage. Le système français est donc de ce point de vue assez abrupt. Il ne permet l'engagement de la responsabilité que si l'ensemble des éléments est considéré comme satisfait au regard des exigences prévues : fait générateur, dommage et lien de causalité. Le dommage constitue donc un élément central et initiateur de la responsabilité pour violation des droits fondamentaux. L'existence de cette dernière lui est conditionnée.

Le troisième élément de la responsabilité représenté par le lien de causalité est également une condition *sine qua non* de la responsabilité. Ce lien de causalité consiste à exiger que le dommage soit la conséquence directe du fait générateur. Le droit français de la responsabilité exige traditionnellement que ce lien soit direct ou

---

[32] V. Lochak (1993).

suffisamment direct pour prouver que l'imputabilité du dommage repose sur ce fait générateur. Cette exigence abstraite, assez simple à comprendre, est évidemment beaucoup plus difficile à appréhender dans la réalité. Si ce lien causal est évident dans nombre d'hypothèses, dans d'autres, il a conduit la jurisprudence à développer des mécanismes de présomption qui permettent de renverser la charge de la preuve de la victime à l'organe ou la personne responsable du dommage.[33] Cette inversion de l'établissement du lien de causalité possède un effet déterminant sur l'engagement de la responsabilité et revient en pratique à exiger de la victime qu'elle rapporte seulement l'existence d'un dommage et d'un fait générateur de la responsabilité. Ceci constitue un mécanisme facilitant l'engagement de la responsabilité et l'indemnisation. La violation des droits fondamentaux n'est pas spécifiquement visée par ces mécanismes de présomption mais elle peut d'une certaine façon en bénéficier lorsque la violation de ces droits rentre dans les matières où elles sont mises en œuvre. Tel est par exemple le cas en matière de responsabilité des services hospitaliers lorsqu'un patient entré pour une opération bénigne en ressort avec de graves séquelles sans commune mesure avec le risque qu'il encourrait.

5.4.2 *La nature du préjudice ou du dommage*

En matière de réparation, le droit français de la responsabilité se fonde, sur le caractère direct, réel et certain du dommage et sur son caractère indemnisable. La réparation du dommage ne peut donc s'opérer sur la seule violation d'un droit, tout au moins en ce qui concerne son caractère pécuniaire. En revanche, l'évaluation du préjudice peut inclure – s'il existe - le dommage moral dès lors que celui-ci se rattache à ce caractère direct, réel et certain du dommage. Cette indemnisation sera toutefois source d'interrogations car elle présente toujours une difficulté d'évaluation malgré les barèmes établis et la prise en compte par les juges d'un spectre d'informations et de critères qui reste le plus large possible. Les juges restent souverains en ce qui concerne cette appréciation.

Le caractère matériel du dommage fait en revanche l'objet d'un consensus plus large, que ce soit devant le juge administratif ou le juge judiciaire. D'une façon générale, le droit et la politique jurisprudentielle des juges consiste à indemniser la victime de toutes les conséquences dommageables du préjudice : tout le dommage mais rien que le dommage ! Cela concerne aussi bien la réparation matérielle, physique ou morale que le manque à gagner si celui-ci est indemnisable et n'a pas fait pas déjà l'objet d'une prise en charge par ailleurs. Le droit français se montre assez englobant de ce point de vue, dès lors que les chefs du préjudice issus du dommage ne font aucun doute. Ces principes, issus du droit de la responsabilité civile, ont été repris par la juridiction administrative dans le cadre du droit de la responsabilité de la puissance publique. On constate néanmoins que si les sources de l'indemnisation sont les mêmes, elles peuvent faire l'objet d'une appréciation

[33] V. Paillard (2013).

variable en fonction de l'ordre juridictionnel, des juges et de la nature de l'affaire à traiter. Si les mots sont les mêmes, les chiffres sont parfois difficiles à interpréter en raison de l'apparente similitude des situations et de la différence d'indemnisation. Il existe toutefois une série de questions marginales sur le type de préjudice indemnisable qui n'a pas reçu – et ne peut à notre avis pas recevoir - de réponse prédéterminée. En effet, dans le cas de la violation d'un droit fondamental, rien n'indique que la nature ou le contexte de la violation ne pourra être pris en compte. Il n'empêche que le contexte de commission de la violation peut avoir une incidence sur la perception que le juge pourra avoir de la réparation. Logiquement, lorsque la violation sera la conséquence d'un comportement fautif, la nature de ce comportement ne devrait avoir aucune incidence sur le montant de la réparation. La réparation du préjudice doit être uniquement calculée sur l'ampleur du dommage et non sur la gravité de la faute. Pourtant, la lecture des arrêts et une analyse synthétique de la jurisprudence amène à s'interroger sur cette déconnexion complète : les circonstances de commission de la faute peuvent inciter le juge à se montrer plus ou moins sévères dans l'évaluation des préjudices et aboutir ainsi à relier la faute et l'évaluation du dommage. Ceci n'est évidemment pas mesurable juridiquement. On relèvera également pour clore cet aspect du débat, que l'exacte comptabilisation de la réparation du dommage peut subir certains atermoiements lorsque le régime de responsabilité est législatif. Dans ce cas, sans qu'il s'agisse d'une obligation, il n'est pas rare que le législateur mette en place un régime d'indemnisation forfaitaire du dommage, notamment lorsque l'évaluation précise du dommage est impossible en raison du moment de la réparation ou d'accès impossible à l'information permettant de calculer la réparation. Tel fût le cas des lois successives d'indemnisation à l'issue de la Deuxième Guerre mondiale. Ce peut notamment être le cas dans l'hypothèse d'une violation d'un droit fondamental.

5.4.3 *Etendue des réparations*

L'étendue des réparations constitue un sujet vaste et complexe qui ne peut recevoir de réponse unique ou caricaturale. Le système français de responsabilité, loin d'être parfait, tente néanmoins d'apporter une réponse adaptée qui a évolué au cours de l'histoire.[34]

Les règles générales d'indemnisation s'appliquent tout d'abord devant les juridictions lorsqu'elles sont saisies d'une demande en réparation. Ce sont ici, comme cela a été mentionné précédemment, les règles générales de l'indemnisation qui s'appliquent, quelle que soit la source de la responsabilité. Lorsque la violation d'un droit ou d'une liberté fondamentales ont donné lieu à un préjudice dont le juge estime le lien avec la violation suffisante, il pourra engager la responsabilité et indemniser le préjudice suivant les règles classiques de la responsabilité.

---

[34] V. Bouchet (2013).

Les règles spécifiques d'indemnisation issues des régimes législatifs peuvent en revanche varier suivant la nature et l'objet poursuivi par la législation. Si cette dernière cherche à cibler un groupe déterminé et inclut dans ses objectifs d'autres éléments que ceux du caractère réel, direct et certain du préjudice, ces régimes spécifiques pourront dépasser les critères et caractères traditionnels de la réparation. Ces régimes sont en réalité indépendants des régimes classiques généraux et n'obéissent pas aux mêmes objectifs. Comme cela a déjà été mentionné, les violations des droits fondamentaux peuvent être également concernés par ces régimes.

Les réparations et indemnités octroyées aux victimes des dommages concernent à la fois le *damnum emergens* et le *lucrume cessans*. Tel est le principe de base.

Toute atteinte physique ou morale peut donc faire l'objet d'une indemnisation dans les différents chefs de préjudice qu'elle comporte : cela inclut la prise en charge médicale pour le traitement, le prix de la douleur, la longueur du traitement, le préjudice esthétique si besoin est, la perte de mobilité, le caractère temporaire ou définitif de l'éventuelle incapacité. L'atteinte à l'intégrité corporelle est de façon générale complètement indemnisable et l'est encore davantage si cette atteinte se double d'une souffrance morale. Le décès n'entraîne pas en revanche d'indemnisation pour la victime directe, compte tenu de l'extinction de la personnalité juridique du défunt. Elle ouvre en revanche un droit à indemnisation pour les proches de la victime qu'il s'agisse des conséquences pécuniaires du décès ou du *pretium doloris* qui est également indemnisable ainsi que du préjudice moral. Si les conséquences du décès peuvent avoir une incidence sur le patrimoine du *de cujus*, elles pourront faire l'objet d'une indemnisation. La situation peut également être légèrement différente d'un ordre de juridiction à un autre en raison de l'origine et des conditions de réalisation du dommage.

La perte de propriété est également indemnisable dans son intégralité dès lors que cette perte est la conséquence du fait générateur. La situation est ici généralement plus facile à gérer car la perte de propriété est plus facilement évaluable que les dommages corporels ou psychologiques. Les principes de l'indemnisation restent toutefois les mêmes que ceux qui prévalent pour ces dommages corporels : le préjudice doit être indemnisé intégralement et dans toutes ses formes mais ne peut aller au delà de l'indemnisation du préjudice. La question s'est notamment posée pour la restitution des biens spoliés aux personnes de religion juive durant la Deuxième Guerre mondiale. La réponse en termes de responsabilité a été double : les personnes qui ont pu retrouver leurs biens ont bénéficié de leur restitution ; en revanche, dans les hypothèses où le bien ne pouvait être restitué à son propriétaire ou à ses ayant-droits, l'indemnisation s'est faite sur la base d'une évaluation du bien et sur l'évolution de sa valeur dans le temps. Le préjudice affectif peut également être indemnisé s'il est prouvé qu'il existe et est intégré à l'indemnisation offerte à la victime. On remarquera qu'en ce qui concerne les dommages liés à la perte ou à la restriction de propriété, ne sont pas intégrées les décisions ou actions légitimes de la puissance publique, telle l'expropriation ou la réquisition pour cause d'utilité publique, qui font l'objet de processus d'indemnisation et de procédures spécifiques. La question se pose d'ailleurs de savoir si le traitement de la responsabilité pour violation des droits fondamentaux ne doit pas tenir compte de l'aspect matériel ou immatériel du dommage causé. Dès lors que le dommage est évaluable dans toutes ses dimensions objectives, il peut être indemnisé beaucoup plus facilement que s'il s'agit d'un dommage comportant de multiples aspects subjectifs.

La privation illégitime de liberté peut donner lieu à indemnisation mais dépendra de sa cause. Le régime français de responsabilité institue un régime spécifique d'origine législative pour les privations de liberté liées à une instance judiciaire pour laquelle la victime serait reconnue innocente.[35] Concrètement, cela vise les hypothèses de détention provisoire avant un procès pour lequel la personne serait acquittée. La France reste, malgré les opportunités offertes par le code pénal et le code de procédure pénale, un Etat dans lequel la mise en détention provisoire reste largement répandue. Les acquittements permettent de demander à la victime une indemnisation fondée sur cette détention. Ce régime législatif prend en considération l'intégralité des préjudices subis par la victime d'une telle détention. Ce régime est un régime de responsabilité sans faute et ne tient évidemment pas compte du fonctionnement défectueux du service public de la justice.

Certaines autres privations de liberté ne sont pas considérées comme des actes illégaux soit par leur durée trop courte (garde à vue), soit par leur nature (rétention de sécurité en zone d'attente pour les étrangers entrés illégalement sur le territoire français). Si l'on peut contester théoriquement ou philosophiquement ces privations de liberté, elles n'en restent pas moins non indemnisables sauf si elles ont été utilisées de façon abusive. Toute autre privation de liberté orchestrée par la puissance publique ou ses agents ne pourrait être justifiée et constituerait donc une violation de la liberté d'aller et de venir qui serait inacceptable en termes de respect de l'Etat de droit. Une telle atteinte pourrait même être qualifiée de « voie de fait », même si cette notion n'a plus aujourd'hui le même intérêt que celui qu'elle possédait en raison d'un rapprochement des jurisprudence administrative et judiciaire en matière d'atteinte aux droits et libertés fondamentaux. Dans l'histoire française contemporaine, ces attitudes extrêmes remontent aux périodes troublées du deuxième conflit mondial ou de la guerre d'Algérie. Ce ne sont donc pas des questions que le juge a l'habitude de rencontrer.

Les violations des règles procédurales de garanties des droits ne peuvent normalement donner lieu à indemnisation sauf s'il s'avère qu'elles ont été à l'origine d'un dommage. Ce cas de figure est exceptionnel car il serait nécessaire de démontrer qu'il existe un dommage dont la cause se trouve dans cette violation procédurale.

[35] La réparation de la détention provisoire est organisée par les articles 149 à 150 et R. 26 à R. 40-22 du code de procédure pénale. Le régime de l'indemnisation de la détention provisoire, issu de la loi n° 70-643 du 17 juillet 1970, a été modifié en profondeur par les lois n° 2000-516 du 15 juin et n° 2000-1354 du 30 décembre 2000. La personne qui a fait l'objet d'une détention provisoire au cours d'une procédure terminée à son égard par une décision de non-lieu, de relaxe ou d'acquittement devenue définitive a droit, à sa demande, à la réparation intégrale du préjudice moral et matériel que lui a causé cette détention. c'est le premier président de la cour d'appel dans le ressort de laquelle a été prononcé le jugement ou l'arrêt d'où résulte l'innocence du détenu, qui statue, à l'issue d'une procédure publique et contradictoire, par décision motivée susceptible de recours devant la commission nationale de réparation des détentions placée auprès de la Cour de cassation (CNRD).

Or, une violation procédurale peut contribuer à la naissance ou reconnaissance d'un dommage mais la plupart du temps, elle participe d'un ensemble plus vaste sur lequel l'ensemble de la responsabilité reposera. Ceci participe également de l'idée selon laquelle le régime français d'indemnisation est largement fondé sur le dommage et son lien de causalité beaucoup plus que sur son fait générateur.

La responsabilité en droit français ne connait normalement pas de régime d'indemnisation pour des dommages qui ne peuvent être évalués pécuniairement. Cela tient tant à l'origine du système de responsabilité examiné antérieurement qu'à l'idée que le dommage ne peut être réparé que s'il est réel, direct et certain. Sans ce caractère, le juge ne peut se transformer en une autorité morale qui distribuerait *satisfecit* et blâmes aux autorités publiques. La réponse de principe est donc négative. Toutefois la situation est certainement en train d'évoluer depuis que le juge français s'est trouvé confronté à des contentieux possédant une portée historique dans lesquels l'attitude générale de l'Etat peut être mise en cause. S'il reste un juge de la responsabilité dont l'instrument principal est l'octroi de dommages-intérêts en cas de violation d'un droit, il a pu être un peu plus prolixe sur l'existence d'une responsabilité de la puissance publique pour des actes qui ne pouvaient donner lieu à indemnisation monétaire. Il a ainsi parfois transposé en droit interne l'idée d'une satisfaction équitable empruntée au modèle de compensation employé en droit international de la responsabilité des Etats.[36] L'attente des victimes en matière de reconnaissance de responsabilité repose parfois davantage dans les lettres et les mots employés que dans les chiffres et montants d'indemnisation attribués.

Les dommages-intérêts octroyés ne sont normalement pas taxables dans la mesure où ils correspondent à la compensation d'un préjudice. L'idée simple de cette règle repose sur l'idée que l'indemnisation ne correspond pas à un gain mais à la réparation d'un dommage subi. Il serait donc anormal de soumettre à l'impôt sur le revenu une somme qui correspond à une remise en état d'une situation qui n'aurait pas du se détériorer. Ce principe trouve toutefois ses limites dans d'autres principes du droit fiscal qui peuvent trouver à s'appliquer lorsque le montant de la réparation a été versé.

Le juge français dispose en théorie d'un large pouvoir d'appréciation dans l'octroi des dommages-intérêts demandés par une victime. Il reste d'abord et avant tout lié par le cas qui lui est soumis et doit apprécier avec les moyens et instruments dont il dispose les situations qu'il doit réparer. On remarquera en premier lieu que le juge ne peut aller au-delà de ce que lui demande les requérants. Ceci explique d'ailleurs partiellement que les sommes réclamées soient nettement supérieures à

---

[36]V. Affaire CPJI, 13 septembre 1928, *Affaire relative à l'usine de Chorzow*, Série A, n° 17, Rec. p. 17; v. égal. « Étude concernant le droit à restitution, à indemnisation et à réadaptation des victimes de violations flagrantes des droits de l'homme et des libertés fondamentales», Rapport final présenté par M. Theo van Boven, Rapporteur spécial » (E/CN.4/ Sub.2/1993/8). Il est généralement admis que le droit à réparation possède une double dimension dans le cadre du droit international : a) une dimension de fond qui doit se traduire par le devoir de donner réparation pour le préjudice subi sous les formes suivantes : *restitution, indemnisation, réadaptation, satisfaction et, le cas échéant, garanties de non-répétition* ; et b) une dimension procédurale permettant d'assurer la réparation de fond en question. V. égal CE Avis ass 16 février 2009 *Hoffman Glemane*, Req n° 315499, op.cit.

celles octroyées. En deuxième lieu, lorsqu'il est confronté à un dommage, le juge peut recourir à l'expertise et demander une évaluation du dommage subi. Même si cette expertise n'est pas le seul élément pris en considération, elle canalise l'évaluation finale. Enfin, le juge dispose de toute une série d'instruments (aides, barèmes, grille…) provenant souvent de systèmes d'assurances, qui l'aident à évaluer l'indemnisation. Le pouvoir du juge existe donc mais il reste encadré par un certain nombre de principes ou de comportements méthodologiques qui l'amènent à affiner son évaluation. En revanche, le juge se trouve dans une situation de compétence liée en ce qui concerne l'octroi de dommages-intérêts en cas d'absence de préjudice : il ne peut pas se transformer en redresseur de torts, quelle que soit la position personnelle qu'il peut avoir sur la situation ou la violation. Le pouvoir discrétionnaire est donc moins large qu'il ne paraît à première vue.

Reposant sur l'indemnisation de l'intégralité du dommage, le droit français de la responsabilité ne devrait normalement pas connaître de limitation si les éléments de la responsabilité sont réunis. Toutefois, les régimes législatifs de responsabilité, qui se sont multipliés ces dernières années, ont amené le Parlement à prévoir certains cas d'indemnisation forfaitaire au cas où le dommage pouvait être difficile à évaluer. On peut donc considérer que dans certains cas, l'indemnisation forfaitaire ne couvre qu'une partie du dommage. Toutefois, deux raisons aisément compréhensibles expliquent cette attitude : d'une part, les éléments nécessaires à l'évaluation d'une indemnisation ne sont pas ou plus toujours disponibles et rendent donc cette évaluation exacte quasi-impossible ; d'autre part, la masse des dossiers à traiter peut parfois rendre le processus impraticable si l'on s'en tenait au régime ordinaire de responsabilité et nécessite un traitement d'ensemble. Au demeurant, rien ne prouve que l'indemnisation forfaitaire ne soit pas plus favorable au demandeur que l'indemnisation exacte du dommage.

Le droit français de la responsabilité ne limite pas non plus les demandes en fonction des violations commises. Comme ce droit repose essentiellement sur une analyse du préjudice et hormis le cas spécifique d'une demande de réparation législative, la question de la multiplication des violations des droits fondamentaux ne pose pas en soi de difficultés. En revanche, elle n'aura aucune incidence sur le montant de l'indemnité ou de la compensation versé à la victime dans la mesure où seul le dommage final sera pris en considération. Ceci s'inscrit dans la logique du système français de responsabilité. En revanche, il n'est pas impossible que le juge voit dans le dommage la conséquence directe de la violation de plusieurs droits ou de multiples droits mais cela n'affecte pas en soi le régime de l'indemnisation du dommage.

La question de la transmissibilité des créances éventuelles pour violation des droits fondamentaux aux ayant-droits d'une victime s'inscrit dans la perspective décrite antérieurement. Les dommages possédant une incidence personnelle sur les victimes (prix de la douleur, effets traumatiques, troubles dans les conditions d'existence) ne peuvent pas être transmis et leur indemnisation ne peut être répercutée sur leurs ayant-droits. En revanche, les dommages patrimoniaux et évaluables peuvent être transmis aux ayant-droits comme cela se ferait dans les règles de dévolution successorale. La transmission de la demande existe donc si la personne les reprend à son nom ou s'est jointe initialement à la procédure. Par ailleurs, les ayant-droits possèdent eux-mêmes un droit d'action pour les préjudices personnels qu'ils auraient pu subir et qui résulteraient de la disparition du demandeur initial. Il s'agit d'une action en responsabilité propre qui se fonde non pas sur une transmission de la demande mais sur l'existence de préjudices personnels liés à la disparition du demandeur ou de la victime. En termes de violations des droits et libertés fondamentaux, ceci est illustré par l'indemnisation de la spoliation des biens immobiliers et mobiliers dérobés par ou avec l'assentiment de l'Etat.

5.4.4 Absence de dommages-intérêts punitifs

Le droit français de la responsabilité étant fondé sur la réparation intégrale du préjudice (*restitutio in integrum*), l'idée d'introduire un caractère punitif à l'indemnisation des préjudices est absente des raisonnements juridictionnels. Si l'action pénale exerce une fonction rétributive, l'action civile ou administrative ne possède dans le cadre de la responsabilité qu'une fonction réparatrice[37] et le mélange des deux n'est guère possible. Cette situation vaut autant devant le juge administratif[38] que devant le juge judiciaire. Toutefois, ainsi que cela a été mentionné antérieurement, il n'est pas exclu que dans certains contentieux de la responsabilité – et alors même que cela n'apparaît pas officiellement – l'attitude de l'auteur du fait générateur de la responsabilité soit pris en compte pour renforcer ou appuyer le caractère anormal et grave du dommage. Il est extrêmement difficile de déterminer dans quelle mesure le poids de la faute est intégré dans le calcul du montant de la réparation. En toute logique, il ne devrait pas l'être. Cependant, une succession de négligences ou de fautes peut avoir renforcé le caractère du dommage et le juge n'y est pas insensible dans le traitement de l'évaluation de l'indemnisation. Ceci résulte néanmoins davantage d'une analyse sociologique du contentieux, beaucoup plus que d'une analyse strictement juridique.

5.4.5 Moyens de limitations et d'exclusion de la responsabilité

La responsabilité pour violation des droits fondamentaux connaît les mêmes modes de partage et d'exclusion que les autres domaines de la responsabilité.[39] Le régime français de responsabilité n'est sur ce point guère original et repose avant tout sur la logique et le bon sens.

[37] Cette idée était pourtant présente à l'origine en droit civil de la responsabilité. La réparation du comportement fautif reposait sur trois éléments: la compensation du dommage, la punition de la faute, la prévention de la répétition. V. Flour (1987).

[38] Il existe quelques exceptions marginales tels que le contentieux des dégradations apportés au domaine public qui possède un caractère quasi-pénal mais qui ne nous concerne pas directement dans le cadre de ce rapport.

[39] V. Sabard (2012).

La faute de la victime est traditionnellement l'un des éléments qui peut être pris en considération. Il est évidemment nécessaire qu'elle soit prouvée et que son degré puisse être évalué. Si la victime a contribué à la production du dommage dont elle demande réparation, elle pourra se voir imputer une part de responsabilité qui pourra diminuer voire supprimer la réparation. Il faut évidemment que cette faute puisse être rattachée à un lien de causalité juridique entre le dommage et le ou les actes générateurs de la responsabilité. Ce principe général s'applique à l'ensemble des régimes de responsabilité.[40] Dans le cadre de la violation des droits fondamentaux, le partage de la faute n'est pas impossible mais devrait logiquement se cantonner à des cas exceptionnels dans lesquels la victime aurait contribué à la violation de ses propres droits (refus d'identification, attitude menaçante, induction volontaire en erreur, par exemple). Le partage de responsabilité n'est donc pas impossible même s'il n'est guère fréquent.

Le droit interne français n'impose pas, par ailleurs, d'épuiser préalablement les autres voies de recours devant les juridictions françaises. Le recours en responsabilité est un recours subjectif indépendant d'autres voies de droit objectives. Il n'y a donc pas d'autres obligations sur ce point que celles du respect des règles procédurales. Il arrive cependant que les deux types de recours soient exercés successivement. Tel est par exemple le cas de la responsabilité de la puissance publique pour illégalité. Si un droit ou une liberté est méconnue et qu'un recours est exercé dans le cadre du contentieux de la légalité, rien n'empêche ensuite le requérant d'intenter une action en responsabilité pour illégalité : les deux types de contentieux sont indépendants mais leur combinaison conserve leur intérêt.[41] En revanche, si la demande d'indemnisation ou de réparation du préjudice est portée devant une juridiction supranationale (européenne), les conditions d'épuisement des voies de recours internes sont normalement exigées pour que la requête puisse être transmise.

Les exclusions complètes de responsabilité sont extrêmement rares.[42] Le principe est aujourd'hui celui de la responsabilité de la puissance publique pour les actes, actions et omissions qui lui sont imputables soit directement, soit au travers de ses agents. Ce principe a pu connaître par le passé des exceptions dès lors que l'activité de la puissance publique apparaissait extrêmement complexe ou ne relevait pas du seul contrôle de la puissance publique nationale. Ces exclusions de responsabilité ont pu intervenir dans la conduite des relations internationales ou pour des

---

[40] Il peut même l'être dans les cas de responsabilité sans faute d'origine législative. Ainsi à titre d'exemple, dans le cas de demande d'indemnisation pour détention provisoire abusive, le texte de la loi prévoit que 'la reconnaissance de l'irresponsabilité du demandeur au sens de l'article 122–1 du code pénal, ou une amnistie postérieure à la mise en détention provisoire ou encore la prescription de l'action publique, si celle-ci est intervenue après la libération de la personne' libère l'Etat de toute forme d'indemnisation.

[41] V. Belrhali-Bernard (2009) 1337.

[42] On peut même considérer aujourd'hui qu'elles ne peuvent qu'être liées à des causes extérieures (v. en ce sens Sabard (2012); les exclusions complètes de nature politique ne sont plus de mise aujourd'hui.

dommages liés à des situations de force majeure.[43] En revanche, la limitation de responsabilité a pu être autrefois mise en œuvre dans le domaine de la responsabilité pour faute en utilisant l'exigence d'une faute lourde de la 'administration. Ce fût notamment le cas pour les services de police, les services fiscaux ou le fonctionnement défectueux du service public de la justice. En réalité, cette théorie qui consistait à exiger une faute lourde pour engager la responsabilité de l'Etat aboutissait à reconnaître une quasi forme d'exclusion de responsabilité. Ces théories ont aujourd'hui disparu ou ne sont plus usitées. Dans la plupart des cas, la jurisprudence ou le législateur ont mis fin à ces régimes d'irresponsabilité ou de responsabilité limitée, ce qui correspond à la volonté d'offrir aux victimes de ces actions une forme de garantie ou une indemnisation équitable que la puissance publique prend à sa charge.

5.4.6 Les titulaires et bénéficiaires de l'obligation de réparer

L'obligation de réparer les dommages nés de la violation de droits fondamentaux variera en fonction de l'origine de l'obligation. Le plus souvent, il s'agira d'une personne de droit public (Etat ou collectivité publique) mais il pourra également s'agir d'une personne privée si celle-ci est chargée de respecter ou de faire respecter un droit fondamental spécifique. A cet égard, on distingue classiquement les personnes privées chargées d'une mission de service public et pouvant exercer des prérogatives de puissance publique[44] et les personnes privées qui dans le cadre de l'exercice d'activités privées doivent respecter et faire respecter certains droits fondamentaux (comme les entreprises par exemple dans le cas du droit du travail). Il n'y a donc pas un seul titulaire de l'obligation de réparer mais plusieurs, en fonction des droits concernés. D'un point de vue pratique, ce sont surtout les juridictions administratives qui sont le plus souvent confrontées à cette violation des droits fondamentaux pour les raisons examinées antérieurement et parce qu'elles sont directement confrontées à l'activité des autorités publiques où les risques de méconnaissance des droits sont les plus nombreux.

La responsabilité administrative, ainsi que cela a été mentionné, repose également sur l'auteur physique de la violation pour autant que celui ci ait contribué par

[43] La force majeure se définit comme un fait étranger, extérieur, imprévisible et irrésistible. L'évènement doit ainsi être réellement insurmontable, tel un séisme ou un catastrophe naturelle. La force majeure exonère la responsabilité de l'administration pour faute et sans faute (CE Sect., 29 juillet 1953, *Epoux Glasner* Rec. 427)

[44] Cette distinction possède un effet sur la compétence mais non sur le fondement même de la responsabilité. Ainsi, le Conseil d'Etat a refusé de reconnaître la compétence du juge administratif pour les contributions apportées par la SNCF (société nationale de chemin de fer) dans le transport en vue de la déportation des juifs (CE 21 déc. 2007, n° 305966, *Lipietz et autres*, Rec. 540) ; Cette situation a cependant conduit ladite société à reconnaître son implication et à présenter ses excuses sans pour autant qu'aucune compensation financière n'ait été octroyée : *Guillaume Pépy reconnaît le rôle de la SNCF dans la Shoah.* Le Monde, 25 janvier 2011.

son comportement à la production de la faute, et ceci même lorsque les dommages ont été causés dans la cadre de l'exercice d'une activité de la puissance publique ou du service public. La responsabilité personnelle de l'agent peut dans ces conditions être engagée mais est en pratique limitée à l'hypothèse où la victime souhaite faire retomber une partie symbolique de la faute sur l'agent lui-même. La demande de dommages-intérêts est, dans un tel cas, souvent limitée à une somme symbolique limitée voire dérisoire, car les bénéficiaires de l'obligation de réparer savent que l'initiateur physique du dommage ne possède pas les garanties de solvabilité d'une personne publique.

Enfin, on soulignera que les personnes étrangères peuvent solliciter des dommages-intérêts dans le cadre d'une action en responsabilité pour violation d'un droit fondamental dès lors que les droits invoqués ne sont pas limités aux seuls nationaux.

5.4.7 Juridictions compétentes et procédures

Le système français de répartition des compétences juridictionnelles aboutit à scinder en deux régimes le droit de la responsabilité, y compris pour les violations relatives à la violation ou méconnaissance des droits fondamentaux. Il a été précédemment mentionné que les régimes reposaient sur des sources et fondements juridiques différents mais reposaient au fond sur la même dynamique. Partis d'un régime de responsabilité pour faute pour admettre des exceptions en fondant la responsabilité sur le risque ou la rupture d'égalité devant les charges publiques, les régimes spécifiques de responsabilité se sont multipliés au point d'admettre assez largement des régimes dérogatoires, créés et organisés par le législateur et fondés sur des considérations d'équité. Il faut souligner que ces règles de répartition des compétences ne sont pas propres à la responsabilité pour violation des droits fondamentaux et que ces derniers n'ont aucune influence directe sur la répartition des compétences.

L'existence de délais-limite pour introduire une action en responsabilité n'est également pas propre à la violation des droits fondamentaux. Il n'existe pas de règle procédurale de forclusion qui empêche l'exercice d'un recours en responsabilité. Toutefois, deux limites externes à ce principe méritent d'être mentionnées. La première a trait au délai du recours pour excès de pouvoir lorsque la violation d'un droit est précédée d'un recours pour illégalité. Le délai de recours est de deux mois à compter de la décision. Certes, il n'est pas opposable en matière de responsabilité mais s'impose lorsque l'action en responsabilité est fondée sur une telle illégalité que le requérant veut faire sanctionner indépendamment de son action en dommages-intérêts. La deuxième limite a trait à la prescription. Le régime de la prescription en droit français varie suivant les juridictions. Il est de cinq ans en matière civile[45] et de

---

[45] Jusqu'à la loi n° 2008-561 du 17 juin 2008 portant réforme de la prescription en matière civile, le délai général de prescription en matière civile était de trente ans. Le délai de droit commun de la

quatre ans en matière administrative.[46] Ces délais de prescription peuvent influer sur le recours en indemnité à partir du moment où la victime avait connaissance de l'origine du fait générateur susceptible d'engager la responsabilité de la personne privée ou de la personne publique et s'est abstenue.

Les actions collectives sont recevables en droit français de la responsabilité si elles sont initiées par des organisations regroupant ou représentant l'intérêt des victimes pou peu qu'elles soient à l'origine de la requête et qu'elles cherchent à défendre l'intérêt collectif de leurs membres. Les associations, les syndicats, les groupements de défense sont ainsi recevables à défendre les droits de leurs adhérents et de les représenter en tant que groupement collectif de défense. En revanche, le droit défendu doit rentrer dans l'objet social du groupement. En revanche, le droit français vient récemment d'évoluer sur les actions collectives en regroupements spontanés,[47] inspiré des *class actions* aux Etats-Unis. Le droit français de la responsabilité reste fondé sur le principe : « pas d'intérêt, pas d'action ».

5.5 L'interaction entre les principes d'indemnisation nationaux et supranationaux en cas de responsabilité pour violation des droits de l'Homme

La multiplication des catalogues de droits fondamentaux mais également celle des juridictions amène à s'interroger sur l'interaction entre les mécanismes de réparation financière tels qu'ils sont prévus par le droit interne et ceux qui peuvent exister au travers de mécanismes internationaux.

Le droit français de la réparation est fondé sur l'indemnisation intégrale du préjudice mais uniquement sur ce seul préjudice comme mentionné antérieurement. Logiquement les victimes de la violation de droits fondamentaux qui estiment avoir subi un tel préjudice se retourneront devant les juridictions nationales mais ces dernières se prononceront pour « solde de tout compte », c'est à dire en estimant que le dommage sera intégralement réparé. Logiquement, les juridictions françaises n'indemnisent pas deux fois le même préjudice : si celui ci a déjà été indemnisé, les juridictions françaises considéreront qu'il y aurait là un enrichissement sans cause.

Cette situation n'est toutefois pas réciproque pour les juridictions supranationales et peut donner lieu à des situations pour le moins contradictoire.

prescription extinctive est désormais fixé à l'article 2224 qui dispose que 'Les actions personnelles ou mobilières se prescrivent par cinq ans à compter du jour où le titulaire d'un droit a connu ou aurait dû connaitre les faits lui permettant de l'exercer'.

[46] La prescription quadriennale, également appelée 'déchéance quadriennale', est une règle selon laquelle les créances pesant sur les personnes publiques sont éteintes au bout d'un délai de quatre ans à compter du 1er janvier de l'exercice qui suit celui de la naissance de la créance.

[47] Loi n° 2014-344 du 17 mars 2014 relative à la consommation, JORF n°65 du 18 mars 2014, p. 5400.

La France est membre du Conseil de l'Europe et de la Convention européenne des droits de l'Homme. A ce titre, un ressortissant français peut actionner le mécanisme de 'demande de satisfaction équitable pour violation d'un droit garanti par la Convention' au titre de l'article 41 de cette dernière.[48] Cet article permet à un requérant dont l'un des droits garantis par la Convention a été violé, en cas d'insuffisance de la réparation ou de l'indemnité versée dans le cadre du système national (que celui-ci soit juridictionnel ou législatif), de demander à la Cour européenne des droits de l'Homme, de lui octroyer une indemnité complémentaire (satisfaction équitable).

La Cour européenne des droits de l'Homme a elle-même défini[49] les conditions de mise en œuvre de cette responsabilité et confirme qu'il ne peut s'agir d'une demande automatique en cas de violation d'un droit garanti par la Convention. La genèse de cet article ne vise donc pas à octroyer des dommages-intérêts systématiques mais à permettre au requérant de recevoir une compensation équitable qu'il ne pourrait ou ne peut recevoir dans son propre système national. La définition de la notion de «satisfaction équitable» est complexe et repose sur une impression d'ensemble dépendant de l'attitude du requérant, du contexte de l'affaire ainsi que de l'attitude de l'Etat. Parfois la Cour considère que la satisfaction équitable réside dans la sanction par la Cour de la violation de la Convention et que ce seul élément peut suffire. Elle peut aussi en revanche considérer que, compte tenu des circonstances de l'affaire et de l'ensemble des dommages subis, il y a lieu d'accorder une compensation pécuniaire qui couvrira l'ensemble du dommage.

Le mécanisme de satisfaction équitable mis en place au sein de la Convention européenne des droits de l'Homme, bien qu'inspirés dans se principes par les mêmes règles que celles prévalant en droit interne,[50] est directement inspiré d'une forme de responsabilité pour violation des droits fondamentaux ou des droits de l'Homme. Ce n'est que parce qu'un droit garanti a été violé que le mécanisme de l'article 41 peut être mise en œuvre. Le système ainsi mis en place par la Convention repose assez largement sur les principes de la responsabilité internationale de l'Etat et se trouve transposé aux droits de l'Homme: la violation d'une obligation internationale oblige l'Etat à la réparer suivant les modalités appropriées.[51] Cette origine internationale de la réparation implique une analyse particulière non pas des chefs de préjudice qui doivent être les mêmes que ceux exigés devant les juridictions nationales mais des rapports entre la violation du droit protégé et ses conséquences. Le mécanisme de l'article 41 n'est clairement pas destiné à réparer exclusivement

---

[48] Article 41 de la Convention 'Si la Cour déclare qu'il y a eu violation de la Convention ou de ses Protocoles, et si le droit interne de la Haute Partie contractante ne permet d'effacer qu'imparfaitement les conséquences de cette violation, la Cour accorde à la partie lésée, s'il y a lieu, une satisfaction équitable.'

[49] Instruction pratique relative aux demandes de satisfaction équitable Edictée par le président de la Cour au titre de l'article 32 du règlement le 28 mars 2007, disponible sur: http://www.echr.coe.int/Documents/PD_satisfaction_claims_FRA.pdf

[50] V. Blay-Grabarczyk (2013).

[51] V. en ce sens Verhoeven (1984) 278 et seq.

les préjudices comme l'est le droit de la responsabilité interne mais à tirer toutes les conséquences de la violation d'un droit garanti par la Convention européenne. D'une certaine façon, la responsabilité repose ici sur la violation du droit fondamental garanti par la Convention alors que les mécanismes internes sont fondés - d'abord et avant tout - sur l'indemnisation du préjudice dans son intégralité. Entre les deux, il existe plus qu'une différence d'approche : les paradigmes sont différents même si le traitement du préjudice reste identique dans les résultats qu'il vise.

Si le mécanisme d'indemnisation de la Convention européenne des droits de l'Homme s'inspire des principes appliqués dans les systèmes nationaux, il reste fondé sur une logique différente de celle précédemment décrite dans le système français de responsabilité. Ce dernier reste autonome dans son appréciation de l'indemnisation du dommage mais s'il est fondé sur le même principe de *restitutio in integrum*, son appréciation peut différer. D'un point de vue théorique, rien n'empêche le système national d'accorder des dommages-intérêts supplémentaires si le juge ou l'organe de compensation estime que le préjudice n'a pas été complètement indemnisé. D'un point de vue pratique, il y a fort peu de chances pour que ce cas de figure se présente car les modalités d'indemnisation devant la Cour se fondent dans leur évaluation sur les pratiques nationales. L'inverse n'est en revanche pas systématiquement exact car la notion de satisfaction équitable donne au juge davantage de marge de manœuvre dans l'évaluation de ce que doit être l'indemnisation complète du dommage. En d'autres termes, si dans les deux cas les principes sont les mêmes, leur appréciation peut diverger…

Cette situation est d'autant plus questionnable qu'une décision récente de la Cour européenne des droits de l'Homme concernant la Belgique et la France amène à s'interroger sur le contenu exact de la notion de « satisfaction équitable » en matière d'octroi de dommages-intérêts. Dans un arrêt du 25 juin 2013 *Trévalec c. Belgique*,[52] la Cour européenne des droits de l'Homme a octroyé au requérant une somme supplémentaire de 50 000 Euro correspondant au solde du préjudice moral 'en sus de tout montant qui lui a déjà été versé'. Dans cette affaire, un reporter français avait demandé et obtenu l'autorisation de suivre une unité spéciale de la police belge luttant contre le grand banditisme et le terrorisme. Au cours d'une de ces opérations, le reporter avait été blessé par balles et en avait conservé des séquelles. N'ayant pu obtenir réparation de son préjudice devant les juridictions pénales belges, il s'était retourné en France devant la Commission d'indemnisation des victimes d'infractions qui permet à ces dernières de bénéficier d'un fonds de garantie (organisme mis en place par la loi) et qui assure une réparation intégrale du dommage. A ce titre, il avait bénéficié d'une telle indemnisation. Si la Cour a considéré qu'en ce qui concerne la réparation du préjudice matériel la Commission avait correctement évalué le dommage, elle a considéré, sans véritablement s'en expliquer,[53] que le dommage moral avait été incomplètement compensé et a accordé

[52] CEDH 25 juin 2013 n° 30812/07, *Trévalec c/ Belgique*, arrêt sur la satisfaction équitable. V. également CEDH, 14 juin 2011, *Trévalec c. Belgique*, n° 30812/07, arrêt sur le fond, notamment aux ns 86 et 87.

[53] V. Marguénaud (2013) 807.

une indemnité supplémentaire à celle déjà versée. Cet exemple démontre que les analyses nationales et les analyses supranationales en matière de dommages-intérêts ne sont pas nécessairement les mêmes. La doctrine – française[54] – notamment a fortement critiqué cette décision en estimant que l'on passait d'une réparation intégrale à une satisfaction équitable. Ce n'est pas la première fois que cette critique est formulée[55] et elle revient à s'interroger sur l'existence d'autres composantes de l'indemnisation dans la notion de satisfaction équitable. Ainsi, il a été relevé[56] dans l'opinion concordante du juge Pinto de Albuquerque que les dommages-intérêts prononcés dans le cadre de la satisfaction équitable possédaient un caractère punitif. Cette adjonction du caractère punitif de la satisfaction équitable ne cadre pas avec la définition qui en avait été donnée par la Cour elle-même. On se trouve donc devant une hypothèse nouvelle, révélatrice des tensions disjonctives qui existent dans le cadre de l'indemnisation pour violation d'un droit fondamental.

L'apparition de nouveaux acteurs de l'indemnisation augmente le risque d'inflation de nouvelles formes d'indemnisation. Il se peut que la concurrence entre mécanismes nationaux et mécanismes supranationaux en matière d'indemnisation correspondent à différentes logiques et que les systèmes nationaux comprennent mal la rationalité qui pourrait exister derrière une logique d'indemnisation qui n'est pas la leur. Ceci témoigne également des tensions et évolutions en matière d'indemnisation des risques et de la volonté de garantir l'individu contre toute forme de dommage qui pourrait survenir dans la sphère publique. Les logiques sont différentes mais les mots demeurent à peu près les mêmes. Tous les Etats ne sont pas logés à la même enseigne et derrière les notions et concepts de la responsabilité se regroupent des appréciations parfois profondément différentes. La question centrale demeure toutefois celle de savoir ce qui engage en premier lieu la responsabilité : l'existence d'un préjudice ou celle d'un fait générateur ? De cette réponse dépendra une conception de l'indemnisation qui ne sera pas nécessairement la même.

5.6 Conclusion

Le droit français de la responsabilité pour violation des droits fondamentaux est avant tout un calqué sur l'existence de la violation d'un droit et d'un préjudice. Si le panorama français a largement évolué ces dernières années – comme probablement celui de bien d'autres Etats – il a opéré cette mutation supprimer en éloignant progressivement les conséquences sociales les plus inacceptables des principes de cette responsabilité. Les systèmes tant de la responsabilité publique que de la responsabilité privée sont suffisamment rôdés pour anticiper les conséquences prévisibles de l'indemnisation. Lorsque se profile une difficulté, le législateur peut pallier les règles générales de la responsabilité en créant des régimes spéciaux dont

[54] V. not. Sabard, D. 2013, 2139, Gautier (2013) 2106, Quézel-Ambrunaz (2014).

[55] V. Flauss et Lambert-Abdelgawad (2011), Flauss (1992b) 1; Flauss (2003) 227.

[56] V. Quézel-Ambrunaz (2014) 5.

la fonction est d'apporter une réponse politique à une question dont la solution juridique ne correspondrait pas nécessairement à ce qu'il estime devoir être pour préserver la paix sociale.

La France n'a pas été confrontée durant ces dernières décennies à des difficultés majeures en matière de responsabilité et d'indemnisation en raison de son histoire et de l'absence – heureuse - de grande catastrophe. La responsabilité, tant du côté des auteurs que des victimes, reste encore largement une question individuelle. L'existence d'une responsabilité collective a cependant été posée dans les années récentes par la résurgence des conséquences de l'histoire contemporaine. Le cadre de la responsabilité de l'Etat durant les périodes troublées a démontré que les critères traditionnels, s'ils pouvaient s'adapter et être appliqués, trouvaient néanmoins leurs limites dans l'exorbitance des conditions de mise en œuvre de la responsabilité. Initiée par une reconnaissance politique de la responsabilité de l'Etat et de la collectivité, la responsabilité juridique a su faire écho à cette exorbitance du dommage et de ses conséquences. Cette situation pourrait peut-être déboucher un jour sur de nouvelles formes et de nouveaux fondements de la responsabilité qui n'existent pas encore.

Le législateur est également devenu un acteur majeur de la responsabilité. Là où les juges avaient construit des régimes généraux, le Parlement est venu ajouter de nouveaux régimes ponctuels ou permanents, tenant compte de l'évolution des normes sociales. La multiplication de ces régimes a pu apparaître comme une source de complexité mais répond à des demandes sociales. Certes, l'édifice, pour le juriste, est moins harmonieux dans sa présentation, mais son fonctionnement répond à une demande d'effectivité et d'efficacité privilégiée par le législateur.

Il reste que la question de la responsabilité pour violation d'un droit fondamental garanti par la Constitution et les conventions internationales reste posée. Une telle responsabilité n'existe pas formellement mêmes si les conséquences dommageables issues du préjudice né d'un tel droit peuvent être indemnisées. La question centrale de l'évolution reste focalisée sur ce point. L'existence d'autres sources d'indemnisation – notamment dans le cadre supranational – pourrait avoir pour effet de faire évoluer cette question sur le plan interne. Il n'en reste pas moins qu'une telle évolution impliquerait un changement de logique qui dépasserait l'indemnisation du préjudice.

Toute la question repose alors sur la définition du droit à réparation. Si la réparation demeure une question purement pécuniaire, le système n'a aucune raison d'évoluer. En revanche, si la question de la réparation se profile dans une autre perspective et inclut la nécessité d'inclure dans les réparations d'autres aspects que l'octroi d'une somme d'argent, la question reprend un intérêt majeur et l'évolution de la réponse une dimension nouvelle. Peut-on envisager la réparation sous le seul prisme de la compensation monétaire ? Si le dommage n'était pas évalué par la situation passée mais à travers ses conséquences sur l'avenir, le raisonnement développé serait-il le même ? En matière de violation des droits de l'Homme, la question de la non-récurrence est aussi importante que celle de l'indemnisation comme celle de la place de la victime dans le processus de réparation. L'argent ne résout pas tout, y compris en matière de responsabilité… Mais s'agit-il là vraiment d'une découverte?

References

Agostini, Frédérique. 2000. Les droits de la partie civile dans le procès pénal. Cour de cassation, protection de la personne, http://www.courdecassation.fr/publications_26/rapport_annuel_36/rapport_2000_98/deuxieme_partie_tudes_documents_100/tudes_theme_protection_personne_102/civile_proces_5858.html. Accédé 15 Mars 2015.

Beaud, Olivier. 2013. Les obligations imposées aux personnes privées par les droits fondamentaux. Un regard français sur la conception allemande. *Jus Politicum* 10. http://www.juspoliticum.com/Les-obligations-imposees-aux.html Accédé 15 Mars 2015.

Belrhali-Bernard, Hafida. 2009. Responsabilité administrative et protection des droits fondamentaux. Tribune, AJDA, juillet 13.

Blay-Grabarczyk, Katarzyna. 2013. L'incertaine présomption de préjudice pour violation d'un droit protégé par la Convention EDH. *Revue des droits et libertés fondamentaux* 2. http://rdlf.upmf-grenoble.fr/?p=3141. Accédé 15 Mars 2015.

Bouchet, Loïc. 2013. Les chiffres de l'indemnisation. In *20 ans d'indemnisation des victimes d'infractions*. Paris: L'harmattan.

Charpentier, Jean. 1986. L'affaire du Rainbow Warrior: le règlement interétatique. *Annuaire français de droit international* 32: 873–885.

Charpentier, Jean. 1990. L'affaire du Rainbow Warrior: la sentence arbitrale du 30 avril 1990 (Nouvelle Zélande c. France). *Annuaire français de droit international* 36: 395–407.

Disant, Mathieu. 2011. La responsabilité de l'Etat du fait de la loi inconstitutionnelle : Prolégomènes et perspectives. *Revue Française de droit administratif* 6: 1181.

Ewald, François. 1992. Responsabilité – solidarité – sécurité. *Risques (Assurance, droit, responsabilité)* 10:12.

Flauss, Jean-François. 1992. Le contentieux de la satisfaction équitable devant les organes de la Cour européenne des droits de l'homme. Développements récents. *Europe* juin: 1.

Flauss, Jean-François. 2003. Réquisitoire contre la mercantilisation excessive du contentieux de la réparation devant la Cour européenne des droits de l'homme. A propos de l'arrêt Beyeler c/ Italie du 28 mai 2002. *Dalloz* 227.

Flauss, Jean-François et Elisabeth Lambert-Abdelgawad (eds.). 2011. *La pratique de l'indemnisation par la Cour européenne des droits de l'homme*. Bruxelles: Bruylant.

Flour, Yvonne. 1987. Faute et responsabilité civile: déclin ou renaissance? *Droits. Revue française de théorie juridique - Fin de la faute ?* 5: 29–36.

Gautier, Pierre-Yves. 2013. La Cour européenne des droits de l'homme poursuit la révolution normative. *Dalloz* 2106.

Instruction pratique relative aux demandes de satisfaction équitable Edictée par le président de la Cour au titre de l'article 32 du règlement le 28 mars 2007, disponible sur: http://www.echr.coe.int/Documents/PD_satisfaction_claims_FRA.pdf. Accédé 15 Mars 2015.

Lochak, Danièle. 1993. Réflexions sur les fonctions sociales de la responsabilité administrative – A la lumière des récents développements de la jurisprudence et de la législation. In *Le droit administratif en mutation*, 275–316. Paris: PUF.

Marguénaud, Jean-Pierre. 2013. Haro sur la motivation des arrêts de satisfaction équitable de la Cour EDH. *Revue trimestrielle de droit civil* 807.

Nahmod, Sheldon. 1990. Constitutional damages and corrective justice: A different view. *Virginia Law Review* 76: 997–1022.

Paillard, Christine. 2013. Droits fondamentaux et présomption de préjudice en droit de la responsabilité administrative. *Revue des droits et libertés fondamentaux* 16. http://rdlf.upmf-grenoble.fr/?p=4168. Accédé 15 Mars 2015.

Quézel-Ambrunaz, Christophe. 2014. Des dommages et intérêts octroyés par la Cour européenne des droits de l'homme. *Revue des droits et libertés fondamentaux* 5. www.revuedlf.com. Accédé 15 Mars 2015.

Sabard, Olivia. 2012. Les causes d'exonération en droit français et dans d'autres ordres juridiques nationaux, In *Le droit français de la responsabilité civile confronté aux projets européens d'harmonisation. Recueil des travaux du Groupe de Recherche Européen sur la Responsabilité Civile et l'Assurance –GRERCA*, 485–506. Paris: IRJS Editions, grerca.univ-rennes1.fr/digital-Assets/267/267960_osabard.pdf. Accédé 15 Mars 2015.

Verhoeven, Joe. 1984. A propos de l'autorité des arrêts de la Cour européenne des droits de l'homme et de la responsabilité internationale liée à leur observation. *Revue critique de jurisprudence belge* 278.

Chapter 6
Damages for the Infringement of Human Rights in Germany

Andreas von Arnauld

6.1 Introduction and Scope of the Report[1]

Claims for damages for the infringement of human rights are a specific way to react to a legal wrong, with the aim of compensating for harm resulting from that infringement. As a legal remedy they are closely connected with numerous other means by which the Constitutional State attempts to enforce a right, or to prevent, redress or compensate for its violation. To mark this connection, in Germany these ways to address a legal wrong are grouped into primary and secondary remedies. The former covers all means directed against the illegal act as such (e.g. actions for annulment of executive decisions) while the latter is directed at its consequences.[2] This distinction is not confined to terminology; as will be explained later, it is paramount for the eligibility of claims. As damages aim at financial compensation they clearly belong to the secondary remedies. For this reason, our report will not deal with primary ones. Furthermore, we will also exclude all secondary remedies that are not aimed at financial compensation. Therefore, claims for restitution will not be dealt with. Rather the question asked here is: When and under which conditions does the German legal order allow claims for financial compensation of human rights

I am greatly indebted to my assistant, *Philipp Stöckle*, for his excellent research.

[1] This chapter was previously published in *The German National Reports on the 19th International Congress of Comparative Law*, (ed) Martin Schmidt-Kessel, Mohr Siebeck 2014, pp. 545–580.

[2] Schmidt-Aßmann (2003), Art. 19 Abs. 4, nos. 281, 283; Maurer (2011) 684; Grzeszick (2002) 66. For a different categorisation see Axer (2001) 1322 (primary remedies include all means aimed at restitution of the situation which would exist in legality; secondary remedies include only means directed at financial consequences).

A. von Arnauld (✉)
Co-Director, Walther Schücking Institute for International Law,
Christian-Albrechts-Universität zu Kiel, Kiel, Germany
e-mail: arnauld@wsi.uni-kiel.de

E. Bagińska (ed.), *Damages for Violations of Human Rights*,
Ius Comparatum - Global Studies in Comparative Law 9,
DOI 10.1007/978-3-319-18950-5_6

violations? In order to answer this question, we will first give a short account of the role international human rights guarantees play in the German legal order in general (6.2.1). Afterwards we will present the system of public authority liability in Germany, focusing of course on liability for the infringement of human rights (6.2.2). Finally, we will expand on three recent and especially pertinent questions (6.3): compensation for violations of the ECHR, historical wrongs, and damages resulting from actions of the German Federal Armed Forces abroad.

6.2 The Legal Framework

6.2.1 International Human Rights in the German Legal Order

6.2.1.1 Commitment to International Law

According to the jurisprudence of the Federal Constitutional Court (FCC), the Basic Law (*Grundgesetz*) conceives the Federal Republic of Germany as a State open for international cooperation ("open statehood").[3] However, in general, taking a dualist stance towards international law, the FCC has coined the principle of "openness to international law" (*Völkerrechtsfreundlichkeit*) in order to avoid any contradiction between Germany's domestic law and its international legal obligations.[4]

6.2.1.2 The Status of International Human Rights

Incorporation and Direct Effect

Germany has signed and ratified all major international human rights instruments.[5] As treaties, they are incorporated into the German legal order by enactment through the two Chambers of Parliament (*Bundestag*, *Bundesrat*) according to art. 59 para. 2 Basic Law, ranking on the same level with federal statutory law, i.e. above tertiary federal legislation and above all law of the federal States (*Bundesländer*). With their adoption into the domestic legal order, human rights treaties become binding, their direct application depending upon whether the norm in question is self-executing

[3] BVerfGE 35, 311, 320; 54, 358, 370; 63, 343, 370; 74, 358, 370; 82, 106, 120; BVerfG (Chamber), Europäische Grundrechte-Zeitschrift (EuGRZ) 2004, 317, 318; BVerfGE 111, 307, 317; 120, 180, 200; 128, 326, 368.

[4] BVerfGE 6, 309, 362; 31, 58, 75; 74, 358, 370; 92, 26, 48; 111, 307, 317; 112, 1, 24 ss; BVerfG (Chamber), Neue Juristische Wochenschrift (NJW) 2007, 499, 501; BVerfG (Chamber), NJW 2011, 207, 208; BVerfGE 128, 326, 326, 328; BVerfG (Chamber), 5.7.2013, file no. 2 BvR 708/12 (juris); BVerfG (Chamber) 18.08.2013, file no. 2 BvR 1380/08, no. 26 (juris). For more detail see Vogel (1964) 51; Bleckmann (1996) 137, 142; Payandeh (2009) 465, 485 ss; Proelß (2009) 553, 564 s.

[5] For a full list see the Human Rights Library of the University of Minnesota, online: http://www1.umn.edu/humanrts/research/ratification-germany.html. Accessed 26 Feb 2015.

(e.g. like most of the ECHR rights) or not (e.g. like most of the ICESCR rights).[6] As far as international human rights are part of customary law, they are received into the domestic legal order via art. 25 Basic Law, ranking above federal statutory law but still below the Federal Constitution (Basic Law).[7] Again, though being binding upon all state organs, non-self-executing rights need to be put into effect by statutory law.

Legal Remedies

According to art. 19 para. 4 Basic Law, everyone who is violated in his/her rights by acts or omissions of the German public authority has a right to a judicial remedy. This right to remedy can be claimed in connection with any subjective right conferred to the individual in the Basic Law or statutory law. Thus it also encompasses international human rights guarantees.[8] Whereas action addressing the violation as such (primary legal remedy, *Primärrechtsschutz*) is brought before the administrative courts, claims for damages (secondary legal remedy, *Sekundärrechtsschutz*) have to be raised before the civil courts. This division between two branches of the law is rooted in history; the administrative judiciary having been established in the second half of the nineteenth century only.

Normative Guidance for Interpretation

In order to avoid any violation of Germany's international obligations, the FCC demands that the other courts (as well as the executive branch) interpret all domestic law in the light of the relevant international treaty law or customary law, including international human rights.[9] Limits to this "inclusive" interpretation are the limits of statutory interpretation (methodological constraints) and basic tenets of the Federal Constitution, which must not be touched upon (constitutional constraints).[10]

---

[6] BVerfGE 74, 358, 370; 82, 106, 114; 111, 307, 317; 112, 1, 24 ss; 120, 180, 200; BVerfG (Chamber), NJW 2007, 499, 501; NJW 2011, 207, 208; BVerfG (Chamber) 18.08.2013, file no. 2 BvR 1380/08, no. 26 (juris); Uerpmann (1993) 46; Simma et al. (1997) 71, 86.

[7] This is the prevailing opinion which has been endorsed by the FCC, see BVerfGE 6, 309, 363; 37, 271, 279; 111, 307, 318; for detail see Geiger (2010) 151; Tomuschat (2009), Artikel 25, no. 83 ff. With regard to human rights recognised in customary international law, the FCC referred to the enumeration of the ICJ in Barcelona Traction, Light and Power Co. Ltd., ICJ Reports 1970, 3, 34 in BVerfGE 112, 1, 28. Other courts also recognised fundamental human rights as rules of customary international law and hence have given direct effect to them pursuant art. 25 Basic Law, e.g. OLG München, InfAuslR 1995, 382, 383; BGHSt 32, 314, 324 and 326 (Prohibition of inhuman treatment as recognised under Art. 7 ICCPR).

[8] BVerfGE 57, 9, at 25 s; Jarass (2012), Art. 19, no. 37; Simma et al. (1997) 86; Uerpmann (2003) 87, 99.

[9] See footnote 4.

[10] This position was first developed with respect to EC Law: BVerfGE 37, 271, 279 ss; 73, 339, 387; 89, 155, 172; BVerfGE 123, 267, 343 ss. It was later taken up with regard to the ECtHR:

Jurisprudence of International Courts and Tribunals

Especially in view of the ECtHR, the FCC underlines a general duty to respect the jurisprudence of international courts and tribunals. Although limited to the *res judicata* and only binding *inter partes* according to art. 46 ECHR, the ECtHR is seen as the primary interpreter of the ECHR and thus of Germany's general obligations following from the Convention. A second line of argument stresses the probability that Germany would incur being sentenced by the ECtHR if acting in a way incompatible with the Strasbourg jurisprudence.[11] This has also been held with regard to the jurisprudence of the ICJ in a case concerning the (human) right to consular protection.[12] The FCC accepts, however, the departure from rulings by international courts and tribunals when these decisions do not conform with the constant jurisprudence of domestic courts, especially with regard to human rights. In this case the obligation to follow international jurisprudence turns into an obligation for thorough reasoning.[13] This exception has to be seen in the light of institutional rivalries between the FCC and international courts in the field of human rights protection.[14]

6.2.1.3 However: Limited Impact on the Practice of German Courts

Despite being incorporated into the German domestic legal order as statutory law or even ranking above federal statutes, international human rights obligations in general play a limited role in the practice of German courts.[15] The main reason is that in the decades since its creation in 1951, the FCC, in a joint effort with other courts and Constitutional legal scholarship, have turned the First Part of the Basic Law (arts. 1 to 19), the part concerning the "Fundamental Rights" (*Grundrechte*), into the cornerstone of the German legal order.[16] They encompass negatory, procedural and institutional dimensions and oblige the State to take action. Despite being limited to a more or less "classic" canon of rights, the FCC interprets the right to free development of the individual (art. 2 para. 1 Basic Law) as a subsidiary right to general freedom and has "invented" a number of rights not expressly guaranteed in the Constitution. The Basic Law's Fundamental Rights influence practically every

BVerfGE 111, 307, 317s.; 128, 326, 326, 368; cited BVerfG of 18.08.2013, file no. 2 BvR 1380/08; see further Schorkopf (2010) 131; Talmon (2013) 12.

[11] BVerfGE 111, 307, 317; 112, 1, 24 ss; BVerfG (Chamber), NJW 2011, 207, 208; BVerfGE 128, 326, 368; cited BVerfG of 18.08 2013, file no. 2 BvR 1380/08. See also BVerwG, Neue Zeitschrift für Verwaltungsrecht (NVwZ) 2000, 810, 812. For more detail cf. Payandeh (2009), 465, 485; Proelß (2009) 564 ss; Schorkopf (2010) 131; Hofmann (2013) 326.

[12] BVerfG (Chamber), NJW 2007, 499, 500.

[13] BVerfGE 111, 307, 324.

[14] See von Arnauld (2012) 12, 24.

[15] Cf. Uerpmann (1993) 118; Simma et al. (1997) 86; Uerpmann (2003) 87, 99; von Arnauld (2012) 24.

[16] For a general analysis see Schuppert and Bumke (2000).

field of law, fundamentally encoding the relationship of the individual with the State and beyond.

As Constitutional rights, these Fundamental Rights possess the highest normative rank within the German legal order, making it more effective to base claims on the Basic Law than on human rights guarantees enshrined in international conventions. Furthermore, there is a special judicial remedy for the protection of these rights in the Constitution. According to art. 93 para. 1 no 4a, every person who claims to have been violated in his or her Constitutional rights by the public authority can, after having exhausted all other judicial remedies, lodge a Constitutional Complaint (*Verfassungsbeschwerde*) with the FCC. These Constitutional Complaints account for almost 97 % of all the cases brought before the FCC. In 2012 alone, there were 194,005 applications. The impressive body of FCC jurisprudence on the Basic Law's Fundamental Rights has been broadly received into everyday legal practice and law school teachings. The central place these Constitutional human rights guarantees occupy in the German legal system leaves little room for a genuine practice relating to international human rights. Thus, the general observation that awareness by German courts of relevant international law is sometimes wanting[17] has little practical effect on the standard of human rights protection in Germany.[18]

Given this dominance of Constitutional rights protection with the central position of the FCC as the foremost interpreter of these rights, international human rights can be of practical importance only in two cases: when they add a new aspect to (international human rights as a source for inspiration), or when they collide with, domestic rights jurisprudence (international human rights as a source of conflict).[19] By demanding that Constitutional rights must be interpreted in the light of the relevant international human rights law, the FCC opens up the domestic legal order for inspiration, but also for adjustment. Conflict arises, however, when judgments of international courts and tribunals run counter to a constant rights jurisprudence of the FCC itself. A major point of conflict was the balancing of privacy rights and the freedom of the press in the case of Caroline of Hanover (*née* de Monaco): When the ECtHR tipped the balance slightly more in favour of the right to privacy than the FCC in its jurisprudence that had evolved over about 12 years, the FCC felt institutionally insulted and reacted with the *caveats* mentioned above. Basic tenets of the Constitution are being touched upon when rights protection is diminished, and if an international court balances colliding rights of private individuals differently than domestic jurisprudence does, German courts may reasonably depart from international adjudication.[20] The Caroline 'trauma' having been sublimated over the years, in its recent judgment on the constitutionality of post-sentence preventive detention (*Sicherungsverwahrung*) the FCC again chose more co-operative terms.[21]

[17] In detail see von Arnauld (2012) 15 ss.

[18] Kirchhof (1994) 16, 36 ff; Uerpmann (2003) 87, 122.

[19] Uerpmann (2003) 87, 122; von Arnauld (2012) 14 (with further references).

[20] BVerfGE 111, 307, 324; von Arnauld (2012) 24.

[21] BVerfGE 128, 326, 366 ss, answering to ECtHR case no. 19359/04, M. v. Germany, judgment of 17.12. 2009, NJW 2010, 2495.

The basic tenets exception still holds, but in general there is an obligation to adjust domestic jurisprudence according to a judgment of the ECtHR. This obligation is not an obligation to receive the Strasbourg ruling in form, but in substance.

Taken together, international human rights only exceptionally influence the domestic legal order in Germany. Therefore, the question of damages for the infringement of human rights must be re-defined as including damages for the infringement of Constitutional rights in order to avoid a largely theoretical essay.

6.2.2 *The System of Public Authority Liability*

6.2.2.1 Main Features

"No System"

The most important and characteristic feature of the German System of State Liability is that, as far as one expects a "system" to possess a coherent structure and a minimum of common rules, there seems to be no system of state liability in German law.[22] Rather, there is a plethora of rules and claims, both customary and statutory, which has grown from different sources over centuries and, if not based completely on case law, is very much shaped by jurisprudence.[23] It appears resilient against legislative reform and against doctrinal systematisation.[24] In fact, a legislative push to reform this diffuse area of law failed in 1982 before the FCC and has until now not been taken up again.[25] In recent years the liability of the state based on violations of EU Law has added yet another dimension struggling to be reconciled with the traditional claims. We will come to this point below. Lastly, the very subject of this report, damages for the infringement of International Human Rights (namely ECHR rights), adds new claims and modifies existing ones.

Constitutional Exigencies

Notwithstanding the confusing legal situation, some guidance can be drawn from Constitutional law. Firstly, the Constitutional principle of the rule of law demands that, in general, a violation of a right shall be prevented, redressed or compensated. This follows from Art. 20 para. 3 Basic Law, according to which all state organs

---

[22] Ossenbühl (1998) 2 – who speaks of a "grown chaos" of rules; see further Bonk (2013) 17, 18 („normatives Defizitgebiet").

[23] See a historical overview on State Liability law in Grzeszick (2001) 10 ss; Detterbeck et al. (1999) 8 ss.

[24] For a recent attempt see Breuer (2011) 113 ss; sceptical Ossenbühl and Cornils (2013) 2.

[25] Staatshaftungsgesetz, 26.6.1981, BGBl. I 553 declared unconstitutional in BVerfGE 61, 149 in 1982 for lack of competence of the federal legislator; this was remedied in 1994 by inclusion of art. 74 para. 1 no. 25 Basic Law; for an overview on legislative action see Maurer (2011) 661.

shall be bound by the Constitution, Art. 19 para. 4 Basic Law, which guarantees an effective remedy against violations of rights, and Art. 34 Basic Law, which provides the liability of the state for tortious acts of its agents.[26] Secondly, the Fundamental Rights of the Basic Law not only protect the individual against governmental interference, but they also contain a subjective claim to restore the legal situation and to compensate for harm sustained when infringed. The latter point, however, has only been raised in literature.[27] The FCC still denies a general obligation to compensate the individual for violations of his or her fundamental rights (human rights). In general, it limits the Constitutional exigencies to specific obligations expressly foreseen in the Basic Law (esp. relating to the right to private property, Art. 14) and otherwise refers to the political discretion of the legislator.[28]

Substantive Legal Framework

Claims for damages face both substantive and procedural restrictions. Most important is a proviso developed by the FCC: the priority of primary remedies and the respective subsidiarity of secondary ones.[29] This means that the individual is not free in the choice of remedies. Inasmuch as the individual was able to prevent harm by challenging an act of state violating her or his rights, she or he is not able to claim damages later. The dictum that "compensation is the *ultima ratio* of the Constitutional State"[30] thus very much applies to the Basic Law and also influences claims for damages for the infringement of human rights.

6.2.2.2 Substantive Claims

With regard to the substantive rules of German State liability law, it is helpful to distinguish two types of claims: claims based on *Amtshaftung* (governmental liability for tortious acts of its agents) and claims based on *Aufopferung* (sacrificial

[26] Windthorst in Detterbeck et al. (1999) 83; Maurer (2011) 664; Breuer (2011) 113; sceptical as to the precise content of the rule of law principle in this regard Grzeszick (2002) 130; Haack (2010), 1475, 1480.

[27] von Arnauld (2002) 394; Grzeszick (2002) 185 ss; Röder (2002) 150 ss; Ossenbühl (2012) 535 ss.

[28] BVerfG, NVwZ 1998, 271; NJW 2006, 1580; NJW 2010, 1943, at 22.

[29] Developed in BVerfGE 58, 300 with regard to infringements of the Basic Right to property, art. 14 Basic Law. It is also explicitly laid down in sect. 839 para. 3 BGB concerning claims for tortious acts of government agents. It is unclear, however, whether this can be generalised with regard to all claims in the law of State liability. In this direction: BGHZ 138, 247, 251: "Entsprechend dem heute allgemein anerkannten grundsätzlichen Vorrang des Primärrechtsschutzes vor dem Sekundärrechtsschutz …"; BVerfG, DVBl. 2000, 350, 351. Favouring a more flexible approach Axer (2001) 1322, 1330; Windthorst in Detterbeck et al. (1999) 188.

[30] Jellinek (1931) 321.

encroachment).[31] These claims have developed over the last centuries mainly independently from each other and form the basis of all other claims in the law of public authority liability.

Governmental Liability for Tortious Acts, Sect. 839 BGB, Art. 34 Basic Law

According to sect. 839 of the German Civil Code (BGB), a civil servant who violates his or her official duties and thereby causes harm to an individual is liable for damages. However, a set of preconditions must be met: Firstly, the violation must concern a duty not only owed to the State, but to the citizen (*drittbezogene Amtspflicht*); in the case of human rights violations this precondition is generally met.[32] Secondly, only intent or negligence give rise to liability. Thirdly, sect. 839 BGB is subsidiary to other titles for damages. Fourthly, according to sect. 839 para. 3 BGB, the claimant himself or herself must have used all available means to avoid the damage. Finally, sect. 839 para. 2 BGB excludes violations of subjective rights by the judiciary from the ambit of this provision. Since the legislator is not understood as being obliged towards specific individuals, but towards the common good (i.e. there is no *drittbezogene Amtspflicht*), violations of individual rights by laws and statutes also do not give rise to compensation according to sect. 839 BGB.

Though widely regarded as an institute of public law, this liability is based on the Civil Code. The reason is once more a historical one: According to Roman legal theory, received into German law in pre-constitutional times (and still enshrined in sect. 13 of the *Reichsbeamtengesetz* of 1873), the Monarch could do no wrong, so if an individual was unlawfully harmed by a State officer, the officer was seen as acting in a private capacity (*extra* or *contra mandatum*).[33] Today, art. 34 Basic Law (as before art. 131 of the Weimar Constitution) provides for the transfer of this personal liability from the acting organ to the State, thus turning it into a title against the State (which is then, in turn, entitled to seek recourse from the civil servant in case of intent or recklessness). The legal basis of this institute in Private Law explains why damages can only be sought if the State official violated his or her obligation, either intentionally or by negligence. While the idea of the rule of law would advocate for holding the State responsible and liable for any violation of individual rights, i.e. for the result alone, here the State takes advantage of the historically based fiction that its civil servant acted in a private capacity only. Ironically, sect. 839 BGB requires that the officer acted in the performance of his or her official (!) duties. Function, not status, is thus the relevant nexus between the act or omission and liability. This is only partly reflected in positive law.[34]

---

[31] Grzeszick (2002)10 ss; Detterbeck et al. (1999) 8 ss; Rau (2006) 701, 710.

[32] Ossenbühl and Cornils (2013) 60; Maurer (2011) 675; Papier (2003) Art. 34, no. 180.

[33] Grzeszick (2002) 10 ss; Detterbeck et al. (1999) 8 ss.

[34] Ossenbühl and Cornils (2013) 7 ss; Bonk (2013) 21.

"Sacrificial Encroachment"

Section 75 of the Introduction to the Prussian General Law of the Land of 1794 (*Preußisches Allgemeines Landrecht*, ALR) determined that the State should compensate citizens who have to sacrifice their rights or possessions for the common welfare. This has been received into the Public Law of the Federal Republic of Germany by jurisprudence, supported by literature. The basis for this principle of "sacrificial encroachment" is disputed[35]: some call it a general principle of law,[36] others base it on customary law,[37] and another view wants to found it on the Fundamental Rights of the individual.[38] The principle encompasses the encroachment of both material and immaterial subjective rights. Since encroachments of personal property follow their own specific paths in German legal dogmatics (see the ensuing subsection), the general principle of "sacrificial encroachment" is relevant today only for non-property-related rights, namely for the right to life, the right to physical and mental integrity, and the right to freedom from arrest. With good reason, some authors argue that encroachments of the general right of personality (*allgemeines Persönlichkeitsrecht*, esp. privacy rights, personal honour, life planning) should also be included.[39] In all cases, it is necessary that the individual is not affected as part of the general public; he or she must have to bear a specific burden (*Sonderopfer*). Originally intended only to cover unequally distributed burdens from lawful State action, the scope of the principle has been widened to include burdens from unlawful action ("quasi-sacrificial encroachment", *aufopferungsgleicher Eingriff*).[40] It is not limited to direct consequences, but also covers indirect effects of State action (or omission). This makes it important to determine the reach of State responsibility and to delineate the spheres of influence. If e.g. a prisoner is physically harmed by his fellow-prisoners in a State prison, this should not be seen as the consequence of a private quarrel (as the Federal Court of Justice did)[41]; instead, the State should be deemed under a positive obligation to ensure as far as feasible that inmates in a state-run institution do not injure each other.[42]

The principle only obliges the State to pay an appropriate compensation, not full damages, and only for the material harm suffered.[43] The latter limitation has come under pressure. A number of authors convincingly argue for the inclusion of

---

[35] For an overview Ossenbühl and Cornils (2013) 130 ss.

[36] RGZ 102, 390; 113, 301; BGHZ 45, 58, 77.

[37] BGHZ 9, 83, 85; 13, 88, 91; 22, 43; 28, 297; 34, 13.

[38] See von Arnauld (2002), 394, 395 ss.

[39] Papier (2003), Art. 34, no. 56 ss; Grzeszick (2002) 340 ss, 358 (in favour); BVerfG, NVwZ 1998, 271; Haack (2010) 1475, 1480 (against). Yet undecided: BGHZ 50, 14, 18; 65, 196, 206.

[40] RGZ 140, 276, 285; BGHZ 45, 46, 77; see also BGHZ 65, 196, 206 ff; 66, 118, 122; Ossenbühl and Cornils (2013) 142.

[41] BGHZ 17, 172; 60, 302.

[42] This would also be more in line with the ECtHR's jurisprudence: ECtHR case no. 44973/04, Premininy v. Russia, judgment of 10.2.2011, no. 71 ss; Ossenbühl and Cornils (2013) 138 ss.

[43] BGHZ 20, 61, 68 ss; 45, 46, 77; Ossenbühl and Cornils (2013) 146 ss; Grzeszick (2013), no. 54.

a compensation also for immaterial harm, at least after the legislator expressly recognised such a compensation in the general law of torts (cf. sect. 253 para. 2 BGB).[44] It is undisputed, however, that the claimant's own negligence in avoiding or diminishing the harmful effects of State action (or omission) curtails or even excludes the title for compensation (by way of analogy to sect. 254 BGB). A claim based on the "sacrificial encroachment" principle can be raised alongside claims based on sect. 839 BGB, art. 34 Basic Law, since both follow different rationales. In relation to statutory provisions that are themselves based on the idea of "sacrificial encroachment" and expressly confer a title to compensation, the judge-made general principle is superseded according to the rule of *lex specialis*.[45] We will deal with the most pertinent of these provisions in the next but one subsection.

Property-Related Claims

Grown out of the logic of "sacrificial encroachment" and today established as a third pillar of the law of public liability in Germany are property-related claims. They lead a separate legal life next to the other two pillars because of their (more or less) express basis in the Constitution. The right to property is guaranteed as a Fundamental Right in art. 14 Basic Law. Paragraph 3 of this article states that expropriation may only be ordered by law or on the basis of a law providing for an adequate compensation. Adequacy has to be determined by a fair balance of interests between the general public and the interested persons. Since the early 1980s, the FCC applies a formal and narrow concept of expropriation, limited to the transfer of property in the common interest ordered by State authority.[46] Thus, it also limits the ambit of the compensation clause in art. 14 para. 3 Basic Law. All other encroachments of personal property are either made by laws defining content and limits of property according to art. 14 para. 1, 2nd sentence, or by decisions based on those laws. Though the legislator, when defining the notion of "property" protected by the Constitution, is bound to strike a fair balance between the ideas of self-interest and common welfare, there is no general obligation to compensate for loss in these cases.

However, the FCC acknowledges that in certain cases a regulation falling under the "content and limits" clause may fail to strike a fair balance if it does not provide for a compensation (*ausgleichspflichtige Inhaltsbestimmung*).[47] Thus, the principle of proportionality demands an adequate compensation for balancing the public purpose with the proprietor's interest in a similar manner as art. 14 para. 3 Basic Law does in the case of expropriation *sensu stricto*. Compensation is necessary espe-

[44] Papier (2003) Art. 14 (July 2010), no. 677 with further references.

[45] BGHZ 13, 88, 92; Maurer (2011) 781; Papier (2003) Art. 34, no.60.

[46] See BVerfGE 58, 300 as the turning point.

[47] BVerfGE 58, 137, 147 ss.

cially in the case where a proprietor is under a specific burden not born by others, e.g. in the case of special duties for the protection of monuments[48] – the FCC having thus "constitutionalised" the received idea of *Sonderopfer* in the context of the right to property. Since it is up to the legislator to define "content and limits" of property, and since in these cases a "definition" without an adequate compensation renders the law unconstitutional, the compensation must be provided for already by the legislator and cannot be left to the administration. And since (certain exceptions notwithstanding) the FCC has a monopoly for invalidating parliamentary statutes, this means that it is the Constitutional Court – not the Civil or the Administrative Courts – that in these cases can award compensation when the legislator failed to provide for it.[49]

Apart from these Constitution-based titles for compensation, there are another two property-related titles that are embedded in the tradition of "sacrificial encroachment".[50] In fact, the so-called "expropriating encroachment" (*enteignender Eingriff*) is nothing more than a "sacrificial encroachment" in the field of property rights. It provides for compensation whenever lawful state action imposes a specific burden (*Sonderopfer*) on the property of the claimant.[51] No specific burden is needed in the case of harm to property effected by unlawful state action: In this case, the institute of "quasi-expropriatory encroachment" (*enteignungsgleicher Eingriff*) gives a title to compensation without the need either to prove a specific burden (as in the case of the expropriating encroachment) or intent or negligence on the side of the responsible state organ (as in the case of sect. 839 BGB).[52] Examples of the former are the adverse effects of traffic noise for adjacent owners[53]; examples of the latter include damages caused to private property by gunfire during an army manoeuvre.[54] As variants of (quasi-)"sacrificial encroachment", the legal basis for both institutes is disputed: sect. 75 ALR as customary law, general principles of law or the right to property in art. 14 Basic Law. This ambiguity translates into confusion about the actual relevance of these institutes.[55] The "quasi-expropriatory encroachment" today is subsidiary to primary legal protection against the act in question and only covers damages that could not be avoided by challenging the (unlawful) act of State. Institutionally, primary legal protection is given by the Administrative Courts, whereas compensation is awarded by Civil Courts. The "expropriating encroachment", in turn, has practically been reduced to cover unforeseeable effects of statutory law or its application – as foreseeable effects must be compensated by the legislator according to the doctrine of the determination of

[48] BVerfGE 100, 226, 244 ss.

[49] von Arnauld (2002) 394, 404 ss.

[50] See von Arnauld (2002) 394. In detail Ossenbühl and Cornils (2013) 259 ss, 325 ss.

[51] See e.g. BGH, NJW 1965, 1907; BGHZ 57, 359.

[52] Ossenbühl (2000) 887, 904.

[53] BGHZ 64, 220.

[54] BGHZ 37, 44.

[55] For an attempt to clarify the debate von Arnauld (2002) 394, 402 ss.

content and limits to property subject to compensation (*ausgleichspflichtige Inhaltsbestimmung*). This is the consequence of the "constitutionalisation" of this institute by the FCC referred to above.

Other Substantive Claims

Hazardous Activity If the State operates a hazardous facility (e.g. power plants or a coal mine) it is liable for damages should they occur according to the principle of strict liability in torts (cf. the general rule in sect. 1 and 2 *Haftpflichtgesetz*, Liability Act).[56] It is irrelevant if the facility is run in forms of public or of private law (in German law, the State can chose the form of operation, but cannot escape its obligations and responsibilities). This liability complements the liability for tortious acts of state agents because, again, they follow different rationales. In most of the articles providing for such a liability, it is independent of any default on the acting state organ's side. Special provisions can be found e.g. in sect. 33, 54 and 55 Civil Aviation Act (*Luftverkehrsgesetz*, LuftVG), sect. 89 Water Management Act (*Wasserhaushaltsgesetz*, WHG), sect. 114 Federal Mining Act (*Bundesberggesetz*, BBergG) and sect. 1, 2 Environmental Liability Act (*Umwelthaftungsgesetz*, UHG). While these provisions protect the rights to life, integrity and property, the liability clauses in laws on data protection primarily seek to protect privacy rights and other rights relating to the general right of personality. Sect. 8 Federal Data Protection Act (*Bundesdatenschutzgesetz*, BDSG) concerning compensation in case of automated data processing by public bodies reads:

1. If a public body harms a data subject through collection, processing or use of his or her personal data, which is unlawful or improper under this Act or other data protection provisions, the body's supporting organisation shall be obligated to compensate the data subject for damage suffered irrespective of any fault.
2. In case of a serious violation of privacy, the data subject shall receive appropriate financial compensation for non-financial damage suffered.
3. Claims under subsections 1 and 2 shall be limited to a total of €130,000. If compensation exceeding the maximum of €130,000 is to be paid to more than one person due to the same incident, the compensation paid to each person shall be reduced in proportion to the maximum amount.
4. If, in the case of automated processing, more than one body is authorised to record data and the injured person is unable to determine which body recorded his/her data, then each body shall be liable.
5. Section 254 of the Civil Code shall apply to contributory negligence on the part of the data subject.
6. The limitation provisions stipulated for tortious acts in the Civil Code shall apply accordingly with regard to statutory limitation.

[56] Ossenbühl and Cornils (2013) 448 ss.

Criminal Prosecution, Arrest and Detention The Law on Compensation for Prosecution Measures (*Gesetz über die Entschädigung für Strafverfolgungsmaß nahmen*, StrEG) compensates for harm from criminal prosecution and punitive arrest. If someone is acquitted after rehearing his or her case (sect. 1) or suffers harm from prosecution measures (pre-trial confinement, search of premises, requisition, etc.) and finally is acquitted (sect. 2), he or she is entitled to compensation for pecuniary loss and – in the case of deprivation of liberty – also immaterial damages (€25 per day in detention or arrest), sect. 7. The compensation is left to the discretion of the Court if the prosecutor closes a case (sect. 3) or where prosecution measures turned out disproportionate with a view to the final verdict (sect. 4). The rationale behind this title to compensation is seen, once again, in the idea of "sacrificial encroachment", because the aggrieved person has to bear a "special burden" for the administration of criminal justice.[57] This is the reason why the StrEG supersedes titles based on sacrificial encroachment, but can be put forward alongside titles based on sect. 839 BGB, art. 34 Basic Law.[58]

The StrEG covers only cases of lawful detention, which afterwards turned out to be based on false suspicion (by the prosecutor) or false reconstruction of events (by the Court handing out the verdict). In cases of unlawful detention – criminal, therapeutic or administrative – the duty to compensate follows from the idea of "quasi-sacrificial encroachment". However, this general institute of State liability is superseded by the provision of art. 5 para. 5 ECHR according expressly to "[e]veryone who has been the victim of arrest or detention in contravention of the provisions of this Article [...] an enforceable right to compensation".[59] In recent years, this title has gained prominence after the ECtHR declared the German system of post-sentence preventive detention for security reasons (*Sicherungsverwahrung*) to be largely incompatible with art. 5 and 7 ECHR.[60] Only claims concerning the unlawful detention as such can be based on art. 5 para. 5 ECHR; claims relating to degrading conditions of detention (art. 3 ECHR, art. 1 para. 1 Basic Law) have to be based on tortious liability (sect. 839 BGB), or on the traditional institute of "quasi-sacrificial encroachment".[61] The title from art. 5 para. 5 ECHR is independent of any default on the acting organs' side.[62] As a comparison with the wording of art. 50 ECHR shows, it covers full damages and also compensation for immaterial harm.

---

[57] BGHZ 72, 302 (305).

[58] Ossenbühl and Cornils (2013) 460; Cornelius (2013), no. 9.

[59] BGHZ 45, 58; Maurer (2011) 781; Elberling (2012) Art. 5, no. 137; Renzikowski (2004) no. 315.

[60] ECtHR case no. 19359/04, M. v. Germany, judgment of 17.12.2009, NJW 2010, 2495; BVerfGE 128, 326. Claims for compensation may be directly based upon art. 5 para. 5 ECHR: BGH (= FCJ), judgment of 19.9.2013, file no. III ZR 405/12 (juris) (no. 11 ff).

[61] As decided recently by the FCJ: BGH, judgment of 4.7.2013, file no. III ZR 342/12 (juris) (no. 29). This question was much disputed in jurisprudence before, cf. OLG Celle, NJW 2003, 2463 s.; NJW-RR 2004, 380, 381; KG, OLGR 2005, 813; OLG Nürnberg, decision of 21.1.2011, file no. 4 U 92/10 (juris); OLG Naumburg, NJW 2005, 514, 515; LG Duisburg, decision of 11.5.2009, file no. 1 O 343/08 (juris) (no. 5); OLG Hamm, decision of 13.6.2008, file no.11 W 78/07 (juris) (no. 26).

[62] BGHZ 45, 58, 65; 122, 268, 282.

There is no fixed amount of compensation; recently, the Provincial Court of Appeal (*Oberlandesgericht*) in Munich awarded €30 for each day in arrest or detention, comparing the compensation for unlawful detention to the rate fixed in sect. 7 StrEG.[63]

Public Security and Hazard Defence That an individual violated in his or her rights (esp. human rights) by the police or other agencies entrusted with the defence of public order and security is entitled to full damages is also based on the idea of "sacrificial encroachment".[64] This is obvious when the police enlist someone not responsible to remove a danger to or disturbance of public security, but also extends to the case of damages from unlawful police action (situation of quasi-sacrificial encroachment). In accordance with this line of reasoning, sect. 56 of the Law on Police Bremen (BremPolG) orders the following:

1. If someone is damaged as a consequence of a lawful enlistment according to sect. 7 (i.e. persons not responsible for a danger or disturbance), he/she shall be awarded an appropriate compensation. This applies also if someone is damaged by an unlawful police measure. There is no title to compensation as far as the measure was taken for the protection of the aggrieved person or his/her property.
2. Compensation is also to be awarded for persons who volunteered – with the consent of the police – in fulfilling police duties or placed objects at the disposal of the police forces and thereby suffered damage.
3. This title is without prejudice to further reaching titles to compensation, especially such titles based on liability for tortious acts of civil servants.

These express titles in the State (*Länder*) Laws on Police supersede any title based on the general principles of "sacrificial encroachment". However, since some State Laws only expressly provide for compensation in the case of enlisting persons not responsible for the danger or disturbance, in these States the principles of "quasi-expropriatory" and "quasi-sacrificial encroachment" apply in cases of unlawful police action.[65]

Infringement by Private Third Parties In general, the violation of individual rights by private third parties is being redressed by means of private law. An infringement of human rights will often amount to a crime and thus will also give rise to prosecution. In this case, sect. 403 Code of Criminal Procedure (*Strafprozessordnung*, StPO) provides the possibility to decide about damages as an annex to criminal proceedings. This so-called "adhesive procedure" (*Adhäsionsverfahren*) has not gained too much practical importance, however. Mostly, civil law suit and prosecution are conducted separately. An important exception to the general rule of compensation *inter partes* is made by the Law on the Compensation of Victims of violence (*Gesetz über die Entschädigung von*

[63] OLG München, judgment of 22.8.2013, 1 U 1488/13 (juris) (no. 62).

[64] Papier (2003), Art. 34, no. 60; Ossenbühl and Cornils (2013) 485.

[65] Ossenbühl and Cornils (2013) 527.

Opfern von Gewalttaten, OEG). Victims of criminal violence are entitled by this statute to a pension in order to compensate for serious harm to their health and their economic situation resulting from the assault. The moral basis for this compensation is mostly seen in the principle of solidarity – which might explain why it is primarily limited to nationals and EU citizens and includes non-EU foreigners only under certain conditions (namely duration and status of residence in Germany).[66] However, since the situation which gives rise to the need for financial aid is the same in all cases, solidarity should rather extend to all victims of criminal violence on German territory – regardless of their nationality and status. In fact, the 1920 Law on Damages from Turmoil (*Tumultschädengesetz*), which is still in force in some States within Germany (although fortunately of no practical importance), does not contain similar restrictions. Its rationale is mostly explained as covering indirect State responsibility: As the State should protect its citizens from turmoil and chaos, it becomes liable because of its failure to award protection. There does not seem to be much difference in the case of victims of violence.[67]

Claims Related to the Violation of EU Law

When applying or implementing EU law or when restricting the fundamental (economic) freedoms guaranteed in the TFEU, the EU Member States are bound to respect the rights now enshrined in the Charter of Fundamental Rights (CFR).[68] Any infringement renders an act of State illegal. If damage results therefrom, the State becomes liable for reparation. With the *Frankovich* judgment, the ECJ famously transferred its jurisprudence concerning the liability of the EC/EU to the liability of the EU's members in order to effectively protect the individual's rights and to further the enforcement of Community (Union) Law. Today, the liabilities of the Union and of its members are part of an overarching general principle of public authority liability in EU law.[69] According to this principle, the aggrieved is conferred a right to reparation when three conditions are met: "the rule of law infringed must be intended to confer rights on individuals; the breach must be sufficiently serious; and there must be a direct causal link between the breach of the obligation resting on the

---

[66] Maurer (2011) 803; Ossenbühl and Cornils (2013) 469 s.

[67] Ossenbühl and Cornils (2013) 469 s.

[68] ECJ, case C-260/89, ERT [1991] I-2925, para. 42; case C-299/95, Kremzow [1997] I-2629, para. 15; case C-309/96, Annibaldi [2007] I-7493, para. 13; case C-94/00, Roquette Frères [2002] I-9011, para. 25; case C-349/07, Sopropé [2008] I-10369, para. 34; case C-617/10, Åkerberg Fransson [2013] ECR I-105, para. 19 ff.

[69] ECJ, joined cases C-6/90 and C-9/90, Francovich [1991] I-5357, para. 35 ff.; joined cases C-46/93 and C-48/93, Brasserie du Pêcheur und Factortame [1996] I-1029, para. 31; case C-392/93, British Telecommunications [1996] I-1631, para. 38; case C-5/94, Hedley Lomas [1996] I-2553, para. 24; joined cases C-178/94 a.o., Dillenkofer [1996] I-4845, para. 20; joined cases C-283/94 a.o., Denkavit [1996] I-5063, para. 47; case C-424/97, Haim [2000] I-5123, para. 26; case C-118/00, Gervais/Inasti [2001] I-5063, para. 34; case C-224/01, Köbler [2003] I-10 239; case C-63/01, Evans [2003] I-14 447, para. 82.

State and the damage sustained by the injured parties."[70] Reparation is due in the form of adequate compensation, but not of full damages. What was previously developed by the ECJ on the basis of a general principle of Community (Union) Law can meanwhile be based on art. 47 para. 2 FRC conferring on the individual a subjective right to an effective remedy, which also includes secondary remedies, i.e. claims for compensation.[71] According to art. 19 para. 1 TEU, the Member States are obligated to introduce the necessary remedies into their domestic legal orders. When doing so, they have to respect the principles of equivalence and effectiveness; especially, the conditions for enforcement of titles based on EU law must not be less favourable than those for the enforcement of comparable "domestic" titles.

For the German legal order, some writers advocated the expansion of the traditional titles (tortious liability and sacrificial encroachment in the broader sense) so as to include the violation of EU law.[72] The FCJ, however, chose to anchor the title to compensation directly in EU law. Nevertheless, the Court will first of all attempt to realise the title within the institutions of the domestic law of State liability. Only to the extent that this does not fulfil the requirements of EU law is the claim directly based on the *Frankovich* principle.[73] As to acts by the executive, there is little need for German courts to refer to *Frankovich*. It is different, however, with violations of individual subjective rights by the judiciary and by the legislator. Apart from extremely rare cases of miscarriage of justice, State liability for judicial or legislative wrongs is alien to the German legal tradition. Thus, if laws or regulations or court decisions infringe individual rights conferred by EU law (such as the CFR rights), the duty to compensate is taken directly from EU law.[74] By keeping these cases apart, the FCJ adds to the patchwork structure of the law of public authority liability in Germany with its plurality of legal bases. With its dualist approach the Court aims to avoid contagious effects, i.e. that the general principles of EU law – in theory derived from the Member States' domestic legal orders – inspire a change in the autochthonous legal tradition.

Claims Related to the Violation by Non-German Public Authority

Human Rights violations by Other States For acts of foreign States the rules on conflict of laws refer to the legal order of that State alone. Thus, the German law of State liability is inapplicable to infringements of rights by another State's public

---

[70] ECJ, joined cases C-46/93 and C-48/93, Brasserie du Pêcheur und Factortame [1996] I-1029, para. 51.

[71] Nowak (2011) no. 18; Schwarze (2012) Art. 19 TEU, no. 51.

[72] For an overview cf. Ruffert (2011), Art. 340 TFEU, no. 70; von Bogdandy and Jacob (2011) no. 192.; Dörr (2012) 86, 87; Papier (2013) § 839, no. 103.

[73] BGHZ 134, 30; 146, 153.

[74] Dörr (2012), 86, 87.

authority.[75] Furthermore, according to the principle of sovereign equality of States and the principle of *par in parem non habet imperium*, German courts are barred from accepting any claim relating to a foreign act of State unless the State in question waives its right to immunity. Only in the case of infringements resulting from *acta iure gestionis*, are German courts allowed to consider a claim against another State.[76] Since human rights violations mostly arise from another State's *acta iure imperii*, in these cases compensation for infringement of human rights must in general be sought outside Germany. Departing from this rule, art. 11 of the European Convention on State Immunity (1972), which Germany signed and ratified, determines the following:

"A Contracting State cannot claim immunity from the jurisdiction of a court of another Contracting State in proceedings which relate to redress for injury to the person or damage to tangible property, if the facts which occasioned the injury or damage occurred in the territory of the State of the forum, and if the author of the injury or damage was present in that territory at the time when those facts occurred."

As the ICJ ruled in the *Germanyvs. Italy* case, this foreign tort exception does not apply to acts of another State's armed forces on the territory of the forum State.[77] Special agreements, however, might provide otherwise. As for troops from other NATO members, Art. 8 para. 5–7 NATO Status of Forces Agreement deals with liability and jurisdictional questions in relation to foreign acts of State on German soil.

Further exceptions have to be made in the EU context. There are special rules on liability and compensation, e.g. in the Framework Decision on Joint Investigation Teams and also in some bilateral agreements with neighbouring Member States on the basis of EU legislation.[78] In particular, by allowing officers from one Contracting State to operate within the territory of another, the 1990 Schengen Convention (Convention implementing the Schengen Agreement) had to distribute liabilities and duties to make reparation. According to art. 43, the State in whose territory a damage was caused has to compensate the victims "under the conditions applicable to the damage caused by its own officers". The State whose officers caused the damage is then under an obligation of full reimbursement towards the former.

While it is usually up to each State to compensate for human rights violations attributable to its own organs alone, the Law on Personal Injuries in War (*Kriegspersonenschädengesetz*) of 1927 stands out in that it gave a subsidiary right to compensation for injuries suffered in World War I, not distinguishing whether the harm was caused by German and allied forces or by forces of the enemy during that war.

---

[75] BGH NJW 2003, 3488, 3499; OLG Köln NJW 1999, 1555; Thorn (2013), Art. 40 EGBGB, no. 11.

[76] BVerfGE 16, 27, 33; 46, 342, 392; 64, 1, 40; 117, 141, 152 ss; BVerfG, NJW 2012, 293, 295.

[77] ICJ, judgment of 3.2.2012, Germany v. Italy, Jurisdictional Immunities of the State, not yet reported, no. 62 ss.

[78] Cf. Baldus (2009) no. 557 ss.

Human Rights Violations by International Organisations Human rights violations by acts attributable to International Organisations are compensated according to their respective Charter or a special agreement. For example, for the EU it incurs liability under the conditions set in art. 340 TFEU with the ECJ being entrusted with adjudicating on these matters, art. 268 TFEU. When the Federal Republic of Germany enters such agreements it is constitutionally bound to observe that basic exigencies of the rule of law are met and that there are effective remedies available.[79] Thus, when in the case of targeted UN and EU sanctions against alleged supporters of *al-Qaeda* the ECJ demanded a fair delisting procedure, the Court also relieved the German judiciary from Constitutional pressure. However, the question of compensation still leaves much to be desired. In its 2012 *Sison* judgment the EU General Court in principle agreed to the EU's non-contractual liability for unlawful damages resulting from its (in this case: autonomous) sanctions, but then awarded a wide margin of appreciation to the acting organs: "The decisive test for a finding that this requirement [a 'sufficiently serious breach'] has been satisfied is whether the institution concerned has manifestly and gravely disregarded the limits of its discretion."[80]

Another problem in connection with human rights violations by International Organisations lies with the attribution of conduct. In its 2007 *Behrami and Saramati* decision, the ECtHR assumed a shift of responsibility from a State to the UNO already with a largely political "overall control" of the UN Security Council regarding an international peacekeeping mission mandated under Chapter VII of the UN Charter.[81] Since, generally, responsibility for human rights violations is a prerequisite for an obligation to compensate,[82] this decision also had implications for the question of liability. The Court having all but overturned that decision in its 2011 *Al-Jedda* ruling,[83] it should by now be clear that "effective control" over the specific act in question is crucial for attribution of conduct. This criterion, however, can sometimes be difficult to ascertain, especially in integrated military units. Here, the idea of multiple attribution of conduct – and thus of multiple international responsibility – to which the *Hooge Raad* of the Netherlands subscribed in its 2013 decision in the Srebrenica case[84] – points in the right direction.[85] A duty for reparation should be incumbent upon all subjects of international law responsible; the question of a possible reimbursement will have to be answered with a view to each specific case.

[79] Cf. BVerfGE 59, 63 – Eurocontrol II.

[80] EU General Court, case T-341/07, Sison v. Council [2011] II-687, no. 35.

[81] ECtHR, case no. 78166/01, Behrami and Saramati v. France a.o., judgment of 2.5.2007, no. 133 ss.

[82] von Arnauld (2014), no. 373.

[83] ECtHR, case no. 27021/08, Al-Jedda v. United Kingdom, judgment of 7.7.2011, no. 80 ss.

[84] Hooge Raad (Supreme Court of the Netherlands), cases no. 12/03324 (The State v. Hasan Nuhanović) and 12/03329 (The State v. Mehida Mustafić-Mujić a.o.), judgments of 6.9.2013, both at 3.11.2.

[85] von Arnauld/Buszewski (2013), 15, 25 ss. An in-depth research is currently conducted by the Amsterdam SHARES project on shared responsibility in International Law: http://www.sharesproject.nl/.Accessed 26 Feb 2015.

Up to now, there is no State practice in Germany in this respect. However, there is a general reluctance of the German judiciary to deal with reparation for violations of human rights and humanitarian law by the Federal Armed Forces (*Bundeswehr*), which will be dealt with in greater focus at the end of this paper.

6.3 Special Questions

6.3.1 The Impact of the ECHR: Compensation for Excessively Lengthy Court Proceedings

The ECHR in two instances has exerted influence on the German law of State liability. The first is the title to compensation based directly on art. 5 para. 5 ECHR in cases of unlawful arrest or detention. In contrast to its autochthonous siblings, it covers full damages and immaterial harm alike, whereas the title based on "quasi-sacrificial encroachment" (*aufopferungsgleicher Eingriff*) only awards an adequate compensation and excludes – according to the still prevailing view in jurisprudence and judiciary – immaterial damages.[86] Thus, the direct reference to art. 5 para. 5 ECHR does have an impact on the standards of State liability in arrest and detention cases.

Another example of that impact is the title to compensation introduced in 2011 in reaction to a series of judgments of the ECtHR. In the 50 years up to 2009, the ECtHR passed more than 40 judgments against the Federal Republic of Germany because of excessively lengthy court proceedings.[87] When Germany ignored the final warning shot in the 2006 *Sürmeli* decision[88] and did nothing to redress the violation of art. 13 ECHR (right to an effective remedy), the Court in its 2010 *Rumpf* judgment[89] took recourse to a further intensified version of its pilote judment procedure: It set a deadline of 1 year for Germany to introduce effective measures against excessively lengthy proceedings before German courts.

The "Act on Legal Redress for Excessive Length of Court Proceedings and of Criminal Investigation Proceedings" (*Gesetz über den Rechtsschutz bei überlangen Gerichtsverfahren und strafrechtlichen Ermittlungsverfahren*) of Nov. 24, 2011 only partly fulfils that order from Strasbourg – although for the time being, the ECtHR seems to be satisfied.[90] Instead of tackling structural problems, Germany has chosen to introduce a new title for compensation into the different codes of

---

[86] BGHZ 45, 58; 122, 268; BGH, judgment of 19.9.2013, file no. III ZR 405/12 (juris), no. 28; Elberling (2012) Art. 5 ECHR, no. 136.

[87] Cf. Ossenbühl (2012), 857; Schenke (2012) 257, 265.

[88] ECtHR, case no. 75529/01, Sürmeli v. Germany, judgment of 8.6.2006, NJW 2006, 2389, 2392.

[89] ECtHR, case no. 46344/06, Rumpf v. Germany, judgment of 2.9.2010, NJW 2010, 3355, 3358.

[90] ECtHR, case no. 53126/07, T. v. Germany, judgment of 29.5.2012, Arbeit und Recht 2012, 363, no. 40.

procedure.[91] The central provision for this new instrument of State liability is sect. 198 of the Courts Constitutive Act (*Gerichtsverfassungsgesetz*, GVG). It accords a title to compensation for material and immaterial "disadvantages" incurred by a participant in unreasonably lengthy proceedings. The reasonableness of the length of proceedings has to be assessed in light of the circumstances of each specific case, in particular its complexity and importance, and the conduct of the participants (para. 1). As to pecuniary disadvantages, art. 198 GVG does not provide for full damages (thus excluding lost profits, in particular), but only for "reasonable" compensation. For the immaterial disadvantages, art. 198 para. 2 GVG accords a sum of €1,200 for every year of the delay; a higher or lower sum can be assessed by the court of compensation (the next higher court) with a view to the particularities of the case concerned. Examples of immaterial disadvantages that were mentioned during the Parliamentary proceedings are damages to reputation, or estrangement between child and parent in custody cases.[92]

Compensation, however, is only awarded if prior to his or her claim a participant in the dispute has complained about the length of the proceedings to the court of proceedings. This censure of delay can be filed only if there is cause to fear that the case will not be concluded within reasonable time, and has to be repeated before each court seized of the case. It does not only serve as a precondition for securing the right to compensation, but is also meant to press for an acceleration of proceedings.[93] If no censure of delay was filed (or if it was filed too early, or not repeatedly when necessary), sect. 198 para. 4 GVG only gives a right to "reparation by other means" – a finding by the court of compensation that the length of proceedings was unreasonable. Thus, a title to compensation can easily be lost and exchanged for mere satisfaction. Given that it is far from clear at what time the earliest and the latest a censure of delay must be filed and repeated, the regulation as a whole comes under the suspicion to be of primarily symbolic relevance.[94]

Next to this new title, therefore, the tortious liability according to sect. 839 BGB remains of importance.[95] The exclusion of the judiciary in its second paragraph is no bar to these cases, because they do not relate to the judicial decision, but to the proceedings.[96] Different from art. 198 GVG, sect. 839 BGB presupposes intent or negligence on the side of the judges or court clerks, and, according to the prevailing view, it also does not entitle to compensation for immaterial disadvantages.[97] However, since it awards full damages for material harm suffered, it is still a necessary complement or substitute to sect. 198 GVG.

---

[91] Critical Ossenbühl (N 87), DVBl 2012, 857, 860.

[92] BT-Drs. 17/7217; Althammer and Schäuble (2012) 1, 2 s.; Rathmann (2013) § 198 GVG, no. 2.

[93] Althammer and Schäuble (2012) 1, 2 s.

[94] Ossenbühl (2012b) 857, 860; Ossenbühl and Cornils (2013) 466.

[95] Althammer/Schäuble (2012) 1, 5; Ossenbühl (2012b) 857, 859.

[96] See however the broad understanding of "judicial decision" in the FCJ's jurisprudence: BGHZ 187, 287.

[97] Ossenbühl (2012b) 857, 859.

6.3.2 *Reparation for Historical Injustice*

The last 25 years have witnessed a shift of perspective in international law: the formerly state-centred system has gradually opened up to include the individual and his or her rights. As a parallel development, the traditional concept of inter-state responsibility has come under pressure to recognise the individual's own right to reparation for human rights violations. This has found expression in the "Basic Principles and Guidelines on the Right to a Remedy and Reparation for Victims of Gross Violations of International Human Rights Law and Serious Violations of International Humanitarian Law" adopted by the UN General Assembly in December 2005.[98] Claims for reparation do not only concern recent cases of human rights violations; on numerous occasions there have been attempts to redress historical injustice by way of compensation claims filed with international and national courts alike.[99]

6.3.2.1 Human Rights Violations During the National-Socialist Rule

In these debates, the reparation Germany paid to victims of National Socialism is often cited as setting a standard.[100] Even though, after unprecedented mass atrocities committed by Germans in the years between 1933 and 1945, Germany has indeed done a lot to compensate (at least financially) for those crimes, the German reparation policy was far from comprehensive. The patchwork of instruments set up soon after the foundation of the Federal Republic of Germany (which defined itself – contrary to the German Democratic Republic – as successor to the German Reich, and thus accepted legal responsibility) was very much characterised by selectivity. Lobby and pressure groups (or a lack of such groups) and the rise of the Cold War left their marks on the outcome.[101]

The central element of the diverse set of reparation instruments was the Federal Compensation Act (*Bundesentschädigungsgesetz*, BEG) of 1956, amended in 1965 by a "Final Act" (*Bundesentschädigungs-Schlussgesetz*, BEG-SG), which, *inter alia*, introduced a deadline for compensation claims (end of 1969).[102] The BEG covered a wide range of harm suffered: violations of the rights to life, to physical

98 U.N. GA Res. 60/147 of 16.12.2005.

99 Shelton (2006) 428 ss.

100 Shelton (2006) 428; Colonomos and Armstrong (2006) 391, 411.

101 Schwarz (1986) 433 ss; Hockerts (2001) 105 ss.

102 For a detailed overview on all relevant compensatory measures see Bericht der Bundesregierung über Wiedergutmachung und Entschädigung für nationalsozialistisches Unrecht sowie über die Lage der Sinti, Roma und verwandter Gruppen, BT-Drs. 10/6287 of 31.10.1986 and Federal Ministry of Finance, Compensation for National Socialist Injustice Indemnification Provisions, August 2011 (http://www.bundesfinanzministerium.de/Content/DE/Standardartikel/Themen/Oeffentliche_Finanzen/Vermoegensrecht_und_Entschaedigungen/Kriegsfolgen_Wiedergutmachung/compensation-for-national-socialist-injustice.pdf?__blob=publicationFile&v=3). Accessed 26 Feb 2015.

and mental integrity, to personal freedom and to property, as well as professional and economic disadvantages resulting from persecution. It awarded reparation by financial compensation, pensions and regular allowances, by subsidies and in other forms. Detailed provisions fixed the sums due. However, the BEG was severely flawed in that it was territorially limited: Only victims of NS persecution living in the Federal Republic of Germany or those emigrants who had been living on the territory of the German Reich within its boundaries of 1937 were entitled to claim reparation. Some exceptions were later made for stateless and displaced persons and for Jewish emigrants from Eastern Europe, but in general the BEG excluded foreign NS victims. These were to be compensated via reparation agreements with their respective State of nationality. Another flaw in Germany's post-World War II reparation policy was that certain groups of victims remained excluded, such as Sinti and Roma (included in a special fund in the 1980s), homosexuals or victims of forced sterilisation, which were not seen as persecuted in the legal sense.

The German reparation policy was (and still is) shielded by the FCC. The Court maintains that under the rules of intertemporality, the law of the period must be applied. In the 1930s and 1940s the individual was still fully mediated by its State of nationality and thus could not claim a right to reparation under international law. As far as foreigners are concerned, questions of reparation must therefore be left to the inter-state level. The domestic law of the Federal Republic of Germany might entitle to individual reparation; this, however, is up to political discretion. This position was upheld by the FCC still in recent years when dealing with (eventually unsuccessful) claims of former forced labourers and war-crime victims.[103]

While the Court's jurisprudence conforms well to the traditional and still prevailing view in Public International Law (at least as historical injustice is concerned), reparation at inter-state level had its flaws, too. In order to support the Federal Republic of Germany in its political and economic recovery, its Western partners agreed in Art. 5 para. 2 of the London Agreement on German External Debts to defer the "[c]onsideration of claims arising out of the Second World War by countries which were at war with or were occupied by Germany during that war, and by nationals of such countries, against the Reich and agencies of the Reich [...] until the final settlement of the problem of reparation". This clause was widely understood as a moratorium on claims against Germany until the conclusion of a peace treaty. However, only some of the States that could have claimed reparation were represented in the negotiations. During the 1960s, Germany concluded lump-sum agreements on reparation with eleven Western European countries. When in 1990 the "Two-plus-Four Treaty" had paved the way for German reunification – and thus for the "final settlement" – Germany started to conclude bilateral agreements on reparation with eight States from the former Eastern Bloc. Already in 1952, the Federal Republic in the Hague Protocols and the ensuing Agreement of Luxemburg had agreed to reparations due to Israel and to the Jewish Claims Conference. Taken together, what (after the integration of Eastern European States in the reparation

[103] BVerfGE 94, 315; BVerfG (Chamber), NJW 2004, 3257; BVerfG, NJW 2006, 2542, 2543; Randelzhofer and Dörr (1994); Hahn (2000) 3521 ss.

scheme) looks like a complete picture does have its drawbacks. Especially in the case of Greece, there remained differences regarding whether or not the bilateral agreement of 1960 was meant as a final settlement on reparations in the bilateral relations.[104]

The reopening of the debate on reparation for war damages and war crimes after the "Two-plus-Four Treaty" met with the awareness that international law could no longer be seen as classic inter-state law but also gave a voice to the individual.[105] This led to the filing of class action before US courts on the basis of the Alien Torts Claims Act, expanding US jurisdiction to human rights-based claims against foreign companies. In particular, the unresolved question of reparation for World War II victims of forced and slave labour was urgently raised. What was also new about these claims was that they did not so much call on the responsibility of the German State, but on the companies that employed forced labourers or even slave labourers during the Nazi period.[106] In order to avert the impending threat of judicial proceedings in the USA, the Federal Government together with German trade and industry associations set up the Foundation "Remembrance, Responsibility and Future" (*Erinnerung, Verantwortung und Zukunft*, EVZ).[107] The EVZ was funded with DM 10 billion, with equal contributions from the Federal Republic of Germany on one side and from more than 6,000 German companies participating on a voluntary basis on the other. From 2000 to 2007 the EVZ paid compensations to those victims of forced and slave labour, who had hitherto been excluded. The foundation of the EVZ was the prerequisite for an agreement with the US Government in July 2000 guaranteeing that any claim before US courts would be quashed by raising the political questions objection.

The loose ends of German post-war reparations also put a severe strain on Germany's relations with Greece and Italy in the first decade of the twenty-first century. Disappointed about the exclusion from reparation in Germany[108] and Germany's reluctance to re-enter into negotiations with the Greek Government regarding further payments, survivors of the massacre committed in Distomo on June 10, 1944 by the Waffen-SS filed a claim against the Federal Republic of Germany with the District Court in Livadeia. The Greek Court awarded damages of €28 million to the claimants, a ruling confirmed in May 2000 by the Areopag.[109] The judgment could not be executed, however, because the Greek Minister of Justice denied his consent, which would have been necessary under Greek law. An appeal

---

[104] Rumpf (1973) 344, 354; Hockerts (2013), 15.

[105] van Boven (2009) 21 s; Brunner et al. (2013) 23.

[106] Hockerts (N 101) 105; Authers (2006) 421, 426 ss; Colonomos and Armstrong (2006) 412.

[107] Bank (2001) 307; Fassbender (2005) 243; Fischer-Lescano (2007), 299, 358 ss.

[108] By applying the principle of non-retroactivity also to the German law of public authority liability, the FCJ had denied that respect of International Humanitarian Law had been incumbent upon State officers vis-à-vis the victims in 1944. Thus the Court had excluded any such claims also under sect. 839 BGB: BGHZ 155, 279, 290 ss.

[109] Aereios Pagos, case no. 11/2000, Prefecture Voiotia v. Germany, judgment of 4.5.2000, ILR 129 (2007), 513.

against that decision to the ECtHR was dismissed in 2002.[110] The claimants then took their title to Germany for execution on the basis of EU legislation on legal cooperation between EU Member States. The German courts, however, denied the execution because German sovereignty had been disregarded by the Greek judiciary.[111] The claimants were successful, however, before the Italian courts, which in 2008 ordered sequestration into the Villa Vigoni, a cultural institution at Lake Como run by the German State, not only on the basis of the Greek titles, but also because of the killing of 250 civilians at Civitella (Tuscany) on June 29, 1944 in reaction to a partisan attack.[112] Finally, Germany took the dispute to the ICJ, which in 2012 decided in favour of the German position and ruled out – in an almost apodictic manner – any possibility of bypassing State immunity in cases of gross violations of human rights and international humanitarian law.[113] Even if these violations should today amount to a breach of peremptory norms of international law, the status of *jus cogens* only belonged to the substantive rules, not to the related procedural duties such as a duty to judicial protection.[114]

In summary, the chequered history of Germany's reparation policy towards victims of the NS period illustrates the possibilities and the limits of human rights litigation. However, even where an immediate legal success was missing (as in the case of class action in US courts or in the Greek and Italian cases),[115] human rights arguments have been of great importance to mount political pressure. This is another, less institutionalised way in which human rights might become instrumental for individual reparation.

6.3.2.2 Human Rights Violations in the German Democratic Republic

Germany had a historical chance to revisit the difficult question of compensation for human rights violations committed under a different political system with the re-unification of October 3, 1990. Of course, the situation differed greatly from that immediately after 1945. The GDR, although being a dictatorial State responsible for numerous and structural violations of human rights, had not committed atrocities comparable to those committed during the Nazi period; the GDR had existed for 40 years (as opposed to the 12 years of the "Third Reich") and thus had formed at least two generations; finally, there was no "point zero" from which to start with the help of Allied authorities after a complete defeat, but rather the task to integrate the former GDR citizens into the political and legal system of the "old" Federal

[110] ECtHR, case no. 59021/00, Kalogeropoulou a.o. v. Germany and Greece, judgment of 12.12.2002, NJW 2004, 273.

[111] BGHZ 155, 279, 290; BVerfG, NJW 2006, 2542, 2543.

[112] See De Sena and De Vittor (2005) 89; Focarelli (2005) 951; El Boudouhi (2010) 747.

[113] ICJ, judgment of 3.2.2012, Germany v. Italy, Jurisdictional Immunities of the State, ICJ Reports 2012, 99.

[114] Ibidem, no. 92 ss.

[115] Authers (2006) 426 ss.

Republic – which in turn was to be transformed in order to build a new *gesamtdeutsch* society.[116]

The attempt to strike a balance between continuity and discontinuity found expression in art. 17 to 19 of the Unification Treaty (*Einigungsvertrag*, EV). In art. 17 EV the Contracting Parties affirmed "their intention to create without delay a legal foundation permitting the rehabilitation of all persons who have been victims of a politically motivated punitive measure or any court decision contrary to the rule of law or constitutional principles". This rehabilitation was also to "be accompanied by appropriate arrangements for compensation". Art. 18 and 19, however, ordered the continued validity of decisions by courts and public administrative bodies, which then could be made subject to recourse for invalidation in each individual case.

Rehabilitation and compensation have been regulated in detail in three statutes, devoted to criminal law, administrative law, and professional disadvantages, respectively. According to the Rehabilitation Act in Criminal Matters (*Strafrechtliches Rehabilitierungsgesetz*, StrRehaG), on request of a victim, a criminal judgment irreconcilable with the rule of law may be quashed. The immediate consequences of such a quashing are that any further enforcement must be stopped, that all fines or costs paid have to be refunded, confiscated property returned, registrations effaced. For immaterial damages, sect. 16 gives a right to "social adjustment payments" (*soziale Ausgleichsleistungen*) to compensate disadvantages suffered from criminal arrest.[117]

The Rehabilitation Act in Administrative Matters (*Verwaltungsrechtliches Rehabilitierungsgesetz*, VwRehaG) gives a right to demand the re-opening of a case and eventually a formal disaffirmation, if the applicant is still seriously and unacceptably impaired by the effects of an administrative decision contrary to the rule of law. In cases of infringements of the rights to life or integrity, the applicant is entitled to specific social security payments and confiscated property must be returned or compensated. If for reasons of political persecution someone suffered considerable disadvantages in his or her professional advancement, the Rehabilitation Act in Professional Matters (*Berufliches Rehabilitierungsgesetz*, BerRehaG) provides for compensation by social security payments and a regularly monthly allowance of €184. Laws on compensation for specific groups of victims concern, *inter alia*, victims of the GDR doping programme, or children separated from their parents and brought up in protectories. Compensation payments under all these statutes are based on the constitutional principle of the welfare state (art. 20 para. 1 Basic Law).[118] Thus, they do not bar compensation claims directed against private individuals responsible under civil law.[119]

---

[116] Papier and Möller (1999) 3289, 3297; Guckes (2008) 24; details in Starck et al. (1992).

[117] These payments are effected either as financial compensation (sect. 17: €306.78 for each month of arrest) or as supportive payments (sect. 18). They do not award full damages. For graver cases, there is a monthly allowance of € 250 or a higher sum, where appropriate (sect. 17a).

[118] BVerfGE 84, 90, 125 ss; Papier (1997) 587 ss; Stern (2000) 2151 ss.

[119] BGH, NJW 1995, 256; Märker (1995) 37.

Another pertinent topic after the reunification of Germany in 1990 was that of the expropriations ordered and effected by the Soviet authorities in the agrarian reform of 1947. In the negotiations for the accession of the GDR to the Federal Republic of Germany and for the "Two-plus-Four Treaty", the Federal Government agreed to accept the outcome of this reform and not to return the land to the former proprietors, mostly owners of big estates belonging to the local nobility. In accordance with the relevant provision of the Unification Treaty, the former proprietors were compensated. They challenged the decision in a number of judicial proceedings with the aim of having their land returned to them. Before the FCC they argued that the confiscatory expropriation by the Soviet authorities violated international law and the right to property as guaranteed in art. 14 Basic Law. By supporting a flagrant violation of human rights, the Federal Government – so the argument ran – breached its own Constitutional obligations and even violated those basic tenets of the Constitution declared peremptory in art. 79 para. 3.[120] The FCC, however, rejected that line of argument in a series of judgments[121]: Art. 79 para. 3 Basic Law does not demand that the German State has to return property confiscated by foreign State authority, even if that confiscation should have been unacceptable according to the Basic Law and also in breach of international legal obligations, namely the Hague Regulation of 1907 on the obligations of an occupying power. That the Federal Republic waived any rights resulting from this breach of international law by the Soviet Union for and on behalf of the former owners was regarded by the Court as a sovereign decision taken in a difficult political setting in the context of making possible the reunification of Germany, and not violating international *jus cogens*, either. In return, the FCC affirmed a constitutional obligation to provide for an adequate compensation, but granted wide discretion to the political bodies.[122] The legislator was accorded the right to determine the compensation with respect to the other financial burdens and needs prompted by the reunification. The compensation regime for the former estate owners in the Soviet Occupation Zone was accepted as a reasonable solution by the Court.[123] The ECtHR, finally, rejected an appeal against this jurisprudence, basically along the same line of argument.[124]

6.3.2.3 Human Rights Violations in Former Colonies

Only recently, Germany was reminded of its short, but violent history as a colonial power. While never being involved in colonialism like the big powers of the time, Germany generally kept a tight reign over its colonies. One of the darkest chapters

[120] This argument was necessary, since the Unification Treaty was adopted by way of a Constitutional amendment. Thus, the Basic Law itself could not serve as a legal standard, but only those elements of the Basic Law that define the substantive limits of Constitutional amendments.

[121] See BVerfGE 84, 90; 94, 12; 112, 1.

[122] BVerfGE 84, 90, 125 ss.

[123] BVerfGE 84, 90, 128 ss.

[124] ECtHR, cases no. 46720/99, 72203/01, 72552/01, Jahn a.o. v. Germany, judgment of 22.01.2004.

of that period in German history must be the "Waterberg battle" in Namibia (then German South West Africa), where the German commander *Lothar von Trotha* in 1904 ordered the (almost) complete extinction of the Herero people. Many hold this incident to be the first genocide in German history, whereas others fear the polemic use of the term and try to avoid speaking of genocide "in the proper sense".[125] The fate of the Herero was again brought to public attention when in 1999 Chief Riruako first turned to the ICJ and then (2001) to US courts in order to sue Germany and German companies for compensation and damages. The application to the ICJ was inadmissible from the beginning (since only States can act as parties before the Court), and the claims in the USA were later withdrawn, not least because the question of how to address the matter properly is still controversial within the Herero community.[126] However, the basic argument is well founded, at least morally. The Herero representatives refer to flagrant violations of the 1899 Hague Regulation on the rules of land warfare and also to modern conceptions of peremptory norms of international law:

> The defendants, and each of them, with Imperial Germany, committed crimes against humanity and violated fundamental principles of international law by committing genocide of the Herero tribe, participating in the intentional extermination and destruction of the Herero tribe, enslaving the Herero tribe, subjecting the Herero tribe to forced labour, and participating in the systematic abuse of Herero women. The defendants, individually and jointly, are liable to plaintiffs for violations of international law and crimes against humanity.[127]

Finally, they stress that for the genocide against the Jews of Europe, Germany assumed not only moral, but also legal responsibility and paid accordingly.[128]

The official German position rejects this claim on legal grounds.[129] By referring to the non-retroactivity of international law, Germany is in the awkward position of relying on Imperialist international law, which from today's point of view is utterly unjust. According to the German position, the 1899 Hague Regulation only applied to wars between States and civilised nations to which the African communities did not belong – according to the *Jus Publicum Europaeum*. Neither did the "Protection Treaties" concluded by the Colonial powers with leaders of African communities award protection; they were simply meant for the demarcation of spheres of influence.[130] Finally, the notion of genocide was as alien to international law in 1904 as was the idea of peremptory norms of international law.

---

[125] Cf. Sarkin-Hughes (2009) 12; Eicker (2009) 173.

[126] Höfelein (2009).

[127] Superior Court of the District of Columbia, Civil Division, Case No. 01–0004447, The Herero People's Reparation Corporation et al. v. Deutsche Bank AG *et al.*, no. 164.

[128] Harring (2001–2002) 393, 396.

[129] Antwort der Bundesregierung auf eine parlamentarische Anfrage der Fraktion Die Linke: Historische, politische und juristische Hintergründe des Massakers gegen die Herero und Nama und Sachstand der Sonderinitiative, 14 August 2012, BT-Drs 17/10481.

[130] On the nature of theses treaties see Kämmerer and Föh (2004), 294, 304 ss; Eicker (2009) 116; Craven (2012) 862, 882 ss.

While all these arguments might be formally correct, they miss the crucial point.[131] It becomes clear that the rule of non-retroactivity of law(s) might be too simple for legally assessing a historical past. While it certainly has a reasonable moral basis in cases of criminal accountability (the principle of *nulla poena sine lege praevia*), in cases of State responsibility and State liability it is unable to grasp that when raising historical claims the claimants do not mean history, but the present. This is not only true for the Herero and Germany, but also for recent attempts to reassess the history of slavery and the brutal submission of the American Indians. In most of these cases, compensation is but a secondary aim, the primary being to make the voice of the victims heard and to "tell one's own story" as a counter-narrative to the hegemonic discourse of the former oppressors. International law should therefore provide a means for giving that opportunity. The very least (and compatible even with a stricter stance on the limits of intertemporality) could be an *obligatio de negotiando*. This could be derived from a violation of the principle of good faith by the so-called "Protection Treaties". However, even such a small step would need to consider the African chiefs of the late nineteenth century as principally equal to their European counterparts. As long as the laws of intertemporality bar even this basic respect, injustice will prevail. For years, Germany has "compensated" by according to Namibia the highest per-capita development aid.[132] This, however, is not the solution on equal footing demanded by the Herero.

6.3.3 Reparation for Violations of Human Rights and IHL by the German Military

When on 30 April 2008 Germany at long last submitted in general to the jurisdiction of the ICJ according to art. 36 para. 2 ICJ Statute, the declaration was furnished with reservations: one concerned a temporal limitation excluding all attempts to institute proceedings against Germany to adjust historical wrongs; another excluded any dispute which "relates to, arises from or is connected with the deployment of armed forces abroad, involvement in such deployments or decisions thereon". This reservation highlights that another sore point for Germany is the possibility of being held liable for the external actions of the Federal Armed Forces.

In a recent decision, the FCC confirmed its jurisprudence according to which International Humanitarian Law does not entitle individual victims of armed violence to reparation. While in general, the Court holds that today individual titles to reparation might be derived directly from International Law (thus overcoming the former complete mediatisation of the individual), it denied that either art. 3 of the Fourth Hague Convention or art. 91 of the First Additional Protocol to the Geneva Red Cross Conventions could serve as a legal basis for individual claims for repara-

---

131 Hinz (2004) 148 ss; Kämmerer and Föh (2004) 294, 317, 325, 327; Shelton (2006) 428 ss.

132 Höfelein (2009).

tion.[133] The main argument relied on the wording of the treaties, thereby following the ICJ's ruling in the *LaGrand* case.[134] As the FCJ had decided before (by also referring to international practice), claims for reparation could only be raised by the victim's State of nationality.[135] As to a possible customary rule of international law, the FCC conceded that there were some examples of state practice; however, these isolated cases did not add up to a general custom.[136]

With respect to national law, the FCC already decided in 1996 (in the context of World War II forced labourers) that the non-existence of an individual title in International Law is no bar to a possible title based on German law.[137] Thereby it refuted the opinion held by some authors that according to International Law war damages were to be exclusively dealt with on the inter-state level.[138] Instead, it is up to the sovereign decision of any State to allow such claims under its own domestic law. While in the case of the Distomo massacre the FCJ had held that in 1944 the rules of International Humanitarian Law had not given rise to any obligations towards the individual,[139] in the case of the bombing of Varvarin by NATO forces during the Kosovo war in 1999 the Provincial Court of Appeal (*Oberlandesgericht*) Cologne accepted as a principle that art. 839 BGB is applicable to the case.[140] Completely suspending the rights of the individual in times of armed conflict would not conform with the system of values instituted by the Basic Law. Furthermore, it would be paradoxical not to apply the principles of public authority liability to situations with a special tendency to produce damages. In an appeal against this judgment, the FCJ left this question unanswered, arguing that in any case by the actions in question the officers had not violated their official duties. The government enjoyed a wide margin of appreciation in the choice of legitimate targets.[141] The FCC rejected this judicial self-restraint and denied that the choice of military targets possessed a political character and could thus justify a lower standard of review.[142] Since the German armed forces were only involved in the targeting process but not in the bombing itself, however, the FCC came to the same conclusion as the FCJ: that German officers had not violated an obligation which – potentially – also was due towards the individual. Also, the FCC criticised the FCJ in its position on the burden of proof: If the claimant had to prove that an obligation was violated on

133 BVerfG, decision of 13.08.2013, 2 BvR 2660/06, 2 BvR 487/07, not yet published, no. 46. See before BVerfG, NJW 2004, 3257, 3258; BVerfGE 112, 1, 32; BVerfG, NJW 2006, 2542, 2543.

134 ICJ, judgment of 27.6.2001, LaGrand, ICJ Rep. 2001, 466, no. 77.

135 BGHZ 169, 348, 353 ss.

136 BVerfG, decision of 13.08.2013, 2 BvR 2660/06, 2 BvR 487/07, EuGRZ 2013, 573, no. 43.

137 BVerfGE 94, 315, 329.

138 Feaux de la Croix (1960) 2268, 2269; Dolzer (1989, 6/90), 199. In this direction also Papier (2009), Art. 34, no. 288a.

139 BGHZ 155, 279, 290 ss.

140 OLG Köln, NJW 2005, 2860, 2862. Concurring Schmahl (2006), 699, 710 ss.

141 BGHZ 169, 348, no. 31. Critical Baufeld (2007), 502 ss.

142 BVerfG, Decision of 13.08.2013, 2 BvR 2660/06, 2 BvR 487/07, EuGRZ 2013, 573, no. 53 ss.

purpose, this would reduce any possible title to nothing.[143] In its recent judgment on the bombing of two road tankers in Kunduz (Afghanistan) in September 2009, the Provincial Court (Landgericht) Bonn also dismissed a claim based on sect. 839 BGB on factual grounds:[144] While it accepted the legal basis as such, the Court stressed that the standards for assessing due diligence in times of armed conflict must be those of International Humanitarian Law and eventually denied negligence on the side of the responsible officer. By linking the German law of public authority liability to the relevant standards of international law of armed conflict the Court has found the most appropriate solution so far.

Summing up, tortious liability according to art. 839 BGB can serve as a legal basis for claims to compensation when someone is damaged by the actions of the German military forces abroad. No title, however, can be derived from the principle of "sacrificial encroachment": Here, the FCC apodictically decreed that historically this principle had been formed to accommodate for damages resulting from everyday State action, not from exceptional circumstances like wars.[145] Although this is certainly true for the principle of "sacrificial encroachment" *sensu proprio* with its basic idea of a "special burden" hardly fitting for times of war, it is different with the more recent idea of quasi-sacrificial encroachment in cases of unlawful State action. By artificially severing those institutes from the rights enshrined in the Basic Law, the FCC deliberately blocked any path that could circumvent the requirements of art. 839 BGB, namely the need for purpose or negligence in the violation of a legal obligation.

6.4 Conclusion

The plurality of rules pertaining to damages and compensation for infringements of human rights in Germany is close to perplexity. They derive from Constitutional law, statutory law and customary law, and are partly directly based on European Union law and Public International Law. Their basic rationales are tortious liability, sacrificial encroachment and solidarity in the welfare state; the fundamental principles, however, are often modified by special regulations. Historically, infringements of individual rights were compensated for only if they constituted a special burden resulting from lawful State action, or, in the case of unlawful action, if a government agent violated intentionally or negligently his/her obligations towards the citizen. By widening the scope of the sacrificial encroachment principle to unlawful State action by an *argumentum a fortiori*, the "quasi-sacrificial encroachment" partly overlapped with situations until then only covered by tortious liability.

143 BVerfG, Decision of 13.08.2013, 2 BvR 2660/06, 2 BvR 487/07, EuGRZ 2013, 573, no. 59 ss.

144 LG (Provincial Court) Bonn, judgment of December 11, 2013, 1 O 460/11, JZ 2014, 411. This judgment has been confirmed by the Court of Appeal (Oberlandesgericht) Cologne on April 30, 2015, I-7 U 4/14, 7 U 4/14 (not yet published)

145 BVerfG, NJW 2006, 2542, 2544.

Further tectonic shifts were introduced in the "system" of public authority liability by the Constitutional guarantee of the right to property, and by the FCC's jurisprudence, especially on the legislative determination of property subject to compensation (*ausgleichspflichtige Inhaltsbestimmung*). Finally, obligations to compensate derived from EU law and from the ECHR, respectively, added further to the complexity of the whole. In general, if claims for damages follow the same basic rationale, the *lex specialis* rule applies. Competing claims then have to be distinguished according to whether they aim at full damages or at compensation, if immaterial harm is covered, whether they depend on intentional or negligent behaviour, etc. Until recently, different periods of limitation also had to be taken into account; after the reform of the German law of torts in 2002, the general period of 3 years (sect. 195 BGB) pertains to all claims, at least according to the prevailing opinion.

What might come as a surprise is that the law on public authority liability seems to be the only branch of law in Germany that until now has escaped the process of constitutionalisation. The Basic Law's Fundamental Rights today pervade almost all legal relations between the individual and the State (as well as between individuals). This has led to a systematic restructuring of German law in practically every field – bar those very rules on public authority liability. These rules still present a patchwork of judge-made law and statutory provisions with little direction from the Constitution. Looking at the reluctance of the judiciary to reform the autochthonous institutions to accommodate European and international legal obligations, the reason becomes clearer. If the Constitution were allowed to add a general obligation to compensate for any infringement of human rights that cannot be redressed otherwise, for the treasury this would open up Pandora's box. To abide with the traditional institutions, adding new titles every now and then in order to conform to transnational obligations, and securing the *interpositio legislatoris*, is the guarantee for a generally high standard of compensation without giving up control of the consequences for the national budget. This is especially important for incalculable risks from liability for new forms of State action (Germany's armed forces abroad) or for the million fold violations of human rights committed by Germany during the course of the twentieth century.

References

Althammer, Christoph, and Daniel Schäuble. 2012. Effektiver Rechtsschutz bei überlanger Verfahrensdauer – Das neue Gesetz aus zivilrechtlicher Perspektive. *Neue Juristische Wochenschrift (NJW)* 65(1): 1–7.

Antwort der Bundesregierung auf eine parlamentarische Anfrage der Fraktion Die Linke: Historische, politische und juristische Hintergründe des Massakers gegen die Herero und Nama und Sachstand der Sonderinitiative, 14 August 2012, BT-Drs 17/10481.

von Arnauld, Andreas. 2002. Enteignender und enteignungsgleicher Eingriff heute. *Verwaltungsarchiv* 93: 394–417.

von Arnauld, Andreas. 2012. Public international law and the role of federal courts in Germany. In *The practice of international law in France and Germany – Les pratiques comparées du droit international en France et en Allemagne*, ed. Christian Tomuschat and Joe Verhoven, 11–25. Paris: Pedone.

von Arnauld, Andreas. 2014. *Völkerrecht. Lehrbuch*, 2nd ed. Heidelberg: C.F. Müller.

von Arnauld, Andreas and Buszewski, Sinthiou. 2013. Modes of legal accountability: the Srebrenica example, *Die Friedens-Warte* 88(3–4):15–44.

Authers, John. 2006. Making good again: German compensation for forced and slave laborers. In *The handbook of reparations*, ed. Pablo de Greiff, 420–448. Oxford: Oxford University Press.

Axer, Peter. 2001. Primär- und Sekundärrechtsschutz im öffentlichen Recht. *Deutsches Verwaltungsblatt (DVBl.)* 116: 1322–1332.

Baldus, Manfred. 2009. Ersatzansprüche gegen juristische Personen ausländischen öffentlichen Rechts. In *Staatshaftungsrecht*, eds. Baldus Manfred, Grzeszick Bernd, and Wienhues Sigrid, 3rd edn. Heidelberg: C.F. Müller.

Bank, Roland. 2001. The new programs for payments to victims of national socialist injustice. *German Yearbook of International Law (GYIL)* 44: 307–352.

Baufeld, Stefan. 2007. Die schadensersatzrechtliche Stellung ziviler Opfer von militärischen Operationen. *Juristen-Zeitung (JZ)* 62: 502–509.

Bleckmann, Albert. 1996. Der Grundsatz der Völkerrechtsfreundlichkeit der deutschen Rechtsordnung. *Die öffentliche Verwaltung (DÖV)* 49: 137–145.

von Bogdandy, Armin and Jacob, Marc. 2011. Art. 340 TFEU. In *Das Recht der Europäischen Union*, eds. Eberhard Grabitz, Meinhard Hilf and Martin Nettesheim. Munich: C. H. Beck.

Bonk, Heinz Joachim. 2013. Betrachtungen zum Staatshaftungsrecht in Deutschland. In *Der Staat im Recht: Festschrift für Eckart Klein*, eds. Marten Breuer et al., 17–36. Berlin: Duncker & Humblot.

van Boven, Theo. 2009. Victim's right to a remedy and reparation: The new United Nations principles and guidelines. In *Reparations for victims of genocide, war crimes and crimes against humanity: Systems in place and systems in the making*, ed. Carla Ferstman, Mariana Goetz, and Alan Stephens, 19–40. Leiden: Nijhoff.

Breuer, Marten. 2011. *Staatshaftung für judikatives Unrecht*. Tübingen: Mohr Siebeck.

Brunner, José, Constantin Goschler, and Norbert Frei. 2013. Die Globalisierung der Wiedergutmachung. *Aus Politik und Zeitgeschichte* 25–26: 23–30.

Colonomos, Ariel, and Andrea Armstrong. 2006. German reparations to the Jews after World War II – A turning point in the history of reparations. In *The handbook of reparations*, ed. Pablo de Greiff, 390–419. Oxford: Oxford University Press.

Cornelius, Kai. 2013. § 1 StrEG. In: *Beck'scher Online-Kommentar StPO*, ed. Jürgen-Peter Graf. Munich: C.H. Beck (via beck-online).

Craven, Matthew. 2012. Colonialism and domination. In *Oxford handbook on the history of international law*, ed. Fassbender Bardo and Peters Anne, 862–889. Oxford: Oxford University Press.

De Sena, Pasquale and Francesca De Vittor. 2005. State immunity and human rights. *European Journal of International Law (EJIL)* 16: 89–112.

Detterbeck, Steffen, Kay Windthorst, and Hans-Dieter Sproll. 1999. *Staatshaftungsrecht*. München: C. H. Beck.

Dolzer, Rudolf. 1989. Entschädigung für NS-Zwangsarbeit, Öffentliche Anhörung des Innenausschusses des Deutschen Bundestages am 14. Dezember 1989. *Zur Sache* 6/90: 199.

Dörr, Claus. 2012. Der unionsrechtliche Staatshaftungsanspruch in Deutschland zwanzig Jahre nach Francovich. *Europäische Zeitschrift für Wirtschaftsrecht(EuZW)* 23(3): 86–92.

Eicker, Steffen. 2009. *Der Deutsch-Herero-Krieg und das Völkerrecht: Die völkerrechtliche Haftung der Bundesrepublik Deutschland für das Vorgehen des Deutschen Reiches gegen die Herero in Deutsch-Südwestafrika im Jahre 1904 und ihre Durchsetzung vor einem nationalen Gericht*. Frankfurt am Main: Lang.

Saïda, El. Boudouhi. 2010. La motivation de la jurisprudence récente de la Corte Suprema di Cassazione italienne sur les immunités juridictionnelles de l'Etat. *Revue Générale de Droit International Public (RGDIP)* 114(4): 747–778.

Elberling, Björn. 2012. Art. 5. In *EMRK-Kommentar*, ed. Karpenstein Ulrich and Mayer Franz C. Munich: C.H. Beck.

Fassbender, Bardo. 2005. Compensation for forced labour in WW II: The German compensation law of 2 August 2000. *Journal of International Criminal Justice* 3(1): 243–252.

Feaux de la Croix, Ernst. 1960. Schadensersatzansprüche ausländischer Zwangsarbeiter im Lichte des Londoner Schuldenabkommens. *NJW* 13:2268–2271.

Fischer-Lescano, Andreas. 2007. Subjektivierung völkerrechtlicher Sekundärregeln - Die Individualrechte auf Entschädigung und effektiven Rechtsschutz bei Verletzungen des Völkerrechts. *Archiv des Völkerrechts (AVR)* 45: 299–381.

Focarelli, Carlo. 2005. Denying foreign state immunity for commission of international crimes: The Ferrini decision. *International and Comparative Law Quarterly (ICLQ)* 54: 951–958.

Geiger, Rudolf. 2010. *Grundgesetz und Völkerrecht*, 5th ed. München: C.H. Beck.

Grzeszick, Bernd. 2002. *Rechte und Ansprüche*. Tübingen: Mohr Siebeck.

Grzeszick, Bernd. 2013. Art. 34. In *Beck'scher Online-Kommentar zum Grundgesetz*, eds. Volker, Epping, and Christian Hillgruber. Munich: C.H. Beck (via beck-online).

Guckes, Ulrike. 2008. *Opferentschädigung nach zweierlei Maß?:Eine vergleichende Untersuchung der gesetzlichen Grundlagen der Entschädigung für das Unrecht der NS-Diktatur und der SED-Diktatur*. Berlin: Berliner Wissenschafts-Verlag.

Haack, Stefan. 2010. Entschädigungspflichtige Grundrechtseingriffe außerhalb des Eigentumsschutzes. *DVBl* 125: 1475–1483.

Hahn, Hugo J. 2000. Individualansprüche auf Wiedergutmachung von Zwangsarbeit im Zweiten Weltkrieg: Das Entschädigungsgesetz vom 2.8. 2000. *NJW* 53: 3521–3592.

Harring, Sidney L. 2002. German reparations to the Herero nation: An assertion of Herero nationhood in the path of Namibian development. *West Virginia Law Review* 104: 393–417.

Hinz, Manfred O. 2004. Der Krieg gegen die Herero, Friedensschluss hundert Jahre danach? In *Völkerrecht statt Machtpolitik: Beiträge für Gerhard Stuby*, ed. Norman Paech et al., 148–171. Hamburg: VSA-Verlag.

Hockerts, Hans Günter. 2013. Wiedergutmachung in Deutschland 1945–1990 – Ein Überblick. *Aus Politik und Zeitgeschichte* 25–26: 15–22.

Hockerts, Hans Günter. 2001. Wiedergutmachung in Deutschland: Eine historische Bilanz 1945–2000. In *Jahrhundertschuld, Jahrhundertsühne: Reparationen, Jahrhundertschuld, Jahrhundertsühne: Reparationen, Wiedergutmachung, Entschädigung für nationalsozialistisches Kriegs- und Verfolgungsunrecht*, ed. Doehring Karl, Bernd Josef Fehn, and Hockerts Hans Günter, 91–142. Munich: OLZOG.

Höfelein, Ralph. 2009. Ein Weg zur Versöhnung: Statt Entschädigungszahlungen fordern Stammesvertreter ein nachhaltiges Herero-Förderprogramm. *Das Parlament* Nr. 48/23.11.2009; http://www.das-parlament.de/2009/48/Themenausgabe/27888393/304208. Accessed 26 Feb 2015.

Hofmann, Tobias. 2013. Der Grundsatz der völkerrechtsfreundlichen Auslegung. *Juristische Ausbildung (JURA)* 35(4): 326–333.

Jarass, Hans D. 2012. Art. 19. In: *Grundgesetz-Kommentar*, eds. Hans D. Jarass and Pieroth Bodo, 12 edn. München: C.H. Beck.

Jellinek, Walter. 1931. *Verwaltungsrecht*, 3rd ed. Berlin: Springer.

Kämmerer, Jörn Axel, and Jörg Föh. 2004. Das Völkerrecht als Instrument der Wiedergutmachung? Eine kritische Betrachtung am Beispiel des Herero-Aufstandes. *Archiv des Völkerrechts (AVR)* 42(3): 294–328.

Kirchhof, Paul. 1994. Verfassungsgrechtlicher Schutz und internationaler Schutz der Menschenrechte: Konkurrenz oder Ergänzung? *Europäische Grundrechte Zeitschrift EuGRZ* 20(1–2): 16–44.

Märker, Klaus. 1995. Unrechtsbereinigung auf dem Zivilrechtsweg? Zur Schadenshaftung bei Denunziationen in der Ex-DDR. *Deutsch-Deutsche Rechtszeitschrif* 6(2): 37–64.

Maurer, Hartmut. 2011. *Allgemeines Verwaltungsrecht*, 18th ed. Munich: C.H. Beck.

Nowak, Carsten. 2011. Europäisches Verwaltungsrecht und Grundrechte. In *Verwaltungsrecht der Europäischen Union*, ed. Jörg-Philipp Terhechte. Baden-Baden: Nomos.

Ossenbühl, Fritz. 1998. *Staatshaftungsrecht*, 5th ed. München: Beck.

Ossenbühl, Fritz. 2000. Staatshaftungsrecht. In *50 Jahre Bundesgerichtshof: Festgabe aus der Wissenschaft*, vol. III, ed. Karsten Schmidt, 887–904. Munich: C. H. Beck.

Ossenbühl, Fritz. 2012. Die vergessene Grundrechtshaftung. In *Der grundrechtsgeprägte Verfassungsstaat: Festschrift für Klaus Stern*, ed. Michael Sachs, 535–549. Berlin: Duncker & Humblot.

Ossenbühl, Fritz. 2012b. Staatshaftung bei überlangen Gerichtsverfahren. *DVBl* 127: 857–861.

Ossenbühl, Fritz, and Mathias Cornils. 2013. *Staatshaftungsrecht*, 6th ed. München: C. H. Beck.

Papier, Hans-Jürgen. 1997. Vergangenheitsbewältigung: Abwicklung, Ahndung, Entschädigung. In *Handbuch des Staatsrechts*, vol. IX, 1st ed, ed. Josef Isensee and Paul Kirchhof, 587–628. Heidelberg: C.F Müller.

Papier, Hans-Jürgen. 2003. Art 34. In *Grundgesetz Kommentar*, ed. Theodor Maunz, Günter Dürig, et al. Munich: C.H Beck.

Papier, Hans-Jürgen. 2013. § 839. In *Münchner Kommentar zum BGB*, eds. Franz-Jürgen Säcker and Roland Rixecker, 6th edn. Munich: C.H. Beck.

Papier, Hans-Jürgen, and Johannes Möller. 1999. Die rechtsstaatliche Bewältigung von Regime-Unrecht nach 1945 und nach 1989. *NJW* 52: 3289–3297.

Payandeh, Mehrdad. 2009. Völkerrechtsfreundlichkeit als Verfassungsprinzip. In *Jahrbuch des öffentlichen Rechts der Gegenwart (JöR)* 57: 465–502. Tübingen: Mohr Siebeck.

Proelß, Alexander. 2009. Der Grundsatz der völkerrechtsfreundlichen Auslegung im Lichte der Rechtsprechung des BVerfG. In *Linien der Rechtsprechung des Bundesverfassungsgerichts – erörtert von den wissenschaftlichen Mitarbeitern*, ed. Hartmut Rensen and Stefan Brink, 553–584. Berlin: De Gruyter.

Randelzhofer, Albrecht, and Oliver Dörr. 1994. *Entschädigung für Zwangsarbeit? Zum Problem individueller Entschädigungsansprüche von ausländischen Zwangsarbeitern während des Zweiten Weltkrieges gegen die Bundesrepublik Deutschland.* Berlin: Duncker & Humblot.

Rathmann, Jens. 2013. § 198 GVG. In *Zivilprozessordnung*, ed. Ingo Saenger. Baden-Baden: Nomos.

Rau, Markus. 2006. State liability for violations of international humanitarian law: The Distomo case before the German federal constitutional court. *German Law Journal (GLJ)* 7: 701–720.

Renzikowski, Joachim. 2004. Art. 5. In *Internationaler Kommentar zur EMRK*, eds. Katharina Pabel and Stefanie Schmahl. Cologne: Carl Heymanns.

Robert, Uerpmann. 2003. Implementation of United Nations human rights law by German courts. *German Yearbook of International Law (GYIL)* 46: 87–122.

Röder, Daniel. 2002. *Die Haftungsfunktion der Grundrechte.* Berlin: Duncker & Humblot.

Ruffert, Matthias. 2011. Art. 340 TFEU. In *EUV/AEUV*, eds. Christian Callies and Matthias Ruffert, 4th ed. Munich: C. H. Beck.

Rumpf, Helmut. 1973. Die deutsche Frage und die Reparationen. *Zeitschrift für ausländisches öffentliches Recht und Völkerrecht (ZaöRV)* 33: 344–371.

Sarkin-Hughes, Jeremy. 2009. *Colonial genocide and reparations claims in the 21st century: The socio-legal context of claims under international law by the Herero against Germany for Genocide in Namibia, 1904–1908.* Westport: Praeger Security International.

Schenke, Wolf-Rüdiger. 2012. Rechtsschutz bei überlanger Dauer verwaltungsgerichtlicher Verfahren, *Neue Zeitschrift für Verwaltungsrecht (NVwZ)* 31: 257–265.

Schmahl, Stefanie. 2006. Amtshaftung für Kriegsschäden. *Zeitschrift für ausländisches öffentliches Recht und Völkerrecht (ZaöRV)* 66: 699–718.

Schmidt-Aßmann, Eberhardt. 2003. Art 19 Abs. 4. In *Grundgesetz Kommentar*, ed. Theodor Maunz, Günter Dürig, et al. Munich: C.H Beck.

Schorkopf, Frank. 2010. Völkerrechtsfreundlichkeit und Völkerrechtsskepsis in der Rechtsprechung des Bundesverfassungsgerichts. In *Der „offene Verfassungsstaat"des Grundgesetzes nach 60 Jahren: Anspruch und Wirklichkeit einer großen Errungenschaft*, ed. Thomas Giegerich et al., 131–157. Berlin: Duncker & Humblot.

Schuppert, Gunnar Folke, and Bumke Christian. 2000. *Die Konstitutionalisierung der Rechtsordnung. Überlegungen zum Verhältnis von verfassungsrechtlicher Ausstrahlungswirkung und Eigenständigkeit des "einfachen" Rechts*. Baden-Baden: Nomos.
Schwarz, Walter. 1986. Das Recht der Wiedergutmachung und seine Geschichte, *Juristische Schulung* 26: 433–440.
Schwarze, Jürgen. 2012. Art. 19 TEU. In *EU-Kommentar*, eds. Jürgen Schwarze, Ulrich Becker, Armin Hatje, and Jürgen Schoo, 3rd ed. Baden-Baden: Nomos.
Shelton, Dinah. 2006. *Remedies in international human rights law*, 2nd ed. Oxford: Oxford University Press.
Simma, Bruno, Khan Daniel-Erasmus, Markus Zöckler, and Geiger Rudolf. 1997. The role of German courts in the enforcement of international human rights. In *Enforcing international human rights in domestic courts*, ed. Benedetto Conforti and Francesco Francioni, 71–109. The Hague: Nijhoff.
Starck, Christian, Wilfried Berg, and Bodo Pieroth. 1992. Der Rechtsstaat und die Aufarbeitung der vor-rechtsstaatlichen Vergangenheit. *Veröffentlichungen der Vereinigung der Deutschen Staatsrechtslehrer* 51: 9–116.
Klaus, Stern. 2000. *Das Staatsrecht der Bundesrepublik Deutschland*, vol. V. Munich: Beck.
Talmon, Stefan. 2013. Die Grenzen der Anwendung des Völkerrechts im deutschen Recht. *Juristenzeitung* 68(1): 12–21.
Thorn, Karsten. 2013. Art. 40 EGBGB. In *Bürgerliches Gesetzbuch*, ed. Palandt Otto, 72th edn. Munich: C. H. Beck.
Tomuschat, Christian. 2009. Artikel 25. In *Bonner Kommentar zum Grundgesetz*. Heidelberg: C. F. Müller.
Uerpmann, Robert. 1993. *Die Europäische Menschenrechtskonvention und die deutsche Rechtsprechung: Ein Beitrag zum Thema Völkerrecht und Landesrecht*. Berlin: Duncker & Humblot.
Vogel, Klaus. 1964. *Die Verfassungsentscheidung des GG für eine internationale Zusammenarbeit*. Tübingen: Mohr Siebeck.

Chapter 7
Damages for the Infringement of Human Rights by the Public Authority in Greece

Ioannis Stribis

7.1 Introduction

In human rights law, over the last decennia, there has been growing responsiveness to victims' rights at the national, regional and international level.[1] Therefore, there is a vibrant discussion about the means that such responsiveness can take and its respective effectiveness. The aim of such a discussion is to find the appropriate way to eliminate the consequences of the violation of human rights in each case. In a general perspective, the Permanent Court of International Justice (PCIJ) held, already in 1928, that the obligation for reparation is not only a principle of international law but also a general principle of law, common in the national legislations, in accordance with art. 38(1)(c) of the PCIJ Statute (now ICJ Statute).[2] This point has been confirmed also in the EU legal order[3] and is enshrined in the Greek legislation (e.g. Art. 297, 914 of the Civil Code, CC).

As it has been rightly pointed out, "Most probably the deepest desire of any victim of a human rights violation is to turn back the clock."[4] Yet returning to the situation before the violation is not always possible; sometimes it may lead to an

---

[1] For a general overview and concrete national experiences, cf. De Feyter et al. (2006); De Greiff (2006); Shelton (2001). Cf. also Bassiouni (2006) 203.

[2] PCIJ, *Factory at Chorzów*, Judgment (Merits), 13.9.1928, PCIJ Reports, Series A 17, p. 29.

[3] European Court of Justice (ECJ), *G. Köbler v. Österreich*, Case C-224/01, Opinion of the Advocate General Leger, 8.4.2003, para. 35, [2003] *ECR*, I-10253, "th[e] obligation to make reparation constitutes a fundamental principle of Community law, which is as fundamental as that of the primacy of Community law or direct effect."

[4] Buyse (2008) 129.

I. Stribis (✉)
Secretariat of the Organization for Security and Co-operation in Europe, Vienna, Austria

University of the Aegean, Rhodes, Greece
e-mail: i_strib@hotmail.com

E. Bagińska (ed.), *Damages for Violations of Human Rights*,
Ius Comparatum - Global Studies in Comparative Law 9,
DOI 10.1007/978-3-319-18950-5_7

injustice or further violations of human rights. As a consequence, other means of reparation have been devised, both in international and in domestic law, to make good for violations of human rights. These means include in general restitution, compensation, rehabilitation, satisfaction and guarantees of non-repetition.[5] The *Basic Principles and Guidelines on the Right to a Remedy and Reparation for Victims of Gross Violations of International Human Rights Law and Serious Violations of International Humanitarian Law* (BPGRR) specify this general enumeration of their principle 18, in the two following principles dealing respectively with restitution (principle 19) and compensation (principle 20). The former, "should, whenever possible, restore the victim to the original situation," before the human right infringement occurred, and "includes, as appropriate: restoration of liberty, enjoyment of human rights, identity, family life and citizenship, return to one's place of residence, restoration of employment and return of property."[6] Compensation, on the other hand, "should be provided for any economically assessable damage, as appropriate and proportional to the gravity of the violation and the circumstances of each case." Such compensation should cover *inter alia*: "(a) physical or mental harm; (b) lost opportunities, including employment, education and social benefits; (c) material damages and loss of earnings, including loss of earning potential; (d) moral damage."[7]

Taking into account that human rights obligations even when assumed through international treaties, do not primarily aim at the reciprocal benefit of the contracting parties, but at the protection of individuals (physical and moral persons) from the exercise of public authority, in human rights law reparation could also include the adoption of normative measures aiming at the disappearance of the provision(s) and practice that are at the source of the infringement of a given human right.

The state authorities responsible for the reparation of human rights violations attributable to them are, in principle, free to choose the means for such reparation among the options mentioned afore.[8] Under the Greek Civil Code monetary compensation (damages) takes precedence over other means of reparation. In accordance with Art. 297 CC, damages are monetary. In exceptional cases only, after

---

[5] *Basic Principles and Guidelines on the Right to a Remedy and Reparation for Victims of Gross Violations of International Human Rights Law and Serious Violations of International Humanitarian Law*, UNGA Resolution 60/147 of 16.12.2005, UN Doc A/RES/60/147, 21.3.2006, Principle 18, p. 7. Comp. PCIJ, *Factory at Chorzów*, Judgment (Merits), 13.9.1928, *PCIJ Reports, Series A 17*, p. 48; Article 34 of the International Law Commission 2001 Draft Articles on Responsibility of States for Internationally Wrongful Acts, *Yearbook of the International Law Commission*, 2001, vol. II (Part Two) (Text reproduced as it appears in the annex to General Assembly resolution 56/83 of 12.12.2001, and corrected by document A/56/49(Vol. I)/Corr.4.); *Report of the International Law Commission on the Work of its Fifty-third Session*, UN Doc A/56/10, 43 (2001), including the ILC Articles on Responsibility of States for Internationally Wrongful Acts, Commentary on Article 35, p. 238, para 3.

[6] BPGRR, UNGA Resolution 60/147 of 16.12.2005, UN Doc A/RES/60/147, 21.3.2006, Principle 19, p. 7.

[7] *Ibid.*, Principle 20.

[8] Cf. ECtHR, *Papamichalopoulos and Others v. Greece* (Art. 50), (Application No. 14556/89), Judgment of 31.10.1995, *Series A 330-B*, para. 34.

assessment of the special circumstances of the case at hand, the competent court may order the *restitutio in integrum*, provided that this type of reparation does not impair the interest of the beneficiary of the damages.

Monetary compensation in the form of "just satisfaction" is also the main option directly available to the European Court of Human Rights (ECtHR) under Art. 41 (formerly Art. 50) of the European Convention of Human Rights (ECHR): "If the Court finds that there has been a violation of the Convention or the protocols thereto, and if the internal law of the High Contracting Party concerned allows only partial reparation to be made, the Court shall, if necessary, afford just satisfaction to the injured party."[9] This is so because the judgments of the ECtHR "are essentially declaratory in nature," leaving it open for the national authorities of the state concerned to choose (under the supervision of the Committee of Ministers of the Council of Europe) the appropriate implementation means which are compatible with the Court's findings.[10] In some cases the Court's declaration that a violation has occurred, is considered sufficient satisfaction for the applicant.[11] However, though the ECtHR is in principle unable to grant other forms of redress for human rights violations it establishes, e.g., cessation, non-repetition, restitution in kind, it can recommend to the violating state to afford restitution in kind to the victim as a primary means of reparation, with monetary just satisfaction as a secondary remedy in cases where the state fails to follow the Court's advice.[12]

Pecuniary fair compensation for violations of human rights is also provided in the Inter-American system, as a secondary remedy to ensuring the enjoyment by the victim of the right or freedom that was violated.[13] In the African regional system, reparation measures made their way in the decisions of the African Commission on Human and Peoples' Rights, despite the lack of a mandate thereto,[14] while an explicit authorisation for "payment of fair compensation or reparation," for a violation of a human or peoples' right was incorporated in Art. 27 para. 1 of the Protocol to the African Charter on Human and Peoples' Rights on the Establishment of an African Court on Human and Peoples' Rights (adopted in 1998, into force since 2004).

---

[9] On the interpretation and application of this provision, see Steiner (2011) 3–26.

[10] ECtHR, *Assanidze v. Georgia* (Application No. 71503/01), Judgment of 8.4.2014, para. 202.

[11] Dannemann (1994) 365–368; Józon (2011) 741–769.

[12] See ECtHR, *Papamichalopoulos and Others v. Greece* (Art. 50), (Application No. 14556/89), Judgment of 31.10.1995, *Series A 330-B*, para. 34; *Brumarescu v Romania* (Art. 4I), (Application No. 28342/95), Judgment of 23.1.2001, *Reports 2001–1*, paras 19–22.

[13] Art. 63, para. 1 American Convention on Human Rights: "If the Court finds that there has been a violation of a right or freedom protected by this Convention, the Court shall rule that the injured party be ensured the enjoyment of his right or freedom that was violated. It shall also rule, if appropriate, that the consequences of the measure or situation that constituted the breach of such right or freedom be remedied and that fair compensation be paid to the injured party." See Inter-American Court of Human Rights, Case of *Benavides-Cevallos v. Ecuador*, Judgment of June 19, 1998 (Merits, Reparations and Costs).

[14] Naldi (2001) 681.

7.2 Public Authority Liability: General Features

In Greece, the liability of public authority in general (including infringements to human rights) is governed by Articles 104–106 of the Introductory Law to the Civil Code (ILCC).[15]

ILCC distinguishes the regime of public authority depending on the nature of its conduct: when the state acts in a private law capacity, as *fiscus*, the legislator subjects the state's civil liability to the provisions of the Civil Code in a way identical to the civil liability of any other legal person (Art. 104 ILCC).[16] Such cases, not involving the exercise of public authority will in principle remain outside the scope of the present inquiry on the public authority liability.

The law introduced a particular regime of liability, distinct from the general system of the CC, for the state when the latter exercises its public law authority: in accordance with Art. 105 ILCC, the state is liable for damages caused by unlawful conduct of its organs[17] and its instrumentalities.[18] Article 105 ILCC (and Art. 106, with respect to local self-governance entities and legal people of public law) establish thus the concept of a *special prejudicial act in public law*, creating public authority non-contractual (or extra contractual) liability.

The recognition of the non-contractual liability of the state for its conduct derives from the constitutional principle of equality and is consequently considered as being a constitutionally guaranteed provision.[19] The compensation for violations of human rights is considered to be a form of the reparation of the infringement aiming at the respect of the principle of legality (rule of law) in the action of the government, in particular regarding the activities of the state agents.[20] Further, it is submitted that the non-contractual liability of the state should be considered as an indirect means that render the rule of law a *lex perfecta* in the Greek legal order contributing thus to the

---

[15] Presidential Decree 456/1984, *Journal of the Government*, vol. A, No. 164 (initially Emergency Law No. 2783/1941). Cf. Stassinopoulos (1949) 507–514.

[16] Art. 104 ILCC: "The State shall be liable in accordance with the provisions of the Civil Code concerning legal persons, for acts or omissions of its organs regarding private-law relations or State assets."; Art. 71 CC: "The legal entity shall be liable for acts or omissions of the organs that represent it, where the act or omission is done in the performance of duties assigned to them by the legal entity and give rise to compensation. The person(s) shall be liable jointly and severally for fault or negligence."

[17] Art. 105 ILCC reads: "The State shall be under a duty to make good any damage caused by the unlawful acts or omissions of its organs in the exercise of public authority, except where the unlawful act or omission is in breach of an existing provision which is intended to serve the public interest. The person responsible shall be jointly and severally liable, without prejudice to the special provisions on ministerial responsibility."

[18] In accordance with Art. 106 ILCC, "The provisions of the two previous articles [104 and 105] apply also to the liability of municipalities and other legal entities of public law for acts or omissions of organs at their service."

[19] Pavlopoulos (1986) 134 ff.

[20] Pavlopoulos (1986) 57 ff.

application in practice of the rule of law in the state activity through the guarantee of an effective judicial protection of the individual.[21]

The civil liability of the state in general is immediate, principal and objective. It requires that a damage has been suffered due to an unlawful action (by commission or omission) of the state through its organs. The illegal character of the action suffices for establishing the liability of the state, the (subjective) fault of the/a particular organ of the state is *not* a constitutive element of the civil liability of the state.[22] This is the major difference of Articles 105 and 106 ILCC compared with the general regime of "delictual liability" (liability in tort), for which Art. 914 ff CC require a subjective fault (wilful wrong, intention or negligence) of the tortfeasor. Fault is also required for the civil liability of the state arising out of its relations of private law nature, in accordance with Art. 104 ILCC, which refers to "the provisions of the Civil Code concerning legal persons," (Art. 71, 914 ff CC). The intention or negligence may also be relevant for the *personal* liability of the organ, jointly and severally with the state. Consequently, the fault of the organ is required also for the right of recourse of the state against the person(s) who committed (or omitted) the unlawful and harmful act that triggered the civil liability of the public authority.

The system of liability provided for by Art. 105 ILCC is restorative, instituting a remedy of purely compensatory character.[23] This is in line with the general provision of the Civil Code with respect of civil liability stipulating that damages owed are pecuniary. Only exceptionally, when assessing the special circumstances of the case, may a competent court order *restitutio in integrum* on the further condition that this type of reparation does not impair the interest of the beneficiary of the damages (Art. 297 CC).

The system of liability of a public authority for human rights violations of Art. 105–106 ILCC stands at the junction of civil law, municipal public law, and public international law. Civil law is relevant because the nature of the liability is civil and the general regime of civil liability and damages apply. Public law is implicated because the debtor of the damages is the state or its instrumentalities acting in the exercise of public authority. In addition, the administrative courts have been the competent jurisdiction for adjudicating claims for damages for human rights violations attributed to the state (or its instrumentalities) for the past three decades;

---

[21] Tachos (2003) 809; Raikos (2010) 3–4, www.esd.gr/eisigiseis/raikos.doc, pp. 3–4. Comp. ECJ, *G. Köbler v. Österreich*, Case C-224/01, Opinion of the AG Leger, 8.4.2003, para. 35, [2003] ECR, I-10254, "The principle of State liability constitutes the necessary extension of the general principle of effective judicial protection or of the right to challenge a measure before the courts, whose importance has been regularly underlined by the Court and whose scope has been constantly extended through its case-law."

[22] Areios Pagos (Court of cassation in civil and criminal matters, hereinafter AP), Judgment No. 449/1972, Juridical Tribune (*Nomiko Vima* – a monthly publication of the Athens Law Bar, hereinafter JT), 1972, p. 1183; Council of State (Supreme court in administrative matters, hereinafter CS), Judgment No. 1413/2006. Greek case-law without reference to law journal or other printed source is to be found in the legal database (Isokratis) of the Athens Law Bar.

[23] Cf. ECtHR, *Tsoukalas v. Greece*, (Application no. 12286/08) and Judgment of 22.7.2010, para. 41 "recours purement indemnitaire".

unsurprisingly, the lower administrative courts, as well as the Council of State, i.e., the supreme court in administrative matters, instill their public law perspective and approaches in through their application of the relevant Civil Code provisions on civil liability. International law is equally implicated because of its obvious importance to the protection of human rights and the permeation of the relevant international rules (customary and conventional, upon ratification by Greece) into the Greek legal order, in which they have pre-eminence over municipal legal provisions, with the exception of the Constitution (in accordance with Art. 28 of the Greek Constitution). As a consequence, the unlawful conduct of the public authority frequently consists of the violation of international (customary and conventional) rules on the protection of human rights, which co-exist and complement the constitutional and other municipal safeguards of human rights.

Article 105 ILCC is a special provision, which however, points to the application of the general principles for non-contractual liability (tort liability) exposed in Art. 914 ff CC.

Specific provisions for the non-contractual liability of the state for specific infringements of human rights exist with respect to victims of unjust or illegal detention, on remand or on conviction, which has been subsequently reversed on appeal (Art. 533–545 of the Code of Criminal Procedure, see *infra*), and also providing for the obligation of the state to make good loss or damage caused by violations to the rights to life, to physical safety and integrity and to private property of individuals due to terrorist acts (Laws Nos. 1897/1990, 1947/1991 and 2093/1992).[24]

7.3 Scope of the Liability Regime

Below we describe the requirements set by Art. 105 ILCC for damages for unlawful and harmful acts of the public authority (including unlawful and harmful violations of human rights).

7.3.1 Positive Requirements

7.3.1.1 Conduct

The liability of the state for violations of human rights results from the conduct of its organs. This conduct includes acts or omissions that entail legal consequences. It further encompasses physical acts of state organs,[25] including acts which are not in

[24] *Journal of the Government*, vol. A, No. 120, 11.9.1990; vol. A, No. 70, 15.5.1991; vol. A, No. 181, 25.11.1992.

[25] E.g. CS, Judgments nos 3042/1992, 736/1994, 3226/1998, 1857/1999. Cf. Mathioudakis (2006)135 ff. and *passim*.

principle enforceable but affect legal rights or interests of private persons.[26] This understanding aims at covering all aspects of the sovereign activity of the state and its organs.[27] The case-law held the state liable in accordance with Art. 105 ILCC in a case, for example of illegal exercise of psychological pressure by police agents in order to make the owner of land to consent to the occupation of his property by a third person.[28]

Civil liability of the state for an omission constituting a violation of human rights arises when there is a duty of the state to act. This duty to act should be stipulated in a legal provision. This happens when the competent public authority was bound by an applicable legal provision to adopt the act it omitted, i.e., when it had no discretionary power to assess the opportunity of the act.[29] Moreover, in accordance with the case-law an omission that can trigger the civil liability of the state is the lack to fulfill specific tasks and obligations imposed to a state organ by the applicable laws and other normative acts or pertaining to a public service in accordance with the teachings of common experience and the principle of good faith.[30] In this way the scope of violation of human rights through omission of state organs becomes broader.

7.3.1.2 By an Organ of the State or of Legal Entities of Public Law

The civil liability of the state for human rights violation requires the attribution to the state of the act, omission or other conduct by which the alleged infringement was caused. Art. 105 ILCC uses the term "organ", deliberately chosen because it is broader than the (likewise suggested) concepts of "civil servant" or "official".[31] Hence, for the purposes of civil liability of the public authority, any person at the service of the state is an organ of the state,[32] provided that he/she has a functional ("organic") link with the state.[33]

---

[26] E.g. omission of the penitentiary agents to conduct physical controls to prevent the introduction into a penitentiary institution of drugs that caused the death of an inmate and the risk to the security and wellbeing of other inmates, Athens Administrative Court of First Instance (ACFI), Judgment No. 1881/2011.

[27] Kyriakopoulos, Article 105 ILCC, no. 23; Stassinopoulos (1950) 150–151; Pavlopoulos (1989) 42 ff., 67–72; Karditsa Court of First Instance (CFI), Judgment No. 772/1964, *JT*, 1965, p. 414. Comp. Gour (1978) no. 193, p. 20.

[28] AP, Judgment No. 1701/1984, *Journal of Greek Jurists*, 1985, p. 686.

[29] E.g. CS, Judgments Nos. 2052/1980, 641/1979, 1601/1982.

[30] CS, Judgments Nos. 1249/2010, 1019/2008, 2146/2004; Piraeus ACFI, Judgment No. 5283/2010; see also Mathioudakis (2004), 1416 ff.

[31] Stassinopoulos (1950) 93; Spiliotopoulos (1986) 217–218;. Pavlopoulos (1989) 77–79.

[32] Thessaloniki CFI, Judgment No. 2238/1969, *Harmenopoulos*, 1970, p. 176. Cf. Thessaloniki Court of Appeal: hereinafter CA, preceded from the district, Judgment No. 1395/1975, *Journal of Greek Jurists*, 1977, p. 445.

[33] Stassinopoulos (1950) 93; Dagtoglou (2004) 966–968.

This "organic" link exists for persons who are at the service of the state in all three branches of the government. A violation of human rights by a state organ of the executive, of the legislative or of the judicial function can be equally attributed to the state and can, in principle, trigger the civil liability of the public authority.

Executive Function

With regard to the executive function in the state, the principle is broadly accepted and the definition of a state "organ" encompasses each and every agent and officer, including the Head of State (President of the Republic), the President of the Council of Ministers (Prime Minister) and the Ministers.[34] Civil liability of the state is possible also for human rights violations by *de fact*o state organs,[35] including organs whose existence is based on violence or an illegal act, as it was held for example with regard to the non-contractual liability of the Greek state for the acts of the regime issued from the *coup d'état* of April 1967.[36]

Finally, people that cooperate with organs of the executive branch, without having an "organic" link with the state (offer their services voluntarily or upon request or order of a state organ) can trigger with their conduct the non-contractual liability of the state towards a third person and also with regard to the people themselves who cooperated and suffered injury as a result of their voluntary or requested cooperation with state organs.[37]

A specific issue is raised by the normative activity of organs of the executive branch, that is from the possibility to attach the civil responsibility of the state for human rights violations that occur in the exercise of normative-legislative competence, in the cases the executive branch is vested with such delegated competence either directly from the Constitution (Art. 43 para. 1; 54 para. 2; 83 paras. 1, 2 Constitution) or through delegation by a law (act of parliament) (Art. 43 paras. 2 and 4 Constitution).

This hypothesis intersects with the germane issue of the civil liability of the state from violations of human rights by the legislative organ(s) and the answers given depend on the developments in the latter issue. The earlier case-law did not accept without hesitations the possibility of the state to incur civil liability for human rights violations through the exercise of delegated normative authority of the executive branch, on the grounds that the normative competence of the executive branch is part of the legislative function of the state organs, and the state should not incur civil

---

[34] Chrysogonos (2003) 565–566; Raikos (2002) 861–862; cf. Athens CFI, Judgment No. 10756/1955, *Harmenopoulos*, 1955, p. 393. See also, Law No. 3126/2003, Art. 15, para. 5; Stassinopoulos (1961) 641 ff.

[35] Stassinopoulos (1950) 143 ff.; Pavlopoulos (1989) 85–87.

[36] See judgments of the Athens CA, Judgments Nos. 4154/1979, *JT*, 1979, p. 1332, and 6898/1977, *JT*, 1978, p. 748.

[37] AP, Judgment No. 316/1983, *JT*, 1983, p. 1571.

liability from acts or omissions of the legislative branch of the government.[38] However, this negative approach, based on the assimilation of the normative acts of the executive branch to the acts of parliament, has been gradually eroded through the recognition of civil liability of the state from the exercise of particular aspects of the normative competence of the organs of the executive branch.[39] It is now accepted that the state can incur civil liability for human rights violations in the exercise of delegated normative competence of the executive branch of the government, mainly through commission but also by omission, if the state organ authorised to issue the normative act is bound by the authorising provision to adopt the act it omitted, i.e., when it has no discretionary power to assess the opportunity of the act.[40]

Legislative Function

In a general perspective, the question of civil liability for violations of human rights through the conduct of legislative organs stumbled originally on the traditional conception that when legislating the state cannot act illegally. The rigidity of this view was highlighted quite early in the *mater parliamentorum*, in which originated the doctrine of parliamentary sovereignty. In a case dating back in 1701, it was held that "an act of parliament can do no wrong though it may do several things that look pretty odd," that is things that are contrary to the axioms of natural justice in all laws.[41] In Greece, where the diffuse (and incidental) control of the constitutionality of the laws adopted by the Parliament is traditionally firmly embedded in the legal culture (cf. Art. 93 para. 4 Constitution), the position that the state cannot incur non-contractual liability for the conduct of the legislative organs was not accepted initially in cases where the legislative conduct constituted a violation of the Constitution,[42] in particular in case of legislative acts which are contrary to the constitutional guarantees of fundamental human rights.[43] For the identity of the *ratio* (hierarchical structure of the legal order), the non-contractual liability of the state should be accepted also, in case the law voted by the Parliament contravened other sources of the Greek legal order, with higher status than the acts of Parliament: the generally accepted rules of international law and international conventions ratified by Greece (Art. 28 para. 1 Constitution) as well as norms emanating from the

---

[38] AP, Judgment No. 665/1975, *JT*, 1976, p. 59; see observations on this decision by Anastassiadis (1976) 163.

[39] See, for example, Athens CA, Judgment No. 2590/1975, *JT*, 1975, p. 773; AP, Judgments Nos. 413/1981, *JT*, 1982, p. 204; 226/1982, *Hellenic Justice*, 1983, p. 22.

[40] E.g. CS, Judgments Nos. 3088/2009, 1601/1982, 2052/1980. See P. Pavlopoulos (1989)109 ff.

[41] Plucknett (1926), 55–56; cf. Helmholz (2009) 325–346.

[42] AP, Judgments Nos. 115/1931, *Themis*, 1931, p. 333; 198/1941, *Journal of Greek Jurists*, 1941–42, p. 280; 37/1957, *JT*, 1957, p. 517. See Kyriakopoulos (1949) Article 105 ILCC, no. 58; Stassinopoulos (1950) 99; Dagtoglou, (1962); Manitakis (1984) 17 ff.; Pavlopoulos (1989)162-163.

[43] Dagtoglou (1992) 825.

EU legal order (Art. 28 paras. 2 and 3 Constitution).[44] However, the case of unconstitutionality was the only exception to the principle that the state cannot act unlawfully when legislating, and the courts at the highest level, remained for a long period (also after the adoption of Art. 105 and 106 ILCC), in general faithful to the position that the state does not bear non-contractual liability for acts (or omissions) of the legislative organs.

Legal doctrine submitted, however, the view that the plain text of Art. 105 ILCC did not distinguish the conduct of the legislative organs from any other organ of the state and that, for the purposes of the civil liability of the state, the legislative acts were not different in their nature from the acts of the other branches of the government;[45] hence, the acts of parliament could in principle trigger the non-contractual liability of the state, provided that the remaining requirements of Art. 105 ILCC were met.

The possibility to attach in principle the civil liability of the state for conduct of the legislature, based on the unqualified language of Art. 105 ILCC, was disputed also by the contention that it would be inconceivable to apply the regime of the civil liability, because Art. 105 ILCC provides that the state can incur non-contractual liability from the violation of a provision that is not aimed at the protection of a general interest.[46] An essential and fundamental feature of a law passed by the Parliament is its abstract and general character; thus, *by definition*, the acts of parliament could not trigger the civil liability of the state under the regime instituted by Art. 105 ILCC. Yet, this objection, even if it were accepted as valid,[47] would fall under the requirement of the violation of a provision that is not aimed at the protection of the general interest and not under the condition that we currently examine of an act (or omission) of a state organ. Consequently, if a law adopted by the Parliament *does in concreto* cause a violation of a protected human right of concrete person(s), the civil liability of the state could not be excluded. The Council of State held the state civilly liable because it had awarded compensation to five farmers expressly named in a law following a natural calamity that destroyed their crops, while omitting to compensate a sixth farmer who had incurred loss in the same conditions.[48]

On the other hand, the applicability of the regime of civil liability of the state for non-legislative acts of the legislative branch which violate human rights did not face the above obstacles.[49] Hence, acts of administrative nature of the parliament, e.g., decisions for the organisation and structure of the services of the parliament, or acts in the process of the parliamentary control of the executive branch are considered conduct attributable to the state for the purposes of triggering the non-contractual liability of the state.

[44] Georgopoulos, (2002).

[45] Cf. Dagtoglou (1962) 13.

[46] Cf. Stassinopoulos (1950) 94–95; Dagtoglou (1962) 16.

[47] See however Pavlopoulos (1989) 145–146.

[48] CS, Judgment No. 2546/2010.

[49] Stassinopoulos (1950) 107–108; Pavlopoulos (1989) 135–137; Dagtoglou (1962) 14–15.

Judicial Branch

With regard to the possibility to consider actions (or omissions) of the judiciary branch as conduct of the state in the meaning of Art. 105 ILCC, the prevailing opinion tends to be disapproving, though a recent development, if consolidated, signals a possible change. Distinct, though intersecting, strands of legal argument have been submitted to deny the possibility of non-contractual liability of the state for infringement of human rights attributable to judicial organs.

It has been disputed, in the first place, that courts and tribunals can be considered as state organs because of the constitutionally guaranteed functional and personal independence of the judiciary (Art. 87 Constitution).[50] In addition, it was submitted that the non-contractual liability of the state for conduct of the judicial organs should be excluded also because of the existence of specific provisions in the Constitution and in the legislation concerning the personal liability of members of judiciary for miscarriage of justice; Art. 99 Constitution and Law No. 693/1977 (Art. 6 para. 1) provide and organise respectively a particular action for damages against a judge for mistrial, in case of intent, gross negligence or denial of justice, on the condition that their intent, gross negligence or denial of justice caused injury to a party in the judicial proceedings. Based on one or both of the above reasons, Greek courts generally admit that in case of the violation of human rights by judicial decisions, the state cannot be held liable, and only the judges are liable in their personal capacity.[51] Based on the same line of reasoning the case-law rejects the existence of civil liability of the state (and admits only the personal liability of the respective agent(s)) for violations of human rights by prosecuting functionaries.[52]

After the introduction of Art. 105 ILCC, legal doctrine has submitted that the state is jointly and severally liable for unlawful acts (or omissions) of the judicial organs because the personal and functional independence of the judiciary is guaranteed in order to prohibit any tentative of other branches of the government to exercise influence on the judicial activity.[53] This position was mainly founded on the language of Art. 105 ILCC which does not distinguish the state organs whose unlawful conduct engages the non-contractual liability of the state.[54] On a subsidiary basis it is further submitted that the conditions of the personal liability of agents of the judicial power in accordance with Art. 99 Constitution and Law No. 693/1977 are very restrictive; therefore, the regime of civil liability of the state under Art. 105

[50] AP, Judgment No. 256/1996, *Hellenic Justice*, 1997, p. 555; Thessaloniki Administrative Court of Appeal (ACA), Judgment No. 2037/2005, *Administrative Trial*, 2007, p. 1536; Thessaloniki ACFI, Judgment No. 1458/2000, *Administrative Trial*, 2000, p. 1011; cf. Kavkas (1946) 859; Korsos (1977) 100–101.

[51] Athens CA, Judgments Nos. 6044/1979, *JT*, 1980, pp. 308–309; 6772/1987, *JT*, 1987, p. 1630.

[52] Thessaloniki ACFI Judgment No. 1458/2000, *Administrative Trial*, 2000, p. 1011.

[53] Pavlopoulos (1989) 175–178, with further references; Macridou (2012) 1349.

[54] On the similar question in the field of the EU law, see ECJ, *Brasserie du pêcheur and Factortame*, Joined Cases C-46/93 and C-48/93, [1996] *ECR*, I-1029, in particular paras. 30–33; *G. Köbler v. Österreich*, Case C-224/01, Opinion of the Advocate General Leger, 8 April 2003, [2003] *ECR*, I-10255, para. 35.

ILCC complements the above provisions, instituting a civil liability of the state for acts or omissions of organs of the judicial branch that are not covered from the language of Art. 6 para. 1 of Law No. 693/1977.[55]

For more than seven decades these arguments have, however, failed to convince the Greek courts which invariably reject the civil liability of the state for the acts or omissions of the judicial organs. A lower administrative court, however, upheld in 2008 the joint and several liability of the state for damages sustained by the violation of the right to have a case adjudicated within a reasonable time, inscribed in Art. 6 para. 1 ECHR.[56]

It is significant to note that the above, rather exceptional[57], decision was rendered with regard to a systemic problem of the judicial system in Greece,[58] the excessive delays in the judicial proceedings.[59] In this respect, under pressure from the ECtHR, specific remedies have been introduced providing just satisfaction for injury sustained due to excessive length of the judicial proceedings. In three pilot judgments, the ECtHR held that the excessive length of proceedings in administrative (*Athanasiou and Others v. Greece*), criminal (*Michelioudakis v. Greece*) and civil (*Glykantzi v. Greece*) proceedings constituted a structural problem, and requested the Greek state to institute effective domestic remedy within 1 year.[60] The Greek authorities complied with the above judgments by enacting Law No. 4055/2012, for excessive delay in administrative proceedings,[61] and Law No. 4239/2014 pertaining to the excessive length of civil and criminal trials as well as of proceedings in the Court of Audits.[62] Articles 53–60 of Law No. 4055/2012 and 1–7 of Law No. 4239/2014 introduce a specific compensatory, legal remedy for just satisfaction in case of "non-reasonable" length of judicial proceedings in civil and criminal

---

[55] D. Korsos (1977) 100.

[56] Athens ACFI, Judgment No. 15006/2008.

[57] See ECtHR, *Tsoukalas v. Greece* (Application no. 12286/08), Judgment, 22 July 2010, para. 34, rejecting the argument of the Greek Government that the domestic remedies had not been exhausted, because the applicants had not lodged an action in accordance with Art. 105 ILCC for their compensation for acts and omissions of the judicial organs that have violated their rights under Art. 6 and 13 ECHR.

[58] Sitaropoulos (2011) 17–25.

[59] For the list of (90) cases against Greece before the EctHR for excessive length of judicial proceedings (Art. 6, para. 1 ECHR), see Council of Europe, Committee of Ministers, Interim Resolution CM/ResDH(2007)74, 6.6.2007, Appendix.

[60] ECtHR, *V. Athanasiou and Others v. Greece* (Application No. 50973/08), Judgment of 21.12.2010, para. 57; *Michelioudakis v. Greece* (Application No. 54447/10), Judgment of 3.4.2012, para. 78; *Glykantzi v. Greece* (Application No. 40150/09), Judgment of 30.10.2012, para. 81.

[61] *Journal of the Government*, vol. A, No. 51 of 12.3.2012, pp. 1397 ff, in particular 1420–1426; cf. *Plan d'action complémentaire (08/04/2013), Communication de la Grèce relative à l'affaire* Athanasiou et autres *(arrêt pilote)* contre Grèce *(requête n° 50973/08)*, Doc DH-DD(2013)758, 04/07/2013, https://wcd.coe.int/ViewDoc.jsp?Ref=DH-DD(2013)758&amp%3bamp%3bamp%3bamp%3bLanguage=lanEnglish&amp%3bamp%3bamp%3bamp%3bSite=CM. Accessed 1 March 2015. This Communication of the Greek Government has as an annex the translation in French of Art. 53–60 Law No. 4055/2012 (pp. 13–17 of the Communication).

[62] *Journal of the Government*, vol. A, No. 43, 20.2.2014, pp. 737–739.

matters,[63] in administrative matters and in auditing matters.[64] In 2013, the ECtHR considered that the domestic remedies introduced by the relevant provisions of Law No. 4055/2012 (administrative justice), enabling proceedings to be speeded up and litigants to obtain compensation under the new Law should be regarded as effective for the purposes of Art. 13 of the ECHR. The Court further noted that the compensatory remedy had already proved its effectiveness in practice, as demonstrated by recent domestic court rulings.[65]

At the general level, a significant change in the negative attitude of the case law occurred in late spring 2014, when the plenary of the Council of State found that the state should be liable for damages due to the conduct of judicial organs.[66] Taking into account the specific nature of the judicial function, the judgment limited however the civil liability of the state only in the case of "manifest error" of the judicial organ, excluding from the scope of such liability damages for erroneous application or interpretation of the law.[67] The highest administrative court did not depart from the prevailing opinion that the system of civil liability organised by Art. 105 did not apply to the conduct of judicial organs; it noted, however, that the omission of the legislator to adopt specific regulation of this type of civil liability of the state is not consistent with the Constitution[68] and therefore it declared that Art. 105 ILCC should apply *by analogy* with respect to civil claims for damages due to a manifest error of judicial organs.[69] This decision constitutes an important shift of the case-law and potentially (it was adopted with a notable minority opinion) will mark a change in the long-standing negative position of Greek courts.[70]

---

[63] In addition to the compensatory legal remedy (action for damages) in criminal proceedings, Art. 7, para. 3 Law No. 4239/2014 provides also the possibility for the competent court to reduce the sentence in an express and measurable manner as an additional remedy to the excessive length of proceedings that is not due to the fault of the accused. The law complies thus with the guidelines of the ECtHR with regard to the unreasonable length of criminal trials, cf. ECtHR, *Michelioudakis v. Greece* (Application No. 54447/10), Judgment, 3.4.2012, para. 77.

[64] The afore-mentioned pilot judgments do not concern the proceedings in the Court of Audits. By the moment of the introduction of the relative legislation (2014) the ECtHR had, nevertheless, rendered one judgment finding a violation of Art. 6 ECHR by Greece for excessive length of proceedings in the Court of Audits (ECtHR, *Kalatzi-Kanata v. Greece* (Application No. 951/10), Judgment, 22.1.2013), while several similar applications were pending, see Ministry of Justice, *Explanatory Memorandum of the draft law "Just satisfaction for excess of the reasonable length of the proceedings in civil and criminal courts and in the Court of Audits,"* Athens, 29.11.2013, para. 13, http://www.ministryofjustice.gr/site/LinkClick.aspx?fileticket=VBmBBBvMj7w%3D&tabid=132. Accessed 1 March 2015.

[65] ECtHR, *Techniki Olympiaki A.E. v. Greece* (Application No 40547/10), Decision of 1.10.2013, paras, 41 ff, in particular para. 58.

[66] CS, Judgment No. 1501/2014.

[67] *Ibid.*

[68] Art. 4, para. 6, "Greek citizens contribute without distinction to public charges in proportion to their means."

[69] CS, Judgment No. 1501/2014.

[70] For a commentary of this decision, see Prevedourou (2014) 411 ff.

Specific provisions exist for damages for violations of the right to liberty, in particular in cases of deprivation of freedom through arrest or detention for acts of which they have been subsequently acquitted. The basis for damages for this specific aspect of conduct of judicial organs is Art. 7 para. 4 of the Constitution, stipulating that "The conditions under which the State, following a judicial decision, shall indemnify persons unjustly or illegally convicted, detained pending trial, or otherwise deprived of their personal liberty shall be provided by law." The constitutional mandate, consonant with international law commitments and standards,[71] has been implemented through relevant provisions of the Code of Criminal Procedure (CCP). Articles 533–545 CCP, as amended by Law No. 2915/2001,[72] organize the regime, conditions and procedure for the award of damages in case of unjust or illegal detention on remand or conviction.[73] In accordance with Art. 533 para 1 CCP, damages from the state for unjust or illegal detention can claim individuals who were placed in provisional detention and were later found not guilty for the offence they were charged with and persons who were detained following a judicial decision, which was subsequently quashed. Damages can also claim persons who were initially convicted of an offence and, after judicial review, were sentenced to a shorter term than that they have actually served. Moreover, in the above cases, compensation from the state can claim, *independently from* the individuals who have been unjustly or illegally deprived of their freedom, the persons who are entitled to alimony from those unjustly or illegally deprived of their freedom (Art. 534 CCP).

The damages for unjust or illegal deprivation of freedom should cover the patrimonial injury and the moral damage sustained by the claimant (Art. 536 para. 2 and 540 CCP). Unlike the general regime of civil liability of the state, entrusting the determination of the compensation due to a successful claimant, Art. 536 para. 2 CCP provides for the award of a *lump sum compensation* which cannot be lower than 8.80 euros nor higher than 29 euros[74] per day of unjust or illegal detention. Within these lower and upper limits, the competent court determines the exact amount of the compensation taking into account the financial and family situation of the claimant (Art. 536 para. 2 CCP).

The criminal courts that have found the claimant not guilty for the offence are competent for the action in damages in these cases (Art. 536, para. 1 CCP). The action for damages can be lodged by the defendant during the criminal proceedings for review of the initial decision. In such a case the competent court decides on the claim in a separate but simultaneous (with the judgment on the innocence of the defendant) judgment (Art. 536 para. 1 CCP). If the action for damages were not

[71] Art. 5 para 5 ECHR ("Everyone who has been the victim of arrest or detention in contravention of the provisions of this article shall have an enforceable right to compensation."); ECtHR, *Sakik and others v. Turkey*, (Application Nos 23878/94, 23879/94, 23880/94, 23881/94, 23882/94, 23883/94), Judgment, 26.11.1997, *Reports of Judgments and Decisions* 1997-VII, no. 58. Comp. ICCPR, Art. 14, para. 6.

[72] *Journal of the Government*, vol. A, No. 109, 29.5.2001.

[73] Margaritis (2001) 750 ff.

[74] These amounts can be modified by joint decision of the Ministers of Finance and Justice.

lodged during the criminal proceedings, the defendant who has been unjustly or illegally deprived of his freedom, can lodge a claim to that effect to the criminal court which has reversed the conviction in a deadline of 10 days after the publication of the judgment in the criminal proceedings (Art. 537 CCP). The defendant who has been acquitted and awarded damages for unjust or illegal deprivation of his/her freedom by the criminal courts, has an additional remedy to the civil courts, in case he/she considers the compensation awarded by the competent criminal court insufficient to cover the material damage and the moral harm actually sustained (Art. 539 CCP). This action can be lodged within 2 years after the award of damages by the competent criminal court. In deciding on such a claim for additional damages, the civil court can *only in exceptional circumstances* grant damages beyond the upper limit provided for in Art. 536 para. 2 CCP (currently 29 euros per day of unjust or illegal deprivation of liberty) (Art. 539 *in fine* CCP).

Finally, the state bears civil liability for infringements to human rights in accordance with Art. 105 ILCC attributable to organs of the judicial branch, when the latter act in the exercise of their administrative functions in the organization of the public service of justice or from the organs of the judicial branch that are not exercising judicial functions (law clerks, officials of the registries of the courts).

7.3.1.3 Conduct in the Exercise of Public Authority

A further condition required by the case-law in order to adjudicate damages for the infringement to human rights by unlawful conduct of organs of the state is that the organ should act in its capacity of public authority, *de iure imperii*, exercising a sovereign power of the state.[75] The exercise of public authority implies the adoption of (in principle[76] unilateral) acts that are mandatory for the private persons and the competence to use public enforcement for the respect of such acts.

In practice, this criterion is fulfilled when the harmful conduct of the state organ (infringement of human rights) relates to the organisation and function of a public service.[77] This close relationship is described in theory and jurisprudence as the "*inner nexus*" between the act or omission causing the harm and the exercise of public authority.[78] The obvious consequence of this requirement is that the state (or a legal entity of public law) cannot incur liability for acts or omissions of its organs undertook in their *private* capacity.[79] By virtue also of the requirement of the

[75] AP, Judgment No. 186/1968, *JT*, 1968, p. 637. Papevangellou et al. (2002) 13 ff., 137 ff.

[76] Cf. Pavlopoulos (1989) 213–220, for the scope of application of Articles 105 and 106 ILCC to administrative contracts. Comp. Amselek (1983) 3–7.

[77] Supreme Special Court, Judgment No. 5/1995, *Administrative Trial*, 1995, p. 311; CS, Judgments Nos. 2763/1999, 740/2001, 1485-1486/2005.

[78] AP, Judgment No. 161/1987, *JT*, 1987, p. 1045. Raikos (2008) 386 ff; Pavlopoulos (1989) 22 ff.; Stassinopoulos (1950) 171 ff.

[79] Already in that sense: Athens CA, Judgment No. 88/1900, *Themis*, 1905–1906, p. 409. As stated *supra* the non-contractual liability of the state when its organs act in their private law capacity, as

"inner nexus" of the conduct and the exercise of public authority, Art. 105 (and 106) do not apply in case of obvious incompetence of the state organ, when the organ acted patently outside its (territorial or material) competence, as well as in cases in which the organ intentionally exceeded its competence for its own illicit private benefit.[80]

The presence of an "inner nexus" between the conduct of a state organ and the exercise of public authority is capable for triggering the civil liability of the Greek state also for conduct of its organs undertaken outside the national territory or outside spaces in which the Greek state exercises competences in accordance with international law. This position is consonant with the scope of the states parties' obligations under the ECHR, in accordance with its Art. 1 ("The High Contracting Parties shall secure to everyone within their jurisdiction the rights and freedoms defined in Section I of this Convention.") In such cases the civil liability of the Greek state towards victims of human rights violations can be triggered also for conduct inconsistent with public international law.

Exceptions to this general principle can be provided for in particular with regard to police and judicial cooperation in the framework of relevant modalities among members of the European Union. Hence, Law No. 3663/2008,[81] adopted in implementation of the Decision of the Council of the European Union No. 2002/187 on setting up Eurojust,[82] organizing the establishment of Joint Research Groups among EU member states for the transboundary investigation of some serious criminal activities (illegal drug trafficking, human trafficking, terrorism), provides that the Greek state is liable for harmful conduct of its officials participating in a Joint Research Group functioning on the territory of another state in accordance with the applicable law of the latter state (Art. 24, para. 1 Law No. 3663/2008).[83] If, on the contrary, the Joint Research Group is active on the Greek territory, the Greek state is liable in accordance with Greek law (Art. 105 ILCC) also for the conduct of the foreign members of the Group (Art. 24, para. 1 Law No. 3663/2008).

fiscus (*acta iure gestionis*), is regulated, in accordance with Art. 104 ILCC, by the general rules of the CC (Art. 71, non-contractual liability of juridical persons) in a way identical to the civil liability of any other legal person, that is it requires the subjective fault of the tort-feasor.

[80] Athens CA, Judgment No. 3541/1954, *JT*, 1954, p. 1197; Stassinopoulos (1950) 180–189; Pavlopoulos, (1989) 244–255.

[81] *Journal of the Government*, vol. A, No. 99, 28.5.2008.

[82] Council Decision of 28.2.2002 setting up Eurojust with a view to reinforcing the fight against serious crime (2002/187/JHA), *Official Journal of the European Union*, L 63/1, 6.3.2002.

[83] In accordance with Art. 19, para. 1 Law No. 3663/2008, applicable law to the activities of a Joint Research Group is the law oft he EU member state in which the relevant activity took place.

7.3.1.4 Conduct Which Is Unlawful

Art. 105 and 106 ILCC further require for the non-contractual liability of the state the unlawfulness of the organs' conduct. The state does not incur civil liability under the regime of Art. 105–106 ILCC for acts that are *lawful*, even if they cause an injury, e.g., expropriation;[84] in such cases the state may be obliged to compensate the injury suffered by private persons though lawful conduct of its organs by virtue of specific provisions, e.g., compensation due for expropriation for reasons of public benefit in accordance with Art. 17 of the Constitution.[85]

The unlawful character of the conduct of the state act can arise from any infringement to the principle of legality in its broad sense, i.e., the violation of any binding legal rule of the judicial order in its hierarchical order, from the Constitution or the public international law (generally accepted rules of international law, i.e., general international customary rules, and international conventions ratified by Greece)[86] and the EU law[87] down to the laws and the normative acts of the administration. The requirement of unlawfulness exists both in case of violation of a legal provision of substantive or procedural character.[88] In reality, Art. 105 and 106 constitute a "blank" reference to the entire *corpus* of legislation, the way Art. 914 CC is for the non-contractual liability in general civil law. Yet contrary to the general regime of non-contractual liability, which requires fault (intention, negligence) of the tortfeasor (Art. 914 CC), the unlawfulness of the conduct of the state organ is sufficient for triggering the civil liability of the state. The latter is *objective* and no fault of the state organ concerned is required. The fault of the state organ can however constitute the unlawfulness of the act (or omission), when related to the failure to organize and operate a public service.[89] In this case, the negligence of the competent state organ to organize and operate a concrete public service is itself an unlawful conduct attributable to the state and, provided that the remaining conditions of Art. 105 are fulfilled, can trigger the non-contractual liability of the state.

---

[84] See AP, Judgment No. 1283/1976, *JT*, 1977, pp. 903–904.

[85] CS, Judgment No. 3751/2003. The Council of State held however that damages in accordance with Art. 105 ILCC may be due for unlawful and harmful acts or omissions of the state organs in the process of the expropriation (not in the determination of the value of the expropriated property), cf. Supreme Special Court, Judgment No. 13/1992.

[86] CS, Judgments Nos. 909/2007, 169 2010.

[87] E.g. Piraeus ACFI, Judgment No. 4768/2010. For the seminal judgment of the ECJ, *Francovich and Others*, Joint Cases C-6/90 and C-9/90, [1991] *ECR*, I-5357, in particular paras. 31–37. Cf. Raikos (2006).

[88] CS, Judgments Nos. 2884/1999, 3411/2009; see generally Mathioudakis (2011), 1071–1086; cf. Lazaratos (2008) 532 ff. Initially, case-law was extremely reluctant to accept the civil liability of the state from unlawful acts of its organs when the unlawfulness consisted in the violation of provisions of procedural/formal character on the ground that the state organ had the possibility, and in many cases the legal obligation, to re-issue the act with the same substantive contents, without the formal default which was at the origin of its unlawfulness; in such cases the courts denied the existence of a causal link between the unlawful act and the harm sustained by the claimant, e.g. AP, Judgment No. 39/1988; Athens ACA, Judgment No. 2117/2001.

[89] Pavlopoulos (1989) 403–404.

7.3.1.5 Conduct Which Has Violated a Provision That Is not Aimed at the Protection of the General Interest

An additional requirement for the success of an action for damages for unlawful conduct of the state violating human rights is that the infringement should consist in a breach of a legal provision that is not aimed at the protection of the general interest. This condition was present since the very beginning of the legislative history of Art. 105 ILCC and was motivated by the idea that a right to compensation should exist in case of violation of a provision aiming at the protection of a concrete person.[90] This conception considered that a breach affecting the general interest of the community (of all citizens, or of the interest of the state, or of the public legal entity responsible for the violation, in the case of Art. 106 ILCC) could not give rise to the non-contractual liability of the state.[91] However, the concern of the drafters of the Civil Code to avoid excessive burden of the state's treasury also motivated the adoption of such a limitation of the state's liability.[92]

This condition is straightforwardly fulfilled when a state organ violates a legal provision stipulating the commission of an act or its omission by a state organ in favour of a private person.[93] The violation of a legal provision gives rise to the civil liability of the state when the provision protects a private right or even a simple interest of a private person.[94] Moreover, the civil liability of the state can be established when the infringed legal provision, while set for the protection of the general interest, simultaneously aims also at the safeguard of the rights or interests of concrete persons envisaged in that legal provision.[95]

7.3.1.6 Conduct Which Has Caused Injury (Harm)

The injury sustained by the claimant is a necessary condition for engaging the civil liability of the state for unlawful conduct of its organs. On this point Art. 105–106 ILCC do not deviate from the general regime of civil liability. The required injury is some form of loss or harm to the victim of a human rights violation. Art. 298 and 299 CC address, respectively, the reparable patrimonial and non-patrimonial injury.

The material harm sustained by the claimant for damages for infringement of human rights by state organs is calculated in accordance with the general rule laid down in Art. 298 CC: it encompasses the decrease of the assets (positive loss) as

[90] See AP, Judgment No. 729/1981, *JT*, 1982, p. 231.

[91] See the explanations of the Rapporteur to the Commission for the drafting of the Civil Code, Maridakis (1936) 79–80. In general, see Tsatsos (1960).

[92] Maridakis (1936) 80–81.

[93] AP, Judgment No. 185/1967, *JT*, 1967, p. 895.

[94] E.g. AP, Judgment No. 103/1985, *Hellenic Justice*, 26, p. 455.

[95] CS, Judgment No. 1183/2013 (provisions regulating air traffic aim at the general interest of the safety of flights but also at the protection of passengers and crew); also CS, Judgment No. 979/2000; Athens ACFI, Judgment No. 5406/2010.

well as lost profits due to the unlawful act or omission of the state organ (*lucrum cessans*).[96] Lost profit is the material benefit that the claimant would probably expect in accordance with the usual course of circumstances or the special circumstances of the case, in particular taking into account the preparatory acts undertaken by the victim of the infringement.[97]

While damages for patrimonial harm are due in any case of unlawful conduct, the reparation of non-patrimonial harm has to be explicitly provided for by a legal provision. The relevant Art. 299 CC stipulates that damages for non-patrimonial harm are awarded in case it is so provided by law. With respect to non-contractual liability in general, such a legal provision is found in Art. 932 CC enabling the court to award a reasonable, in its own assessment, pecuniary satisfaction in respect of non-patrimonial damage, irrespective of any compensation due in respect of the pecuniary damage. The beneficiaries of such a reasonable, in the assessment of the court, pecuniary satisfaction for non-patrimonial harm include those whose health has been impaired, whose honour has been infringed, who have been subjected to indecent assault or who have been deprived of their liberty. In particular, in the event of loss of life, the compensation may be paid to the victim's family in the form of damages for pain and emotional suffering. The beneficiaries may also encompass moral persons, to whom reasonable pecuniary satisfaction has been awarded for conduct of state organs having caused harm to the authority, reputation or development of the activities of the moral person concerned.[98]

By virtue of the above provisions,[99] case-law holds the state liable for damages that cannot be related to a person's financial estate, for moral harm, suffering, etc. Reasonable satisfaction is due also by the state for the reversal of an existing favourable situation.[100] Damages may be awarded also exclusively for moral harm (when the claimant does not allege or cannot prove any patrimonial harm).[101] This is the case when the authorities have remedied the human rights infringement (revocation of the harmful act with retroactive force): in such cases reasonable pecuniary satisfaction is due for the moral harm caused for the period the harmful act was in force.[102]

The calculation of the damages due by the state for human rights violations follows the general rules of the CC (Art. 298–299, 914 ff):

---

[96] CS, Judgments Nos. 3214/2004; 2171/2000.

[97] CS, Judgment No. 4913/1998. Generally on *lucrum cessans* in the framework of Art. 105 ILCC, see Mathioudakis (2009) 708–709; Chryssanthakis (2010) 5–9.

[98] Athens ACA, Judgment No. 3216/2009.

[99] By direct or analogical application of Art. 932 CC, see CS, Judgment No. 1249/2010.

[100] CS, Judgment No. 2732/2004 (unlawful closure of a law office).

[101] Athens ACA, Judgment No. 3216/2009; Piraeus ACFI, Judgment No. 450/2010.

[102] CS, Judgments Nos. 1210/2008, 122/2011 (acts offending the honour or reputation of a civil servant, e.g. initiation of disciplinary proceedings, reprimand, transfer to a post of lower level); Athens ACFI, Judgment No. 7020/2000 (unlawful designation of the victim as a debtor of the public treasure, which prejudiced his professional reputation and prospects, by decline in business clientele and opportunities).

The damages due in case of patrimonial injury should be full, i.e., to remedy all and every loss sustained. The decrease of the assets of the victim also encompasses any indirect or consequential damage, to the extent that there is a causal link between such type of damage and the unlawful and harmful act or omission of the state.[103] Specific rules are laid down for the scope of damages due in the event of loss of life, bodily harm or health impairment, disability or disfigurement (costs of medical treatment, of funeral, future expenses and losses due to the unlawful act, or alimony that was due by the victim, Art. 928, 929, 931 CC).[104] With regard to the reasonable, in the assessment of the court, pecuniary satisfaction, for moral harm, there are no set criteria of general application.[105] Faced with the difficulty to calculate a non-patrimonial injury, courts rely on the severity of the injury for the computation of the reasonable pecuniary satisfaction. Art. 932 CC explicitly refers to the court's assessment in such cases and qualifies the reparation due as reasonable satisfaction. The discretion of the courts is therefore quite large; the tendency however, was not to award extensive damages for moral harm, with the exception of loss of life.[106]

Punitive or exemplary damages are not allowed.

In the calculation of damages the court can fully or partially accept the claim of the defendant (public authority) for set-off of damages due to the plaintiff and benefit of the latter due to the unlawful, harmful act or omission.[107] Any profit or benefit (material or moral) that the claimant in damages for civil liability of the state enjoyed as a consequence of the unlawful act or omission of the state is also taken into account by the competent court as a ground for mitigation/reduction or exclusion of the damages due.[108]

The damages for violation of human rights as any other damages awarded by judicial organs are tax exempt. Tax exempt is also the just satisfaction awarded by the ECtHR under Art. 41 ECHR.

7.3.1.7 A Causal Link

The compensation of the state for human rights infringements, further require the existence of a causal link between the unlawful conduct of the state organs and the harm sustained by the applicant.

Causation is a general feature of the regime of civil liability in Greek law. Several theories are proposed by the civil law theory and practice in order to assess the existence of a causal link between the unlawful conduct and the injury of an individual. Greek courts overwhelmingly adhere to the doctrine of the *adequate condition* or

[103] See Athens ACFI, Judgment No. 7020/2000.

[104] CS, Judgment No. 1249/2010; Athens ACA, Judgment No. 7775/2005; Piraeus ACFI, Judgments Nos. 2505/2011; 3576/2010; Athens ACFI, Judgment No. 1933/2005.

[105] Karakostas (2008) 379–385.

[106] Cf. CS, Judgment No. 1183/2013.

[107] CS, Judgment No. 2733/2010.

[108] CS, Judgments Nos. 3214/2004; 2171/2000.

adequate causation (*causa adequata*), following which there exists a casual link between those aspects of the conduct in which the usual and normal course of events tend to cause an effect and in the concrete case actually produced that effect.[109] This case-law approach marks the dismissal of the outdated doctrine of the equivalence of the conditions (*conditio sine qua non*), but has also been criticised by parts of the civil law doctrine for lack of foundation in the positive law and for its alleged inconsistency. For those opponents the right doctrine of causation would be the approach based on the objective of the infringed legal provision, so that the existence of the causal link in each case should be assessed in relation with the scope of the legal provision that has been violated.[110]

The doctrine of the adequate condition prevails also in the field of the civil liability of the state.[111] Applied in the field of damages for civil liability of the state, this approach affirms that a causal link exists between the unlawful conduct and the injury when in accordance with the teachings of common experience, the conduct is sufficiently capable (adequate) to bring about, in the usual course of events or due to the specific elements of the concrete case, the damage sustained.[112] The case law has tried to adjust the doctrine of the adequate condition in the case when the damage consists in lost profits. In such cases, due to the hypothetical nature of this type of damage (*lucrum cessans*), it is almost impossible to affirm beyond any doubt that the victim of the human rights infringement would have reaped the profit (he/she claims he/she has been deprived of), but for the unlawful conduct of the state organ. To overcome this difficulty, the courts consider it sufficient that for lost profits the causal link should consist in the probability that the profit would have been obtained by the victim in the usual course of events.[113] Another obstacle that this doctrine had to overcome when applied in the civil liability of the state for violations of human rights is when the unlawfulness of the state conduct consisted in the omission of its organs: here again the case law accepts that, while it is not possible to establish beyond doubt that the damage would have been caused, had the state organ committed the act that unlawfully omitted to do, the existence of a causal link between the omission and the injury can be affirmed, if the former were, in accordance with the teachings of common experience and in the usual course of events, objectively capable to bring about the injury.[114] Finally, in accordance with recent case law, the causal link continues to exist even in case of *force majeure*, when the harm is in any case due to the unlawful conduct of the state organ.[115]

---

[109] E.g. AP, Judgments Nos. 680/2007, 1230/2007, 1197/2005; CS, Judgment No. 1893/2000.

[110] Stathopoulos (2004) nos. 129–130.

[111] Only occasionally some lower courts have applied in the framework of the civil liability of the state the theory of the objective of the legal provision, Rodos CFI, Judgment No. 102/1994, *Harmenopoulos*, 1996, p. 564; Athens ACFI, Judgment No. 7020/2000.

[112] CS, Judgments Nos. 1248/2010, 1024/2005; AP, Judgment No. 316/1983, *JT*, 1983, p. 1571.

[113] CS, Judgment No. 289/1995.

[114] CS, Judgments Nos. 4776/1997, 3027/1998.

[115] Athens ACFI, Judgments Nos. 12150/2011 (collapse of a building during an earthquake, which was due to the unlawful acts and omissions of the public urban planning authority); 11196/2011

7.3.2 *Negative Requirements*

7.3.2.1 Contributory Fault

In accordance with the general rule of Art. 300 CC the contributory fault may lead to the rejection of the claim to reparation or to the award of partial damages.[116]

7.3.2.2 "Legitimate Illegality"

In public law it is widely accepted that under special and specific circumstances, e.g., state of necessity, the violation of the principle of legality is legitimate, if such infringement is necessary to satisfy the public interest or to avert an imminent danger and is also proportional to the public interest it aims to satisfy or to the danger it aims to avert.[117] In such cases of so-called "legitimate illegality", the public authority is in principle exonerated from the responsibility and the liability arising from such violations of legal provisions (*salus populi suprema lex*).

This negative requirement can significantly impact on claims for compensation due to violations of human rights and fundamental freedoms in case of application of the Art. 44, para, 1 and 48 of the Constitution. These provisions allow derogations from constitutional fundamental rights in case of extraordinary circumstances or urgent and unpredictable necessity (Art. 44, para. 1) or in case of war, direct threat to the national security or armed rebellion against the democratic regime (Art. 48): in principle the acts (or omissions) of the state organs in such state of necessity or siege cannot trigger the civil liability of the state.[118] It has been, however, submitted that acts of legislative content taken in accordance with Art. 44 and 48 of the Constitution can trigger the civil liability of the state in case of violation of the constitutional principles of equality and proportionality, if the other conditions of Art. 105 ILCC are fulfilled.[119] In general, it is admitted that the state may be liable for damages to the victim of such a "legitimate illegality" in accordance with the provisions of Art. 285 and 286 CC (state of necessity).[120] The scope of these provisions are nevertheless limited as they stipulate that only reasonable (instead of full) compensation may be granted for the destruction of an object belonging to a third party, if such destruction was indispensable to avert an imminent danger threatening disproportionally greater damage than the destruction of the said object.

Unlike the cases of "legitimate illegality" above, *force majeure* does not provide a blanket exoneration for the civil liability of the state. This principle is restrictively

(omission of the competent state organs to take protective measures against flooding).

[116] CS, Judgments Nos. 2100/2006; 2796/2006; AP, Judgment No. 13/2002; Piraeus ACFI, Judgment No. 5283/2010.

[117] CS, Judgment No. 2774/1999.

[118] Pavlopoulos (1989) 295–296.

[119] Stassinopoulos (1950) 170; Tachos (1973) 159; Pavlopoulos (1989) 293.

[120] CS, Judgment No. 2774/1999.

interpreted and applied by the case-law to cover only cases where the harm was due to an unforeseeable external event, despite the fact that the competent state organs had taken all adequate measures in their disposal to avert or limit the harm.[121]

7.3.2.3 International Law Commitments

Finally a specific exoneration of the civil liability of the public authority for unlawful conduct is provided for harmful conduct of the state authorities in complying with international treaties, judgments of international courts or international arbitral awards.[122]

7.4 Procedural Issues

Before the adoption of the Constitution of 1975, civil courts had jurisdiction over actions for damages for civil liability of the state. Since June 1985 that jurisdiction was transferred to the administrative courts by virtue of the Law No. 1406/1983, adopted in execution of Art. 94 of the Constitution prescribing that disputes of administrative character where the judicial organ exercises full jurisdiction[123] should be adjudicated by the administrative courts (Administrative Court of First Instance, Administrative Court of Appeals and, in cassation, Council of State). Only with respect to damages owed by the state for unjust or illegal detention on remand or after conviction, the competent court is, as we have seen *supra*, the criminal court that pronounced the acquittal of the claimant, and in case the damages awarded by that court are considered insufficient by the acquitted defendant, the latter can lodge an action for additional damages in civil courts (see *supra*, Art. 536, 537 and 539 CCP).

The action for damages of Art. 105 and 106 ILCC is an independent legal remedy. Neither lodging nor the success of another remedy constitute a condition for the action for damages for civil liability of the state.[124] The Council of State had, however, introduced an exception with regard to the legal remedy of complaint against an administrative act. Based on Art. 26 of the Presidential Decree No. 341/1978 (providing for the *possibility* of aggregation of the legal remedies of complaint against an administrative act and of action for damages arising out of the

[121] Athens ACFI, Judgments No. 12150/2011 (upholding state liability in case of earthquake) and No. 11196/2011 (upholding state liability in case of flooding); CS, Judgment No. 1590/2010 (rejecting state liability in case of violent street manifestations). See Mathioudakis (2006) 119; Katsigiannis (2008) 398.

[122] Emergency Law No. 202/1936, Art. 2.

[123] See Constitution, Art. 94; Law No. 1406/1983, Art. 1, paras 1, 2(h); Papayannopoulos (1985) 5 ff.

[124] AP, Judgment No. 704/1982, *JT*, 1983, p. 207; see Pavlopoulos (1989) 50–51.

same administrative act),[125] the Council of State held that the success of an action for damages for civil liability of the state depended on the earlier or simultaneous lodging of a complaint against the administrative act that caused the damage.[126] This understanding of the highest administrative court has been persuasively criticised as misreading the positive law (explicitly providing only for the possibility to join the two legal remedies) and conflicting with provisions of higher hierarchical standing in the legal order, in particular Art. 20 para. 1 of the Constitution (effective judicial protection) and Art. 6 para. 1 ECHR.[127] This difference of approach was addressed by legislative deed, which reiterated the independence of the action for damages for civil liability of the state and clarified that this action can be joined with other legal remedies or lodged separately at the choice of the person concerned.[128] As a consequence, the decision of the court competent for the action for damages neither affects the status of the act of the state organ, nor creates *res juricata* for the court(s) competent in the framework of remedies against the validity of the acts of state organs.

The action in damages is not subject to a time limit from the procedural point of view. Only the substantive right giving rise to the claim for damages is subject to (extinctive) prescription. With respect to non-contractual liability, as it is the case for the civil liability of the state for human rights infringements, claims are generally time-barred in 5 years[129].

This rather short period of prescription could raise some problems in particular in the cases of claims arising from serious human rights infringements. In recent years, there has been a growing concern in international law over the risk of impunity due to short periods of extinctive prescription and limitations of action applied to gross violations of international human rights law and serious violations of international humanitarian law. The legally non-binding, UN BPGRR,[130] include a section IV entitled "Statutes of limitations," which distinguishes between "gross violations of international human rights law and serious violations of international humanitarian law which constitute crimes under international law," and other types of human rights infringements, "that do not constitute crimes under international law." With respect to the former category of violations (crimes under international law), the BPGRR provide that statutes of limitations shall not apply to crimes under international law "where so provided for in an applicable treaty or contained in other international legal obligations" (principle 6 BPGRR). The two principal international law instruments that prohibit the application of statutes of limitations to international crimes are the Convention on the Non-Applicability of Statutory Limitations to War Crimes and Crimes against Humanity[131] and the Rome Statute of

[125] *Journal of Government*, vol. A, No. 71, 10.5.1978.

[126] CS, Judgments Nos. 1084/1984, *JT*, 1985, p. 338; 2238/1988.

[127] Pavlopoulos (1989) 309–315.

[128] Law No. 1868/1989 (Art. 19), *Journal of the Government*, vol. A, No. 230, 10.10.1989.

[129] AP, Judgment No. 904/1982, *JT*, 1983, p. 982

[130] UNGA Resolution 60/147 of 16.12.2005, see *supra*, fn. 5.

[131] *United Nations Treaty Series*, vol. 754, p. 73.

the International Criminal Court (ICC).[132] Greece has ratified the ICC Statute,[133] but it is not a party to the Convention on the Non-Applicability of Statutory Limitations to War Crimes and Crimes against Humanity.

With respect to the second category of human rights infringements envisaged in the BPGRR (violations that are *not* crimes under international law), principle 7 provides that "Domestic statutes of limitations…, including those time limitations applicable to civil claims and other procedures should not be unduly restrictive."

The application of the above principles in concrete cases is not straightforward, taking into account the current uncertainty and existing gaps in the regulation of the prescription/statutes of limitations in modern international law, in particular, with regard to civil claims arising from the violation of international norms,[134] where the original tension between the principle of legal certainty and the growing wish to avoid impunity remains deep-seated. Originally, statutes of limitations were not admitted in international law.[135] Gradually the notion of time limits for the exercise of rights paved its way into this field of law,[136] yet the introduction of a statute of limitations, if at all valid in international law, was not accompanied by the adoption of specific time limits applicable in concrete cases.[137]

The judicial practice in Greece provides a recent example where action in civil liability of a (foreign) state was admitted for serious violations of human rights law and international humanitarian law that occurred during World War II. A civil claim for damages was lodged in 1995 against the Federal Republic of Germany (as the successor of the German *Reich*) for damages due to atrocities that were committed by German troops in Greece in 1944 (war crimes, crimes against humanity, gross violations of international human rights law). In the judgments rendered both at first instance and also on cassation, the issue of a possible time limitation of the claims *did not* come up.[138] It is, therefore, allowed to infer from that case-law that a statute of limitations will not apply to claims for damages due to gross violations of international human rights law and serious violations of international humanitarian law.

Both under the Code of civil procedure (Art. 67, 74) and the Code of administrative procedure (Art. 64, 71) it is not allowed for someone to be a party in civil proceedings (*locus standi*), unless he/she acts in his/her own name as a party. In the afore

[132] *United Nations Treaty Series*, vol. 2187, p. 3; Art. 29 of the Statute of the ICC stipulates: "The crimes within the jurisdiction of the Court shall not be subject to any statute of limitations."

[133] Law No. 3003/2002, *Journal of the Government*, vol. A, No. 75, 8.4.2002.

[134] Cf. Roucounas (1999) 223–240.

[135] *Pious Fund* (USA/Mexico), Arbitral Award, 14.10.1902, *RIAA*, vol. IX, p. 13; *Alsop* (USA/Chile), *Amiable Composition* (King George V of Great Britain), 5.4.1911, *RIAA*, vol. XI, 1911, p. 356.

[136] See Mixed Arbitral Tribunal Bulgaria-Greece, *Sarropoulos v. Etat bulgare*, 14.2.1927, *Recueil des décisions des tribunaux arbitraux mixtes*, vol. VII, p. 47.

[137] ICJ, *Certain Phosphate Lands in Nauru (Nauru v. Australia)*, Preliminary Objections, Judgment, 26.6.1992, *ICJ Rep.*, pp. 253–254, para. 32; Stribis (2009) 423–425. Comp. Doehring (2007) 385–394.

[138] Livadia CFI, Judgment No. 137/1997, *JT*, 1998, p. 246; AP, Judgment No. 11/2000. On this case, cf. Micha, (2000), 511–516.

mentioned civil action against the German state (war crimes, crimes against humanity, gross violations of international human rights law committed in occupied Greece at the end of World War II), the court of the first instance, rejected a self-standing claim of the Local Self-Administration authority of the place where the violations were committed for lack of *locus standi*. Yet, it declared admissible the claim lodged by the same Local Self-Administration authority as an *agent* of 118 victims and victims' successors, who were recognised as the principals in this agency, voluntarily established (agency in fact, not agency created by law) between the Local Self-Administration and the victims, in accordance with Art. 713 CC,[139] in order to facilitate the victims in seeking damages from the foreign state.[140] This pattern, in line with the agency provisions of the Civil Code may be further used in civil actions for damages for unlawful conduct of the state violating human rights of larger group of individuals.

With regard to the people against whom an action for damages for human rights violations can be lodged, Art. 105 ILCC *in fine* explicitly provides that, "The person responsible [public official or agent] shall be jointly and severally liable," with the state. This provision allows for recourse for recovery by the state against the official(s) author(s) of the unlawful conduct that triggered the non-contractual liability of the state.

A specific provision exists with respect to miscarriage of justice: the personal civil liability of agents of the judicial power for their conduct in the exercise of their judicial tasks can be triggered only if the harm sustained by an individual is due to intent, gross negligence or denial of justice of the judges (Law No. 693/1977, Art. 6 para. 1).

In case of unlawful and harmful conduct of a state organ *and* of a legal entity of public law, Art. 105 and 106 ILCC apply cumulatively and the central administration and the decentralized administration or other legal entity of public law are severally and jointly liable towards the claimant.[141]

In general aliens are entitled to claim compensation for infringements to their protected human rights. Limitations can be adopted by law (act of parliament). However, such limitations cannot affect citizens of EU member states. In addition, Art. 5, para. 2 of the Constitution stipulates: "Every person found on Greek territory enjoy absolute protection of their life, honour and liberty, without distinction based on nationality, race, language and religious or political convictions." This provision circumscribes thus *rationae materiae* those fundamental human rights that are guaranteed also for aliens. It ensues that for the same constitutional intent, the procedural right to lodge an action for damages for the violation of the above fundamental human rights cannot be denied to any category of persons found on Greek territory.

---

[139] Livadia CFI, Judgment No. 137/1997, *JT*, 1998, p. 246, with further references (AP, Judgments Nos. 1551/1991, 981/1973; Athens CA, Judgment No. 806/1980).

[140] Lodging individual claims would have been costly and unwieldy, see Decision of the Council of the Self-Administration of Viotia, *Minutes of Deliberation No. 9* of 15 May 1995, not published, in file with the author.

[141] Athens ACFI, Judgment No. 642/1011.

There has been in recent times a tendency to limit existing exceptions for aliens to claim reparation for human rights violations. Most significant was the evolution with respect to damages for unjust or illegal detention on remand or on conviction which was subsequently reversed (*supra*). Until the amendment of the relevant provisions of the CCP (Art. 533–545) in 2001 through Law No. 2915/2001,[142] the aliens could claim compensation for their unjust or illegal detention under the condition of reciprocity (the same right being recognised in their countries of nationality for Greek citizens, old formulation of Art. 543 CCP). The new wording of this provision stipulates that Art. 533–542 CCP apply equally to aliens and stateless.

7.5 The Interplay Between Principles of National and International Human Rights Law (Concerning Financial Compensation)

As already exposed, Art. 105 (and 106) ILCC provides for full reparation of the pecuniary and non-pecuniary harm sustained by a victim of human rights violations, as opposed to "just satisfaction", that the ECtHR may award, on a subsidiary basis, in accordance with Art. 41 ECHR. Just satisfaction is also provided for in the Greek law as reparation in the case of "non-reasonable" time of judicial proceedings in the administrative courts (see Law No. 4055/2012, *supra*).

In *Z.A.N.T.E. – Marathonisi A.E. v. Greece*, the ECtHR held that the action in damages for non-contractual liability of the state under Art. 105 ILCC constituted an appropriate legal remedy as it afforded the claimant the possibility of reparation for the damage caused. Consequently, it considered that this action fulfilled the requirement of the exhaustion of domestic remedies.[143] This finding in conjunction with subsidiary character of the just satisfaction awarded by the ECtHR ("If the internal law of the High Contracting Party concerned allows only partial reparation to be made," and "if necessary"), would probably contribute to avoiding clashes between the national and ECHR regimes of full reparation and just satisfaction. If the Greek courts had adjudicated an action in damages before an application was lodged in the ECtHR, their final decision would be covered by *res judicata* and could not be reopened. If the action in damages is introduced in a national court after the determination by the ECtHR of a violation of a protected human right, and if the competent Greek court establishes the civil liability of the state in accordance with Art. 105 (or 106) ILCC, full compensation could be granted. However, the amount of the "just satisfaction", if such a just satisfaction has been adjudicated by the ECtHR and paid to the applicant by the Greek state, will be deducted from the full compensation due to be paid in accordance with Art. 105 (or 106) ILCC.

---

[142] *Journal of the Government*, vol. A, No. 109, 29.5.2001.

[143] *Z.A.N.T.E. – Marathonisi A.E. v. Greece*, Application No. 14216/03, Judgment (just satisfaction) of 28.5.2009, para. 25.

The nature of the entitlement to just satisfaction awarded by the ECtHR in the domestic Greek legal order remains debatable, in particular in the (unlikely[144]) case the state authorities do not voluntarily comply with a decision of the ECtHR awarding just compensation. In such a case, it may be reasonably submitted that the illegality of the state conduct (required for the establishment of the civil liability of the state in accordance with Art. 105 ILCC) would be the failure or omission to comply with the obligation under art. 41 ECHR to pay the just satisfaction awarded by the ECtHR.[145] However, such illegality of the failure to pay the just satisfaction would require the obligation of the state, under national law, to pay. The debate whether the right to just satisfaction awarded by the ECtHR is a subjective entitlement under national Greek law or a right under public international law is not definitively settled. At first sight the entitlement to receive the just satisfaction awarded by the ECtHR stems from a treaty body (a body operating under an international convention, in the case at hand, the ECHR). It would be therefore a right primarily under the public international legal order. However, in states that have incorporated the Convention into their domestic legal orders, which is the case of Greece,[146] the persons under their jurisdiction can invoke the rights guaranteed by the ECHR before national authorities, including the national courts. From this standpoint, it has been submitted that people under the jurisdiction of a state party to the ECHR can invoke in their national legal orders the rights recognised to them by the ECtHR, an organ provided for by the ECHR and deciding in accordance with that Convention. If such a point of view were to be accepted, the entitlement to just satisfaction awarded by the ECtHR would be a *quasi* "secondary right" recognised by the ECHR as a personal claim of the victim of the violation of a human right against the state which violated it. Based on this reasoning, it is submitted that the right to the just satisfaction awarded by the ECtHR is also vested the character of a right under the domestic Greek law.[147] As such, this subjective right would have the exact scope it has under public international law, which is without executory force. It could however constitute a right, the violation of which could trigger, provided that the conditions of Art. 105 ILCC are fulfilled, non-contractual liability of the public authority.

References

Amselek, Paul. 1983. La qualification des contrats de l'administration par la jurisprudence. *L'Actualité juridique-Droit administratif* 29: 3–7.

Anastassiadis, Konstantinos. 1976. Observations on AP, Judgment No. 665/1975. *Journal of Greek Jurists* 43: 162–164.

---

[144] The compliance of the States parties to the ECHR is closely followed by the organs of the Convention and the monitoring mechanisms put in place are sophisticated and effective. In addition there is always the possibility of international responsibility of the state for lack of compliance with an award by the ECHR.

[145] See Iliopoulos-Strangas (1996) 79–80. In this sense, cf. Micha (2012), 607–626.

[146] Legislative Decree No. 53/1974, *Journal of the Government*, vol. A, No. 256, 20.9.1974.

[147] Iliopoulos-Strangas (1996) 72.

Bassiouni, M. Cherif. 2006. International recognition of victims' rights. *Human Rights Law Review* 6: 203–279.

Buyse, Antoine. 2008. Lost and regained? Restitution as a remedy for human rights violations in the context of international law. *Zeitschrift für ausländisches öffentliches Recht und Völkerrecht (ZaöRV)* 68: 129–153.

Chrysogonos, Konstantinos. 2003. *Constitutional law*. Thessaloniki: Sakkoulas Publ.

Chryssanthakis, Charalampos. 2010. Civil liability of public hospitals due to medical malpractice as a field of osmosis between medical and legal science. *Theory and Practice of Administrative Law* 3: 1–7.

Dagtoglou, Prodromos. 1992. *General administrative law I*. Athens/Komotini: Ant. N. Sakkoulas.

Dagtoglou, Prodromos. 2004. *General administrative law*, 5th ed. Athens/Komotini: Ant. N. Sakkoulas.

Dagtoglou, Prodromos. 1962. *The liability of the state out of a delictual legislative act*. Athens: [s.e.] [= *Ersatzpflicht des Staates bei legislativem Unrecht*, 1963. Tübingen : J. C. B. Mohr (Paul Siebeck)].

Dannemann, Gerhard. 1994. *Schadenersatz bei Verletzung der Europäischen Menschenrechtskonvention. Eine rechtsvergleichende Untersuchung zur Haftung nach Art. 50 EMRK*. Köln : Carl Heymanns Verlag.

De Feyter, Koen, Stephan Parmentier, Marc Bossuyt et al. 2006. *Out of the ashes. Reparation for victims of gross and systematic human rights violations*. Antwerpen: Intersentia.

De Greiff, Pablo. 2006. *The handbook of reparations*. Oxford: Oxford University Press.

Doehring, Karl. 2007. Statusverwirkung im Völkerrecht. *ZaöRV* 67: 385–394.

Georgopoulos, Theodore. 2002. *La responsabilité du législateur hellénique en cas de violation du droit communautaire*. Athens/Bruxelles: Sakkoula/Bruylant.

Gour, Claude. 1978. Faute de service. In *Dalloz Encyclopédie de Droit Public: Répertoire de la Responsabilité de la Puissance Publique*, ed. F. Gazier and R. Drago. Paris: Ed. Dalloz.

Helmholz, Ruth Wyat. 2009. Bonham's case, judicial review, and the law of nature. *Journal of Legal Analysis* 1(1):325–354.

Iliopoulos-Strangas, Julia. 1996. *The executory force of the judgments of the ECtHR*. Athens/Baden-Baden: Ant. N. Sakkoulas/Nomos Verlag.

Józon, Monika. 2011. Satisfaction by finding a violation. In *Tort Law in the jurisprudence of the European Court of Human Rights*, ed. Atilla Fenyves et al., 741–769. Boston/Berlin: Walter De Gruyter.

Karakostas, Ioannis. 2008. Pecuniary compensation for moral injury in the case of civil liability of the public authority. *Applications of Civil Law* 1: 379–385.

Katsigiannis, Fotios. 2008. The liability of the state for damages in accordance with art. 105 ILCC for unlawful acts or omissions of police agents in the exercise of their service or in case of abuse thereof. *Theory and Practice of Administrative Law* 1: 398–409.

Kavkas, Konstantinos. 1946. The liability of the state for acts or omissions of its organs. *Themis* 57: 857–863.

Korsos, Dimitrios. 1977. *Institutions of administrative law*, vol. A, instal. B. Athens/Komotini: Ant. N. Sakkoulas.

Kyriakopoulos, Ilias. 1949. Article 105 ILCC. In *Commentary of the Civil Code*, no. 23. Athens: I. Zacharopoulos.

Lazaratos, Panos. 2008. The civil liability of the state from rescinding administrative acts. *Theory and Practice of Administrative Law* 1: 532–543.

Macridou, Kalliopi. 2012. Rendering a judicial decision on the merits within a reasonable time in civil trial. *Juridical Tribune* 60: 1345–1356.

Manitakis, Antonis. 1984. L'illicéité comme élément de la responsabilité de l'état en droit hellénique. *Journeés de la Société de Législation Comparée* 6:17–24 [= *Revue Hellénique de droit international*, 1985–1986, pp. 487–499].

Margaritis, Lambros. 2001. Damages for persons detained and subsequently found not guilty and the recent Law 2915/2001: A first approach of the new provisions. *Criminal Justice* 4: 750–761.

Maridakis, Georges. 1936. *Explanatory report of the Rapporteur on the law of persons*. Athens: Ministry of Justice.
Mathioudakis, Iakovos. 2004. Reflections on to the omission of due lawful act of the administration. *Administrative Trial* 16: 1416–1432.
Mathioudakis, Iakovos. 2006. *Civil liability of the state from physical acts of its organs in accordance with articles 105–6 ILCC*. PhD Dissertation, Law School, University Aristoteles of Thessaloniki, Thessaloniki.
Mathioudakis, Iakovos. 2009. Loss of opportunity in the law of state liability. *Journal of Administrative Law* 4: 700–714.
Mathioudakis, Iakovos. 2011. Formal illegality and reparation of injury in state liability. *Harmenopoulos* 65: 1071–1086.
Micha, Eleni. 2000. A guide to state practice concerning International Humanitarian Law: Greece. *Yearbook of International Humanitarian Law* 3: 509–519.
Micha, Eleni. 2012. Article 41 ECHR as basis of extra-contractual liability in Greek law. In *Public law in evolution: Essays in honour of P. Pararas*, 607–626. Athens/Komotini: Ant. N. Sakkoulas.
Naldi, Gino. 2001. Reparations in the practice of the African Commission on Human and Peoples' Rights. *Leiden Journal of International Law* 14(3): 681–693.
Papaevangellou, Thomas, et al. 2002. *Civil liability of the state: Case-law of years 1990–2001*. Athens/Komotini: Ant. N. Sakkoulas.
Papayannopoulos, George. 1985. Full jurisdiction administrative disputes and the law 1406/1983. *Review of Public Law and of Administrative Law* 29: 5–26.
Pavlopoulos, Prokopis. 1986. *Civil liability of the public authority, I: General review*. Athens/Komotini: Ant. N. Sakkoulas.
Pavlopoulos, Prokopis. 1989. *Civil liability of the public authority, II: In accordance with the rules of public law*. Athens/Komotini: Ant. N. Sakkoulas.
Plucknett, T.F.T. 1926. Bonham's case and judicial review. *Harvard Law Review* 40: 30–70.
Prevedourou, Eugénie. 2014. Administrative law remains predominantly 'Case-Law'? Reflections on CS, Judgment No. 1501/2014. *Theory and Practice of Administrative Law* 7: 411–421.
Raikos, Athanassios. 2002. *Constitutional law*, vol. I, 2nd ed. Athens/Komotini: Ant. N. Sakkoulas.
Raikos, Dimitrios. 2006. *The jurisdiction of the administrative courts in Greece over cases of state liability for breach of EC law by public authorities*. Presentation at the annual meeting of administrative judges, Beaulieu-sur-Mer, 10–11 Mar 2006.
Raikos, Dimitrios. 2008. Aspects of the requirement of Art. 105 ILCC of inner relationship for the establishment of the civil liability of state. *Theory and Practice of Administrative Law* 1: 386–397.
Raikos, Dimitrios. 2010. *The road accident: Civil liability of involved actors*. Presentation at the conference on issues of civil liability of the state and of organization of local self-administration from road accidents, Patras, 24–25 Sept 2010, www.esd.gr/eisigiseis/raikos.doc, pp. 3–4. Accessed 1 Mar 2015.
Roucounas, Emmanuel. 1999. Time limitations for claims and actions under international law. In *Liber Amicorum M. Bedjaoui*, ed. Emile K.M. Yakpo and Tahar Boumedra, 223–240. The Hague: Kluwer Law International.
Shelton, Dina. 2001. *Remedies in international human rights law*. Oxford: Oxford University Press.
Sitaropoulos, Nicholas. 2011. Delayed justice in Greek administrative courts and lack of an effective domestic remedy – Comment on Interim Resolution CM/ResDH(2007)74. *Essex Human Rights Review* 7(2): 16–31.
Spiliotopoulos, Epaminondas. 1986. *Manual of administrative law*, 4th ed. Athens/Komotini: Ant. N. Sakkoulas.
Stassinopoulos, Michel. 1949. La responsabilité civile de l'Etat d'après le nouveau code civil grec de 1946. *Revue de Droit public et de la science politique en France et à l'étranger* 65: 507–514.
Stassinopoulos, Michel. 1950. *Civil liability of the state, the public servants and the legal persons of public law*. Athens: [s.e.].

Stassinopoulos, Michel. 1961. Responsabilité civile de l'état des actes de gouvernement ayant trait aux relations internationales. In *Mélanges Séfériadès,* t. II, 641–681. Athens: Panteios Superior School of Political Science.

Stathopoulos, Michel. 2004. *General law of obligations*, 4th ed. Athens/Thessaloniki: Sakkoulas Publ.

Steiner, Elisabeth. 2011. Just satisfaction under Art 41 ECHR: A compromise in 1950 – Problematic now. In *Tort Law in the jurisprudence of the European Court of Human Rights*, eds. Attila Fenyves et al., 3–26. Berlin/Boston: Walter De Gruyter.

Stribis, Ioannis. 2009. *La manifestation des lacunes en droit international.* Athènes: Académie d'Athènes.

Tachos, Anastassios. 1973. *Modern trends of the principle of legality in administrative law.* Thessaloniki: University of Thessaloniki.

Tachos, Anastassios. 2003. *Greek administrative law.* Athens/Thessaloniki: Sakkoulas Publ.

Tsatsos, Dimitrios. 1960. *The concept of the provision in favour of the general interest in accordance with Article 105 of the Introductory Law of the Civil Code*. PhD Dissertation, University of Athens, Athens.

Chapter 8
Damages as Compensation for Human Rights Violations in Ireland

Noelle Higgins

8.1 Introduction

Ireland is a common law jurisdiction, and the government's approach to human rights has been duly influenced by common law principles, but in addition, the Irish government has adopted numerous pieces of legislation which focus on, or affect, human rights in various ways (Dewhurst et al. 2012). The foundation stone of Ireland's legal framework is, however, its Constitution (*Bunreacht na hÉireann*), which was adopted in 1937 and which protects various explicit and implicit human rights (Hogan et al. 2003). The human rights framework in Ireland has also been influenced by Ireland's membership of, and participation in, various regional and international organisations, especially the Council of Europe and the United Nations (Schabas 2007).

While certain pieces of Irish legislation set out the remedies that apply in situations of human rights infringements in their text,[1] the issue of remedies for infringement of human rights which are set out in the Constitution is not addressed in the Constitution text, and therefore, the Courts have quite a lot of discretion in deciding the appropriate remedy, including damages, for infringements.

Section 2 of this chapter discusses the issue of damages and compensation for violations of non-Constitutional rights. Section 3 then focuses on the Irish Constitution and how the Courts have dealt with the issue of damages for infringements of its human rights provisions. Section 4 discusses the types of damages that are available in Irish law. Section 5 deals with the European Convention on Human

[1] See, for example, the European Convention on Human Rights Act 2003 (ECHR Act 2003), which incorporates the rights enshrined in the European Convention of Human Rights (European Convention on Human Rights) into domestic law.

N. Higgins (✉)
Department of Law, Maynooth University, Maynooth, Co. Kildare, Ireland
e-mail: noelle.higgins@nuim.ie

E. Bagińska (ed.), *Damages for Violations of Human Rights*,
Ius Comparatum - Global Studies in Comparative Law 9,
DOI 10.1007/978-3-319-18950-5_8

Rights Act 2003 (ECHR Act 2003) and the remedy of damages under this piece of legislation. Section 6 provides a short discussion of Ireland's relationship with international human rights law and the role of damages in this sphere.

8.2 Damages for Breaches of Non-constitutional Rights

The law of torts is the main method provided by common law for dealing with infringement of civil rights. As highlighted by Quill (2009, 565–566), in Ireland "the remedy of damages at common law is the principal one used to redress tortious wrongs" however, damages may also be used for "secondary purposes, such as the vindication of rights, deterrence and public censure of undesirable behaviour." Damages can be awarded for tortious actions which are committed by private individuals, corporations and also by the State and which infringe human rights. In the case of *Byrne v Ireland* ([1972] IR 241) it was held by the Supreme Court that the Irish State was not immune from tortious liability (Cooney and Kerr 1981). In addition to common law principles, the Irish government has adopted various pieces of legislation which seek to provide remedies, including damages, for human rights infringements in certain areas of the law, which can amend or supplement the common law. This approach to damages can be seen in the context of claims of negligence, defamation, miscarriages of justice and malicious prosecution, as will be discussed below.

8.2.1 Common Law and Legislative Remedies, Including Damages

8.2.1.1 Negligence

According to Quill (2009, 17), negligence "is the most extensively used form of tortious action in modern legal practice." In order to succeed in an action for negligence a plaintiff must prove that he was owed a duty of care by the defendant that arose from the proximity of the parties, that the damage was foreseeable and that there is an absence of any compelling exemptions based on public policy (*Glencar Exploration PLC v Mayo County* [2002] 1 ILRM 481). Furthermore he must prove that the duty of care was breached and that this breach caused damage.

However, Irish law also accepts that damages in cases of negligence must be apportioned between the parties in the event where the damage which was suffered by the plaintiff results in part from the plaintiff's wrong and in part from the defendant's wrong. Section 34(1) of the Civil Liability Act 1961 sets out Irish law on contributory negligence. This states:

> Where, in any action brought by one person in respect of a wrong committed by any other person, it is proved that the damage suffered by the plaintiff was caused partly by the neg-

ligence or want of care of the plaintiff or of one for whose acts he is responsible (in this Part called contributory negligence) and partly by the wrong of the Defendant, the damages recoverable in respect of the said wrong shall be reduced by such amount as the Court thinks just and equitable having regard to the degrees of fault of the plaintiff and Defendant: provided that –

(a) If, having regard to all the circumstances of the case, it is not possible to establish different categories of fault, the liability shall be apportioned equally;
(b) This subsection shall not operate to defeat any defence arising under a contract or the defence that the plaintiff before the act complained of agreed to waive his legal rights in respect of it, whether or not for value; but, subject as aforesaid, the provisions of this subsection shall apply notwithstanding that the Defendant might, apart from this subsection, have the defence of voluntary assumption of risk;
(c) Where any contract or enactment providing for the limitation of liability is applicable to the claim, the amount of damages awarded to the plaintiff by virtue of this subsection shall not exceed the maximum limit so applicable.

This legislation amends the common law principle that contributory negligence is a complete defence to the plaintiff's claim (Jennings et al. 2010).

8.2.1.2 Defamation

Irish law recognises a right to freedom of speech, however, individuals also have a right to protect their reputation. While the Irish Constitution does deal with the right to a good name, the law on defamation in Ireland is also found at the common law and the Defamation Act 2009 (which repealed the earlier Defamation Act 1961).[2] Article 40.6.1.i of the Irish Constitution provides that the State guarantees the right of citizens to express freely their convictions and opinions. However, the Article also goes on to say that, because of the importance of educating public opinion, the State will try to ensure that the organs of public opinion such as the radio and the press keep their right to freedom of expression, but they shall not be used to undermine public order, morality or the authority of the State. The Defamation Act 2009 abolished the separate torts of libel and slander and replaced them with the "tort of defamation". An actionable defamatory statement has three elements: it must be published, it must refer to the complainant and it must be false.

Part 4 of the Defamation Act 2009 deals with remedies for defamation, including damages. In determining the amount of damages to be awarded in any defamation proceedings, the High Court shall give direction to the jury. General, aggravated or punitive damages can be awarded. Section 13 provides that on appeal the Supreme Court may substitute an "appropriate amount" for any High Court jury award Section 13(1) (Defamation Act 2009).

[2] The right of freedom of speech is also guaranteed by Article 10 (1) of the European Human Rights Convention subject to certain restraints.

8.2.1.3 Miscarriages of Justice

The Criminal Procedure Act 1993 introduced a statutory right to compensation where it has been established that a newly discovered fact proves that there has been a miscarriage of justice by virtue of a conviction. Section 2 of the Act allows the Court of Criminal Appeal to quash a conviction or review a sentence imposed in a previously decided case where the convicted person claims that a new or newly-discovered fact shows that there has been a miscarriage of justice in relation to the conviction or that the sentence imposed was excessive. Section 9 (1) deals with the issue of compensation, which is payable to the convicted person or, if he is deceased, to his legal personal representatives. Subsection 2 of section 9 states that an individual may apply for compensation under the Act or institute an action for damages arising out of the conviction. The Minister for Justice, Equality and Law Reform determines the amount of compensation payable (Section 9(4)), but if a person is unhappy with the amount of compensation then he may apply to the High Court to determine the award. In *Francis Shortt v The Commissioner of An Garda Síochána Ireland and the Attorney General* ([2007] 4 IR 587) it was discovered that Mr Shorrt had been convicted based on perjured evidence of two members of the Irish police force. Mr Shorrt successfully appealed for damages to the Supreme Court and was awarded €4,623,871. In the case of *DPP v Hannon* ([2009] 4 IR 147) the Court of Criminal Appeal held that under the Criminal Procedure Act 1993 there was no requirement for a State official to be involved in the miscarriage of justice in order for damages to be awarded.[3]

8.2.1.4 Malicious Prosecution

In order to prove a case of malicious prosecution, it must be shown by the plaintiff that: (i) the criminal proceedings terminated in his favour; (ii) the defendant instituted and/or participated in the proceedings maliciously; (iii) there was no reasonable or probable cause for such proceedings; (iv) the plaintiff suffered damage (*McIntyre v Lewis* [1991] 1 IR 121). In 2007 Frank McBrearty settled his action against the State for damages for malicious prosecution, wrongful imprisonment, defamation and wrongful arrest for €3 million, although the State did not admit liability.[4]

[3] The applicant was convicted of committing sexual assault and common assault against his 10 year old neighbour. However, the neighbour subsequently admitted that she had lied. The Office of the Director of Public Prosecutions argued that the applicant was not entitled to damages as there was no State involvement in the miscarriage of justice, however this argument was rejected by the Court of Criminal Appeal.

[4] See website of the Morris Tribunal. The Tribunal of Inquiry into complaints concerning some members of the Irish police force. The Morris Tribunal was created by Resolution passed by Parliament on the 28th of March 2002, and by Instrument entitled Tribunals of Inquiry (Evidence) Act 1921(Establishment of Tribunal) Instrument 2002 made by the Minister for Justice, Equality and Law Reform on the 24th of April 2002.

8.2.2 Statute of Limitations

In Ireland, the time limit within which a wronged party must take action in a civil claim is dealt with my means of the Statute of Limitations and other pieces of legislation, and is therefore important to note in the context of damages.[5] Generally, the time within which one can bring an action begins from the date of the incident giving rise to the claim. However, in the context of personal injury cases, the 'date of knowledge' principle can apply (Section 2, Statute of Limitations (Amendment) Act 1991) where the date of the injury differs from the date upon which the injury is discovered by the plaintiff. The 'date of knowledge' principle ensures that time limits do not run out before a person realises they have been injured and is especially relevant in medical negligence cases. Medical negligence cases have to be filed within two years of the 'date of knowledge' that an injury has been sustained due to medical negligence (Section 7 of the Civil Liability and Courts Act 2004).[6] Children under the age of 18 have a period of 2 years from the date of their 18th birthday to take a claim or a 'next friend' may take a claim on their behalf. A person who has a mental disability has a period of 2 years from the date they recover from such disability to take a claim or their 'next friend' may take a claim on their behalf (Section 48 of the Statute of Limitations Act 1957, as amended by the Civil Liability & Courts Act 2004). In defamation cases the Statute of Limitations is one year, but this limit may be extended to two years at the discretion of the Court (Section 38 Defamation Act 2009).

The Irish Courts have tended to interpret the Statute of Limitations strictly and have not tolerated an inordinate delay in bringing a claim even in cases concerning those of unsound mind. However, there has been some divergence in the case law on this point. In *Kelly v O'Leary* ([2001] IR 526) a delay of 50 years in bringing an action for child sexual abuse was held to be inexcusable but in the case of *McH v M* ([2004] 3 IR 556) a delay of 54 years was not statute barred under the Statute of Limitations (Amendment) Act 2000 due to the severe psychological and psychiatric damage suffered by the plaintiff as a result of sexual abuse (Ring 2009).

8.2.3 Irish Compensation and Redress Schemes

The Irish government has delegated the responsibility of managing certain claims against the State and of the underlying risks to the National Treasury Management Agency (NTMA) by means of the National Treasury Management Agency (Amendment) Act 2000. In carrying out its duties in this regard the NTMA is known

[5] See Statute of Limitations 1957, the Statute of Limitations (Amendment) Act 1991; Statute of Limitations (Amendment) Act 2000; Civil Liability and CourtsAct 2004; Civil Liability Act 1961 and the Defamation Act 2009.

[6] Prior to the coming into force of Section, the period of limitation was 3 years.

as the State Claims Agency (SCA). The SCA manages personal injury, property damage and clinical negligence claims brought against the State itself and certain State authorities (including Government ministers, the Attorney General, the Commissioner of the Garda Síochána (police force), prison governors, community and comprehensive schools).[7] In 2012 the Government decided to establish a Legal Costs Unit within the SCA to deal with third party costs arising from certain Tribunals of Inquiry. The aims of the SCA are twofold:

1. In cases where the State is considered liable or which involve an apportionment of liability as between the State and the claimant, the SCA's approach is to settle such claims expeditiously as far as possible
2. In cases where liability is disputed by the State, all necessary resources are used in defending such claims.

Under the Act, all State authorities must report adverse incidents in a prompt manner to the SCA, provide relevant evidence and facilitate the SCA's investigations. From the point of first notification of the incident up until its resolution, the SCA assumes ownership of claims. The SCA uses panels of service providers to advise the State, such as solicitors, medical consultants and engineers. Each claim is allocated a notional reserve that is updated as new medical and other expert information becomes available. The SCA then decides whether a claim should be contested in the Courts or whether settlement negotiations should begin.

A number of classes of claims are, however, excluded from the remit of the SCA either because alternative compensation arrangements have already been put in place by the Government or because they give rise to issues of legal policy which require the ongoing close involvement of the Attorney General. These are: claims which gives rise to Constitutional issues, claims for compensation under the Garda Síochána (Compensation) Acts, claims against the Minister for Justice, Equality & Law Reform, the Garda Commissioner or a prison governor in respect of alleged assault by a member of the Garda Síochána or a prison officer, claims under the non-statutory scheme providing compensation for personal injury criminally inflicted on prison officers, claims arising from infection with Hepatitis C through the administration of blood or blood products and claims in which torts other than negligence are pleaded.

According to the SCA, 61 % of claims are from State employees, including prison officers, civil servants, members or former members of the Defence Forces and members of the Garda Síochána. Thirty-three percentage of claims are made by members of the public. Six percentage of claims relate to property damage (particularly damage to third party damage vehicles by vehicles owned by the State). Almost one third of claims are from employees or former employees of the State who allege that they were exposed to asbestos during the course of their employment with a State agency. A number of recent high profile claims have cost the SCA €400 m.

[7] A full list of State bodies is listed in a schedule to the Act.

8.2.3.1 Compensation Under the Garda Síochána (Compensation) Acts (Garda Síochána (Compensation) Act 1941 and Garda Síochána (Compensation) (Amendment) Act 1945)

Two groups of people can receive compensation under these acts. These are:

1. Members of the Garda Síochána who sustained personal injuries (not causing death) maliciously inflicted upon them in the performance of their duties or acting in their general capacity as a member when off duty or merely because of their being a member of the Garda Síochána.
2. Dependants of deceased members who were fatally injured while on duty or while acting in their general capacity as a member or merely because of their being a member of the Garda Síochána. Section 3(1) of the Garda Síochána (Compensation) Act 1941 states that the following dependants may be awarded compensation: the widow, children, step-children, parents, siblings, half brothers or sisters, grandparents of the deceased member or adopted children under the age of 21 years who were supported, maintained and educated wholly or partially by the deceased person (Garda Síochána (Compensation) Act 1941 Section 2(1)(c)).

Compensation is assessed by the High Court, upon the initiation of proceedings against the Minster for Finance which are authorised by the Minister for Justice (Garda Síochána (Compensation) Act 1941 section 7). The application for an authorisation from the Minister for Justice must be made within three months of the injury or death, however this period may be extended (Garda Síochána (Compensation) Act 1941 section 5). The Garda Compensation Acts set out several criteria for assessing compensation for both injured members of the Garda Síochána or dependants of deceased members of the force. Section 19(1) of the Garda (Compensation) Act as amended provides that the High Court can have regard to the financial loss suffered by the applicant, the financial benefits the applicant would have reasonably expected in the future, the non-financial loss suffered by the applicant, the funeral and medical costs sustained due to the death of the member etc. Section 19(2) of the Garda Síochána (Compensation) Act 1941 states that when assessing compensation for injuries sustained by members of the Garda Síochána the Court can take into account the actual medical and surgical expenses of the injured person, any reduction in earnings in the future due to injury and any pain and suffering inflicted on the member.

8.2.3.2 Hepatitis C and HIV Compensation Tribunal

In the 1980s the State's blood supply, which was under the responsibility of the Irish Blood Transfusion Service, was contaminated with Hepatitis C and Human Immunodeficiency Virus (HIV), which affected a large number of people (Kelly 1993–94). A Tribunal of Inquiry (Lindsay Tribunal) was set up along with a non-statutory compensation scheme. Then under the Hepatitis C Compensation Tribunal

Acts 1997, amended and extended by the Hepatitis C Compensation Tribunal (Amendment) Act 2002, a statutory compensation scheme was established and all previous claims made to the non-statutory tribunal were transferred to the new tribunal. The Tribunal assesses compensation on the same grounds as the High Court assesses damages in tort (Hepatitis C Compensation Tribunal Acts 1997–2006, section 5). There are, however, specific provisions concerning awards to dependants, awards for loss of consortium and society and awards for aggravated or exemplary damages (Jennings et al. 2010).

8.2.3.3 Other General Compensation Schemes

A number of schemes have been set up by the government to provide compensation in various spheres. For example, the Criminal Injuries Compensation Tribunal has responsibility for the administration of the Scheme of Compensation for Personal Injuries Criminally Inflicted and the Scheme of Compensation for Personal Injuries Criminally Inflicted on Prison Officers. This is a non-statutory criminal injuries compensation scheme and provides for an award of *ex gratia* compensation for personal injuries or deaths arising from a crime of violence, from coming to the aid of a member of the Garda Síochána or from the prevention of crime or saving a human life (Jennings et al. 2010, 350). In a similar vein, Section 6 of the Criminal Justice Act 1993 provides that a court exercising criminal jurisdiction, upon convicting a defendant, can make an order for compensation in respect of any personal injury or loss resulting from the offence (Jennings et al. 2010, 351).

In addition, a recent ECtHR judgment – *O'Keeffe v Ireland* (Application No. 35810/00, Grand Chamber Judgment 28 January 2014) – has required the Irish government to review its compensation policy. This case concerned victims of abuse in the Irish education system. Ms O'Keeffe was sexually abused by her primary school principal in the 1970s. She has previously been given an *ex gratia* payment by the Criminal Injuries Compensation Tribunal. In 1998, she initiated a civil action in the Irish High Court against her abuser, the Minister for Education and Science as well as against Ireland and the Attorney General, claiming damages for personal injuries suffered as a result of assault and battery, including sexual abuse, in an Irish primary school. The State argued that the Board of Management of Ms O'Keeffe's school was in fact liable, an argument with which the High Court and Supreme Court (*O'Keefe v Hickey* [2008] IESC 72) agreed. She brought proceedings against Ireland before the ECtHR, claiming that the State had breached Articles 3, 6, 13, 14 of the ECHR and Article 2 of Protocol No. 1. The Grand Chamber found that there had been a breach of Article 3 and Article 13. The Court held that there was an inherent obligation on a government to employ special safeguards to ensure the protection of children from ill treatment in schools, particularly at the primary education level where the children were under the exclusive control of school authorities. The Court stated that a State could not release itself of this obligation by delegating it to private bodies or individuals, such as the Board of Management. It found that the State had been aware that sexual abuse of children by adults in the education system prior to the time when Ms O'Keeffe was abused. The court rejected the finding of the Irish Supreme Court that Ms O'Keeffe should fail for not first exhausting all legal remedies in Ireland as she had not sued the Bishop of Cork and Ross who was responsible for running the school and held that Ms O'Keeffe was entitled to choose from a variety of legal remedies available to her. The government's Draft Action Plan (Action Plan (24/07/2014) in response to the O'Keefe judgment was submitted to the Council of Europe in July 2014. This sets out the individual and general measures which have been taken by the government in response to the judgment. The State made a payment of €134,550 to Ms O'Keefe's solicitor, including €30,000 in pecuniary and non-pecuniary damages. In addition, the State Claims Agency has reviewed similar cases relating to day school abuse in an attempt to identify those which fall within the scope of the judgment. This judgment could have significant implications for the State in both legal and financial terms, given the large number of similar cases in Ireland. A further Action Plan is to be filed by 28 January 2015 in relation to the actions identified in the first plan.

8.2.3.4 Other Specific Compensation Schemes

The government has also put in place various *ad hoc* compensation schemes which address specific issues. For example, the Residential Institutions Redress Act was adopted in 2002 to provide a system of compensation for people who suffered physical and sexual abuse while resident in these institutions. The Residential Institutions Redress Board was thus established in 2002. Under section 7 of the 2002 Act an application can be made by a former resident of an institution which is listed in a schedule to the Act or which is specified by a ministerial order (Jennings et al. 2010, 358–60). Initially, the closing date for applications to the Residential Institutions Redress Board was 15 December 2005. However, an extension of the time period was allowed in exceptional circumstances up until 17 September 2011.

There has been recent controversy concerning the government's proposed redress scheme for women who underwent symphysiotomy procedures. Symphysiotomy is a childbirth procedure that unhinges the pelvis, severing the symphysis joint or sundering the pubic bones. In Ireland it is estimated that 1,500 women unknowingly and without consent underwent symphysiotomies during childbirth between 1944 and 1984. This type of procedure was utilised in a number of hospitals in Ireland with a Catholic ethos as it facilitated future vaginal deliveries (Survivors of Symphisiotomy 2014). Approximately 200 women who underwent this procedure survive today, many of them permanently disabled and in pain. Some babies died or were brain damaged or otherwise injured during the process. Significant pressure had been placed on the government to amend the Statute of Limitations in respect of survivors of symphysiotomy (O'Connor 2013 and Survivors of Symphisiotomy 2014) allowing for claims for compensation to be made through the High Court, rather than implement a compensation scheme. However, following the publication of an Independent Review of Issues relating to Symphysiotomy ('the Murphy Report') in addition to the government-commissioned Report on Symphysiotomy in

Ireland, 1944–1984 ('the Walsh Report), in July 2014, the Government announced its intention of launching an *ex gratia* redress scheme to be administered by the State Claims Agency. This is despite the fact that the Murphy report was rejected by members of the 'Survivors of Symphysiotomy', a group which represents the vast majority of symphysiotomy survivors and indeed, the Murphy proposals on redress were also criticised by the United NationsHuman Rights Committee in August 2014. However, the scheme was approved by the Government on 29 October 2014 and published on November 10th. It provides for payments of between €50,000 to €150,000 to survivors of symphysiotomy.

8.3 Damages for Breaches of Human Rights Protected by the Irish Constitution

8.3.1 Human Rights Protection in the Irish Constitution

Ireland has strong constitutional protection of civil and political rights (Dewhurst et al. 2012) and the Constitution takes precedence over Irish legislation. The current Constitution, adopted in 1937, deals with the protection of human rights in Articles 40–44. These provisions seek to protect a wide variety of rights including the right to life, good name, property, liberty, expression, assembly, association, family, education, religion, and a fair trial (Dewhurst et al. 2012). The Constitution is also the source of certain latent or unenumerated rights arising out of the wording of Article 40.3 which states that "[t]he State guarantees in its laws to respect, and, as far as practicable, by its laws to defend and vindicate the personal rights of the citizen" and "[t]he State shall, in particular, by its laws protect as best it may from unjust attack and, in the case of injustice done, vindicate the life, person, good name, and property rights of every citizen". Starting in 1965 with the case of *Ryan v The Attorney General* (*Ryan v Attorney General* [1965] IR 1 at 294) Irish Courts have, therefore, 'discovered' a number of unenumerated rights, including, the right to bodily integrity, to travel, to earn a livelihood, to legal aid, to individual privacy and marital privacy, to litigate and have access to the courts, to justice and fair procedures, to marry and procreate, to communicate and to freedom from torture and from inhuman or degrading treatment or punishment (Doolan 1994). While the flexibility provided by Article 40.3 for constitutional protection of human rights to keep in line with modern day developments in society and interpretations of human rights has led to the extension of the Constitutional protection of rights well beyond its textual limits, this method of constitutional protection has been criticised for creating a "certain blurring of definition, a certain bursting of conceptual banks, rather as though legal rivers finding their confluence in the estuary of liberty and justice, had had their courses confused by flooding further upstream, leaving a somewhat trackless delta for the constitutional geographer" (Hogan et al. 2003, 1413).

Another difficulty with the protection of constitutional rights is that it is unclear from its text if the Irish Constitution bestows rights on both citizens and non-citizens. Some of its provisions specifically states that they relate to citizens, e.g. Article 40.4.1° which states that "no citizen" can be deprived of his liberty except in accordance with the law. Other provisions however, do not explicitly limit their application to citizens. There is also conflicting jurisprudence on this point with the High Court finding in *The State (Nicolaou) v An Bord Uchtála* ([1966] IR 567, 616–617) that Article 40 did not apply to non-citizens as the provision referred specifically to citizens ([1966] IR 567, 645). More recent cases, such as *Northants Co Council v ABF* ([1982] ILRM 164) and *Finn v Attorney General* ([1983] IR 154) seem to have taken a more expansive view with regard to the application of Constitutional rights to non-citizens. In *Northants Co Council v ABF* it was held that natural law applies to all persons, regardless of citizenship, and therefore a non-citizen could rely on Article 41. In a similar vein, in *Finn v Attorney General* it was held that constitutional rights derive from one's nature as a human being rather than from citizenship and that the State promises to protect them. Casey (2000, 448) suggests that "non-nationals will, in practice, be able to invoke the Constitution for most purposes", however, a level of doubt remains concerning rights that have not as yet been considered by the Courts.

As to whether legal persons such as companies have Constitutional rights, "[t]he answer to this question would appear to depend on the nature of the right being claimed" (Dewhurst et al. 2012, 7). Some jurisprudence indicates that the equality guarantee in Article 40.1 is applicable only to human persons, given its wording (*Quinn's Supermarket Ltd v Attorney General* [1972] IR 1). Similarly, both Article 40 and Article 43 have been deemed to be confined to the protection of human persons (*PMPS Ltd and Moore v Attorney General* [1983] IR 339). However, certain provisions, such as Article 44.2.3°, and those relating to property rights are not restricted and can be applied to legal persons (*Quinn's Supermarket Ltd v Attorney General* [1972] IR 1 and *Iarnród Éireann v Ireland* [1996] 3 IR 321). Indeed, in situations where constitutional provisions explicitly mention "citizens" or "persons" the courts have at times dealt with the problem by attempting to identify a "person'" who could be legitimately held to be affected for the purposes of the case.[8]

8.3.2 *The Horizontal Effect of Irish Constitutional Norms*

Irish Constitutional norms are capable of being applied directly to both private individuals and corporations or, in other words, Irish Constitutional rights have direct horizontal effect. Violations of constitutional rights by non-State actors can engender a cause of action known as a 'constitutional tort' (Butler 1993; O'Cinneide 2007). However, unfortunately, the exact parameters of application of this constitutional tort are unclear and uncertain. O'Cinneide (2007, 215) comments that "[t]he existence of

[8] In *PMPS Ltd and Moore v Attorney General* [1983] IR 339 the High Court held that while a corporate entity could not rely on Arts 40 or 43, a shareholder could claim that his constitutional rights had been violated.

the constitutional tort is widely seen as an essential safety net to protect fundamental rights from violations instigated by non-state bodies, if legislation and other forms of legal regulation do not do the job." Nevertheless, as O'Cinneide (2008), 215) proceeds to highlight, "the impact of the direct horizontal effect doctrine has often been muted and even nullified by the adoption of a cautious approach by the judiciary towards developing private law remedies to reflect rights norms, in particular where existing private law rules clearly apply to the matter at issue". Although, in situations where private law is not clearly applicable "constitutional rights have been promiscuously treated as binding private individuals, without any real consideration of the appropriateness of blurring the public / private distinction in this context." Clearly, the uncertainty surrounding when, and in what manner, constitutional rights will have horizontal effect is unsatisfactory for individuals and entities as they cannot be sure of the constitutional obligations which attach to them. In addition, the vagueness surrounding this issue leaves a lot of room for judicial discretion.

8.3.3 Remedies for Breach of Constitutional Rights

The Irish Constitution does not explicitly set out the consequences for breach of its provisions. However, it has been well established in the jurisprudence of the Irish Courts that the Irish Constitution creates a remedy for the violation of the rights set forth within its text. This is the case even when that right is not protected under any domestic legislation or under common law. This is clearly seen from the statement of Walsh J in *Byrne v Ireland* (*Byrne v Ireland* [1972] IR 241 at 264):

> In several parts in the Constitution duties to make certain provisions for the benefits of citizens are imposed on the State in terms which bestow rights upon the citizens and, unless some contrary provision appears in the Constitution, the Constitution must be deemed to have created a remedy for the enforcement of these rights.

Similarly, in *Meskell v Córas Iompar Éireann* ([1973] IR 12, 132–3), the same judge stated that "a right guaranteed by the Constitution or granted by the Constitution can be protected by action or enforced by action even though such action may not fit into any of the ordinary forms of action in either common law or equity and that the constitutional right carries within it its own right to a remedy or for the enforcement of it." However, it should be noted that if a constitutional right is also protected by means of legislation then the Constitution cannot be exclusively relied upon by the Courts in dealing with the issue of remedies. This is highlighted by the statement of Barrington J in *McDonnell v Ireland* (*McDonnell v Ireland* [1998] 1 IR 134, 148) that "constitutional rights should not be regarded as wild cards which can be played at any time to defeat all existing rules. If the general law provides an adequate cause of action to vindicate a constitutional right it appears to me that the injured party cannot ask the court to devise a new and different cause of action."

In *The State (Quinn) v Ryan* ([1965] IR 70, 122), Ó Dálaigh CJ seems to indicate that the Irish Courts had unfettered discretion as to remedies for violations of constitutional rights, stating:

> It was not the intention of the Constitution in guaranteeing the fundamental rights of the citizens that these rights should be set at nought or circumvented. The intention was that rights of substance were being assured to the individual and that the courts were the custodians of these rights. As a necessary corollary, it follows that no one can with impunity set these rights at nought or circumvent them, and that the courts' powers in this regard are as ample as the defence of the Constitution requires.

However, subsequent jurisprudence has drawn some limits as to how the Irish Courts deal with remedies for breaches of Constitutional rights. In *Sinnott v Minister for Education* ([2001] 2 IR 545, 709), Hardiman J stated that the above quoted statement by Ó Dálaigh CJ had to be read in the context of the specific facts of the case in question and that it was "not an assertion of an unrestricted general power in the judicial arm of government but rather a strong and entirely appropriate statement that a pettyfoggong, legalistic response to an order in terms of Article 40.4 of the Constitution will not be permitted to obscure the realities of the case or to preclude appropriate action by the courts." In *Hanrahan v Merck Sharp and Dohme* ([1998] ILRM 629) the Supreme Court clarified that Irish courts "will not develop the parameters of an existing tort or provide a supplemental remedy under their jurisdiction to uphold constitutional rights, unless the existing scope of the tort in question is 'basically ineffective' or 'plainly inadequate' to secure the protection of the constitutional rights at issue" (O'Cinneide 2007, 237).

It is therefore the case that it falls within the remit of Irish courts to ensure performance of constitutional obligations and to provide a remedy for constitutional rights which have been infringed (Casey 2000).[9] Similar infringements of rights are generally responded to with a similar remedy under Irish law, for example, "[i]ssues of personal liberty are most commonly litigated in the *habeas corpus* procedure under Article 40.4" (Hogan et al. 2003, 1302) of the Constitution, although other remedies, including injunctions (*O'Boyle and Rodgers v Attorney General* [1929] IR 558) and damages (*Dunne v Clinton* [1930] IR 366) have also been granted and awarded for infringement of this right. Similarly, an infringement of the constitutional right to fair procedures is generally remedied by means of an order which quashes the relevant decision, but again, other remedies have been deemed to be more appropriate in certain cases, such as in *Healy v Minister for Defence* (7 July 1994, HC) when damages were granted.

8.3.4 Damages for Breach of Constitutional Rights

The Irish Courts have distinguished between rights that are protected under common law and by statute as well as under the Constitution on the one hand and rights which are just protected under the Constitution on the other. However, damages can be awarded for breach of either category of rights. This was affirmed in the case of *Hayes v Ireland* (*Hayes v Ireland* [1987] I.L.R.M. 651, 655), with Carroll J stating:

[9] See *O'Shiel v Minister for Education* [1999] 2 ILRM 241 at 264.

"A plaintiff who establishes unlawful interference with a constitutional right must be in as strong a position as a plaintiff whose statutory rights have been infringed, and is entitled to recover damages for injury suffered by him."

Along similar lines, in *W v Ireland (No 2)* ([1997] 2 IR 165) Costello J stated:

> The courts have . . . pointed out that the Constitution guarantees the exercise and enjoyment of other rights which are not regulated by law and for which no legal provision exists, either to prohibit an anticipated infringement or to compensate for a past one. It is now established that for this class of rights, the Constitution is to be constructed as providing a separate cause of action for damages for breach of a constitutional rights.

As highlighted by Hogan et al. (2003, 1304–5), however, "in most cases, the damages were calculated in accordance with common law principles and, in particular, the breach of constitutional rights did not, per se, result in the award of punitive damages."

In *Blasacod Mór Teo v Commissioners of Public Works (No 4)* ([2000] 3 IR 565, 591) Budd J held that damages could be recovered where constitutional rights had been infringed as a result of a piece of invalid legislation once the damage "is proved to have flowed directly from the effects of the invalidity without intervening imponderables and events."

8.4 Types of Damages

In *Kennedy v Ireland* ([1987] IR 587, 594), the issue of the types of awardable damages in Irish law was considered. The case centred on journalists whose phones had been tapped by government officials. Hamilton P stated:

> In determining the damages to which the plaintiffs are entitled, I must have regard not only to the distress which was suffered by the plaintiffs as a result of the infringement of their constitutional right to privacy, the implications thereof and the publicity consequent thereto, but also to the fact that the infringement was carried out deliberately, consciously and without justification by the executive organ of the State which is under a constitutional obligation to respect, vindicate and defend that rights.
>
> The plaintiffs are in my opinion entitled to substantial damages and it is, in the circumstances of this case, irrelevant whether they be described as 'aggravated' or as 'exemplary' damages.

The various levels of damages available for a breach of a constitutional right were also considered by the Supreme Court in *Conway v Irish National Teachers Organisation* ([1991] 2 IR 305). The case arose from the interruption to teaching in certain primary level schools in the county of Cork due to an industrial dispute. In the High Court, damages of £11,500 were awarded to the plaintiff who was one of the pupils in the affected schools. £1,500 of this amount was deemed to be exemplary damages. The defendants appealed to the Supreme Court, claiming that exemplary damages should not have been awarded, and that if they were awarded that the amount was too high. Finlay CJ set out three categories of damages (*Conway v INTO* [1991] 2 IR 305, 316):

In respect of damages for tort or for breach of constitutional right, three headings of damage in Irish law are, in my view, potentially relevant to any particular case. They are:

(1) ordinary compensatory damages being sums calculated to recompense a wronged plaintiff for physical injury, mental distress, anxiety, deprivation of convenience, or other harmful effects of a wrongful act and/or for monies lost or to be lost and/or expenses incurred or to be incurred by reason of the commission of the wrongful act.
(2) Aggravated damages, being compensatory damages increased by reason of:

   (a) the manner in which the wrong was committed, involving such elements as oppressiveness, arrogance or outrage, or
   (b) the conduct of the wrongdoer after the commission of the wrong, such as a refusal to apologise or to ameliorate the harm done or the making of threats to repeat the wrong, or
   (c) conduct of the wrongdoer and/or his representatives in the defence of the claim of the wronged plaintiff, up to and including the trial of the action.
   Such a list of the circumstances which may aggravatecompensatory damages until they can properly be classified as aggravated damages is not intended to be in any way finite or complete. Furthermore the circumstances which may properly form an aggravating feature in the measurement of compensatory damages must, in many instances, be in part a recognition of the added hurt or insult to a plaintiff who has been wronged, and in part also a recognition of the cavalier or outrageous conduct of the defendant.

(3) punitive or exemplary damages arising from the nature of the wrong which has been committed and/or the manner of its commission which are intended to mark the court's particular disapproval of the defendant's conduct in all the circumstances of the case and its decision that it should publicly be seen to have punished the defendant for such conduct by awarding such damages, quite apart from its obligation, where it may exist in the same case, to compensate the plaintiff for the damage which he or she has suffered.

Finally CJ highlighted the difficulty in differentiating between punitive and exemplary damages and then went on to discuss if exemplary / punitive damages could correctly be awarded for a breach of constitutional rights. He stated:

> It seems clear to me that the court could not be availing of powers as ample as the defence of the Constitution and of constitutional rights requires unless, in the case of the breach of those rights, it held itself entitled to avail of one of the most effective deterrent powers which a civil court has, the awarding of exemplary or punitive damages.

Finlay CJ clarified that the Courts could consider the award of exemplary damages in a case where constitutional rights have been violated, but that this was not to be seen as an automatic course of action. According to the Chief Justice, as a general principle, "exemplary damages should not be awarded if, in the opinion of the court, the amount necessarily payable by the wrongdoer in the form of compensatory damages constituted a sufficient public disapproval of and punishment for the particular form of the wrongdoing" ([1991] 2 IR 305, 321–322). Given the facts of the case Finlay CJ was satisfied that exemplary damages should be awarded due to the severity of the wrongful act. In *Healy v Minister for Defence* (*Healy v Minister for Defence* (7 July 1994) HC) Barron J stated that exemplary damages could not be awarded when a conscious and wilful disregard of the plaintiff's constitutional rights could not be proven.

Other types of damages awarded in Irish law, apart from those ones identified in the case of *Conway* ([1991] 2 IR 305) are nominal damages (the award of a token amount of money in a case where the plaintiff has established a wrong but has not suffered any harm) and contemptuous damages ("where the plaintiff establishes a technical wrong, but is considered not to have a sufficient reason for bringing litigation" (Quill 2009, 575).

Damages for infringement of constitutional rights are generally assessed "on the same basis as damages in tort, not on any higher basis" (Cooney and Kerr 1981) even though the rights breached are constitutional, as opposed to merely common law or legislative, rights. Cooney and Kerr (1981, 10) question whether such an approach is adequate, stating that "this common law backdrop is inappropriate, in that it fails to pay respect to the intrinsic worth of constitutional rights."

8.5 Ireland and the European Convention on Human Rights

Ireland operates a dualist system (Article 29.3.1 of the Irish Constitution) of law and in order for an international treaty to be justiciable in Ireland it must be ratified and then directly incorporated into the domestic legal system, either as an amendment to the Constitution or by an Act of Parliament. Ireland became a member of the Council of Europe in 1949 and the Irish government subsequently signed the European Convention on Human Rights and Fundamental Freedoms (ECHR) in 1950 and ratified it in 1953 (Schabas 2007). However, given the dualist nature of the Irish legal system, the ECHR was binding only on Ireland but not within Ireland. Despite calls for the incorporation of the ECHR into domestic law dating back to 1975[10] there was a certain amount of reticence to enact legislation in this regard because it was felt that the Irish constitutional protection of human rights was sufficient and a fear existed that the incorporation would be considered an encroachment on sovereignty (de Londras and Kelly 2010). However, the Good Friday Agreement 1998, which was signed in the hope of bringing peace to Northern Ireland, required an equivalency of human rights protection between Northern Ireland and Ireland. The ECHR was viewed as a "politically neutral template for sensitive cross border dealings" (Hogan 1999, 210) and thus its provisions became part of Irish law by means of the European Convention on Human Rights Act 2003 (ECHR Act 2003). Despite the recommendations made by the Irish Human Rights Commission, the Irish government incorporated the rights set out in the ECHR into Irish law at a sub-constitutional level which was regarded as constituting a "minimalist" approach to human rights protection (Irish Human Rights Commission 2002, 7). As a result of the ECHR Act 2003, Irish Courts are now obliged to interpret Irish laws in a way that gives effect to Ireland's obligations under the ECHR. In addition, organs of State (such as government ministers and State bodies) are

[10] It was Fianna Fáil who originally called for incorporation of the Convention in 1975 and this was also recommended by the Constitutional Review Group in 1996.

required to act in compliance with the ECHR.[11] This was underscored in the case of *Foy v An tArd Chláraitheoir & Ors* ([2007] IEHC 470, 93), where McKechnie J stated:

> It is misleading to say that the Convention was incorporated into domestic law. It was not. The rights contained in the Convention are now part of Irish law. They are so by reason of the 2003 Act. That is their source. Not the convention. So it is correct to say, as I understood in this way, that the Convention forms part of the law. The method employed b the Oireachtas was the interpretative method. Section 2 of the 2003 Act compels this court to interpret and apply any and every statutory provision and rule of law, insofar as is possible in a manner compatible with Ireland's obligations under the Human Rights Convention.

Section 3(1) of the ECHR Act 2003 states: "Subject to any statutory provision (other than this Act) or rule of law, every organ of the State shall perform its function in a manner compatible with the State's obligations under the Convention provision."[12] Section 3(2) then deals with the issue of damages and states that a person who has suffered injury, loss or damage as a result of breach of the Act may, if no other remedy in damages is available, institute High Court proceedings. The High Court may then award damages if it deems it to be the appropriate remedy for the breach. However, a limitation is placed on the damages under subsection (3) which states that "[t]he damages recoverable under this subsection in the Circuit Court shall not exceed the amount standing prescribed, for the time being by law, as the limit of that Court's jurisdiction in tort."

In addition to the option to award damages, Section 5 of the Act provides that the High Court or Supreme Court can make a declaration that a statutory provision or common law rule is incompatible with the Convention. While such a declaration does not render the law at issue invalid, prevent the continuing operation or enforcement of the provision or rule, or prevent a party to proceedings to make submissions or representation in any European Court of Human Rights (ECtHR) proceedings, the Taoiseach (Irish Prime Minister) is obliged to lay any such declaration before both houses of Parliament within 21 days of the next sitting of the Parliament.

Section 5(4) of the Act requires a set of criteria be met before damages can be awarded in any given case. First, there must be a declaration of incompatibility made in respect of the particular case. Then, the injured party must make a written

---

[11] Section 4 requires Irish courts to take judicial notice of the provisions of the ECHR and of any declaration, decision, advisory opinion or judgment of the ECtHR, any decision of the European Commission of Human Rights and any decision of the Committee of Minister on any question in respect of which it has jurisdiction. In addition, Irish Courts are required to take due account of the principles set out in these declarations, decisions, advisory opinions, opinions and judgments when interpreting and applying the provisions of the Convention.

[12] The ECHR 2003 Act levies a general obligation on all "organs of State" to perform their duties in a manner compatible with the Convention. Section 1 of the Act defines an organ of State as a tribunal or any other body (other than the President, the Oireachtas (Parliament) or either house of the Oireachtas or a Committee of either House or a Joint Committee of both houses) which is established by law or through which any of the legislative, executive, or judicial powers of the State are exercised. As Kenna (2010, 5) highlights "[t]his amounts to a new tortious action (where no other remedy exists) for breaches of statutory duty by organs of the State, for which damages or equitable relief can be granted."

application to the Attorney General for compensation in respect of an injury or loss or damage suffered by him or her as a result of the incompatibility. The Government may then, at its discretion, make an *ex gratia* payment of compensation. Once these requirements are met the Government can request the advice of an advisor appointed to it with regard to the amount of compensation appropriate in the given case. The Government, however, has discretion to pay the amount recommended by the advisor or any other amount it deems appropriate. Section 5(5) of the Act requires that the advisor, in recommending the amount of compensation, should take into consideration the principles and practice applied by the ECtHR in relation to affording just satisfaction to an injured party under Article 41 of the Convention. Very few declarations of incompatibility have been made in respect of Irish legislation[13] and as yet the issue of compensation has not been dealt with, but it is likely that this compensation would be at a lower level than regular awards in civil courts in Ireland (Farrell 2009).

8.6 Ireland and International Human Rights Law

Ireland has ratified six of the nine core international human rights treaties: the International Covenant on Civil and Political Rights 1966 (ICCPR); the International Covenant on Economic, Social and Cultural Rights 1966; the International Convention on the Elimination of All Forms of Racial Discrimination 1965; the Convention on the Elimination of All Forms of Discrimination against Women 1979; the Convention against Torture and Other Cruel, Inhuman or Degrading Treatment or Punishment 1984; and the Convention on the Rights of the Child 1989, and has incorporated the Torture Convention into domestic law by means of the Criminal Justice (United Nations Convention against Torture) Act 2000. Ireland has signed but not ratified the International Convention of the Protection of All Persons from Enforced Disappearance 2006 and the Convention on the Rights of Persons with Disabilities 2006. Ireland has neither signed nor ratified the International Convention on the Protection of the Rights of All Migrant Workers and Members of their Families. Ireland has also ratified the Optional Protocol to the ICCPR, and thus Irish citizens who feel that their human rights have been violated by the State can make an individual communication to the Human Rights Committee. This has not been a very popular option for Irish citizens, with only five such communications having been sent to the Committee, two of which relate to the same individual, Mr Kavanagh. On 4 April 2001, the Human Rights Committee adopted its Views on Communication 819/1998, and held that Mr Kavanagh's right to equality before the law, guaranteed in article 26 of the ICCPR, had been violated because the Irish Director of Public Prosecutions had directed him to be tried before a Special

[13] Declarations of incompatibility have been made in the cases of *Foy v An tArd Chláraitheoir & Ors* [2007] IEHC 470; *Donegan v Dublin City Council, Ireland and the Attorney General* and *Dublin City Council v Gallagher* [2012] IESC 18.

Criminal Court, which is a juryless court provided for by the Offences against the State Act 1939, without providing grounds justifying the selection of that particular trial procedure. The Committee stated in its Views that Mr Kavanagh was entitled to an "effective remedy" and that the Irish government was under an obligation to ensure that similar violations did not occur in the future. The Committee stated that the Irish government should ensure that persons are not tried before the Special Criminal Court unless reasonable and objective criteria for the decision are provided (Communication 819/1998, para 12). The day after Mr Kavanagh received the Committee's Views, his counsel wrote to the Irish Minister for Justice, Equality and Law Reform seeking his release, indicating that in the alternative legal action to vindicate his rights would be pursued. Mr Kavanagh then applied *ex parte* to the High Court seeking release on bail pending the outcome of proceedings, the quashing of his conviction, a declaration that Section 47 (2) of the Offences Against the State Act 1939 was incompatible with the ICCPR and repugnant to the Irish Constitution, in addition to costs and damages. The application was based on the doctrine of legitimate expectation and the claim that the Irish government should act on the Committee's Views. Mr Kavanagh's application for leave to seek judicial review was heard in the High Court in June 2001, and was refused, with the High Court holding that in the absence of direct incorporation of the ICCPR, the Covenant was only relevant in the domestic legal system via Article 29(3) of the Irish Constitution which states that "Ireland accepts the generally recognised principles of international law as its rule of conduct in its relations with other States" (*Kavanagh v Governor of Mountjoy Prison* ([2002] 3IR 97)). Mr Kavanagh appealed to the Supreme Court. In March 2002 the Supreme Court rejected the appeal, holding that neither the Covenant nor the Committee's Views could be given effect in domestic law and that the Committee's Views could not prevail over the Offences against the State Act. However, in August 2001, the Minister for Justice, Equality and Law Reform had offered Mr Kavanagh £1,000 in response to the Committee's View, although he did not specify the purpose of this money or identify it as damages or compensation or a contribution towards legal costs. However, Mr Kavanagh subsequently returned the cheque stating that this did not amount to an effective remedy. The 'damages' issue did not arise in Court proceedings. Therefore, it is uncertain if any future complaints made to the Human Rights Committee would result in the Irish government awarding money to Irish citizens in response to human rights infringements in the form of damages.

8.7 Conclusion

As can be seen from this discussion, the issue of damages as a remedy for human rights abuses is complex and lacking in clarity in parts. While some pieces of Irish legislation clearly set out when damages are available for a breach of human rights, the situation is not so precise in the case of a breach of constitutional rights and much is left to the discretion of the Courts. One of the most controversial aspects of the damages regime in Ireland in the context of human rights violations is the way in which the government has set up compensation regimes for human rights abuses, such as in the context of claims by survivors of symphysiotomy. It has been suggested that a claim for damages may be a more appropriate way to deal with such abuses, rather than through a compensation scheme (Survivors of Symphisiotomy 2014). However, the government has very recently proceeded with a compensation scheme in spite of extensive criticism (Human Rights Committee 2014). In addition, while the ECHR Act 2003 does provide for damages in case of a breach of its provisions, the Irish Courts have not, as yet, dealt with this issue and so an assessment of the benefits of this regime is impossible. Similarly, there is a lack of practice, and therefore, unfortunately a level of uncertainty, with regard to damages for breaches of international human rights treaties.

References

Butler, A.S. 1993. Constitutional rights in private litigation: A critique and comparative analysis. *Anglo-American Law Review* 22: 1.

Casey, James. 2000. *Constitutional law in Ireland*, 3rd ed. Dublin: Round Hall Sweet and Maxwell.

Cooney, Thomas A.M., and Tony Kerr. 1981. Constitutional aspects of Irish Tort Law. *Dublin University Law Journal* 3: 1–16.

de Londras, Fiona, and Cliona Kelly. 2010. *European Convention on Human Rights Act*. Dublin: Round Hall Thomson Reuters.

Dewhurst, Elaine, Noelle Higgins, and Los Watkins. 2012. *Principles of Irish Human Rights Law*. Dublin: Clarus Press.

Doolan, Brian. 1994. *Constitutional law and constitutional rights in Ireland*, 3rd ed. Dublin: Gill & MacMillan.

Farrell, Michael. 2009. Recent Developments in Human Rights and Judicial Review: The Role of the European Convention on Human Rights Act, 2003. https://www.google.ie/url?sa=t&rct=j&q=&esrc=s&source=web&cd=1&ved=0CCIQFjAA&url=http%3A%2F%2Fwww.flac.ie%2Fdownload%2Fdoc%2F210509_recent_developments_in_human_rights_judicial_review_final16may9.doc&ei=9lN8VPWUJMrQ7AanrYGoAg&usg=AFQjCNGh12YL7gunIVs1B9l47kv4dnj22w&sig2=gP0olViu3WRe3DnIFXRApw. Accessed 28 Nov 2014.

Hogan, Gerard. 1999. The Belfast Agreement and the Future Incorporation of the European Convention of Human Rights in the Republic of Ireland. *Bar Review* 4: 205.

Hogan, Gerard W., and Gerry F. Whyte. 2003. *J.M. Kelly: The Irish Constitution*, 4th ed. Dublin: Tottel.

Independent Review of Issues relating to Symphysiotomy, requested by the Irish Minister for Health, Dr James Reilly, 11 March 2014. http://health.gov.ie/wp-content/uploads/2014/07/Scanned-Murphy-report-redacted-version1.pdf. Accessed 28 Nov 2014.

Irish Human Rights Commission, Submission on the European Convention on Human Rights Bill to the Joint Oireachtas Committee on Justice, Equality, Defence and Women's Rights (June 2002).

Jennings, Colin, Barry Scannell, and Dermot F. Sheehan. 2010. *The law of personal injuries*. Ireland: Thomson Reuters (Professional) Ireland Ltd.

Kelly, Joseph. 1994. The liability of blood banks and manufacturers of clotting products to recipients of HIV-infected blood: A comparison of the law and reaction in the United States, Canada, Great Britain, Ireland, and Australia. *The John Marshall Law Review* 27: 465–492.

Kenna, Padraic. 2010. Local authorities and the European Convention on Human Rights Act 2003. *Irish Human Rights Law Review* 1: 1–31.

Murphy, Yvonne (Judge). 2014. Independent review of issues relating to symphysiotomy. http://health.gov.ie/wp-content/uploads/2014/07/Scanned-Murphy-report-redacted-version1.pdf. Accessed 28 Nov 2014.

O'Cinneide, C. 2007. Irish constitutional law and direct horizontal effect – A successful experiment? In *Human rights and the private sphere*, ed. Oliver Dawn and Fedtke Jőrg, 213–251. London: Routledge.

O'Cinneide, C. 2008. The European convention on human rights and the Irish constitutional system of rights protection: Complementary or divergent? In *The Irish Constitution: Governance and values*, ed. Doyle Oran, 507–530. Dublin: Thomson Round Hall.

O'Connor, Marie. 2013. Symphisiotomy and the statute of limitations. *Human rights in Ireland*, blogpost June 06 2013. http://humanrights.ie/civil-liberties/symphisiotomy-and-the-statute-of-limitations/. Accessed 28 Nov 2014.

Quill, Eoin. 2009. *Torts in Ireland*, 3rd ed. Dublin: Gill & MacMillan.

Ring, Sinéad. 2009. Beyond the reach of justice? Complainant delay in historic child sexual abuse cases and the right to a fair trial. *Judicial Studies Institute Journal* 2: 162–203.

Schabas, William. 2007. Ireland, the European Convention on Human Rights and the personal contribution of Seán MacBride. In *Judges, transition and human rights*, ed. Morison John, 251–274. Oxford: Oxford University Press.

Survivors of Symphisiotomy. 2014. Report to the UN Committee Against Torture (2014). http://cdn.thejournal.ie/media/2014/03/symphysiotomy-submission-to-uncat-10-march-2014.pdf. Accessed 29 Nov 2014.

UN Human Rights Committee. 2014. Concluding observations on the fourth periodic report of Ireland (2014). CCPR/C/IRL/CO/4, 19 Aug 2014.

Walsh, Oonagh. 2014. Report on Symphysiotomy in Ireland, 1944–1984. http://health.gov.ie/wp-content/uploads/2014/07/Final-Final-walsh-Report-on-Symphysiotomy1.pdf Accessed 29 Nov 2014.

Irish Cases

Blascaod Mór Teo v Commissioner of Public Works (No 4) [2000] 3 IR 565
Byrne v Ireland [1972] IR 241
Conway v Irish National Teachers Organisation [1991] 2 IR 305
Director of Public Prosecutions v Hannon [2009] 4 IR 147
Director of Public Prosecutions v Shortt [2002] 2 IR 696
Donegan v Dublin City Council, Ireland and the Attorney General and *Dublin City Council v Gallagher* [2012] IESC 18
Dowman v Ireland [1986] 1 ILRM 111
Dunne v Clinton [1930] IR 366
Finn v Attorney General [1983] IR 154
Foy v An tArd Chláraitheoir & Ors [2007] IEHC 470
Glencar Exploration PLC v Mayo County [2002] 1 ILRM 481
Hanrahan v Merck Sharp and Dohme [1998] ILRM 629
Hayes v Ireland [1987] I.L.R.M. 651
Healy v Minister for Defence (7 July 1994) HC
Iarnród Éireann v Ireland [1996] 3 IR 321
Kearney v Minister for Justice [1986] IR 116
Kelly v O'Leary [2001] IR 526
Kennedy v Ireland [1987] IR 587

McDonnell v Ireland [1998] 1 IR 134
McH v M [2004] 3 IR 556
McIntyre v Lewis [1991] 1 IR 121
Meskell v Córas Iompar Éireann [1973] IR 121
Nicolaou v An Bord Uchtála [1966] IR 567
Northants Co Council v ABF [1982] ILRM 164
O'Boyle and Rodgers v Attorney General [1929] IR 558
O'Keefe v Hickey [2008] IESC 72
O'Shiel v Minister for Education [1999] 2 ILRM 241
PMPS Ltd and Moore v Attorney General [1983] IR 339
Quinn's Supermarket Ltd v Attorney General [1972] IR 1
Ryan v Attorney General [1965] IR 1
Shortt v The Commissioner of An Garda Síochána Ireland and the Attorney General [2007] 4 IR 587
Sinnott v Minister for Education [2001] 2 IR 545
The State (Quinn) v Ryan [1965] IR 70
W v Ireland (No 2) [1997] 2 IR 165

ECtHR Cases

O'Keeffe v Ireland (Application No. 35810/00). Grand Chamber Judgment 28 January 2014

UN Human Rights Committee Communications

Communication No 819/1998 (Kavanagh v Ireland No 1)
Communication No. 1114/2002 (Kavanagh v Ireland No 2)

Irish Legislation

Garda Síochána (Compensation) Act 1941
Garda Síochána (Compensation) (Amendment) Act 1945
Civil Liability Act 1961
Hepatitis C Compensation Tribunal Acts 1997-2006
Civil Liability and Courts Act 2004
Defamation Act 2009
European Convention on Human Rights Act 2003
Offences against the State Act 1939
Statute of Limitations 1957
Statute of Limitations (Amendment) Act 1991
Statute of Limitations (Amendment) Act 2000

Council of Europe

European Convention on Human Rights 1950

UN Instruments

International Covenant on Civil and Political Rights 1966
Optional Protocol to the International Covenant on Civil and Political Rights 1966

Chapter 9
Litigating Human Rights Violations Through Tort Law: Israeli Law Perspective

Iris Canor, Tamar Gidron, and Haya Zandberg

9.1 Introduction

Israeli law offers multiple legal sources for the protection of human rights: constitutional protection, criminal protection, administrative protection and civil law – mostly tort law – protection. These sources supply protection against both public (state and public authorities, bodies, officers) and private (personal as well as legal entities) violations of human rights. This papers deals with the relevant causes of action by which compensation for harm caused by human rights violations can be achieved. The discussion will focus on tort law, but since the interplay among the multiple sources of protection is sometimes complicated and unclear, issues relating to constitutional/penal law will also be briefly discussed when directly relevant to the main issue of the paper.

Most of the legal tools applied by Israeli law to protect against human rights violations were supplied by a very active judiciary, acting in a common law system, which, by way of "interpretation", widened the scope of statutory provisions that were not originally aimed at the protection of human rights. Thus, although Israeli

I. Canor (✉)
The Haim Striks School of Law, The College of Management, Academic Studies, Rishon LeZion, Israel
e-mail: canor@colman.ac.il

T. Gidron
The Haim Striks School of Law, The College of Management, Academic Studies, Rishon LeZion, Israel

School of Law, Zefat Academic College, Safed, Israel
e-mail: tgidron@netvision.net.il

H. Zandberg
Civil Litigation Department, Attorney General Office
e-mail: HayaZ@Justice.gov.il

E. Bagińska (ed.), *Damages for Violations of Human Rights*,
Ius Comparatum - Global Studies in Comparative Law 9,
DOI 10.1007/978-3-319-18950-5_9

law does show an impressive list of basic laws that are intended eventually to produce a formal constitution, when it comes to compensation for damages to human rights, explicit statutory provisions are not only scarce, but also limited to certain aspects of human rights only. Thus, as Israeli civil law is also, as yet, not codified, the overall picture of the system reflects a more "pocket protection approach" rather than a holistic comprehensive approach to this very important issue that is so fundamental to a modern democratic society like Israel. The new decision of the Supreme Court on the issue of "*ubi jus ibi remedium*, that opened the gate – alas very narrow and still unclear – to the right to compensatory damages in certain cases of human rights" violation that are not adequately compensated by other legal means or through other legal sources, will definitely cause a huge change, if properly developed and tailored to become a general source of private law liability.

9.2 Overview of Basic Rules Governing Human Rights Protection in the Israeli Legal System

9.2.1 The Israeli State Is not Immune to Tortious Liability

The Civil Wrongs Ordinance (1947)[1] reflected the then general and well-known (English) principle that "the King can do no wrong." Thus, the State of Israel was immune from tort liability. However, this principle was rescinded by the Civil Wrongs (Liability of the State) Act of 1952, which stated explicitly that state liability in tort should be equivalent to the liability of any other corporate body. The only exceptions this act allows relate to liability for damage caused by war actions and for damage caused by a non-negligent act within the scope of lawful authority. This "equality rule", set by the Liability of the State Act, also applies to public authorities, such as municipalities and local councils, as well as corporations serving government functions originally within the power of the state.

In addition to the explicit immunities from tortious liability granted to the Israeli state by the State Liability Act, the Israeli Civil Wrongs Ordinance (New Version) (hereafter the "CWO"), also introduces a very important immunity that reflects a legal/moral/social value choice. Following a long academic debate, the CWO now grants immunity to civil servants, including state organs, for acts performed in the course of government duty and in a public capacity. Only a few exceptions are available. This immunity, however, does not apply to the state itself. The State or the public authority is entitled to indemnification only in certain circumstances, when the civil servant gravely deviates from the proper public norms.

The CWO grants two additional general immunities: an immunity from liability for an act performed within the scope of lawful authority, unless the act was negligent, and an immunity to the judiciary *and* to the state in cases of negligence in a judicial

[1] Originally a British Ordinance, which was adopted by the Israeli legislator in 1948 when the state of Israel was founded.

process, something that has sparked intense debate during the last decade. The Liability of the State Act also moved to abolish the highly contentious immunity of the state from liability in defamation cases and the restricted vicarious liability in assault and unlawful imprisonment.[2] All in all, the Israeli legislator aims to impose liability on the state with very few exceptions, and, as we shall see, the Israeli Supreme Court is even more anxious to pursue this course.

9.2.2 *Specific No-fault Liability Sources: Public and Private Defendants. 'Particular Accountability'*

The Israeli legal system offers a number of specific acts, which protect against specific violations of human rights. These acts accord compensatory damages against the state and public authorities.

Some of these acts, like the ones dealing with land requisition,[3] are public in nature and explicitly afford damages in cases of harm to the right to property. A good example to this type of pinpointed protection is a recent case dealing with compensation for damage caused to the complainant's agricultural crops in the Gaza Strip near the Israeli border. A formal statutory decree banning flights (including agricultural –civilian- spraying flights) over the area for fear of potential retaliatory war actions prevented the spraying of pesticides on crops, which were eventually infected and damaged. The owner of the corps relied on a specific act explicitly covering damage caused by war actions, [4] and although the damage was not caused directly by an act of war, the Supreme Court granted him full payment for the damaged, unsprayed crops,[5] stressing that the said specific act was clearly intended to protect the right to property and to accord compensation in cases of its breach.

Other acts protecting human rights reflect a "dual identity"; a mixed – public and private – nature. The Prohibition of Discrimination in Products, Services and Entry into Places of Entertainment and Public Places Act (2000) is a good example of the latter. It states that a violation of the right to equality in public services may give rise to an action in tort, and can lead to liability of up to 50,000 NIS[6] without proof of harm.[7] Another example is the Environmental Risks Prevention Act (Civil Claims) (1992). This law protects the right to a clean environment. The right to minimum

---

[2] For additional discussion, see Loubser and Gidron (2011).

[3] See: Land Ordinance (Acquisition for Public Purposes) (1943); Design and Construction Act (1965). (hereinafter: Design and Construction Act).

[4] The Property Tax and Compensation Fund Act (1961).

[5] MCA 5902/12 *Menahel Keren Pitzuim Vepeolot Eiva v. Kibutz Nirim* (23/01/2014).

[6] Approximately 10,400 Euro.

[7] 5(b) the Prohibition of Discrimination in Products, Services and Entry into Entertainment Sites and Public Places Act (2000).

wages is yet another example.[8] All three acts allow for a "class action" suit,[9] thus attaching an additional constitutional-like effect to the human rights protected therein, making the process more affective and cost worthy.

It is important to stress that although many of the class actions approved by Israeli courts in the last few years are based on consumer protection notions,[10] and the issue of human rights as such was not really a central issue in both the arguments and the decisions, ultimately most of these actions did touch upon human rights protection at least in part.[11] One of the most well known examples is the class action against *Strauss,* a large Israeli milk product marketer, which presented un-kosher (not "dairy only") products as "kosher". [12] This class action suit involved, largely, the issue of freedom of religion. *Strauss* eventually agreed to pay 8.5 million NIS[13] worth of kosher milk products to needy children. Another known class action was submitted against *Tnuva*, another large milk product marketer, for having marketed milk that contained silicone. Although the amount of the silicone was insignificant, *Tnuva's* consumers asserted that they should have been informed. The court ruled[14] that *Tnuva* indeed infringed its consumer's fundamental right to autonomy, and ordered *Tnova* to pay an unprecedented amount of 38.5 million NIS,[15] paid to some extent by supplying free milk to needy populations.

The Consumer Protection Act) until recently an almost forgotten piece of legislation), as well as other specific acts, thus supplies a combination of criminal, administrative and tortious safeguard which – enforced by the class action procedure – protects basic human rights against all violations and entails compensatory damages that are sometimes very high and deterring. However, it should be noted that, according to the Class Actions Act, the state and other regulating public authorities are immune from class actions.[16] The Israeli Supreme Court had ruled that this immunity is proportional and reasonable according to leading public policy.[17]

Most of these acts that explicitly impose legal liability – be it criminal, administrative or other – whereby liability for human rights violations is a secondary outcome, ("pocket accountability"), also produce a potential tort liability. This liability is based on the general tort of breach of statutory duty in sec. 63 of the Tort Ordinance 1968.[18] Here, the liability stems from a breach of a duty imposed by statute, whether criminal, civil or sometimes even tort (legislated) law. Liability in

---

[8] Minimum Wage Act (1987).

[9] Class Action Act (2006), 2nd supplement. (hereinafter: Class Action Act).

[10] See, in general: CA 1977/97 *Barzani v. Bezek Inc.*, PD 55(4) 584 (2001); CA 7808/06 *Sarah Levi v. Israel* (2012); CA 458/06 *Shtendel v. Bezek Int'l Inc.* (2009).

[11] See: Class Action Act, 2nd supplement, which includes consumers' claims.

[12] CC (Tel Aviv) 2061-06 *Negler v. Strauss-Elite Inc.* (10.01.2011).

[13] Approximately 1,780,000 Euro.

[14] CA 10085/08 *Tnouva v. Rabi Estate* (04.12.2011), hereinafter as *Tnouva.*

[15] Approximately 8,100,000 Euro.

[16] §3 Class Action Act.

[17] HCJ 2171/06 *Cohen v. Chairman of the* Knesset (2011).

[18] Tort Ordinance [New Version]. (hereinafter: Tort Ordinance).

breach of statutory duty mirrors the terms of the breached legislation and may reflect fault and no-fault liability. One of the leading considerations applied by the courts in deciding this potentially very wide liability is the identity of the defendant. Public defendants – the state and other public harm inflicting entities – are usually assessed differently than private defendants, and the nature of the public defendant as well as its powers usually call for special attention concerning competing consideration for and against imposition of liability. The well-known case in which an insurance company collapsed allegedly due to the negligence or breach of statutory duty of the Israeli Comptroller of Insurance, thus leading to economic harm to an insured road accident victim, supplies a summary of these competing interests. The state liability was denied in both counts.[19] In recent years, this line of claims against public defendants is becoming more and more popular although the Supreme Court has already indicated that the balance of interests should be reconsidered.[20]

9.2.3 *Infringement of Internationally Protected Human Rights*

Israel has ratified seven of the main human rights conventions.[21] Yet, Israel made several important reservations to some conventions and became party only to one protocol.[22] Israel has also not accepted the jurisdiction of any of the treaty body committees; thus, individual communications cannot be considered. Finally, Israel did not agree to subject itself to the jurisdiction of any regional human rights court.

However, international treaties and conventions, although ratified by the government, are not directly incorporated as enforceable in Israeli law until they are either formally imported by parliamentary legislation or recognised as customary international law.[23] As of now, no legislation has been passed to formally incorporate any of the treaties,[24] and therefore only human rights that were recognised as having the status of customary international law form part of Israeli domestic law. All other human rights mentioned in the treaties are not directly applicable to Israeli law. Despite this, the judiciary is obligated to interpret legislation, whenever possible, in

[19] CA 915/91 *Israel v. Itzhack Levy*, PD 48(3) 45 (1994), hereinafter: *Levy*.

[20] CA 7008/09 *El Rakhim v. El Kader* (2012), §47; CA 2648/09 *Gil Import Inc. v. Israel* (2011), §14.

[21] International Convention on the Elimination of All Forms of Racial Discrimination; International Covenant on Civil and Political Rights; International Covenant on Economic, Social and Cultural Rights; Convention on the Elimination of All Forms of Discrimination against Women; Convention against Torture and Other Cruel, Inhuman or Degrading Treatment or Punishment; Convention on the Rights of the Child; Convention on the Rights of Persons with Disabilities.

[22] Except the Optional Protocol on Children in Armed Conflicts.

[23] See, Chief Meir Justice Shamgar in S.C 785/87 *Affo v. Commander of l.D.F Forces* P.D. 42(2)4,40.

[24] As mentioned above, the basic rights explicitly included in the Basic Laws are limited. They do not include many of the constitutional rights mentioned in the charters, despite article 2 of the ICCPR stating that all State Parties are required to adopt measures necessary to give effect to the rights recognised.

a way consistent with Israel's international obligations, in general, and in accordance with international treaties, ratified by the government, in particular.[25]

Nevertheless, to the best of our knowledge Israeli courts have never decided a tort claim based on customary international law human right. Additionally, Israeli courts have never relied on international treaties when defining the scope of protection of human rights granted by specific legislation such as the above-mentioned acts.[26]

9.2.4 *General Liability Sources: Open-Ended Accountability. Both Public and Private Defendants. Both Fault and No-fault Based Liability in Tort*

As we have already explained, the Israeli legal system has abandoned the "The King Can Do No Wrong" ancient value. It has been replaced by the "same status" norm.[27] The state is not immune from tort liability except in specific cases.[28] Accordingly, the state might be found liable in tort for human rights violations. Public officers are sometimes immune[29]. Then the state takes responsibility and ultimately the harm to human rights is covered.

9.2.4.1 The Tort Ordinance (1968)

The general tort of negligence,[30] originally a copy of the Donoghue vs. Stevenson[31] common law rule, is the most common source of tort liability in the Israeli legal system. Liability is imposed on both public and private wrongdoer when the injurious action deviated from a reasonable standard of care. As we shall see below, here, as in cases of breach of statutory duty, liability is imposed on public defendants only when policy considerations justify such liability. The reach of this fault-based

[25] See particularly in regard to tort legislation, AC (Tel-Aviv) 4289/89 *Shalom v. Attorney General*, para. 22.

[26] This was the argument put forward in CC 1461/00 *The State of Israeli v. Dirani*; however, the Court of Appeal and in an appeal also the Supreme Court (CA 993/06 *The State of Israel v. Dirani*) did not have a chance to decide on the merits as they were preoccupied rejecting an arguments that the applicant (Dirani) was an alien enemy and therefore did not have standing before Israeli courts. This decision is now awaiting judgment before a panel of the Supreme Court.

[27] See §2 Civil Tort (State liability) Act (1952) (hereinafter: Civil Tort Act) states that the State is liable as any incorporated body.

[28] §3-5B Civil Tort Act; CC (Haifa) 371/05 *Rachel Aliene Corrie Estate v. Israel* (2012), available at ukhumanrightsblog.com/2012/10/18/ask-and-you-shall-receive-finally-an-english-translation-of-the-rachel-corrie-judgment. Accessed 4 March 2015.

[29] See §7A, 7B Tort Ordinance.

[30] See §35–36 Tort Ordinance.

[31] [1932] UKHL 100.

liability has become very wide and encompassing during the last few years, especially in cases of human rights violations, and the courts tend to set a very high price tag on an increasing number of acts of negligence in a growing number of human rights injuries.

The second general source of liability in the Tort Ordinance is the breach of statutory duty, which we have already mentioned. This tort has huge potential for further development of additional sources of liability on which an obligation to pay damages to the injured plaintiff can be based. We shall further explain these liability sources in the next chapter.

9.2.4.2 The Criminal Code (1977)

Apart from supplying potential protection for human rights via the breach of statutory duty tort, which enables victims of criminal action to impose liability in tort, the Israeli Criminal Code also offers an additional tool for compensatory damages for violations of human rights. According to sec. 77 of the Code, when, at the end of a criminal proceeding, the defendant is convicted, the Court may require him/her to pay the person who sustained damage through the offense an amount up to 84,400 NIS[32] as compensation for the loss.[33] This rule also applies to civil servants and employees of the state when convicted of a criminal act. Here are two typical examples for such liability: a police officer using unreasonable force against a person who was taking part in a protest action in a public place[34]; a person convicted of human trafficking.[35] Both were obliged to pay for the victims' various losses.

9.2.4.3 The Basic Law: Human Dignity and Liberty

Although Israel lacks a formal constitution, Israeli law has always sought to protect human rights especially through constitutional law and criminal law, and to compensate for violations of human rights mostly through private law. In 1992 the Israeli Knesset launched a "constitution forming process" and legislated the Basic Law: Human Dignity and Liberty, and other subsequent Basic Laws. Israel currently has 12 basic laws, which will eventually create a formal constitution. Their constitutional impact mostly speaks to a higher hierarchical standing given to constitutionally protected interests when balanced with competing interests. Moreover, the Basic Laws provide private law with values and concepts such as "reasonableness", "good faith", and "public interest," which the courts apply not only to contracts and property claims but also to tort claims, especially in negligence. Following intense academic discussion, and notwithstanding the diverse opinions regarding the effect

[32] Approximately 17,655 Euro.

[33] See §77 Criminal Act (1977).

[34] See CA (beer Sheva) 228/09 *Israel v. Ran Tzuref* (2010).

[35] CA 3806/06 *Ploni v. Plonit* (2009).

of the Basic Laws on private law in general and on tort law in particular, the accepted wisdom is that the Basic Laws do not constitute a new source of tort liability, neither through constitutional claims nor through the tort of breach of statutory duty. Nevertheless, the Basic Law's notions, values and choices, although lacking direct application on private litigants, still filter into the whole of the legal system and are constantly affecting human rights protection across the board.[36]

The impact of the Basic Laws on the liability of the state and public authorities may be traced mainly with regard to the issue of balancing between private interests protected by the Basic Laws and conflicting duties and interests of public authorities. The Israeli Supreme Court had stated more than once that by protecting public interests, the interests of the individuals that comprise the "public" are being protected as well. Thus, the tort of negligence, for example, which is undoubtedly the most important source of human rights protection in private law, when applied to public authorities, clearly reflects the constitutionally affected balancing process between both the constitutionally protected rights of the individuals as such *and* the (usually opposing) collective private interests. The meaning of this is that the Basic Laws can be used to limit the state's ability to harm or restrict its citizen's basic human rights. Consequently, the rights protected under the basic laws are now elevated, compared to rights that are still not protected under the basic law.[37]

9.2.4.4 A General State Duty to Compensate for Human Rights Violations?

A new decision by the Supreme Court begs to be introduced at this point although its impact is yet unclear. The Court was called to decide on the liability of the state for damages caused by human rights violations in no-fault cases. There was no specific legislation imposing liability or granting compensation, so if the Court chose to impose liability it had to decide that a mere violation of human rights is sufficient to invoke the right to compensation: *Ubi remediu, ibi jus* (" when there is a right then there should be a remedy as well").[38] We shall address the issue below.

9.2.4.5 Ex Gratia Compensation

In addition to the above, the state sometimes pays "ex gratia" compensation for violation of human rights. Such compensation, executed by administrative rather than legal proceedings (and thus open to judicial review concerning the administrative

[36] CA 294/91 *Kadisha inc. v. Kastenbaum*, PD 46(2) 464 (1992).

[37] Loubser and Gidron (2011); Barak-Erez and Gilead (2007) 252–275; Barak-Erez and Gilead (2009) 11–37.

[38] "It is a settled and invariable principle in the laws of England, that every right when with-held must have a remedy, and every injury its proper redress." (Blackstone, William. 1765. Commentaries on the Laws of England 23).

decision only,[39] is not based on fault, negligence or any other form of misconduct. Sometimes there is not even an explicit legally binding duty to pay such compensation, which is normally lower than the usual compensatory damages.

For example, the Israeli ministry of agriculture compensates, ex gratia, farmers who, following the ministry's regulations, vaccinated their livestock and suffered damages caused by such vaccination. Such absolute liability is imposed notwithstanding the lack of negligence on the part of the state and its servants. Violation of the constitutional right to property, supported by the need to encourage farmers to vaccinate their livestock, justifies this no-fault compensation mechanism. The logic behind such laws is sometimes associated with the general governmental obligation "to do on behalf of the state, and subject to the law, any action that is not under the responsibility of other public authority". It also explains the varied range of circumstances and the wide scope of the gratia compensations in Israel.[40]

The above overview of the various protections that the Israeli legal system supplies in cases of harm caused to human rights portrays a very well equipped toolkit. It also calls for a more detailed presentation of some of the leading liability sources we have listed.

In the next chapters, we shall focus on the two main avenues open before a plaintiff claiming that his/her human rights have been violated. We shall first explain the leading aspects of liability in Israeli tort law generally and the Tort Ordinance specifically, and second, the various special statutory tortious provisions that aim to cover interests and rights that do not fall within the protection of the Tort Ordinance. A short explanation of the potential no-fault new liability will follow.

9.3 The Israeli Law of Torts

In spite of many changes inserted during the last 30 years in the originally British Tort Ordinance,[41] it still conveys the spirit of English law and English common law way of thinking. Nevertheless, in many ways the interpretation of the Ordinance by the Israeli Courts during the last decades and the interpretation of British Courts on similar topics have led to different decisions. The interpretation of the tort of negligence in general and liability of public defendants in negligence in particular is quite different in Israeli law as compared to other common law legal systems, especially the English common law. Thus, the existing Israeli law of compensatory damages for human rights violations portrays a mixed picture of both English *and* Israeli tort law, which is the product of both legislation *and* case law.

The Tort Ordinance historically had a very important mission in the evolution of the protection of human rights in the Israeli (then very young) legal system. It had –

[39] See §15(d) of Basic Law: The Judiciary.

[40] See §32 Basic Law: The Government.

[41] §2 Tort Ordinance; and compare with Palmer (2012) 577.

at least until the first two Basic Laws came into force[42] – a double mission. The first was to set a list of norms that can coordinate daily human life in a modern society and define allocation of accidental damages, and the other mission, the most important one, was to declare, define and protect human rights and compensate for their violation within Israeli civil law.

Against this background, we shall now look into the various torts listed in the Tort Ordinance.

9.3.1 The Tort Ordinance. A General Overview of the Various Torts

The various torts in the CWO are divided into two categories:

1. The general torts – negligence and breach of statutory duty.
   In negligence, liability is imposed in cases of an unreasonable deviation from standards – intentional or negligent, and in breach of a statutory duty liability is based on breach of legislation. These two general torts will be addressed below.

2. The particular torts – assault, imprisonment, trespass, negligence, harm caused by dogs, nuisance, misappropriation and conversion, fraud, malicious prosecution, causing breach of contract, breach of statutory duty. These torts are characterised by having distinctly described elements that, if met, entail liability. The particular torts reflect, to some extent, the ancient "writs" through which liability was developed in the English common law [43] The particular torts allow for compensation for the violation of specifically named human rights.[44] These torts were originally intended to apply to private litigants and were not designated to regulate the relationship between individuals and the state.[45] However, today, when liability of public defendants is mainly similar to liability of other defendants, private or corporate,[46] it is common practice to impose liability on the state and public servants and/or officials based on the Ordinance. In fact, Israeli case law of the last few decades clearly shows that public defendants have become the most "popular" defendants in tort litigation. Some academics even say that recent tort law can no longer be viewed as "private law" when most of the litigants, especially defendants, are public tortfeasors.[47]

---

[42] 1992.

[43] See CA 243/83 *Jerusalem Municipality v. Gordon*, PD 39(1) 113, 123–124 (1985), hereinafter: *Gordon*; Mishael.Cheshin (1968) 346.

[44] Except for the tort of fraud and causing breach of contract, which were designated to protect commercial interests rather than any specific human right.

[45] See Tadesky et al. (1977) 401.

[46] §2 Civil Tort.

[47] Gidron (2012) 443–512; Zandberg (1994) 591.

Nevertheless, the particular torts still protect only certain "pockets" of human rights. For instance, the right to elect or to be elected is not protected. Neither is the right to freedom of speech – which is protected implicitly by the Basic law, Human Dignity and Liberty – or the right to equality. These important human right interests, and a few more, have no trace within the particular torts. Thus, given the fact that Israeli tort law is a statute law, and bearing in mind that the list of torts in the CWO is exhaustive, the most important question in Israeli law in this regard is whether a plaintiff may use one of the general torts – negligence and breach of statutory duty – in place of a particular tort, be it as a substitute or a safeguard or a completion of the particular tort in cases where the particular tort supplies only a partial protection and/or in cases where the particular tort is factually and legally insufficient. The working assumption of recent Israeli case law is that the general torts can in fact be applied on every "orphan" right and interest that is not explicitly protected by the particular torts. The only question applies to the scope of protection and the terms of its application.[48]

9.3.2 *The General Torts*

9.3.2.1 Negligence

As in other common law systems, negligence is an open-ended tort. Liability is founded on the following elements:

Duty of Care Duty of care stems from reasonable expectation of injury. Both actual-technical foreseeability (*could* the defendant actually foresee the occurrence of the injury) and normative foreseeability (*should* the defendant have foreseen the injury) must be proved.

Traditionally this duty concept was built in two stages: a conceptual duty followed by a particular duty. In most cases of "hard-core" negligence: medical negligence, landowner's negligence, abuse of rights to personal safety, product liability cases (most of these cases are strict liability cases), Israeli courts tend to recognise a duty of care and impose liability.

Only on rare occasions, is a duty of care negated. The same is true even in "problematic circumstances": a duty of care is recognised in cases of negligence by public defendants notwithstanding the type of loss caused by the public negligence and also in cases in which the loss is ("only") pure economic loss.[49]

Fault (Also Known as "Negligence") Fault represents a breach of duty of care. Fault includes both intentional and unintentional (negligent) acts and omissions,

[48] *Gordon*, *supra* note 43; CA 558/84 *Carmeli v. Israel*, PD 41(3) 757 (1987); CA 593/81 *Mifaley Rekhev Ashdod v. Adam Tzizik*, PD 41(3) 169 (1987); FA (Jerusalem) 29170/05 *Anat Elimelekh's estate v. David Apotha's estate* (2011); CA 8489/12 *Ploni v. Ploni* (2013), hereinafter: *Ploni*.

[49] Gidron (2008) 95–185; Gidron, supra note 43; Zandberg (1994); Loubser and Gidron (2011).

which deviate from a standard that, according to public considerations and the court's view of optimal professionalism and desirable criterion, is reasonable, both from a moral and economical point of view.

Causal Connection Liability in negligence is imposed only when the plaintiff can prove a causal connection between the breach of the duty of care (the "fault" or the "negligence") and the type of harm sustained. Thus, the plaintiff needs to show both factual causal connection ("condition sine qua non") and legal causal connection.[50] As previously noted, Israeli courts tend to be quite lenient with plaintiffs in cases of problematic causation situations.[51]

Harm Israeli case law tends to recognise liability for almost all types of loss, even those that other legal systems tend to libel "problematic". Pure economic loss, pure consequential mental loss, harm to personal autonomy, abuse of other personal interests that are part of human dignity – it seems as if unlike other legal systems the width and depth of the protection of negligence is impressive. Liability covers loss that results from the "natural course of things" and which "flows directly from the defendant's actions.[52]

9.3.2.2 A Budding New Perspective: Only Time Will Tell

Recently, the Supreme Court has suggested a new model, which is supposed to be much simpler and easier to apply.[53] This model assumes that if negligence, i.e. deviation from reasonable standard when unreasonable risk is foreseeable, is proven, then a duty of care is recognised. Only in some problematic cases, where special policy considerations are called for, will the court delve into the delicate task of balancing between competing interests and opposing interests. The following are some such problematic cases, which traditionally were outside the realm of "core" tort liability: cases where a special problematic loss occurred, (pure economic loss); certain types of plaintiffs (children, workers) or defendants (public defendants); certain problematic circumstances (omissions, joint causes) – all present difficulties in tort theory. These are just a few illustrations given by the court, and the list is not exhaustive.[54] In these cases, the court must apply special policy considerations very

[50] "The reasonable expectation test: could the plaintiff, as a reasonable person, anticipate that his/her recklessness will cause the damage" (CA 4486/11 *Ploni v. Ploni* [2011] §10, hereinafter: CA 4486/11).

[51] Gilead and Guttel (2004) 385.

[52] §76(1) Tort Ordinance.

[53] Meanwhile, most courts, including the majority of the judges of the Supreme Court, continue to rule according to the original accepted model.

[54] *Ploni, supra* note 48.

similar to the well-known House of Lords' *Caparo*[55] reasoning and ask whether it is "fair, just and reasonable to impose liability".[56]

Following this new negligence agenda an excellent example of how this model works was presented by the Supreme Court: two couples found themselves in an awkward situation in which husband A fell in love with woman B. They became lovers. Husband B sued his wife and husband A in contract and tort. The plaintiff relied on the tort of causing breach of contract[57] and on negligence. In a sweeping and convincing speech, Justice Amit explained that the circumstances of the case presented a good example for restraint and thus a rejection of duty of care. Due to philosophical, social, cultural and religious considerations, "we should not allow tort law into our bedrooms," concluded the Supreme Court.[58]

9.3.3 The Tort of Negligence as the Main Source of Protection of Human Rights in Israeli Civil Law

During the last three decades, the tort of negligence has become the most important source of liability in the protection of human rights in Israel. The reason is clear: the tests and terms of the tort of negligence, although statutory, apply "loose end" definitions. Courts have a very wide field for policy consideration, especially when it comes to issues of duty, reasonableness and causation. The list of considerations that Israeli courts apply is long and diverse.

The leading concerns mainly relate to slippery-slope consequences, which may lead to excessive professional/public liability, litigation costs, over-flooding the courts, over-burdening the public resources and clashes with other legal sources of liability (contract law, unjust enrichment, property law). Together with traditional concerns regarding equality, justice, risk allocation, fairness and reciprocity, it is not surprising to see that the discourse among the Israeli Supreme Court judiciary reflect important social, cultural, economic and sometimes even political deliberations.[59]

When it comes to public authorities, the problems are even more pressing. As we have already seen, negligence law applies to public defendants. As negligence covers all types of human activities, it also covers all types of public negligence including omissions and negligent supervision – two very typical problematic features of public negligence. It protects all type of interests and rights including those that some jurisdictions find "difficult" to sustain a duty of care. Pure emotional loss, pure economic loss and harm to human autonomy are the best examples

---

[55] *Caparo Industries plc. v. Dickman* [1990] UKHL 2.

[56] *Ploni, supra* note 48; Compare with *Levy,* supra note 19.

[57] §62 Tort Ordinance.

[58] *Ploni, supra* note 48.

[59] *Ploni, supra* note 48, §13 to Justice Amit ruling.

of recent years. Public defendants are liable in the same way as other defendants, even though policy considerations sometimes tend to produce a different outcome.

Indeed, the number of claims against public defendants is growing rapidly. The popularity of the new "harm to autonomy" type of damage and the wider agenda in pure economic loss caused by the state and its agents both contribute to this trend. Thus, favourable treatment of human rights violation cases, and eventually payments of large compensational damages, has become typically characteristic of recent Israeli case law.

One of the best illustrations of last year's case law is the *Refaelov* case.[60] This case involved a prisoner convicted of sexual assault against his wife. While in prison he experienced a psychotic episode and claimed that it was caused by an attack by other prisoners. He claimed that his schizophrenia was the outcome of the state's failure to safely guard him. The Supreme Court ruled that the state was indeed liable in negligence and had to pay him damages of 560,000 NIS.[61] The most significant feature in the Supreme Court's decision is the deep commitment to protection of human rights in general, physical and mental wellbeing of its citizens in particular.[62]

The Court clarifies that the scope of negligence is wide enough to accommodate suitable protection for human rights against abuse by private as well as public tortfeasors, even though such protection was not originally the end aim of this tort. It is worthy to note in conclusion that although the Israeli Supreme Court tends to use comparative law, particularly common law precedents in negligence law, it has significantly deviated from the much stricter view the British Supreme Court has adopted in this issue.

9.3.4 Autonomy as a Protected Interest via the Tort of Negligence

Violation of human rights may cause all types of loss: physical as well as pure economic and pure emotional loss. The latter is typical to many cases of harm to human rights: virtual non-physical interests, such as reputation, dignity, privacy, equality. Yet this type of loss was, for many years, constantly rejected by the courts. Similar to other common law legal systems, Israeli negligence jurisprudence was reluctant to compensate for pure mental / emotional damage. The virtual nature of the harm coupled with additional policy considerations was used as justification for the unremitting rejection of liability in negligence in cases of pure emotional loss.[63]

[60] CA 8650/08 *Refaelov v. Israel* (2013), hereinafter: *Refaelov*.

[61] Approximately 117,145 Euro.

[62] *Refaelov*, *supra* note 60, §18 of Justice Meltzer ruling.

[63] CA 2781/93 *Daaka v. "Carmel" Hospital*, PD 53(4) 526 (1999), hereinafter: *Daaka*.

The change occurred in the mid 1990s in a very famous medical negligence case[64] in which the court decided to impose liability on a doctor for breach of his patient's right to autonomy – the right to know, understand and consent to a medical treatment. In this case, the treatment – although not faulty – caused physical harm to the patient. Since the court was not convinced that the patient would have refused the treatment had she known the dangers involved, there was no causal connection, hence liability should have been rejected. Nevertheless, the court decided that the patient's autonomy was violated and she was paid 15000 NIS as compensation.[65] This new "type of harm" caused by failure to warn, explain, inform and consult has become very popular in Israeli tort law during the last 15 years. Liability is now imposed almost in every negligence claim, and the volume of damages paid under this heading is increasing constantly. The latest (modern liberal) examples to the width and depth of protection of human rights through negligence law are cases of human trafficking,[66] refusal to divorce,[67] dignity/autonomy/emotional distress,[68] sexual assault[69] and discrimination.[70]

Moreover, protection of autonomy in current Israeli law is proliferating. "Proprietary autonomy",[71] "financial autonomy"[72] and "parental autonomy"[73] are all recognised by the courts as giving rise to liability in negligence. Hence, although the Supreme Court is constantly stating that violation of autonomy does not constitute a "new" cause of action but "only" a special type of harm, which may produce a duty to compensate if negligence is proved, the realm of protection of human rights via the tort of negligence has been greatly expanded.

---

[64] *id.*

[65] *id.*

[66] For example: CA 11152/04 *Ploni v. Migdal Insurance Inc.*, PD 61(3) 310 (2006); CC (Tel Aviv) 2727/06 *Plonit v. Ploni* (2011); CC (Tel Aviv) 55775/05 *Plonit v. Ploni* (2013); CA 3806/06 *Ploni v. Plonit* (2009); LA 628/07 (State) *Almoni v. Plonit* (2009).

[67] For example: MFA 7071/13 *Ploni v. Plonit* (2013); FA (Haifa) 23464-10-09 *A. S. v. D. S.* (2011); FC (Jerusalem) 39371-09-12*S. B.A. v. I. T. B. A.* (2013); FC (Jerusalem) 22970-11-11 *A. S. v. M. S.* (2013); FC (Jerusalem) 46820-03-10 *Almoni v. Plonit* (2012); FC (Jerusalem) 22158/97 *M. T. v. M. T.* (2011); FC (Tel Aviv) 24782/98 *N. S. v. N. I.* (2008).

[68] For example: CA 4584/10 *Israel v. Shovar* (2012); *Tnouva*, supra note 14; CA 2781/93 *Daaka v. Carmel Hospital*, PD 53(4) 526 (1999); CA 2034/98 *Amin v. Amin*, PD 53(5) 69 (1999); ACA 4693/05 *Carmel Hospital v. Malool* (2010); CA 4690/04 *Sidi v. Clalt*, PD 60(3) 590 (2005); CA 1303/09 *Kadosh v. Bikor Kholim Hospital* (2012).

[69] For example: *Refaelov, supra* note 60; CC (Beer Sheva) 3001/09 *A. K. v. Israel* (2013); CC (Tel Aviv) 42400/05 *A. N. v. A. A.* (2013); FC (Tel Aviv) 82377/99 *D. M. S. v. T. S.* (2011); FC (Krayot) 1330/01 *A. v. Ploni* (2009).

[70] For example: CA (Haifa) 51160-06-11 *Hai v. Ramot Menasheh* (2012); CA (Merkaz) 39345-07-12 *K inc. v. Shraga* (2013); CC (Jerusalem) 5901/09 *Yaakobovitz v. Yad HAshmonah* (2012); CC (Tel Aviv) 42617-02-11 *Tzizis v. Vita Inc.* (2012); CC (Kfar Saba) 5244/02 *Nathan v. The Minister of Education* (2006).

[71] CA 153/04 *Robinovitz v. Rozenboim* (2006).

[72] CA 1081/00 *Avnaal Distribution Company Inc. v. Israel* (17.01.2005)

[73] In CC 3590-02-11 (Haifa) *Plonit v. Israel* (2013) the compensation was set for 87,000 Euro.

9.3.5 *International Treaties as Constituting Negligence*

To the best of our knowledge, no Israeli court has ever decided that a duty of care exists between the State and an individual in cases of infringements of an obligation stemming from international treaties which protect human rights and to which Israel is a signatory. To the contrary, the Israeli Supreme Court has dismissed such an allegation in the past, relying on procedural reasoning. The Court ruled that the right procedure in case of violation by the State of its duties stemming from international treaties, *including the obligation to compensate* in specific circumstances, would not be a civil lawsuit. Such cases should be referred to the Israeli Supreme Court sitting as a High Court of Justice as an administrative action.[74] The Israeli Court perceives the question of alleged violation of an international treaty as a question regarding the *scope* of competences and the *legality* of the exercise of such competences and therefore directed plaintiffs to the administrative law path, while foreclosing a direct tort lawsuit based on the violation of international treaty.[75]

9.3.6 *Breach of Statutory Duty*

9.3.6.1 Liability in Tort for Breach of Statutory Duty

Liability in tort for breach of statutory duty is justified – morally, economically and socially – by a concept quite similar to the *ubi jus ibi remedium* (where there is a right there should also be a remedy) principle. Tort law (sec. 63 of the CWO) compensates harm caused by breach of a legal statutory duty. Unlike other legal systems in which breach of a statutory provision is considered as *prima facia* negligence, the CWO regards the tort of negligence and the tort of breach of statutory duty as two separate liability sources, each based on different perceptions and values. Liability in negligence may sometimes be concurrent to liability for breach of statutory duty, yet the fact that a statutory duty had been breach does not, in itself, attest to negligence on the part of the defendant.[76]

Following many years of negative case law (reflecting reservations from "the untamed horse"),[77] breach of statutory duty had lately become a favourable source

[74] Given the fact that the lawsuit was based on the activity of the Israeli Defense Forces in the occupied territories, an alternative procedure would be to sue at the occupied territories for violation of decrees issued by the military commander. AC 3675/09 *The State of Israel v. Daud*, 109 PD 879 (2011).

[75] See also RAC 6665/11, *Daud v. the State of Israel*, PD (2012); Yet one judge (Meltzer) has expressed in a separate opinion a wish that the State will grant ex gratia compensation, AC 3675/09 *The State of Israel v. Daud*, 109 PD 879 (2011).

[76] Lewinsohn-Zamir, Daphna and Bar-Shira, Ada (1989); Tadesky et al. (1977); Gidron and Iluz (2013).

[77] CA 245/81 *Sultan v. Sultan*, PD 38(3) 169, 175 (1984).

of protection of human rights in the Israeli legal system. The Patient's Rights Act (1996),[78] for example, which protects the basic right to physical integrity, the right to informed consent, and many other basic human rights, does not mention any procedural means through which a patient can claim damages in cases of harm caused by breach of the Act's provisions. Neither does it contain a specific referral to the CWO. Thus, the joint application of the Act and sec. 63 of the CWO may produce an important avenue through which these important human rights can find protection and redress. Legislation dealing with licensing, building construction,[79] as well as environmental law and labour law,[80] are also potential sources of tort liability via the general tort of breach of statutory duty.

Liability in breach of statutory duty is imposed if the following terms are met:

1. a breach of a statutory (outside the CWO) duty occurred;
2. the said duty was intended to protect the plaintiff;
3. the harm caused by the defendant was the harm the legislator intended to avoid and it stemmed from the defendant's breach.
4. The breached statute, when properly interpreted, does not contradict application of sec. 63.[81]

Liability for breach of statutory duty is imposed on public defendants just as it applies on other defendants; hence the huge aptitude of protection of human rights. Similar to liability in negligence, the nature of the defendant – public, private, corporate – is very important in breach of statutory duty cases too. The nature of the breached statute (for example: does the statute mean to supply an exhaustive solution or does it still leave place to a tort action) is heavily dependent upon the fact that the tortfeasor is a public defendant. The nature of the breached duty (is it a private or a public duty?) is also built upon the question of who the defendant is. In most of the cases, the fact that liability is being imposed on a public figure or the state does not cause too much reservation. For the last two decades Israeli case law has tended to impose liability on public defendants for breach of statutory duty in a growing number of cases. Most of these cases are human rights cases. For instance, certain provisions of the Water Act (1959),[82] guarantee supply of water (under several conditions). The Supreme Court recently decided that if an individual was unlawfully denied water supply, contrary to the Water Act, he/she has the right to sue the water authority for damages for breach of a statutory duty[83].

---

[78] Patient Rights Act (1996).

[79] Design and Constructing Act; Business Licensing Act (1968); Risks Prevention Act (1961).

[80] Environmental Risks Prevention Act (Civil Claims) (1992)

[81] CA 1661/09 *Shinberger v. Hava'ada Hamekomit* (27.10.2011), §36, hereinafter: *Shinberger*.

[82] CA 8664/06 *Havat Tzabari Orly v. Israel* (2012).

[83] CA 9535/06 *Abu Mesad v. Netziv Hamaim* (2011).

9.3.6.2 Basic Laws: A Source of Liability in Breach of a Statutory Duty?

Where an explicit statutory provision protects a certain human right then the application of sec. 63 of the CWO is clear. The situation is more problematic when we deal with human rights, which are protected by the Basic Laws. Explicit private law statutory provisions concurrently protect some of these rights: defamation law, privacy law and sexual harassment law, so the protection by Basic Law is less relevant for sec. 63 purposes. Yet the problem is much more pressing when we deal with human rights, which are protected "only" by the Basic Laws, which, as common wisdom states, do not supply a private cause of action and do not have direct application outside the realm of constitutional law. Thus, the possible use of a breach of a Basic Laws' provision as grounds for liability according to sec. 63 of the CWO is of immense importance. The potential protection of human rights here is huge on the one hand, yet on the other hand the potential problems should not easily be disregarded.[84]

The Basic Law: Human Dignity and Liberty grants explicit statutory protection to various human rights: sections 2 and 4 protect life, body and dignity; section 3 protects the right to liberty; and section 7 protects the right to privacy. Case law has added the protection of freedom of speech, which is not explicitly mentioned, as part of human dignity. However, the Basic Laws do not provide any working tools. Protection of human rights is achieved through constitutional declaration only, and their implementation as practical means is limited to an indirect filtration into private law and limited change of hierarchy between constitutionally named and unnamed rights when the balancing of opposing interests by the courts is called for. On this background, the issue of interplay between the Basic Laws and the tort of breach of statutory duty is almost crucial from a human rights' protection perspective.

The Supreme Court in the case of Dor Zahave briefly discussed the issue.[85] The Court rejected the attempt to use the Basic Laws as a source for indeterminate expansion of tort law through sec. 63 of the CWO. It declared that the duties listed in the basic law cannot be regarded as "duties" for sec. 63 purposes and that policy considerations dictate a restricted practical use of Basic Laws' statutory protection especially where the danger of over-deterrence is substantive, real and imminent.[86]

Despite the firm position of the Supreme Court, the issue is still under discussion. Following an academic debate – mostly in line with the Supreme Court's decision – the issue is now again pending before the Supreme Court in an appeal on the Tel Aviv district court's decision (the Pri-Metola cae) in which the court favoured the view that violation of a Basic Law's human right's protection may well supply a cause for action based on sec. 63 of the CWO. The matter before the district court focused on the right to property and the right to freedom of occupation.[87] This district court's decision was, of course, decided before the Supreme Court

[84] In Israel there are 12 Basic Laws that should, in time, and with additional future Basic Laws that might be legislated, become its constitution.

[85] CA 10508/08 *Dor Zahav v. Hava'ada Hamekhozit* (04.02.2010), hereinafter: *Dor Zahav*.

[86] *id.*; §54; *Shinberger, supra* note 81.

[87] CC (Nazeretz) 1135/04 *Pri Metulah v. Rashoot Sedot Hateofa* (12.03.2009).

decided to the contrary in Dor Zahav. Therefore, it remains to be seen which of the two options the second round will favour. Furthermore, the entire legal situation in this case is particularly problematic due to the following circumstances: first, the Supreme Court is asked to deviate from its own former decision; second, various Israeli district courts have already decided for and against the line adopted by the Supreme Court in Dor Zahav, and third, and most important, the issue goes to the heart of one of the most important value decisions on human rights protection in Israeli private law.[88]

9.3.6.3 International Treaties as Forming a Statutory Duty

We have seen that the use of the basic laws as a source for liability in breach of statutory duty is problematic. The potential use of international treaties as a source of liability in breach of statutory duty is equally problematic. This issue has yet to be addressed by the Israeli courts. A case in which the issue was recently raised was eventually decided based on different reasons, which are outside the scope of this paper.[89]

It would have been reasonable to predict that the same problems that complicate the use of the Basic Law as a source for breach of statutory duty liability will also complicate the same use of international treaties as an origin for breach of statutory duty claims. Both types of legislation – basic laws and international treaties – impose "general" public sphere duties, whereas liability for breach of statutory duty requires a specific and concrete statutory duty. Yet, recently, in a lawsuit of an Israeli citizen against the Palestinian Authority, in which the applicant argued that he was unlawfully imprisoned by the Palestinian Authority, the district court was willing to deduce a "legal duty" stemming from an international treaty ruling that, according to international treaty, the Palestinian authority did not have competence to imprison Israelis and therefore was violating Article 63 of the Tort Ordinance.[90] Given the fact that this is only an obiter dictum by a district court decision, and taking into account the uniqueness of the facts, it is premature to predict a meaningful change. In any case, it is clear that the issue is pertinent only where the relevant treaties are part of the customary international law, and only regarding treaties that Israel had joined as a party. Treaties that are not obligatory according to the Israeli system will under no circumstances be considered as potential statutory duty for sec. 63 purposes.[91]

---

[88] It should be noted that the legal construction by which a breach of a Basic Law is a breach of a statutory duty is a construction that was developed by current Supreme Court Justice Dafna Barak-Erez in her academic writing previous to her appointment. It is reasonable to assume that she will voice her opinions in due time.

[89] CC (Jerusalem) 19157/08 *Allatif v. Israel* (2012).

[90] CC 4071/02 *Anonym v. The Palestinian Autority*, Judge Drori, 115 PD 1057 (2012), para. 370. The international treaty referred to was the Interim Agreement on the West Bank and the Gaza Strip.

[91] See a similar discussion on whether the European Right Charter applies to private disputes English (2014) ukhumanrightsblog.com/2014/01/22/does-the-eu-rights-charter-apply-to-private-disputes-sometimes-sometimes-not.. Accessed 4 March 2015.

9.4 Faultless Constitutional Tort?

9.4.1 The Dilemma

As we have seen, Israeli private law offers various forms of protection for human rights. However, each of these forms of protection supplies a specific and limited remedy, a post factum remedy (such as negligence and breach of statutory duty), and none of them was originally targeted at addressing human rights *per se* at large.

Therefore, the issue of liability for breach of human rights in cases that involve no negligence and no specific statutory provision applicable to the harmful situation, is of great importance. This question was recently addressed by an extended panel of the Israeli Supreme Court. The following is a brief summary of the facts, the legal debate and the decision.

9.4.2 The Factual Circumstances and the Legal Setting: The Law of Disengagement

9.4.2.1 The Decision to Evacuate

The two merged appeals[92] before the Supreme Court raised the issue of state responsibility for damages sustained by Israeli citizens who were evacuated from their homes in 2005 according to a formal political democratic state resolution.[93] As part of this resolution, the Knesset (the Israeli Parliament) legislated the Implementation of the Disengagement from the Gaza Strip and the North of Judea and Samaria law (2005) (hereafter "The Disengagement Act"). This Act stated that the evacuees should be fairly and appropriately compensated by the state treasury in accordance with the Act. The Act also stated that the evacuees would not be entitled to additional compensation from any other public source.

9.4.2.2 The Petition Against the Legality of the Act

Following a petition by a few of the evacuees, an expanded panel of 11 judges of the Supreme Court reviewed the disengagement act. The main arguments evoked by the petitioners suggested that their human rights – dignity, liberty, property and the right to freedom of occupation – were violated.

The Supreme Court rejected, by a majority of 10 to 1, both claims concerning the legality of the evacuation. According to the majority opinion, the disengagement

[92] CA 7703/10 *Yeshuah v. Minhelet Tenufa*; CA 5212/11 *I. S, Ezrah Inc. v. Minhelet Tenufa*; for the district courts' decision see: CC (Jerusalem) 2131/08 *Yeshuah v. Israel*, (05.08.2010). (hereinafter: *Yeshuah*); CA 4550-01-08 *I. S, Ezrah Inc. v. Israel* (23.05.2011), hereinafter: *Ezrah*.

[93] See §1(1) Application of the Disengagement Plan Act (2005).

interfered with the plaintiff's human rights. It interfered with their right to property (their homes), their right to freedom of occupation (most of them were working in the evacuated territory) and their right to dignity.[94]

Nevertheless, the Supreme Court was ready to validate the disengagement and the evacuation as long as the following terms were met: A. compensations were fair and reasonable; B. the disengagement and the evacuation were "proportional"; C. the violation of human rights was consistent with the values upon which the Israeli state was founded; D. the violation was formulated for a proper cause and did not exceed the necessary volume.[95]

9.4.2.3 The Compensation Issue

Concerning the issue of proper compensation, the Supreme Court was much less in favour of the statutory arrangement. It decided that it was disproportionate and unconstitutional.[96] Thus, the evacuees could use any legal tool offered by the Israeli legal system to claim their damages.

9.4.2.4 The Subsequent Tort Claims

This Supreme Court decision (the Supreme Court was sitting here as a High Court of Justice), which opened the doors of tort law for the evacuees to claim their damages exceeding the compensation dictated by the Law of Disengagement, was the trigger of two claims for compensation. These claims were based on the general law of torts. The plaintiffs were former inhabitants of the evacuated territory. They received statutory compensation according to the Act, and yet they argued that they were entitled to additional tortious compensation. Both claims were declined by the district courts.

The District Court's Decision: Recognition of a Very Limited Constitutional Tort

The district court decided that:

1. There was no negligence on the part of the defendants;
2. There was no breach of statutory duty because the tort of breach of statutory duty could not be based on violations of the Basic Law[97];

---

[94] HCJ 1661/05 *Haezorit Hof Aza v. Rosh Hamemshala*, PD 59(2) 481, 560–561 (2005), hereinafter: *Hof Aza*.

[95] These are the conditions set by the Basic Laws.

[96] *Hof Aza*, *supra* note 94, 594, 616–621.

[97] *Yeshuah*, *supra* note 92, §39.

3. The only possible avenue through which liability can be imposed would be by an explicit adoption of the principle of *ubi jus ibi remedium*. According to this principle, the courts would be able to fully protect human rights even if no tort had been committed, and would be able to compensate for all types of violations of human rights even when no negligence or breach of statutory duty had been proved, as was the case in both instances before the courts; [98]
4. This meaningful change in basic legal, economic and social accepted values may seem appropriate in some circumstances, but it might raise serious concerns of over deterrence and unlimited liability, especially in public defendants' cases.

The district court adopted a safe, reasonable, logical and mainstream solution. First, it decided that the right to property should be fully protected and its violation – even a no-fault violation – will normally entail liability. Distributive justice dictates that in cases of property expropriation tort law must follow property law's notions and fill the gap between the statutory damages and the amount of loss proved by the plaintiff. As to the two cases in question, the court noted that this gap was minimal.

The trivial divergence of the actual value of the property in question from the statutory compensation granted by the disengagement law led to the conclusion that the compensation granted by the law was indeed reasonable, fair and proper. Thus, no violation was shown and no constitutional tort was recognised.[99]

The Appeal and the Supreme Court's Decision

Both plaintiffs appealed to the Supreme Court. The State, of course, presented the conservative position opposing recognition of a constitutional tort – even within the limits accepted by the district courts. This position is in line with the accepted position regarding the limited applicability of the basic laws in private law and with the additional common view, which leaves the basic laws outside the reach of the tort of breach of statutory duty. The Supreme Court, in a very short dictum relating to the issue of liability in a no-fault situation of violation of basic human rights, adopted the District Court's decision and declared that in certain limited circumstances in which it is unreasonable to deny compensation, a no-fault claim might be applied. It still remains to be seen how this potentially revolutionary decision will be applied by the Supreme Court in future controversial circumstances.

9.5 Concluding Remarks

The arsenal of legal tools offered by Israeli legal systems for protection of human rights is impressive. Compensation can be achieved through various causes of action, and the Israeli courts are very plaintiff friendly when it comes to claims

---

[98] id., §60–64.

[99] id., §61–80; *Ezrah, supra* note 92, §22–25.

against the state and other public defendants. The last decision of the Supreme Court is certainly in line with the overall trend of imposing tortious liability – mostly in negligence – in cases of human rights violations, which in other legal systems would have entailed different conclusions.

References

Barak-Erez, Daphne, and Israel Gilead. 2009. Human rights in tort and contract law: The silent revolution. *Kiryat Hamishpat* 8: 11–37.

Barak-Erez, Daphne, and Israel Gilead. 2007. Human rights in private law: The Israeli Case. In *Human rights and the private sphere – A comparative study*, eds. Dawn Oliver and Jorg Fedtke, 252–275. New York: Routledge-Cavendish.

Blackstone, William. 1765. *Commentaries on the laws of England*. Oxford: Clarendon.

Cheshin, Mishael. 1968. Tort law and the law of the fathers. *Mishpatim* 1: 346–371.

English, Rosalind. 2014. Does the EU Rights Charter apply to private disputes? UK human rights blog. ukhumanrightsblog.com/2014/01/22/does-the-eu-rights-charter-apply-to-private-disputes-sometimes-sometimes-not. Accessed 4 Mar 2015.

Gidron, Tamar. 2008. Between Bank's Neglagence (UK) and The State's Negligence (Israel): Pure economic damage in light of new ajudification – Analysis and evaluation in a comparative perspective. *Hapraklit* 50: 95–185.

Gidron, Tamar. 2012. The state, public bodies, and public officials in negligence – A slippery sloap. *Hapraklit* 51: 443–512.

Gidron, Tamar and Roi Iluz. 2013. Breach of statutory duty. In *Sefer Or*, eds. Aharon Barak, Ron Sokol, and Oded Shaham, 141–201. Nevo.

Gilead, Israel, and Ehud Guttel. 2004. On broadening tort liability in the causation dimension – A critical analysis. *Mishpatim* 34: 385–441.

Lewinsohn-Zamir, Daphna, and Ada Bar-Shira. 1989. Breach of statutory duty. In *The law of civil wrongs – The particular torts*, ed. Tedeschi Gad, 1–96. Jerusalem: The Harry and Michael Sacher Institute for Legislative Research and Comparative Law.

Loubser, Max, and Tamar Gidron. 2011. Liability of the state and public authorities in Israel and South Africa. *Loyola Law Review* 57: 727–780.

Palmer, Vernon. 2012. *Mixed jurisdictions worldwide: The third legal family*. Cambridge: Cambridge University Press.

Tadeschi, Gad, Aharon Barak, and Mishael Cheshin. 1977. *The law of civil wrongs: General part*, ed. Gad Tedeschi, 2nd ed. Magnes.

Zandberg, Haya. 1994. Tort claims against the executive authority – The pendulum movement. *Hapraklit* 52: 591–627.

Chapter 10
Looking Back in Anger and Forward in Trust: The Complicate Patchwork of the Damages Regime for Infringements of Rights in Italy

Graziella Romeo

10.1 Introductory Remarks: Three Issues Surrounding the Regime Governing Human Rights Infringements in Italy

The issue of damages for human rights infringements in Italy needs to be addressed from a threefold perspective. Firstly, it should be pointed out that the regime applicable to violations of *constitutional* rights differs from the rules on "State liability", which primarily concern *human* rights violations. Secondly, it should be stressed that there is nothing like a general system of rules prescribing compensation in cases involving human rights violations, with the sole exception of violations perpetrated by the fascist regime. Finally, focusing for a moment on a rough synthesis of a far more problematic issue, it should be highlighted that the damages regime for infringements of human rights has been ambiguously influenced by international[1] and supranational law.[2] Indeed, international courts contributed to the matter either in the direction of adding grounds for compensation for damages occurred in

[1] International obligations result in different consequences under Italian domestic law, depending both on the type of international legal order that established them and the binding status of the relevant rules. Human rights enshrined in supranational legal instruments, such as the European Convention on Human Rights (hereinafter: ECHR), that are the "outcome" of integrated legal systems deserve a more intensive and, from the State's point of view, "intrusive" protection compared to those stemming from other international charters. In other words, rules prescribing compensation for human rights violations are more likely to result from an integrated international legal order than from the international community as normally understood. On the notion of integrated legal order see McCormick (1993) 17.

[2] For the purposes of this study, the word "supranational" is used to identify legal systems that are characterised by high level of integration among their Member States, even though they result purely from international agreements. Indeed integration implies that these legal orders create

G. Romeo (✉)
Department of Legal Studies, Bocconi University, Milan, Italy
e-mail: graziella.romeo@unibocconi.it

E. Bagińska (ed.), *Damages for Violations of Human Rights*,
Ius Comparatum - Global Studies in Comparative Law 9,
DOI 10.1007/978-3-319-18950-5_10

specific circumstances or in the direction of limiting State's responsibility under customary law.

The three aforementioned issues describe the general features of the regime on the award of damages for human rights violations in Italy; at the same time, each of them defines peculiar features of the Italian "model", which in some sense have a disparate impact on the overall regime.

This chapter looks at the regime applicable to human rights violations through the lenses of those three issues, which provide the *fils rouge* for the present study. Consequently, the essay will be organised as follows: Section 10.2 will analyse the differences between the liability regime applicable in cases involving violations of constitutional rights and State liability in cases involving human rights violations. Section 10.3 will focus on compensation for historical injustices, examining separately the payment for infringements occurred during the fascist regime (Sect. 10.3.1) and the judicial compensation for the (other) violations of human rights included in the so-called international *jus cogens* (Sects. 10.3.2 and 10.3.3). Section 10.4 will address the interplay between principles of domestic jurisdiction and international human rights law. Finally, Sect. 10.5 will draw some conclusions regarding the general liability regime in Italy, arguing for the need to provide for more effective redresses for violations of human rights.

10.2 The Liability Regime in Cases Involving Infringements of Rights

The regime for infringement of rights consists of different sets of rules, whose applicability is determined by the kind of right that has been allegedly violated. With a view to summarising the composite framework, one can distinguish two categories of rights and four different types of remedy available in cases of infringement. Indeed, it must be underlined that the category of constitutional rights, that is rights expressly enshrined in the Constitution, falls within a specific discipline set forth in Art. 28 of the Italian Constitution for infringements committed by the State or its public officials and agents. On the contrary, a separate regime is applicable to human rights[3] violations perpetrated either by the State or by foreign countries towards Italian citizens. This set of rules does not create a comprehensive framework for violations of human rights. It simply provides for remedy in very specific cases.

norms that are more effectively legally enforceable than "ordinary" international norms. See Gerards (2008) 407.

[3] For the purpose of this study, human rights are defined as rights that are enjoyed by all individuals subject to a State's jurisdiction, as also protected by international legal tools: see Feldman (2002). Human rights therefore present themselves as absolute subjective claims that are valid per se and irrespective of their statutory recognition within states: see Zagrebelsky (1992).

Moreover, the two regimes are unconnected, in the sense that they refer to different kind of violations. The first one entails infringements perpetrated by State officials and agents, but it leaves out of its scope those violations that are not specifically imputable to a single person. The second one pertains to violations that do not result purely from the exercise of administrative power, but more broadly from acts that can be described as political or that even imply the use of force (so-called *acta iure imperii*).

The two systems works independently and once a given right, being at the same time both a constitutional and a human claim (such as the right to life), is violated it is the kind of violation that controls the applicable rule.

10.2.1 Infringements of Rights and Infringements of Constitutional Rights

As far as liability for violations of rights and/or constitutional rights, Art. 28 of the Italian Constitution lays down the general provisions on the responsibility of public authorities, prescribing that: "Officials of the State or public agencies shall be directly responsible under criminal, civil, and administrative law for acts committed in violation of rights". Furthermore, the constitutional provision specifies that civil liability extends to the State as well as to the specific public agencies in such cases.

Art. 28, which is probably one of the less explored provisions of the Italian Constitution, defines the four main features of the liability regime, which may be inferred from a literal interpretation of the constitutional provision. The first is that the State and public agents are *directly* responsible for violation of rights. The second concerns the type of rights the violation of which implies a form of liability for the State and/or public agents. From this perspective, it should be pointed out that the provision is construed to refer essentially to the rights of individuals enshrined in the Constitution. The third characteristic of the general liability regime is that detailed rules on criminal, civil and administrative accountability need to be established by means of ordinary legislation. Finally, the fourth element is that public officials and the State are jointly liable for infringements of rights.[4]

Constitutional scholars do indeed establish a link between State liability and that of public officials for the violation of constitutional rights and the democratic principle, which does not tolerate any exemption from liability for those who are in charge of public functions of any kind.[5]

This kind of liability does not cover all possible violations of rights. It does not apply to infringements resulting from the exercise of legislative authority.[6]

[4] See Merusi and Clarich (1991) 362.

[5] See Colzi (1950) 247.

[6] See Cerbo (2009) 1363.

Parliamentary privilege prevents the application of Art. 28 of the Constitution and, consequently, of any laws seeking to establish liability of MPs for votes cast.[7]

Even though the provision clearly asserts the liability of public officials and the State, the traditional and prevailing interpretation among Italian scholars was that Art. 28 encompassed a tautological expression.[8] In other words, legal doctrine (especially administrative law scholars) attached a kind of "minimal meaning" to the provision, which was generally believed to be incapable of asserting anything more than a restatement of the accountability regime established under all ordinary legislation directly addressing specific instances of liability on the part of public authorities. Furthermore, Art. 28 was construed as a constitutional mandate to Parliament to enforce constitutional rights by essentially strengthening the provisions of the criminal law that punish illegal conduct by public officials.

Constitutional law scholars tend to construe the provision in a different way.[9] They favour an interpretation of Art. 28, read in conjunction with Art. 2, which in turn prescribes that "the Republic recognises and guarantees the inviolable rights of the person, both as an individual and in the social groups where human personality is expressed". In other words, the State liability and that of officials safeguards the inviolability of the rights protected by the Constitution against government action. In light of this assumption, Art. 28 is linked to the classical theory of liberal constitutionalism that interprets the proclamation of rights as a reaction against executive action that is intended to infringe upon them.[10] The main consequence of this thesis is that Art. 28 prevents Parliament from excluding or excessively restricting State liability or that of public officials, even in limited circumstances.

However, until the recent rethinking of the position by the courts, "Constitutional torts"[11] were not considered either within contemporary constitutional theory, which has largely stood aloof of the issue, or in constitutional litigation.[12] There are at least two reasons for this. The first is related to the features of Italian system of constitutional adjudication: since there is no direct right of appeal to the Constitutional Court, this generally prevents the initiation of proceedings in which the potential violation of constitutional rights by public authorities is directly addressed.[13] The second reason is that specific statutes have been enacted to regulate the liability of public officials, which do not constitute a coherent system of regulation, with some falling entirely under criminal law and others, in limited cases, under administrative law.

---

[7] See Arts. 68 and 122 of the Italian Constitution.

[8] See Merusi and Clarich (1991) 356.

[9] See Grossi (1972) 176.

[10] According to the liberty/authority dialectic: see Barbera (2007) 4 ff. See also Peces-Barba Martinez (1993).

[11] See Cooper Stephenson (2003) 4.

[12] See Merusi and Clarich (1991) 393.

[13] Constitutional adjudication in Italy involves the scrutiny of legislative acts and the conflicts between powers or between the State and the Regions or between Regions (see Art. 134, Italian Const.); as far as the constitutional review of legislation is concerned, in the event that a declaration of unconstitutionality is issued, Parliament is not legally responsible.

Against this backdrop, the administrative courts sanctioned violations of rights committed by public authorities in the exercise of their powers, whilst the ordinary judges were responsible for assessing damages for infringements of rights. In other words, the system was organised into a sort of "two-stage" scheme[14]: the violation was recognised by Administrative courts, which could at most annul the act that perpetrated the violation, whilst the award of damages was an exclusive matter for the civil courts.

This situation changed dramatically in 1999 when the Court of Cassation handed down a pivotal decision on the issue of damages awards in cases involving infringements of rights. In judgment no. 500 of 1999[15] the Supreme Court clarified that an individual may bring a claim for compensation for the violation of rights and legitimate interests even if he has not previously filed an action seeking the annulment of the act by the public authority that violated the individual's right. The Court identified the three main features of the regime: (a) the existence of damage (of either tangible or intangible nature), which must be alleged; (b) the actual infringement of a legally relevant interest, which can take the form of a subjective right or a legitimate interest; (c) negligence on the part of the public officials, whose conduct breached principles of impartiality and fairness. Finally, the Court held that it was not possible to state in absolute terms the full range of protected interests; on the contrary, the ordinary judges should decide on a case-by-case basis and award compensation according to equity considerations.

This approach was later affirmed in decision no. 157 of 2003,[16] in which the court reiterated the fact that an award of compensation does not require the annulment by the administrative courts of the public authority's act that encroached upon rights or protected interests.

From a theoretical point of view, the justification may be found in the notion that civil liability is inherent in the principle of the rule of law. In other words, the exercise of power implies that it should be possible to challenge it, to annul administrative acts and, if appropriate, to award damages.

The doctrine benefits from a broad interpretation[17] of Art. 2043 of the Italian Civil Code. Originally intended as a provision applicable to actions for pecuniary damages, the Art. has been construed more broadly by the Constitutional Court. It has been interpreted as providing the legal basis (*inter alia*) for actions seeking non-pecuniary damages, provided that the infringements "possibly prevent those acts through which an individual realises himself".[18] This approach is coherent with the doctrine of the effectiveness of constitutional rights,[19] which implies that the State should take any measure needed in order to guarantee the actual exercise of

[14] See Lanzi (2005) 2773 and 2775.

[15] Court of cassation, dec. no. 500, of 22.7.2000, available in *Foro italiano*, 1999, I, 2487 ff.

[16] Court of Cassation, dec. no. 157 of 10.10.2003, available in *Foro italiano*, 2003, I, 78 ff.

[17] See Abbamonte (2000) 743 ff.

[18] See Constitutional Court, dec. no. 184 of 1986. See Ponzanelli (1986) 2053 ff. and Abbamonte (2000) 760 ff.

[19] See Silvestri (2009) 10–11.

those rights. Indeed the reference to self-realisation recalls the Arts. 2 and 3 of the Italian Constitution in which both the recognition of the "inviolable rights of the human being" and the fulfilment of the principle of equality are directly linked to the development of the person both as individual and as a member of a social and political community.

In order to be consistent with this construction, the Court of cassation seems to apply specific criteria when the potential violation of constitutionally recognised rights is concerned. Indeed, in decision no. 7713 of 2000, the Court apparently distinguished between infringements of constitutional rights and infringements of *other* rights, arguing that in the former case damages should be recognised irrespective of the actual existence of pecuniary consequences of the violation. Furthermore, with a view to affording special consideration to the violations of constitutional rights, the Court specified that the claimant should not bear the burden of proof.[20]

10.2.2 Infringements of Human Rights

As previously touched on in the introduction, there is no general regime specifically regulating compensation for human rights violations committed by the State and its officials or agents in Italy.[21] However, the development of international law and particularly of supranational legal orders such as the EU and the Council of Europe strongly influenced domestic law as far as the enforcement of internationally recognised rights is concerned. Since when those two systems have been integrated with domestic legal orders, the problem of guaranteeing the effectiveness of treaty provisions have been perceived as an issue of enforcement of legal norms through some kind of sanction. Both the EU and the Council of Europe indeed pushed towards a more effective protection of those rights enshrined under the respective normative parameters through the provision of compensation for infringements of rights.

This kind of sanction originally intended as a violation of an international obligation with internationally prescribed sanction has been progressively transformed under domestic law in a kind of State responsibility arising under specific

---

[20] See Court of Cassation, dec. no. 7713 of 6.6.2000. Legal scholars criticised the criteria developed by the Supreme Court. They seem to favour a different doctrine, which identifies the rights that merit protection *inter alia* through compensation on the basis of their content and on the type of violation committed, rather than on the basis of their mere classification as "constitutional rights". On this point see the arguments offered by Principato (2001) 4176 ff. From this perspective only "personal rights" exempt the claimant from the burden of proof. Personal rights are rights that are not absolute, not amenable to pecuniary assessment, and not susceptible of disposal, transferral or prescription: see Messineo (1957) 142.

[21] However the existence of the ECtHR, which is charged with the scrutiny of violations of such rights and decisions of which apply within domestic jurisdiction, provides for an alternative instrument, at least in some cases. See *infra* 10. 4.

circumstances.[22] As a result there are three different types of compensation for infringements of rights: the first is the case of responsibility deriving from the exercise of judicial functions (L. no. 89 of 2001); the second is the responsibility arising from the inhuman conditions of the detention; finally, the third is the State responsibility for omitted enforcement of EU directives.[23] The latter is only partially relevant in the realm of human rights violations as it covers a wide range of cases not likely concerning human rights. For this reason, it is preferable to concentrate the analysis on the formers.

Indeed due to the large number of European Court of Human Rights' (hereinafter: ECtHR) decisions condemning Italy for the violation of both the right to a fair trial (Art. 6, European Convention on Human Rights, hereinafter: ECHR) and the right not to be subjected to inhuman or degrading treatment or punishment (Art. 3, ECHR), Parliament was brought to adopt appropriate measures to regulate the cases involving compensation for the violation of (at least some) human rights.

The legal basis for State liability for the violation of ECHR was initially found in Art. 2043 of the Civil Code, i.e. the provision on liability under tort. The thesis, which was supported by ordinary courts,[24] was based on upon Art. 2043, Civil Code and Art. 5(5) ECHR, which expressly provides that "everyone who has been the victim of arrest or detention in contravention of the provisions of this article shall have an enforceable right to compensation". The Court of Cassation eventually reversed this interpretation in 1992, arguing that the ECHR could not be construed as self-executing source of law under domestic law.[25]

Almost ten years later, the Italian Parliament finally decided to enact Law no. 89 of 24 March 2001, known as the "Pinto Act",[26] which laid down the first complete legislative framework that covers just compensations in case of violation of rights protected in the ECHR. Nevertheless, the Law addresses only the rights to trial in a reasonable time (Art. 6 ECHR).

In the broader framework of a trend towards a rethinking of the relationship between domestic and international law,[27] in 2005 the Court of Cassation held that the violation of the rights enshrined in the ECHR has immediate relevance within the domestic legal order.[28] In other words, the *Pinto Act* asserts a legal position (the right to compensation) which was already recognised under domestic law. The

[22] This process has something do to with the *constitutionalization* of international law: see Cohen (2012) XVff.; Jarmul (1996) 334 and Nardin (1987) 416.

[23] Pursuing to the well known *Francovic* case, ECJ, dec. 19.11.1991, C-6/90 e C-9/90.

[24] Court of Rome, *Mustacchia v. Ministero di grazia e giustizia*, dec. of 7.8.1984, *Temi Romana*, 1985, 977. See Francioni (1997) 16 ff.

[25] See dec. of 27.5.1992, in Rivista internazionale dei diritti dell'uomo, 1992, 1151 ff. See also Vezzani (2010) 1148 ff.

[26] See Izar (2002) 957 ff.

[27] Which was eventually completed by the Italian Constitutional Court: see Ruggeri (2008) 217.

[28] See dec. no. 28507 of 23.12.2005; on this issue Vezzani (2010) 1149.

legislation was then designed to guarantee an effective and immediately applicable restoration of the infringement of Art. 6 ECHR.[29]

In other words, even though Italian judges did have interpretative instruments to immediately enforce the ECHR provisions, the enactment of Law no. 89 of 2001 was perceived to be required in order to align the domestic system to the ECHR. The *problem italien*[30] pushed the national Parliament to enact legislation designed to offer a domestic remedy for those alleging the infringement of the right to a trial within a reasonable time.

The law covers both pecuniary and non-pecuniary damages caused by the violation of the right enshrined in Art. 6 ECHR.[31] Art. 2-bis of Law no. 89 of 2001 stipulates the minimum as well as the maximum amount of the compensation,[32] hence circumscribing the discretion of the courts.[33] Compensation covers both actual damage and loss of profit, according to the ordinary liability regime for compensation laid down by Art. 1223 of the Civil Code.[34] The Law also sets out the criteria that must be followed in order to calculate the amount of the compensation. More precisely, Art. 2-bis(2) specifies that the judge must consider: (a) the final outcome of the trial in which the violation occurred; (b) the conduct of the judge and the parties; (c) the type of interests involved in the case; and (d) the value and the relevance of the dispute in relation to the personal situation of the claimant. By contrast, the principle of foreseeability does not apply, according to a constant interpretation of Italian tort liability regime.[35]

As regards the type of damages for which compensation may be recognised, the case law does not regard non-pecuniary damages as mandatory elements of the amount of the indemnity. On the contrary, the claimant must expressly assert that such damages occurred as consequence of the undue delay to the judicial procedure.

---

[29] See Court of Cassation, dec. no. 15746 of 11.7.2006 and no. 16284 of 10.7.2009.

[30] See Fabri (2009) 10 ff. See also Angelini (2010) 89 ff. spec. 97 and Corongiu (2001) 1003 ff.

[31] As far as the matter of jurisdiction is concerned, the Law specifies that the complaint must be addressed to the president of the court of appeal responsible for deciding on judicial liability within the district in which the case alleged to constitute violation was settled: see Art. 4(1), which refers to Art. 11 of the Code of Criminal Procedure. One of the most controversial issues, which lies partially beyond the scope of this study, is the classification of the "process", the excessive duration of which caused the harm: see Focarelli (2005) 5163 ff.

[32] In any case, Art. 3 stipulates that the amounts shall be liquidated insofar as possible taking account of actually available resources. Indeed, with a view to granting effective compensation but also safeguarding public resources, Art. 5-quinquies lays down specific rules on foreclosures and seizures of public goods. On the uncertainties and difficulties of the law enforcement, see Sanna (2011) 160 ff.

[33] The minimum amount is 500 euros, while the maximum is 1500 euros. In both cases, the amounts are compensated for each year or part thereof (subject to a minimum of 6 months) in excess of the reasonable duration of the trial concerned. Initially, the Law provided that non-pecuniary losses should be compensated also through "appropriate forms of publicity of the decision holding that a violation has occurred": see Art. 2(3). The provision was eventually repealed by Art. 55(1)(a)(3) of Decree-Law no. 83 of 22.6.2012, converted into Law no. 134 of 7.8.2012.

[34] While punitive damages are normally not awarded to the successful claimant.

[35] See Court of Cassation, judgment no. 6725 of 2005.

However, the courts do not require claimants to explain in detail any suffering experienced or their individual personal circumstances.[36]

The majority opinion in both legal scholarship and case law is that non-pecuniary damages are excluded when the delay in the trial *de facto* causes beneficial consequences for the claimant.[37]

Moreover, there is a statutory limitation to the awarding of damages which directly concerns the claimant: no compensation is awarded to claimants who have acted in bad faith or with a view to deliberately delaying the procedure in which they were involved.[38]

The Law was substantially amended in 2012,[39] with a view to revising the rights and duties of the claimant.[40] In particular, he now bears the burden of proof, that is he is required to allege all documents showing both the development of the trial and his specific procedural position.

It has been pointed out in the literature that the new requirement on the responsibility for filing evidence, combined with the rule on bad faith, requires the petitioner to demonstrate specifically that he was the *victim* of an unreasonably long trial.[41]

According to the prevailing interpretation, the compensation required under the *Pinto Act* should be regarded as an indemnity, rather than a restoration,[42] as it is a statutory obligation. In other words, the duty to compensate damages results direct from the law rather than from an actual offence. This kind of interpretation has consequences for the quantification of fair compensation.

Italian scholars generally criticise Law no. 89 of 2001 on the grounds that it is not implemented in full as regards the award of damages. The reason may be found in the inconsistency between the domestic courts and the ECtHR's position on both the amount of the compensation and also on the type of violation which the remedy is supposed to cover.[43] Indeed, as far as the calculation of the indemnity is concerned, until 2012 the Italian courts insisted in considering only the length of time in excess of the reasonable duration of the trial, rather the overall period in which judgment was pending. The amendments to the *Pinto Act* expressly stipulate that any trial not resolved within six years shall be considered to be unreasonably long.[44]

---

[36] See Court of Cassation, judgment no. 1999 of 14.10.2005.

[37] Court of Cassation, judgment no. 8716 of 13.4.2006. See Azzalini (2012) 1707B.

[38] See Art. 2-quinques(a)-(f). Moreover the Act extends to heirs who have standing to sue in order to claim damages for the violation of the right to a trial in a reasonable time suffered by a deceased relative.

[39] See Decree-Law no. 83 of 22.6.2012, converted into Law no. 134 of 7.8.2012.

[40] See Azzalini (2012) 1702 ff.

[41] See Azzalini (2012) 1707.

[42] See Chindemi (2008) 690 ff.

[43] See Azzalini (2012) 1707B.

[44] The Law provides that the court hearing the civil proceedings seeking compensation shall consider the specific circumstances of the case as well as the complexity of the legal issues to be decided: see Art. 1.

As will be explored in greater detail below,[45] notwithstanding its efforts to afford restoration of damages for human rights violations, Law no. 89 of 2001 encounters a series of problems within its concrete implementation.

10.2.3 The Case of Compensation for Inhuman Condition of Detention

The Parliament enacted another piece of legislation in order to address the violations of Art. 3, ECHR and comply with the Court of Strasburg's decisions. Law no. 117 of August 11 2014 specifically concerns the cases of detainees suffering from inhuman or degrading conditions of detention. The compensation provided for is not of a pecuniary kind at a first step. Detainees who suffered from an inhuman imprisonment that has been continued for at least fifteen days have the right to claim the cutback of their conviction, which will be equal to one day per every ten days of impairment they have experienced.[46] Only in those cases in which the remaining time of the punishment is not sufficient to cover the compensation, the law prescribes the restoration of the damages,[47] according to a prefixed amount calculated on a day basis.[48]

Some scholars argued that this measure, awarding compensation irrespective of the assessment of State's responsibility, arises constitutional issues as for the compliance with Art. 28, which would require at least the evaluation of the actual negligence.[49] In other words, behind the enactment of Law no. 117 of 2014 there have apparently been political drives which have something to do with the inability of the Italian Parliament to deal with the issue of overcrowded prisons, which would entail the long-awaited reform of the penitentiary policy.

10.3 Compensation for Historical Injustices

Whilst the regime of State liability for human rights violations is a recent acquisition, somehow necessitated by international obligations (the ECHR), the statutory right to compensation for historical injustices has a peculiar history within the Italian legal system.

---

[45] See Sects. 10.4 and 10.5.

[46] See Art. 35 ter, L. no. 354 of 1975 as amended by Art. 1, l. no. 117 of 2014, in O.G. 20.8.2014, n. 192.

[47] Thus pushing commentators to qualify this measure as part of the compensation regime: see Gori (2014) 1.

[48] The law prescribes that the judge shall award eight euros for each day of impairment suffered by the detainee.

[49] See *supra* 10.2.1.

After the Second World War, the newly-born Italian Republic faced the difficult task of restoring a society that has been violated by the atrocities of the global conflict. The solution was found during a constituent period in which the dictatorial regime was rejected and specific constitutional provisions enacted in order to prevent possible authoritarian tendencies.[50] The repudiation of the fascism (and the restoration of the democratic order) was completed by a series of statutes, which were expressly designed to make good the human rights violations committed by the authoritarian regime.[51] In other words, statutory remedies were primarily intended to restore the integrity of human society, which had been destroyed by the injustices of Fascism and the subsequent atrocities of the world war.

10.3.1 Compensation for the Racial Laws Enacted by the Fascist Regime

The first piece of legislation concerning compensation for historical injustices was Law n. 96 of 10 March 1955 (so called "Terracini Law"), which provides for compensation[52] for Italian citizens who had been victims of persecution due to their political activities in opposition to the Fascist regime and who had become unable to work.[53] Art. 2 recognises the same form of compensation to the heirs of the victims of racial and political persecution. The law expressly classifies victims as those who died during detention or banishment, unless and until proven otherwise, i.e. until it has been proved death was caused by unrelated circumstances. The amount of compensation is calculated according to requirements and criteria laid down by the Law, as amended over time.[54]

In other cases, and specifically where the violation was committed by occupying troops during the Second World War, Parliament amended the legislation on pensions, mainly in the 1960s and 1970s, in order to provide for specific measures

---

[50] The summary is, to some extent, approximate. The constituent phase was indeed more problematic and has its own unclear points as regards the full and effective rejection of the authoritarian regime. Some of the constitutional provisions remained unenforced for a long time; at the same time, many of the statutory provisions of codes and laws approved during the Fascist period remained in force until their progressive demolition by the Italian Constitutional Court. On this issue see Paladin (1997) 102 ff. and Mortati (1931). See also Bognetti (1982) 435 ff.

[51] See Speciale (2012) 115 and Falconieri (2012) 139 ff.

[52] A series of provisions concerning pensions for the surviving victims of Fascism: see Arts. 4–7 of Law no. 96 of 1955. In the aftermath of the Second World War and before the *Terracini Law* was passed, the transitional government issued a series of decrees repealing all of the decrees and laws that had previously been directed at and discriminated against the Jewish population. Furthermore, the new measures fully restored the civil, political and economic rights of Jewish citizens: see Royal Decree-Laws no. 24 of 1944 and no. 26 of 1944. On this point see Falconieri (2012) 139.

[53] See Art. 1 of Law no. 96 of 1955.

[54] See Art. 6 of Law no. 12 of 25.1.1962.

addressing the requirements of survivors and victims.[55] Those measures require survivors to show that they were still suffering a disease at the time when they applied for a pension.

The theoretical framework surrounding both the *Terracini Law* and the measures related to other kinds of human rights violations committed during the Fascist period was based on the notion that compensation should be linked to the pension system and, as far as the quantification of the amount was concerned, related to the loss of capacity for work.

The Constitutional Court expressly rejected this theory in 1987 when it ruled unconstitutional a provision of the compensation regime[56] that linked the recognition of a certain benefit exclusively to pecuniary harm suffered by the victims of violations.[57]

Although Law no. 96 of 1955 was the first piece of legislation to specifically address the situation of the victims of Fascist persecution, it left open the question of the scope of the compensation regime, that is the categories of victims that were entitled to claim compensation as well as the type of compensation. The *Terracini Law* was in fact primarily dedicated to the victims of political prosecution, and was later extended to those who had fallen victim to racial hatred.

In an effort to introduce greater efficiency into the mechanism of compensation for historical injustices, the case law of the Court of Auditors (*Corte dei Conti*) clarified that as far as Jewish citizens were concerned, there were two classes of victims. The first group included all the Jewish citizens, insofar as racial laws passed in the 1930s and 1940s generically addressed them; the second group comprised those Jewish citizens who had suffered specific and concrete harm during Fascism. While the latter group of people needed to demonstrate the harm they experienced as a result of racial persecution, the former are entitled to benefits *ex lege*, i.e. Jewish citizens are entitled due to the "mere fact" of being Jewish under the Fascist dictatorship.[58]

The distinction between the two categories is based on the theory that conceives of compensation as the consequence of two different kinds of harm: moral harm (*danni morali*) and moral detriment (*pregiudizi morali*). The formers result from conduct that specifically hurt someone, whilst the latters relate to the *generic* limitations and restrictions imposed by racial legislation, which applied to Jewish citizens as a whole.[59]

---

[55] This was the case for the so-called "marocchinate", that is the gross violation of human rights perpetrated by Moroccan-French troops in central Italy in May 1944. See Speciale (2012) 117.

[56] See Arts. 10(1) and 22 of Law no. 648 of 10.8.1950; Arts. 9(1) and 11 of Law no. 313 of 18.3.1968; Arts. 1, 8(1), 11 and 83 of Presidential Decree no. 915 of 28.12.1978.

[57] See Constitutional Court, dec. no. 561 of 18.12.1987.

[58] Art. 1 of Law no. 17 of 16.1.1978 specifies that the word "Jewish" written down on the registry office certificate shall be held as proof of moral damages.

[59] See Court of Auditors, 1st Division, judgment of 27.1.2003, central appellate instance and of 11.11.2002, central appellate instance.

However, this judicial trend is fluctuating in the sense that it does not appear to be able to provide completely satisfactory answers to some of the fundamental questions relating to the recognition of compensation for historical violations of human rights committed by States and public officials, including the kind of remedy victims are entitled to, apart from the provisions of statutory compensation mostly linked to pensions and, more broadly, to the welfare system.

10.3.2 The Germany v. Italy Saga

The situation is slightly different for human rights violations committed by foreign countries against Italian citizens.

In fact, the Court of Cassation (*Corte di Cassazione*) developed remarkable case law regarding the violations of rights perpetrated by the Nazi regime. The judicial trend was inaugurated by the decision in the *Ferrini* case.[60] The dispute was initiated by a complaint made by an Italian citizen who alleged that he had been deported to Germany in 1944 and later held in forced labour. Specifically, Mr Ferrini sued the Federal Republic of Germany, claiming damages for infringements of his right to liberty and alleging that German military forces had captured him in August 1944, deported him and then forced him to work for a German company.

The Supreme Court held that such conduct involved serious violations of human rights and found Germany to be responsible for such violations, even though the theory of acts performed *iure imperii* prevented the application of States civil liability. In the court's opinion, the specific actions performed by German military forces constituted systematic infringements of rights, which took *inter alia* the form of slavery. In cases involving serious violations of human rights, the State cannot claim immunity from jurisdiction in order to avoid paying compensation to victims.

After the *Ferrini* judgment, the Court handed down another decision which was based on similar grounds. In the *Mantelli* case,[61] the Court was asked to issue an interlocutory regarding the jurisdiction of the Italian courts over claims for compensation for human rights violations committed in Italy by the Nazi military forces between 1943 and 1945. The Court of Cassation upheld the jurisdiction of the Italian courts to hear the compensation claim for three reasons: a. the mere fact that the unlawful conduct took place in Italy; b. the fact that jurisdiction was not barred either by the Treaty Peace of 1947 or by the Bilateral Treaty of 1961; c. there was no inderogable principle of customary international law asserting State immunity from civil actions.

As far as the treaties are concerned, the judges specified that the two agreements only related to substantive rights, that is whether the right to compensation existed

---

[60] See Court of Cassation, Joint Divisions, *Ferrini v. Germany*, dec. no. 5044 of 11.3.2004, available in *Rivista di diritto internazionale*, 2004, 539 ff.

[61] See Court of Cassation, Joint Divisions, *Mantelli v. Germany*, dec. no. 14201 of 29.5.2008. See Gaeta (2011) 305 ff. See also De Vittor (2008) 632 ff. and Persano (2008) 2259 ff.

or not; consequently they did not cover the issue of the jurisdiction, much less the exclusion of the jurisdiction of the Italian courts.

As regards the existence of principles of customary international law that prevented the instauration of civil actions, the Supreme Court held that serious violations of fundamental rights as well as infringements of peremptory norms (the so called *ius cogens*) must be interpreted as a derogation from the principle of State immunity. Furthermore, the supreme judges maintained that the case law of the European Court of Human Rights (ECtHR)[62] shows the emergence of a customary rule denying immunity when the respondent State is accused of crimes against humanity.[63]

Similar cases arose within criminal proceedings in 2009.[64] Once again the Supreme Court held that the German armed forces were liable for crimes against humanity committed during the occupation, maintaining that the principle of State immunity does not apply to cases involving gross violations of human rights. Although, the Italian court acknowledged both the existence of the principle of State immunity and the incomplete consensus over the rule excluding immunity in cases involving crimes against humanity, they argued that the rulings against Germany will contribute to the formation of customary international law affirming the non-operability of State immunity at least in cases involving gross violations of human rights.

After the series of verdicts, handed down between 2004 and 2011, Germany brought a suit against Italy before the International Court of Justice (ICJ), alleging the violation of the principle of State immunity, which cannot be subject to derogations even in cases involving crimes against humanity.[65] The Italian Court of Cassation is alleged to have denied systematically the jurisdictional immunity the Federal Republic of Germany enjoyed under international law, holding it liable under civil law for infringements of human rights and enforcing the judgments of foreign courts that had found Germany liable for similar actions,[66] and finally adopting measures of enforcement against Germany's properties situated in Italy.

---

[62] See *Al-Adsani v. United Kingdom*, App. no. 35763/97, 21.11.2001 (joint dissenting opinion of judges: Rozakis, Caflish, Wildhaber, Costa, Cabral Barreto, Vajić, par. 3) and *Kalogeropoulou and ors. v. Greece and Germany*, App. no. 59021/00, 12.12.2002.

[63] This conclusion is highly arguable: indeed Italian international scholars have argued that the Supreme Court used the general categories of crimes against humanity, serious violations of human rights and international individual crimes in an inconsistent and not entirely appropriate manner: see Pisillo Mazzeschi (2012) 310 ff.

[64] The case arose in relation to the massacre committed at Civitella, Cornia and S. Pancrazio on 26.6.1944. The massacre caused the death of 203 civilians and was committed by the German armed forces as a reprisal for the murder of 4 German soldiers. See Frulli (2009) 442 ff.

[65] This seems to be the position of the majority of international law scholars: see *ex multis* Zimmerman (1995) 438 ff. and Brömer (1997) 195 ff. Among Italian scholars see Marongiu Buonaiuti (2011) 236 ff. Furthermore, the derogation from the principle of State immunity was substantially undisputed in the 1930s and 1940s: see Verdross (1937) 571 ff. and Lauterpacht (1937) 306 ff.

[66] See for example Court of Cassation, *Repubblica federale di Germania c. Amministrazione regionale della Vojotia*, dec. no. 14199 of 29.5.2008, in *Rivista di diritto internazionale*, 2009, 594 ff. On this issue see Gavouneli (1997) 595 ff. and Bordoni (2009) 496 ff.

The ICJ finally settled the dispute in 2012 with its pivotal ruling in *Germany v. Italy*.[67] The international tribunal had to clarify whether the Italian courts were obliged to grant Germany immunity from civil liability in proceedings regarding claims for compensation arising out of violation of human rights. In order to assess the case, the international judges considered the existence of "international custom, as evidence of a general practice accepted as law" conferring immunity on States and analysed the scope and extent of that immunity.

The ICJ set out its reasoning in detail. First of all, the Court pointed out that the "tort exception", that is the rule excluding State immunity in relation to civil proceedings for acts occasioning death, does not apply to the so called *acta iure imperii*,[68] which constitute the exercise of pure sovereign powers. The judges then considered whether the seriousness of the human rights violations committed by the German armed forces required the exclusion of State immunity, notwithstanding the nature (*iure imperii*) of the actions carried out. In order to reach a conclusion, the Court examined the current status of development of international customary law, finding that State practice, in the form of judicial decisions as well as national legislation, shows that the gravity of violations does not affect the applicability of the principle of State immunity.[69]

The ICJ's ruling immediately deployed its effects on international human rights law. Indeed the ECtHR was asked to issue a judgement on violations of Art. 6 ECHR in the case *Jones v. UK*. Four applicants of British nationality alleged to have suffered torture and other inhuman and degrading treatment from Saudi Arabia public officials. They had sought restoration before UK courts, which granted immunity in civil proceedings to both the Kingdom of Saudi Arabia and the individual defendants. The applicants claimed that this decision amounted to a disproportionate interference with their right of access to court under Art. 6 of the Convention. The Court of Strasbourg acknowledged the status of international customary law certified by the ICJ and dismissed the case concluding that UK courts correctly uphold Saudi Arabia immunity claim, which "cannot ... be said to have amounted to an unjustified restriction on the applicant's access to a court" because it complies with international law principles.[70]

[67] Jurisdictional Immunities of the State (*Germany v. Italy*: Greece intervening), Judgment, I.C.J. Reports 2012, p. 99. The decision raised a significant scholarly debate: see *ex multis* Marongiu Buonaiuti (2011) 232 ff. For the effects of the decision in the Italian legal order, see Salerno (2012) 350 ff.

[68] As opposed to acts *iure gestionis*, that is those concerning non-sovereign act of the State, especially private and commercial acts.

[69] See Jurisdictional Immunities of the State (*Germany v. Italy*: Greece intervening), Judgment, par. 70–81. The only exceptions to the aforementioned State practice seem to be the cases of Italy and Greece.

[70] See *Jones v. UK*, dec. 14.1.2014, App. nos. 34356/06 and 40528/06, par. 198.

10.3.3 *Questioning State Immunity Principle: The "Last Word" to the Italian Constitutional Court?*

Most of the Italian Courts immediately acknowledged the ICJ's judgment. They have accordingly started to rule inadmissible any civil actions brought against armed forces alleged to have infringed human rights. To cite an example, the Court of Appeal of Turin, in the *De Guglielmi* case,[71] found that the ICJ's decision prevents the Italian ordinary courts from ordering Germany to compensate victims of human rights violations. A compensation verdict indeed would have raised Italy's international responsibility for violation of the duty to respect and apply ICJ's rulings.

In order to avoid further civil actions to be brought before Italian courts,[72] the Parliament enacted law 14 January 2013, no. 5 (ratifying United Nations Convention on the Jurisdictional Immunities of States and Their Property) compelling Italian judges to recognise the ICJ's decisions when the latter exclude the domestic jurisdiction over a proceeding concerning a foreign State's civil liability.

Art. 3 of the newly adopted statute indeed states that when the ICJ issued a judgment within a proceeding to which Italy has taken part concerning the exclusion of a foreign State's civil liability, the Italian court before which a dispute relating to the same conduct is pending shall declare *ex officio* (and also when it has issued a final judicial judgment which recognised the existence of jurisdiction) the lack of jurisdiction at any stage and level of the proceeding. Furthermore the statute prescribes that final judgments not open to appeal and contrary to the ruling of the ICJ may be challenged to claim their revision (*revocazione*).[73] Final judgments can be impugned when they conflict with an ICJ's decision preventing Italy from exercising jurisdiction (even when the ICJ's ruling comes after the domestic judgment).

However, in the meantime claims concerning the compensation for historical injustices have been lodged. The Tribunal of Florence has accepted to hear three of them and, instead of simply declaring the claim inadmissible, the Tribunal[74] suspended the proceeding and raised the question of constitutionality (*questione di costituzionalità*) before the Constitutional Court (hereafter the CC). The referring judge questioned the compatibility with Art. 24 and Art. 2, Italian Const.[75] of: (a) the norm concerning the foreign State immunity from civil jurisdiction that has been incorporated within the Italian legal system pursuant to the automatic adaptation to

[71] Court of Appeal of Turin, 3rd Civil Division, *Germany v. De Guglielmi*, dec. of 14.5.2012, reg. no. 1470/10.

[72] As it is clearly evident from the *travaux préparatoires*: see Third Commission for Constitutional Affairs, 19.9.2012 – Chamber of Deputies, act no. 5434.

[73] See Art. 3, par. 2, Law no. 5/2013, adding new grounds for the reopening of a proceeding other than those provided for in the Arts. 395 and 306, Code of Civil Procedure.

[74] Tribunal of Florence, dec. of 21.1.2014.

[75] Stating that "[a]nyone may bring cases before a court of law in order to protect their rights under civil and administrative law".

international law via Art. 10, cl. 1, Italian Const.[76]; (b) the statute ratifying the UN Charter, insofar as it compels Italy to obey the ICJ under Art. 94 of the Charter even when it requires Italian judges to decline jurisdiction; (c) the newly enacted statute.

The CC[77] dismissed the first issue as unfounded clarifying that the norm reflecting the international customary rule has not actually been incorporated into the Italian legal system as the domestic incorporation does not operate with respect to those rules that breach fundamental principles of the constitutional order and inalienable rights of the human being.[78] In particular, the norm infringes upon the guarantee of inalienable rights and the right to access to justice, respectively enshrined in Arts. 2 and 24, Italian Const., which falls within the fundamental principles of the Italian legal order.[79] The Court acknowledges the right to access to justice is not absolute; nevertheless limitations need to be justified by a countervailing public interest, which may override Art. 24 in a given case. In other words, the sacrifice of the constitutional rights must be assessed according to a proportionality test. The CC however does not intend to deny *in toto* the norm mirroring customary international law on State immunity from civil actions. Arts. 2 and 24 bar the norm insofar it includes within the State immunity the *acta iure imperii* that violate international law as well as international human rights law.

Following the same line of reasoning the CC declared unconstitutional the statute ratifying the UN Charter insofar it compels Italian judges to deny their jurisdiction over civil rights actions brought against a foreign State for violations of human rights, without prejudice for the Italian obligation under the UN Charter as a whole.

Finally, concerning the third issue the Court declared unconstitutional the newly enacted statute, partially relying upon the argumentation already developed and focusing on the *ratio legis* of law no. 5 of 2013. Specifically, the purpose of the statute, that is to avoid civil actions to be brought against Germany, contrasts a number of the constitutional principles. In other words, the complete sacrifice of Art. 2 and 24 cannot be justified when it is designed to shelter the unlawful exercise of State sovereign powers.

The CC resorted to the counter-limits doctrine (*dottrina dei controlimiti*),[80] a theory that has been formulated with regard to the obligation deriving from the European integration process and very seldom invocated in constitutional case law.[81] According to the aforementioned doctrine, the State can resist the incorporation of those international customary norms that violate fundamental principles of the constitutional order. The CC indeed seems to foster two complementary aims, the first of purely legal nature, and the second of presumably "political" kind. The former is

[76] According to which "[t]he Italian legal system conforms to the generally recognised principles of international law".

[77] See Italian Constitutional Court, dec. 22.10.2014, no. 238, available in Italian at http://cortecostituzionale.it. Accessed 24 March 2015. For a comment see Fontanelli (2014) and Passaglia (2014).

[78] See dec. 238/2014, par. 3.2.

[79] See CC dec. 98/1965; 18/1982; 82/1996; 26/1999; 29/2003; 386/2004 and 120/2014.

[80] On this issue see Passaglia (2014).

[81] See Ruggeri (2006) 398.

the promotion of a change in what it has called an alarming evolution of international law.[82] The latter is to urge both Italy and Germany to reach an agreement on compensation of historical injustices, preventing the end of the saga with the surrendering of the Nazi's victims.

It is not by chance however that the CC insisted upon fundamental rights as qualifying feature of the domestic constitutional order. This mention can reveal one of the driven forces behind the decision that seems to be the re-affirmation of the Italian constitutional identity, which was ultimately built upon the reaction to the atrocities of the Second World War.

10.4 The Interplay Between Principles of Domestic Jurisdiction and International Human Rights Law: The Quest for Uniform Standards

The set of rules and principles concerning the compensation for infringements of human rights has been inconsistently applied by domestic court on the one hand and international courts on the other. National judges indeed offered different interpretations of those rules and principle even when the domestic regime simply mirrors international case law.

Indeed, it should be pointed out that the interplay between domestic and international courts becomes almost unfeasible for human rights violations that are direct consequences of acts of war. While the national courts tend to recognise the right to compensation even for infringements caused by air raids or other acts of war,[83] both the ICJ[84] and the ECtHR[85] developed a completely different approach, maintaining that acts that constitute an expression of sovereign power, that is those which qualify themselves as *political actions* (or *decisions*), should be removed from the ambit of judicial review. The conclusion reached by the ICJ prevented the emergence of a State practice out of the decisions of the Italian and Greek courts establishing State liability under criminal and civil law in cases involving serious human rights violations. At the same time the Italian CC seems to push toward the opposite direction, even though it is unlikely that the attempt can gain some sort of success under international customary law.

Turning to the supranational level, despite the special nature of the international obligations stemming from the ECHR, which belong in the category of super-primary law[86] under the Italian system of the sources of law, the domestic and

[82] See dec. 238/2014, par. 3.1.

[83] See *supra* note 60.

[84] See *supra* 10.3.2.

[85] Randazzo (2007) 673 ff. and Amato (2007) 126 ff.

[86] The Italian Constitutional Court has clarified that the ECHR represents an interposed principle of constitutional review of domestic legislation conflicting with the ECHR: see Const. Court, judgements no. 348 and 349 of 2007. On this issue see Ruggeri (2008) 217 ff. and Bartole (2008)

supranational courts encountered significant problems in adjusting their respective parameters applicable to monetary remedies for human rights violations.

The Court of Cassation has pointed out that domestic judges retain an autonomous margin of appreciation, which allows them to reasonably distance themselves from ECtHR case law.[87] However, whilst domestic courts cannot completely depart from the supranational judges' interpretation, they must nonetheless provide adequate justification for their decisions.

There are at least two examples of this non-alignment. First of all, as far as the calculation of the indemnity is concerned, up until 2012 the Italian courts insisted in considering only the length of time in excess of the reasonable duration of the trial, while the ECtHR assessed compensation on the basis of the overall period in which the judgment was pending.[88] In recent years, especially after the 2012 reform of the *Pinto Act*, the Court of Cassation has tried to align its case law with ECtHR precedents.[89]

Secondly, the supranational court tended to award damages for non-pecuniary harm just as much as for pecuniary losses. On the contrary, the Italian courts seem to be more reluctant to award damages not specifically connected to a visible impairment.[90]

As a result, the Strasbourg Court, which were initially adverse to awarding compensation to claimants who has successfully enforced internal remedies, made a kind of judicial U-turn (justified under Art. 41 ECHR) and started to award additional compensation to appellants who had not obtained appropriate and satisfactory redress before the domestic courts.[91]

The practice of the international awards of compensation (along with the required parallel rulings against Italy) rendered substantially ineffective the *Pinto Act*, which has long since been consigned to a kind of ancillary role by legal actors, and only established new opportunities for effective application after the 2012 reform.

10.5 Concluding Remarks: Problems and Open Questions within a Composite Patchwork

The Italian State's liability regime for human rights violations is built on three main "pillars".

---

291 ff. For a broader perspective on the interplay between constitutional courts and the European Court of Human Rights as far as the ranking of the ECHR in domestic systems is concerned see Eissen (1990) 137 ff.

[87] See Court of cassation, dec. no. 10894 of 11.5.2006.

[88] See Court of cassation, dec. no. 14 of 3.1.2008. See also Angelini (2010) 97.

[89] See Gitti (2009) 645 ff.

[90] The issue is analysed in a broader perspective by Ponzanelli (2012) 611 ff.

[91] See Chindemi (2008) 690 ff.

The first is the constitutional regime, which is essentially grounded in the criminal and administrative law provisions sanctioning violations of rights that are enshrined in the Constitution. In these cases, the legal basis for compensation is to be found in the Constitution and in the Civil Code and is only applicable if a claim for damages has been filed before the competent court according to the ordinary procedures.

The second pillar is the special regime for historical infringements of human rights. This statutory system has two distinctive features: a. it involves the interpretation of international law concerning States' immunity; and b. for the most part it is comprised of legislative provisions on pensions and social welfare rather than compensation for harm or losses awarded following litigation. The efforts made by Italian courts to assert the right to obtain redress for gross and systematic violations of human rights were ultimately frustrated by the ICJ's decision in *Germany v. Italy* and apparently restored by the CC's judgment. In any case, the principle of State immunity is still construed as a bulwark against the assertion of a right to compensation in cases involving human rights violations perpetrated as iure imperii acts, and the ruling of the Italian CC is not likely the last word on this issue.[92]

Finally, the third pillar is the *Pinto Act*, which does not cover all possible violation of human rights committed by the public authorities, but only breaches of the right to trial in a reasonable time enshrined in Art. 6 ECHR. The Law was intended to enforce the right to a speedy trial, and to some extent was even required owing to the status of international law obligations contained in the ECHR. Indeed, in 2007 the Italian Constitutional Court held that the Convention provisions have the status of "interposed norms" for the purposes of judicial review of legislation. In other words, the Court may strike down a law as unconstitutional on the grounds that it violates the rights enshrined in the ECHR. Consequently, the Convention "supplements" the principle of constitutional law. It is therefore the ranking of the ECHR provisions that requires Parliament to afford enhanced protection to the rights provided for thereunder.

However, even prior to the enactment of Law no. 89 of 2001, both the Italian courts and scholars tried to find a legal basis for compensation in cases involving violations of the rights enshrined in the ECHR. There were at least three possible theses. The first derived the right to compensation directly from Art. 2043 of the Civil Code[93]; the second assert it on the basis of Art. 1 of Protocol no. 1 to the ECHR[94]; the third inferred the direct effect of Art. 6 ECHR from the peculiar status of the international law obligations enshrined in the European Convention.[95] Despite these efforts to justify the right to compensation for violations of Convention rights, the majority opinion of legal scholars considered that legislation would be required

[92] See Bianchi (2012) 307 ff.

[93] See Court of Rome, *Mustacchia v. Ministero di grazia e giustizia*, dec. of 7.8.1984, *supra* note 24.

[94] See Vezzani (2010) 1153 ff.

[95] See Court of cassation, dec. no. 28507 of 23.12.2005. See *contra* dec. no. 17650 of 2002 and dec. no. 360 of 2003.

in order to ensure the effective enforcement of the right to compensation.[96] In other words, damages for infringements of rights can be recognised irrespective of domestic law only for rights the violation of which expressly requires (inter alia) pecuniary compensation.[97] As a result, with the exception of the right to a speedy trial, the violation of human rights enshrined in the ECHR will merit compensation only if a claim has been brought before the ECtHR.[98]

Although it is the most comprehensive legislation on the redress for harm caused by human rights violations, the *Pinto Act* encountered a series of difficulties in relation to its specific implementation.

From a broader perspective, both the *Scordino* case[99] and the *Sulejmanovic* case[100] show that Italian legislation is still not properly enforced, or at least it is implemented in a manner that is inconsistent with the case law of the ECtHR's. In the former case, the Court held that in order to constitute an effective remedy, compensation granted under domestic law must be *adequate*.[101] In the latter, the ECtHR awarded 1,000 euros to the applicant, who had accused Italy of violating Art. 3 ECHR on the ground that the redress provided by the Italian courts was inadequate. In order to offset the failures of domestic case law and legislation, the European Court held that an applicant may directly lodge a claim before the ECtHR where he has concrete reasons to believe that the domestic courts do not comply with the Strasbourg Court's standards.

These three pillars cover different kinds of violations of rights, whilst only the third can actually be interpreted as a coherent scheme of legislation specifically intended to provide redress for human rights violations.

Thus, if considered from an overall perspective, the general picture of the regime of State liability resembles a patchwork complicated by inconsistencies between national and international standards.

In the framework of rules concerning reparations for historical injustices, the inconsistency is even more problematic when one considers the double standards that the Italian law seems to apply to domestic as opposed to foreign-made violations of human rights. Indeed infringements of rights perpetrated by Italian public officials have been mostly addressed with legislative provisions pertaining to welfare policy and only insufficiently restored, while a general regime concerning the restoration for human rights violations is still missing.

In the end the desirable change in international law and practice that the CC fostered in her ruling needs to be paired with a similar effort on the side of Italian Parliament and courts.

---

[96] See Salerno (2010) 663 ff.

[97] See Vezzani (2010) 1152 and Bartolini (2009) 501 ff.

[98] On this point see Sironi (2012) 32 ff.

[99] ECtHR, dec. of 29.3.2006, application no. 36813/97, *Scordino v. Italy*. See Azzalini (2012) 1711.

[100] ECtHR, dec. of 16.7.2009, application no. 22635/03, *Sulejmanovic v. Italy*. See Angelini (2010) 97.

[101] See also ECtHR, dec. of 23.2.2012, application no. 27765/09, *Hirsl Jamaa et al. v. Italy*. On this issue see Napoletano (2012) 436 ff.

References

Abbamonte, Giuseppe. 2000. L'affermazione legislativa e giurisprudenziale della risarcibilità del danno derivante dall'esercizio illegittimo della funzione amministrativa. Profili sostanziali e procedurali. *Consiglio di Stato* 4: 743–787.

Amato, Fabrizio. 2007. Se la Corte europea rinnega i diritti dell'uomo. *Foro italiano* 3: 126–129.

Angelini, Niccoló Guido. 2010. Detenzione e divieto di tortura. *Responsabilità civile e previdenza* 1: 89–103.

Azzalini, Marco. 2012. L'eccessiva durata del processo e il risarcimento del danno: la legge Pinto tra stalli applicativi e interventi riformatori. *Responsabilità civile e previdenza* 5: 1702–1737.

Barbera, Augusto. 2007. Le basi filosofiche del costituzionalismo. In *Le basi filosofiche del costituzionalismo*, ed. Augusto Barbera, 3–42. Roma-Bari: Laterza.

Bartole, Sergio. 2008. Integrazione e separazione della tutela costituzionale e convenzionale dei diritti umani. *Diritti umani e diritto internazionale* 2: 291–300.

Bartolini, Giulio. 2009. *Riparazione per violazione dei diritti umani e ordinamento internazionale*. Napoli: Jovene.

Bianchi, Andrea. 2012. Il tempio e i suoi sacerdoti. Considerazioni su retorica e diritto a margine del caso Germania c. Italia. *Diritti umani e diritto internazionale* 6: 293–309.

Bognetti, Giovanni. 1982. Direct application and indirect impact of the Constitution in the Italian legal system. In *Italian national reports to the XIth international congress of comparative law*, 429–448. Milano/Caracas: Giuffrè.

Bordoni, Matteo. 2009. L'ordine pubblico internazionale nella sentenza della Cassazione sulla esecuzione della decisione greca relativa al caso *Distomo*. *Rivista di diritto internazionale* 2: 496–503.

Brömer, Jürgen. 1997. *State immunity and the violation of human rights*. The Hague: Kluwer Law International.

Cerbo, Pasquale. 2009. Leggi idonee a ledere posizioni giuridiche di soggetti individuati (o individuabili) e responsabilità dei pubblici agenti nell'art. 28 Cost.: alla ricerca di un equilibrio. *Giurisprudenza costituzionale* 2: 1363–1415.

Chindemi, Domenico. 2008. "Legge Pinto": questioni processuali, sostanziali e di "etica del diritto". *Responsabilità civile e previdenza* 3: 690–721.

Cohen, Jean L. 2012. *Globalization and sovereignty: Rethinking legality, legitimacy, and constitutionalism*. Cambridge: Cambridge University Press.

Colzi, Giorgio. 1950. La responsabilità dei pubblici funzionari. In *Commentario sistematico alla Costituzione Italiana*, vol. I, ed. Piero Calamandrei and Alessandro Levi, 247–279. Firenze: Barbera.

Cooper Stephenson, Ken. 2003. Theoretical underpinning for reparations. A constitutional tort perspective. *Windsor Y. B. Access Justice* 22: 3–40.

Corongiu, Serena. 2001. L'equa riparazione dei danni derivanti dalla durata irragionevole del processo nella «legge Pinto»: prime riflessioni. *Studium Iuris* 9: 1003–1009.

De Vittor, Francesca. 2008. Immunità degli Stati dalla giurisdizione e risarcimento del danno per violazione dei diritti fondamentali: il caso Mantelli. *Diritti umani e diritto internazionale* 3: 632–637.

Eissen, Marc A. 1990. L'interaction des jurisprudences constitutionnelles nationales et la jurisprudence de la Cour européenne des droits de l'homme. In *Conseil constitutionnel et Cour européenne des droits de l'homme*, ed. Dominique Rousseau and Frédéric Sudre, 137–215. Paris: STH.

Fabri, Marco. 2009. The Italian Maze towards trial within a reasonable time, in the right to trial within a reasonable time and short-term reform of the European Court of Human Rights. Publication of the Council of Europe. http://www.coe.int/t/dghl/standardsetting/cddh/Publications/bledproceedings_book.pdf. Accessed 24 Mar 2015.

Falconieri, Silvia. 2012. Riparare e ricordare la legislazione antiebraica: la reviviscenza dell'istituto della discriminazione (1944–1950). In *Riparare Risarcire Ricordare. Un dialogo tra storici e giuristi*, ed. Resta Giorgio and Zeno-Zencovich Vincenzo, 139–155. Napoli: Editoriale Scientifica.

Feldman, David. 2002. *Civil liberties and human rights in England and Wales*. Oxford: Oxford University Press.

Focarelli, Carlo. 2005. La Legge Pinto e l'applicabilità del diritto alla durata ragionevole del processo alle indagini preliminari e ai giudizi tributari. *Giurisprudenza costituzionale*. 6: 5163–5178.

Fontanelli, Filippo. 2014. I know it's wrong but I just can't do right. First impressions on judgment no. 238 of 2014 of the Italian Constitutional Court. http://www.diritticomparati.it/2014/10/i-know-its-wrong-but-i-just-cant-do-right-first-impressions-on-judgment-no-238-of-2014-of-the-italianconstitutional.html Accessed 24 Mar 2015.

Francioni, Francesco. 1997. The jurisprudence of international human rights enforcement: Reflections on the Italian experience. In *Enforcing international human rights in domestic courts*, ed. Benedetto Conforti and Francesco Francioni, 15–34. The Hague: Kluwer Law International.

Frulli, Micaela. 2009. La "derogabilità" della norma sull'immunità degli Stati dalla giurisdizione in caso di crimini internazionali: la decisione della Corte di cassazione sulla strage di Civitellla della Chiana. *Diritti umani e diritto internazionale* 2: 442–448.

Gaeta, Paola. 2011. Are victims of serious violations of international humanitarian law entitled to compensation? In *International humanitarian law and international human rights law*, ed. Orna Ben Naftali, 305–327. Oxford: Oxford University Press.

Gavouneli, Maria. 1997. War reparation claims and state immunity. *Revue hellénique de droit international* 50: 595–608.

Gerards, Janneke. 2008. Judicial deliberations in the European court of human rights. In *The legitimacy of the highest courts' rulings*, ed. Nick Huls, Maurice Adams, and Jacco Bomhoff, 407–436. The Hague: Asser Press.

Gitti, Angelo. 2009. Riparazione del danno non patrimoniale in caso di violazione del termine ragionevole del processo: la sentenza della Corte europea nel caso *Simaldone. Diritti umani e diritto internazionale* 3: 645–650.

Gori, Pierpaolo. 2014. Art. 3 CEDU e risarcimento da inumana detenzione. http://www.questionegiustizia.it/articolo/art_3-cedu-e-risarcimento-da-inumana-detenzione_02-10-2014.php. Accessed 24 Mar 2015.

Grossi, Pierfranceso. 1972. *Introduzione ad uno studio sui diritti inviolabili nella Costituzione italiana*. Padova: CEDAM.

Izar, Simone. 2002. Prime applicazioni giurisprudenziali della legge n. 89/2001 (c.d. Legge Pinto) sulla responsabilità dello Stato per violazione del termine ragionevole del processo. *Responsabilità civile e previdenza* 4: 957–978.

Jarmul, Holly D. 1996. The effect of decisions of regional human rights tribunals on national courts. *New York University Journal of International Law and Politics* 28: 311–366.

Lanzi, Fabrizio. 2005. Fermo amministrativo di veicolo e risarcimento del danno. *Giurisprudenza di merito* 12: 2773–2777.

Lauterpacht, Hersch. 1937. Règles générales du droit de paix. In *Recueil des cours de l'Académie de droit international*, vol. 62, 95–422. The Hague: Martinus Nijhoff.

Marongiu Buonaiuti, Fabrizio. 2011. Azioni risarcitorie per la commissione di crimini internazionali ed immunità degli Stati dalla giurisdizione: la controversia tra la Germania e l'Italia innanzi alla Corte internazionale di giustizia. *Diritti umani e diritto internazionale* 5: 232–270.

McCormick, Neil. 1993. Beyond the Sovereign State. *Modern Law Review* 56: 1–18.

Merusi, Fabio, and Marcello Clarich. 1991. Art. 28. In *Commentario alla Costituzione italiana. Rapporti civili*, ed. G. Branca, 356–393. Bologna: Zanichelli.

Messineo, Francesco. 1957. *Manuale di diritto civile e commercial*. Milano: Giuffré.

Mortati, Constantino. 1931. *L'ordinamento del governo nel nuovo diritto pubblico*. Roma: ARE.

Napoletano, Nicola. 2012. La condanna dei "respingimenti" operati dall'Italia verso la Libia da parte della Corte europea dei diritti umani: molte luci e qualche ombra. *Diritti umani e diritto internazionale* 2: 436–447.

Nardin, Terry. 1987. Realism, cosmopolitanism and the rule of law. *American Society of International Law Proceedings* 81: 416–419.

Paladin, Livio. 1997. *Diritto costituzionale*. Padova: CEDAM.

Passaglia, Paolo. 2014. Una sentenza (auspicabilmente) storica: la Corte limita l'immunità degli Stati esteri dalla giurisdizione civile. http://www.diritticomparati.it/2014/10/una-sentenza-auspicabilmente-storica-la-corte-limita-limmunit%C3%A0-degli-stati-esteri-dalla-giurisdizion.html#sthash.GIZYCHzF.dpuf. Accessed 24 Mar 2015.

Peces-Barba Martinez, Gregorio. 1993. *Teoria dei diritti fondamentali*. Milano: Giuffré.

Persano, Federica. 2008. Immunità statale dalla giurisdizione civile e violazione dei diritti fondamentali dell'individuo. *Responsabilità civile e previdenza.* 11: 2259–2274.

Pisillo Mazzeschi, Riccardo. 2012. Il rapporto tra norme di ius cogens e la regola sull'immunità degli Stati: alcune osservazioni critiche sulla sentenza della Corte internazionale di giustizia del 3 febbraio 2012. *Diritti umani e diritto internazionale* 6: 310–326.

Ponzanelli, Guido. 1986. La Corte costituzionale, il danno non patrimoniale e il danno alla salute. *Foro italiano* 9: 2053–2062.

Ponzanelli, Giulio. 2012. La Cassazione bloccata dalla paura di un risarcimento non riparatorio. *Danno e responsabilità* 6: 611–613.

Principato, Luigi. 2001. Risarcimento. Responsabilità aquiliana e lesione di diritti costituzionali. *Giurisprudenza costituzionale* 6: 4170–4181.

Randazzo, Barbara. 2007. Responsabilità dello Stato per atti di guerra: la «ragion di stato» alla Corte di Strasburgo? *Quaderni costituzionali* 3: 673–675.

Ruggeri, Antonio. 2006. Le pronunzie della Corte costituzionale come controlimiti alle cessioni di sovranità a favore dell'ordinamento comunitario. In *Id. Itinerari di una ricerca sul sistema delle fonti*, vol. IX. Torino: Giappichelli.

Ruggeri, Antonio. 2008. La CEDU alla ricerca di una nuova identità, tra prospettiva formale-astratta e prospettiva assiologico-sostanziale d'inquadramento sistematico. *Diritto pubblico comparato ed europeo* 1: 215–220.

Salerno, Francesco. 2010. La garanzia costituzionale della Convenzione europea dei diritti dell'uomo. *Rivista di diritto internazionale* 3: 637–665.

Salerno, Francesco. 2012. Gli effetti della sentenza internazionale nell'ordinamento italiano: il caso *Germania c. Italia. Diritto internazionale e diritti umani* 6: 350–370.

Sanna, Cecilia. 2011. Il ritardato pagamento degli indennizzi per la durata irragionevole dei processi: una violazione strutturale destinata a restare tale. *Diritti umani e diritto internazionale* 1: 160–164.

Silvestri, Gaetano. 2009. *L'effettività e la tutela dei diritti fondamentali nella giustizia costituzionale*. Napoli: ESI.

Sironi, Alice. 2012. La tutela della persona in conseguenza di danni all'ambiente nella giurisprudenza della Corte europea dei diritti umani. *Diritto internazionale e diritti umani* 6: 5–33.

Speciale, Giuseppe. 2012. Il risarcimento dei perseguitati politici e razziali: l'esperienza italiana. In *Riparare Risarcire Ricordare. Un dialogo tra storici e giuristi*, ed. Resta Giorgio and Zeno-Zencovich Vincenzo, 115–138. Napoli: Editoriale Scientifica.

Verdross, Alfred V. 1937. Forbidden treaties in international law. *American Journal of International Law* 31: 571–577.

Vezzani, Simone. 2010. Sul fondamento del diritto dell'individuo al risarcimento dei danni subiti in conseguenza della violazione degli obblighi posti dalla Convenzione europea. *Rivista di diritto internazionale* 4: 1148–1154.

Zagrebelsky, Gustavo. 1992. *Il diritto mite. Libertà, diritti, giustizia.* Torino: Einaudi.

Zimmerman, Andreas. 1995. Sovereign immunity and violation of international Jus Cogens. Some critical remarks. *Michigan Journal International Law* 16: 433–440.

Chapter 11
Damages for Fundamental Rights Violations, Dutch Perspectives

Jessy M. Emaus

11.1 Liability for Fundamental Rights Violations Under Current Dutch Law

11.1.1 Introduction

In Sect. 11.1 current Dutch law on liability for fundamental rights violations will be outlined. Liability for fundamental rights violations is based on the general provision governing liability arising from an unlawful act, the general tort clause, as laid down in article 6:162 Dutch Civil Code (hereinafter: DCC; *Burgerlijk Wetboek*). For this reason, the general tort clause will be dealt with briefly at Sect. 11.1.2.1 first. In Sects. 11.1.2.2 and 11.1.2.3 the liability of non-state actors and public authorities for fundamental rights violations will be explained respectively. Lastly, three current issues will be addressed, being: state liability for excessive length of proceedings (at Sect. 11.1.3.1), the participation of victims in criminal proceedings (at Sect. 11.1.3.2) and the Netherlands Institute for Human Rights' decisions on quantifying damages and gender discrimination (at Sect. 11.1.3.3).

J.M. Emaus (✉)
Utrecht Centre for Accountability and Liability Law (Ucall), Utrecht Centre for Regulation and Enforcement in Europe (Renforce), Utrecht University,
Janskerkhof 12, 3512 BL Utrecht, The Netherlands
e-mail: J.M.Emaus@uu.nl

E. Bagińska (ed.), *Damages for Violations of Human Rights*,
Ius Comparatum - Global Studies in Comparative Law 9,
DOI 10.1007/978-3-319-18950-5_11

11.1.2 Liability for Fundamental Rights Violations

11.1.2.1 Liability Arising from an Unlawful Act

Article 6:162 DCC provides a general basis for liability arising from an unlawful act. It reads:

1. "A person who commits a *tort* against another *which is attributable to him*, must repair the *damage* suffered by the other *in consequence thereof.*
2. Except where there are grounds for justification, the following are deemed tortious: the violation of a right and an act or omission breaching a duty imposed by law or a rule of unwritten law pertaining to proper social conduct.
3. A tortfeasor is responsible for the commission of a tort if it is due to his fault or to a cause for which he is accountable by law or pursuant to generally accepted principles. [emphasis added, *JE*]"[1]

Liability on the basis of this provision thus requires an unlawful act (*i.e.*, tortious conduct / an act or omission), damage, a causal link between the damage and the unlawful act, and attribution of the unlawful act to the wrongdoer. Additionally, article 6:163 DCC requires that the standard breached is intended to protect the person suffering the loss and that the standard moreover is intended to protect against the damage suffered and how it was caused.[2] An unlawful act or omission can be either the violation of a right, the act or omission in violation of a statutory duty, or the act or omission of what, according to unwritten law, has to be regarded as improper social conduct (the general duty of care). This last category seems to be most relevant in practice. Also in cases of fundamental rights violations by non-state actors, it is mostly the general duty of care that is relied on, since the first category, the violation of someone else's right, is interpreted strictly. Only when a person's conduct itself constitutes a violation of a right, this requirement is fulfilled.[3]

Once someone is held liable, the aggrieved party has a right to damages as stipulated in art. 6:95 ff DCC. According to art. 6:95 DCC, one can claim compensation for pecuniary loss and for non-pecuniary loss, the latter, however, only to the extent that the law confers a right to damages therefor.[4] Damages for fundamental rights violations *per se*, are based on article 6:106 DCC. This provision offers a legal basis for damages in different situations, including the situation where the aggrieved party's person has been otherwise afflicted.[5] Apart from the damages for the violations *per se*, the aggrieved party can of course claim compensation for other losses once liability has been established.

---

[1] Translation from: Warendorf et al. (2013).

[2] See on the requirements extensively: Hartkamp and Sieburgh (2011) chapter 3.

[3] Sieburgh (1997) 628–635, Sieburgh (2000) 62–68.

[4] Translation from: Warendorf et al. (2013).

[5] Translation from: Warendorf et al. (2013).

It is generally accepted that the main function of non-contractual liability arising from an unlawful act, from an individual's point of view, is to offer compensation to an aggrieved party who has suffered harm as a consequence of one's unlawful conduct or negligence (*compensatie*).[6] It is not exactly clear, however, what the main goal of liability is from a wider perspective. According to *Sieburgh* the main goal is to find an answer to the question whether it is just to shift the loss that is suffered by the aggrieved party to the alleged wrongdoer.[7] *Engelhard* and *Van Maanen* argue that the main goal of liability law is to offer redress to guarantee a person's rights and to prevent that people take the law into their own hands.[8] Liability law also has side effects. According to *Engelhard* and *Van Maanen* these side effects include: encouraging prevention (*preventie*), proper cost allocation (*zuivere kostenallocatie*), punishment (*straffen*), recognition and satisfaction (*erkenning en genoegdoening*), and finding out the truth (*waarheidsvinding*).[9]

The law of damages, following liability law, is aimed at offering redress once liability is established. A basic principle in the law of damages, therefore, is the principle of *restitutio in integrum*. Damages should thus reflect the loss and offer compensation for the loss suffered. Although compensation was considered the only main function of damages law for a long time, today rights vindication may be considered another main function. In its landmark judgment in *Gemeente Groningen* v. *X*, the Supreme Court of the Netherlands (hereinafter: Supreme Court; *Hoge Raad*) seems to have accepted "rights vindication" as an independent function in addition to the compensatory function.[10] In *Gemeente Groningen* v. *X* a family in Groningen had sued the Gemeente Groningen, *i.e.*, the municipality Groningen, for refraining from interference in time when the family was menaced by rioters during the night of 30 to 31 December 1997 three times. The family called the police for the first time at 9:50 p.m., but the authorities, at 11:00 p.m., had decided not to take action. Around midnight, after having contacted the mayor, who is in command of the police, the authorities had decided to call in the anti-riot squad to assist. The anti-riot squad arrived at the family's home at around 2:30 a.m. The family stated they had suffered psychological harm, as they experienced serious threats to their body and property during the night. The Supreme Court decided that the district court had rightly considered that a serious breach of one's integrity and the safety of their home can be described as harm under article 6:106 DCC (right to damages for non-material harm), *i.e.*, a violation of personality (*persoonsaantasting*). It thus allowed a right to damages for fundamental rights violations *as such*. The Supreme Court afterwards has confirmed its considerations in a wrongful life case, holding

[6] Engelhard and Van Maanen (2008) 11.

[7] Sieburgh (2000) 9–21.

[8] Engelhard and Van Maanen (2008) 11–13.

[9] Engelhard and Van Maanen (2008) 13–20.

[10] Hoge Raad 9.7.2004 (2005) NJ: 391. See Lindenbergh (2008) 3–16, Verheij (2013) 94, Rijnhout and Emaus (2014) 106. Note: the idea of rights vindication as an independent function of the law of damages was strongly advocated by Verheij years before: Verheij (2002) chapter 10 *passim*. See also: Hartlief (2008) 34.

that a serious breach of a critical fundamental right indeed constitutes a violation of personality.[11]

11.1.2.2 Liability of Non-State Actors

The liability of non-state actors for fundamental rights violations is based on article 6:162 DCC. Particular norms, the so-called personality rights, give substance to the requirement of unlawful conduct or negligence in this regard.[12] These unwritten rights are considered fundamental rights governing private law relationships[13] and derive from a general right to personality that has been accepted by the Supreme Court in its landmark judgment in *Valkenhorst*.[14]

Valkenhorst concerned the application of De R. (applicant) to Stichting Valkenhorst (defendant) to reveal information about her father, whom she did not know. De R. was born in an institution that aimed to assist young unmarried pregnant women during the last stages of pregnancy in 1935. The legal predecessor of defendant Stichting Valkenhorst managed that institution. Stichting Valkenhorst, according to De R.'s mother's wish, refused to hand over information to De R. about her father. The Supreme Court, to start with, stated that rights such as the right to respect for one's private life, the right to freedom of thought and religion, and the right to free speech derive from a general right to personality that also encloses a right to know one's genetic origins.[15] This right to know one's origins, however, is not an absolute right. The right must give way to other rights and freedoms if these rights and freedoms come before the right to know one's origins. The Supreme Court in *Valkenhorst* decided that the De R.'s right to know her genetic origins is superior to the mother's right to respect for her private life.

After *Valkenhorst*, other personality rights have been denominated in academic literature, among which the right to life, the right to mental integrity, the right to free movement, the right to private life and also, for example, the right to property.[16] In short and following *Lindenbergh*, personality rights can best be described as personal rights that refer to different aspects of the core of one's personality. Personality rights, says *Lindenbergh*, aim to guarantee the value of a human being as a person, including his integrity, identity and autonomy.[17]

---

[11] Hoge Raad 18.3.2005 (2006) NJ: 606. See par. Sect. 11.1.2.3.

[12] See on personality rights in great detail: Lindenbergh (1999) 1665–1707. Nehmelman (2002) 103–108.

[13] Lindenbergh (1999) 1665–1707.

[14] Hoge Raad 15.4.1994 (1994) NJ: 608.

[15] See on this right extensively: Blauwhoff (2009).

[16] Although proprietary interests of course also find protection in personality rights, one must realise that the right to property *per se* is of course highly regulated in private law, in the law of property. As regards their proprietary interests it is thus first property law that serves to protect against infringements. See on Dutch property law e.g. Bartels and Van Mierlo (2013).

[17] Lindenbergh (1999) 1701.

The liability of non-state actors for fundamental rights violations on the basis of article 6:162 DCC is also increasingly related to fundamental rights in the Dutch constitution and the ECHR, most significantly in the sphere of freedom of expression. The Supreme Court in several cases has explained and reiterated that when one of the parties in a private law dispute relies on the right to freedom of expression and the opposing party relies on the right to privacy, as a basic principle none of the rights prevails.[18] In these cases a decision has to be made on which right does prevail in the matter at hand. That decision must be found in all circumstances of the case. The Supreme Court in 1983 listed different factors, including for example the gravity, from a public interest point of view, of the malpractice that was presented in a publication. Today, the Supreme Court, and the lower courts, also refer to ECHR rights and considerations of the ECtHR play an important and explicit part. The Supreme Court, for example, referred to a distinction made by the ECtHR under article 10 ECHR between statements of facts and value judgments, and more particular to the Court's finding that, "However, even where a statement amounts to a value judgment, the proportionality of an interference may depend on whether there exists a sufficient factual basis for the impugned statement, since even a value judgment without any factual basis to support it may be excessive."[19] In conclusion, the Supreme Court in these cases, when European fundamental rights law became further developed, has thus sought harmonization with European fundamental rights law.

It must be noted that fundamental rights provisions do not always play a clear role in proceedings concerning actions for damages. Their role seems to depend, among other things, on whether or not the ECtHR in its case-law has provided for concrete elements to be taken into consideration in determining whether someone has acted unlawfully. Fundamental rights in these cases hold a more prominent role. In contrast, fundamental rights provisions seem to play a less important role, for instance, when the Supreme Court in previous judgments has given other points of reference.

At Sect. 11.1.2.1 it has been said that, today, one of the functions of the law of damages is rights vindication. The Supreme Court in *Baby Kelly* accepted this with regard to private law relationships. The *Baby Kelly* case concerned the birth of a severely handicapped baby, Kelly. The parents of the child sued the obstetrician and the hospital as legal representatives of Kelly and also on their own behalf. The claims of the parents were based on their right to self-determination. The parents argued that their right to self-determination was violated as the parents were deprived of the option of deciding to carry out an abortion for the reason that the baby was handicapped, since the parents had not known that she was. The obstetrician had failed to initiate a medical examination once she was informed by the mother of hereditary abnormalities. The Supreme Court decided that the serious breach of a critical fundamental right constitutes a right to damages on the basis of article 6:106 DCC, *i.e.*, constituting a violation of a personality. More recently, the

[18] Hoge Raad 6.1.1995 (1995) NJ: 422. See also: Hoge Raad 18.1.2008 (2008) NJ: 274.

[19] Hoge Raad 18.1.2008 (2008) NJ: 274. See ECtHR 19.12.2006, no. 18235/02.

Supreme Court reiterated the rule in a case concerning a personal injury (a bruised eye resulting from hitting), caused by a violent group.[20] The Supreme Court stated that a right to damages for non-pecuniary loss may exist on the basis of a severe violation of standards, also taking into account the consequences for the victim.

11.1.2.3 Liability of Public Authorities

Public authority liability for fundamental rights violations is based on the general rule on liability arising from an unlawful act.[21] Although art. 6:162 DCC is part of Dutch *civil law*, it is said that there is no reason not to apply it to *public law* relationships, as far as no explicit general public law provision exists to deal with damages for unlawful acts of public authorities substantively.[22] According to *Scheltema* and *Scheltema*, it is in fact a general principle of law, which is reflected in art. 6:162 DCC that constitutes the basis for an unwritten public law doctrine that greatly resembles the private law provision.[23] This means that it is not the private law provision that is applied, but an unwritten rule that derives from the common principle. However, when a public authority commits a tort, which is attributable to it, it is obliged to repair the damage suffered by the other in consequence thereof.[24]

Since public authorities, as opposed to non-state actors, are expected to serve the public interest, the weighing of interests between the wrongdoer and the aggrieved party in these cases is different than the balancing exercise in private law relationships. More specifically, the attributability of the unlawful act to the public authority is assumed[25] or is not considered a requirement for liability.[26] Another illustration is the general duty of care being replaced by the principles of good governance.[27]

As regards fundamental rights violations, public authorities have explicit duties under several sources of fundamental rights, most important the Dutch constitution and the ECHR. The ECHR is of direct relevance in the Dutch legal order, since the legal order is a monist one. On the basis of art. 93 and 94 Dutch Constitution (DC; *Grondwet*) provisions in treaties that may be binding on all parties become binding

[20] Hoge Raad 29.6.2012 (2012) NJ: 410.

[21] Note that liability of public authorities is also based on European law. This part is excluded in this contribution. See Hartkamp and Sieburgh (2011) 298–300.

[22] See e.g. article 8:88ff General Administrative Law Act on liability for unlawful decision-making. These provisions, however, hold procedural rules.
See also Hartkamp and Sieburgh (2011) 297–298, Snijders (2011) 27–28.

[23] Scheltema and Scheltema (2013) 330 ff. See also Afdeling Bestuursrechtspraak Raad van State 29.11.1996 (1997) AB: 66.

[24] Scheltema and Scheltema (2013) 330 ff.

[25] Hartkamp and Sieburgh (2011) 315.

[26] Scheltema and Scheltema (2013) 350.

[27] Scheltema and Scheltema (2013) 347 ff.

after publication and have precedence over conflicting statutory provisions.[28] When public authorities breach these duties the criterion of an unlawful act or omission is in principle fulfilled. It is the second category of unlawful acts or omissions, *i.e.*, an act or omission breaching a duty imposed by law, that is thus of relevance.[29]

A broad range of fundamental rights issues has arisen in court over the years, including: violations of the right to liberty and security (e.g., in a criminal law case concerning a hospital order patient that had to await transfer to forensic hospital in prison too long),[30] of the right to private life (e.g., in a private law case concerning security risks after removal of a threatened politician),[31] and of the right to respect for family life (e.g., in a family law case concerning maintenance obligation Dutch state for foster child).[32] A recent category of cases is the category of excessive length of proceedings cases. In line with case law of the ECtHR, and even more far-reaching, the highest courts in the Netherlands have developed rules for claiming damages for excessive length of proceedings from the Dutch state. These rules will be elaborated at Sect. 11.1.3.1.

Also in cases concerning fundamental rights violations by public authorities it is not always clear what role fundamental rights play. Sometimes a standard of care is discussed extensively while only referring briefly to a fundamental rights provision. As mentioned at Sect. 11.1.2.2 with regard to liability of non-state actors, fundamental rights provisions in this regard are also discussed more comprehensively when concrete standards for the present case can be derived from case law of the ECtHR or other courts.

11.1.3 Focus: Three Current Topics

11.1.3.1 State Liability for Excessive Length of Proceedings[33]

The first current topic concerns state liability for excessive length of proceedings based on the right to a fair trial within a reasonable time. Over the last decade the highest courts in the Netherlands have developed general rules based on principles underlying article 6 ECHR concerning state liability for excessive length of proceedings.[34] The Administrative Jurisdiction Division of the Council of State (hereinafter: Administrative Jurisdiction Division; *Afdeling Bestuursrechtspraak*

[28] See www.government.nl/documents-and-publications/regulations/2012/10/18/the-constitution-of-the-kingdom-of-the-netherlands-2008.html. Accessed 26 March 2015.

[29] See Sect. 11.1.2.1.

[30] Hoge Raad 21.12.2007 (2008) NJ: 242. See also ECtHR 11.5.2004, no. 49902/99.

[31] Hoge Raad 20.10.2006 (2007) NJ: 3.

[32] Hoge Raad 30.11.2007 (2008) NJ: 143.

[33] See e.g. Lindenbergh (2014) 636–642. Van Kessel (2014) 266–274, Lindenbergh (2013) 15, Dijkshoorn (2010) 1346–1351, Barkhuysen and Van Ettekoven (2009) 129–141.

[34] See Emaus and Keirse (2014) 442–446.

Raad van State), the highest general administrative court in the Netherlands, has led the way in this development. The Administrative Jurisdiction Division has decided that the case law of the ECtHR, with regard to length of proceedings, also applies to cases that are not strictly covered by article 6 ECHR on the basis of judgments of the ECtHR.[35] The Administrative Jurisdiction Division grounded its decision on the universally accepted principle of legal certainty, underlying article 6 ECHR. In line with case law of the ECtHR the Administrative Jurisdiction Division accepted that feelings of distress and frustration can be presumed to flow from the failure to settle a case within a reasonable time.[36] The damages amount to 500 euros per 6 months that the proceedings have exceeded the reasonable period of time. In public law proceedings claims for damages for excessive length of proceedings can be submitted in the current proceedings.

The Supreme Court, following the case-law of the Administrative Jurisdiction Division, has decided that also in private law disputes excessive length of proceedings are remedied on the basis of the principle of legal certainty.[37] Also the presumption of feelings of distress and frustration applies in this regard and the amount of compensation is 500 euros per 6 months delay. It is, however, and differently from public law cases, not possible to involve the state in the current proceedings. The state must be sued in separate proceedings.

The judicial development of a system for damages for excessive length of proceedings raises constitutional issues. Some years ago a legislative proposal was created to regulate claims for excessive length of proceedings. In accordance with that intention, the government had expressed before the ECtHR, "That they are in the process of drafting legislation which is aimed at providing an effective remedy for the litigious complaint," (*Voorhuis v. the Netherlands*). However, the legislator eventually announced that it was not necessary anymore to introduce a law.[38] The Minister for Security and Justice referred to the case law of the Administrative Jurisdiction Division and concluded that a satisfactory solution had been found to handle claims for excessive length of proceedings in public law. It remains to be seen, however, whether things can go on like this.[39] One practical and important drawback was raised by Van Kessel, who pointed to the fact that the Supreme Court is not able to rule in all different types of cases.[40] The legislation is thus in this regard more capable of monitoring the uniformity of law.

[35] ABRvS 17.4.2009, ECLI:NL:RVS:2009:BI2283.

[36] *Riccardi Pizzati v Italy*, ECtHR 29.3.2006, no. 62361/00. Hoge Raad 11.1.2013 (2013) NJ: 99.

[37] Hoge Raad 11.1.2013 (2013) NJ: 99.

[38] ECtHR 3.3.2009, no. 28692/06.

[39] Staatsblad (2013) 162, p 4.

[40] Van Kessel (2014).

11.1.3.2 Participation of Victims in Criminal Proceedings

A second current topic concerns the increased participation of victims in criminal proceedings. Victims of criminal offences, who can be assumed to be victim of fundamental rights violations, can claim damages in criminal proceedings for a long time. In the past few years the legislator has taken several measures to support victim participation in criminal proceedings. To ensure that the accused party does not transfer his properties, in 2013 the proposal for Prejudgment Attachment of the Assets of the Accused for the Benefit of a Victim was passed. Since 2005, in addition to a right to claim damages before the criminal court, victims of crimes have a right to speak in court. This right is restricted in that victims are only allowed to talk about the consequences of the crime. In 2014, the State Secretary of Security and Justice issued a proposal in which he presented his intention to lift these restrictions.[41]

11.1.3.3 The Netherlands Institute for Human Rights' Decisions on Quantifying Damages and Gender Discrimination

One last recent development not exactly concerning damages for fundamental rights violations, but related to this theme is the development concerning gender discrimination when calculating damages. A recent decision of the Netherlands Institute for Human Rights (hereinafter: NIHR) on equal treatment in personal injury cases has confirmed that the settled practices as regards calculating damages in the Netherlands cannot pass in light of the right to equal treatment.[42] In this paragraph the decision of the NIHR and the tensions it reveals between liability and damages law on the one hand and fundamental rights law on the other will be discussed briefly. For a clear understanding of the matter it is necessary to spend a few words on the Netherlands Institute for Human Rights first.

Since 2012, the Netherlands Institute for Human Rights has been in operation.[43] The institute is entrusted with the tasks, "to protect human rights, including the right to equal treatment, in the Netherlands, to increase awareness of these rights and to promote their observance,"[44] and is the national human rights body referred to in *Resolution A/RES/48/134 of the General Assembly of the United Nations of 20 December 1993*.[45] The Equal Treatment Commission was incorporated in this new human rights body. Amongst other tasks, the NIHR may institute an investigation, forward its findings and may make recommendations, although compliance with these recommendations cannot be enforced.

---

[41] See www.overheid.nl. Accessed 26 March 2015.

[42] College voor de Rechten van de Mens 19.8.2014. Judgment 2014–97.

[43] See www.mensenrechten.nl. Accessed 26 March 2015.

[44] Section 1 (3) Netherlands Institute for Human Rights Act.

[45] Section 1 (2) Netherlands Institute for Human Rights Act.

In a recent case, the calculation of damages for a young woman (aged 18) who was hit by a car while walking on the street, was called into question.[46] As a consequence of the accident the woman had become paralysed and suffers brain damage. The young woman (applicant) complained that the insurance company (defendant) had breached the equal treatment act, more particular, the prohibition on discrimination on ground of gender. The NIHR decided that on the basis of the facts that were presented by the applicant a violation of the prohibition on discrimination could be presumed. These facts included calculations of the insurance company on the basis of statistics that were clearly related to women career planning.

Although it is clear that insurance companies need to calculate risks on the basis of statistics, from this case it has become clear that insurance companies are not allowed to include in the calculations the gender of the aggrieved party concerned. Hence, the decision reveals an area of tension between the law of damages and fundamental rights law.

Before the creation of the NIHR the Equal Treatment Commission had decided three times on equal treatment and quantifying damages.[47]

11.2 Reflections on Dutch Law, with an Emphasis on Violations by Non-State Actors[48]

11.2.1 Introduction

In Sect. 11.2 the author will reflect upon current Dutch law and will consider how Dutch liability and damages law can contribute to the enforcement of fundamental rights, in particular the rights in the European Convention on Human Rights.[49] The emphasis is on the liability of non-state actors on the basis of private law, as the author has considered this most urgent. The urgency is based on the observation that the liability for non-state actors for fundamental rights violations was never analysed from a systemic point of view, although private parties more and more rely on fundamental rights in legal disputes. Whereas the liability of public authorities follows from the hard obligations of public authorities envisaged in the fundamental rights documents (such as the ECHR), it is still less clear what exactly is expected from non-state actors in this regard. Furthermore, it was observed that the general

---

[46] College voor de Rechten van de Mens 19.8.2014. Judgment 2014–97.

[47] Commissie Gelijke Behandeling 5.11.1996, Judgment 1996–90. Commissie Gelijke Behandeling 1.4.2004, Judgment 2004–37. Commissie Gelijke Behandeling 1.12.2009, Judgment 2009–117. See the report of the Equal Treatment Commission: Commissie Gelijke Behandeling (2012) Onderscheid naar geslacht bij de vaststelling van letselschade. Een verkennend onderzoek. 2012.

[48] This part of the article has been published before, as a part of the English summary of the author's dissertation. See Emaus (2013).

[49] The European Convention on Human Rights has proven to be the most relevant source of fundamental rights in the Dutch (monistic) legal system.

tort clause was aimed at dealing with losses. Although the emphasis is on the liability of non-state actors, the final conclusions may also be useful in public law relationships.

To start with, considerations on the desirability of the constitutionalisation of liability and damages law will be elucidated at Sect. 11.2.2. At Sect. 11.2.3, the author will show that liability and damages law on the one hand and European fundamental rights law on the other are built on distinctive principles. The analysis at Sect. 11.2.4 will demonstrate that, although liability and damages law can contribute to the enforcement of fundamental rights, the nature of fundamental rights justifies a new basis in liability law in addition to the unlawful act, creating a specific approach to enforce fundamental rights. That approach will be introduced in Sect. 11.2.5 and will be named "the breach of a fundamental right".

11.2.2 The Desirability of Constitutionalising Liability and Damages Law

The constitutionalisation of Dutch private law started several decades ago.[50] Following extensive debates in legal academic literature regarding the manner in which constitutionalisation should be realised, it now seems justified to draw the (preliminary) conclusion that fundamental rights provide private law with a constitutional foundation in various ways. The legislator and the courts, each in their own way and within their own competence, have worked to advance the constitutionalisation of private law. The concepts of direct and indirect horizontal effect are leading in the qualification of how constitutionalisation has developed.

The law governing liability and damages should also be constitutionalised. Constitutionalisation of liability and damages law, for the purpose of this text, is interpreted as providing fundamental rights with a statutory basis in this branch of law. Constitutionalisation of liability and damages law is not an isolated phenomenon, but is part of the constitutionalisation of private law in a broader sense. It would not just be desirable to give fundamental rights an explicit, more specifically defined position in liability and damages law, but also to give fundamental rights a "broader" statutory basis in private law. There are various arguments to support these propositions.

The first argument to support these propositions is based on the nature of fundamental rights: they are rights that support the protection of citizens' interests that most deserve protection. Fundamental rights are rights that contain "the normative basic principles that serve to assess society." [51] Looking at it from this perspective, it is difficult to see why the specific protection of the interests as supported by these rights should be restricted to public-law relationships. Second, this is even more

[50] See e.g. Maris (1969) 9–67, Drion (1969) 585–594, Boesjes (1973) 905–916, Kortmann (1984) 301–302, Elders and Biesheuvel (1986), Groen (1995) 131–173.

[51] Nieuwenhuis (2000) 204.

difficult to see if on balance fundamental rights have a different, fairer result than the more specific private-law legislation. I believe, following *Lindenbergh*, that a new perspective on the "beaten track" of private law may be reason to take a different turn.[52] The third and final important argument is that private parties are to respect each other's freedom and that it is difficult to see why their fundamental freedom should not be protected in the most effective way possible. It is true that fundamental rights are relatively open provisions, but they are necessarily so in view of their function. The advantage of fundamental rights over other open provisions in private law is that fundamental rights express which interests they serve to protect.

Objections against constitutionalisation of private law mainly originate from the textual provisions of fundamental rights. Relatively often, the formulation of fundamental rights is of such nature that it is difficult to find concrete clues in the text as to their application in private-law relationships.[53] However, the textual provisions *do* include concrete clues for their application in public-law relationships. These clues are found in the restrictive clauses that are part of the provisions and that serve to determine how to assess the cases that need a decision on whether the government's interference in the protected interest was justified.

The second paragraph of art. 8 ECHR is such a restrictive clause and serves as a good example, since it sets out the conditions on which interference *by a public authority* is justified, which are subsequently specified further to cover the public law relationship. The author believes that the fact that the restrictive clauses are not very useful, being geared towards the public-law relationship, does not alter the idea that the fundamental interests as expressed in art. 8 ECHR (the right to respect for private and family life, the home and correspondence) are interests that deserve protection in the private-law relationship as well. This is all the more true when considering that fundamental rights are based on human dignity and fundamental freedoms. It is important to realise that in private law, fundamental rights need specific accommodation, but their open nature does not prevent these rights from deserving and needing a statutory basis in private law. Private law itself also includes open norms. As described, the advantage of fundamental rights over other open norms in private law is that they convey information regarding the interests that they aim to protect.

In the constitutionalisation of private law it is rather natural to, also, focus on liability and damages law, since these regulations are by nature an open system, and as such serve to put an end to unfair situations in private law. The open norm of due care is an obvious starting point in current liability and damages law to cover situations where an unfair situation that has arisen, is the consequence of the violation of one or more fundamental rights.[54] The law on liability for unlawful acts provides the basis for the remedy of damages, which is important in private law.

---

[52] Lindenbergh (2010) 368.

[53] Smits (2003) 49.

[54] Nieuwenhuis (2000) 204.

11.2.3 *Two Distinctive Fields of Law*

11.2.3.1 Two Legal Spheres

The questions arises how Dutch liability and damages law can contribute to the enforcement of ECHR rights, assuming as a starting point that liability and damages law should be constitutionalised. In other words, one can ask oneself how ECHR rights should be enforced through liability and damages law. The answer to this question needs reference to the nature of liability and damages law and the nature of ECHR law. The author has identified five key themes that support the description of the nature of both sets of regulations.

These themes are the basic principles, the basis, the legal rule, the criteria, and enforcement. *Basic principles* are individual principles, ideas, normative starting points that in themselves are simply propositions. The basic principles are the foundations for a *basis*. The basis expresses a clear moral attitude with respect to a certain situation, but it is too vague to be applied as a rule in actual practice, lacking further definition; lacking criteria. A basis is the foundation for a *legal rule*, which *does* serve practical application, since the basis has been defined by normative choices. The legal rule includes *criteria* that define its field of application. The basic idea is that adjustments to legal rules for reasons of changes in society, request a reconsideration with regard to the basic idea and a basic principle to see whether it is necessary to construe a new rule, based on different principles, *i.e.*, to see if a legal rule still responds to the underlying principles and ideas. The development of legal rules on the basis of basic principles and a basis must guarantee consistency in a certain area of law.

11.2.3.2 Dutch Liability and Damages Law

When describing current liability and damages law it must be emphasised that liability law and the law of damages have been studied in mutual coherence, as one set of regulations. This choice was made because the author believes that this ties in with legal practice, where liability law and the law of damages often go hand in hand.

The characteristics of liability and damages law, as we currently know it, show that the regulations are based on basic principles that all constitute starting points that in some way include *harm*. The basic principles "each shall bear his/her own damage, not to injure another, to live honestly and to give to each one that which belongs to him/her" support the basis of liability and damages law,[55] which reads as follows: "any person who disadvantages another, thus acting contrary to fairness, is obliged to remedy the disadvantage caused by their act or omission". The basis for current liability and damages law serves as foundation for the rule that we nowadays

[55] See on these basic principles: Sieburgh (2000) 5 ff, Keirse (2003) 13 ff, Engelhard and Van Maanen (2008) 4–5, Nieuwenhuis (2008) 22–23.

read in art. 6:162 DCC and further in arts 6:95 ff DCC. The legal rule ensures a good balance and allows the weighing of many more factors than just the protection of the disadvantaged party's interests. One of the core elements is harm, which is not just one of the independent constitutive criteria resulting in a compensation obligation based on the unlawful act, but also is a component in the other constitutive criteria. The relativity criterion requires, for example, that the norm violated by the act or omission concerned serves to protect from the *harm* as actually suffered by the disadvantaged party.

11.2.3.3 European Fundamental Rights Law

The characteristics of ECHR law reveal differences with liability and damages law that are fundamental and refer to the basic principles and basis of the two systems. Contrary to current liability and damages law, the basic principles in ECHR law are *human dignity* and *fundamental freedom*. These basic principles have resulted in regulations that are primarily aimed at protecting fundamental rights. Violations of fundamental rights in itself will warrant action based on ECHR law. In the way that "harm" is a core element in liability and damages law regulations, "violation of rights" is a core element in ECHR law.

In ECHR law, the violation of rights is established in two steps. The first step is to establish interference with an interest that qualifies for protection under the ECHR. The interest of the disadvantaged party interest must be an interest that is protected by one or more ECHR rights. If this is true, this means that interference can actually be established. The second step is to assess this interference using the assessment framework constituted by the restrictive clauses accompanying the ECHR rights. These restrictive clauses in the ECHR are specific for a public-law relationship, as illustrated above under art. 8 para. 2 ECHR. This means that the ECtHR case-law only includes limited clues to support the development of fundamental rights in a private-law relationship. These clues are mainly found in the case law establishing the interests deserving protection.

11.2.4 Enforcing Fundamental Rights Through Current Dutch Liability and Damages Law

The comparison of the nature of liability and damages law and the nature of ECHR law has resulted in a twofold conclusion. The first part of this conclusion states that we should not look for the solution regarding the enforcement of fundamental rights in the liability for unlawful acts law only; a conclusion that cannot be read without the second part, which is that a new basis in liability law, in addition to the law governing liability for unlawful acts, can be used more directly and be more specifically geared towards ECHR rights in order to enforce ECHR rights.

An important point in the comparison is the observation that the bases in the two sets of regulations are essentially different. Liability and damages law, on the one hand, is based on the basic principles of "to live honestly, not to injure another, to give to each one that which belongs to him and each shall bear his own damage". The basic principles reveal that harm is a core element in liability and damages law as it is currently structured.

ECHR law, on the other hand, is based on the basic principles of human dignity and fundamental freedom. These basic principles have made ECHR law a system that aims to prevent rights violations and, where no longer possible, to sanction violations. Protection of fundamental interests is therefore the core element. Current liability and damages law, as opposed to ECHR law, more specifically aims to remedy an unfair situation which consists of harm caused by the wrongdoer on the aggrieved party through the shift of property from the former to the latter. Harm and the correlative relationship between the harmed and harm-inflicting party are therefore the core elements.

Although current liability and damages law shows that the core element of harm has a broad interpretation and also includes non-pecuniary damage, and that moreover the application of the criteria is sufficiently wide to take into account the fact that fundamental rights have been violated, the criteria of the unlawful act result in a clear definition. The criteria of unlawful act, attribution of fault, harm, causal connection and relativity create barriers that are easily explained in the law governing liability for unlawful acts, but which in certain cases prevents access to a remedy, whereas a remedy is necessary for the enforcement of rights.

The author believes that the nature of fundamental rights justifies a new basis in liability law in addition to the unlawful act, creating a specific approach to enforce fundamental rights: the breach of a fundamental right. The above considerations lead to the conclusion that the difference between the bases of liability and damages law as it is currently structured and of ECHR law will necessitate adaptation of liability law when the two systems are intertwined. Adaptation of liability law creates a new basis to support the concept of the breach of a fundamental right.

11.2.5 Introducing a New Legal Concept: The Concept of a Breach of a Fundamental Right

As a concept in civil law, the breach of a fundamental right contributes to the enforcement of fundamental rights in the private-law relationship. A breach of a fundamental right is an unjustified interference in individuals' interests most worthy of protection, that are protected within the framework of personal rights. Like the concept of an unlawful act, the breach of a fundamental right concept is a central set of regulations that also includes remedies designed to prevent harm, and remedies to impose fines in the event of breach. As opposed to the regulations governing unlawful acts, which answer the central question of, "Who bears the damage?" the fundamental rights breach answers the central question of, "Is a person affected in their dignity or fundamental freedom?" In view of the nature of the rights and the consequent impact automatically caused by a breach, there is strong emphasis, more than in liability for unlawful acts law, on preventive remedies, where remedies are concerned. The justification of providing a person with a remedy against the party causing the breach of a fundamental right is not in the act or omission causing harm, but in the fact that this party, by their act that caused the fundamental rights breach, has crossed the line of respect for another person's fundamental rights.

In Dutch civil law therefore, the breach of a fundamental right is to fulfil a role that is closely related to that of the unlawful act. Whereas the unlawful act provides a basis for the compensation of harm, the breach of a fundamental right provides a basis for the enforcement of rights. The legal rule that regulates the fundamental rights breach includes two constitutive requirements. The first requirement is the interference with an interest of the disadvantaged party that is protected by one or more fundamental rights, *i.e.*, interference with a fundamental right. The second requirement is that the interference has affected human dignity or fundamental freedom.

To satisfy the first requirement, the interests that are protected by fundamental rights need to be established and the interests as claimed by the disadvantaged party also need to be established, in order to decide whether interference with a fundamental right has occurred. The second requirement further restricts the protection based on the fundamental rights breach, because it needs to be established that the interference was so serious that it affected the disadvantaged party's human dignity or fundamental freedom. This will at least apply when a person has been affected in the very substance of their right.

The legal rule also includes a justification ground, stating that the wrongdoer is not liable if the interference was necessary to protect their own right or to exercise one of their rights or freedoms. To invoke this justification, it is also necessary that the prohibition of the wrongdoer's action would cause such breach of his or her own right or freedom that this would result in their own human dignity or fundamental freedom being affected. In the process of making of the choice to include this justification the starting point was that only circumstances that are at least as weighty as the interests of the disadvantaged party may justify interference.

If the court rules that, in principle, an unjustified breach has occurred, but that the infringing party has rightly invoked the justification, it is up to the court to weigh the conflict of interests. The court should do so using the assessment formula as introduced by *Gerards*, which the author believes would also be suitable in this private-law consideration.[56]

This formula states that the interests involved should first be defined. The court should take an active stance, meaning that it can process the parties' statements, but also needs to continue to ask questions if these statements do not offer sufficient information to define the interests involved. To ensure effective deliberations the court will then have to "approximate" the interests involved concerning their degree

[56] Gerards (2006).

of abstraction. After all, *Gerards* states, the more general the formulation of the interests, the higher the value that is usually attached to them. Approximating the interests will therefore make the consideration more neutral regarding values, *Gerards* states.

After approximating the interests as to their degree of abstraction, the question arises whether they should first be weighed individually, or whether they should immediately be weighed in comparison to each other. *Gerards* argues in favour of the former, and weighs the interests individually, before comparing the weight of the interests with each other. As to weight, it is easier to detect the weight in the severity of the extent to which the interest has been affected and the interest's significance in the realisation of purposes and interests, rather than in the established interest itself. The former is apparently easier to establish than the intrinsic value of the interests involved.

References

Barkhuysen, Tom, and Bart Jan Van Ettekoven. 2009. De compensatie voor schending van de redelijke termijn van art. 6 EVRM door de bestuursrechter. *Nederlands Tijdschrift voor Bestuursrecht* 23: 129–141.

Bartels, Steven E., and A.I.M. Van Mierlo Toon. 2013. *Mr. C. Assers Handleiding tot de beoefening van het Nederlands burgerlijk recht. 3-IV. Vermogensrecht algemeen. Algemeen goederenrecht.* Deventer: Kluwer.

Blauwhoff, Richard J. 2009. *Foundational facts. Relative truths. A comparative law study on children's right to know their genetic origins*. Antwerp: Intersentia.

Boesjes, J. 1973. De horizontale werking van grondrechten. *Nederlands Juristenblad* 49: 905–916.

Dijkshoorn, Walter. 2010. Overschrijding van de redelijke termijn: moet de burgerlijke rechter het EHRM of de bestuursrechter volgen? *Nederlands Juristenblad* 86: 1346–1351.

Drion, Huib. 1969. Civielrechtelijke werking van de grondrechten. *Nederlands Juristenblad* 45: 585–594.

Elders, Jacobus L.M., and Mark B.W. Biesheuvel. 1986. *Burgerlijk recht en grondrechten (preadviezen Vereniging voor Burgerlijk Recht)*. Lelystad: Koninklijke Vermande.

Emaus, Jessy M. 2013. *Handhaving van EVRM-rechten via het aansprakelijkheidsrecht* (with a summary in English). Den Haag: Boom Juridische uitgevers.

Emaus, Jessy M., and Anne L.M. Keirse. 2014. The Netherlands. In *European Tort law yearbook 2013*, ed. Ernst Karner and Barbara C. Steininger, 442–465. Berlin: De Gruyter.

Engelhard, Esther F.D., Van Maanen, and E. Gerrit. 2008. *Aansprakelijkheid voor schade: contractueel en buitencontractueel*. Deventer: Kluwer.

Gerards, Janneke H. 2006. *Belangenafweging bij rechterlijke toetsing aan fundamentele rechten (rede Leiden)*. Alphen aan den Rijn: Kluwer.

Groen, Bart H.A. 1995. De reikwijdte van fundamentele rechten in burgerlijke zaken. In *De reikwijdte van fundamentele rechten (Handelingen Nederlandse Juristen-Vereniging 1995-I)*, ed. Evert A. Alkema, Bart H.A. Groen, Peter J. Wattel, and Jan Naeyé, 131–173. Zwolle: Tjeenk Willink.

Hartkamp, Arthur S., and Carla H. Sieburgh. 2011. *Mr. C. Assers Handleiding tot de beoefening van het Nederlands burgerlijk recht. 6-IV*. De verbintenis uit de wet*. Deventer: Kluwer.

Hartlief, Ton. 2008. Handhaving met smartengeld. *Aansprakelijkheid Verzekering & Schade* 8: 237–247.

Keirse, Anne L.M. 2003. *Schadebeperkingsplicht: over eigen schuld aan de omvang van de schade*. Deventer: Kluwer.

Kortmann, Costantijn AJM. 1984. Horizontale werking van grondrechten? *De Nederlandse Gemeente* 38: 301–302.

Lindenbergh, Siewert D. 1999. De positie en de handhaving van persoonlijkheidsrechten in het Nederlandse privaatrecht. *Tijdschrift voor Privaatrecht* 37: 1665–1707.

Lindenbergh, Siewert D. 2008. *Smartengeld: tien jaar later*. Deventer: Kluwer.

Lindenbergh, Siewert D. 2010. Fundamental rights in private law. Anchors or goals in a globalizing legal order? In *Globalization and private law. The way forward*, ed. Michael Faure and André Van der Walt, 367–382. Cheltenham: Edward Elgar.

Lindenbergh, Siewert D. 2013. De prijs van vertraging. *Aansprakelijkheid Verzekering & Schade* 13: 15.

Lindenbergh, Siewert D. 2014. Effectieve remedie bij overschrijding redelijke termijn *in civilibus*. Over doorwerking, inpassing en verdere doorwerking van het EVRM in het privaatrecht. *Ars Aequi* 63: 636–642.

Maris, Guus. 1969. Dient de wet bijzondere regelen te bevatten ten aanzien van de civielrechtelijke werking van de grondrechten, en, zo ja, welke? In *Dient de wet bijzondere regelen te bevatten ten aanzien van de civielrechtelijke werking van de grondrechten, en, zo ja, welke? (Handelingen Nederlandse Juristen-Vereniging 1969-I)*, ed. Guus Maris and Jim M. Polak, 9–67. Zwolle: Tjeenk Willink.

Nehmelman, Remco. 2002. *Het algemeen persoonlijkheidsrecht. Een rechtsvergelijkende studie naar het algemeen persoonlijkheidsrecht in Duitsland en Nederland*. Deventer: Kluwer.

Nieuwenhuis, Hans. 2000. De Constitutie van het burgerlijk recht. *Rechtsgeleerd Magazijn Themis* 161: 203–211.

Nieuwenhuis, Hans. 2008. *Onrechtmatige daden. Délits, Unerlaubte Handlungen, Torts. Buitencontractueel aanpsrakelijkheidsrecht in Europees perspectief*. Deventer: Kluwer.

Rijnhout, Rianka and Emaus, Jessy M. 2014. Damages in wrongful death cases in the light of European human rights law: Towards a rights-based approach to the law of damages. Utrecht Law Review 10: 91–106.

Scheltema, Martijn W., and Michiel Scheltema. 2013. *Gemeenschappelijk recht. Wisselwerking tussen publiek- en privaatrecht*. Deventer: Kluwer.

Sieburgh, Carla H. 1997. Wat is een rechtsinbreuk? *Nederlands Juristenblad* 73: 628–635.

Sieburgh, Carla H. 2000. *Toerekening van een onrechtmatige daad*. Deventer: Kluwer.

Smits, Jan. 2003. Constitutionalisering van het vermogensrecht. In *Preadviezen uitgebracht voor de Nederlandse Vereniging voor Rechtsvergelijking*. Deventer: Kluwer.

Snijders, Gerbrand. 2011. *Overheidsprivaatrecht, algemeen deel. Monografieën BW A26a*. Deventer: Kluwer.

Staatsblad. 2013. Besluit van 22 April 2013 tot vaststelling van het tijdstip van inwerkingtreding van de Wet nadeelcompensatie en schadevergoeding bij onrechtmatige besluiten en gedeelten uit het Besluit van 20 December 2012 tot wijziging van het Besluit proceskosten bestuursrecht in verband met indexering van de bedragen en toevoeging van enkele proceshandelingen (Stb. 2012, 683), voor zover het betreft schadevergoeding wegens onrechtmatig bestuurshandelen.

Van Kessel, Laura W.C.M. 2014. HR 28 maart 2014, ECLI:NL:HR:2014:736 (Eiser c.s./Gemeente De Bilt): Redres van schendingen van het recht op berechting binnen redelijke termijn in civiele procedures. *Nederlands Tijdschrift voor Burgerlijk Recht* 31: 266–274.

Verheij, Albert J. 2013. Twee benaderingen van vergoeding van immateriële schade. *Verkeersrecht* 61: 269–276.

Verheij, Albert J. 2002. *Vergoeding van immateriële schade wegens aantasting in de persoon*. Nijmegen: Ars Aequi.

Warendorf, Hans C.S., Thomas Richard, and Curry-Sumner Ian. 2013. *The civil code of the Netherlands*. Alphen aan den Rijn: Kluwer Law International.

Chapter 12
Damages for the Infringements of Human Rights Under Norwegian Law

Bjarte Thorson

12.1 General Notes on the Norwegian Tort Law and Human Rights Regulation

12.1.1 Norwegian Tort Law

Norwegian tort law is largely built upon the ideas of reparation, prevention and risk spreading, sometimes supplemented by an analogy to expropriation, i.e. that where public interests prevail to the detriment of individuals, the latter should be compensated. The body of law developed in order to support these ideas is a mixture of written and unwritten law, derived from, respectively, dispersed legislative measures and, first and foremost, jurisprudence from the Norwegian Supreme Court.[1] Given the unwritten nature of much of the law, it is also a common view that doctrine plays a certain role in the development of it.[2]

This law on torts, ordinarily designated as concerning liability for *delicts*[3] or on non-contractual grounds, is generally to be considered as private law, even if the alleged tortfeasor is a civil servant or a public authority as such. As a starting point, the same rules and principles will therefore apply to private and public actors. There

[1] Published in a law report named *Norsk Retstidende*, commonly and hereinafter abbreviated as 'Rt.'.

[2] The three textbooks on Norwegian tort law, as of today, are Nygaard Nils. 2007. *Skade og ansvar*, Universitetsforlaget, Bergen, Lødrup Peter. 2009. *Lærebok i erstatningsrett*, Gyldendal akademisk, Oslo and Stenvik Are and Hagstrøm Viggo. 2015. *Erstatningsrett*, Universitetsforlaget, Oslo.

[3] This implies that the phrase 'liability for *delicts*' in a Norwegian context, does not always point to, e.g. negligence, unlawfulness, infringements of criminal codes, *et cetera*. It is often used merely as a general reference to a number of common liability rules that are not dependent upon breaches of contracts.

B. Thorson (✉)
Department of Private Law, Faculty of Law, University of Oslo, Oslo, Norway
e-mail: bjarte.thorson@jus.uio.no

E. Bagińska (ed.), *Damages for Violations of Human Rights*,
Ius Comparatum - Global Studies in Comparative Law 9,
DOI 10.1007/978-3-319-18950-5_12

may, however, be variations as to *how* the rules and principles are interpreted and applied with regard to the two. Neither are infringements of human rights – as a starting point – subject to a special regime; they are largely governed by the same rules and principles, and, consequently, it is first and foremost via interpretation and application that the particular features of human rights infringements must be taken into account. Therefore, this paper will, to some extent, address and present the general regime that is Norwegian tort law, and seek to illustrate its application in cases concerning human rights infringements. Already at the outset, it may be mentioned that the court cases apt to illustrate these issues are scarce. Nor are there any doctrinal works on Norwegian tort law that go in-depth on human rights infringements; contrarily, human rights are for the most part only briefly mentioned.

The abovementioned is, however, not the whole picture. First, there are also – albeit still a limited number of – judgments that seem to regard at least some human rights infringements as giving a, more or less, *per se* right to damages. Secondly, some legislative acts governing particular areas related to human rights also contain liability rules, e.g. the Act relating to Gender Equality.[4] Thirdly, Norwegian tort law consists of an interplay between the general liability rules on the one hand, and specific rules providing for rights and duties derived from legislation on the other. This also holds true as regards human rights. It is therefore useful to provide an overview of the general human rights regulation before going into details on the liability regime.

12.1.2 Norwegian Human Rights Regulation

At the outset it should be mentioned that Norway has a tradition of dualism as regards the relationship between international and national law. There are of course not necessarily any clear borders between dualism and monism, e.g. as emphasising conformity and loyalty *vis-à-vis* international treaties may affect interpretation of domestic rules. All in all, one may even question how useful this dichotomy is with respect to Norway today. The simple *starting point* is, however, at least that international law will not form part of the internal Norwegian legal order on the same terms as acts sanctioned by the Parliament, without participation of the legislator.

The Norwegian Constitution of 17 May 1814 has always contained certain specific rules that address different – first of all civil and political – human rights. The Constitution was, however, altered in 2014, when, *inter alia*, a more extensive catalogue of human rights was inserted in, what is now, its Section E, a novelty titled 'human rights'. In this Section, not only numerous civil and political rights, but also several economic, social and cultural rights are set out. Thus, it has become a true 'catalogue', in the sense that it starts with a provision which vests the State with the obligation to ensure and secure the human rights as they are accorded in the

[4] Parliamentary act 21 June 2013 no. 59, Article 28 (entry into force 1 January 2014, replacing Parliamentary act 9 June 1978 no. 45, Article 17).

Constitution and treaties binding upon Norway (Article 92), followed by provisions on the right to life and ban of torture *et cetera* (Article 93), *habeas corpus* and ban of arbitrary detentions *et cetera* (Article 94), fair trial (Article 94), the principle of *in dubio pro reo* (Article 95) – and so on. Some rights are still found in other parts of the Constitution where they functionally relate to specific areas; for instance, there is a provision in the Section dealing with the electoral system that sets out that elections of members of Parliament shall be free and secret (Article 49).

Before the major revision of the Constitution, which took place this year (2014), the Constitution had relatively few specific Articles setting out human rights, but contained, instead, a general rule in then-Article 110c, after which it was the responsibility of the authorities of the State to respect and ensure human rights, and after which specific provisions for the implementation of treaties thereon should be determined by law. In line with this, an Act on human rights was adopted in 1999.[5] The legislative technique chosen with respect to that Act was to set out a rule in its Article 2, according to which a number of international conventions should, fully or partly, immediately be regarded as domestic law. Without going into all details as to which protocols, this generally goes for the Convention for the Protection of Human Rights and Fundamental Freedoms (ECHR) of 4 November 1950, the International Covenant on Economic, Social and Cultural Rights (ICESCR) of 16 December 1966, the International Covenant on Civil and Political Rights (ICCPR) of 16 December 1966, the Convention on the Rights of the Child (CRC) of 20 November 1989 and the Convention on the Elimination of All Forms of Discrimination against Women (CEDAW) of 18 December 1979. Article 3 of the Act on human rights lays down that in cases of discrepancy between provisions in the conventions and the protocols mentioned in Article 2 and other legislative provisions, the former shall prevail. This Act can be updated by amendment acts when changes in the related treaties so demand, or if new inclusions should prove desirable. At present, it was last altered in May 2014 due to the adoption of ECHR Protocol 15.

Additionally, the Norwegian legislator will, naturally, pay recourse to human rights in general, as well as obligations under specific international treaties in particular, when developing any kind of legislation. This is often reflected in the preparatory works, which under Norwegian law are important sources of arguments when interpreting a legislative act. *Par exemple*, the CRC is reflected in the Norwegian Child Welfare Act[6] and highlighted in the preparatory works of this act[7]; the CEDAW is today reflected in the Norwegian Act relating to Gender Equality and highlighted in the preparatory works to amendments of this act[8]; there is a separate Act on

[5] Parliamentary act 25 May 1999 no. 30.

[6] Parliamentary act 17 July 1992 no. 100.

[7] Cf Proposition to the Parliament 2012–2013 no. 88 L, and, for the previous act, e.g., Proposition to the Odelsting (Parliament) 1991–1992 no. 44.

[8] Cf, e.g., Proposition to the Odelsting (Parliament) 2000–2001 no. 77.

prohibition of discrimination based on ethnicity, religion, etc.,[9] which is adopted also in order to ensure the protection of human rights[10]; *et cetera*.

When, for instance, the Act relating to Gender Equality and the Act on prohibition of discrimination based on ethnicity, religion, etc. additionally have special rules on damages, this of course directly affects the protection of human rights in tort law. Reflecting human rights in legislation will, however, also indirectly aid the protection of human rights in tort law in general because legislation plays a role under, particularly, the general rules of *culpa liability* and *vicarious liability* for employers. This will be further explained below.

12.1.3 Brief Notes on Proof and Procedures

Norwegian courts are as a rule not specialised, and so there are normally not different courts for, e.g., judicial review in administrative matters, civil claims of damages, criminal cases, *et cetera*, notwithstanding whom the addressees of the claims should be. As of today, the courts also usually handle the different types of cases under the same designation. That is '*tingrett*' for the 65 district courts,[11] '*lagmannsrett*' for the six appeal courts and '*Høyesterett*' for the Supreme Court. This means that the same courts merely apply different codes of procedure in civil and penal cases, respectively the Act relating to mediation and procedure in civil disputes[12] and the Act relating to legal procedure in criminal cases.[13] The latter also governs, *inter alia*, certain cases concerning eventual committal to compulsory mental health care.

A party claiming damages for a human rights infringement may instigate ordinary civil proceedings against the alleged tortfeasor. Yet, if the public prosecutor initiates criminal proceedings, the victim will also normally be able to have his/her claim for damages handled during the same proceedings, and be ruled in the same judgment, as that concerning the eventual penal sanctions.[14] In this way the victim may obtain a ruling on his/her damages claim simply, without cost, and without, at least in a great deal of such cases, playing any central role in the proceedings, a matter which may be appealing to the victim e.g. if he/she has only suffered minor losses. Such inclusion in criminal proceedings of a claim against the person charged by any person who has suffered direct damage from the criminal act, may only be refused

[9] Parliamentary act 21 June 2013 no. 60 (entry into force 1 January 2014, replacing Parliamentary act 3 June 2005 no. 33).

[10] Cf Proposition to the Parliament 2012–2013 no. 88 L, and, for the previous act, e.g., Proposition to the Odelsting (Parliament) 2004–2005 no. 33.

[11] Which, along with *one* special court in Oslo (*Oslo byfogdembete*), make up for the 66 courts of the ordinary first instance.

[12] Parliamentary act 17 June 2005 no. 90.

[13] Parliamentary act 22 May 1981 no. 25.

[14] Parliamentary act 22 May 1981 no. 25, Chapter 29.

if the said claim is obviously unjustified or if it would cause disproportionate inconvenience for the hearing of the criminal case if the claim were pursued in connection with it.[15]

The standard of proof as regards a damages claim is normally 'more likely than not', i.e. over 50 % likelihood.[16] With such lenient standards of proof, there is relatively little need for such concepts as loss of a chance under Norwegian law. The Supreme Court has, however, held that if the imposition of some sort of civil law sanction implies putting severely onerous or burdensome characteristics on the defendant's conduct, it should be proven that the alleged conduct has *significantly* more likely than not taken place. There is no general rule that such proof is needed where civil liability also indicates that the defendant may have acted in breach of penal provisions, but this is arguably an area in which this elevated requirement of proof plays an important role.[17] Nonetheless, it does not have to pass the threshold for imposing criminal sanctions, which is 'beyond reasonable doubt' in accordance with the principle of *in dubio pro reo*. Thus, a person may be acquitted of criminal charges yet held to pay damages due to a *delict* that in fact is the same as that which the criminal charges were based upon. This may also happen in the same judgment.[18]

It may also be added that Norway has a Parliamentary Ombudsman for Public Administration, an institution of which the purpose is, *inter alia*, to help to ensure that human rights are respected.[19] If the Ombudsman finds that there are matters that may entail liability to pay compensation, he/she may also, depending on the circumstances, suggest that compensation should be paid.[20] This is, however, not binding upon the authorities.

12.1.4 Extra-Legal Compensations

Also at the outset, before turning to the rules on liability, it should be mentioned that there have been some cases in which the Norwegian State has taken upon itself to compensate individuals claiming to have had their human rights infringed, without necessarily paying recourse to questions of eventual liability in law. With roots that may be traced back to the time when the Norwegian Constitution had just been established in 1814, a tradition of *ex gratia* payments from the State has developed. This is also an appropriate way to handle historical injustices, as there are, normally, no prescription rules, given the nature of *ex gratia* compensation, while an ordinary

[15] Parliamentary act 22 May 1981 no. 25, Article 427.

[16] Cf, e.g., Rt. 1992 page 64.

[17] Cf, e.g., Rt. 1995 page 1641; Rt. 1999 page 1363; and Rt. 2005 page 1322.

[18] The case in Rt. 1987 page 1495, cf, below, chapter 2.2.4.2, gives an indication that the courts may operate with rather lenient standards of proof as regards the hypothetical assessments that have to be made in order to determine eventual loss of income due to unlawful detentions.

[19] Parliamentary act 22 June 1962 no. 8, Article 3.

[20] Parliamentary act 22 June 1962 no. 8, Article 10.

claim for damages in tort will generally be barred after three years according to the Act relating to the prescription of claims.[21]

On some occasions the *ex gratia* payment system has also been specifically adapted in order to deal appropriately with claims for certain groups of claimants. Some examples are claims from citizens of the Romani people due to maltreatment following from an assimilation policy that was, at some point, the policy of the Norwegian State; citizens of the Sami and Kven people, both minorities in Norway, due to lack of schooling in their own language; and claims from Jewish people due to confiscations of properties during the occupation of Norway during World War II.[22]

12.2 Liability Conditions

12.2.1 Legally Relevant Damage

Historically, Norwegian tort law was linked to a notion of subjective rights. This link gradually disintegrated during the first part of the twentieth century, and what is left is a more generally shaped requirement of a legally relevant damage. All in the doctrine, jurisprudence and legislative measures, there are, in this regard, some distinctions made between personal injuries and property damages on the one hand, and pure economic losses on the other.

As concerns personal injuries and property damages, a further distinction may be made between the physical or, in the case of personal injuries, mental injury, and the losses flowing therefrom. First, the physical or mental injury has to represent an infringement of a legally protected interest. In practise, bodily health and property are, however, considered as *per se* protected, meaning that there are only a few situations in which a physical or mental injury will not fulfil this requirement, and these may, thus, for practical purposes be considered as exceptions. The latter has so far been the case with, *inter alia*, wrongful birth, as held by the Supreme Court in the case Rt. 1999 page 203, in which a claim for damages due to an ineffective vasectomy was dismissed. The decision reported in Rt. 2013 page 1689 concerned a woman who had given birth to a child with Down syndrome, wherefore she developed an anxiety/depression disorder. In accordance with the Act on patient injury compensation,[23] the hospital was accountable for this mental injury due to the fact that it had not offered the woman an amniocentesis. It was undisputed that this test would have revealed that the child had Down syndrome, and that the woman upon this revelation would have aborted the pregnancy. The Supreme Court, by three to two votes, held that psychological distress related to giving birth to a child could not

[21] Parliamentary act 18 May 1979 no. 18, Article 9.

[22] Cf on these specially adopted payment systems, Report to the parliament 2003–2004 no. 44 ("White paper") 2 July 2004.

[23] The Act on patient injury compensation, 15 June 2001 no. 53.

be considered as a legally relevant damage. The Court also added, following considerations on jurisprudence by the European Court of Human Rights,[24] that neither ECHR Article 3 nor ECHR Article 8 had been violated.

Following the doctrine, this will also be the case with directly unlawful interests, e.g. damage to illegal drugs. It is a subject of debate whether, and if so to what extent, other interests may be excluded on moral grounds.

Secondly, personal injuries and property damages must, as a general rule, have led to some kind of economic loss in order to be recoverable. There are, however, some special regimes governing non-economic losses, some of which will be dealt with in the following, and some exceptions stemming from case law, regarding, *inter alia*, preventive costs, which will not be handled further.

Pure economic losses are not subject to a general exclusionary rule under Norwegian law, but cannot, unlike personal injuries and property damages, for practical purposes be considered as *per se* protected. Determination of whether a particular purely economic interest is protected depends on a broad assessment in which key factors are, on the one hand, eventual expressions in favour of protection that may be found in legislative measures or may otherwise be derived from, an arguably more vague notion of, legitimate or reasonable expectations, and on the other hand, more openly policy-oriented questions of risk-placement and eventual benefits of private enforcement. Under given circumstances the test for unravelling whether a pure economic loss represents an infringement of a protected interest may bear some likelihood to the assessment of whether there is a sufficiently close and adequate causal connection (see infra at Sect. 12.2.3.2). There are therefore numerous examples of cases in which the courts *de facto* skip the questions concerning protected interest when there is no sufficient normative causation anyway. Moreover, there are many cases in which the courts simply have not raised the question of whether a pure economic loss enjoys protection in tort, seemingly because the question has been considered as giving no rise to doubts. The latter may also serve to indicate that Norwegian law is not very 'strict' as regards recoverability of pure economic losses.

Part of the question of a protected interest concerns public services or supervision, *et cetera*. In such cases the claimant may meet a particular obstacle notwithstanding the nature of the damage, be it a personal injury, property damage or a pure economic loss. The typical issue in these contexts is whether establishing some sort of public service, say, lighthouse services along the coast, also implies liability in tort when someone relying on the service experiences damage because his/her expectations are not met, e.g. the ship crashing because the lighthouse lamp is erroneously off. The conclusion may be a compromise, for instance that only grave or manifest departures from the standard prescribed by the act establishing the service may be followed by liability. The latter has led to a practise by the Supreme Court according to which it often discusses this question not as a question of protected interests, but rather as a question of which 'standard' of negligence that should be applied.

[24] Namely, *R.R.* v *Poland* (26 May 2011); and *Draon* v *France* (6 October 2005).

As regards human rights infringements, the abovementioned implies that the requirement of a legally protected damage should not on a general basis be problematic. The strong expression of the worthiness of protection of human rights given via the Constitution and the general human rights act would, in itself, largely suffice as a foundation for concluding that the interest at issue enjoys protection under the law of liability for *delicts*.

12.2.2 Accountability

12.2.2.1 General Notes on the Accountability Rules

Reasons of accountability under Norwegian law are partly set out in legislation, some of which are general – i.e. they may, as a starting point, give rise to liability for any kind of injury –, some of which only cover particular injuries or heads of damage, *par exemple* by positively covering 'pollution damage',[25] or by positively covering personal injuries and property damages,[26] by which *a contrario* ruling out pure economic loss. Partly, reasons of accountability are derived from case law only, some of which have a general application, while some liability rules or principles may be confined to specific areas or situations. In general it should be noted that the different rules on accountability do not, in the absence of particular rules laying down otherwise,[27] rule each other out or canalise the liability to particular subjects, i.e. they may overlap.

A part of the accountability rules is also the issue of *who* the addressees are, i.e. who may be sued and ordered to pay the damages. In the judgment reported in Rt. 2010 page 291, cf, as to the facts, below, chapter 2.2.4.2, the damages claim was directed towards a municipality, and partly based on ECHR Articles 1 and 41. The Supreme Court noted that only the States are subjects of duty under ECHR, and from this, drew the conclusion that only the State level may be sued and held to pay damages. It is submitted that this is, at best, not an advisable approach. As it is clear that the municipalities are included in the notion of a State under ECHR, this finding of the Norwegian Supreme Court *de facto* means that the State level must be held liable for breaches committed at the municipality level, which contradicts the general principles under Norwegian law. The Swedish courts have arrived at different conclusions.[28] It has, nonetheless, been upheld by the Norwegian Supreme Court in the decision reported in Rt. 2011 page 1166.

---

[25] Cf, e.g. Parliamentary act 13 March 1981 no. 6 (Pollution control Act), Article 53.

[26] Cf, e.g. Parliamentary act 23 December 1988 no. 104 (Products liability Act), Article 2–3.

[27] Some examples of rules laying down otherwise are to be found in Parliamentary acts 16 June 1989 no. 65 (Act on industrial injury insurance), Article 8 and 15 June 2001 no. 53 (Act on patient injury compensation), Article 4(3).

[28] Cf, e.g. the judgment by the Swedish Supreme Court (*Högsta Domstolen*) reported in the Swedish Law Report *Nytt juridiskt arkiv* (NJA) 2009 page 463.

12.2.2.2 Culpability

The most general rule of accountability is that of *culpa* or negligence. The general rule on *culpa* is unwritten, but nonetheless also codified in many different acts, partly out of purely informational purposes.

Under Norwegian law culpability is normally considered to consist of an objective and a subjective element.

The objective element concerns the *unlawfulness* of the act or omission at issue. As regards personal injuries and property damages, the creation of a given degree of risk of damage will normally suffice to constitute unlawfulness. Non-elimination of a given degree of risk of damage may also suffice, depending on how, factually and legally, close the alleged tortfeasor is considered to be to the risk. Such a general duty not to create unacceptable risks for others' personal integrity and property is, however, not applicable when dealing with purely economic interests. As regards pure economic loss, unlawfulness must therefore normally be construed as a violation of some other specific written or unwritten norm, and eventually as an infringement of the claimant's legitimate expectations.

The subjective element refers to the fact that objective unlawfulness is not sufficient to establish culpability. The tortfeasor must additionally be *to blame* for his/her act or omission. As the subjective element is an addition to the objective element, the content may vary depending on what constitutes the unlawfulness in the first place. If the unlawfulness consists of a violation of the prohibition of creating an unacceptable risk for other persons or their property, it will generally suffice for the subjective element that the tortfeasor could, with sufficient ease, have avoided or eliminated the risk by acting differently. This is an assessment of, *inter alia*, the costs involved and the time available. When unlawfulness is construed as primarily a violation of a more specific legal provision, which is generally the matter when dealing with pure economic loss, the subjective element mainly concerns the question of whether the tortfeasor may be excused due to an – excusable – error of facts or in law.

The *culpa* rule governs liability for legal persons including public authorities under a theory of identification between the legal person and its representatives, comparable to the German '*Organtheorie*'. Breaches of statutory duties are not considered as a separate tort or liability type under Norwegian law. However, statutory duties and other written norms are relevant both in cases of personal injuries or property damages, and in cases concerning pure economic loss. In the former, statutory duties and other written norms are considered to shed light on the standard of duty of care the tortfeasor's behaviour will be tested against, and, as regards pure economic loss, breaches of statutory duties and other written norms will, as just mentioned, often amount to *culpa* unless the tortfeasor can show that his/her act or omission was due to an excusable error of facts or in law, of which particularly, errors in law will generally seldom be considered excusable. It follows from this that not only provisions expressly laying down duties for the tortfeasor may be relevant. If it is possible to, via interpretation, derive duties for the tortfeasor from provisions that expressly only grant rights to the claimant, such may also be relevant.

The test for relevance is, first and foremost, that the provisions must be interpreted as to address the relationship between the tortfeasor and the claimant, as well as to have the purpose to regulate situations such as the one in which the damage occurred. These will generally be the same rules that the claimant invokes in order to justify that his/her losses represent an infringement of a legally relevant interest (cf, supra at Sect. 12.2.1).

Culpa liability will govern infringements of human rights. Moreover, the human rights regulation may shed light on the standard of care that the tortfeasor's conduct will be tested against. Thus, as the human rights regulation gives strong expressions of the level of protection of the interests concerned, there may only be limited options for the tortfeasor to argue that he/she is not to blame for an unlawful act. This type of reasoning may contribute to blurring the differences between *culpa* and strict liability, but it is well recognised by the Supreme Court that the delineation between different accountability regimes may at times be rather vague.[29]

12.2.2.3 Vicarious Liability for Employers

Vicarious non-contractual liability is codified in the Compensation Act,[30] after which employers may be held liable for injuries caused by their employees in the course of work, conditional upon negligence at the hands of the employee and, briefly put, a sufficient connection between the employee's negligent act or omission and his/her work duties. This Article governs liability for the public for injuries caused by civil servants, and it is in this regard important that also so-called 'anonymous and cumulative' faults fall within the scope of the Article. This implies that it does not rule out liability if one cannot point to a fault of one specific employee, and that several faults may be considered as a whole when assessing whether the requirement of negligence is fulfilled. In practise, this gives room for liability in cases of 'systemic errors' in the public authority or private company at issue.

The rule on vicarious liability for employers will govern infringements of human rights. Also in this regard, human rights regulation will form part of the legal basis when establishing the standard of duty of care against which the employee's conduct will be tested. The situation as regards this is, for the most part, comparable to that under the rule of *culpa*.

The judgment reported in Rt. 2012 page 146 concerned claims for damages from a person who had been the victim of bullying for several years in a municipal preliminary school, a matter which later led to post-traumatic stress disorder, social phobia and depression, which in its turn led to the claimant having to quit his higher studies. The claims were directed towards the municipality as responsible for the school, on the basis, foremost, that the school staff had not taken sufficient steps to stop the bullying.

---

[29] Cf, e.g. Rt. 1970 page 1192; and Rt. 2000 page 388.

[30] Parliamentary act 13 June 1969 no. 26, Article 2–1.

The Supreme Court ruled in favour of the claimant. All judges agreed on the need for a very high standard of care in order to combat bullying. This has to be seen in light of, *inter alia*, the fact that school implies an obligation of staying in a particular environment over a long period of time. This may at least be considered as a duty *de facto* on the child, and undoubtedly *de jure* at the hands of the parents, punishable by law.[31] One judge, notably, also drew upon the CRC before concluding that there was a 'massive' legal foundation for ordering schools to do whatever is within their means to combat and stop bullying. Thus, the judgment illuminates how the human rights regulation may impact the general rules on liability.

12.2.2.4 Strict Liability Regimes

Liability for High-Risk Sources

A particular type of strict liability has been developed through case-law, namely liability for, e.g., businesses, arrangements, properties or, simply, any kind of 'things' which are seen to constantly represent a particular degree of risk – exceeding the *'tolerance limit'* of those in their surroundings – which is also especially characteristic for the relevant source of the risk. Historically, this liability form is a product of the new types and degrees of risks that came along with the industrialisation of Norway in the late 1800s, but as of today it is not confined to industrial factories or the likes. It may, for example, just as well cover injuries due to loose roof tiles of city tenements. This type of liability will normally be restricted to the owner of the source of the risk, e.g. the building, but may in exceptional circumstances also include others with sufficient connections to the source, e.g. tenants. The liability issue has primarily to be solved via a broad assessment of the risks stemming from the source at issue, particularly whether there is a continuous risk for injuries, whether this risk is particularly characteristic for the source at issue and whether this risk to a sufficient degree exceeds the risks that anyone are exposed to in their everyday life. This risk assessment is, however, supplemented by broad policy considerations.

This unwritten rule on liability for high-risk sources is also general, and thus will also govern human rights infringements. It seems that the practical implications of this are, at least so far, limited. The European Court of Human Rights' judgment in *Vilnes and Others* vs. *Norway*,[32] (see infra at Sect. 12.2.2.5) may, however, indicate that this type of liability serves a certain role also with respect to ensuring an adequate remedy to violations of, in that case, ECHR Article 8.

---

[31] Parliamentary act 17 July 1998 no. 61, Article 2–1.

[32] *Vilnes and Others* v *Norway* (5 December 2013).

Strict Liability for Public Authorities

If the State acts, as a legal person, on equal terms as a private legal or physical person, it will be subject to the *culpa* rule and, eventually, the rule of vicarious liability for employers. Whether, and if so, to what extent, public authorities have to be evaluated under a strict liability regime when they exercise public authority, has been, and still is, the subject of some debate among Norwegian scholars. It is clear that the Supreme Court has held public authorities liable on a non-fault basis in several rulings; the discussions concern whether these are expressions of a general rule of strict liability, or exceptions from the general rules of culpa liability and vicarious liability.

The public Norway is divided into state level, county level and municipality level. Legal actions may be taken against each. The abovementioned doctrinal discussions as of today mostly revolve around the issue of liability for the state-level. The case Rt. 2010 page 291 (supra at Sect. 12.2.2.1) concerned liability for a municipality for its refusal of an application to alter the allowed type of usage of a property, a matter which, at the time of the facts, was governed by an Act of 14 June 1985 no. 77 on planning and building, Article 93. The judgment's *ratio decidendi* clearly shows that liability for municipalities is not, as a main rule, strict. The judgment also contains *obiter dicta* indicating that the same holds true for state liability.

Even if this should be the correct interpretation of the *obiter dicta*, there are many exceptions from this starting point, i.e. where strict liability will be imposed. Thus, notwithstanding what is the correct approach to the question of what is the main rule and what are the exceptions, infringements of human rights will nonetheless often be cases in which one can easily picture the *delict* as being regarded to fall within an area governed by strict liability.

The decision reported in Rt. 1987 page 1495 concerned claims of damages put forward by a person who had been the victim of unlawful retention in a psychiatric hospital for a number of years. The claims covered both economic and non-economic losses.

The Supreme Court established that, due to the degree of intervention in a person's most essential interests, i.e. personal freedom and integrity, cases of unlawful detention and retention in psychiatric hospitals should, as a main rule, be governed by a strict liability regime. The claim was therefore successful. No remarks were given as to an eventual infringement of ECHR Article 5.

Some rules on strict liability in cases of arrests or detainment, *et cetera,* are laid down in the Act relating to legal procedure in criminal cases,[33] cf, below, chapter 2.2.6.

12.2.2.5 Autonomous Accountability Rules for Human Rights Infringements

The Supreme Court has not been entirely clear as to whether human rights infringements may also give rise to a liability *sui generis*. Such liability may possibly be built upon the basis of, e.g., ECHR Articles 13 or 41, in conjunction with the Norwegian Act on human rights,[34] Article 2, cf, above, chapter 1.2.

[33] Parliamentary act 22 May 1981 no. 25.

[34] Parliamentary act 25 May 1999 no. 30.

ECHR Article 13

It is well settled, following the European Court of Human Rights, that the right to effective remedies defined in ECHR Article 13 may also include a right to compensation if appropriate.[35] What is less clear is the question of whether the Norwegian Supreme Court considers this as a separate basis of liability under Norwegian law, or whether this is foremost a standard to 'test' the domestic liability rules against.

The case reported in Rt. 2010 page 291 concerned, as mentioned above, liability for a municipality for its refusal of an application to alter the allowed type of usage of a property. The claimant also argued that the municipality's liability could be based on an infringement of ECHR Article 1 of Protocol no. 1 combined with an infringement of the right to an effective remedy in ECHR Article 13. The Supreme Court found that there had been no violation of ECHR Article 13, as the claimant had obtained a ruling on the validity of the refusal and would be entitled to compensation should the conditions for vicarious liability set out in the Compensation Act[36] Article 2–1 be fulfilled. This judgment indicates that the Supreme Court does not consider ECHR Article 13 as a separate ground of liability under Norwegian law, as long as one of the ordinary liability rules appears adequate.

The Court in the case Rt. 2013 page 588 adjudicated claims from a woman who had been the victim of a long and terrifying persecution by a man whom she had previously had a brief relationship with. The claim was directed towards the State, on the basis that the State had not fulfilled its obligations to protect her against the persecution. The Supreme Court found that the man's acts substantively amounted to a violation of ECHR Article 8. It did not conclude as to whether they also substantively amounted to an infringement of ECHR Article 3. On the decisive question of whether the State had failed to comply with ECHR Article 1, i.e. the duty to secure the rights and freedoms defined in ECHR Section 1, the Supreme Court gave extensive reasons when elaborating the rule, taking into account a number of rulings by the European Court of Human Rights.[37] Referral was also made to the Council of Europe Convention on preventing and combating violence against women and domestic violence of 11 May 2011. Ultimately, the Supreme Court found that the State had failed to fulfil its obligations under ECHR Article 1.

Nonetheless, the implications of the ruling as regards the liability issue are unclear. This is due to the fact that the District Court, i.e. the court of first instance, had used an option under the Act relating to mediation and procedure in civil

---

[35] Cf, e.g., *Leander* v *Sweden* (26 March 1987) para 77.

[36] Parliamentary act 13 June 1969 no. 26.

[37] Namely, *H.L.R.* v *France* (29 April 1997) para 40; *Osman* v *United Kingdom* (28 October 1998) paras 115–116; *Opuz* v *Turkey* (9 June 2009) paras 159 and 164; *Valiuliene* v *Lithuania* (26 March 2013) paras 75–76 and 85; *Wilson* v *United Kingdom* (23 October 2012) para 37; *Kontravá* v *Slovakia* (31 May 2007) para 50; *Milanovic* v Serbia (14 December 2010) para 84; *Dordevic* v *Croatia* (24 July 2012) para 139; *Kalucza* v *Hungary* (24 April 2012) para 64; *Kowal* v *Poland* (18 September 2012) para 51; *A* v *Croatia* (14 October 2010) paras 78–79; *Bevacqua* v *Bulgaria* (12 June 2008) paras 64–65; *Hajduová* v *Slovakia* (30 November 2010) para 50; and *E.M.* v *Romania* (30 October 2012) para 58.

disputes,[38] to split the proceedings into two, whereafter the question of whether the ECHR had been breached was judged separately. This is arguably an option under Article 16-1(2) of this act, yet the normal case would be that the proceedings are split so that *all conditions for liability* are determined first, whereafter there will be separate proceedings on – and only on – *the extent of the damages* if the first ruling goes in favour of the claimant. In the current case, however, only the issue of eventual breach of the ECHR was dealt with, even though the Supreme Court as well as the court of first instance expressly mentioned that the proceedings were split so that only 'the basis for liability' was at issue. It is possible that the judgment has to be interpreted to presuppose that violations of ECHR Article 1 will *per se* amount to liability. This also makes it possible that the Supreme Court considers ECHR Article 13 as a separate ground of liability, although this provision is not mentioned in the judgment. In sum, it is difficult to draw a certain conclusion from this judgment.

The judgment reported in Rt. 2001 page 428 concerned claims for non-economic losses. The plaintiff had applied for a job at a court, and in this context the director of the court had gathered information and records of his penal convictions from, *inter alia*, the Ministry of Justice. This collecting and handing out of information was unlawful, as it had required consent from the claimant. The Supreme Court found that ECHR Article 8 had been infringed. It then considered whether the applicant could base a claim on ECHR Article 13. This was answered in the negative. In this regard, the Supreme Court took notice of how the civil servants had sought to act carefully, and that the fact that the information had been more widespread was a result of the plaintiff's own conduct. This ruling arguably indicates that ECHR Article 13 may constitute a basis of liability in itself under Norwegian law.

The case in Rt. 2009 page 1237 dealt with claims from deep sea divers who had been employed by the petroleum industry operating in the North Sea during the so-called 'pioneer' time, i.e. from approximately 1965 to 1990. The divers suffered from different health injuries, such as, *inter alia*, post-traumatic stress disorders, and argued that this was causally connected to the diving and their working conditions.[39]

Their claims for damages relied, firstly, upon strict liability for high-risk sources. This was dismissed because the Supreme Court found that such a claim should eventually have been made *vis-à-vis* the operators in the North Sea, and not the Norwegian State. Secondly, the divers argued that representatives of the State had acted negligently, primarily in the supervision of the industry, and that that should lead to vicarious liability, a matter that the Supreme Court also disagreed with. Also at this point the Court indicated that it would have been more appropriate to direct such claims towards the operators. Thirdly, a number of human rights provisions were invoked: ECHR Articles 2, 3, 8 and 14; and ICCPR Articles 2, 6, 7 and 17. The

[38] Parliamentary act 17 June 2005 no. 90, Article 16-1(2).

[39] The Norwegian State had previously established different sorts of *ex gratia* schemes for the deep sea divers. Particularly, in 2004, a compensation regime was established that gave each diver the right of up to 2,300,000 NOK, today approximately 280,190 EUR. Around 600,000,000 NOK, circa 73,000,000 EUR, has been paid over through this system.

Supreme Court discussed possible infringements extensively, drawing upon a number of rulings from the European Court of Human Rights.[40] Ultimately it found none to have taken place, and therefore briefly mentioned that it was not necessary to look into whether – and if so, to what extent – the applicants could base a claim for damages on breaches of human rights. The case was brought before the European Court of Human Rights, that in *Vilnes and Others* vs. *Norway*[41] held, by five votes to two, that there had been an infringement of ECHR Article 8. The violation lay, briefly put, in the fact that the authorities, when authorising diving operations and protecting the safety of such operations, should have ensured that the diving operator companies observed full transparency about the diving tables used (because the use of 'too rapid' diving tables is likely to cause decompression sickness), so that the divers would have been able to assess the risk to their health and to give informed consent to the risks involved. The applicants were each awarded a lump sum of 8 000 EUR in accordance with ECHR Article 41, alongside compensation for some expenses. The European Court of Human Rights rejected claims for economic losses by referral to uncertain causality. In the aftermath, the State of Norway has offered to make out-of-court settlements with the applicants; still not based on liability in law; reportedly these have already been accepted, according to which the divers and bereaved families have received another 2 200 000 NOK, roughly 270 000 EUR.

In sum, the role played by ECHR Article 13 in Norwegian tort law is not entirely clear. Yet, the most plausible interpretation is that the ordinary liability rules should first be applied on the facts. If the result of this application does not fulfil the requirements stemming from ECHR Article 13, a claim may be based directly on this provision, which is directly applicable Norwegian law. This is coherent with the decision in Rt. 2010 page 291, and implies that ECHR Article 13 may constitute a separate basis for liability, but secondary to other liability rules.

ECHR Article 41

ECHR Article 41 may also theoretically form a legal basis of a *sui generis* liability. ECHR Article 41 formally deals only with the European Court of Human Rights' competence to afford 'just satisfaction' to victims of convention infringements. Yet, the general aim that eventual infringements should primarily be rectified in the national court systems suggests that domestic liability law should provide for liability in cases where the European Court of Human Rights would plausibly impose liability in accordance with ECHR Article 41.

---

[40] *Budayeva* v *Russia* (20 March 2008), paras 128–131, 134–136 and 146; *Guerra and Others* v *Italy* (19 February 1998); *LCB.* V *United Kingdom* (9 June 1998), para 38; *Öneryildiz* v *Turkey* (30 November 2004), paras 100–101; *Niemietz* v *Germany* (16 December 1992); *Giacomelli* v *Italy* (2 November 2006), para 76; *Roche* v *United Kingdom* (19 October 2005), paras 155–169.

[41] *Vilnes and Others* v *Norway* (5 December 2013).

The decision reported in Rt. 2004 page 1868 points in this direction, although not with much clarity. Leading up to this ruling was a former appeal court ruling, in which criminal prosecutions against two individuals for tax offenses were dismissed because the prosecution was thought to have contradicted the protection against double jeopardy in ECHR Protocol 7, Article 4; this was because the persons involved had already been imposed surcharged taxes due to the offenses. The current Supreme Court case only concerned their claims for damages. However, the Supreme Court ultimately did not need to address the issue of liability directly based on ECHR Article 41 as it found that there was a sufficient basis for liability in the Norwegian Act relating to legal procedure in criminal cases.[42] It may be noted that the lawyer representing the Norwegian State in the case held that ECHR Articles 13 and 41, in conjunction with the Act on human rights,[43] Article 2, could not form a basis of liability within the Norwegian legal system, and under no circumstances when there are already established liability rules governing the situation at hand.

Also, the judgment reported in Rt. 2010 page 291 arguably indicates that ECHR Article 41 may form a legal basis for damages claims under Norwegian law, but in this case the claim was dismissed as directed *vis-à-vis* the wrong legal subject, cf, above, chapter 2.2.1.

On the basis of this scarce jurisprudence, there is undeniably some legal uncertainty as regards the options of building a damages claim directly upon ECHR Article 41 and the Act on human rights Article 2. Until the Supreme Court takes a clearer stand in favour of such claims, they should arguably be considered as implausible. [44]

12.2.2.6 Special Liability Rules

Certain special liability rules may be mentioned for the sake of completeness, as they are at least closely connected to the issues of violated human rights.

First, the Act relating to legal procedure in criminal cases provides for objective rules on recovery of expenses incurred for the defence after acquittal or discontinu-

[42] Parliamentary act 22 May 1981 no. 25, Articles 445 and 446.

[43] Parliamentary act 25 May 1999 no. 30.

[44] A ruling from the Oslo district court in the summer of 2014 spawned much media attention. On two occasions in 2013 a man had been arrested and kept isolated in a police detention cell for several days. The district court found that violations of ECHR Article 8 had taken place due to the isolation (the principle of *habeas corpus* had seemingly been respected and was not the object of the proceedings). On the issue of compensation, the court reasoned firstly that ECHR Article 41 could not form the basis of an action under Norwegian law. On the question of ECHR Article 13, the court concluded that this provision could form a basis of liability with respect to economic losses. It justified this by referral to how Norwegian tort law had already established compensation rules governing such losses, and according to which the applicant indeed had a legitimate claim in this case. On redress for non-financial injury, on the other hand, this could not be awarded according to the Compensation Act, Article 3–5, cf, below, chapter 5.2, as this is normally dependent upon gross negligence or intent. The court, however, awarded 25 000 NOK (today 3000 EUR) on the basis of ECHR Article 13. It has been reported that the State has lodged an appeal, but no further judgments have yet been delivered. Cf Oslo tingrett (District court) 2 June 2014 (Case No. TOSLO-2013-103468).

ation of a public prosecution, as well as rules imposing liability on the State for both economic and non-economic losses.[45] This is occasionally seen in context with ECHR Article 13. For instance, in a case concerning (very briefly put) the time spent on handling applications of a preventive detention, the Supreme Court found that ECHR Article 5 had been breached. The Supreme Court thus, under referral to the Norwegian Act relating to legal procedure in criminal cases[46] as well as ECHR Article 13 and the Norwegian Act on human rights,[47] ordered the State to pay a sum of 50 000 NOK, a sum which today equals approximately 6500 EUR.[48] This Act also contains a rule of liability in so far as the person charged has been arrested or detained in custody contrary to ECHR Article 5 or ICCPR Article 9.[49]

Secondly, there is an act on compensation to victims of violence.[50] This is not truly a regulation of liability as such, but a system in which the State pays out compensation to victims of violence and subsequently seeks recourse from the individual responsible for the violent acts. This regime was introduced in the 1970s, and in 1992 Norway ratified the European Convention on the Compensation of Victims of Violent Crimes of 24 November 1983. The current act is thought to fulfil Norway's obligations under the convention.

A set of acts concerning equality and anti-discrimination should also be mentioned here as they contain rules on strict liability where the discrimination has taken place within the framework of employment, but otherwise merely codify *culpa* liability.[51] This technique has been used for some time within the anti-discrimination legislation.

12.2.3 Causation

The rules on causation under Norwegian law are generally seen to be twofold.

12.2.3.1 Legal Requirements Concerning the Factual Causation

Firstly, there is a rule concerning the legal assessment of the factual causation. The contours of this rule are not clear in all regards, but it is a well settled law that if the causal factor under scrutiny was *conditio sine qua non* for the injury, this will normally suffice to fulfil its requirements, i.e. a positive but-for test is performed. It

[45] Parliamentary act 22 May 1981 no. 25, Article 438 and Chapter 31.

[46] Parliamentary act 22 May 1981 no. 25, Article 447(2).

[47] Parliamentary act 25 May 1999 no. 30, Article 2.

[48] Rt. 2006 page 577.

[49] Parliamentary act 22 May 1981 no. 25, Article 446.

[50] Parliamentary act 20 April 2001 no. 13.

[51] Parliamentary acts 21 June 2013 no. 58, Article 24; no. 59, Article 28; no. 60, Article 25; and no. 61, Article 31 (all will enter into force 1 January 2014).

is also arguably settled law that if the causal factor under scrutiny was not *conditio sine qua non*, the conditions inherent in this rule concerning the factual causation are *often* not fulfilled. The precise extent of the applicability of such a negative but-for test is, however, not fully clear.

Given that Norwegian law at least has greatly relied on the but-for test, injuries or damages may often be traced back to multiple tortfeasors, who may then be held jointly liable in accordance with the Compensation Act.[52] Nonetheless, the Supreme Court has held that causal contributions may be considered to be of such minor importance that they cannot justify being considered as a factual cause at all.[53] The latter is particularly relevant in cases where the complete causal picture is complex, involving a multitude of contributing factors.

12.2.3.2 Legal Assessment of the Adequacy of the Factual Causation

Secondly, there is a rule containing an assessment of whether the factual connection can be considered as adequate. This rule calls for a broader evaluation of the links between the injuries at issue and the conditions giving rise to liability. Key factors are foreseeability, directness and proximity, and the overriding issue is often described as whether it would be unreasonable to hold the tortfeasor liable for the consequence at hand.[54] Norwegian tort law largely accepts the 'you take your victim as find him' principle, thus limiting the possibility for tortfeasors to successfully argue that the victim's injuries should be dismissed as inadequate where they, e.g., may be connected to pre-existing vulnerability *et cetera*.

No cases on the requirement of normative causation between acts and consequential human rights infringements have been judged by the Supreme Court. A series of cases before the courts of first instance have concerned damages claims due to a change in the rules on taxation of shipowners. Interim rules on the transmission from the old to the new taxation regime were, by a majority of the judges in the Supreme Court, found to contravene the ban on retroactive legislation in the Norwegian Constitution Article 97 in Rt. 2010 page 143. Due to this finding, this majority did not assess whether ECHR Article 1 of Protocol no. 1 had also been breached. A minority of judges found that neither the Norwegian Constitution Article 97 nor ECHR Article 1 of Protocol no. 1 had been violated. As regards ECHR Article 1 of Protocol no. 1, a minority referred to a number of judgments by the European Court of Justice,[55] and ultimately found the new, intermediary tax regime as a proportional interference with the property rights of the claimants. In this regard, ECHR Article 14 was also taken into consideration.

In the subsequent cases with claims for damages, both the Norwegian Constitution Article 97 and ECHR Article 1 of Protocol no. 1 have been invoked. Oslo District

---

[52] Parliamentary act 13 June 1969 no. 26, Article 5–3.

[53] Cf, e.g., Rt. 1992 page 64.

[54] Cf, e.g., Rt. 2010 page 24.

[55] Namely, *Burden* v *United Kingdom* (29 April 2008) paras 59–60; *Sporrung and Lönnroth* v *Sweden* (23 September 1982) para 69; *Jokela* v *Finland* (21 May 2002) para 57; and *The National & Provincial Building Society* v *United Kingdom* (23 October 1997) para 80.

Court has on one occasion ruled that losses due to the change of taxation rules are not recoverable because they are too remote consequences.[56] Judgments from District Courts are not considered to create precedence in Norwegian law, and it is possible that there was no violation of ECHR Article 1 of Protocol no. 1 at all. Nonetheless, the ruling is arguably apt to illustrate that the requirement of normative causation holds equally valid where the claim for damages is based on infringements of human rights. The concrete circumstances will nonetheless be defining. For instance, the eventual gravity of the tort may be taken into consideration. One may then easily picture that where the *delict* implies a human rights infringement, depending on the circumstances, this may also lead to a relatively lenient standard as regards the requirement of an adequate causal link.

12.3 Contributory Negligence

Contributory negligence is codified as a general rule in the Compensation Act,[57] which sets out that negligent contribution may, on the basis of discretion, lead to a reduction or complete loss of the claim.

No cases on contribution to infringements of human rights have been judged by the Supreme Court. The aforementioned case reported in Rt. 2001 page 428 (supra at Sect. 12.2.2.5) suggests that there is in principle no hindrance to applying the rules on contributory negligence. In the case leading up to the abovementioned case Rt. 2004 page 1868 (supra at Sect. 12.2.2.5) the *appeal court* had awarded the claimants damages on the basis of ECHR Articles 13 and 41, but substantially reduced the amounts due to their own contributory conduct. The fact that a human right has been infringed may in some cases be apt to impact the discretion as to whether negligent contribution should have any, and if so, which, consequences. Yet, this will again depend on the circumstances of the particular case.

12.4 Rules and Principles Governing the Calculation of Damages

12.4.1 General Notes on the Rules and Principles of Calculation

The rules and principles governing the calculation of damages are largely based on the idea of reparation, i.e. aim to ensure that the *victim*'s *financial situation* is *restored* as it was pre-injury. From this focus on the *victim* it follows that penal considerations are, as of today, normally not relevant, and there has, in general, been

[56] *Fred Olsen Shipping* v *The Ministry of Finance,* Oslo District Court, Judgment 27 September 2011. The ruling was confirmed upon appeal, and the appeal court reasoned along similar lines, cf *Fred Olsen Shipping* v *The Ministry of Finance*, Borgarting Appeal Court, Judgment 20 June 2013.

[57] Parliamentary act 13 June 1969 no. 26, Article 5–1.

a shift towards putting little weight to the idea of prevention when it comes to the amount of damages. There are, however, some exceptions from this as regards certain types of compensation for non-economic losses, and perhaps one can also assume that there will be somewhat of a shift towards emphasising the idea of prevention more strongly in some cases of pure economic loss. The concern with the *financial situation* points to the general lack of rules implying reparation in kind. It also points to the main principle that only injuries that represent economic losses may call for damages. The reference to *restoration* implies that the principle of *compensatio lucri cum damno* is acknowledged, i.e. that eventual benefits flowing from the injury must be taken into account when calculating the damages.

Additionally, a general principle is that the plaintiff cannot claim compensation for losses he/she should him/herself have avoided, often designated as a duty to mitigate or limit the losses. This also governs the question whether the claimant should have exhausted other remedies before claiming financial compensation. It may also be added that the claimant *de facto* must also exhaust ordinary public sources of financial compensation, e.g. social security, as such compensation is deducted from the amounts claimable from the tortfeasor.[58]

12.4.2 Personal Injuries

The amounts of damages in cases of personal injuries have to be calculated individually.[59] Loss of income, both that already suffered and that which will occur in the future, is to be covered in its whole. Increased expenses, also both those already suffered and those that will occur in the future, due to the injury are as well to be covered in whole, as far as they may be regarded as reasonable and necessary expenses.

Human rights may only impact this in an indirect way. If, for instance, a child is injured, the right to respect for family life, enshrined, *inter alia*, in ECHR Article 8, may perhaps contribute to justifying that the child is awarded a sum that actually makes it possible to live with his/her parent/s. This may, however, imply, albeit indirectly, expanded obligations upon individuals. There seems to be no Supreme Court jurisprudence reflecting this sort of reasoning. It is still not entirely absent in practise.[60]

---

[58] Parliamentary act 13 June 1969 no. 26, Article 3-1(3).

[59] Parliamentary act 13 June 1969 no. 26, Article 3–1. In 2011, a group appointed by the Government made suggestions for a set of rules implying, to some extent, standardisation of the damages in cases of personal injuries, published in *Norges offentlige utredninger* 2011 no. 16.

[60] There exists, for instance, an Appeal Court judgment in which the court briefly noted that not awarding sufficient compensation so that a child could stay at home during nights, by reference to the existence of a municipal service of night respite care, could not amount to an infringement of the ECHR or the CRC, cf Eidsivating lagmannsrett (Appeal court) 13 June 2006 (Case no. LE-2005-80803).

Payments of social security have to be deducted from the compensation, ensuring that the claimant does not benefit financially from the injury.

12.4.3 Property Damages

Also when property damages are at issue, the compensation has to be calculated individually.[61] If the damaged property may be repaired, reparation costs will be recoverable. Where it is damaged beyond repair, the damages should amount to the costs of purchasing a similar good. If neither reparation nor repurchase is possible, one will generally have to look at the sale value of the property or good before the damage. Moreover, consequential losses are recoverable.

12.4.4 Pure Economic Loss

As regards pure economic loss, the simple rule is that the actual loss suffered due to the infringement of a protected interest is what should be covered. This is also very briefly codified.[62] In practise, this often calls for rather uncertain hypotheses concerning some sort of a contra-factual development. The judge is therefore empowered to calculate the damages in a somewhat discretionary way. This empowerment was previously codified in the act on civil procedure but is now unwritten law.

12.5 Special Regimes Governing Non-economic Losses

12.5.1 Compensation for Loss of Life Quality

A special rule on compensation for loss of life quality is to be found in the Compensation Act.[63] This rule lays down that the person who has been imposed a notable and lasting medical injury shall have the right to such compensation. The injuries may be of a psychological or mental as well as a physical nature.

Although these conditions are phrased in rather vague wordings, and the assessment of the compensation, according to the wording of the Article, would seem to be based on a very broad discretion, this is in fact rather standardised, both in the assessment of whether an injury is notable and in the amount of damages. Relevant factors are the degree of the medical invalidity of the claimant, his or her age, and

---

[61] Parliamentary act 13 June 1969 no. 26, Article 4–1.

[62] Parliamentary act 13 June 1969 no. 26, Article 3–1.

[63] Parliamentary act 13 June 1969 no. 26, Article 3–2.

the expected length of the injury. In practise, medical experts will be consulted as regards the medical invalidity.

Whether human rights have been violated or not will not affect this compensation.

12.5.2 Compensation (Redress) for Non-financial Injury

There is a special rule on compensation (redress) for non-financial injuries.[64] The rule serves as a legal basis for liability where the claimant has been imposed a personal injury intentionally or by gross negligence, but also provides for compensation where the tortfeasor is guilty of particular criminal offences or misconducts. Furthermore, it provides for compensation for certain, close family members where the victim has died.

The sums are awarded discretionarily. As regards certain types of violations, the Supreme Court has nonetheless given indicators of the appropriate level of compensation, a practice that in fact serves as a type of standardisation, although open to adjustments depending on the case at issue.

Whether human rights have been violated or not will not necessarily *directly* affect this compensation. Given that it leaves room for discretion when fixing the amount, the concrete circumstances will, however, determine the extent. It may therefore happen that the court can refer to, e.g., a human rights convention as part of its justification for a particular level of compensation.

The case reported in Rt. 2011 page 769 concerned liability for a father who had dropped his son onto a concrete floor, causing severe injuries to the boy's head. The father later omitted to inform the medical professionals of the accident, although such information would have contributed to them understanding the boy's condition and thus ultimately have prevented, or at least reduced, the injuries that developed. The Supreme Court awarded the son a sum of 300,000 NOK, today amounting to approximately 37 500 EUR. When justifying this amount, which is fairly high by Norwegian standards, the Court referred to, *inter alia*, CRC Articles 3, 4 and 19, and it was said that the sum should reflect the need to protect children against neglect and misconduct.

12.5.3 Compensation for Defamation and Infringement of Privacy

The Compensation Act contains a special rule on compensation in cases of libel or slander, or infringements of the privacy of another person.[65] Compensation may cover both economic and non-economic losses, but is discretionary. Dogmatically the question of liability for defamation is addressed as a question of unlawfulness,

[64] Parliamentary act 13 June 1969 no. 26, Article 3–5.

[65] Parliamentary act 13 June 1969 no. 26, Article 3–6.

while the liability for infringement of privacy calls for an assessment of whether the disputed conduct amounts to an infringement. As the rule interferes with several questions of human rights, its application is *de facto* largely a matter of deciding whether liability would be compliant to the human rights of the parties.

12.5.3.1 Defamation

As regards defamation, the task of the courts has generally been seen, first and foremost, to assess whether imposing liability upon the defendant accords primarily to ECHR Article 10, i.e. whether it contradicts ECHR Article 10(1) and, if so, whether it may be acceptable under ECHR Article 10(2). As of today the task is rather seen to be one of balancing ECHR Articles 8 and 10.

The judgment reported in Rt. 2014 page 152 dealt with a claim from a previous paramedic versus a newspaper. A Somali-born man had been punched by a third-party on a sunny day in the park. The ambulance arrived and assessed his medical situation as not representing any medical emergency, thus departing without bringing him along. Upon the man himself taxing a taxi to a medical centre, it was, however, discovered that he had suffered a serious head injury. The media started heavy coverage implying that the incident related to ethnic discrimination. The Supreme Court opened by referring to how ECHR Articles 8 and 10 had to be balanced, as illustrated by practise from the European Court of Human Rights.[66] Upon reliance on a large number of further rulings by that Court,[67] a majority of the Supreme Court judges ultimately concluded that allegations of negligence with respect to the medical assistance were protected by ECHR Article 10, while allegations of racism were not. The applicant was awarded 200,000 NOK, as of today approximately 24,000 EUR.

12.5.3.2 Infringement of Privacy

Also, regarding infringements of privacy, the courts have to balance ECHR Article 8 and ECHR Article 10. Some rulings by the Supreme Court will exemplify[68]:

The case Rt. 2005 page 1677 regarded claims against a newspaper which had indicated that the plaintiff was a suspect in a case concerning the rape and murder of two young girls. The Supreme Court considered the present state of law on freedom of speech, cf ECHR Article 10, which could be deduced from rulings by

[66] *Delfi* v *Estonia* (10 October 2013).

[67] Namely, *Bladet Tromsø and Steinsaas* v *Norway* (20 May 1999); *Bergens Tidende and Others* v *Norway* (2 May 2000); *Jersild* v *Denmark* (23 September 1994); *Lingens* v *Austria* (8 July 1986); *Blaja News SP. Z.O.O.* v *Poland* (23 November 2013); *Ovchinnikov* v *Russia* (16 December 2010); *Tonsberg Blad AS and Haukom* v *Norway* (1 March 2007); *Selisto* v *Finland* (16 November 2004); *A* v *Norway* (9 April 2009); and *Ungváry and Irodalom KFT* v *Hungary* (3 December 2013).

[68] Others are Rt. 2002 page 764; Rt. 2003 page 914; Rt. 2003 page 928; Rt. 2003 page 1190; and Rt. 2009 page 265.

the European Court of Human Rights.[69] Ultimately it was found by the majority of judges that there was no infringement. The European Court of Human Rights later found that ECHR Article 8 had been breached.[70]

The decision reported in Rt. 2007 page 687 concerned two former participants in the reality-show 'Big Brother', who claimed compensation from a magazine which had published several articles about them after they had made it clear that they were not interested in further articles. The Supreme Court took into consideration the jurisprudence of the European Court of Human Rights,[71] found that ECHR Article 8 had been breached, and awarded each of the applicants 160,000 NOK, which today amounts to approximately 20,000 EUR.

The judgment reported in Rt. 2008 page 479 dealt with a claim from a person who had been caught by a security camera as he was handled by the police after buying illegal drugs. At the time, he was accompanied by a little girl – the daughter of his partner. A news/documentary show by the State-held TV station used the footage without, e.g., blacking out their faces sufficiently to make them non-identifiable. The Supreme Court again looked at the practise of the European Court of Human Rights,[72] and found that the TV-station had operated within the borders of ECHR Article 10.

The case Rt. 2008 page 1089 concerned claims from a singer and an actress against a 'gossip magazine' that, without their consent, had made a *reportage* about their wedding. Again the Supreme Court looked at how the relevant provisions have been interpreted by the European Court of Human Rights, and the majority of judges found that there had been no breach. The couple sought to bring the case before the European Court of Human Rights, and after a considerable waiting time – possibly due to how some clarifications brought by the *Axel Springer* and *Von Hannover* vs. *Germany* judgments[73] were awaited –, the European Court of Human Rights found that there had not been any violations of the Convention.[74]

[69] *Cumpana and Mazare* v *Romania* (17 December 2004), para 88; *Radio France and Others* v *France* (30 March 2004); *von Hannover* v *Germany* (24 June 2004); *Chauvy and Others* v *France* (29 June 2004), para 70; *Pedersen and Baadsgaard* v *Denmark* (17 December 2004), para 71, referring to *Jersild* v *Denmark* (23 September 1994), *Janowski* v *Poland* and *Nilsen and Johnsen* v *Norway* (25 November 1999); and *Selistö* v *Finland* (16 November 2004).

[70] *A* v *Norway* (9 April 2009).

[71] *Von Hannover* v *Germany* (24 June 2004); and *Karhuvaara and Others* v *Finland* (16 November 2004).

[72] *Von Hannover* v *Germany* (24 June 2004); and *Peck* v *United Kingdom* (28 January 2003).

[73] *Axel Springer* v *Germany* (7 February 2012); *Von Hannover* v *Germany* (no. 2) (7 February 2012); and *Von Hannover* v *Germany* (no. 3) (19 September 2013).

[74] *Lillo-Stenberg and Sæther* v *Norway* (16 January 2014).

12.6 General Clause on Lifting the Duty to Pay

For the sake of completeness, it should be mentioned that the Norwegian law on *delicts* contains a general clause on lifting the duty to pay.[75] The rule, which has some characteristics of a 'fairness rule', is interpreted as a narrow exception.

12.7 Correlation of Norwegian Court and European Court of Human Rights Decisions

Some particular issues arise due to how the Norwegian courts and the European Court of Human Rights may both take decisions on the issues of liability as well as those of compensation.

These issues may be considered as having two aspects, one having a substantive and the other more of a methodological/procedural character. With respect to the latter, there is, e.g., as yet no experience regarding how a national court, in a subsequent damages claim eventually involving the same parties, will relate to findings by the European Court of Human Rights dealing directly with the claim for just satisfaction under ECHR Article 41. This may, for instance, be findings such as that in *Vilnes and Others* vs. *Norway*, where the European Court of Human Rights found a breach of ECHR Article 8, yet still rejected/dismissed claims in respect of pecuniary damage due to uncertainty as to which losses had been suffered.[76] This specific case has later been settled out of court, cf, above, chapter 2.2.5.1. The European Court of Human Rights also ruled against Norway in *Lindheim and Others* vs. *Norway*,[77] in which it found that national statutory legislation on ground lease contracts ran counter to ECHR Article 1 of Protocol no. 1. This case also illustrates possible methodological/procedural issues, as compensation for pecuniary damage was not afforded due to, *inter alia*, the complexity of the issues with which the Norwegian Parliament had been confronted, as it was held:

> In the particular circumstances of the instant case, the Court finds that the respondent State should be dispensed from liability with regard to legal acts or situations that antedate the present judgment … and accordingly dismisses the applicants' above-mentioned claims for compensation for pecuniary damage.[78]

It remains to be seen how this eventually affects subsequent damages claims before the Norwegian courts. Several proceedings have been instigated before the

---

[75] Parliamentary act 13 June 1969 no. 26, Article 5–2.

[76] Cf *Vilnes and Others* v *Norway* (5 December 2013), para 270.

[77] *Lindheim and Others* v *Norway* (12 June 2012).

[78] *Lindheim and Others* v *Norway* (12 June 2012), para 141.

first instance courts in the aftermath of *Lindheim and Others* vs. *Norway*, implying that some clarification can soon be expected.[79]

On the more substantive aspects, there are to this date also no judgments from the Supreme Court dealing directly with the issue of how to eventually correlate sums awarded by the European Court of Human Rights in accordance with ECHR Article 41, with damages according to the Compensation Act.[80] Norwegian tort law, as mentioned, recognises the principle of *compensatio lucri cum damno*, and generally correlates the different payments from either one or several debtors, but there is a general idea that damages claims may only be coordinated as far as they aim to compensate the same matter.[81] Doctrine occasionally coins this as a requirement of '*kompensasjonsrelevans*'. How far this idea is represented in the law of *delict* is not in all regards completely clear, but as far as sums awarded in order to compensate non-pecuniary damages go, it is submitted that it may – as these are matters of discretion – be correct to take such sums into account when assessing whether, and eventually to what extent, the victim should be awarded compensation (redress) for non-financial injury, for instance in accordance with Articles 3–5 or 3–6 of the Compensation Act,[82] cf, above, chapters 5.2 and 5.3, or the rules on such losses in the Act relating to legal procedure in criminal cases,[83] cf, above, chapter 2.2.6. Some support for this may also be found in decisions by the Supreme Court.[84] Apart from this, compensation for economic losses in accordance with ECHR Article 41 will have to be coordinated to eventual compensation for economic losses founded upon another legal basis, so that the indemnity principle is respected.

A rather different procedural aspect relates to that of *res judicata*. Although a Norwegian judgment may amount to an infringement of a human right, it still formally settles the matter. Under given circumstances, this may involve some procedural complications, which are well illustrated by one of the most infamous Norwegian criminal court cases.[85] A man who, in 1993, was wrongfully charged of sexual abuse versus a vast number of children in the kindergarten where he worked,

[79] Cf, e.g., judgment by Oslo tingrett (District court) 9 April 2014 (Case No. TOSLO-2013-176193), which was, however, solved on the basis of an interpretation of *Lindheim and Others* v *Norway* which led to a distinguishing of that case versus that before the district court. Subsequently the district court found that no breach had taken place in its case. This judgment is currently under appeal. A different variation was in fact at issue in the aforementioned Rt. 2013 page 588. While this case dealt with the question of whether the State had fulfilled its obligations under ECHR Article 1, cf the Norwegian Human Rights Act, it appears from the *dicta* that the victim had already been afforded compensation under the system of compensation to victims of violence, cf, above, chapter 2.2.6. This system is, however, in one sense based on the underlying liability of the 'direct' infringer, as the State will seek recourse from him or her.

[80] Parliamentary act 13 June 1969 no. 26.

[81] Cf, particularly, Rt. 2007 page 1415; and Rt. 2005 page 769.

[82] Parliamentary act 13 June 1969 no. 26.

[83] Parliamentary act 22 May 1981 no. 25.

[84] Cf Rt. 2010 page 396.

[85] Which, *inter alia*, formed one of the inspirations for the Danish 2012 award-winning movie 'The Hunt' ('*Jagten*'), directed by Thomas Vinterberg.

was, by an appeal court in 1995,[86] after being acquitted of the accusations in a previous ruling in 1994, awarded 45,000 NOK (today circa 5500 EUR) for lost income and 125,000 NOK (EUR today approximately 15,000) as redress for non-financial injury. He appealed this decision on the damages to the Supreme Court, arguing that the *dicta* in the appeal court decision violated ECHR Article 6, as they indicated that he was guilty of the criminal offenses for which he had previously been acquitted. The Supreme Court dismissed the appeal, as it found that the appeal court *dicta* did not run counter to the presumption of innocence.[87] Upon a complaint to the European Court of Human Rights, the judgment in *Hammern* vs. *Norway* was eventually handed down, in which that Court asserted that the disputed *dicta* indeed contained a 'voicing of suspicion against the applicant with respect to the charges of sexual abuse for which he had been acquitted'.[88] Thus, ECHR Article 6 no. 2 had been infringed. The man subsequently filed for further damages from the State before a Norwegian court, partly damages he argued that he should have been awarded in the original judgment from 1995, partly damages due to losses that he argued that that same original judgment had inflicted upon him. This application was dismissed from all instances as a claim for damages was considered to interfere with the binding effect of the original judgment.[89] This dismissal was then the basis of a new complaint to the European Court of Human Rights in 2007, which was, however, dismissed by that Court the same year. Arguably, the man should rather have applied to have the original damages case *reopened* as soon as the judgment in *Hammern* v. *Norway* had been delivered. He ultimately tried this in the aftermath of the last dismissal by the European Court of Human Rights in 2007. This was, however, well over the time limits prescribed for applications of reopening cases, and, hence, that application was also ultimately dismissed.[90] It should be recalled that if the basis of liability does not lie directly in a – kind of 'wrongful' – judicial decision itself, one will not be faced with these sorts of procedural implications.

12.8 Concluding Remarks

In summary, there are not many rules that specifically address issues of liability for infringements of human rights under Norwegian law. It is rather mostly a matter of interpreting and applying the general principles of the law of non-contractual liability. In this regard, the fact that human rights have been violated may, firstly, mean that one is faced with a legally relevant interest and, secondly, be particularly apt to impact the rules on accountability. This does, however, not mean that losses will be

[86] Frostating lagmannsrett (Appeal court) decision 28 February 1995 (LF-1994-244).

[87] Supreme Court decision 8 June 1995 (HR-1995-1155-S), based on a rule now placed in the Act relating to the Courts of Justice of 13 August 1915 No. 5, Article 200.

[88] *Hammern* v *Norway* (11 February 2003).

[89] Cf Rt. 2005 page 730.

[90] Cf Rt. 2008 page 1719.

recoverable should they be inadequate, i.e. too remote. Nonetheless, the Norwegian law of *delict* is, at least formally, relatively 'liberal' and calls for concrete assessments of what would be fair and just in each specific case.

Furthermore, there is still a relatively modest amount of case law on damages for human right violations. Many cases, in which one could think that the claimant would also perhaps invoke human rights, are ruled on different grounds. For instance, Rt. 2003 page 1468 concerned liability for a person's developed dysfunctionality and schizophrenia allegedly caused by a municipality's negligent omission of assuming care of him as a child. The Supreme Court assessed whether there was vicarious liability on the hands of the municipality, and answered this in the negative. Moreover, it found that there would be no causal connection nonetheless. In light of several judgments by the European Court of Human Rights,[91] one could have thought that the plaintiff would also have invoked infringements of ECHR Articles 3 and 8, at least in light of the fact that this proceeding preceded the finding of the Supreme Court in 2010 that only the State level is the appropriate addressee for damages claims founded upon breaches of the ECHR.[92] Another, newer, example is a judgment of the Supreme Court reported in Rt. 2013 page 805, where the Court found that a non-adopted stepchild, unlike a biological child, could not claim compensation (redress) for non-financial injury after her stepfather had been brutally murdered, although she had been living with him since she was two years old, and did not even know she was not his daughter until she was approximately ten or eleven years old. One would perhaps expect some remarks on the human rights regime in such a case. At least as an – albeit anecdotal – comparison, one may look to the lengthy discussions of the Court of the Queen's Bench of Alberta in *Dares* vs. *Newman*,[93] which regarded a rule concerning step children's lack of rights to bereavement damages, and this rule's constitutionality in light of the prohibition of discrimination laid down in the Canadian Charter of Rights and Freedoms, Section 15. The main current controversy is primarily that concerning the status of ECHR Articles 13 and 41. As these provisions are invoked in an extending number of cases, clarification by the Supreme Court should not lie too far ahead.

The overall picture shows, it is submitted, a liability regime in development. All in all, human rights may not have played any dominant role with respect to most areas of Norwegian tort law so far, but concurrently, firstly, development seems to have been intensified lately, and secondly, it completely dominates the picture in some areas, such as compensation for defamation and infringement of privacy. The jurisprudence with respect to the latter also shows the importance of tort law as a tool for the victims to simply obtain an authoritative decision holding that somebody else has acted wrongly and infringed one's right, as the sums of monies actually awarded are often so modest that the prospect of the damages in itself can hardly explain the motivation to initiate usually lengthy and expensive proceedings.

---

[91] Cf, e.g., *Z and Others* v *United Kingdom* (10 May 2001); *D.P. and J.C.* v *United Kingdom* (10 October 2002); and *E and Others* (26 November 2002).

[92] Cf, above, chapter 2.2.1.

[93] *Dares* v *Newman*, 2012 ABQB 328.

Lastly, it is arguably notable how human rights have been highlighted in connection with such a number of different aspects of the liability rules – on the different conditions for obtaining damages, as well as on the different rules concerning the calculation; at least this illustrates the diversity of the impact of human rights. Due to the combination of Norway ratifying a growing number of conventions and, arguably, an increasing consciousness amongst Norwegian jurists as regards human rights and their possible impact on liability law, one may assume that human rights will continue to gradually play a greater role. This does not alter the fact that it seems clear that traditional domestic tort law also in the future will be the dominant tool in order to remedy infringements of human rights, but there are also some – albeit few – signs of a more distinct liability law in cases of human rights violations.

References

Nils, Nygaard. 2007. *Skade og ansvar*. Bergen: Universitetsforlaget.
Peter, Lødrup. 2009. *Lærebok i erstatningsrett*. Oslo: Gyldendal akademisk.
Are, Stenvik, and Hagstrøm Viggo. 2015. *Erstatningsrett*. Oslo: Universitetsforlaget.

Chapter 13
Polish Domestic Remedies Against Human Rights Violations and Their Interaction with 'Just Satisfaction' Awarded by the European Court of Human Rights

Michał Balcerzak

13.1 Introductory Remarks and Clarifications

Before addressing in detail the issues raised in the questionnaire, it appears essential to clarify what is meant by "human rights" for the purposes of the present paper. While it is not this author's intention to dwell on theoretical background or meaning of the term, it needs to be underlined that "human rights" do not lend themselves to a simple and commonly accepted definition. In this context terminological ambiguities and contemporary dilemmas concerning human rights in the Polish legal system have also been invoked (Łętowska 2010, 267). Yet, there is little doubt that this research project and questionnaire refers to "human rights" in a normative rather than philosophical sense, i.e., to legally recognized entitlements of law subjects vis-à-vis public authority within its jurisdiction.

Human rights in the normative sense may be perceived as a catalogue of norms which create obligations binding for public authorities and entrusting individuals with recognized rights or freedoms. These catalogues are usually enshrined in national constitutions and international treaties (or other international law instruments). It is assumed that irrespective of being assembled in normative catalogues, human rights are to be implemented at a national level, both as a matter of domestic law and as a practice of state organs.

The primary version of this text (as a country report) has been published in: B. Lewaszkiewicz-Petrykowska (ed.), *Rapports polonais. XIXe Congrès international de droit comparé*, Łódź University Press, Łódź 2014, pp. 283–300.

M. Balcerzak, Ph.D. (✉)
Human Rights Department, Faculty of Law and Administration, Nicolaus Copernicus University, Toruń, Poland
e-mail: michal.balcerzak@law.umk.pl

E. Bagińska (ed.), *Damages for Violations of Human Rights*,
Ius Comparatum - Global Studies in Comparative Law 9,
DOI 10.1007/978-3-319-18950-5_13

"An infringement of human rights," should be understood as an act (action or omission) of state which violates at least one legal obligation binding on that state towards an individual (or other entitled subject), provided that the violated obligation resulted from the norm denominated as a "human rights norm." At this point it is crucial to distinguish between domestic and international consequences of such an infringement. Even for states with a monistic approach to international law, as is the case of Poland, the same human rights norm may cause effects both within the domestic legal system (*pro foro interno*) and within the international one (*pro foro externo*). In the latter case we deal with the law of international state responsibility which constitutes part and parcel of public international law (Crawford 2013, *passim*). In this sphere the term "responsibility" is widely recognized in international law and doctrine to denote prerequisites and consequences of acts prohibited by international law, e.g., infringements of human rights norms, as distinguished from the term "liability" used with reference to damage caused by actions not prohibited by international law.

It seems evident that the questionnaire focuses on domestic consequences of human rights infringements, and more particularly on domestic remedies allowing to claim and obtain pecuniary damages in domestic law. However, the project also includes the interaction between national and international human rights law. There seems to be no limitation of the scope of the project to human rights norms as reflected in the constitutional, i.e., domestic, catalogue or the national legislation. The so-called "international human rights," i.e., human rights norms enshrined in instruments of international law, are equally important in defining the material scope of states' obligations. Even where norms of international law treaties are directly applicable in the domestic law system (which is in the case of Poland), it is understandable that they would only rarely be of use as a direct base of compensatory claims before domestic courts. More often than not, norms of international human rights law would be directly applied to claim damages within international control mechanisms, the European Convention on the Protection of Human Rights and Fundamental Freedoms (hereinafter as "ECHR") being the most notable example.

To avoid any misunderstanding it needs to be stressed that direct applicability of human rights treaties ratified by Poland is of a fundamental importance. Human rights norms enshrined in these treaties may be effectively referred to both in parties' submissions as well as in judicial decisions. Polish courts do invoke and apply international human rights norms although the frequency of such references is another matter (Łętowska 2010, 275). Generally speaking, the rate of referrals to human rights treaties is uppermost at the highest level of judiciary, with the Supreme Court and Constitutional Tribunal having the leading position. But notwithstanding their significance and practical application, international human rights norms would not be applied by Polish courts as the sole basis for adjudicating compensation or satisfaction.

International human rights law norms serve as a direct source of international obligations whose violation may lead to state responsibility and compensatory claims submitted to international control organs. It can be submitted that satisfying the claims which originate in human rights law (both international and domestic) is primarily to be sought in the domestic legal order. The principle of subsidiarity is widely recognized in human rights law as such and has also many normative manifestations, including the principle of exhaustion of domestic remedies prior to recourse to international ones, as well as the right to an effective domestic remedy as provided *inter alia* in Art. 13 of the ECHR.[1]

It follows that the project's focus on domestic compensatory remedies for infringement of human rights reflects the logic of subsidiarity: human rights protection starts "at home" and it is in the domestic system where any victim of human rights violation should be offered compensation and/or other forms of reparation. It is however also important to remember that this protection does not stop "at home" and includes international remedies derived from instruments of international law. Therefore, the full picture of compensatory remedies for infringements of human rights needs to encompass both areas mentioned above (Shelton 2005, 22–49, 291–353).

13.2 Liability Regime for Human Rights Violations: General Remarks

Arguably, there is no separate "system" of public authority liability for violations of human rights in Poland. In particular, the Polish legal system does not recognize any general (unique) remedy for human rights violations and there appears to be no tendency in this direction although the idea of introducing a "general domestic remedy" has been discussed in the context of increasing the effectiveness of procedural protection of human rights in the Polish legal system (Balcerzak 2010, 42–44). In any event, the liability of public authority for infringements of human rights in Polish domestic law should be perceived as a part of the law of public authority liability. Compensatory remedies for a violation of human rights would normally be sought on the basis of private law, though compensation may also be obtained under other branches of law, i.e., criminal law (see below).

The general concept and rules of liability for damage caused by public authority has been very intensively discussed in Polish civil law doctrine, especially since the entry into force of the Polish Constitution in 1997 and subsequent legislative and jurisprudential changes which brought a truly new approach (Safjan 2004; Bagińska 2006; Banaszczyk 2012). The origins of this attitude come from Art. 77 para. 1 of the Constitution which provides:

> Everyone shall have the right to compensation for any damage (*szkoda*) done to him by any action of an organ of public authority contrary to law.

[1] Art. 13 ECHR provides: *Everyone whose rights and freedoms as set forth in this Convention are violated shall have an effective remedy before a national authority notwithstanding that the violation has been committed by persons acting in an official capacity.*

As regards explicit legal basis for claiming damages for violations of human rights, it can be indicated that insofar as these violations caused pecuniary or non-pecuniary damage in the sense of Polish civil law, the relevant legal basis can be found in the Polish Civil Code (CC) and in particular in the following provisions (as amended by the Act of 17 June 2004 in an amendment of the Civil Code and some other acts):

Art. 417 § 1. The State Treasury or a unit of local self-government or other legal person exercising public authority on the basis and within limits of law shall be liable for damage caused by an unlawful action or omission in exercising that authority.

§ 2. Where the performance of the tasks from the scope of public authority has been commissioned by virtue of an agreement to a unit of local self-government or other legal person referred to in § 1, both the performer and the commissioning unit of the self-government or the State Treasury are liable for the damage.

Art. 417^1 § 1. If damage was caused by issuance of a normative act, the reparation of the damage may be sought after an establishment in relevant proceedings that the act is not in conformity to the Constitution, ratified international agreement or statute.

§ 2. If damage was caused by issuance of a legally valid judgment or a final decision, a person may seek reparation of the damage after an establishment in relevant proceedings that the judgment or the decision is unlawful. The above rule shall also apply in a case when a legally valid judgment or a final decision was issued on the basis of a normative act that was not in conformity to the Constitution, ratified international agreement or statute.

§ 3. If damage was caused by non-issuance of a legal order or a decision and if an obligation to issue them was provided by law, a person may seek reparation of the damage after an establishment in relevant proceedings that the non-issuance was unlawful, unless the separate provisions provide for otherwise.

§ 4. If damage was caused by non-issuance of a normative act and if an obligation to issue it was provided by law, the unlawfulness of the non-issuance is declared by the court examining the case concerning the reparation of the damage.

Art. 417^2 If damage to a person was caused by lawful exercising of public authority, the victim may seek full or partial reparation of the damage and a pecuniary just satisfaction when the circumstances – and especially the inability of the victim to work or his or her financial situation – show that it is required by the principles of equity.

The above provisions could be regarded as a general legal regime of public authority liability, including for violations of human rights. According to Art. 421 CC the provisions of Arts. 417, 417^1 and 417^2 shall not apply if the liability for damage caused by exercising public authority is regulated elsewhere by detailed provisions.

In view of the above it can be submitted that whenever a human rights violation resulted in damage caused to an individual (or other entitled subject) by an unlawful action or omission in exercising that authority, a claim based on Art. 417 of the Civil

Code, can be brought to civil court by the victim of the violation. Let us however note that it is usually non-pecuniary damage rather that material one which results from a human rights violation, with the exception of violations of the protection of property where material damage seems to be the most "natural" consequence of these violations.

Therefore it is vital to ask, how can an individual or other entitled subject claim damages in Polish domestic system if an infringement of human rights results in non-pecuniary damage? For the sake of precision it needs to be recalled that this question is relevant both in the cases of human rights guaranteed by international law instruments as well as human rights norms enshrined in the Polish Constitution (i.e. its Chapter II – "Freedoms, rights and duties of people and citizens"). In both instances human rights norms are directly applicable and may be invoked in Polish courts. Nevertheless, from the perspective of Polish civil law there is a difficulty in claiming compensation for non-pecuniary damage caused by violation of human rights, unless the violation can be considered an infringement of personal rights (*dobra osobiste*) in the meaning of Art. 23 CC. This provision sets out an open catalogue of protected interests,[2] however, it cannot be assumed that all human rights norms are covered by Art. 23; in other words – some rights protected by constitutional and/or international human rights norms remain outside the scope of protected rights in the meaning of Civil Code (Kaliński 2011, 2365). This apparently leads to a legal lacuna which can only partly be filled in by *leges speciales*, i.e., compensatory remedies outside the regime of civil law (see below).

There is an alternative point of view expressed in the civil law doctrine which advocates to consider all human rights as personal rights in the meaning of Art. 23 CC, having regard to the fact that human rights and freedoms originate in human dignity which as such should be regarded as a personal right protected by Civil Code (Kaliński 2011, 2365). The author provides arguments in favour of this approach but eventually takes a more cautious stance and argues this concept has not yet been recognized and requires further studies, also in the context of works on a new Civil Code. Nevertheless, the general idea behind this approach seems reasonable since there is no doubt as to the central position of human dignity as a normative, and philosophical, explanation of human rights' origins. Further arguments in favour of this concept include the fact that the catalogue in Art. 23 CC is open-ended and – moreover – a possibility to claim damages for non-material damage caused by human rights violations would even go beyond what is required by the right to an effective remedy as enshrined in Art. 13 ECHR (which requires an availability of a remedy to "a competent organ," not necessarily a judicial one). Although the above idea is so far not implemented in judicial practice, there are sound reasons to pursue it, at least with respect to human rights guaranteed in the ECHR and its Protocols. It must however be noted that human rights norms enshrined in the inter-

[2] See Art. 23 of Polish Civil Code which provides: *Personal human interests, and in particular health, freedom, reputation, freedom of conscience, family name or nickname, secrecy of correspondence, inviolability of home, scientific, artistic, inventive or rationalizing creation, remain under protection of civil law irrespective of protection provided by other provisions.*

national treaties should not be categorized into "more" or "less" important groups. It needs to be recalled in this regard that all human rights are regarded as universal, indivisible, inter-dependent and inter-related. Despite differences in their normative structure, contents of international obligations and the sometimes used division into "generations", human rights constitute a system of state obligations and may not be picked à la carte. On the other hand, providing an individual with the right to claim compensation for non-pecuniary damage in the case of every violation of international human rights norm would be of far-reaching and unpredictable consequences for the state budget.

The legal basis for claiming a violation of personal rights and compensation for non-pecuniary damage resulted therefrom is Art. 448 CC which provides:

> In case of infringement of a personal right the court may award the subject affected by the infringement an appropriate sum as pecuniary satisfaction for harm or adjudicate upon request of the affected subject an appropriate sum for a social purpose indicated subject, irrespective of other measures necessary for eradicating the consequences of the infringement. (…)

It has been generally accepted in Polish jurisprudence that claiming damages for non-material violations of personal rights under Art. 448 CC requires to prove the defendant's fault (at least *culpa levissima*) (Bagińska 2006, 416–417). Of course, this requirement may seriously undermine the effectiveness of invoking Art. 448 as a legal basis for claiming an infringement of human rights recognized as personal interests in the meaning of the Polish Civil Code. It should be noticed that normally fault is not a prerequisite of international state responsibility for human rights violations.

Nevertheless, some compensatory claims for human rights violations may be successfully brought to the Polish civil courts under this head and are considered as "effective remedies" for the purpose of the ECHR. There is a notable example involving the so-called "systemic problem" identified in the case-law of the ECtHR in cases against Poland. In a number of cases Polish civil courts found a violation of the claimants' personal interests due to the fact that they were detained in overpopulated prison cells.[3] This kind of cases gave rise to numerous complaints against Poland to the Strasbourg Court and judgments founding violations of the applicants' rights under Art. 3 ECHR (prohibition of inhuman and degrading treatment). It has been only in recent years that the Polish civil courts started to award compensations for violation of the claimants' personal rights, and notably their dignity and health, due to overpopulation in prisons. Following a ground-breaking judgment of the Polish Supreme Court delivered on 17 March 2010,[4] the European Court of Human Rights found that *a civil action under Art. 24 taken in conjunction with Art. 448 CC*

[3] See *inter alia* the ECHR judgment in *Orchowski v. Poland* case of 22.10.2009.

[4] Case no. II CSK 486/09. Having examined and allowed a cassation appeal, the Supreme Court restated a principle already expressed in its earlier judgment (of 28.2.2007, case no. V CSK 431/06) that the right to be detained in conditions respecting one's dignity undoubtedly belonged to the catalogue of personal rights. Therefore actions infringing this right could involve the State Treasury's liability for the purposes of Arts. 24 and 448 of the Civil Code.

could be considered an "effective remedy" for the purposes of Art. 35 § 1 of the Convention as from 17 March 2010 and having regard to the 3-year limitation period for lodging such an action, the Court held that essentially in all cases in which in June 2008 the alleged violation had either been remedied by placing the applicant in Convention-compliant conditions or had ended ipso facto because the applicant had been released, the applicants concerned should bring a civil action for the infringement of personal rights and compensation.[5] It follows that the compensatory claim based on the infringement of personal rights should be considered a primary domestic remedy in cases involving violation of human rights due to overpopulation in prisons. However, it should be stressed that not all applicants are successful in pursuing their rights under this head in Polish courts.[6]

As has already been noted above, the general regime of public authority liability has been set out in Art. 417, 417^1 and 417^2 CC. Its basic features can be summarized as follows:

- The principle of strict liability (risk) for damages caused by an unlawful action or omission constitutes the basis of the general regime (Bagińska 2006, 217). Fault used to be the basis of this regime prior to the ruling of the Constitutional Court of 2001 (case no. SK 18/00) which found such an approach as unconstitutional. An unlawful action or omission of public authorities is considered a delict according to Polish civil law.
- With respect to liability for damage to a person caused by lawful exercising of public authority, the leading principle is equity. It has been indicated that public authority liability under this head had been commonly applied to damage caused in public health care facilities, particularly in the 1990s, but nowadays it is debatable whether such strict liability should be borne by health facilities, which are in fact considered "self-governing" (*samodzielne publiczne zakłady opieki zdrowotnej*) (Bagińska 2006, 223). This is important also from the human rights perspective as it is doubtful whether in the current regime the actions of public health facilities should be considered actions of public authorities and as such be attributed to state for the purposes of international human rights law.[7]
- Damage is a prerequisite of a claim for pecuniary or non-pecuniary compensation. The notion of 'damage' (*szkoda*) covers both material and non-material harm. It is necessary that the damage be caused by an act (action or omission) in exercising public authority. The public authority liability is not excluded in case of actions ultra vires.

[5] See ECHR judgment in *Kurkowski v. Poland* case of 9.4.2013, § 53, referring to the ECHR decision in *Łasak v. Poland* case of 12.10.2010, § 85 and 76.

[6] See for instance the judgment of the Warsaw Court of Appeal delivered on 4.7.2013 (ref. no. I ACa 31/13).

[7] Cf. *Z. v. Poland* case in which the European Court of Human Rights referred to "an established case-law of the Polish courts to the effect that this liability of the State also includes liability for damage caused by medical treatment in a public system of medical care, run either by the State or by the municipalities" (judgment of 13.11.2012, § 60). The facts of the case concerned events of 2004.

13.3 Liability Regimes for Human Rights Violations: *Leges Speciales*

The Polish legal system provides for several remedies which could be availed of, in order to compensate selected human rights violations, outside the general regime of the Civil Code. Having regard to the scope of the research, the analysis is focused on two such remedies which have a compensatory nature. Thus the comments do not concern the Polish constitutional complaint (*skarga konstytucyjna*) which is undoubtedly a very important remedy but has no compensatory function.

Special ('tailored') remedies having compensatory nature include:

- A complaint against undue length of judicial proceedings (including preparatory criminal proceedings as well as civil execution proceedings)
- A complaint against damage caused by wrongful conviction and execution of punishment or manifestly wrongful detention or detention on-remand.

13.3.1 A Complaint Against Undue Length of Judicial Proceedings

In 2004 the Polish Parliament adopted an Act on a complaint against undue length of judicial proceedings. In 2009 the Act was amended to include also preparatory criminal proceedings.[8] The Act introduced into Polish legal system a new remedy to combat the unreasonable length of proceedings and at the same time to provide the injured party with an adequate compensation for non-pecuniary damage which, interestingly, was not explicitly called "satisfaction" in the sense of the Polish Civil Code, but "a sum of money." While it is quite similar to compensation for non-material damage and considered as such by the Supreme Court, the doctrine of civil law does not seem to be unanimous in recognizing the "sum of money" referred to in the 2004 Act as a "pure" compensation for non-material damage (Kaliński 2011, 2575 et seq.). Nevertheless, as provided in Art. 12(4) of the 2004 Act, if the court allows a complaint it shall afford, upon the complainant's request, a sum of money in the amount between 2000 and 20,000 PLN. The award is thus obligatory if a violation of the right to have a case examined without undue delay was violated. This principle was introduced by the 2009 amendment whereas the original Act provided that any financial award was up to the court examining the complaint.

[8] Ustawa z dnia 17 czerwca 2004 r. o skardze na naruszenie prawa strony do rozpoznania sprawy w postępowaniu przygotowawczym prowadzonym lub nadzorowanym przez prokuratora i postępowaniu sądowym bez nieuzasadnionej zwłoki, Dz.U. z 2004 r. nr 179 poz. 1843 ze zmianami [Act of 17.6.2004 on a complaint against violation of the right to have a case examined without undue delay in preparatory proceedings conducted or supervised by prosecutor or judicial proceedings, Journal of Laws no. 179 of 2004, item 1843, amended].

According to Art. 15(1) of the 2004 Act, the party whose complaint has been allowed may, in separate proceedings, seek reparation from the State Treasury or jointly from the State Treasury and the court enforcement officer for the damage resulted from the established undue delay. Moreover, the order that allows a complaint shall be binding on the court in civil proceedings concerning reparation (*odszkodowanie*) or satisfaction (*zadośćuczynienie*) as regards the establishment of an undue delay of the proceedings (Art. 15(2)).

An important feature of the complaint against undue delay of proceedings is that it can be lodged only while the delayed proceedings are pending. However, the failure to lodge the complaint during the delayed proceedings does not in any way influence the party's right to seek reparation of the damage that resulted from the delay on the basis of Art. 417 CC, after the final completion of the proceedings as to the merits (Art. 16 of the 2004 Act). As follows from Art. 15(1) referred to above the party whose right to proceedings without undue delay was violated, has also the full possibility to seek compensation for material or non-material damage in separate proceedings, based on the general regime of public authority liability.

The remedy against undue length of judicial (or other) proceedings is a principal example of the influence of the ECHR standards on the Polish law system. Its introduction was a direct consequence of the *Kudła v. Poland* judgment delivered by the ECtHR on 26 October 2000. The remedy has been recognized by the Court as "effective" within the meaning of Art. 13 of the ECHR. While the interpretation and application of the 2004 Act sometimes gives rise to legal debates, it can be argued that the remedy against undue delay generally proved successful, at least insofar as it allowed an injured party to claim damages for undue delay and at the same time obtain some acceleration of the proceedings. With respect to the legal character of the compensation ("sum of money" referred to in Art. 12(4) of the 2004 Act), it can be considered as having a *sui generis* character since it was aimed both at providing a redress for an established violation of the party's human rights, and at having a punitive effect on a court (or other relevant organ conducting proceedings). The latter function of the compensation results from the fact that the compensation awarded for undue length of proceedings is to be paid from the budget of the court (or other relevant organ) which was conducting the proceedings that was complained of.[9]

Last but not least, it should be noted that the 'special' compensatory remedy provided for in the 2004 Act concerns just one aspect of the right to fair trial guaranteed by Art. 6(1) of the ECHR and reflected in Art. 45(1) of the Polish Constitution, and notably the right to have a case examined by a court "in reasonable time" (ECHR) or "without undue delay" (Polish Constitution). The 2004 Act was drafted in direct consequence of the Kudła judgment and with the sole intention of providing a remedy for this particular aspect of the right to a fair trial, so it would be pointless to criticize the Act for restricting the material scope of the remedy to that aspect. It goes without saying that the right to have a case examined in a reasonable time has been the most problematic, i.e., the most frequently invoked basis of complaints against Poland to the European Court of Human Rights. However, it

[9] See Art. 12(5) of the 2004 Act.

should be stressed that the remedy against undue delay is the only one in the Polish legal system which explicitly allows for obtaining compensation for non-pecuniary damages. The problem arises if a party demands such compensation for a violation of other aspects of the right to fair trial, i.e., the right of access to a court, the right to have a case examined in a fair and public hearing, or by 'an independent and impartial tribunal established by law.'

As was already mentioned, not every human right can easily be considered as a 'protected right' in the meaning of the Polish Civil Code. It appears that whereas a party may successfully claim non-pecuniary damages for a violation of the right to have a case examined without undue delay, he/she cannot do so in the case of other aspects of Art. 6(1) ECHR even if there are other domestic remedies available to an individual in cases where his/her rights under Art. 6(1) are in danger, e.g., a motion for exemption from court fees if a party is not able to cover the costs himself/herself; a motion for exclusion of a *iudex suspectus*, etc. This may be seen as favouring one aspect of the right to a fair trial against the others regarding the possibility to claim and obtain non-pecuniary damages. On the other hand, since the domestic system allows for preventing or restoring the individual in his/her rights under Art. 6(1), it could be asked whether non-pecuniary compensation is really essential in every single case. Be it as it may, the Polish legal system explicitly allows for claiming non-pecuniary compensation for an undue delay of judicial (or other) proceedings and not for other aspects of the right to a fair trial. Let us also recall that no such distinction exists when it comes to claiming compensation for material damage caused by violation of this right.

13.3.2 A Complaint Against Damage Caused by Wrongful Conviction and Execution of Punishment or Manifestly Wrongful Detention or Detention On-Remand

According to Art. 552 of the Polish Code of Criminal Procedure:

§ 1. An accused who, as a result of reopening of proceedings or cassation appeal has been acquitted or re-sentenced for a milder penalty, shall be entitled to compensation from the State Treasury for pecuniary and non-pecuniary damage which he has suffered as a result of having served all or part of the sentence unjustifiably imposed on him.

(…)

§ 3. A right to compensation for pecuniary and non-pecuniary damage shall also arise if a precautionary measure (*środek zabezpieczający*) has been applied (…).

§ 4. A right to compensation for pecuniary and non-pecuniary damage shall also arise in the event of clearly unjustified pre-trial detention (*tymczasowe aresztowanie*) or arrest (*zatrzymanie*).

The above provision could be regarded as basis for claiming compensatory remedies with respect to several human rights standards enshrined in international treaties as well as the Polish Constitution. The right to compensation and satisfaction for wrongful conviction provided in Art. 552 § 1 of the Code of Criminal Procedure (CCP), reflects the guarantee included in Art. 3 of Protocol no. 7 to the ECHR (compensation for wrongful conviction).[10] The right to compensation or reparation for wrongful conviction differs in its scope and conditions from the general regime of Art. 417 CC, nevertheless, it clearly provides an individual with a compensatory remedy if his/her conviction has been established as wrongful following a reopening proceedings or cassation appeal. Art. 552 § 3 CCP allows for claiming compensation and satisfaction also when precautionary measures (*środki zabezpieczające*) have been wrongfully applied. These measures are usually imposed on a convicted person whose mental health or other medical condition, e.g., alcohol addiction, requires isolation in specific conditions.[11]

Although the direct prerequisite of a compensatory claim based on Art. 552 § 1 and 3 of the CCP is wrongful conviction, it should be noted that this kind of claims is supposed to redress human rights violations in the broader context. Assuming that a wrongful conviction included imprisonment or other form of isolation, it is hard to argue that the person's right to freedom and security of person (Art. 5(1) of the ECHR) was fully respected, even though prior to declaring the conviction as wrongful all guarantees concerning the right to freedom and security might have been observed. From a purely legal point of view however, the legality of detention does not depend on a subsequent finding that the conviction had been wrongful (Hofmański 2011, 643). Nevertheless, in a broader sense and if the conviction included other penalties (or precautionary measures) than deprivation of liberty, the compensatory remedy provided in Art. 552 § 1 and 3 of the CCP may indirectly concern also other human rights guarantees than the right to freedom and security of person. For instance, compensation for wrongful conviction may concern the right to free elections in Art. 3 of Protocol no. 1 to the ECHR (when the court ruled on the deprivation of public rights) or the right to privacy in Art. 8 of the ECHR (for instance when the court imposed a prohibition of certain activities or certain kind of employment, or indicated public announcement of the criminal judgment). Needless to mention, all material loss caused by wrongful conviction is to be compensated just as non-pecuniary damage.

Art. 552. § 4 of the CCP provides for the right to compensation and satisfaction in the case of manifestly unjustified (wrongful) pre-trial detention or arrest. This corresponds or actually fulfills the requirements of Art. 5(5) of the ECHR which stipulates: *Everyone who has been a victim of arrest or detention in contravention of the provisions of this Article shall have an enforceable right to compensation.* This

[10] Art. 3 of Protocol no. 7 to the ECHR provides: *When a person has by a final decision been convicted of a criminal offence and when subsequently his conviction has been reversed, or he has been pardoned, on the ground that a new or newly discovered fact shows conclusively that there has been a miscarriage of justice, the person who has suffered punishment as a result of such conviction shall be compensated according to the law or the practice of the State concerned, unless it is proved that the non-disclosure of the unknown fact in time is wholly or partly attributable to him.*

[11] See Art. 93 *et seq.* of Polish Criminal Code.

standard is reflected also in Art. 41(1) of the Polish Constitution which provides for the right to compensation for unlawful deprivation of liberty. Importantly, Art. 552 § 4 of the CCP allows an individual to obtain compensation and satisfaction only for selected violations of the right to freedom and security of person, and notably wrongful arrest or detention referred to in Art. 5(1) "b", "c" and "f". It is hardly possible to a find legal basis in Polish law for claiming damages and executing the right provided in Art. 5(5) of the ECHR when an individual claims violation of his/her rights under Art. 5 para. 2 (the right to be informed promptly and in an understandable language of the reasons of the arrest and any charges against the person arrested), Art. 5 para. 3 (the right of an arrested or detained person to be brought promptly before a judge or other officer authorized by law to exercise judicial power and be tried within a reasonable time or released pending trial), Art. 5 para. 4 (the right of an arrested or detained person to take proceedings by which the lawfulness of the detention shall be decided speedily by a court and his/her release ordered if the detention is unlawful).

It has been pointed out in the doctrine that this is particularly problematic in the case of undue length of pre-trial detention contrary to Art. 5 para. 3 of the ECHR, since these types of cases are not covered by Art. 552 of the CCP and at the same time the complaints based on this provision of the ECHR are relatively frequently examined by the ECtHR (Hofmański 2010, 239). Indeed, there is no 'tailored' compensatory remedy in cases where the length of pre-trial arrest is claimed to be contrary to Art. 5(3) of the ECHR. So far there has also been no visible tendency in the practice of the Polish civil courts to consider such cases under the general regime of public authority liability. But such possibility have been invoked by the Polish government before the European Court of Human Rights and the latter seemed prepared to consider it as a remedy fulfilling the requirements of Art. 5(5).[12] However, the Court expects the compensatory remedy against violation of Art. 5(3) based on the general regime to be confirmed in domestic judicial practice before considering it as effective and satisfactory.[13]

The special compensatory remedies provided in Art. 552 CCP do not apply in the case of minors whose wrongful convictions or detentions are to be compensated within the general regime (Banaszczyk 2012, 277).

[12] See *ibidem*, with reference to ECHR judgments in cases of *Ryckie v. Poland* of 30.1.2007 and *Bruczyński v. Poland* of 4.11.2008.

[13] See the judgment of the ECHR in the case of *Wereda v. Poland* of 26.11.2013, § 55: (…) [E]ven assuming that an action for damages could be an effective remedy in the context of a complaint about the allegedly excessive length of detention, it is first noted that this can be said to be the case only when that detention has come to an end and when the availability and practicability of such a remedy under the domestic system must be convincingly established, either by reference to a specific provisions of domestic law or to established and consistent practice of national courts.

13.4 Interaction Between Domestic Compensatory Remedies and "Just Satisfaction" Awarded by the European Court of Human Rights

The following remarks concern the availability of domestic compensatory remedies in the Polish legal system after the ECtHR found a violation of the European Convention. The remarks do not tackle all effects of the judgments of the European Court of Human Rights in Polish law, though it should be mentioned that one of them is a possibility to re-open criminal proceedings which is provided *expressis verbis* in Art. 540 § 2 CCP. Such a possibility has not been proved possible within civil proceedings: following a period of swinging jurisprudence, the Supreme Court held in 2010 that a judgment of the European Court of Human Rights does not constitute a basis for the re-opening of civil proceedings.[14] Let us recall that the judgments of the Strasbourg Court cannot quash any domestic judicial decisions *per se* or oblige domestic courts to re-open proceedings, nevertheless, in some cases the re-opening of civil proceedings might happen to be the most suitable way of providing redress and apply the principle of *restitutio in integrum*. Be it as it may, the current position of the Polish Supreme Court as regards impossibility to re-open civil proceedings following the judgment of the Strasbourg Court is a valid reason for pursuing alternative ways of redress. Obviously, the most appropriate alternative to re-opening is to be found in the general regime of public authority liability, however, it is premature to say whether this option would be really feasible and effective.

The judgment of the Strasbourg Court finding a violation of the Convention usually specifies what kind of action or omission by state authorities was found to be an internationally wrongful act and caused the violation complained of. Although every act of state may be subject to the Court's scrutiny under the ECHR, it is extremely rare that the Court finds that the adoption of a domestic normative act (or the act itself) violates the Convention. But assuming that the Court finds such a violation, then it can be argued that it opens the door for the application of Art. 417^1 § 1 CC, which provides for the possibility to seek reparation of damage caused by the issuance of a normative act after an establishment, in relevant proceedings, that the act is not in conformity with inter alia "ratified international agreement".

It is far more common that the European Court of Human Rights finds a violation of the ECHR due to a domestic judicial or administrative decision. It has been rightly suggested in the doctrine of civil law that also in this case the general regime of public authority liability would be applicable (Bagińska 2006, 359; Banaszczyk 2012, 349 et seq.). According to Art. 417^1 § 2 CC, the reparation for damage caused by a (final) judgment or decision may be sought after establishing "in relevant proceedings" that the judgment or decision complained of had been unlawful. The proceedings before the Strasbourg Court should then be regarded as "relevant" for the purposes of the above mentioned provision.

---

[14] See judgment of the Supreme Court of 30.11.2010 (ref. no. III CZP 16/10).

The very possibility of claiming damages following a judgment of the European Court of Human Rights which found a judicial decision (or, rarely, a domestic normative act) unlawful under the Convention, needs to be reviewed in the context of possible award to the applicant (victim of the violation) of "just satisfaction" under Art. 41 of the Convention. Let us note that this is an optional and discretional competence of the Strasbourg Court. Art. 41 of the ECHR allows the Court to award "just satisfaction" when a violation of the ECHR was found and "if the internal law of the High Contracting Party concerned allows only partial reparation to be made." It should be recalled that "just satisfaction" in the meaning of Art. 41 ECHR might be awarded both for pecuniary and non-pecuniary damage. In practice there are two (or three) possible scenarios: the Strasbourg Court may rule that the very finding of the violation "constitutes in itself just satisfaction" (option I), or may award just satisfaction for pecuniary and/or non-pecuniary damage in the same judgment which established a violation (option II), or finally, the Court may adjourn its decision as to an application of Art. 41 after finding a violation of the Convention (option III).

Let us review the above mentioned options in the background of the Polish general regime of public authority liability. As regards option I, it appears that the Court's decision not to award any just satisfaction to the victim of a violation and considering the very judgments as "just satisfaction" is not binding on the domestic courts. It is the unlawfulness of the domestic judicial ruling or decision – found in "relevant proceedings" as well as existence of damage – which is crucial in this context, and not the Court's decision under Art. 41 ECHR. Nevertheless, it is uncertain to what extent the domestic court would be influenced by the fact that the Court decided not to make any awards under Art. 41.

In option II, which seems to be most common in the Court's judicial practice, the victim of a violation is awarded compensation for pecuniary or (most frequently) non-pecuniary damage. For reasons of space limits it is not possible to discuss here the Court's policy and jurisprudence under Art. 41. Suffice it to say, that while compensation for pecuniary damage is awarded to the full extent of damage (*damnum emergens* and *lucrum cessans*) proven by the applicant and directly caused by the violation, the compensation for non-pecuniary damage is generally based on the principle of equity (Oliphant and Ludwichowska 2011, 397–447). With regard to the possibility to claim compensation for pecuniary or non-pecuniary damage in the Polish general regime of public authority liability, I share the view that an award of "just satisfaction" under Art. 41 does not deprive the applicant to submit further claims under Art. 417 et seq. CC (Bagińska 2006, 359; Banaszczyk 2012, 349 *et seq.*). This is justified in view of the principle of full compensation which is not in any way limited in respect to damage caused by actions of public authorities (Banaszczyk 2012, ibid.). The sums awarded by the Strasbourg Court under Art. 41 would in all probability need to be taken into account by the Polish courts in assessing claims submitted under Art. 417 et seq. CC.

Let us now comment on option III mentioned above, and notably when the Court finds a violation of the Convention but adjourns its ruling under Art. 41. This situation is rather uncommon though it occasionally happens in the Court's practice.

An adjournment of this kind would usually be necessary when the issues under Art. 41 are not ready for decision. It is expected that the respondent State and the applicant in such cases would submit further observations and/or enter into negotiations as to the compensatory issues. The parties may arrive at a friendly settlement as regards to compensatory claims. Such a settlement is subject to the Court's approval. In theory it is advisable that no claims under the domestic regime of public authority liability be examined by domestic courts while the application of Art. 41 is still unresolved in Strasbourg. However, following the Court's judgment which found a domestic ruling contrary to the Convention, the prerequisite of establishing unlawfulness "in relevant proceedings" is fulfilled. Thus it is hard to indicate a reason for a civil court to dismiss a claim under Art. 417^1 § 2 CC is such a situation. As a matter of fact it could be argued that the domestic proceedings should be considered as the best way to resolve compensatory claims of the applicants. This is justified by the principle of the subsidiarity which is underpinning the Convention since its adoption and has recently been agreed to be included into its Preamble.[15]

This brings us to the last point and notably a brief evaluation of compensatory remedies available in Poland under the general regime of public authority liability against the current practice of the Court concerning the application of Art. 41 of the ECHR. In other words, it is worth considering whether the remedies offered under the general regime of Polish civil law to victims of human rights violations may successfully "replace" the awards on the basis of Art. 41. Generally speaking, it is unlikely that domestic compensatory remedies would indeed induce the Court to restrict its application of Art. 41 after finding a violation of the Convention. There are several reasons behind this supposition and only some of them are related to the domestic remedies themselves. The European Court of Human Rights has considerably departed from the original wording of Art. 41 which stipulates, as was mentioned above, that the competence to award "just satisfaction" depends on whether the internal law of the respondent State allows for the full reparation to be made. If the internal law does allow it then according to the literal meaning of Art. 41 the Court can hardly be entitled to award "just satisfaction".

In the Court's jurisprudence of the 1970s and 1980s there was more adherence to the exact meaning of the then Art. 50 of the Convention.[16] The Court usually cared to verify if domestic law allowed for full reparation if the issue was far from obvious. But over the years the application of Art. 41 of the ECHR started to be more automatic in the sense that the Court seemed less interested in the literal meaning of this provision. Instead, the Court opted for elaborating its own doctrine of reparation for the violation of the Convention. The Court's judicial policy is of course rooted in

---

[15] See Art. 1 to Protocol no. 15 to the Convention adopted on 16.5.2013 (not yet in force), which shall add the following paragraph at the end of the Preamble to the ECHR: *Affirming that the High Contracting Parties, in accordance with the principle of subsidiarity, have the primary responsibility to secure the rights and freedoms defined in this Convention and the Protocols thereto, and that in doing so they enjoy a margin of appreciation, subject to the supervisory jurisdiction of the European Court of Human Rights established by this Convention.*

[16] Protocol no. 11 to the ECHR which entered into force on 1.11.1998 slightly changed the then Art. 50 and renumbered it into Art. 41.

Art. 41, however, the part of this provision referring to availability of "full reparation" in domestic law is not a priority when the Court applies Art. 41 and awards just satisfaction. Arguably, the Court developed specific (secondary) rules of state-parties' responsibility under the Convention which include the determination of the consequences of the violation without the necessary reference to compensatory remedies available in domestic law. This might be partly explained by the fact that the Court is fully entitled to determine the consequences of the violation of the ECHR, within the limits provided by the Convention itself as well as the rules of general law of international state responsibility. It can be expected that the Court continues to apply Art. 41 of the ECHR this way since so far there seem to be no plans within the Council of Europe member states to amend this provision or introduce other changes as regards "just satisfaction". It could be mentioned however that there has been an interesting proposal to "repatriate" compensatory claims under the Convention, i.e. to entrust domestic courts with the competence to determine compensation for pecuniary and non-pecuniary damage following the judgment of (and instead of) the Court (Steiner 2011, 24).

Against this background it needs to be observed that the availability of compensatory remedies in Polish civil law in the case of damage caused by actions of public authority is not likely to radically change the attitude of the Court as to the application of Art. 41 in cases against Poland. The reasons for this assumption lay more on the part of the Court itself than on the deficiencies of compensatory remedies available in the Polish legal system. Nevertheless, it should be noted that so far there is hardly any jurisprudence of the Polish courts applying general regime of public authority liability after a violation of human rights was found by the European Court of Human Rights.

References

Bagińska, Ewa. 2006. *Odpowiedzialność odszkodowawcza za wykonywanie władzy publicznej* [Compensatory liability for exercising of public authority]. Warszawa: C.H. Beck.

Balcerzak, Michał. 2010. The improvement of domestic remedies in the post-interlaken process. In: *Concepts of general domestic remedy and simplified procedure for amending the convention in the post-interlaken process*. 4th Warsaw Seminar. In memory of Professor Krzysztof Skubiszewski, 38–47. Warsaw: Krajowa Szkoła Administracji Publicznej

Banaszczyk, Zbigniew. 2012. *Odpowiedzialność za szkody wyrządzone przy wykonywaniu władzy publicznej* [Liability for damage caused in exercise of public authority]. Warszawa: C.H. BECK.

Crawford, James. 2013. *State responsibility. The general part*. Cambridge: Cambridge University Press.

Hofmański, Piotr. 2010. Art. 5 [Prawo do wolności i bezpieczeństwa osobistego]. In: Konwencja o Ochronie Praw Człowieka i Podstawowych Wolności. Komentarz do artykułów 1–18 [Convention on the Protection of Human Rights and Fundamental Freedoms. Commentary to Articles 1–18] t. I, ed. Lech Garlicki, 152–241. Warszawa: C. H. Beck.

Hofmański, Piotr. 2011. Protokół nr 7 do Konwencji ochronie praw człowieka i podstawowych wolności. In: Konwencja o Ochronie Praw Człowieka i Podstawowych Wolności. Komentarz do artykułów 19–59 oraz Protokołów dodatkowych [Convention on the protection of human rights and fundamental freedoms. Commentary to Articles 19–59 and additional protocols] t. II, ed. Lech Garlicki, 617–669. Warszawa: C. H. Beck

Kaliński, Maciej. 2011. O naprawieniu szkody wynikłej z naruszenia praw człowieka [On reparation of damage resulting from violation of human rights]. In: Aurea praxis, aurea theoria. Księga pamiątkowa ku czci Profesora Tadeusza Erecińskiego, vol. II, eds. Jacek Gudowski and Karol Weitz, 2345–2378. Warszawa: Lexis Nexis.

Łętowska, Ewa. 2010. Human rights – universal and normative? (a few remarks from the Polish perspective). In: Rapports polonaise. XVIII Congrès International de Droit Comparé, ed. Biruta Lewaszkiewicz-Petrykowska, 267–283. Łódź: Wydawnictwo Uniwersytetu Łódzkiego.

Oliphant, Ken, and Katarzyna Ludwichowska. 2011. Damage. In: *Tort law in the jurisprudence of the European Court of Human Rights*, ed. Fenyves Attila, Karner Ernst, Koziol Helmut, and Steiner Elisabeth, 397–447. Berlin/Boston: De Gruyter.

Safjan, Marek. 2004. *Odpowiedzialność odszkodowawcza władzy publicznej za szkodę* [Compensatory liability of public authority for damage]. Warszawa: Lexis Nexis.

Shelton, Dinah. 2005. *Remedies in international human rights law*. Oxford: Oxford University Press.

Steiner, Elisabeth. 2011. Just satisfaction under Art 41 ECHR: A compromise in 1950 – Problematic now. In: *Tort Law in the Jurisprudence of the European Court of Human Rights*, ed. Fenyves Attila, Karner Ernst, Koziol Helmut, and Steiner Elisabeth, 3–26. Berlin–Boston: De Gruyter.

Chapter 14
Damages for Violations of Human Rights: The Portuguese Legal System

Maria José Reis Rangel de Mesquita

14.1 General Features of the Liability Regime

1 Regarding the main features of the general Law on public authority liability insofar as it concerns the liability for violations of human rights (HRs) both constitutional and infra-constitutional levels are most relevant.

The evolution observed in the Portuguese Legal Order led to the consecration in the 1976 Constitution (last revised in 2005[1]) of a general constitutional principle of "liability of public entities" meaning the State and other public entities, as well as their officials, public officers and agents, arising out of functional acts or omissions causing violation of "rights, freedoms and guarantees" or damage to someone. This general principle, placed within Part I of the Constitution "Fundamental Rights and Duties", is laid down in Art. 22 of the 1976 Constitution, which states as follows:

> Jointly with their officeholders and their staff and agents the state and other public entities are civilly liable for actions or omissions that are committed in or because of the exercise of their functions and result in a breach of rights, freedoms or guarantees or in a loss to others.

The liability for violations of HRs is therefore within the scope of application of this general constitutional principle, either through the express reference to "the violation of rights, freedoms and guarantees" or through the reference to damages caused to a third party. Although the first notion "the violation of rights, freedoms and guarantees" refers only to one category of fundamental rights laid down by the Constitution, the notion of damaged caused by public authorities includes the cases of damages due to the violation of the other main category (and sub-categories) of

[1] Available in http://www.parlamento.pt. Accessed 15 March 2015.

M.J.R. Rangel de Mesquita (✉)
Faculty of Law, University of Lisbon, Lisbon, Portugal
e-mail: mjrangeldemesquita@gmail.com; mjrangeldemesquita@fd.ulisboa.pt

E. Bagińska (ed.), *Damages for Violations of Human Rights*,
Ius Comparatum - Global Studies in Comparative Law 9,
DOI 10.1007/978-3-319-18950-5_14

fundamental rights "economic, social and cultural rights and duties"[2] foreseen in the Constitution as well as other fundamental rights, also foreseen through the open-clause on fundamental rights (art. 16, 1 of 1976 Constitution) that are laid down either in the infra-constitutional law or in the applicable international law rules.

The above mentioned general constitutional principle is understood as a principle that implies direct liability of the State and other public entities irrespective of the State function (legislative, administrative or judicial), the way in which they carry out their activity (public or private) and the cause of the obligation to compensate (unlawful conduct and fault, lawful conduct implying sacrifice or mere risk inherent to hazardous things, activities or services). Moreover, such principle is considered to be an expression of the rule of law principle (art. 2 of 1976 Constitution) which implies a general duty to compensate even in cases which may not be covered by the general principle of State liability laid down in Art. 22 of the Constitution. The principle is considered to be a general principle regarding fundamental rights and has been considered by the Constitutional Court to be directly applicable at least regarding liability for unlawful and faulty acts or omissions (decision no 107/92[3]) meaning that it can be invoked against the law or in the absence of law.

The intervention of the legislator to develop the constitutional principle is therefore desirable although not indispensable, namely to establish the regime of the public liability and the requirements of the obligation to compensate. Only in 2007, a new law on the liability of the State and other public entities, according to the constitutional principle, was approved by the Parliament, which is the law in force (Law no 67/2007 of 31.12.2007, modified by Law no 31/2008 of 17.7.2008). The 2007 Law on Public Authorities Liability (PAL) laid down four different regimes of public authority liability, three according to the State function involved (administrative, judicial and political-legislative) and one regarding of liability in case of sacrifice imposed by public authorities on grounds of public interest (See further *infra* 14.3 at 9).

In addition of the general principle of State liability, the 1976 Constitution foresees, in the framework of the rules on Public Administration, a general principle of liability of the State's political office holders as well as public officers, agents and employees, civil as well as criminal, disciplinary and political liability (Arts. 117 and 271), which is further developed by law (Law 34/87 of 16.7.1987 and Law 67/2007).

2 Public authority liability, including liability for violations of HRs falls therefore under public law, except in the case of liability, including liability for violation of HRs, deriving from private activities undertaking by public authorities which falls under private law (the law of tort, or civil responsibility, as foreseen in the Civil Code – art. 501).

[2] The 1976 Portuguese Constitution establishes a main distinction between the following categories of fundamental rights: "rights, liberties and freedoms" (including *personal* rights, liberties and freedoms, rights, liberties and freedoms regarding *political participation* and *worker's* rights, liberties and freedoms) and 'economic, social and cultural rights and duties' – arts. 24–57 and 58–79.

[3] Available in http://www.tribunalconstitucional.pt. Accessed 15 March 2015.

Compensation is nevertheless also available under criminal procedural law to the extent that a request for compensation can be presented within criminal proceedings when such request is based in the practice of a crime, including in cases of crimes implying the violation of fundamental rights, e.g. right to life or right to personal integrity. In fact, the request for compensation for damages (civil liability) based in the practice of a crime must be formulated within a criminal procedure (art. 71–84 of the 2013 Criminal Procedural Code (CrimPC)) except in a few cases foreseen by the law where the request for compensation can be presented separately in civil courts (art. 72 of the CrimPC). In the special case of civil liability in connection with criminal liability of the political office holders (see further *infra* 3), the applicable (special) Law on "crimes of liability of political office holders" (Law 34/87) foresees an option between a liability request presented in the criminal action or in a separate liability action in civil courts (art. 47 of Law 34/87).

3 The explicit legal basis for claiming damages for violations of HR's can be found both in constitutional law (either general or special rules – *infra* 3.1) and in the infra-constitutional 2007 Law (*infra* 14.3) as well as in (infra-constitutional) special legal rules (*infra* 3.2). Accordingly, a claim for financial compensation arising from infringement of HRs may involve either the application of general principles laid down both in the constitution and in the (general) 2007 Law on PAL or in special legal rules. In some cases the 2007 Law on PAL (as well as some special legal rules on PAL) foresees the application of some general principles and rules of tort law (non-contractual tortuous liability) as laid down in the Civil Code – to the extent that such statutory (general or special) rules refer to them (see *infra* 14.3).

3.1 Constitutional Law foresees not only a general principle applying to public authority liability for violations of "personal rights, freedoms and guarantees," those consecrated in arts. 24–47 of the 1976 (or for damages caused to third parties, including in case of violation of other fundamental rights), but also several rules on special cases of state liability that may involve violation of HRs: liability for unlawful privation of one's liberty and for unjust criminal judicial decisions (arts. 27(5) and 29(6)), both cases meaning violation of specific fundamental rights under the category of "p*ersonal* rights, freedoms and liberties"; liability (political, civil and criminal) of the holders of political offices (art. 117) and liability (civil, criminal, disciplinary and political) of the State's and public authorities' public officers, agents and employees (art. 271); compensation in case of requisition and expropriation (art. 62(2)); compensation in case of public appropriation of the "means of production" (art. 83); liability for damages within the "popular action" (art. 52(3)), all cases further developed by law.

3.1.1 The first two special constitutional legal basis for claiming damages refer to compensation in case of deprivation of liberty in breach of constitutional and legal rules (art. 27, 5 of 1976 Constitution) and in case of criminal unjust sentence (art. 29, 6 of 1976 Constitution), cases in which the right to freedom and the *nullum crimen sine lege* rule are involved, and are developed by the CrimPC, respectively in art. 225 (namely deprivation of liberty being illegal or due to a gross error in the analysis of the facts on which it depends[4]) and in arts. 449 and 462 (implying revision of a definitive court decision (*res judicata*) and absolution of the condemned person) of the CrimPC.[5] Both regimes are excluded from the scope of application of the 2007 Law on PAL (art. 13, 1) and involve exclusive liability of the State. In both cases the request for compensation can only be presented in the competent court within a term of 1 year after the release of the person detained or imprisoned or after the final decision of the case.

3.1.2 The case of civil liability of political offices holders, related with the practice of the so-called "crimes of liability of political office holders" is further developed in Law 34/87 of 16 July, which is applicable both to office holders of the sovereignty organs established by the Constitution and to holders of "high public offices" (*altos cargos públicos*) as defined in Arts. 3 and 3-A of Law 34/87. Such civil liability is ruled by civil law and the State is jointly liable with the political office holder (external relations) tough having the right of recover against the office holder (art. 45 (1 to 3) of Law 34/87).

However, the Constitution foresees the immunity of the members of the Portuguese Parliament (*Assembleia da República*) who cannot be held civil, criminal or disciplinary liable in relation to their votes or the opinions they express in the exercise of their functions (art. 157(1) of the 1976 Constitution).

3.1.3 The Portuguese Constitution in art. 62 (2), also foresees special legal rules on financial compensation arising from the "infringement" of the fundamental (economic) right to property in the cases of requisition and expropriation on the grounds of public utility (public interest), although both cases depend on lawful public acts foreseen (previously) by the law, and they depend on the payment of a "fair compensation." The special legal rules regarding the procedure of expropriation (and requisition) on the grounds of "public utility" and the consequent payment of such "fair compensation" are laid down in the Expropriations' Code (EC), approved by Law 168/99 of 18th September (as subsequently modified in 2002, 2003, 2007 and 2008), namely in arts. 23 to 32, 67–73 (and art. 84 concerning requisition), and arts. 38–57 and 58–66.

3.1.4 The Constitution also foresees the compensation in case of "public appropriation of the means of production," i.e., of nationalization of the (private) ownership of enterprises (art. 83 of 1976 Constitution), that occurred after the 1974 revolution and more recently in 2008. The possible means and terms of such

[4] The case law of the Supreme Court of Justice (*Supremo Tribunal de Justiça*, STJ) that applied art. 27 of the Constitution and art. 225 sec. 1, b), of the CPC – according to which liability depends on the existence of a gross error (*erro grosseiro*) – is rather strict in the interpretation of such requirement of the duty to compensate – see decisions of the STJ of 1.10.2004 (case 04B2543), of 22.1.2008 (case 07A2381) and also of 11.9.2008 (case 08B1747) – see http://www.dgsi.pt/jsts.nsf. Accessed 15 March 2015. According to such case law liability and the duty to compensate in the case of deprivation of liberty due to gross error in the judgment on the factual framework on which depends the deprivation of liberty can only be declared in exceptional cases when a really ostensive error was committed by the judge.

[5] On the relationship between such norms of the CrimPC and the 1976 Constitution see Catarino (2002), no. 11, 274 ff.

appropriation as well as the criteria to determine the respective financial "compensation" were laid down by the law that approved such nationalizations and presently in a general law approved in 2008 when the nationalization of a private bank took place, Law 62-A/2008 of 11 November.

3.1.5 Finally, special constitutional rules on liability for damages within the "*actio popularis*" in order to promote the prevention, cessation or judicial prosecution of offences against public health, consumer's rights, quality of life or the preservation of the environment and cultural heritage and to ensure the safeguard of property of the public domain of the State, the autonomous regions or of the municipalities (art. 52(3) are further developed in Law no 83/95 of 31st August which foresees both (subjective) civil liability and (objective) no fault liability (arts. 22 and 23)).

3.2 Some explicit legal basis for claiming damages for violations, including the violation of HR's, can also be found, as mentioned, either in Law 67/2007 (see *infra* 14.3), or in other (infra-constitutional) special legal rules (*infra* nos 3.2.1 and 3.2.2).

3.2.1 Regarding the liability of the Bank of Portugal, the Portuguese Central Bank which functions are determined both by national and international (EU) rules (Art. 102 of the 1976 Constitution and Organic Law 5/98 of 31 January), since it is a "legal person of public law" (*pessoa colectiva de direito público*) the regime laid down by the Law 67/2007 (rules on liability deriving from the exercise of the administrative function and on the compensation for the sacrifice imposed by reasons of public interest) fully applies (see *infra* 14.3). However, the General Regime of the Credit Institutions and Financial Societies (approved by Decree-Law no 298/92 of 31st November and subsequently amended) foresees a special rule (Art. 12(3), as modified lastly by Decree-Law no 31-A/2012) regarding the personal liability of the office holders of the Bank of Portugal thus implying the exclusive liability of the Bank of Portugal (external relations). Since this rule (exclusive liability) is previous to the Law 67/2007, the main question is whether such special rule is applicable after the entering into force of Law 67/2007. Some doctrine seems to defend the application of the mentioned special rule considering, in special, the existence of cases of exclusive liability in the Law 67/2007, and the special nature of the Bank of Portugal namely while acting as an element of the European System of Central Banks (see Art. 3 and Art. 27(2) regarding office holders of the Administration Council, of Organic Law 5/98) and while acting as an Independent Administrative Authority foreseen in Art. 267(3) of the 1976 Constitution.

3.2.2 A new sphere of PAL regarding the administrative function has developed in the field of market regulation. Some of the more recent infra-constitutional acts, that create independent regulatory entities within several areas, foresee a specific (special) general rule on the liability of such entity as well as of their public office holders, agents and workers, by acts or omissions committed in the exercise of its functions, and according to the constitutional and (general) legal statutory rules in force. That is the case of the Regulatory Authority for Health (art. 56 of Decree-Law 127/2009 of 27th May).

4 Considering both constitutional and infra-constitutional statutory law in force on Public Authority Liability, including for violation of HRs, the main purpose of the public authority liability, and the compensation for damages within, in cases of infringement of HRs, is the re-establishment of the situation prior to the violation (principle of "natural restoration" or "natural reconstitution" (of the hypothetical current situation)) and, if this is not possible or it does not provide for compensation of all damages (full compensation) or is too onerous, to pay financial compensation for all the damages caused by such infringement (art. 3, 1 and 2, of Law 67/2007).

Therefore, a full compensation of damages principle applies, except in some specific cases expressly foreseen that may lead to a non-full compensation of damages, e.g. liability arising from State political and legislative power, compensation for sacrifice in the name of the public interest or fault of the injured person (see *infra* 14.3).

In some of the special constitutional regimes of liability for lawful acts, namely the case of expropriation and nationalization, the purpose of the respective special compensatory schemes laid down in infra-constitutional law is to pay a "fair compensation" (expropriation) or a "compensation" (nationalization) that may however not correspond to the general rule of natural reconstitution (of the situation prior to the "violation" or lawful act) or to the full compensation rule.

5 In some circumstances, in a comprehensive overview, other remedies besides financial reparation (compensation), through the means of public authority liability, may be available, in the Portuguese legal order, in cases of infringement of HRs. Such is the case of ordinary declaratory actions and judgments in civil and administrative courts (that can be used to obtain a declarative judgment on the existence of a violation of a HR) and of an autonomous urgent procedure in administrative courts in order to obtain the protection of Fundamental Rights entering the constitution-based category of all (personal, political participation and workers') "rights, liberties and guarantees" by the means of obtaining a judicial decision (injunction (*Intimação para protecção de direitos, liberdades egarantias*) against public (or private) authorities).[6] *Provisional measures* (both in civil and administrative procedures) can also be used in order to obtain interim protection against violation of HRs, to prevent or avoid the infringement or the aggravation of the damage caused by such infringement.

The law does not establish, as a rule, a specific correlation or precedence between those remedies available in case of infringement of HRs. However, the use of the autonomous urgent procedure in administrative courts to obtain protection of "rights, liberties and freedoms" depends on the impossibility or insufficiency, considering the circumstances of the case, to obtain (previously) an interim measure.

6 From the constitutional perspective, the basic concept upon which a claim for financial compensation of damages caused by the violation of HRs is based is firstly the concept of violation of "rights, liberties and guarantees" (*Direitos, liberdades e garantias*). The "rights, liberties and guarantees" correspond to one of the (two) categories of fundamental rights foreseen in the 1976 Constitution and include three sub-categories (*supra*, footnote 2). This category of fundamental rights benefits from a special constitutional regime and therefore special rules of protection, such

[6] Arts. 109–111 of the (2002) Code of Procedure in the Administrative Courts (*Código de Processo nos Tribunais Administrativos*, CPTA) approved by Law no 15/2002, of 22.2.2002 and modified afterwards – the Code is in course of revision and the approved project is available at www.portugal.gov.pt. Accessed 15 March 2015.

as rules on the special legal force of norms foreseeing such category of rights (including direct applicability and binding force on public and private entities), on its suspension and on the right of resistance in case of offences to such category of fundamental rights and on its restriction (arts. 18, 19 and 21 of 1976 Constitution).

However, in the Law 67/2007 on PAL, including liability in case of infringement of HRs, the requirement of "unlawfulness" requires both unlawfulness of conduct and unlawfulness of the result (see further *infra* 14.3 at 1.2.2). Therefore, according to the statutory law a claim for financial compensation is supported in the doctrine of offence of (subjective) rights and "legally protected interests."

14.2 Scope of the Liability Regime

1 The types of rights that have been infringed (by an unlawful act or omission), and given place to a financial compensation on the grounds of liability of public authorities, are covered by explicit liability rules – either general rules on PAL (both constitutional and legal rules – art. 22 of 1976 Constitution and Law 67/2007) or special rules on specific cases of liability (foreseen in constitutional rules and developed in infra-constitutional rules) – the ones mentioned above (*supra* 14.1 at 3).

2 The general constitutional rule on State and other public authorities' liability as well as the 2007 Law that lays down its regime do not foresee a distinction in treatment of claims stemming from violations of international norms/duties ("State responsibility") and from violations of domestic, e.g. constitutional or legal norms. However, the Law 67/2007 expressly foresees liability arising out of the political-legislative function of the State in case of violation of international law and of European Union law, the legal regime, as well as the requirement to be met, being the same as in the case of violation of the relevant internal legislative acts. Consequently, compensation of historical injustices as well as compensation in the case of gross and systematic violations are available (in theory) under the same rules both the general constitutional rule and the 2007 Law on PAL. Nevertheless, the statutory rules and therefore the requirements on which depends the financial compensation and its extent vary according to the (administrative, judicial or political-legislative) function of the State in the origin of the damage (*infra* 14.3).

3 The purpose of public authorities liability is, as a rule, the one mentioned above although some special cases do exist (*supra* 14.1 at 4).

14.3 Specific Features of the Liability Regime

1 Concerning the foundation of claims for damages (grounds and premises of liability), the 2007 Law on PAL develops the constitutional principle of PAL and therefore lays down the types of liability and the conditions that, in each case, must be met in order to obtain compensation for damages, including in the case of violations of HRs.

The Law 67/2007 has defined its subjective scope of application to the State and other public entities (Public Sphere) therefore including: (I) the State and other public entities liability for damages arising out of the exercise of legislative, judicial and administrative functions (and compensation for sacrifice imposed on grounds of "public interest"); (II) their respective office holders, staff and agents regarding compensation arising out of acts or omissions adopted in the exercise of both the administrative and judicial functions and due to such exercise (functional action); (III) other workers of the State and other public entities as if they were office holders, staff or agents; (IV) only regarding the exercise of the administrative function (see definition *infra* 1.1), also private entities performing such function on behalf of public authorities for damages arising out of such function, either private entities created by the State itself, namely under a private form or private parties with which the administration enters into a contract or to which commits a public activity; (V) office holders, legal representatives and workers of the latter private entities (Arts. 1(1) and (2)–(5) of Law 67/2007). However, the 2007 Law provides neither for a definition of the 'State' nor of "public entity" and the former distinction of the previous 1967 law between "private" and "public" management (*acta iure imperii* vs *acta iure gestionis*) has been abandoned.

1.1 According to Law 67/2007 state liability can arise out of all three State functions, administrative, judicial and political/legislative, and private entities (while performing public functions) liability can arise out of administrative function only. Therefore the 2007 Law provides for three legal regimes for liability arising out of administrative, judicial and political/legislative functions.

The first one provides for different rules regarding liability of the administration for unlawful acts or omissions and fault (presumed in some cases) and for activities, things or administrative services "especially hazardous," i.e. involving a risk. The Administrative function is defined as the "actions or omissions adopted in the exercise of prerogatives of public power or ruled by principles or rules of administrative law" (Art. 1(2) of Law 67/2007). The 2007 Law applies to all the administrative activity (acts/omissions) namely under the form of regulations and plans, administrative acts, other legal acts, material conducts and operations and even informal actions.

The second provides for rules regarding liability for unlawful acts and omissions and fault arising out of the judicial function, except in the case of judicial error the regime of State liability arising out of the administrative function applies to liability arising out of the judicial function, e.g. delay to give a court decision; unjust non-criminal court decision, *faute du service*. The third provide rules on liability for unlawful acts and one case of legislative omission, fault being irrelevant.

Moreover, the 2007 Law provides for a fourth special (no fault) regime for damages caused to private parties by the "sacrifice" imposed by the State or other public entities for "public interest reasons," irrespectively of the State function involved (Art. 16 of Law 67/2007).

Concerning the (four) different legal regimes foreseen the 2007 Law provides for a certain number of (explicit or implicit) remissions to the general rules on non-contractual (tortuous) liability, e.g. duty to compensate, as well as specific rules that differ accordingly to the state or public entity activity and the existence of a unlawful or lawful action or omission, e.g. assessment of fault of public officers and agents.[7]

1.2 Concerning liability in respect of unlawful activities or fault, some basic principles must be firstly underlined.

PAL relies basically upon special public law (constitutional and infra-constitutional) rules. However, State liability also implies, to some extent, the application of basic principles and rules of tort law to State defendants in two aspects: the application of the rules of tort law (Civil Code) when a *gestão privada* (private management) of the State or public entity is at stake; the remissions of the Law 67/2007 to the rules and principles of tort law foreseen in the Civil Code both explicitly (prescription term and its suspension and interruption; fault in case of breach of vigilance duties and in case of a plurality of responsible (arts. 5 and 10(3) and (4) of Law 67/23007)) and implicitly (duty to indemnify, fault of the injured person (arts. 3 and 4 of Law 67/2007)).

1.2.1 In establishing the liability both unlawfulness of the conduct *and* fault of the responsible public officer or agent are in principle relevant: the unlawfulness is relevant as a requisite of liability in some of the PAL regimes (administrative, judicial and political functions). Unlawfulness of the conduct is especially relevant as a condition of the presumption of fault in the case of liability arising out of the administrative function (and partially of liability arising out of judicial function) – presumption of existence of *culpa leve* (mere fault, *faute légère*) in the case of an unlawful juridical act (art. 10(2)).

However, there are three cases in which unlawfulness of the conduct *only* (act/omission) is relevant: (i) within liability deriving from administrative function, the case of *faute du service* (damages caused by an "abnormal functioning of the (public) service" – which is considered to exist "whenever according to the circumstances and to medium patterns of result it would have been reasonably demanded from the service an action that could avoid the incurred damages" (Art. 7 (3) and (4) of Law 67/2007); (ii) also within liability deriving from administrative function, the case of pre-contractual liability for damages originated by a violation of a rule within the procedure of formation of public contracts ruled by EU Law on public contracts ('*marchés publics*') and mentioned specifically in art. 100 of the CPTA (Arts. 7(2) of Law 67/2007), the compensation for damages is to be paid according to the conditions laid down by EU law itself (namely under the terms foreseen in Directives 89/665/CEE (arts. 2(1), c)) and 92/13/CEE (art. 2(1), d)); (iii) the case of liability deriving from the political/legislative function of the State (Art. 15 of Law 67/2007).

1.2.2 Concerning unlawfulness the 2007 Law requires both unlawfulness of conduct and unlawfulness of the result.

Unlawfulness of conduct regarding the exercise of an administrative function relates to "actions and omissions in breach of constitutional, legal or executive norms or principles and the violation of technical rules or duty of care" (Art. 9(1) of Law 67/2007) – as well as, tough not expressly foreseen, in breach of international and European Law (unlawfulness of the conduct of the public officer or agent), as

[7] See further on the 2007 Law, Cadilha (2011) and VVAA (2011).

well as to the *faute du service;* unlawfulness of the *result* regarding the exercise of an administrative function relates to the offence of rights (subjective rights) or legally protected interests (Art. 9(2) of Law 67/2007).

Unlawfulness of conduct regarding the exercise of the State judicial function also relates (since the rules on liability arising out of the State administrative function apply to liability arising out of the judicial function except in the case of judicial error) expressly, to the "breach of the right of obtaining a judicial decision within a reasonable time" (art. 12 of law 67/2007).

Finally unlawfulness of conduct regarding the exercise of the State political and legislative function relates to "acts adopted in breach of the Constitution, international law, European Union law or of a legislative act with reinforced value" as well as to the "omission of the necessary legislative providences in order to make constitutional rules executable" (art. 15(1) and (3) of law 67/2007). The fact that such definition of unlawful omission does not expressly include omission of approval of legislative acts required by the duty to transpose EU secondary legislation into the national legal order does not prevent the State legislative power from being held liable for having breach EU Law by failure to act according to the EU principle of liability of the member States as Portuguese supreme courts have already decided regarding the omission of complete transposition of Directive 84/5/CEE.[8]

1.2.3 Concerning fault, the degree of fault, "culpa leve" or "culpa grave" (mere fault/*faute légère* or *faute lourde*) and "dolo" (malice), is mainly relevant to determine the exclusivity of State and other public entities liability or the joint liability of the State and other public entities and their office holders, staff and agents. In the latter the possibility of a recovery action exists but only within liability for damages caused by the administrative function and by the judicial function, including the duty of recovery, since liability for damages arising out of hazardous activities or services (risk) run by the State-Administration (risk), as well as liability for political/legislative activity and compensation due to sacrifices imposed by the pursuit if public interest, do not require fault.

The law foresees two cases of presumption of "culpa leve" (mere fault/*faute légère*), the adoption of an unlawful juridical act (as the administrative courts had previously admitted) and the non-fulfillment of duties of surveillance (*culpa in vigilando*) as foreseen in Art. 10(2) and (3), that imply an *exclusive* liability of the State (judicial function) and of the State or other public entities (administrative function). After compensating the injured party (external relations), the public entity is bound to recover what they have paid from their officers or agents (internal relations) that acted with *culpa grave* or *dolo* (*faute lourde* or malice) within the fulfillment of their functions (functional acts), the right of recovery being conceived as a juridical obligation except, for some doctrine, in the case of recovery against magistrates.

1.3 Concerning liability in respect of lawful activities, two cases are foreseen in the 2007 Law on PAL.

---

[8] See *infra* fn10.

1.3.1. Firstly (no fault) liability of the State and other public entities (or private entities to which the 2007 Law applies) within administrative activity for damages caused by "activities, things or services especially dangerous."

1.3.2 The Law 67/2007 provides for a general rule on compensation for the sacrifice (no fault liability) imposed to private parties by reasons of public interest and irrespective of the State function causing damage (Art. 16 of law 67/2007) that applies where no special rules exist (*supra* in 14.1 at 3.1.3 and 3.1.4), although, only the imposition of charges or special and abnormal damage imply a duty to compensate.

1.4 In conclusion the same principles and rules of public law (and whenever expressly foreseen, some tort law rules) apply to compensatory (and non-compensatory) remedies for violation of HRs.

1.5 Although the constitutional principle of state and other public entities liability imposes the duty to compensate whenever there is violation of "rights, liberties or guarantees" or damage caused to someone, the infra-constitutional Law developing the constitutional principle imposes harm (loss), to property or person, as a prerequisite of a claim for damages (requisite of the obligation to compensate). "Pure violation" (in general and in the case of violation of HRs) is therefore not sufficient to claim compensation although in the case of violation of "rights, liberties and guarantees" the "damage" resides in the violation of such category of fundamental rights (as well as fundamental rights that have an analogue nature according to art. 17 of the 1976 Constitution).

1.6 Regarding the burden of proof concerning damage/harm the general rule on the burden of proof (Art. 487(1) of the Civil Code), according to which is the injured party that must prove the elements of his right to receive compensation and so each of the elements of the obligation to compensate, applies to liability of public authorities except in the two cases of *juris tantum* presumption of fault within liability arising out of the administrative function where the Law 67/2007 foresees a legal inversion of the burden of proof (arts. 10(2) and (3)), unlawful juridical acts and omission of duties of vigilance.

1.7 Regarding the doctrine of causation, three main theories are to be considered, the doctrine of the adequate causation, the doctrine of the sphere of protection of the norm and the doctrine of the connection of the risk. The doctrine of adequate causation is the dominant doctrine within the law of civil liability in the Portuguese legal order to access the relationship between the unlawful or lawful action or omission and the damage incurred (art. 563 of the Civil Code). This doctrine must be adapted in the case of the non-fault liability (objective liability) of the State and other public entities in order not to consider the intention of the agent (since not relevant).

2 Regarding the nature of harm (damage/injury) although the Constitution foresees a liability principle whenever there is a violation of "rights, freedoms and guarantees" or damage to someone, the 2007 Law on PAL foresees special rules concerning the nature of the damage that may lead to financial compensation. Accordingly to its general rule the liable entity must restore the situation prior to the occurrence of the event causing damage. If this is not possible, as well as if the restoration is not possible, does not compensate fully the damage or is "excessively onerous" the compensation is fixed in money (art. 3, 1 and 2, of Law 67/2007). The

2007 Law expressly states, regarding the obligation to compensate damages, that public authority liability includes compensation for both patrimonial and non-patrimonial damages (moral harm), as well as incurred damages and future damages, under the "general terms of law," i.e., under the general principles applying to liability arising out of private acts or omissions. The principle of full compensation allows therefore compensation for real loss, lost profits (*lucrum cessans*), loss of chance and costs and expenses.

3 Regarding the scope of damages (compensation) special rules laid down in the 2007 law on PAL are applicable.

3.1 The scope of damages (compensation) includes, as a general principle, compensation for *all* damages caused by an act or omission of the state or other public authority arising out of the different functions of the state (administrative, judicial or political-legislative) or when the administrative function is at stake, also private entities performing public functions, except in the two cases where only special and abnormal damages or abnormal damages can be compensated through a liability action and the right to compensation is, besides other requirements, dependent on the scope of the damage (see *infra* 3.2 and 3.3).

3.2 The 2007 Law on PAL foresees two categories of damages: special damages and abnormal damages, respectively those which "fall upon a person or a group without affecting the generality of the people" and those which "go beyond the costs of living in society and deserve by its gravity the protection of the law" (Art. 2 of Law 67/2007). These definitions are only relevant regarding both liability arising out of the political-legislative function where only abnormal damages can be compensated (arts. 15 and 16 of Law 67/2007) and liability arising out of the sacrifice (lawful acts) for reasons of public interest where only special and abnormal damages can be compensated.

3.3 Exclusively regarding liability arising out of the exercise of the political-legislative function of the State or the autonomous regions (Azores and Madeira), the compensation may not correspond to a full compensation of the (abnormal) damages suffered (art. 15, 4 and 6, of Law 67/2007).

On one hand, there are legal criteria to assess the "existence" itself and the "extension" of such liability (and therefore of the obligation to compensate), which is based on the "concrete circumstances of each case and, namely, the degree of clarity and precision of the breached rule, the type of unconstitutionality and the fact that diligences that could avoid the illicit situation were adopted or omitted" (Art. 15(4) of Law 67/2007). The first of the mentioned (non-exclusive) criteria to assess such (non-fault) liability clearly relates to some of the criteria enounced by the EUCJ to access the "manifest breach" of EU Law within the principle of State liability for breaching EU law.[9] On the other hand, such liability can be limited in the case there are a large number of injured persons. The Law foresees that, "When the injured are in such a number that, by reasons of public interest of exceptional relevance, the limitation of the scope of the duty to compensate may be justified, such duty can be equitably fixed in an amount lower than the amount that would

[9] See among other Case C-224/01, *Köbler* [2003] ECR I-10239 55 ff.

correspond to the integral reparation of the caused damages," (Art. 15(6) of Law 67/2007) and a court decide on the financial compensation on the basis of equity.

3.4 Regarding taxation of damages and interests, the Code on the taxation of the revenue of non-juridical persons (CIRS) foresees that indemnities (compensation for damages) are (if not included in other categories) a sub-category of the "patrimonial increases" category of revenue (art. 1, 1, Category G) and art. 9, 1, b) of the CIRS). Its respective amount is a part of the total revenue subject to taxation on the basis of a percentage that may vary between 14.5 % (total revenue up to 7,000€) and 48 % (total revenue over 80,000€) – to which a supplementary "solidarity tax" of 2.5–5 % (respectively revenue over 80,000 and 250,000€) may be added (arts. 68 and 68-A of the CIRS).

3.5 The legal rules on PAL do not foresee in principle, a limitation/cap on damages so whenever financial compensation to the person suffering damage is due its limits relates only to the limits of the principle of full indemnity of damages.

Besides the cases mentioned above in 3.2 and 3.3, financial compensation can be limited by the court decision in the specific case of fault of the injured person (see *infra* 5.1).

3.6 There is no express rule on the accumulation of claims (damages) in cases of multiple violation. Therefore, such accumulation is permitted under the terms of general law.

3.7 Pecuniary claims survive the death of a direct victim if he/she dies during the proceedings to the extent that the right to obtain financial compensation is transmitted to legal heirs of the deceased victim. The claim for financial compensation can be presented directly by the legal heirs of the victim also in the case when the death occurs previously to the beginning of the (judicial) proceedings. The CrimPC foresees one specific rule (art. 226) on the legitimacy to present a claim for damages in case of death of the victim that was detained or deprived of its freedom in breach of the law or in an unjustified manner although the financial compensation to be paid to those who claim it cannot, in its whole, exceed the financial compensation that would be paid to the detained or imprisoned deceased victim.[10]

4 Punitive or exemplary damages are not expressly foreseen in the case of state and other public authorities' liability, neither at constitutional nor at infra-constitutional level.

5 Defenses foreseen in the 2007 Law on State and other public entities liability regarding unlawful conduct are foreseen both as a general principle applicable to all State functions and as specific rules within the regime of State liability deriving from the exercise of the judicial function and from the exercise of political/legislative function.

5.1 According to the general rule on the relevance of the fault of the injured person when the conduct of the person suffering damage has contributed to the

[10] That is the case of a liability action introduced by a victim's heirs (deceased in a car accident where no fault of the driver existed) against the State (as legislator) in case of incomplete transposition of a EU motor insurance directive regarding no-fault liability – decision of the STJ of 27.11.2007 (case 07A3945), in http://www.dgsi.pt/jstj.nsf. Accessed 15 March 2015.

production of the damage or to its aggravation, namely by not using the competent action in court to eliminate the act causing damages, it is up to the competent court to decide whether compensation must be paid in full, reduced or even excluded on the bases of two criteria, the gravity of the fault (when relevant) of both parties and their respective consequences (Art. 4 of Law 67/2007). The failure to exhaust all the adequate procedural means to eliminate the unlawful act causing damage (use of a procedural means to obtain the annulment or declaration of nullity of a juridical act) is not a requisite or pre-condition of the liability action. The same judgment applies to the omission to use any other possible procedural means related to the action or omission causing damages, e.g. an action to condemn the Administration to adopt a legal act or a conduct. Moreover within liability arising out of the administrative function and regarding activities involving risk the court can also reduce or even exclude the financial compensation whenever there is fault of the injured person or a case of *force majeure* (art. 11, 2 of Law 67/2007).

5.2 Within liability arising from the exercise of the judicial activity of the State related to a judicial error a specific rule on defenses is foreseen (art. 13(2) of Law 67/2007) since the request for indemnification (within a liability action against the State – exclusive liability in external relations) "must be based on the previous revocation of the [judicial] decision causing damages by the competent jurisdiction." This rule raises three main questions: (I) whether such legal requirement is to be considered a specific procedural requirement to bring a liability action in Court or a requirement of the obligation to compensate, the first seeming the adequate interpretation; (II) if such requirement violates the Constitution, namely the principle of State liability and the right to accede to court to exercise the right to seek for compensation for damages (principle of effective legal protection), since the revocation of the judicial causing damages implies a right of judicial recourse which may not exist in all cases, namely due to reasons related to the value fixed for the case; (III) if such requirement violates EU Law and the principle of liability of member states for breach of EU Law since it lays down a further requirement besides those laid down by the relevant CJEU case law. Concerning the last two questions such a requirement is considered by the doctrine to be contrary to the Constitution since it is disproportionate and can prevent to exercise the right to seek for compensation from the State and other public bodies as well as contrary to EU Law on member States liability since it violates, especially the principle of effectiveness (of judicial remedies) leading to turning the right to compensation in case of breach of EU Law excessively difficult or even impossible.

5.3 Within liability arising from the exercise of the political/legislative activity specific rules on defenses are also foreseen (Art. 15(4), (5) and (6) of Law 67/2007). Firstly liability arising out of the omission of exercise of legislative power to make a constitutional rule executable depends on the previous judgment of the unconstitutionality of such omission by the Constitutional Court through the specific constitutional procedure aimed at such judgment (Art. 283 of the 1976 Constitution). Such condition seems to violate the constitutional principle of liability, since a private party can never meet such requirement and since the procedural legitimacy to bring an action before the Constitutional Court to declare the unconstitutionality of the relevant legislative omission is limited to a few constitutional organs foreseen in Art. 283(1), of the Constitution, as well as the fundamental right of access to a court to exercise a fundamental right (to compensation), thus being disproportionate regarding the scope of the liability principle and of the fundamental right to obtain compensation from the State and other public entities. Secondly, the assessment of the existence and of the extension of the liability accordingly to the "concrete circumstances of each case" (see *supra* 3.3).

6 The answer to the questions, "Who to sue?" and "Who may sue?" arises out of the Constitutional text as well as of the 2007 statutory law on PAL.

6.1 As regards the question who incurs liability in damages for infringement of HRs, both constitutional and infra-constitutional levels must be considered.

6.1.1 Under constitutional law, and according to the state function that is at the origin of the damage as well as on the degree of fault, either the State itself or other public entities (autonomous regions, local government, public institutes and public bodies, other) themselves, the State or other public entity and their respective officeholders, staff and agents or these only can be sued.

6.1.1.1 Three special cases of the State itself liability (or duty to compensate) are foreseen in the Constitution within judicial or the executive/administrative functions: unconstitutional or illegal deprivation of freedom; unjust conviction in criminal proceedings; requisitions and expropriations in the public interest (lawful act) and nationalizations – see *supra* 14.1 nos 3.1.1, 3.1.3 and 3.1.4).

6.1.1.2 The Constitution lays down a principle of joint responsibility of the State and other public entities with their respective officeholders, staff and agents although some exceptions are foreseen in the Constitution, immunities of some officeholders (members of Parliament (art. 157)) and the fact that in principle judges may not be held personally liable for their decisions (art. 216(2), see also *infra at* 6.1.2).

6.1.1.3 The Constitution also provides for a general principle on the organization of the political Power according to which, "Political officeholders are politically, civilly and criminally liable for their actions and omissions in the exercise of their functions," (Art. 117(1)) further developed in the Law 34/87 of 16 July 1987 (*supra* 14.1 at 3.1.2.)) and a general rule on civil (and criminal) liability of the staff and agents of the State and of other public entities for their actions and omissions in the exercise of their functions and for any such exercise that leads to a breach of those citizens' rights or interests that are protected by law (Art. 271(1) – see *supra* 14.1 at 1).

6.1.2 At infra-constitutional level, the 2007 Law on PAL defines the Public Sphere as mentioned above (*supra* at 1). Two notes must be added: first, the public sphere concerning liability arising out of the exercise of political-legislative functions includes both the State and the autonomous regions of Azores and Madeira and these may be held liable since they also have political and legislative competence foreseen in the Constitution[11]; second, the case law on court jurisdiction for liability actions (administrate courts vs. common courts), especially when the administrative action of private entities performing administrative function is involved, shows the

[11] See art(s) 6(2) and 225 ff of the 1976 Constitution. The Portuguese doctrine is not however unanimous concerning (autonomous) liability arising out of the exercise of the legislative power by the autonomous regions.

difficulties inherent to the extension of the subjective scope of application of Law 67/2007 to private entities performing an administrative function (for example private concessionaries of public services).[12]

6.1.3 In conclusion, regarding the question "Who can be sued?" institutional and/or individual liability may occur and therefore, either the state or public authorities (or private entities performing administrative function) alone, or these and their respective officers and agents, or the latter themselves can be sued in order to obtain financial compensation, according to the rules laid down by (the Constitution and) Law 67/2007 which state as follows depending: (I) on the nature of the state function which is in the origin of the damage; (II) the unlawful (or lawful) nature of the public act or omission; (III) and the degree of fault involved (namely *faute légère, faute du service* or *faute lourde*). Except in the case of judicial error the rules on who to sue regarding liability arising out of the administrative function also apply to liability arising out of the judicial function (see 1.1).

6.2 Also regarding "Who may sue?" both constitutional and infra-constitutional rules are relevant. At constitutional level, the state and other public entities, as well as their respective officeholders, staff and agents or private entities performing public functions can be sued by those who suffered a violation of their "rights, liberties or guarantees" or who suffered damage, caused by acts or omissions committed in the exercise of their functions and because of such exercise (therefore including compensation for damages caused by a lawful act). As the 2007 Law on PAL foresees a right to obtain compensation for "damages arising out of the exercise of the administrative, judicial and political-legislative function" as well as in the case of a sacrifice on grounds of public interests, an action for damages can be introduced in the competent court by those who suffered such damage.

7 Regarding courts and procedures, it must be underlined that a dual system exists in the Portuguese legal order and therefore, two categories of courts may be competent to judge upon public authorities' liability, including in case of liability due to the violation of human rights – administrative courts and general (civil) courts.

7.1 After the reform of the administrative procedural law (2002–2003) and the approval of a new Code of Procedure in the Administrative Courts (CPTA)[13] and a new Statute for Administrative and Tax Courts (*Estatuto dos Tribunais Administrativos e Fiscais*, ETAF) the rule regarding courts and procedures is the unity of jurisdiction and competence of courts for all matters and actions on State liability and all State liability, on other public entities liability, as well as liability of their public office holders, staff and agents and other public servants, including recovery actions (Art. 4(1), g) and h) of ETAF).

Therefore, public authorities (State and public entities) liability claims must, in principle, be brought before administrative courts, foreseen in the Constitution as a

[12] See e.g. decisions of the Court of Conflicts of 5.6.2008 (case 21/06) of 4.11.2009 (case 6/09 and case 13/09) of 20.1.2010 (case 25/09) or of 28.9.2010 (case 10/10); decisions of the STJ of 14.1.2010 (case 1450/06.4 TBALM-A.S1) and of 10.4.2008 (case 08B845); or decision of the Central Administrative Court-North of 6.5.2010 (case 1566/08) – http://www.dgsi.pt. Accessed 15 March 2015.

[13] *Supra*, fn 6.

special category of Courts (Arts. 209(1), b), and 212). This principle of competence of the administrative courts applies to the State (and other public and private entities liability) both irrespective of the function which may cause damages and the right for compensation (administrative, judicial or legislative function),[14] and irrespective of public or private nature of the act or omission[15] of the public authorities and the substantive applicable law (public law on public authorities liability or private law). However one exception is foreseen: the exclusive competence of the (general) courts of law (first, second and last instance) to rule on State liability actions for damages (and recovery actions) arising out of a judicial error of non administrative courts (Art. 4(3) of ETAF).

The type of action to bring a state liability claim before the competent administrative court is, in principle, the (autonomous) "common administrative action" (Art. 37 and the following, CPTA, 37(2), f) and 38(1)), except in the case of joint procedural requests where the "special administrative action" must be used (Art. 46 and the following, CPTA). The common administrative action is also the adequate procedural means to obtain the condemnation in the payment of indemnities due to the imposition of a sacrifice by reasons of public interest (Art. 37(2), g), CPTA and Art. 16 of Law 67/2007; Art. 1(1), ETAF and Art. 212(3), of the Constitution), except when there is exclusive competence of the common courts of law to rule (ruling on indemnities to compensate expropriations in the public interest (lawful act)).

7.2 There is no time limit to bring a common administrative action before administrative courts (Art. 41(1), CPTA) although the term (time limit) for the exercise of the right for compensation and to issue a liability action foreseen in the substantive (tort) Law (Art. 498 of the Civil Code) applies; however, the term to bring a special administrative action against an act that can be annulled and caused damages is 3 months from its notification (and 1 year for the public prosecutor – Art. 58, CPTA).

7.3 Group claims are not expressly foreseen in the 2007 law on PAL but they may exist within the *actio popularis* through the associations of defense of the relevant violated interests (*supra* 14.1 at 3.1.5) and to the extent that procedural rules allow them.

14.4 The Interplay Between Principles of National and International Human Rights Law Concerning Financial Compensation

1 In respect to violations of Human Rights the definition of unlawful action or omission relates not only to such rights protected by the Constitution, but also by transnational catalogues of Human Rights, by which the Portuguese State is bound according to its international obligations including deriving from its participation in

[14] STJ of 10.7.2008 (case 07B740) – see http://www.dgsi.pt. Accessed 15 March 2015.

[15] *Tribunal de Conflitos* (Court of Conflicts), 18/12/2003 (conflict no 15/03).

the European integration process. Besides universal international catalogues of Fundamental Rights that Portugal must respect (for example Universal Declaration on Human Rights or the UN 1966 Covenants) the most relevant regional catalogues which breach can imply State liability for damages are the European Convention on Human Rights (ECHR) and the Charter of Fundamental Rights of the European Union.

The only relevant transnational system of protection of HR's that may (also) award financial compensation directly to victims in case of violation of HR's by which Portugal is bound by an international treaty is the system of the European Convention on Human Rights (ECHR) and the European Court of Human Rights (ECtHR).[16]

Although the access to such jurisdictional transnational system is subsidiary and implies the exhaustion of the national remedies, when a case has been ruled by an ECtHR decision and just satisfaction is awarded to the victim of the violation, compensation under national is not automatically excluded. In fact, in the Portuguese Legal Order there is no rule on the correlation between monetary remedies (financial compensation) available to victims of violations of HRs under the ECHR and under national law. Therefore, a claimant who has already been awarded compensation by the ECtHR ("just satisfaction" on the grounds of art. 41 of the ECHR) is in principle entitled to seek further compensation in the domestic system according to the rules above mentioned (*supra* 14.3) to the extent that full compensation of damages was not awarded by the Strasbourg Court. However, the following limitations apply: (I) the possibility to obtain further compensation will depend mainly on the rules on prescription and on the delay to bring an action for damages against the State or the public authority involves in the violation (*supra* 14.3 at 7.2); (II) national competent courts cannot award (further) financial compensation in breach of the national rules (full compensation rules) and in breach of the general (civil law) rule according to which nobody can enrich without a just cause. Therefore the financial compensation already awarded by the ECtHR must be taken into consideration by national courts when deciding on a claim for compensation in case of violation of HR's – either by reducing the compensation claimed by the victim or even excluding it if full compensation has already been awarded by the Strasbourg Court.

It must also be underlined that the decision of the ECtHR awarding financial compensation – as consequence of the declaration of a breach of the ECHR – will be particularly relevant for the decision of national courts in the case where the decision of the ECtHR is contrary to a previous (*res judicata*) decision of national courts – in order to assess the unlawful action of the State (or public entity) that may lead to further financial compensation after the national *res judicata* court decision is reviewed on that ground. So, the right to obtain further (besides 'just satisfaction'

[16] Although Portugal is bound by other international systems of (direct or indirect, administrative and jurisdictional) protection of HR's – that is the case of the systems of the UN Covenants of HR's and of the jurisdiction of the International Criminal Court laid down by the Rome Statute. However, in practice, only the system of the ECHR is relevant regarding the interplay with national law and domestic jurisdiction.

awarded by the Strasbourg Court) compensation at the national level is particularly relevant in the case where the "victim" of violation was condemned in national criminal proceedings, e.g. crimes related to the freedom of press, and the ECtHR finds subsequently that the State has breached the ECHR. After the 2007 reform of the Civil and Criminal Procedural Law both CrimPC and Civil Procedural Code provide for a legal basis for an exceptional revision recourse against definitive internal court decisions whenever there is, among other, an international or regional court contrary decision on the violation of human rights such as a decision of the ECtHR or of the CJEU (respectively Art. 449, g) of the CrimPC and art. 771, f) of the Civil Procedural Code), allowing under some conditions, the extraordinary revision of an internal court decision with *res iudicata.* This revision procedure may not be enough to compensate the damage suffered by the injured party. Therefore, further compensation can be further awarded at the national level in such cases. Recent cases judged by the ECtHR against Portugal for violation of art. 10 of the ECHR (freedom of expression) led to the revision of national criminal court decisions.[17] In those cases the ECtHR condemned Portugal to pay for material damages as well as for expenses, consequently it cannot be excluded that a liability action can be brought action against the state to seek for compensation of other relevant damages.

2 The policy considerations that have exerted the greatest influence on the development of the national legal system in the discussed area are national policy considerations regarding the financial cost of state liability and both EU secondary law on liability within public procurement law and the case law of the CJEU on state liability for infringement of EU law. The first led, after a political veto of the President of the Republic, to a modification of the original project of the 2007 Law in order to restrain the liability of the State itself arising out of the legislative function in the case of legislative omissions (see supra 14.3 at 5.3). The second lead to both an explicit and implicit consideration of such case law in the text and features of the Law 67/2007, explicit regarding liability arising out of the administrative function (art. 7, 2) and implicitly regarding liability arising out of the legislative function (art. 15, 4) and *supra* 14.3 at 3.3).

Three main aspects must be underlined in what concerns the influence exerted by other systems, national or transnational: on one hand, the special (non-constitutional) rules on State and other public entities liability sometimes refer expressly to the general system of tort law and the general rules on tortious liability, that is, non-contractual liability, which are foreseen in the Civil Code; on the other hand in the non-constitutional rules in force on State and public entities liability it is possible to identify expressly or implicitly, a few cases of (explicit and implicit) influence of

---

[17] ECtHR, Case 20620/04, *Azevedo c. Portugal* of 27.3.2008, and STJ Case 104/02.5TACTB-A.S1 of 23.4.2009; ECtHR, Case 17107/05, *Campos Dâmaso c. Portugal*, 24/4/2008, and STJ Case 55/01.OTBEPS-A.S1 of 27.5.2009 (in http://echr.coe.int and in http://dsgi.pt/jsts.nsf. Accessed 15 March 2015). Although there are also examples of decision of the Supreme Court (STJ) that did not allow the exceptional revision of a national (criminal) court decision on the grounds of contradiction with a previous ECourtHR decision against Portugal.

EU Law and of the case law of the CJEU on state liability; moreover, the influence of ECHR case law is explicitly considered in procedural law in the framework of an extraordinary appeal for revision of a definitive court decision *caso julgado* (see *supra* at 1).

14.5 Final Remarks

Considering that a new Law on State Liability (approved in 2007 and amended in 2008) entered into force in 2008, it is not foreseen that further legislative reforms will be approved in a near future. Nevertheless, two main aspects of the system deserve further consideration and eventually require modification.

Firstly, the fact that the system laid down in the Law 67/2007 does not considers fully in an explicit manner the obligations deriving from EU law on state liability: not only because the case of legislative omissions to comply with EU law is not foreseen but also because some of the explicit features of the system are contrary to EU Law, mainly the requisite of previous revocation of the court decision causing damages (in the case of judicial error) and the features of the damages that may lead to compensation in case of liability arising out of the political-legislative function, since only abnormal damages may be compensated.

Secondly, the relationship between the national and transnational system of compensation in the case of violation of HR's. Since the relevant regional transnational catalogues which breach can imply State liability for damages are the ECHR the Charter of Fundamental Rights of the European Union, the protection in the case of violation of such rights in general, and consequent compensation for liability, can take place at a transnational level to which private parties can accede (until the adhesion of the EU to the ECHR, either the EUCJ regarding violations committed by the EU itself or the ECtHR regarding violations committed by a member State of the Council of Europe). On one hand, the protection at the level of the European Union is still not adequate enough since private injured parties can complain to the Commission but still cannot bring a direct action against a member State within the EUCJ on the grounds of breaching EU law. On the other hand, recent ECtHR and EUCJ cases have demonstrated that the protection of Human Rights at a national level may not be enough and also that the presumption of compliance with the obligations derived from the ECHR or the Charter can be rebutted.[18]

[18] ECtHR, Case 30696/06 of 21.1.2011 and Case 27765/09 of 23.2.2012 (in http://echr.coe.int); CJEU, Case C-411/10, *N.S. v Secretary of State for the Home Department* [2011] (available in http://curia.europa.eu Accessed 15 March 2015).

References

Cadilha, Carlos Alberto Fernandes. 2011. *Regime da Responsabilidade Civil Extracontratual do Estado e demais Entidades Públicas Anotado*. Coimbra: Coimbra Editora.

Catarino, Luís. 2002. Responsabilidade por facto jurisdicional – Contributo para uma reforma do sistema geral de responsabilidade civil extracontratual do Estado. In *Responsabilidade Civil Extra-contratual do Estado, Trabalhos preparatórios da reforma*, ed. VVAA, 267–287. Coimbra: Coimbra Editora.

Rangel de Mesquita, M.J. 2009. *O regime da responsabilidade civil extracontratual do Estado e demais entidades públicas e o Direito da União Europeia*. Coimbra: Almedina.

VVAA. 2011. XIII Seminário de Justiça Administrativa. *Cadernos de Justiça Administrativa* 89: 1.

Chapter 15
Monetary Compensation for Violations of Human Rights and Fundamental Freedoms in Slovenia

Samo Bardutzky

15.1 Introduction

In comparing law of monetary compensation for human rights violations, Slovenia presents an interesting comparative system for three main reasons. First, from the general human rights aspect, it can serve as a case study of a society in transition. Little more than two decades ago, Slovenia radically changed its political system (from single party to democratic government) and economic system (from "self-managed" to market based). It also left the multi-ethnic Yugoslav federation and became an independent state. These changes are reflected in the new (1991) constitution, a document with an accentuated legal character and strong focus on the protection of human rights and fundamental freedoms. At the same time, it took serious supranational commitments that are very relevant to this report (first and foremost, it signed the European Convention on Human Rights). All of these recent large-scale developments are the reason that legislative solutions are new and prone not only to frequent change but also contestation in front of courts.

The author expresses his gratitude to Martina Greif, Zoran Skubic, Saša Zagorc, Peter Pavlin, Maria Gomes and Ewa Bagińska. All potential mistakes, errors and blunders are nevertheless attributable solely to the author. The unofficial translations of the Obligations Code and of the Civil Procedure Act into English prepared by the Slovenian Ministry of Justice were of great help in looking for adequate terminology; I, however, did not follow it in all instances.

S. Bardutzky (✉)
University of Kent Law School, Canterbury, Kent, UK
e-mail: bardutzky@gmail.com

E. Bagińska (ed.), *Damages for Violations of Human Rights*,
Ius Comparatum - Global Studies in Comparative Law 9,
DOI 10.1007/978-3-319-18950-5_15

Secondly, Slovenia, somewhat paradoxically, has a decent human rights record, speaking *generally.*[1] However, it has already, since the beginning of its existence as an independent state, experienced two systemic, large scale human rights violations that resulted in condemnations in the European Court of Human Rights. In both cases, the Strasbourg judgments led to the establishment of comprehensive compensatory schemes. In addition to that, Slovenia has taken on the responsibility to provide redress for persons who were victims of states and regimes that existed, functioned and trampled on human rights during the twentieth century. The reflection of this paradox is that after two decades, Slovenia has experienced interesting and noteworthy legal developments when it comes to creating special compensatory schemes. However, it has not seen a development of a consolidated body of law dealing with day-to-day human rights violations.

Thirdly, the body of law that deals with the pecuniary aspect of human rights violations, as we will portray below, is strongly linked to the general rules of private law of non-contractual liability. This is principally a laudable approach as it positions the state, when it has to answer for damage incurred, on the same plane with every individual or legal person. As we will explain below, it has already also proven itself to be inadequate.

In Part 1, we will lay out the constitutional provisions central to our discussion and link it to other relevant norms. This is predominantly in order to position the law of monetary compensation for human rights violations in the space between private and public law. In Part 2, to help us comprehend the scope of the liability regime(s), we pay attention to the special compensatory schemes.

The purpose of Part 3 is in presenting the main features of the liability regime. The account in Part 3 focuses on the general rules of private law of non-contractual liability in the case law of Slovenian courts in discussing the basis of liability, burden of proof and causation. We mention the solidarity-inspired inclination of the system to recognize claims for monetary redress even where there is no breach of law. We further discuss the scope of compensation, describing the general approach to compensating immaterial damages which we found to be more pertinent to our report. We briefly present the relevant rules of the personal income tax legislation. In discussing the possible counterarguments (or "defences") that could be presented, we mention the institute of shared liability and the limitations on public liability regarding legislative acts and judicial conduct. We try to illuminate some of the interesting features of the issue of, "Who may sue and who may be sued?" The

[1] The annual report of the global NGO Amnesty International for 2012, in its country chapter on Slovenia (p 301), only mentions two issues: the first one are the erased persons (see below). The other issue is discrimination against Roma, in particular with regard to the Roma's right to access water and housing. To my knowledge, the discrimination against Roma has so far not yet been discussed in the context of monetary compensation. The US state department in its 2012 country report for Slovenia highlighted the same two issues, adding that there are problems regarding "prison overcrowding; government corruption; domestic violence against women and children; trafficking in men, women, and girls; and discrimination against lesbian, gay, bisexual, and transgender (LGBT) persons." Far from underestimating these issues that are worthy of continuous attention in their own right; the point that is being made here is that human rights violations in Slovenia seem to strike identifiable groups in the society or can be linked to a structural problem.

Section concludes with a discussion of some of the institutional characteristics of the system and a note on the time limits.

In writing this report, I relied on the analysis of relevant case law and legislation undertaken in order to submit a country report to the *Public Liability in Europe/ Staatshaftung in Europa* project of the University of Osnabrück. The analysis was the work of Saša Zagorc and me, with the assistance of Martina Greif. The Osnabrück report focused on the topic of public liability, thus the research undertaken was of direct relevance to the report before us. This is because human rights violations can be understood as a species of illegal action of public authority and thus law of liability for human rights violations can be seen as a sub-area of public liability law. The practical consequence is that the case-law that we have presented below will be taken in account by courts adjudicating similar claims where the alleged illegality of the act in question can be link to one of the human rights or fundamental freedoms.

At the same time, the law of compensation for human rights violations seems, in part, to live a life of its own. We have outlined below a number of special, *"ad hoc"* compensation schemes.[2] "Special" compensation laws diverge from "general" public liability law in a number of features. As the most recent examples shows, e.g., persons erased from the registry of permanent residents, such divergence is in fact necessary if compensation is to be awarded at all, in compliance with international human rights law.

15.2 Liability Regime: In General

The highest legal act in the Slovenian legal order, the 1991 Constitution of the Republic of Slovenia (hereinafter: URS) contains an extensive catalogue of human rights norms in its Chapter II, "Human Rights and Fundamental Freedoms".[3] The

[2] There have been (or were) other special compensatory schemes in force in Slovenia that, regarding their institutional and procedural features, resemble the ones presented below. Among them are for example the compensatory scheme for persons who fell ill as a result of working with asbestos (Act Concerning Remedying the Consequences of Work with Asbestos [Zakon o odpravljanju posledic dela z azbestom], Official Gazzette no. 15/2007 and 51/2009) and the monetary compensation for persons whose assets were nationalized by the communist regime after World War II (Denationalization Act [Zakon o denacionalizaciji], the original version of the statutory text published in the Official Gazzette no. 27I/1991). The Denationalization Act is to be distinguished from the Redress of Injustices Act scheme described below. The claims admissible under the asbestos scheme stem from labour relations and illnesses resulting from certain working conditions. Although it was the state that took over the responsibility for the damages and acknowledging that the damages were often very severe, we considered the scheme to be quite distant from the subject matter of human rights violations. On the other hand, the denationalization process was a very complex symptom of the transition from the socialist system to a society based on rule of law and respect for private property. The monetary compensation in the process of denationalization was perceived as a secondary option in cases where it was not possible to return the assets in nature. A thorough discussion of this complex phenomenon would reach beyond the scope of this report and probably contribute considerably little given that the process is coming to an end anyway.

[3] Constitution of the Republic of Slovenia [Ustava Republike Slovenije], Official Gazzette no. 33I/1991; subsequent amendments published in the Official Gazzette nos. 42/1997, 66/2000, 24/2003, 69/2004, 69/2004, 69/2004, 68/2006, 47/2013 and 47/2013. For an overview of the

Slovenian Bill of Rights contains a cross-cutting provision of Art. 15, which sets limits *(Schranken-schranken)* to the limitations and statutory regulation of human rights (Paragraph III) and envisages an inception of human rights protected by international instruments into the human rights regime of the Slovenian constitution (Paragraph V). What is more central to this discussion is that it guarantees judicial protection and the right to obtain redress for the violation of human rights and fundamental freedoms (Paragraph IV).

Judicial protection of human rights and fundamental freedoms stands in the centre of the human rights protection system. The correlation between different possibilities of redress available through the judicial avenues depends on the nature of the individual human rights violation. The most common way is through civil litigation courts which have jurisdiction over non-contractual damages litigation pursuant to Art. 52 of the Civil Procedure Act (hereinafter: ZPP).[4] On the other hand, the judicial review of administrative action, with the primary function of ruling on the legality of the contested act and if necessary, annulling it, lies with the specialized administrative courts that adjudicate administrative disputes (*upravni spor,* Art. 157/I URS). Aggrieved parties in an administrative dispute have the possibility to claim damages in addition to contesting the act (Arts. 7/II and 67/I of the Administrative Dispute Act, hereinafter: ZUS-1).[5] However, the administrative court may refer the plaintiff to start a procedure for the compensation of damages before a civil litigation court if it assesses that the fact-finding regarding the damages would excessively delay the proceedings.

The constitutional complaint *(ustavna pritožba)* to the Constitutional Court, alleging that an individual act of public authority violates of human rights or fundamental freedoms is only available under quite rigorous admissibility criteria after all other possible remedies had been exhausted (Art. 160/I, III URS; and Arts. 51, 55.a and 55.b of the Constitutional Court Act).[6] In effect, this means that a case might find its way to the Constitutional Court, but only after it had been through the available instances, be that in an administrative dispute, civil litigation or both. The Constitutional Court can, exceptionally, decide in the matter itself (and could technically award damages), but the case law shows that the Court, as a rule, when annulling contested decisions, returns them to the lower court for repeat procedure.

While the right to redress for human rights violations is a cross-cutting, structural element of the human rights regime that applies to all the individual human rights and fundamental freedoms in Chapter II (and beyond), the URS also recognizes a self-standing right to compensation as provided by Art. 26:

---

historical development of the constitutional basis for public liability pre-1991 see Bardutzky and Zagorc (2013), 663 ff.

[4] Civil Procedure Act (official consolidated text) [Zakon o pravdnem postopku (ZPP-UPB3)], Official Gazzette no. 73/2007.

[5] Administrative Dispute Act [Zakon o upravnem sporu (ZUS-1)] Official Gazzette no. 105/2006, 62/2010, 109/2012.

[6] Constitutional Court Act (official consolidated text) [Zakon o ustavnem sodišču (ZUstS-UPB1)], Official Gazzette no. 64/2007.

> [E]veryone has the right to compensation for damage caused through unlawful actions in connection with the performance of any function or other activity by a person or authority performing such function or activity within a state or local community authority or as a bearer of public authority.
>
> Any person suffering damage has the right to claim, in accordance with the law, compensation also directly from the person or authority that has caused such damage.[7]

The guarantee of Art. 26 is in compensation for damages caused by *unlawful* action. The notion of unlawfulness *(protipravnost)* is wider than only human rights violations, covering a wider scope. The legal rule infringed by the public authority could be a statutory rule or even a rule from an executive regulation.

Article 26 is a part of the "Bill of Rights", i.e., Chapter II of the Constitution "Human Rights and Fundamental Freedoms" and therefore the right to be compensated for damage caused by public authorities is considered to be a human right. As a human right, the right to compensation is thus subject to constitutional protection against discrimination (Art. 14/I URS) and can only be limited or further regulated pursuant to the rules of Art. 15 URS. A violation of the right to compensation, being a human right, can be the basis of a constitutional complaint to the Constitutional Court (Art. 160/I URS) and subjected to the scrutiny of the Human Rights Ombudsman (Art. 159 URS). In addition to being a human right, the Supreme Court described the provision of Art. 26, Paragraph I as a "substantive reflection" of the constitutional principle of the rule of law.[8]

The provisions overlap to some extent but also differ in scope and purpose. While the right to obtain redress (Art. 15/IV URS) is limited in scope to human rights, it is quite broadly worded: the Slovenian phrase *odprava posledic kršitev* could also be more literally translated as "eliminating the consequences of the violation," and could be understood as any kind of *restitutio in integrum*, wider than monetary compensation. Art. 26, on the other hand, extends to all unlawful action of public authorities (violations of statutes, executive regulations etc.) and go beyond the Chapter II rights and freedoms. At the same time, its phrasing of "compensation for damage" uses the language of Slovenian law of obligations (Art. 133/I of the Obligations Code, hereinafter: OZ[9]) and immediately alludes to monetary compensation.

The link between Art. 26 and the liability rules of private law goes beyond semantics. As Art. 26 does not answer all the relevant questions that can come up in a liability litigation the Slovenian courts have been consistently applying the private law rules of liability to public liability cases. The Supreme Court finds that in the "unfortunate" absence of statutory rules on public liability, the provisions of private obligations law are used by analogy in public liability cases.[10] In addition to that,

[7] English translation is from the website of the Slovenian Constitutional Court (http://www.us-rs.si/en/about-the-court/legal-basis/constitution/. Accessed 24 February 2014).

[8] Judgment II Ips 505/2003. We started our discussion on public liability law with thoughts on the rule of law in Bardutzky and Zagorc (2013), 661.

[9] Obligations Code (official consolidated text) [Obligacijski zakonik (OZ-UPB1)], Official Gazzette no. 97/2007.

[10] Judgment of the Supreme Court in II Ips 387/97. For a critical appraisal of this stance, see Zagorc (2013).

public liability cases, as a general rule, are adjudicated by courts of general jurisdiction (civil litigation judges) rather than specialized administrative courts.[11]

What needs to be mentioned is a special regime of the Criminal Procedure Act (hereinafter: ZKP) in its Chapter XXXII on monetary compensation for unjustifiable conviction or unfounded arrest.[12]

The above presented fundamental traits of damages for human rights violations in the Slovenian legal order lead us to the conclusion that the response of the legal system floats between the domains of public and private law, with the roots of the legal basis for relevant claims firmly in constitutional law,[13] and with many of the operational aspects that can be traced back to the rules of private law.

15.3 Scope of Liability Regime

The provision of Art 26 is broad in scope and is applicable to all cases of human rights violations attributable to the public authorities. As we have shown, the more precise statutory rules may vary depending on the specific situation, forming several subsystems that in turn, combined, form the Slovenian system of monetary compensation for human rights violations. What the subsystems presented so far have in common is their permanent nature. They were built to entertain claims by the aggrieved on a day-to-day basis. In this section, we will identify compensatory schemes that were put in place in order to deal with large scale violations of human rights, arising from combinations of historical events and systemic errors, but, all in all, temporally finite phenomena (in the language of the European Court of Human Rights, ad hoc compensation schemes).[14] Studying these special schemes, we observe *leges speciales* that differ to a varying extent from the rules under the general system presented in the previous section.

Victims of World War II The provision of Art. 50/III URS guarantees special protection to war veterans and victims of war. This provision serves as a

[11] The administrative dispute *(upravni spor)*, a mechanism of judicial review of administrative action, also makes it possible for the party aggrieved by acts of public authority to claim redress but this seems to be a considerably less important option. See Arts. 17 and 67 ZUS-1 and Bardutzky and Zagorc (2013) 686.

[12] Criminal Procedure Act (official consolidated text) [Zakon o kazenskem postopku (ZKP-UPB8)], Official Gazzette no. 32/2012. According to the Supreme Court, the Art 26 damages can be claimed pursuant to the procedural avenues and conditions laid down in the law of obligations, "however it is up to the legislature to enact different rules for specific situations, as for example in the Criminal Procedure Act (damages for unjust conviction or unfounded deprivation of liberty)..."

Judgment II Ips 879/2008 (para. 7).

[13] In Judgment II Ips 505/2003, the Supreme Court found that the fact that public liability claims are based on Art 26 Constitution puts such claims firmly in the domain of public law.

[14] The European Court of Human Rights (Grand Chamber) Judgment in *Kurić and Others v Slovenia*, Application no. 26828/06, para. 415.

constitutional basis for the establishment of a special compensatory scheme for victims of war violence.[15]

Initially, the 1995 passing of the Victims of War Violence Act (hereinafter: ZZVN) brought to life a compensatory scheme for people who suffered from the aggression of the Nazi and fascist occupiers and their local collaborators on the territory of Republic of Slovenia during the Second World War.[16] The circle of persons entitled to compensation under ZZVN was subject to constitutional controversy, where the Constitutional Court principally held that the question of eligibility for compensation under the Act was an area where the legislature enjoyed broad discretion. Nevertheless, it was judicial intervention that led the legislature to expand the eligibility of the scheme, most importantly, to those people who were as civilians exposed to violent acts or involuntary measures imposed by freedom fighters, allied forces or other armed forces. The compensatory scheme is also available to persons who were deprived of liberty by the Yugoslav forces during the 1991 Independence War.[17] The compensatory scheme represents a very particular situation as the award of damages cannot be directly linked back to the liability of the state. Under the scheme, the eligible persons can claim monthly life annuity the value of which is prescribed by ZZVN, e.g., 1.25 EUR for every month a person spent in a concentration camp) and other entitlements connected to the pension, social security and health system (Chapter II ZZVN). The Constitutional Court held that the compensation is not based on the obligation of the Republic of Slovenia. The Republic of Slovenia, as well as its predecessor, the Kingdom of Yugoslavia, were themselves victims of aggression. The constitutional commitment is based on the recognition that the persons affected by war require special attention by the society and that the society is capable of paying special attention to them. The commitment is based on solidarity, which is one of the elements of the principle of social state (Art. 2 URS).[18]

Post-War Injustices After the liberation of the territory of Slovenia from German occupation in 1945, a single-party communist regime was effectively established in all of Yugoslavia. In many cases, the human rights of persons who were, or were perceived as, political opponents of the communists were severely breached. After the democratization and independence of the country in 1991, the legislature passed the Redress of Injustices Act, introducing a special compensatory scheme for victims of such human rights violations.

[15] Bardutzky and Zagorc (2013) 664.

[16] Victims of War Violence Act [Zakon o žrtvah vojnega nasilja (ZZVN)]. The original version was published in the Official Gazzette no. 63/1995. An official consolidated version of the text (ZZVN-UPB1) was published in the Official Gazzette no. 18/2003.

[17] Decision of the Constitutional Court no. U-I-266/04, Official Gazzette no. 118/2006. The finding of unconstitutionality brought to the adoption of Act Amending the Victims of War Aggression Act [Zakon o spremembah in dopolnitvah zakona o žrtvah vojnega nasilja ZZVN-H)], Official Gazzette no. 72/2009.

[18] Decision of the Constitutional Court U-I-327/96, para. 11, Official Gazzette no. 68/96. Also Supreme Court, Judgment and order II Ips 449/2007.

Persons eligible to redress under the Redress of Injustices Act are persons who were convicted "unjustly and in contradiction to rule of law, for class, political or ideological reasons, in judicial or administrative procedures" between 15 May 1945 and 2 July 1990 and whose freedom was restricted (including persons who were limited in their choice of place of residence or sentenced to forced labour) relatives of such convicts that were executed, and relatives of persons executed extrajudicially (Arts. 2–4).[19]

The Redress of Injustices Act provided for indirect monetary compensation for former prisoners (the time when their freedom was restricted counts towards their pension entitlements) and recognized the rights of the relatives of the executed people to issue death certificates and mark the graves (Arts. 6–8). In Art. 5, it also granted the right to monetary compensation and envisaged that the eligible person and the state would conclude a friendly settlement *(poravnava)*. It envisaged that there would be a second piece of legislation regulating the fund from which the compensations would be paid, not only to the persons eligible pursuant to the Redress of Injustices Act, but also to the persons eligible under the above mentioned Victims of War Violence Act. However, the Payment of Compensation to the Victims of War and Post-war Aggression Act was adopted in 2001,[20] after the Constitutional Court had found twice that the legislative omission (not adopting this act) amounted to a violation of the Constitution.[21]

People Infected with HIV In 1997, the National Assembly established a special compensatory scheme for persons (and, under certain conditions, their relatives) who became infected with the human immunodeficiency virus (HIV) through blood transfusion or blood products before 6 January 1986.[22] As was explained by the members of parliament who signed the proposal to adopt a statute, before 1986 blood products were not tested and persons that required constant treatment involving transfusion or blood products, mostly persons suffering from haemophilia, were exposed to the risk of infection by HIV. This called for, in the words of the parliamentarians, strict liability *(objektivna odgovornost)* of the state. The main arguments of the advocates of this measure were, firstly, the comparative practice in other European countries that have similarly compensated infected persons and, secondly, the fact that the time limits for compensatory claims under general rules

[19] Article 2/III contains a provision on persons convicted in courts based on the territory of other Yugoslav republics but with a link to Slovenia. The attempts of the legislature to try to limit the circle of eligible persons with regard to their origin and/or link to Slovenia were subject to constitutional controversy. See Decision of the Constitutional Court U-I-371/96, Official Gazzette no. 68/1998.

[20] Payment of Compensation to the Victims of War and Postwar Aggression Act[Zakon o plačilu odškodnine žrtvam vojnega in povojnega nasilja (ZSPOZ)]. In its current version (the official consolidated text ZSPOZ-UPB2), it was published in the Official Gazzette no. 21/2011.

[21] Decision no. U-I-86/94, Official Gazzette no. 68/96, and Decision no. U-I-114/98, Official Gazzette 61/1999.

[22] Act on compensation for persons, infected with the HIV due to blood transfusion or blood products [Zakon o povrnitvi škode osebam, okuženim z virusom HIV zaradi transfuzije krvi ali krvnih pripravkov (ZPŠHIV)], Official Gazzette no. 36/1997.

of non-contractual liability have long expired.[23] The parliamentarians saw the awards under the proposed statute as "material compensation for mental distress suffered and reduced life functions," the formulation that made it into the text of the statute (Art. 3/I). The ZPŠHIV envisages fixed monthly award sums depending on whether the claimant was himself infected or is a person close to an infected person and depending on whether the person was infected by HIV only or had in fact suffered from AIDS. Such circumstances also define the length of entitlement. For example, a child of an infected person is entitled to receive a sum of 90,000 Slovenian tolars every month until he/she completes regular education but not longer than his/her 25th year of age (Arts. 4 – 6 ZPŠHIV).[24] Art. 7 foresees that the award shall be reduced by 30 % if the income of the claimant exceeds a certain threshold. This means that the only determinant influencing the otherwise fixed compensation sum is rooted in social and economic egalitarianism.

Trial Without Undue Delay In 2005, the ECtHR handed down the quasi-pilot judgment in *Lukenda v. Slovenia*, finding that Slovenia had violated Mr Lukenda's right to trial within a reasonable time (Art. 6 European Convention on Human Rights) as well as his right to an efficient remedy (Art. 13 ECHR) and that these violations "have originated in the malfunctioning of domestic legislation and practice." The Court ordered Slovenia to "…through appropriate legal measures and administrative practices, secure the right to a trial within a reasonable time." As was commented, this came as a "wake-up call" for the Slovenian authorities.[25]

What followed was the enactment of what became known as *"Lex Lukenda,"* the Protection of Right to Trial without Undue Delay Act.[26] The Act in Chapter II envisages mechanisms (special remedies) to prevent undue delay in judicial proceedings and in Chapter III, the possibility of obtaining "just satisfaction" *(pravično zadoščenje)* for the parties that have suffered undue delay in judicial proceedings.[27] One of the possibilities for just satisfaction is also monetary compensation for immaterial damage. The Act lays down the criteria for setting the sum of the damages (most important are: complexity of the case, the activity of the state, the activity of the aggrieved party and the importance of the matter for the party) and sets the floor for the damages award at 300 EUR and the ceiling at 5,000 EUR (Art. 16 ZVPSBNO). The party can also file a separate lawsuit claiming monetary

[23] National Assembly – Committee for Health, Labour, Family and Social Policy, record of the 9th session, 8 May 1997, available at: http://www.dz-rs.si/wps/portal/Home/deloDZ/seje/evidenca?mandat=II&type =magdt&uid=C84C127862F88F47C1256491004505ED. Accessed 24 February 2015.

[24] For illustration, in January 1997 the average net monthly salary in Slovenia was 87.961 tolars according to the Statistical Office of the Republic of Slovenia (see http://www.stat.si/indikatorji.asp?id=7. Accessed 24 February 2015.

[25] Zagorc (2005).

[26] Protection of Right to Trial without Undue Delay Act (official consolidated text) [Zakon o varstvu pravice do sojenja brez nepotrebnega odlašanja (ZVPSBNO-UPB2)], Official Gazzette no. 67/2012. More on the context of the adoption and the adoption of the ZVPSBNO see Pavlin (2009) 43 ff.

[27] For an overview of the system of remedies under ZVPSBNO see Pavlin (2009) 52 ff.

compensation for material damage caused by delay in judgment. In adjudicating the claim for material, the courts are likewise instructed to take into account the substantive criteria listed above (Art. 21 ZVSBNO). Notably, the ZVSPBNO provides an avenue for redress even where the violation has already ceased and the party has already claimed just compensation before the ECHR (Art. 25 ZVSBNO).

The Erased In 1992 (shortly after the declaration of independence), Slovenian authorities erased approximately 25,000 non-citizens from the registry of permanent residents of the newly founded country without any notification, let alone a chance to be heard.[28] The erasure had severe consequences for the affected persons, including but not limited to loss of social security, barred access to health and education, evictions, often also forced removal from the state territory. The Constitutional Court found the erasure to be unconstitutional in 1999.[29] This was only the beginning of a fight for compensation that awaited the erased. It was more than 10 years later, in 2010, that the National Assembly passed amendments to the Legal Status Act which opened a partial avenue for the victims of the erasure to obtain permanent residence in Slovenia.[30]

In the meantime, some of the victims of the erasure attempted civil litigation against the state for monetary compensation to no avail. Their claims were dismissed predominantly due to the expiration of time limits.[31] The time limits, of course, were the ones laid down by private law of obligations that was used, as was discussed above, by analogy by the courts in these cases. The decision of the courts to stick to the analogous the rules of Obligations Code rather than identify the constitutional shortcomings was convincingly criticized by Zagorc.[32]

In *Kurić and Others*, the central case regarding the erased persons, the European Court of Human Rights (first sitting as a section, then in 2012 as the Grand Chamber) with regard to the violation of ECHR Art. 8 found that:

---

[28] Affected by erasure were people who were citizens of the (former) Yugoslavia, resident in the territory of Slovenia, but who within Yugoslavia's federal order were not citizens of Slovenia and then did not acquire the citizenship of the newly formed Slovenian state under 1991 legislation. *Kurić and Others*, paras. 21–39.

[29] Decision of the Constitutional Court U-I-284/94, Official Gazzette no. 14/99.

[30] Act Amending the Act Regulating the Legal Status of Citizens of Former Yugoslavia Living in the Republic of Slovenia [Zakon o spremembah in dopolnitvah Zakona o urejanju statusa državljanov drugih držav naslednic nekdanje SFRJ v Republiki Sloveniji (ZUSDDD-B)], Official Gazzette no. 50/2010. *Kurić and Others*, paras. 71 ff.

[31] "All the compensation claims were in the end dismissed, mostly for failure to comply with the prescribed time-limits, although the courts had in some cases initially established that the compensation claims were well-founded. At that time, proceedings in eleven cases brought by "erased" persons were pending before the Supreme Court. Finally, on 7 November 2011 the Government submitted a new decision delivered by the Constitutional Court on 26 September 2011 (Up-108/11) in a case brought by one of the "erased" who had claimed compensation for pecuniary and non-pecuniary damage. In that case the first-instance court had initially held in an interim judgment that there were grounds for holding the State liable for damages. However, the Supreme Court upheld the second-instance decision dismissing the claim on account of the expiry of the statutory time-limit. That decision was endorsed by the Constitutional Court." *Kurić and Others*, para. 83.

[32] Zagorc (2013).

> Despite the efforts made after the Constitutional Court's decisions of 1999 and 2003, as well as recently with the enactment of the amended Legal Status Act, the Slovenian authorities have failed to remedy comprehensively and with the requisite promptness the blanket nature of the "erasure" and its grave consequences for the applicants.[33]

The Court also found Slovenia to be in violation of the right to efficient remedy, as the "Government failed to establish that the remedies available to the applicants were 'adequate' and 'effective' in order to redress, at the material time, the alleged violation of Art. 8 of the Convention."[34]

The applicants in the *Kurić and Others* case were awarded 20,000 EUR each in respect of non-pecuniary damage. The decision on pecuniary damages that were also claimed by applicants was reserved by the Court. The Court held that Slovenia should set up an ad hoc domestic compensation scheme.[35]

An *ad hoc* compensatory scheme was set up with the enactment of the Act on restitution of damage for persons who were erased from the Register of Permanent Population (hereinafter: Erased Restitution Act).[36] The Government asserted that the goal of the act was to, "Introduce a systemic solution for just satisfaction and/or monetary compensation into the legal system of the Republic of Slovenia... the jurisprudence of Slovenian courts of general jurisdiction has shown that the general rules of private law, i.e., the Obligations Code are inadequate and inappropriate..." to be used in cases involving monetary compensation of the erased persons.[37]

The Act in Arts. 2 and 3 contains elaborate rules to determine eligible persons and the time period during which they are considered to be erased. Given that the European Court of Human Rights in *Kurić and others* did not recognize as victims the two applicants that were erased but never attempted to remedy their situation, the Government stated that it followed the jurisprudence of the Court when it limited the eligibility to persons that have already succeeded in obtaining either citizenship or permanent resident status.

The Act opens an administrative and a judicial avenue through which claims for compensation can be made. The Act instructs the administrative authority to award 50 euro damages for each month when the claimant was erased (Art. 7). The judicial avenue is through civil litigation courts that are instructed to apply private law of obligations by analogy, except for the rules on time limits. The damages awarded cannot exceed the threefold of the sum that can be awarded by the administrative authority (Arts. 10–12). When awarding damages, the administrative authority and the court are instructed in Art. 5 to lower the damages by the sum that had already been awarded in any kind of prior proceedings. The provisions of Chapter V of the

[33] *Kurić and Others,* para. 361.

[34] *Kurić and Others,* para. 371.

[35] *Kurić and Others,* points 9–11 of the operative part of the judgment and para. 415 of the grounds for the judgment.

[36] Act on restitution of damage for persons who were erased from the Register of Permanent Population [Zakon o povračilu škode osebam, ki so bile izbrisane iz registra stalnega prebivalstva (ZPŠOIRSP)], Official Gazzette no. 99/2013.

[37] Government proposal for the adoption of the Erased Restitution Act, section 2.1.

Act aim to facilitate the claimants' access the social security, housing and health systems, and set them on equal footing with the citizens with regard to the educational system in Slovenia.

The Government presented reasons for the ceiling on monetary compensation. As the grand total of the required funds for the monetary compensation alone (not counting the funds required to implement the provisions of Chapter V) will probably be around 100 million EUR,[38] taking into consideration the impact of the global financial crisis on Slovenia and the critical situation in Slovenia's public finances, not limiting the monetary compensation would possibly lead to such a drain on the state budget that the protection of other human rights and fundamental freedoms in Slovenia would be made impossible.[39]

15.4 Liability Regime in Detail

15.4.1 The Foundation of Claims for Damages

15.4.1.1 Basis of Liability

As a general rule of Slovenian obligations law, whoever inflicts damage on another shall be liable unless the injurer can prove that she or he was not culpable (fault liability – Art. 131/I OZ). The law provides for cases of strict liability *(objektivna odgovornost)*, such as liability for a dangerous object (Art. 131/II and III OZ).

The above cited Art. 26 URS, however, does not contain an exculpatory clause. This has led the scholarship to the conclusion that public liability is a form of strict liability (Virant 2002, 499–512; Pirnat 2005, 27). On the other hand, some of the scholarship has insisted on maintaining culpability as one of the cornerstones of public liability and instead offered an alternative solution (Juhart 2005, 12, footnote 6). Under this concept, the culpability would be "objectivised" via the institute of liability for other persons *(odgovornost za druge)*. In that sense, the state would be liable for the actions of the people exercising state authority.[40] Juhart finds that often

[38] In the first proposal of the government that we are referring to throughout this section, the sum per month of erasure was set at 40 EUR – in the version of the text that was adopted, it is 50 eur. The proposal, counting with the 40 EUR per month, estimated the costs at 75.6 million EUR.

[39] Government proposal for the adoption of the Erased Restitution Act, section 2.2. The Government relied on the decision of the Constitutional Court in U-I-60/98 regarding the restitution of the property confiscated by the communist regime after World War II. The Court, based on the principles of social state and equality, found that the legislature was not acting contrary to the Constitution in setting a ceiling on the restitution.

[40] In its Judgment in II Ips 337/2005, the Supreme Court assessed culpability in a public liability case. The incident dates back to the time when military service was in principle obligatory. The plaintiff was injured by a fellow recruit on military premises during physical exercise. The state failed to prove that the recruit acted in accordance with the football rules and with due care of an average person while exercising. As fault is presumed by law, the court found the state to be liable for damage resulting from the sport injury. See more Bardutzky and Zagorc (2013) 676.

the outcome of a particular legal issue is the same regardless of which of the two competing concepts we apply (Juhart 2005, 13).

As illustrated by the Supreme Court case II Ips 357/97, public authorities are strictly liable in situations where according to the general rules strict liability applies, e.g. liability for damage caused by a dangerous object or dangerous activity.

Also, special compensatory schemes often employ the language of strict liability, e.g., Art. 16/I and 21/II ZVPSBNO; Art. 3/I ZPŠHIV, presumably to emphasize that it was not intended for the state to invoke defences related to the conduct of the responsible officials.[41]

15.4.1.2 Burden of Proof

As we have expounded above, the primary avenue for a claim of monetary compensation will be the civil litigation procedure. It is therefore necessary to take into account the evidentiary rules of civil procedural law (i.e., ZPP) combined with the substantial rules stemming from OZ.

ZPP's general evidentiary rule is laid out in Art. 7/I and, in slightly greater detail, in Art. 212 ZPP. The party has to state, firstly, the facts and adduce the evidence upon which she or he bases claims, and secondly, by means of which she or he contests the facts stated and evidence adduced by the opposing party. This is to be read together with Art. 215 ZPP: "If the evidence produced in respect of a particular fact does not induce a sufficient degree of persuasion (Art. 8 ZPP), the court's conclusions on such fact shall be drawn pursuant to rules on the burden of proof." *Onus proferendi* as well as *onus probandi* thus lay with the plaintiff.

The above cited provision of Art. 131/I OZ establishes a reversed burden of proof with regard to culpability (fault). The Supreme Court case referred to above (II Ips 337/2005) shows us that the court will expect the state to provide proof when it wishes to exonerate itself using arguments rooted in the conduct of the person that directly inflicted damage.

ZUS-1, which applies to the procedures before the specialized administrative courts (see above) has a different rule on evidentiary matters. The court is not bound by evidentiary motions of the parties and may use whatever evidence it deems useful to contribute to the clearing of the matter and to a legal and correct decision (Art. 20/II ZUS-1). The court therefore seeks for material truth *(načelo materialne resnice)*, which necessarily alleviates the burden of the parties to a certain extent. On the other hand, the provision of Art. 20/I ZUS-1 binds the court to the arguments of the parties when assessing the facts of the case and thus maintains the burden on the parties. The provisions of Paragraph I and II stand in contradiction, as was recognized by scholarship and the judges.[42]

---

[41] With regard to the ZVPSBNO scheme, see Pavlin (2009) 75.

[42] Janez Breznik, who presided over the Administrative Court of the Republic of Slovenia and contributed to the commentary of ZUS-1, acknowledges the internal contradiction between these

If we are to resolve the contradiction by interpreting broadly the power of the court to gather evidence, this may lead to different evidentiary systems when comparing civil litigation and administrative dispute.

15.4.1.3 Causation

A causal link is necessary to establish a liability for damages. This stems from the general rules on non-contractual liability and applies to cases of public liability. The OZ does not envisage a specific rule of causation and Bukovec has found that the courts interpret causation quite freely (Bukovec 2002, 235) An analysis of case law gives us an insight into the theories used by the courts when dealing with the issues of causation (Bardutzky and Zagorc 2013, 676). Mostly employed are the *ratio legis* theory of causation, "only the cause that is at the same time a violation of a legal norm can count as a legally relevant cause," and the theory of adequate causation, "would an act of the injurer have this result in normally expected consequences."[43] These two theories are joined by the prospective theory of causation that has been becoming more important recently and seems to be applicable predominantly in cases where there are two parties that both act in a way that inflicts damages. According to the prospective analysis, causation is established if a certain act increases the probability of an event.[44]

The burden of proof regarding the causal link rests with the plaintiff. Also, in cases of minor procedural errors on the side of the public authorities the courts consider whether the outcome of the decision-making of the authority would be the same even if it had complied with the procedural rules. If it was, there is no causal link.[45]

15.4.1.4 "Pure Violation" or "Pure Harm"?

As a general rule, monetary compensation is awarded when there is a legally recognized form of harm. The existence of a violation only will not suffice.

It should be noted that at the same time, the legal system recognizes some instances where a person is entitled to compensation for the grievance that he/she had to endure even though the action of the public authority that had led to his/her grievance is not contrary to the law.

two norms and advocates a wide reading of the restrictions on the assessment of facts by the court. Breznik (2008) 118–121.

[43] For the comparison of the theories (albeit not in a public liability case), see for example the Supreme Court judgment in II Ips 588/99.

[44] Judgment of the Higher Court in Ljubljana in III Cp 1093/2009.

[45] In the judgment and order of the Supreme Court in the case II Ips 434/2009, the execution of pigs was found unlawful as it took place before the clinical tests for swine plague had been conclusive. The Supreme Court nevertheless upheld the objection of the state based on this 'hypothetical causation' since the tests turned out positive.

The concept of human rights in Slovenian constitutional law, derived from the provision of Art. 15 URS, distinguishes an encroachment *(poseg)* upon a human right (or fundamental freedom) from a violation *(kršitev)*. Encroachments, depending on whether or not they pass the proportionality test, can be either permissible or impermissible. Only impermissible encroachments of human rights and fundamental freedoms are tantamount to violations of human rights (Testen 2002, 198).

Using the language of human rights doctrine, we can then speak of material compensation for encroachments upon human rights and fundamental freedoms rather than for violations.

A classic example is expropriation *(razlastitev)*. The right to private property is a human right (Art. 33 URS). However, in the chapter establishing the nature of social and economic system of the country, the Constitution introduces the notion of the "economic, social and environmental function of property" (Art. 67 URS) and additionally provides that ownership rights to real estate *may be revoked or limited* in the public interest, whereas compensation in kind or monetary compensation must be provided (Art. 69 URS; emphasis added).[46]

A specific case of state liability for damage without breach of law was effectively created by the Constitutional Court. In 2004, the Constitutional Court ruled that the legislature must adopt a set of rules that will cover cases where compulsory vaccination of (all) children causes harmful side effects. The Court found that there was a general interest in the protection of public health which legitimized the laying down the rules making certain vaccinations compulsory. However, the Court found that the principle of solidarity requires also that the state compensates the damages suffered due to the measure.[47]

15.4.2 The Nature of Harm

The general rule of liability for damage under Slovenian obligations law in Art. 132 OZ is that damage comprises:

- Diminution of one's property (ordinary damage – *damnum emergens*)
- Prevention of the appreciation of one's property (lost profits – *lucrum cessans*)[48]
- Infliction of physical or mental distress or fear on another person
- Encroachment upon the reputation of a legal person.

[46] The »monetary compensation or compensation in kind« is better conceptualized as restitution than compensation for damages (Virant 2002, 683). This does not change the essential logic of providing material consideration to the person who endured a burden for the benefit of the community, whereas these actions at the same time invaded his protected personal sphere yet were not contrary to the law (or to the Constitution).

[47] Decision of the Constitutional Court U-I-127/01, Official Gazette, no. 25/2004. See also Bardutzky and Zagorc (2013), 678.

[48] See Art 168/IOZ.

The last two elements are considered immaterial damages *(nepremoženjska škoda)*. The OZ rules on immaterial damages are further outlined in a number of provisions. Most importantly, Art. 179/I recognizes the right to just monetary compensation (independent of the reimbursement of material damage and dependent on the level and duration of the fear or distress) for: fear, physical distress and for mental distress suffered due to a reduction in life activities, disfigurement, defamation of good name or reputation, truncation of freedom or a personal right, and the death of a person close.[49]

As a side note on *lucrum cessans*: assessing a claim for lost profit, the court will take into consideration "the profit that could justifiably have been expected given the normal course of events or given the special circumstances but could not be achieved owing to the injurer's action or omission" (Art. 168/III OZ).

An illustrative case of how profit was perceived by the judiciary in the context of public liability is case I Cpg 1004/2006.[50] An owner of a bar claimed for his loss of profit to be compensated. He had suffered loss of profit after his bar had been closed because of road works. The first instance court took the stance that the state can expect from a company to lose profit due to the activities of common benefit under the auspices of the state. The Higher Court of Ljubljana, on appeal and applying Art. 155 of Zakon o obligacijskih razmerjih (which translates into Art. 179 OZ), held that, "Profit was an essential for the development of a market subject in addition to being a legally recognized form of damage." It remanded the case and instructed the lower court, first, to assess the loss of profit compared to the same period in the previous year; second, find the acceptable limit of state interference with the profit of the claimant. The Higher Court in Ljubljana considered Art. 133/3 OZ which states that, "If damage arises during the performance of generally beneficial activities *(splošno koristne dejavnosti)* for which permission has been given by the relevant authority it shall only be possible to demand the reimbursement of damage that exceeds the customary boundaries *(običajne meje)*." The Higher Court put an emphasis of the principle of solidarity which needs to be considered when the legal activities of the state produce certain negative externalities. We can submit that the lawgiver has introduced the "customary boundaries" test into the equation of sharing the burdens of public activities to imbibe this legislative provision with a sense of what is perceived normal in a community which pursues common goals and values (Bardutzky and Zagorc 2013, 683).

We can observe that the legislation setting up the different special compensatory schemes has already employed, very obviously, the language of OZ and the different types of harm the Code recognizes (see above Art. 3/I ZPŠHIV). The compensatory schemes under ZVPSBNO and the scheme for the erased persons, however, worded their provisions on harm using the terms *premoženjska* and *nepremoženjska*

---

[49] This legally recognized ground for mental distress is further elaborated upon in Art 180 OZ, including the possibility that an event that would cause heavy disabledness would give rise to a claim for monetary compensation of the relatives of the disabled person for their mental distress (Paragraph III).

[50] Judgment and Order of the Higher Court in Ljubljana in I Cpg 1004/2006.

škoda (material and immaterial harm), without diving deeper into the different forms of immaterial harm, applying the language of OZ. The dichotomy of material and immaterial damage is more likely to be traced to the judgments of the European Court of Human Rights (*Lukenda* and *Kurić and Others*, respectively).

15.4.3 Scope of Compensation

The essential provisions to be discussed with regard to the scope of compensation are the general rules on scope of compensation in non-contractual liability laid down in OZ. The approach of the lawgiver was different depending on the nature of damages (material or immaterial). In the case of material damage, the primary obligation of the injurer is *restitutio in integrum (vzpostavitev prejšnjega stanja)*; the award of *adequate (ustrezna)* monetary compensation is, if we follow the structure of the legal norm of Art. 164 OZ, a subsidiary option. In awarding monetary compensation for immaterial damage, on the other hand, the provision of Art. 179 OZ instructs the judges to award *just (pravična)* monetary compensation. In an attempt to provide an insight into the perception of this notion among the higher ranks of judges, we refer to the work of Dunja Jadek Pensa in the Commentary to the OZ.[51]

15.4.3.1 Just Monetary Compensation for Immaterial Damage

The legislation instructing the judges to award *just* monetary compensation should be understood as the introduction of a certain *legal standard* (Jadek Pensa 2003, 1036). To decide on the sum in an individual cases is to substantiate this legal standard. The substantiation of the legal standard is supposed to reflect value judgments, based on societal reality. The elements of the value judgment are partly rational and partly irrational (Jadek Pensa 2003, 1037). Such understanding of the law leads to a high level of individualization of it. However, it cannot result in arbitrariness (Jadek Pensa 2001, 7).

There are two elements combined in the understanding of just monetary compensation. The first element is the moral satisfaction of the injured person. This should not be understood neither as the revenge of the injured person nor as punishment of the injurer. The monies paid can contribute to the efforts of the injured person to recover psychologically, he/she can perhaps indulge in something that would otherwise remain unavailable. The second element of just monetary compensation is objective: what is taken into account is the importance of the damaged immaterial good.[52] The threat of having to pay just monetary compensation has equally a pre-

[51] Dunja Jadek Pensa is at present a judge of the Slovenian Constitutional Court; at the time of the publishing of the Commentary, she served as a judge of the Higher Court of Ljubljana and later as a judge of the Supreme Court of the Republic of Slovenia.

[52] Jadek Pensa (2003), 1034. See also Supreme Court judgment in case II Ips 76/2007.

ventive purpose. The latter is almost indistinguishable from the considerations discussed above (Jadek Pensa 2003, 1035).

Dunja Jadek Pensa, who contributed to the commentary of the relevant article of the Obligations Code, also participated in preparing a handbook entitled *Monetary Compensation for Immaterial Harm*. This can be considered a standard work of reference for judges and attorneys, and widely used in their everyday practice. The handbook presents the summaries (approximately one page each) of several hundreds of cases where monetary compensation for immaterial damages was awarded. In the vast majority of the cases, we cannot speak of human rights damages as the harm originated in horizontal relationships between private individuals and entities (most commonly, traffic accidents). The sum of the damages is indexed using the "ODSKODN" index, that is, the total sum is divided by the average net salary in Slovenia in the month when the first instance judgment was issued. The purpose of this is to facilitate the comparison between similar cases regardless of the changes in purchasing power (Jadek Pensa 2001, 18–19). This is expected to safeguard important values in law: equality, the general character of law and its impartiality, and foreseeability (Jadek Pensa 2001, 8). However, the reader is warned not to digest the collection of cases as a set of tables that can be directly used in a concrete case. Using the handbook like that would run counter the understanding of the just monetary compensation as a legal standard that needs to be carefully substantiated in every individual case, taking into account all the specific characteristics of the case (Jadek Pensa 2001, 9).

15.4.3.2 Taxation

Pursuant to Art. 27 of the Personal Income Tax Act (ZDoh-2), there is no personal income tax on:

- Compensation paid to persons that were unjustly convicted or arrested (in accordance with ZKP).
- Compensation paid based on the asbestos compensatory scheme and the HIV compensatory scheme.
- Compensation paid to victim of war and post-war violence.
- Compensation paid on the basis of court judgment (and, under certain conditions, on the basis of settlement) for bodily harm, illness, death or damage to personal assets, but not the compensation for lost income.
- Compensation for immaterial damage paid pursuant to the ZVPSBNO.[53]

[53] Personal Income Tax Act (official consolidated text) [Zakon o dohodnini (ZDoh-2-UPB7)], Official Gazzette no. 13/2011. See Pavlin (2009) 76.

15.4.4 Defences

15.4.4.1 Contributory Conduct

When there is a case of contributory fault, the provision of Art. 171 OZ, laying down rules on "shared liability" *(deljena odgovornost)* has to be applied. Pursuant to Art. 171/I OZ, an injured party that contributed to the occurrence of the damage or increased the damage is only entitled to proportionately reduced compensation (See also Bardutzky and Zagorc 2013, 684).

15.4.4.2 Direct Access to Litigation

There is no general requirement to exhaust other procedures before claiming monetary compensation in a civil litigation. The above mentioned *caveat* regarding the role of the state attorney is to be taken into account.[54]

15.4.4.3 Limitations of Liability

Legislative Acts In the Slovenian constitutional system, it is within the jurisdiction of the Constitutional Court to adjudicate on the constitutionality of statutes adopted by the National Assembly (Art. 160 URS). This existence of a system of judicial review leads to a conclusion that parliament is not sovereign; the laws that it passes must be in conformity with the higher law, and the most important corpus of hierarchically superior norms are of course human rights and fundamental freedoms. This opens the question whether there is a possible claim against the state for monetary compensation in cases of violations of human rights by adoption of a legislative act (or, for that matter, failure of the legislature to act[55]).

Case law has taken the position that a plaintiff cannot succeed with a claim for public liability only by arguing that a statute of the parliament has been annulled by the Constitutional Court. The Supreme Court accepts the liability of the legislature and at the same time limits it. Only the most severe infringements of constitutional provisions or basic civilized standards may give way to public liability for damage occurred by a legislative act.[56] We have criticised this solution before. It effectively means that when courts entertain a claim for monetary compensation based on a violation of human rights by an act of the legislature, they are expected to distinguish

[54] For a more extensive account of procedural avenues in Slovenian public liability law, please consult Section D in Bardutzky and Zagorc (2013).

[55] See for example Judgment of the Supreme Court in II Ips 344/2004.

[56] *See* judgment of the Higher Court in LjubljanaII Cp 3427/2009 and judgment of the Supreme Court in II Ips 800/2006. The latter dealt with unlawful act of the legislature concerning the so called Erased people. See also *Kurić and Others*.

different violations of different constitutionally protected human rights (and the paramount principles such as the rule of law) assessing their severity, regardless of the fact that the constitution- giver did no such thing in laying down rules of public liability in Art. 26 URS (Bardutzky and Zagorc 2013, 672 ff and Zagorc 2013).

Judicial Conduct Similarly, liability for wrongful conduct of judges is recognized but limited by case-law. The jurisprudence of the Supreme Court demands that the nature of judicial work needs to be taken into account, particularly free assessment of evidence (Art. 8 ZPP) and independence of judiciary on all levels (Art. 11/II of the Courts Act) when assessing liability of the state for erroneous judicial decisions.[57] In II Cp 2837/2006, the plaintiff demanded monetary compensation for the damage inflicted by a wrongful decision of the court, claiming that the court had deviated from established practice of the courts when interpreting applicable substantive law. The Higher Court of Ljubljana (the one that was ruling on the damages claim) found that courts are in principle not liable for the way they use substantive law "except in cases of severe violations and abuse of power."[58] We have argued before that what should be considered as an alternative path is for the court entertaining the claim for monetary compensation to assess whether the judge in question followed established professional standards in the exercise of his judicial function (Bardutzky and Zagorc 2013, 671).

15.4.5 *Who to Sue and Who May Sue?*

Three remarks are in order with regard to the issue of who may sue and who may be sued.

15.4.5.1 Bearers of Public Authority

Article 26 URS in Paragraph 1 enshrines the right to compensation for damage caused by persons or bodies exercising (or in connection with) the office or authority of the state, local community or as bearers of public authority. Pursuant to Art. 121 URS, legal entities and natural persons may be vested with the public authority to perform certain duties of the state administration. Bearers of public authority *(nosilci javnih pooblastil)* may issue general legal acts (that need to be in conformity with the Constitution and statutes pursuant to Art. 153/III URS) and individual administrative decisions (that are reviewable by way of administrative dispute pursuant to Art. 157/IURS). Actions of bearers of public authority are explicitly covered by the constitutional right to equal protection (Art. 22 URS) and the constitutional right to legal remedy (Art. 25 URS). There is no accessible case-law on the

[57] Legal opinion of the plenum of the Supreme Court of 15 December 1998, no. 2/98, p 5–7.

[58] Judgment of the Higher Court in Ljubljana in II Cp 2837/2006.

liability claims against bearers of public authority; however, in Pirnat's opinion, the State cannot be fully liable for damages caused by them. The relationship of the State towards the bearers of public authority is not the same as the relationship towards the organs of the State; the control over their activity is limited. Hence, suggests Pirnat, the state should only be liable for deficient control over the bearer of the public authority (Pirnat 2005, 23. See also Bardutzky and Zagorc 2013, 672).

15.4.5.2 Direct Claim

Paragraph II of Art. 26 URS provides that, "Any person suffering damage has the right to demand, in accordance with the law, compensation also directly from the person or body that has caused damage."

Regarding judges, the above cited provision needs to be read in conjunction with Art. 134/I URS that grants immunity from all accountability for an opinion expressed during decision-making in court to all persons participating in making judicial decisions. This, according to the Higher Court in Ljubljana, has to be understood as an expression of the fundamental right to judicial protection (Art. 23 URS).[59] Compensatory claims directly against judges are therefore inadmissible (Bardutzky and Zagorc 2013, 671).

The provision of Art. 26/II URS expressly authorizes the legislature "in accordance to the law" to lay down the rules governing the claims for compensation aimed directly at the persons responsible. With regard to civil servants, the general rule is that the employer, e.g., the Republic of Slovenia in the case of state civil servants, is liable to the injured person (Art. 135/II Civil Servants Act). The injured party has the right to claim compensation directly from the person who caused the damage only when it was caused with intent (Art. 135/III Civil Servants Act).[60]

15.4.5.3 Foreigners and Stateless Persons

Foreigners and stateless persons are entitled to compensation for damage under Art. 26. This was explicitly confirmed by *Vrhovno sodišče* in II Ips 387/97, which is an interesting case with regard to the status of foreigners in public liability law. The plaintiff was a foreigner who was during the 1991 armed conflict ordered by the Slovenian military to participate with his truck in creating a road obstacle that would stop the advancing Yugoslav troops. His claim was based on the provision of Art. 26 which is not limited to citizens. To demonstrate illegality of the acts of the public authority as a necessary condition to establish liability, however, the plaintiff was

[59] Order of the Higher Court in Ljubljana in II Cp 20/2009 and Order of the Higher Court in Ljubljana II Cp 3736/2007.

[60] Civil Servants Act (official consolidated text) [Zakon o javnih uslužbencih (ZJU-UPB3)], Official Gazzette no. 63/2007; the Slovenian word for 'with intent' is *naklepno*; usually, the legal notion is equated with the Latin term *dolus*. See also Bardutzky and Zagorc (2013) 674 and 680.

able to rest on the premise that the duty to defend the country can only be imposed on citizens and not on foreigners.[61]

15.4.6 Courts and Competent Bodies

As we have explained above, the jurisdiction over claims for monetary compensation for human rights violations is primarily vested in courts of general jurisdiction, the courts that hear civil litigation cases regardless of who the parties are. The specialized administrative courts are also invested with powers to award monetary compensation when ruling on the validity of an individual administrative act.

A notable procedural and institutional feature of public liability law in Slovenia is the institution of the State Attorney. The state and its organs are represented by the State Attorney's Office *(državno pravobranilstvo)* in judicial and other legal procedures (Art. 7/I State Attorney Act,[62] hereinafter: ZDPra). Pursuant to Art. 14/I ZDPra, whoever intends to start litigation against the subjects represented by the State Attorney's Office, must propose to the State Attorney's Office that the dispute be resolved before instigating court procedures.[63] The State Attorney's Office must respond in 30 days and should they come to an agreement, the state attorney is authorized *ex lege* to conclude an out-of-court settlement (Art. 14/II ZDPra). Should the attempt to conclude settlement with the state attorney fail, the aggrieved party is of course at liberty to start litigation.

Worth noting is the particular institutional solution of the compensatory scheme established by the Redress of Injustices Act (see above). The Act in Art. 9 established a special administrative board *(komisija)* appointed by the Government. The board decides on the applications filed by individuals and has the power to recognize the status of, e.g., former political prisoner. With a positive decision, the board grants a monetary award (Redress of Injustices Arts. 10 and 17). Similarly, the compensatory scheme for persons infected with HIV created an administrative avenue for claimants, vesting the power to decide on the award in the minister in charge of health, acting upon the recommendation of an expert board. A possibility of judicial review of the minister's decision is via the administrative dispute (Art. 11 ZPŠHIV).

---

[61] Judgment of the Supreme Court in II Ips 387/97. See also Bardutzky and Zagorc (2013) 682.

[62] State Attorney Act [Zakon o državnem pravobranilstvu (ZDPra-UPB2)], Official Gazette, no. 94/2007. By law, the State Attorney's Office *(državno pravobranilstvo)* is an independent authority (Art 2/IZDPra). The State Attorney's office is not an organ of criminal prosecution and is thus separate and independent from the State Prosecutor's Office *(državno tožilstvo)*. It is true that the state attorneys follow the guidelines of the represented authority in the exercise of its functions (Art 7/I ZDPra), however the status of the state attorneys is such to guarantee them professional independence: the rules regarding the rights and duties of judges apply to state attorneys *mutatis mutandis* (Art 3/II ZDPra).

[63] Note that by virtue of ZUS-1, there are special rules in force in the administrative dispute, where the State Attorney plays a different role and does not represent the defendant. Also, the State Attorney does not play a role in the pre-trial phase.

15.4.7 Time Limits

The time limits that apply are the generally prescribed time limit rules *(zastaranje)* of OZ (see Arts. 352–354).[64] Pursuant to the provisions of Paragraphs I and II of Art. 352 OZ, the time limit for a claim for compensation of damages is 3 years since the injured person learnt about the harm and the injurer; in any case, the time limit expires within 5 years of the emergence of the harm. The ZKP provides in Art. 539 that in the case of a person demanding compensation for unjust conviction or unfounded arrest, the 3 year period commences with the finality of the relevant judicial decision, e.g. the acquittal judgment.

It goes without saying that the majority of the special compensatory schemes for human rights violations arising out of wars etc. have had to lay down different temporal rules (e.g. Art. 10/II of the Redress of Injustices Act provides the exact day until which applications can be filed with the Board). At the same time, the compensatory scheme of ZVPSBNO has laid down specific (and relatively short) procedural time limits for the filing of a lawsuit for compensation, tying them to other remedies available under the Act (the compensation lawsuit is to be filed within 18 months since the decision has been made on whether the right to speedy trial had been violated).

The recent events regarding the establishment of a special compensatory scheme for the erased persons have shed light on the unsuitability of the application of general rules of OZ to another instance of systemic violation of human rights.[65]

15.5 Concluding Thoughts: Slovenian System of Monetary Compensation for Human Rights Violations Between Private and Public Law, Between National and Supranational

In its annual reports, the State Attorney's Office reported on a successful claim for monetary compensation for mental distress caused by unacceptable living conditions (first and foremost overcrowding) in the Ljubljana prison. The first instance (civil litigation) court referred extensively to European Court of Human Rights case law "for lack of domestic jurisprudence." The appeal lodged by the State Attorney to the

---

[64] There are different kinds of time limits (or, more broadly speaking, temporal rules) in Slovenian law. *Zastaranje* is an issue of substantive law whereas the limits mentioned with regard to special compensatory schemes are more procedural in nature.

[65] Zagorc summarizes the debate on the appropriateness of application of general rules on time limits between former Constitutional Court Judge Matevž Krivic, Amnesty International's Blaž Kovač and the Vice President of the Supreme Court Nina Betetto (Zagorc 2013).

higher court was dismissed.[66] It is not entirely certain whether the case is (perhaps indirectly) linked to the European Court of Human Rights case of *Mandić and Jović v. Slovenia*.[67]

In October 2011, the Court in *Mandić and Jović* awarded each of the applicants 8,000 EUR in respect of the non-pecuniary damages. This was based on the finding of the Court that the applicants, who were detained on remand *(pripor)* in the Ljubljana Prison, "for the most part of their detention they had less than 3 m^2 of personal space inside their cell for almost the entire day and night, the Court considers that the distress and hardship endured by the applicants exceeded the unavoidable level of suffering inherent in detention and went beyond the threshold of severity under Art 3 and therefore amounted to degrading treatment."[68]

It is noteworthy that the overcrowding in Ljubljana Prison has been flagged both by regional human rights monitoring mechanisms, i.e., the European Committee for the Prevention of Torture and Inhuman or Degrading Treatment or Punishment (CPT)[69] as well as by the Slovenian Human Rights Ombudsman.[70]

The State Attorney's Office reports that in 2012, it received several lawsuits based on sets of facts very similar to the ones in the cases where the Slovenian court and the European Court of Human Rights had awarded damages to persons held in the Ljubljana Prison. In the view of the State Attorney's Office, it is therefore very likely that in those cases, plaintiffs' requests would also be granted. The State Attorney's Office therefore advocates for out of court settlements to be brokered with the plaintiffs.[71]

We propose to take the prison overcrowding to get a cross-section view into the current state of Slovenian law of monetary compensation for human rights violations. What we can observe is the appeals from the international and national human rights monitors were not enough to trigger the action of the executive and the legislative branch of the government. They have, however, made an impact on the European Court of Human Rights when ruling on the case.[72] And it was the case law of the latter that the Slovenian court borrowed to adjudicate a similar case when it came before it, "for lack of domestic jurisprudence". This particular development in the judicial branch is encouraging. It may mean that the domestic courts in the future will look increasingly at Strasbourg for guidance. This could 1 day substitute

[66] DPRS Annual Report 2012, p 46. The report does not cite the docket number of judgment of the Slovenian court and it seems not to be retrievable from the case law website of the Slovenian courts (www.sodnapraksa.si). This report therefore has to rely on the information provided on the judgment by the State Attorney's Office.

[67] European Court of Human Rights (Fifth Section), Judgment in the case of *Mandić and Jović v Slovenia*, Application nos. 5774/10 and 5985/10.

[68] *Mandić and Jović*,para. 80.

[69] *Mandić and Jović,* paras 41 ff. And it most likely made its way from there into the US State Dept report, see above footnote no. 2.

[70] *Mandić and Jović,* paras. 47ff.

[71] DPRS Annual Report 2012, p 47.

[72] See, for example, para. 127 of the judgment.

the current *modus operandi* of special compensatory schemes built based on an ECHR judgment for an alternative model of creative judicial rule-making, inspired by ECHR case law.

Depending on the volume of prison overcrowding cases reaching the Slovenian courts, it is of course possible that the executive and legislative branch will consider establishing a special compensatory scheme, most likely with a ceiling on monetary compensation for immaterial damage as we have already seen in several cases. In the current situation of financial difficulties, limiting the monies spent on monetary compensation would certainly be an attractive idea to the government and taxpayers. More importantly, given how vocal the ECHR was in its demands for the improvement of the conditions in prison, a ceiling legislation would possibly receive Strasbourg approval if the government was to show that it was channelling the money into better prison conditions. This opens a number of political and moral questions.

At the same time, there is a strong argument for Slovenia to put the tool of special compensatory schemes to deal with human rights issues to the side and refrain from using it. When we look at the majority of the special compensatory schemes, we see that the injustices can mostly be traced back to the violent and radical changes of the political regime and power. Even the massive court backlogs are indirectly a legacy of the change in the political system that brought with it a new role for the judicial system. While of course prison overcrowding is linked to a myriad of societal factors too, it is nevertheless a very real example of a human rights problem. The desirable response in such a case is not to rely on the politicians to broker a compromise among themselves and with the international human rights community that they translate into legislation, but rather for the legal system to adequately respond through the independent judiciary, which has at its disposal rules open ended enough to be able to accommodate effective redress of human rights violations as required by the Constitution and international human rights law.

References

Bardutzky, Samo, and Saša Zagorc. 2013. Slowenien [Slovenia]. In *Staatshaftung in Europa – Nationales und Unionsrecht [State liability in Europe – Domestic and union law]*, ed. Dörr Oliver, 661–700. Berlin: de Gruyter.

Breznik, Janez, et al. 2008. *Zakon o upravnem sporu s komentarjem [Administrative dispute act: commentary]*. Ljubljana: GV Založba.

Bukovec, Martina. 2002. *Odškodninska odgovornost države [State liability for damage]*. Doctoral dissertation. Ljubljana: Pravna fakulteta Univerze v Ljubljani.

Jadek-Pensa, Dunja. 2001. *Denarna odškodnina za nepremoženjsko škodo: pregled sodne prakse [Monetary compensation for immaterial harm: Overview of case law]*. Ljubljana: GV Založba.

Jadek Pensa, Dunja. 2003. Komentar 179. člena Obligacijskega zakonika [Commentary of Article 179 Obligations Code]. In Obligacijski zakonik (OZ): (splošni del): s komentarjem [Obligations code (OZ): (General Part): Commentary]. ed. Plavšak et al., 1035–1037. Ljubljana: GV Založba.

Juhart, Miha. 2005. Odgovornost države za nepravilno (protipravno) odločbo [The liability of the state in cases of a wrongful (illegal) decision]. In Odgovornost države, lokalnih skupnosti in drugih nosilcev javnih pooblastil za ravnanje svojih organov in uslužbencev [Liability of state,

local communities and other bearers of public authority for acts of organs and employees], ed. Mojca Seliškar Toš, 11–18. Ljubljana: Inštitut za primerjalno pravo pri Pravni fakulteti.
Pavlin, Peter. 2009. Pilot judgments and systemic human rights violations – the need to establish an effective remedy in the domestic system – the Slovenian experience. Overview of the contents of the act on the protection of the right to a trial without undue delay of the Republic of Slovenia and follow-up to the Lukenda v Slovenia Judgment. In *Pilot judgment procedure in the European Court of Human Rights: 3rd informal seminar for government agents and other institutions*, 41–80. Warszawa: Krajowa Szkoła Administracji Publicznej.
Pirnat, Rajko. 2005. Protipravnost ravnanja javnih oblasti kot element odškodninske odgovornost javnih oblasti [Unlawfullness of acts of public authority as an element of public liability for damage]. In *Odgovornost države, lokalnih skupnosti in drugih nosilcev javnih pooblastil za ravnanje svojih organov in uslužbencev [Liability of state, local communities and other bearers of public authority for acts of organs and employees]*, ed. Mojca Seliškar Toš, 21–27. Ljubljana: Inštitut za primerjalno pravo pri Pravni fakulteti.
Testen, Franc. 2002. Komentar 15. člena Ustave [Commentary of Article 15 of the Constitution]. In *Komentar Ustave Republike Slovenije [Commentary of the constitution of Republic of Slovenia]*, ed. Lovro Sturm, 197–205. Ljubljana: FPDEŠ.
Virant, Gregor. 2002. Komentar 69. člena Ustave [Commentary of Article 69 of the constitution]. In *Komentar Ustave Republike Slovenije [Commentary of the constitution of Republic of Slovenia]*, ed. Lovro Šturm, 662–687. Ljubljana: FPDEŠ.
Zagorc, Saša. 2005. Dvojna predramitev za slovensko oblast: odprava kršitev pravice do sojenja v razumnem roku - kako naprej? [Double wake up call for the Slovenian authority: Redressing the violations of the rights to trial within reasonable time – What should be the next steps?]. *Revus* 5: 45–53.
Zagorc, Saša. 2013. *Odškodninska odgovornost za kršitev človekovih pravic [Liability for human rights violations]*. XI. dnevi civilnega in gospodarskega prava, 11–12 April 2013, Conference Proceedings, 67–70. Ljubljana: Inštitut za primerjalno pravo.

Legislative Materials and Reports (All Accessed on 24 February 2015)

Amnesty International (2012) The state of the world's human rights. files.amnesty.org/air12/air_2012_full_en.pdf.
Državni zbor – Odbor za zdravstvo, delo, družino in socialno politiko [National Assembly – Committee for Health, Labour, Family and Social Policy], Records of the 9th session, 8 May 1997. http://www.dz-rs.si/wps/portal/Home/deloDZ/seje/evidenca?mandat=II&type=magdt&uid=C84C127862F88F47C1256491004505ED.
Državno pravobranilstvo [State Attorney's Office] (2012) Poročilo o delu za leto 2012, [Annual Report 2012]. http://www.dp-rs.si/fileadmin/dp.gov.si/pageuploads/LETNO_POROCILO/Letno_porocilo_2012_splet.pdf
Predlog Zakona o povračilu škode osebam, ki so bile izbrisane iz registra stalnega prebivalstva [Proposal of the Act on restitution of damage for persons who were erased from the Register of Permanent Population] (1345 – VI) of 29 July 2013. http://www.dz-rs.si/wps/portal/Home/deloDZ/zakonodaja/izbranZakonAkt?uid=C12565D400354E68C1257BB70049A695&db=kon_zak&mandat=VI&tip=doc
United States Department of State (2012) Country Reports on Human Rights Practices for 2012 – Slovenia. http://www.state.gov/j/drl/rls/hrrpt/humanrightsreport/index.htm?year=2012&dlid=204339.

Chapter 16
Special Compensation Regimes for Violations of Human Rights in Turkish Law: A Fast Track Remedy or No Remedy at All?

Zeynep Oya Usal Kanzler

16.1 Introduction

International human rights law recognises that States have an obligation to offer remedies to victims of human rights violations. The right to an effective remedy lies at the core of human rights protection and is an essential pre-condition for an effective human rights policy. The formulation of the right to an effective remedy enunciated in the Universal Declaration on Human Rights[1] has been reinforced and expanded by several subsequent binding treaties[2] as well as soft law.[3] It encompasses not only a substantive right to remedies, but also a set of procedural rights necessary to facilitate fair, effective and prompt access to remedies. In other words, the right to an effective remedy requires the provision of a domestic mechanism, which is *effective* in law as well as in practice, to deal with the substance of an arguable complaint

An earlier version of this article was published in the Turkish Reports to the XIXth International Congress of Comparative Law, (eds) R. Serozan/B. Basoglu, Vedat Kitapcilik, January 2015.

[1] Article 8 of the Universal Declaration on Human Rights (UDHR).

[2] E.g. Article 2(3) of International Covenant on Civil and Political Rights (ICCPR); Article 2 of Convention on the Elimination of All Forms of Discrimination Against Women (CEDAW); Article 6 of International Convention on the Elimination of All Forms of Racial Discrimination (CERD); Article 14 of Convention Against Torture and Other Cruel, Inhuman or Degrading Treatment or Punishment (CAT); Article 39 of Convention on the Rights of the Child (CRC); Article 13 of European Convention on Human Rights (ECHR); Article 47 of EU Charter of Fundamental Rights.

[3] E.g. Basic Principles and Guideline on the Right to a Remedy and Reparation for Victims of Gross Violations of International Human Rights Law and Serious Violations of International Humanitarian Law, UN General Assembly Resolution 60/147, 16 December, 2005.

Z.O.U. Kanzler (✉)
Assistant Professor in Human Rights Law, Koç University Law School, Istanbul, Turkey
e-mail: zusal@ku.edu.tr

E. Bagińska (ed.), *Damages for Violations of Human Rights*,
Ius Comparatum - Global Studies in Comparative Law 9,
DOI 10.1007/978-3-319-18950-5_16

and to grant appropriate reparation.[4] This means that, at the procedural level, victims of human rights violations must be guaranteed access to justice through a competent and independent authority in order to successfully obtain reparations. Such an authority must have the power to investigate and decide whether a human rights violation has taken place, and if so, to enforce reparations. In general, as appropriate and proportional to the gravity of the violation and the circumstances of each case, full and effective reparation includes the following forms[5]: restitution,[6] compensation, rehabilitation,[7] satisfaction[8] and guarantees of non-repetition.[9]

In this article, I will analyse the special financial reparation, or in other words compensation, regimes introduced into the Turkish legal system as a remedy for different forms of human rights violations. For the purposes of the article, I will firstly describe the general law of public authority liability insofar as it concerns the liability for violations of human rights under Turkish law. I will then set out the main features of each particular compensation regime. While doing so, I will focus particularly on the important structural change that took place in the judicial system with the introduction of the individual complaint mechanism before the Turkish Constitutional Court ("ConstCt") for the violations of fundamental rights and freedoms. I will further focus on the extent to which the available compensation regimes are regarded as an effective remedy in light of the relevant jurisprudence of the European Court of Human Rights ("ECtHR").

16.2 General Law of Public Authority Liability for Violations of Human Rights

The protection of human rights is constitutionally guaranteed in the Turkish legal system. As stated in the Constitution of the Republic of Turkey 1982 ("Constitution"), "everyone whose constitutional rights and freedoms have been violated has the right

[4] Different terms (e.g. redress, damages) are being used to imply the notion of reparation in different legal systems. For a thorough analysis of domestic remedies for international human rights law violations see Stephens (2002).

[5] Basic Principles on the Right to a Remedy, principle no. 18.

[6] Ibid, principle no. 19 that reads as follows: "Restitution should, whenever possible, restore the victim to the original situation before the gross violations of international human rights law or serious violations of international humanitarian law occurred. Restitution includes, as appropriate: restoration of liberty, enjoyment of human rights, identity, family life and citizenship, return to one's place of residence, restoration of employment and return of property". For a more extensive treatment of restitution under international law, see Buyse (2008).

[7] Ibid, principle no. 21 that reads as follows: "Rehabilitation should include medical and psychological care as well as legal and social services".

[8] Ibid. principle no. 22. e.g. cessation of violations, judicial and administrative sanctions against perpetrators.

[9] Ibid. principle no. 23. e.g. investigation, prosecution and sanctioning of perpetrators, human rights education.

to request prompt access to the competent authorities".[10] Guaranteeing the procedural limb of right to an effective remedy, this provision entails the possibility to lodge a complaint before a judicial, administrative or other body against the alleged violation in order to redress the harm done and as means to ensure adequate sanctions for the perpetrators. The same constitutional provision further secures the substantive limb of the right holding the State responsible for compensation in the event of damages incurred to any person through unlawful treatment by public officials. The state, however, reserves the right of recourse to the official responsible.[11]

The general law of public authority liability in Turkey is primarily governed by public law and is explicitly enshrined in the Constitution. Pursuant to Article 125, "recourse to judicial review shall be available against all actions and acts of administration. The administration shall be liable to compensate for damages resulting from its actions and acts." The obligation to compensate for damages incurred by individuals is regarded as a fundamental duty of a rule of law state.[12]

Notwithstanding that the general principle is holding the administration liable to compensate damages on account of its actions (*eylemler*) and acts (*işlemler*), activities of the administration that are subject to private law fall within the compensation regime under private law, e.g. contractual liability or tort liability, in case damage occurs in the course of this activity.[13] These activities are thus not subject to the jurisdiction of administrative law, which in principle establishes the rules regarding the compensation regime for damages resulted by the actions and acts of the administration.

Turkish Administrative Law lays twofold public authority liability: fault based liability (*kusurlu sorumluluk*) and strict liability (*kusursuz sorumluluk*). In case an individual claims that his/her rights were infringed by the administration through its actions and acts, he/she may then lodge a full remedy action (*tam yargı davası*) against the latter in order to seek compensation. Full remedy action is a law suit where the "liability" of the administration is reviewed; to decide in favour of the claimant, the court should either find a service fault (*hizmet kusuru*) committed by the administration,[14] or should base its judgement on the theory of strict liability.

Fault-based liability requires a service fault on part of the administration, meaning that the service must involve defect, delay or failure in the establishment or operation of the public service in question. In other words, there is nonfeasance, late feasance or malfeasance. Service fault[15] also appears when mishandling of public

---

[10] Article 40 (1) of the Constitution of the Republic of Turkey 1982 ("Constitution").

[11] Article 40 (3) of the Constitution.

[12] Article 2 of the Constitution states that the Republic of Turkey is a democratic, secular and social state governed by rule of law. See also Conseil D'Etat of Turkey (Danıştay) Decision, Danıştay 10. D, T.09.10.1995, E.1994/1682, K. 1995/4256.

[13] For instance, damages resulting from unlawful confiscation or from industrial and commercial service or from operation of private property belonging to the administration.

[14] Güran (2005) 81.

[15] As an interesting example, see the decision of Conseil D'Etat (10. D., T. 28.11.1996, E. 1996/3423, K. 1996/7923) in which the claimant complained following the death of her diplomat husband whom was shot dead on his way to his office. In this case, service fault was established as

affairs has expressed itself in an illegal decision. While determining the service fault, the burden of proof remains with the claimant. In addition to service fault, there may be a fault of the administration's official, e.g. due to the latter's wilful misconduct, gross negligence, or imprudence, which is personal but not severable from service (*görev kusuru*). In this case, the official and the administration are regarded as "jointly liable" (*cumul*). The person aggrieved, however, must sue the administration and collect damages. The administration, in turn, should bring charges against the official before ordinary courts for the ultimate division of responsibility through securing the recourse. In parallel to Article 40 of the Constitution, this principle is clearly stated in Article 129 of the latter, which reads as follows: "Compensation cases concerning damages arising from faults committed by public servants and other public officials in the exercise of their duties shall be filed only against the administration in accordance with the procedure and conditions prescribed by law, as long as the compensation is recoursed to them".

Strict liability, on the other hand, requires holding the administration legally responsible irrespective of its culpability (*fault*). According to this principle, what is done in the general interest, even if done lawfully, may give rise to a right to compensation when an exceptional burden falls on one particular person, the claimant. Besides, the activities of the state, even when conducted without fault, may in certain circumstances constitute a risk. It is thus that the fundamental principle of *equality in bearing public burdens* and the principle of equity or *social risk* are applicable for holding the administration liable for damages caused by its acts or actions without fault.[16]

As far as the procedural rules in order to initiate a full remedy action are concerned, the claimant should have a *locus standi*, meaning the existence of concrete, personal, actual and direct damage arising from the act or action of the administration. There is a 60-day time limit for lodging full remedy action, and the determination of its beginning varies according to the origin of the damage and whether it is an act or action.

16.3 Special Compensation Regimes as a Remedy for Particular Human Rights Violations

As defined in UN Basic Principles and Guideline on the Right to a Remedy and Reparation for Victims of Gross Violations of International Human Rights Law, financial reparation or compensation should be provided for any economically assessable damage, such as: (a) physical or mental harm; (b) lost opportunities, including employment, education and social benefits; (c) material damages and loss of earnings, including loss of earning potential; (d) moral damage; (e) costs required

the State failed to provide with an armored vehicle on account of budget constraints despite the diplomat was explicitly shown as a target by extreme groups.

[16] Güran (2005) 81.

for legal or expert assistance, medicine and medical services, and psychological and social services.[17] It is observed that Turkish law opted for establishing special compensation regimes for particular human rights violations in Turkey, primarily as a remedy for the systemic issues underlined by the judgements of the ECtHR. Hence, while general features of these regimes will be explained in this section, the interaction between the ECtHR and the Turkish domestic law will also be shown.

16.3.1 The Law on Compensation for Damage Arising from Terror and Combating Terror (Law No. 5233)

16.3.1.1 Background

The armed conflict between the Turkish Armed Forces and the PKK (The Kurdistan Workers Party, an illegal organisation), which took place in southeastern Turkey from 1984 onward, raised very important social, political and legal challenges in Turkey. The Law on Compensation for Damage Arising from Terror and Combating Terror, Law no. 5233 ("CDTL"),[18] which was adopted by the Turkish parliament and went into effect in July 2004, was intended to indemnify victims of this armed conflict. Most of the victims were local villagers—mainly Kurdish farmers and their families—who were forcibly displaced from their homes and livelihoods by the conflict, particularly by village evacuations in the context of the fight against the PKK. While it was evident from the debates in Turkish Parliament that the law was to be adopted for remedying this internal displacement, its beneficiaries were not limited to the people who were displaced. [19]

According to the CDTL, anyone who incurred pecuniary losses as a result of terrorist acts or of measures taken by the authorities to combat terrorism is entitled to compensation. In particular, it aims to indemnify the pecuniary/material damage sustained by natural or legal persons who have migrated or have been displaced due to terrorism or anti-terrorist activities. It also aims to partially compensate the damage sustained by civil servants who cannot be considered as part of the internally

[17] para. 20.

[18] Law no. 5233 adopted on 17 July, 2004 and entered into force on 27 July, 2004. On 28 December, 2005 the Turkish Parliament enacted Law no. 5442 and amended several provisions of Law no. 5233.

[19] The government deliberately portrayed the law not as a reparation effort for the displacement but rather as a compensation mechanism for all "victims of terrorism". As stated in the Preamble to Draft Law of 19 April, 2004, the Turkish government stated that the intent of the law was "to deepen trust in the State, to strengthen the State-citizen relationship, to contribute to social peace and the fight against terrorism," and committed itself to seeing that it was effectively implemented. As further explained in the scope of the Law, payments under the CDTL to the displaced people were intended to cover losses arising from the original displacement, as well as those incurred during the decade or more that these families were unable to return to their property.

displaced population or migrants, but who have been affected by terrorism or by anti-terrorist activities carried out by the security forces.

The law is based on the principle of strict liability derived from the concept of *no-fault responsibility* under the constitution, and it does not require proof of any fault on the part of the administration but rests on the doctrine of *social risk based on the objective responsibility of the state*.

16.3.1.2 Scope

At the outset, the CDTL provides compensation for damage to livestock, trees, agricultural products and all property, as well as for physical harm to individuals such as injury, disability and death, including the costs for treatment and funerals. It further covers financial loss of those citizens who could not access their properties. In this regard, Damage Assessment and Compensation Commissions[20] ("Commissions") are set up in 76 provinces in compliance with the CDTL. Commissions base their assessments on standard application forms that require the claimants to state only their economic losses, without implicating anyone as responsible.

As far as the procedure regarding the compensation claim is concerned, anyone who has suffered damage as a result of terrorism or of measures taken by the authorities to combat terrorism can lodge an application with the relevant commission. The application must be lodged within 60 days of the date on which knowledge was obtained of the incident causing damage and, in any event, within 1 year of the impugned incident. The commission must reach a decision within a maximum period of 6 months after the application is lodged. Where necessary, this period can be extended by the governor for another 3 months.

The commissions assess the damages suffered by claimants and prepare friendly-settlement declarations (*sulhname*) for payment of compensation to the claimants in cash or in kind. The amount of compensation is determined on the basis of equity and current economic conditions. Expert opinion can also be obtained with a view to determining whether compensation should be awarded. Following payment of the compensation, the State has a right to bring proceedings against the perpetrators of the acts that caused the damage in question.

Following an amendment made to the CDTL in 2012,[21] its scope was expanded entitling the persons who became disabled, as well as the family members of the persons that lost their lives, due to a terror related incident to receive a monthly social allowance.

[20] Chaired by Deputy Governors, these Commissions are composed of six experts on finance, public works and settlement, agriculture, sanitation, industry and commerce, who work in each province, as well as a lawyer appointed by the Administrative Board of each Bar.

[21] Law no. 6353 adopted on 4 July, 2012 and entered into force on 12 July, 2012.

16.3.1.3 Effectiveness of the CDTL

Albeit the compensation regime was mostly welcomed, it was also subject to criticism for providing extremely low amounts of pecuniary damages in cases of death and bodily harm. Consequently the CDTL was heavily criticised by the victims and their legal representatives, claiming that providing a predetermined, fixed amount of compensation for death and bodily harm contradicts the general principles of law of damages. Another criticism lay in the non-provision of compensation for non-pecuniary damages, i.e. pain and suffering.[22]

The burden of proof on the victims/claimants to prove their claims used to be a major problem in its implementation. However, subsequent to a later decision[23] of the Council of Ministers, claimants can prove their allegations by means of any information or document.

As to the implementation, the substantial delays of up to 18 months–contrary to 3 months requirement in CDTL–in the payment of compensation awards also appeared to be a significant problem.

CDTL, however, has been an efficient tool for the ECtHR to dismiss the pending applications on the same matter. Following its adoption, with its *İçyer*[24] decision, ECtHR rejected almost 1,500 similar applications for non-exhaustion of domestic remedies as the CDTL was regarded as an effective domestic remedy that was introduced by Turkey and to which the applicants should resort prior to lodging their applications before the ECtHR in Strasbourg.

After the *İçyer* decision, some NGOs monitoring the implementation of CDTL argued that the work of the Commissions had deteriorated. In a study from December 2006,[25] it was claimed that the Commissions started to work arbitrarily by dictating the terms of settlements more freely as well as by deciding on lower sums than was previously typical and by excluding more applicants from coverage under the CDTL. Hence, over 200 applications were lodged before the ECtHR after having resorted to the Commissions, in which the applicants primarily complained about the lack of non-pecuniary damages and the poor assessment of the Commissions. Declaring these applications to be manifestly ill founded,[26] the ECtHR underlined

[22] For an extensive analysis of the implementation of the CDTL, see Kurban (2012) https://www.ictj.org/sites/default/files/ICTJ-Brookings-Displacement-Reparations-Turkey-CaseStudy-2012-English.pdf. Accessed 12 Feb 2015.

[23] Decision no. 9239 of the Council of Ministers on 15 September, 2005.

[24] İçyer vs. Turkey (inadmissibility decision, no. 18888/02, 12 January, 2006).

[25] Human Rights Watch (2006) Unjust, Restrictive and Inconsistent: The impact of Turkey's Compensation Law with respect to Internally Displaced People. See http://www.hrw.org/legacy/backgrounder/eca/turkey1206/turkey1206web.pdf. Accessed 12 Feb 2015.

[26] Fidanten and Others vs. Turkey (no. 27501/06, 28 June, 2011); Bingölbalı and 54 Other Applications vs. Turkey (no. 18443/08, 28 June, 2011); Bogus and 91 Other Applications vs. Turkey (no. 54788/09, 28 June, 2011); Akbayır and Others vs. Turkey (no. 30415/08, 8 July, 2011). These applications represented four separate groups of cases, each raising different issues. The first group concerned individuals who had accepted friendly settlements but whose compensations were paid with 6–15 months of delay, resulting in up to a 7 % loss of the initial value, and who

that most of the applications to the Commissions across the country were resolved, and that more than one billion euros had been paid to more than 133,000 applicants. Holding that the effectiveness of a remedy does not depend on the certainty of a favourable outcome for the applicants, the ECtHR also did not assess whether the amount of compensation paid–an average of only 7,500 euros per person–was appropriate.

In the light of these circumstances, one can argue that the effectiveness of the CDTL is already well established by the ECtHR as it did not revise its *İçyer* judgment against the allegations regarding rapid deterioration in the performance of the Commissions.

16.3.2 Right to Compensation for Unlawful Detention Under the Code of Criminal Procedure (Law No. 5271)

Under Turkish law, the right to liberty is guaranteed under a special compensation regime in case it is violated by the State in a wrongful manner. Pursuant to the Turkish Code of Criminal Procedure (Law no. 5271) ("CCP"),[27] anyone who claims that he or she has been unlawfully detained on remand or whose detention on remand has been unlawfully extended may claim damages for pecuniary and non-pecuniary damages incurred under Articles 141–144 of the CCP. However, the issue of the effectiveness of this remedy has already been brought before the ECtHR. In its *Kürüm vs. Turkey*[28] judgment, the ECtHR held that while Articles 141 and 142 CCP introduced the possibility of compensation for unlawful detention, including cases where the detained person has not been judged in a reasonable period or acquitted, the applicant had no possibility, even under these new provisions, to demand compensation before the conclusion of the trial and the delivery of a final judgment. It therefore concluded that the CCP is not an adequate domestic remedy for challenging the lawfulness of detention and thus does not satisfy the requirements of the ECtHR concerning compensation for unlawful detention under Article 5 § 5 of the European Convention on Human Rights ("Convention").[29]

---

were not then given payments for default interest. The second group consisted of those who claimed that their applications were rejected unfairly by the commissions, that their emotional pain and suffering were not compensated, or that their pecuniary losses were wrongly assessed. In the third group were individuals who were not granted legal aid to bring a court action. The fourth group was comprised of those who claimed they had missed the statutory deadline for appealing against the commissions' decisions because they had not been provided with correct information by the authorities.

[27] Law no. 5271 adopted on 17 December, 2004 and entered into force on 1 April, 2005.

[28] Kürüm vs. Turkey (no. 56493/07, 26 January, 2010).

[29] As known, according to Article 5, paragraph 5, of the Convention, "everyone who has been the victim of arrest or detention in contravention of the provisions of this Article shall have an enforceable right to compensation". The right to compensation presupposes that a violation of one of the other paragraphs of Article 5 has been established by either a domestic authority or the Court itself.

Likewise, in the *Altınok vs. Turkey* judgement,[30] the ECtHR further observed that Article 141 of the CCP did not provide, in any of the circumstances to which it referred, for the possibility of claiming compensation for damage suffered as a result of the lack of an effective remedy for challenging pre-trial detention. It hence was considered as a non-effective remedy for the purposes of Article 5 § 5 of the Convention.

Currently, at domestic level, a claim for compensation is admissible only after a final decision is given. It thus means that if the proceedings are still pending in the domestic courts, the applicants claiming unlawful detention cannot have opportunity to avail themselves of the remedy in question. In line with its previous conclusions in *Kürüm* and *Altınok*, the ECtHR, in its inadmissibility decision of *Demir vs. Turkey*,[31] recalled that the right to compensation can be exercised effectively if a claim for compensation is made after criminal proceedings are terminated and detention on remand is ended either by acquittal or conviction. The ECtHR, however, noted that it still remains to be clarified whether the right to compensation can also be exercised effectively while detention on remand is continuing and proceedings are pending under the CCP.

In the light of these circumstances, it appears that CCP provisions regarding compensation, as it stands, cannot be regarded as an effective remedy for the violations of the right to liberty. Underlying a systemic problem in the Turkish criminal justice system, the deficiencies in domestic law require Turkey to take general measures in remedying the situation. It is particularly crucial considering that some 300 applications concerning similar complaints that are likely to give rise to findings of a violation of the Convention are currently pending before the ECtHR. In this regard, the implementation of the recently adopted so-called "Fourth Reform Package",[32] which extended the scope[33] of the right to compensation, should be monitored to conclude on the effectiveness of the compensation for the violations of right to liberty.

It creates a direct and enforceable right to compensation before the national courts. In order to amount to an effective remedy, an award of compensation for unlawful detention must not depend on the ultimate acquittal or exoneration of the detainee. The national authorities must interpret and apply their national law without excessive formalism.

[30] Altınok vs. Turkey (no. 31610/08, 29 November, 2011).

[31] Demir vs. Turkey (no. 51770/07, 16 October, 2012).

[32] Adopted by the Turkish Parliament on 11 April, 2013 and entered into force on 30 April, 2013.

[33] Following the amendment to the CCP, compensation claims can further be made in two other stages of proceedings: firstly, a detainee would be entitled to request compensation if he/she is prevented from exercising his/her right to challenge the lawfulness of detention in adversarial proceedings. Secondly, it will be possible to make a claim for compensation even if the detention period (which might be considered to be excessive) is deducted from the final sentence.

16.3.3 Law on the Establishment and Rules of Procedure of the Constitutional Court[34] *of Turkey (Law No. 6216)*

16.3.3.1 Scope

On a constitutional basis, Turkish law requires that in the case of a conflict between international agreements in the area of fundamental rights and freedoms duly put into effect and the domestic laws due to differences in provisions on the same matter, the provisions of international agreements shall prevail. Pursuant to this rule, which gives direct effect to the European Convention on Human Rights ("Convention"), courts of general jurisdiction are now required to enforce the supremacy of the Convention over domestic laws. While the Court of Cassation and the Council of State referred in some of their judgments to specific provisions of the Convention, it is not possible to speak about a uniform, consistent and principled judicial approach to the direct effect of the ECtHR judgments.

Since 23 September, 2012, the introduction of an individual complaint procedure before the Constitutional Court ("ConstCt") created a structural change in the landscape of the human rights protection system and the perception of the ECtHR in Turkey. Following the adoption of the Law on the Establishment and Rules of Procedure of the Constitutional Court[35] (Law No. 6216) ("CCL"), individuals are required to exhaust domestic judicial remedies prior to filing a petition with the ConstCt. The scope of the complaint is limited to those rights and liberties protected under the constitution, which fall within the scope of the Convention and its additional protocols to which Turkey is a party.[36] Individuals can file a complaint for the infringement of any of these rights by public authorities. Although non-Turkish nationals can also petition the ConstCt, they cannot do so on the basis of those rights that are only granted to Turkish citizens.

The assessment of the complaints is subject to a two-tiered process: admissibility and substantive review. Inadmissibility decisions are final; individuals whose complaint is found to be inadmissible reserve their right to petition the ECtHR. In case of a violation, when the violation stems from a judicial decision, the case is to be referred to the competent court with a view to the re-opening of the proceedings for the purposes of remedying the violation and addressing its consequences. The court that is responsible for rendering the re-trial procedure gives its decision to remove – to the extent possible – the violation and its consequences that have been stated in the ConstCt's decision determining the violation.

According to Article 7 of the CCL, the ConstCt receives complaints filed against judicial decisions and administrative actions that have become final after 23 September, 2012.[37] Complaints must be filed within 30 days after the exhaustion of

---

[34] Article 90 of the Constitution.

[35] Law no. 6216 adopted on 30 March, 2011 and entered into force on 23 September, 2012.

[36] Article 45 of Law no. 6261.

[37] As to the introduction date of the individual complaint mechanism, the inadmissibility decision of *Hasan Uzun vs. Turkey* (no. 10755/13, 30 April, 2013) of the ECtHR must be mentioned. In this

domestic judicial remedies or the occurrence of the alleged human rights violation where there are no remedies available.

16.3.3.2 Compensation Awards by the ConstCt

Following the finding of a violation, in cases where there is no legal interest in re-opening the proceedings, the ConstCt can award compensation.[38] There is, however, no explicit rule designated as to the nature and scope of the compensation in the CCL. It is only indicated in the Rules of Procedure of the Court[39] that in case the determination of compensation requires a more thorough examination, the Chamber of the ConstCt in charge, without deciding on the amount of compensation, might refer the subject to the general courts and direct the applicant to bring proceedings before the appropriate court to this effect.

Since the introduction of the individual complaint mechanism, the ConstCt has rendered numerous decisions in which it has awarded compensation for pecuniary as well as non-pecuniary damages[40] following the finding of a violation. The subject of compensation awards given by the ConstCt has also already been a matter of discussion before the ECtHR. In the inadmissibility decision of *Olcay Koç vs. Turkey*,[41] in light of the evidence at its disposal, the ECtHR found that the amount awarded by the ConstCt to the applicant for non-pecuniary damage was an adequate remedy.[42] In this regard, the ConstCt, with its evolving case law, stands as a new mechanism that provides compensation for human rights violations.

---

case, the final decision of the domestic court (Court of Cassation) was 25 September, 2013, i.e. immediately after the individual complaint mechanism became operative. The ECtHR reiterated that the rule of the exhaustion of domestic remedies was an indispensable part of the functioning of the Convention mechanism. Having examined the main aspects of the new remedy before the Turkish Constitutional Court, the ECtHR found that the Turkish Parliament had entrusted that court with powers that enabled it to provide, in principle, direct and speedy redress for violations of the rights and freedoms protected by the Convention. It thus declared the application inadmissible for non-exhaustion of domestic remedies and confirmed that the individual complaint before the ConstCt is a must for the purposes of non-exhaustion rule.

[38] Article 50(2) of Law no. 6216.

[39] Rules of Procedure of the Court (Anayasa Mahkemesi İçtüzüğü); 12 July, 2012, no. 28351, Art. 79. see http://www.anayasa.gov.tr/files/pdf/ictuzuk.pdf. Accessed 12 Feb 2015.

[40] As an interesting example, see the application lodged on account of the loss of lives in the earthquake which hit the city of Van in 2011. In its decision, the ConstCt held that the State failed to investigate whether the legal duties of public officials–e.g. to assess the damage after the earthquake, to determine if buildings have been damaged and if so, evacuate them immediately, and to take measures to give homeless people shelter–were duly conducted, and whether the misconduct arising from the failure to carry out the duties resulted in the death of 24 people. Finding a violation on the procedural limb of right to life, the ConstCt also awarded compensation amounting to 20.000 TL for non-pecuniary damages. (Turkish ConstCt Second Section, B. 2012/752; K. 2012/54, 17 September, 2013).

[41] Olcay Koç v. Turkey (no.8362/14; 24 June, 2014).

[42] ibid, para. 26–27.

16.3.4 *Law on the Settlement of Some Applications Lodged with the European Court of Human Rights by Means of Paying Compensation (Law No. 6384)*

16.3.4.1 Background

For a long time, Turkey has been one of the two countries[43] with the highest number of applications pending against before the ECtHR. This tremendous backlog of cases, which has been built up over the years, was primarily as a result of systemic problems in the functioning of the Turkish judiciary. Thus the ECtHR found in numerous cases that the length of proceedings in Turkey–in administrative, civil, criminal and commercial cases and before the employment and land tribunals–was excessive. Having reiterated that States should organise their courts in such a way as to administer justice without delays that might jeopardise its effectiveness and credibility, the ECtHR had found repeated violations of the right to have a fair trial (Article 6 § 1 of the European Convention of Human Rights) in Turkey, underlining a clear structural and systemic problem with the legal system.

Against that background, the ECtHR decided to apply the pilot-judgment procedure, in view of the growing number of applicants and potential judgments finding a violation. In its judgment of *Ümmühan Kaplan*,[44] the ECtHR held, with regard to the applications pending before it and those lodged between now (the date of *Ümmühan Kaplan* judgment) and 22 September, 2012 (until the individual complaint before the ConstCt becomes operative), that Turkey had to put in place, no later than 1 year from the date on which this judgment became final, an effective remedy affording adequate and sufficient redress in cases where judicial proceedings exceeded a reasonable time. The ECtHR further decided to adjourn examination of similar applications not yet communicated to the Turkish Government and those lodged between the date of *Ümmühan Kaplan* judgment and the beginning of the individual complaint before the ConstCt – i.e. 22 September, 2012. Applications already communicated continued to be examined by the ECtHR under the normal procedure.

Subsequently, Law on the Settlement of Some Applications Lodged with the European Court of Human Rights (ECtHR) By Means of Paying Compensation (Law No. 6384) ("ECtHRLaw") was adopted.[45] This law was designed as a domestic remedy primarily concerning the length of judicial proceedings and non-enforcement or delayed enforcement of judicial decisions[46] as required in *Ümmühan Kaplan* judgment.

[43] After Russia with most applications. This ranking remained the same until the end of 2013.

[44] Ümmühan Kaplan vs. Turkey (no. 24240/07, 20 March, 2012).

[45] Law no. 6384, adopted on 9 January 2013 and entered into force on 19 January, 2013.

[46] Article 2(1) of the Law No. 6384 reads as follows: "This Law includes the applications lodged with the European Court of Human Rights with the allegations that:

16.3.4.2 Scope

Under Law No. 6384 (ECtHRLaw), the Human Rights Compensation Commission ("Commission") was set up and started working in February 2013. The applicants are able to make a request to the Commission within 6 months after the entry date of the law. Those who fail to make the request within this period are able to make a request to the Commission within 1 month after the inadmissibility decision of the ECtHR, relying merely on the grounds that domestic remedies have not been exhausted, is communicated to them. The law has been implemented on the applications registered as of 23 September, 2012, the entry date of the individual complaint mechanism before the Constitutional Court (ConstCt), before the ECtHR.

Recently, with the decision of the Council of Ministers on 10 February, 2014,[47] the scope of the applications has been extended. Accordingly, the applicants who lodged their cases before the ECtHR on the basis of claims concerning the loss of value in expropriation payments due to: lengthy proceedings and high inflation rate, the restrictions on the right to defence for disciplinary sanctions applied to prisoners, and the inability of prisoners to communicate in a language other than Turkish are able to avail themselves of this special compensation regime under ECtHRLaw.

16.3.4.3 Effectiveness of the ECtHRLaw

The recent ECtHRLaw has also been confirmed by the ECtHR as an effective domestic remedy to be exhausted. In *Müdür Turgut and Others vs. Turkey*,[48] the ECtHR noted that the instant case had been lodged with it before ECtHRLaw had come into force, at a time when the applicants had not had an effective remedy under Turkish law by which to complain about the length of the proceedings in question. The ECtHR, however, reiterated that the remedy introduced by ECtHRLaw was a direct and practical consequence of the pilot-judgment procedure applied in Ümmühan Kaplan judgment, which was designed to deal with repetitive length-of-proceedings cases brought against Turkey, and that the domestic authorities had finally instituted a domestic remedy.

With regard to the nature of ECtHRLaw and to the context in which it had been enacted, the ECtHR concluded that there were grounds for departing from the general principle that the requirement of exhaustion of domestic remedies had to be assessed with reference to the time when the application was lodged. The ECtHR accordingly held that it was not in a position to state, at this stage of the proceedings, that the remedy instituted was not effective and accessible. Thus it concluded

(a) the investigations and prosecutions within the scope of the criminal law and the proceedings within the scope of the private and administrative law have not been concluded within a reasonable time,

(b) the Court's judgments have been executed late or unsatisfactorily, or have not been executed."

[47] Entered into force on 16 March, 2014.

[48] Müdür Turgut and Others vs. Turkey (inadmissibility decision, no. 4860/09, 11 April, 2013).

that the applicants should apply to the Compensation Board set up by ECtHRLaw in so far as this was an accessible remedy capable of offering them a reasonable chance of redress for their complaints. It followed that the complaint had to be rejected for failure to exhaust domestic remedies.

Despite this conclusion, the ECtHR stated that this decision did not in any way prejudice a possible re-examination of the issue of the effectiveness and reality of the remedy introduced by that Law in the light of decisions given by the Compensation Board and the domestic courts. In parallel to this conclusion, the decisions of the Compensation Board have been a subject matter before the ECtHR as well. In the recent inadmissibility decision of *Ahmet Erol vs. Turkey*,[49] the applicant complained that the amount of compensation awarded by the Board was inadequate. The ECtHR, however, held that the applicant should have introduced an individual complaint before the Turkish ConstCt after having appealed before the Regional Administrative Court against this decision. It thus rejected the application for the non-exhaustion of domestic remedies.

By implementing the ECtHRLaw, the settlement of some applications lodged with the ECtHR are secured by means of paying compensation to the applicants. As of 1 April, 2014, 5,390 applications have been made before the Compensation Board.[50] Furthermore, as it stands, ECtHRLaw seems to have been an effective tool in decreasing the number of applications before the ECtHR. It almost reduced[51] by around 4,000 the number of pending cases against Turkey at the ECtHR following its adoption.

16.4 Conclusion

It is observed that special compensation regimes introduced into Turkish law have generally been adopted following the judgments of the ECtHR that reveal widespread systemic and structural problems arising out of the malfunctioning of the Turkish justice system as well as the state of Turkish legislation. In this respect, these regimes, particularly under CCP and ECtHR law, can be regarded as general measures taken at national level in order to resolve the systemic issue and thus fully execute the respective ECtHR judgments.

[49] Ahmet Erol vs. Turkey (no. 73290/13, 6 May, 2014).

[50] Out of these 5,390 applications, 3,086 of them were accepted and 653 of them were rejected. 1,653 applications were pending at the time of given data.

[51] Since 2013, there has been a significant decrease in number of pending applications against Turkey. As of September, 2014, Turkey stands as the fifth country-following Russia, Italy, Ukraine and Serbia with over 10,451 pending applications, whereas the number of applications was over 20,000 by the end of 2012. The Court dealt with 9,198 applications concerning Turkey in 2013, of which 9,008 were declared inadmissible or struck out. This drop is a direct result of individual complaint mechanism (Law no. 6216-CCL) as well as the settlement of some applications lodged with the ECtHR by means of paying compensation (Law no. 6384-ECtHRLaw) introduced in the Turkish legal system.

Developing a collective approach to systemic human rights problems and establishing effective domestic tools to stop similar violations recurring are certainly to be noted as progressive developments in Turkey. Observing the implementation thus far, special compensation regimes have also reduced, or almost fully absorbed, the number of applications registered on the ECtHR's list of cases against Turkey for particular human rights violations. In this sense, some human rights violations are currently being resolved more quickly for more people in Turkey and thus, these regimes bring better justice. However, it still remains answered whether or not these fast track remedies deny individual justice as they signify a deviation predicated primarily on individual justice to a more collective strategy, particularly after the expansion of the scope of ECtHRLaw. Therefore, Turkey has to focus further on the impact of special compensation regimes in order to ensure that "better justice" is indeed delivered to people whose human rights were violated. Additionally, it must be noted that the fully functioning individual complaint mechanism before the Turkish ConstCt is likely to help Turkey a great deal in providing effective remedies for the violations of human rights.

References

Buyse, Antoine. 2008. Lost and regained? Restitution as a remedy for human rights violations in the context of international law. *Heidelberg Journal of International Law* (Zeitschrift für ausländisches öffentliches Recht und Völkerrecht) 68: 129–153.

Güran, Sait. 2005. Administrative law. In *Introduction to Turkish law*, 5th ed, ed. Tuğrul Ansay and Don Wallace, 47–84. The Hague: Kluwer Law International.

Human Rights Watch. 2006 (1). Unjust, restrictive and inconsistent: The impact of Turkey's compensation law with respect to internally displaced people. See http://www.hrw.org/legacy/backgrounder/eca/turkey1206/turkey1206web.pdf. Accessed 12 Feb 2015.

Kurban, Dilek. 2012. Reparations and displacement in Turkey: Lessons learned from the compensation law. Case studies on transitional justice and displacement. International Centre for Transitional Justice (ICTJ)/Brookings-LSE Project on Internal Displacement. See https://www.ictj.org/sites/default/files/ICTJ-Brookings-Displacement-Reparations-Turkey-CaseStudy-2012-English.pdf. Accessed 12 Feb 2015.

Stephens, Beth. 2002. Translating *Filártiga*: A comparative and international law analysis of domestic remedies for international human rights violations. *Yale Journal of International Law* 27(1): 1–57.

Chapter 17
Damages for Violations of Human Rights Law in the United Kingdom

Merris Amos

17.1 Introduction

The Human Rights Act 2000 (HRA), giving further effect to the European Convention on Human Rights (ECHR) in United Kingdom (UK) national law, came into force on 2 October 2000. Prior to this the common law, primary and secondary legislation and European Union law provided legal protection for human rights. International human rights law, including the ECHR, whilst not directly enforceable in national law given the UK is a dualist system, provided an important reference point for Parliament, the courts and government. The UK has no codified constitution, therefore, like Ireland and Canada, a special stand-alone regime for human rights protection is provided by the HRA. This is in contrast to the majority of legal systems considered in this book which lack a specific human rights law granting a direct claim for compensation or an explicit constitutional guarantee to have the damage redressed.

The HRA was designed to essentially 'mirror' the treatment a claimant would receive before the European Court of Human Rights (ECtHR), its purpose 'to make more directly accessible the rights which the British people already enjoy under the Convention' 'in short' to 'bring those rights home'.[1] UK courts have the power to determine whether or not the activities of public authorities are compatible with the 'Convention rights' which are the articles of the ECHR to which the HRA gives further effect in national law.[2] The exact wording of each Convention right is utilised in the HRA and UK courts are also instructed by s.2 of the HRA to 'take into

[1] *Rights Brought Home: The Human Rights Bill* (Cm 3782) (London, TSO, 1997) at [1.19].

[2] Articles 2–12 and 14 of the ECHR, Arts. 1–3 of Protocol No.1 to the ECHR, and Arts. 1 and 2 of Protocol No.6 to the ECHR (as read with Arts. 16–18 of the ECHR).

M. Amos (✉)
Department of Law, Queen Mary University of London, London, UK
e-mail: m.e.amos@qmul.ac.uk

E. Bagińska (ed.), *Damages for Violations of Human Rights*,
Ius Comparatum - Global Studies in Comparative Law 9,
DOI 10.1007/978-3-319-18950-5_17

account' relevant ECtHR jurisprudence when determining a Convention rights issue. There is no other comprehensive legal protection for human rights in the UK such as a bill of rights, so almost all human rights claims at the national level come via the HRA route.

Where a court finds that a public authority[3] has acted in a way which is incompatible with a Convention right contrary to section 6 of the HRA, section 8(1) provides that the court may grant such relief or remedy, or make such order, within its powers as it considers just and appropriate. As with other key features of the HRA, the remedies available closely mirror those which would be available to a claimant before the ECtHR under Article 41 of the ECHR, which enables the Court to award 'just satisfaction to the injured party' for Convention violations.[4] It has been held that the approach of the UK courts should be no less liberal than that applied at the ECtHR or one of the purposes of the HRA will be defeated and claimants will still be put to the expense of having to go to Strasbourg to obtain just satisfaction.[5]

Where an infringement of a person's human rights has occurred, the concern will usually be to bring the infringement to an end. Any question of compensation is often considered to be of secondary importance.[6] The remedies most frequently sought for an act incompatible with Convention rights are the 'orders which are the descendants of the historic prerogative orders or declaratory judgments'. These enable the court to order a public body to refrain from or to take action, or to quash an offending decision. 'Declaratory judgments usually resolve disputes as to what is the correct answer in law to a dispute.'[7] However, whilst in practice this is the position, and damages are rarely awarded, the focus of section 8, and HRA jurisprudence in this area, is primarily on the award of damages for a breach of Convention rights. It is not actually stated in section 8 of the HRA that a court may award damages for a breach of Convention rights although damages are defined in section 8(5) as 'damages for the unlawful act of a public authority'[8] and much of section 8 concerns limits on the award of damages indicating that such an award is possible. There is also considerable extra statutory evidence that this is the position. For example, the Lord Chancellor commented during the Parliamentary debates on the Human Rights Bill that the aim was that people should receive damages equivalent to what they would have obtained had they taken their case to the ECtHR.[9]

[3] Included within the definition of public authority in section 6 are 'any person certain of whose functions are functions of a public nature'. Therefore, private bodies, exercising public functions, perhaps pursuant to a contracting out arrangement, are obliged to act compatibly with Convention rights in the exercise of these functions.

[4] 'If the Court finds that there has been a violation of the Convention or the protocols thereto, and if the internal law of the High Contracting party concerned allows only partial reparation to be made, the Court shall, if necessary, afford just satisfaction to the injured party.'

[5] *Anufrijeva v Southwark LBC* [2003] EWCA Civ 1406, [2004] QB 1124, [57].

[6] *Anufrijeva*, ibid, at [53].

[7] *Anufrijeva*, ibid, at [53].

[8] 'Unlawful act' is defined in section 8(5) as 'unlawful under section 6(1)'.

[9] Lord Chancellor, HL Deb, Vol 582, col 1232 (3.11.1997).

Furthermore, since the HRA has been in force although small in number, some damages awards have been made by courts to victims under section 8.[10]

There is no right to damages for a violation of a Convention right and the award is entirely discretionary.[11] A number of preconditions and principles relate to such awards making it clear, in contrast to most of the other jurisdictions considered in this book, that courts contemplating an award must ignore other rules of civil liability. These preconditions and principles are discussed and assessed in the following paragraphs.

17.2 The Unlawful Act of a Public Authority

First, in order for a damages award to be made, a public authority must have acted unlawfully within the meaning of section 6 of the HRA. Section 6(1) provides that it is unlawful for public authorities to act incompatibly with a Convention right. This appears straightforward – a public authority, such as the police, breaches a Convention right and damages can be a remedy. However, the peculiarities of UK constitutional arrangements make matters a little more complex. The HRA has been carefully drafted to preserve the sovereignty of Parliament.

> Parliamentary sovereignty means that Parliament can, if it chooses, legislate contrary to fundamental principles of human rights. The Human Rights Act 1998 will not detract from this power. The constraints upon its exercise by Parliament are ultimately political, not legal.[12]

Although section 6(1) provides that it is unlawful to act in a way which is incompatible with a Convention right, section 6(2) provides that section 6(1) does not apply to an act if: (a) as a result of one or more provisions of primary legislation the authority could not have acted differently; or (b) in the case of one or more provisions of, or made under, primary legislation which cannot be read or given effect in a way which is compatible with the Convention rights, the authority was acting so as to give effect to or enforce those provisions.[13] Therefore, where the incompatibly with a Convention right is contained in primary legislation, there is no unlawful act within the meaning of section 6 of the HRA and damages cannot therefore be awarded under section 8. But rather than leaving the victims of such unlawful acts without a remedy, the HRA provides in section 4 that a court can make a declaration of incompatibility in relation to the primary legislation. Once a provision of legislation has been declared to be incompatible, a minister, if he or she considers that there are compelling reasons, may by order make such amendments to the legislation

---

[10] See, for example, *R. (Bernard) v London Borough of Enfield* [2002] EWHC (Admin) 2282.

[11] *Anufrijeva*, op cit, at [55].

[12] *R. v Secretary of State for the Home Department, ex p Simms* [2000] 2 AC 115 per Lord Hoffmann.

[13] This makes provision for section 3 of the HRA allowing courts to adopt a Convention rights compatible interpretation 'so far as it is possible to do so'.

as considered necessary to remove the incompatibility.[14] However, the court has no power under the HRA to also make an award of damages to the victim. A victim of a breach of Convention rights contained in primary legislation can only hope that he or she receives an *ex gratia* payment from the public authority, compensating for any loss or damage suffered. Should this not be forthcoming, a victim can bring proceedings relating to the breach in the ECtHR with the possibility of receiving a damages award from that court. This was the position of the claimants in *A v Secretary of State*[15] who were eventually released from over 3 years of prison detention after a change in the law following from a declaration of incompatibility made by the House of Lords. They received no compensation from UK public authorities but the ECtHR eventually awarded them their costs and expenses from bringing the proceedings to the ECtHR, and damages ranging from €1,700 to €3,900 each.[16]

17.3 Court Must Have Power to Award Damages

Secondly, damages may be awarded only by a court which has the power to award damages, or to order the payment of compensation in civil proceedings.[17] It is therefore not possible for a criminal court to award damages. Victims who consider that their Convention rights have been breached must pursue their claim for damages through the civil courts where this type of issue is normally dealt with and the court is 'accustomed to determining whether it is necessary and appropriate to award damages and what the proper amount should be.'[18] Damages may be awarded by the High Court on an application for judicial review[19] and this is the most common way those seeking damages for a violation of Convention rights will recover.

17.4 Just Satisfaction

Once the two forgoing procedural requirements are satisfied – there has been an unlawful act of a public authority within the meaning of section 6 and the court has the power to award damages, the focus of section 8 shifts to determining the level of the award to be made. Section 8(3) of the HRA provides that no award of damages is to be made unless, taking account of all the circumstances of the case, including: (a) any other relief or remedy granted, or order made, in relation to the act in

[14] Section 10(2) HRA.

[15] [2004] UKHL 56, [2005] 2 AC 68.

[16] *A v United Kingdom*, Grand Chamber, ECtHR, 19.2.2009.

[17] Section 8(2) HRA.

[18] Lord Chancellor, HL Deb, Vol 583, cols 854–55 (24.11.1997).

[19] Supreme Court Act 1981 section 31(4).

question (by that or any other court) and (b) the consequences of any decision (of that or any other court) in respect of that act, the court is satisfied that the award is necessary to afford just satisfaction to the person in whose favour it is made.

It has been observed that the phrase 'just satisfaction' is distinct from the approach in common law where a claimant is entitled, so far as money can achieve this, to be restored to the position he or she would have been in had the violation of Convention rights not occurred.[20] 'Just satisfaction' is an ECHR concept and appears in the wording of Art. 41 of the ECHR. However, rather than leaving matters completely to chance, as noted above two important considerations for a court contemplating an award of damages are explicitly set out in section 8: any other relief or remedy granted; and the consequences of any decision.

It is likely that when a violation of Convention rights occurs, the victim will have a number of alternative remedies available to him or her including damages for a private law wrong such as breach of contract or negligence, or damages for breach of a different law. Section 8(3)(a) is designed to prevent such victims being able to recover twice, or more, for the same injury. It is unlikely that any further compensation will be required under the HRA if the victim has already received just satisfaction via an alternative route. For example, in its judgment in *Dobson*[21] the Court of Appeal considered whether just satisfaction demanded that compensation be awarded to a claimant under the HRA where common law damages had already been awarded to his parents, the property owners, with whom he lived. The claim was that he was affected by odours and mosquitoes caused by the negligent operation of a sewage treatment works. The Court did not reach a final conclusion on the issue, noting that it would depend on the trial judge's findings in relation to his pare nts. At trial it was concluded that an award of damages under the HRA was not necessary to afford just satisfaction to the claimant as he had no proprietary interest in the property and remedies had already been afforded to his parents.[22]

Section 8(3)(b) also obliges the court to take into account the consequences of any decision (of that or any other court) in respect of that act. It is not stated in the HRA what is meant by 'consequences' although it is likely that what the drafters had in mind is that when contemplating an award of damages, the court should take into account that it might be opening the floodgates to a number of similar claims. To make an award of damages in respect of that act may mean that hundreds, even thousands, of potential applicants will have a similar claim, representing a considerable strain on the public purse.[23] It is also possible that 'consequences' might include the impact on public authorities generally and society as a whole. For example, in its judgment in *Bernard* the Administrative Court stated as follows:

---

[20] *Anufrijeva*, op cit, at [55].

[21] *Dobson v Thames Water Utilities* [2009] EWCA Civ 28, [2009] 3 All ER 319.

[22] *Dobson v Thames Water Utilities* [2011] EWHC 3253 (TCC).

[23] Floodgates arguments have their roots in the law of tort. See, for example, *X v Bedfordshire County Council* [1995] 2 AC 633.

> [On] a simplistic view of local authority accounting, the larger the award to the claimants under section 8 the less there will be for the London Borough of Enfield to spend on providing social service facilities for the many others in need of care within the borough.[24]

However, it was also noted that it was very much in the interests of society as a whole that public authorities should be encouraged to respect human rights. In the view of the court, a 'restrained' or 'moderate' approach to quantum would provide the necessary degree of encouragement whilst not unduly depleting the funds available to the defendant for the benefit of others in need of care.[25]

17.5 Other Circumstances

Whilst the two circumstances discussed above must be taken into account by a court contemplating an award of damages under section 8 of the HRA, it is open to a court to also take into account other circumstances. Two circumstances of particular relevance have arisen from the jurisprudence to date. First, it is important for the court to take into account the any action the respondent public authority has taken following the finding of a violation of a Convention right. For example, a government minister may rescind a deportation order following a judgment that it is in breach of Art. 3 of the ECHR or allow a public assembly to proceed following a decision that to ban it would be in violation of Art. 11 of the ECHR. Outcomes such as these suggest the victim has already been afforded just satisfaction and in effect, the violations of the Convention rights have been corrected. It may also reduce the amount of damages awarded if the public authority has taken action once the violation is drawn to its attention. In its judgment in *Bernard* the Administrative Court confirmed that it may reduce the level of damages awarded if the public authority acknowledged that something had gone wrong and provided an explanation, an apology and an assurance that steps had been taken to ensure the same mistake would not happen again.[26]

Second, it may be important for the court to take into account the question of fault. It can make a difference to the award of damages if the breach was intentional, negligent or innocent. In its judgment in *Wainwright*[27] the House of Lords stated that although Art. 8 guaranteed a right of privacy, a remedy in damages for breach of this right was not guaranteed irrespective of whether the defendant acted intentionally, negligently or accidentally:

> Article 8 may justify a monetary remedy for an intentional invasion of privacy by a public authority, even if no damage is suffered other than distress for which damages are not ordinarily recoverable. It does not follow that a merely negligent act should, contrary to

[24] *Bernard*, op cit, at [58].

[25] *Bernard*, op cit, at [59].

[26] *Bernard*, op cit, at [39]. See also *W v Westminster City Council* [2005] EWHC (QB) 102.

[27] *Wainwright v Home Office* [2003] UKHL 53, [2004] 2 AC 406.

general principle, give rise to a claim in damages for distress because it affects privacy rather than some other interest like bodily safety.[28]

In addition to these two circumstances, there are the overarching requirements. As already noted, section 8(1) provides that remedies for breaches of Convention rights must be 'just and appropriate'. Therefore, an award of damages must also be just and appropriate in the circumstances. There has been little consideration of the meaning of 'just and appropriate' in the jurisprudence to date. The notion that a remedy must be 'just' implies that it is fair to all who are affected by it, including persons other than the person whose right was violated.[29] In its judgment in *Anufrijeva*[30] the Court of Appeal held that in considering whether to award compensation, and, if so how much, there was a balance to be drawn between the interests of the victim and those of the public as a whole.[31]

'Appropriate' remedies are those which effectively address the grievance brought about by the violation from the standpoint of the person whose Convention right was violated.[32] For example, in its judgment in *M*[33] the Administrative Court determined that the appropriate remedy was the return of a family to the UK so as to restore them to the position they would have been in but for their unlawful deportation in breach of their Convention rights. An order was made, directed at the Secretary of State, for their return.

The final overarching requirement is effectiveness. However, Art. 13[34] of the ECHR, the right to an effective remedy, is not one of the Convention rights given further effect in national law by the HRA. Nevertheless, in the debates as the Human Rights Bill progressed through Parliament, the Lord Chancellor stated that courts may have regard to Art. 13 when interpreting and applying section 8.[35] In the case law it has also been suggested that despite this omission, and the absence of any reference to effectiveness in section 8 of the HRA, any remedy awarded for an act incompatible with Convention rights should also be effective. Lord Rodger has held as follows:

> Since the aim of the Act is that the domestic courts, rather than the Strasbourg court, should be able to remedy violations of the Convention, it can readily be inferred that a remedy will be just and appropriate if it constitutes the kind of effective remedy required by art 13 of the Convention.[36]

---

[28] Per Lord Hoffmann at [51].

[29] *Saskatchewan Human Rights Commission v Kodellas* (1989) 60 DLR (4th) 143 per Bayda CJS at 162. This concerned the interpretation of the Canadian Charter of Rights and Freedoms which empowers the court to award appropriate and just remedies for the infringement of rights.

[30] Op cit.

[31] See also *Bernard*, op cit, [58]–[59].

[32] *Attorney General's Reference No.2 of 2001* [2003] UKHL 68, [2004] 2 AC 72 per Lord Bingham at [24].

[33] *R. (M) v Secretary of State for the Home Department* [2011] EWHC 3667 (Admin).

[34] 'Everyone whose rights and freedoms as set forth in this Convention are violated shall have an effective remedy before a national authority notwithstanding that the violation has been committed by persons acting in an official capacity.'

[35] HL Deb, Vol 583, col 477 (18.11.1997).

[36] *Attorney General's Reference No.2 of 2001*, op cit, at [175].

An effective remedy should adequately compensate those who have suffered damage as a result of the act of a public authority incompatible with Convention rights, emphasise the importance of Convention rights and deter future violations. However, there has been little evidence of the impact of these principles in the case law. In those instances where Art. 13 has been referred to by the courts, it has been to lament its non-inclusion as one of the Convention rights given further effect by the HRA.[37] A part of the HRA vulnerable to challenge under Art. 13 would be the declaration of incompatibility under section 4. As noted above, there is no obligation to pay damages to a person where the breach of Convention rights is contained in primary legislation and the court can only make a declaration of incompatibility. The argument was actually made before the ECtHR in *A v UK*[38] that the remedies available to those detained under primary legislation were not compatible with Art. 13. But this was rejected, the Grand Chamber of the ECtHR finding that Art. 13 did not guarantee a remedy allowing a challenge to primary legislation before a national authority on the ground of being contrary to Convention rights.

17.6 The Principles Applied by the European Court of Human Rights

Once the domestic procedural and substantive requirements relating to an award of damages under section 8, as discussed above, are taken into account by a court contemplating an award, section 8 directs that the court's attention must then turn to the principles applied by the ECtHR. Section 8(4) provides that in determining whether to award damages, or the amount of the award, the court must take into account the principles applied by the ECtHR in relation to the award of compensation under Art. 41 of the ECHR. Whilst there is nothing in the HRA or the jurisprudence of the ECtHR to prevent national courts from awarding greater, or lesser, damages than the ECtHR,[39] this has not been the approach taken and when making awards, any relevant guidance from the ECtHR has been closely followed. However, the observation is often made that the assistance to be derived from the ECtHR jurisprudence in this area is limited. In his judgment in *Faulkner*[40] Lord Reed pointed out the differences between an international court and national court's assessment of damages for a violation of Convention rights. First, the ECtHR did not often articulate clear principles explaining when damages should be awarded or how they should be measured. Second, the ECtHR did not normally undertake detailed fact finding in relation to damages in the way in which a national court of first instance would do. National courts may be able to resolve disputed issues of

[37] See, e.g.: *R v Lambert* [2001] UKHL 37, [2002] 2 AC 545 and *Re S* [2002] UKHL 10, [2002] 2 WLR 720.

[38] ECtHR Grand Chamber, 19 February 2009.

[39] *HM Advocate v R* [2002] UKPC D3, [2004] 1 AC 462 at [58].

[40] *R. (Faulkner) v Secretary of State for Justice* [2013] UKSC 23, [2013] 2 WLR 1157 at [34]–[38].

fact in ways in which the ECtHR would not, and hence decisions in relation to the award of damages under section 8 may have a different factual basis from that which the ECtHR would have adopted. Third, the awards made by the ECtHR reflect the relative value of money in the contracting states. Awards made to applicants from countries where the cost of living was relatively low tended to be low by comparison with awards to applicants from countries where the cost of living is much higher. In Lord Reed's view, the focus of UK national courts should be on awards made to applicants from the UK or from other countries with a comparable cost of living.

The ECtHR itself has held that its role under Art. 41 is not to function akin to a national court determining a tort claim by apportioning fault and compensatory damages between civil parties. In its judgment in *Al-Skeini v UK*[41] the Grand Chamber confirmed that its guiding principle is equity 'which above all involves flexibility and an objective consideration of what is just, fair and reasonable in all the circumstances of the case including not only the position of the applicant but overall context.'[42]

Despite the problems with relying on ECtHR Art. 41 jurisprudence, Lord Reed observed that it was possible, over time, for the remedy to become 'naturalised':

> . . over time, and as the practice of the European court comes increasingly to be absorbed into our own case law through judgments such as this, the remedy should become naturalised. While it will remain necessary to ensure that our law does not fall short of Convention standards, we should have confidence in our own case law under section 8 once it has developed sufficiently, and not be perpetually looking to the case law of an international court as our primary source.[43]

In the meantime, national courts have extracted, and applied, the broad principles utilised by the ECtHR. Certain principles are clear. The ECtHR treats its power as purely discretionary and the amount of compensation awarded, or whether compensation is awarded at all, depends very much on the circumstances of the case. 'Just satisfaction' can only take the form of compensation[44] and the Court will not award damages not based strictly on compensation such as nominal damages or exemplary damages. The ECtHR's awards for compensation are generally divided into an award for pecuniary damage and an award for non-pecuniary damage although where it is difficult to make a distinction, the Court will sometimes award an aggregate sum.[45] Where a violation of the Convention is found, the ECtHR may make an award for both types of damage, only one or neither depending on its judgment of what is

---

[41] 7 July 2011.

[42] See also the judgment of the Grand Chamber in *Al-Jedda v United Kingdom*, 7 July 2011.

[43] At [29]. See also the judgment of Lord Dyson in *Rabone v Pennine Care NHS Foundation Trust* [2012] UKSC 2, [2012] 2 AC 72 at [84].

[44] See, for example, *Vacher v France* (1997) 24 EHRR 482. The ECtHR may also award costs, expenses and interest.

[45] See, for example, *Allenet de Ribemont v France* (1996) 22 EHRR 582 and *Svinarenko v Russia,* 17.7.2014. In *O'Keeffe v Ireland,* 28.1.2014 the Grand Chamber awarded a global figure of €30,000 for pecuniary and non-pecuniary damage resulting from violations of Arts. 3 and 13. It had been found that the system of primary education failed to protect the applicant from sexual abuse by a teacher. She had already been awarded €305,104 at the national level.

'necessary' and what is 'just satisfaction'. Different considerations apply to the assessment of both types of damage and these are considered below.

It is also important to note that the ECtHR can conclude that a finding of violation is, in itself, just satisfaction for the violation of Convention rights found. In its judgment in *Greenfield*[46] the House of Lords noted that this reflected the fact that the focus of the ECHR is on the protection of human rights and not the award of compensation. It observed that in exercising its former jurisdiction under the original Art. 32 of the Convention, the Committee of Ministers did not, before 1987, award compensation at all, even when a violation was found.[47] However, from a survey of recent decisions of the Grand Chamber, the non-award of compensation for a breach of Convention rights is becoming far rarer and will often only occur where no damages are sought[48] or where the applicant is a serving prisoner.[49]

17.6.1 Pecuniary Damage

In assessing compensation for pecuniary damage, the ECtHR endeavours to put the applicant as far as possible in a situation equivalent to the one in which he or she would have been in had there not been a breach of the ECHR.[50] The principle of *restitutio in intergrum* is also familiar to UK lawyers as the principle applied when assessing damages in tort law.[51] There must be a causal link between the violation complained of and the alleged pecuniary damage.[52] In applications concerning a violation of Art. 6, often the ECtHR has refused to speculate on what the outcome of the proceedings would have been had there been compliance with Art. 6. For example, in *Saunders v UK*[53] the Court would not speculate on whether the outcome of the trial would have been different had the prosecution not used the contested transcripts. The ECtHR found no causal connection between the losses claimed by the applicant and the finding of violation. However, in *Sabeh El Leil v France,*[54] finding a violation of Art. 6 in that the applicant had been denied access to court, the Grand Chamber held that whilst it would not speculate on the outcome of the trial if

[46] *R v Secretary of State for the Home Department, ex p Greenfield* [2005] UKHL 14, [2005] 1 WLR 673 at [9].

[47] See also the observations made by the Court of Appeal in *Anufrijeva*, op cit at [53].

[48] See, for example, *X v Latvia*, Grand Chamber, 26.11.2013 and *Neulinger and Shuruk v Switzerland*, Grand Chamber, 6.7.2010.

[49] See, for example, *Maktouf v Bosnia and Herzegovina*, Grand Chamber, 18.7.2013 and *Vinter v UK*, Grand Chamber, 9.7.2013. Damages were awarded to a serving prisoner in *Idalov v Russia*, 22.5.2012.

[50] *Papamichalopoulos v Greece* (1996) 21 EHRR 439 at [38]. See also *Anufrijeva*, op cit, at [59].

[51] *Livingstone v Rawyards Coal Co* (1880) 5 App Cas 25 per Lord Blackburn at 39.

[52] *Vacher v France*, op cit.

[53] (1997) 23 EHRR 313 at [86].

[54] 29.6.2011.

he had had the benefit of Art. 6, it was not unreasonable to regard the applicant as having incurred a real loss of pecuniary opportunities. In addition, it was found that he had sustained non pecuniary damage and €60,000 was awarded for all heads of damage combined.[55]

Claims of pecuniary damage must be supported by evidence and the burden is on the claimant to prove his or her damage.[56] If there is no evidence, but it is clear that pecuniary loss has occurred, the ECtHR makes a speculative assessment, assessing it as a whole and on an equitable basis.[57] There is no limit on the amount that may be awarded for this type of damage, provided the causal link is established. Applications concerning the expropriation of land in violation of Art. 1 Protocol 1 often result in large pecuniary damages awards by the ECtHR.[58] This is also reflected at the national level. Recently in its judgment in *Infinis*[59] the Court of Appeal confirmed the decision of the High Court to award £94,393 for a violation of Art. 1 of Protocol No.1. The Gas and Electricity Markets Authority had unlawfully refused accreditation to the claimant company denying it a pecuniary benefit to which it was statutorily entitled.[60]

Awards have been made for a reduction in the value of property,[61] loss of past and future earnings,[62] and pecuniary damage suffered through loss of opportunities. For example, in *Weeks v UK*[63] the ECtHR awarded the applicant compensation for the loss of opportunities he suffered by reason of the absence of proceedings to challenge the lawfulness of his re-detention in violation of Art. 5(4). The House of Lords has held that in such instances, the key is to establish a sufficient causal connection:

> [T]he Court will award monetary compensation under Art.41 only where it is satisfied that the loss or damage complained of was actually caused by the violation it has found, and it has repeatedly stressed that it will not speculate on what the outcome of the proceedings would have been but for the violation, it has on occasion been willing in appropriate cases to make an award if of the opinion the applicant has been deprived of a real chance of a better outcome.[64]

---

[55] See also *Cudak v Lithuania*, Grand Chamber, 23.3.2010 and *Ramanauskas v Lithuania*, Grand Chamber, 5.2.2008.

[56] *Incal v Turkey*, 9.6.1998.

[57] *Selçuk and Asker v Turkey*, 24.4.1998. See also *Kurić v Slovenia*, Grand Chamber, 12.3.2014.

[58] See, for example, *Vistiņš v Latvia*, Grand Chamber, 253.2014 where pecuniary damages of €339,392 and €871,271 were awarded.

[59] *Gas & Electricity Markets Authority v Infinis plc* [2013] EWCA Civ 70.

[60] See further Tabori (2013)194.

[61] *Pine Valley Developments v Ireland* (1993) 16 EHRR 379.

[62] *Young, James and Webster v UK* (1982) 4 EHRR 38.

[63] (1988) 10 EHRR 293.

[64] *Greenfield*, op cit, at [64]. See also *Guiso-Gallisay v Italy*, ECtHR, 22.12.2009 where damages of €45,000 were awarded for the loss of opportunity occasioned by land being unavailable for a period in violation of Art. 1 Protocol No 1.

17.6.2 Non-pecuniary Damage

In many instances the ECtHR has found that an applicant has suffered non-pecuniary damage (also referred to as moral damage) as a result of a breach of the Convention where the mere finding of a violation does not constitute sufficient reparation. The ECtHR may make an award for this type of damage even where it has not made an award for pecuniary damage. It has held that the impact of the violation may be regarded as being of a nature and degree as to have 'impaired so significantly the moral well-being of the applicant as to require something further' and that non pecuniary awards 'give recognition to the fact that moral damage occurred as a result of breach fundamental human rights'. Such awards 'reflect in broadest terms the severity of the damage'.[65]

The applicant must also show a causal link between the violation and the non-pecuniary damage suffered.[66] The ECtHR has granted compensation for many types of non-pecuniary damage including distress and anxiety,[67] loss of reputation,[68] bouts of depression,[69] enduring psychological harm,[70] feelings of helplessness and frustration[71] and feelings of injustice.[72] The fact that a claimant is particularly vulnerable may also be taken into account. In *KB*[73] the Administrative Court took into account that the claimants had been detained as a result of their mental health and were therefore in a vulnerable condition. It concluded that damages may be awarded to such persons under Art. 5(5) although in analogous circumstances no award would be made to a healthy person.

Such damage may have been caused by ECHR violations such as inordinately lengthy proceedings,[74] the deprivation of property for a long period of time,[75] failure to provide a fair hearing,[76] ill treatment whilst in custody,[77] and deprivation of liberty.[78] The ECtHR assesses compensation on an 'equitable basis' and tends to be conservative with awards ranging from €5,000 to €15,000. However, on occasion it does make large awards for this type of damage. For example, in *Aydin v Turkey*[79]

[65] *Varnava v Turkey*, 18.9.2009.
[66] *Halford v UK* (1997) 24 EHRR 523
[67] *Incal v Turkey*, 9.6.1998.
[68] *Doustaly v France*, 23.4.1998.
[69] *Estima Jorge v Portugal*, 21.4.1998.
[70] *Aydin v Turkey* (1998) 25 EHRR 251.
[71] *Papamichalopoulos v Greece* (1996) 21 EHRR 439; *Ališić v Bosnia*, 16.7.2014.
[72] *Keegan v Ireland* (1994) 18 EHRR 342.
[73] *R. (KB) v Mental Health Review Tribunal* [2003] EWHC (Admin) 193, [2004] QB 936 at [72].
[74] *Cazenave de la Roche v France*, 9.6.1998.
[75] *Vasilescu v Romania*, 22.5.1998.
[76] *Papageorgiou v Greece*, 22.10.1997.
[77] *Aydin v Turkey* (1998) 25 EHRR 251.
[78] *Tsirlis and Kouloumpas v Greece* (1998) 25 EHRR 198; *Al-Jedda v United Kingdom*, 7.7.2011.
[79] (1998) 25 EHRR 251.

the applicant was awarded £25,000 for the serious violation of Art. 3 suffered while she was in custody and the enduring psychological harm she suffered on account of being raped. In *Del Rio Prada v Spain*[80] €30,000 was awarded to a woman detained in prison in breach of Art. 5(1) and 7 for more than 5 years. In *Cyprus v Turkey*[81] the Grand Chamber awarded the Cypriot Government €30 million for non-pecuniary damage suffered by the surviving relatives of 1,456 missing persons and €60 million for the non-pecuniary damage suffered by the enclaved Greek Cypriot residents of the Karpas peninsula.[82]

When assessing non-pecuniary damage, the ECtHR takes into account principles such as mitigation and contributory fault. For example, in *Johnson v UK*[83] the ECtHR awarded £10,000 non pecuniary damages to Mr Johnson for damage sustained when he was detained in breach of Art. 5(1) although no longer suffering from mental illness. The amount would have been greater but the Court took into account the facts that the delay in his release could not be attributed entirely to the authorities:

> In the first place, some period of deferment of release was inevitable having regard to the need to locate a hostel suited to the applicant's situation . . . Secondly, the applicant's negative attitude towards his rehabilitation did not facilitate their task . . he refused to co-operate further with the authorities in finding a suitable hostel.[84]

It is possible for a company to be made an award for non-pecuniary damage suffered. For example, in *Centro Europa 7 SRL and Di Stefano v Italy*[85] the Grand Chamber found breaches of Art. 10 and Art. 1 Protocol No.1 in the failure of the state to allocate necessary frequencies for broadcasting. It held that the violations must have caused the company prolonged uncertainty in the conduct of its business and feelings of helplessness and frustration. Non pecuniary damages were awarded for 'reputation, uncertainty in decision planning, disruption in management, anxiety and inconvenience.' As the Court was unable to precisely assess pecuniary damage, an aggregate sum of €10m was awarded for all heads of damage.

17.6.3 Exemplary Damages

The ECtHR does not award aggravated or punitive (exemplary) damages even for serious violations of Convention rights.[86] Exemplary damages are also not available under the HRA.[87] However, on occasion the ECtHR has made an award for non-

[80] 21.10.2013.

[81] 12.5.2014.

[82] The awards were to be distributed by the Cypriot Government to the individual victims.

[83] 24.10.1997.

[84] At [77]. See also *R. (Richards) v Secretary of State for the Home Department* [2004] EWHC (Admin) 93.

[85] 7.6.2012.

[86] *Tekin v Turkey*, 9.6.1998.

[87] *Anufrijeva*, op cit and *KB*, op cit.

pecuniary damage 'bearing in mind the seriousness of the violation'[88] indicating that an element of aggravated awards has entered the awards of the Court although not labelled as such. For example, in *Askoy v Turkey*[89] the Court held:

> .. in view of the extremely serious violations suffered by Mr Zeki Askoy, and the anxiety and distress that these undoubtedly caused to his father, who has continued with the application after his son's death .. the Court has decided to award the full amounts of compensation sought as regards pecuniary and non-pecuniary damage.

Similarly in *El-Masri v FYR Macedonia,*[90] regard being had to the extreme seriousness of the violations, the Grand Chamber awarded the applicant €60,000 in non-pecuniary damages for breaches of Art. 3, 5, 8 and 13. This practice on the part of the ECtHR has also been the subject of comment by national courts. In *KB*[91] that Administrative Court held that it was not in general the function of an award of damages to mark the court's disapproval of the conduct complained of or to reflect the importance of the right infringed. However, it noted that there was a tendency on the part of the ECtHR to award greater damages where it disapproved of the conduct of the State in question or where there had been repeated infringements. In the view of the Court, this might also be reflected in the awards of national courts:

> .. it may be that it can be accommodated by the latitude (or 'margin of discretion') available to the court in awarding damages for non-pecuniary loss, or even, in an exceptional case of deliberate or persistent infringement, by an award of aggravated damages, which in principle are compensatory rather than penal.[92]

17.6.4 The Level of Damages

The final principle applicable when award of damages is contemplated under section 8 of the HRA is the appropriate level of damages. It is important that a national court should know where to start when assessing the amount to award. In its judgment in *Greenfield*[93] the House of Lords held that the domestic scale should not be applied to damages awards under section 8 of the HRA. Three reasons were given for this approach. First, in the view of their Lordships, the HRA is not a tort statute:

> Its objects are different and broader. Even in a case where a finding of violation is not judged to afford the applicant just satisfaction, such a finding will be an important part of his remedy and an important vindication of the right he has asserted. Damages need not

[88] *Selçuk and Asker v Turkey*, 24.4.1998.

[89] (1997) 23 EHRR 553 at [113].

[90] 13.12.2012.

[91] Op cit.

[92] At [50].

[93] *R. v Secretary of State for the Home Department, ex p Greenfield* [2005] UKHL 14, [2005] 1 WLR 673.

> ordinarily be awarded to encourage high standards of compliance by member states, since they are already bound in international law to perform their duties under the Convention in good faith, although it may be different if there is felt to be a need to encourage compliance by individual officials or classes of official.[94]

Secondly, it was observed that the purpose of the HRA was not to give victims better remedies at home than they could recover in Strasbourg but to give them the same remedies without the delay and expense of resort to Strasbourg. Finally, it was noted that section 8(4) of the HRA required a domestic court to take into account the principles applied by the ECtHR under Art. 41. In the view of the House of Lords, there 'could be no clearer indication that courts in this country should look to Strasbourg and not to domestic precedents'. It concluded that the ECtHR described its awards as equitable which meant they were judged by the Court to be fair in the individual case:

> Judges in England and Wales must also make a similar judgment in the case before them. They are not inflexibly bound by Strasbourg awards in what may be different cases. But they should not aim to be significantly more or less generous that the Court might be expected to be, in a case where it was willing to make an award at all.[95]

17.7 Applying the Principles: The Award of Damages in Practice

Since the HRA came into force on 2 October 2000, in a small number of claims courts have applied the principles set out above to determine the amount, if any, which should be awarded for the breach of Convention rights found. As already noted, this is a small body of jurisprudence. Where a finding of a serious violation of Convention rights, and a substantial damages award, is expected, it is likely that the matter will be settled by the parties and the amount of compensation agreed in settlement not disclosed. Public authorities, particularly the police, are wary of courts adjudicating on HRA claims having the opportunity to further develop the principles applied when making such awards. There is a particular concern that the level of damages awarded will increase, perhaps outpacing the awards possible at common law, and encourage new victims to come forward with clear breaches of Convention rights. Furthermore, cuts to legal aid have meant that legal aid is routinely refused where HRA damages are sought.[96] Nevertheless, there are some reported cases where damages have been awarded for a breach of Convention rights and a selection of these is considered in the following paragraphs.

---

[94] At [19] per Lord Bingham.

[95] Ibid.

[96] Clayton (2005) 436.

17.7.1 Article 2 – Right to Life

In *Savage*[97] the Divisional Court found that the defendant NHS Trust was in breach of its positive obligation under Art. 2 when staff at one of its hospitals allowed a detained patient (the claimant's mother) to escape, resulting in her suicide shortly afterwards. Bearing in mind the claimant's statement that she had not brought the claim for financial reward, as well as the fact that there had been a full inquest which properly investigated the death, the court awarded £10,000 for non-pecuniary loss. The Court observed that the amount granted could never compensate the claimant for the loss of her mother and 'can only be a symbolic acknowledgment that the defendant ought properly to give her some compensation to reflect her loss.'[98] The Art. 2 duty to safeguard life was also at issue in the case of *Rabone*.[99] Here the parents of a young woman, a non-detained mental health patient, was allowed home leave by the hospital where she was receiving treatment and during this time she committed suicide. The NHS Trust admitted negligence but did not admit a breach of Art. 2. The Supreme Court found a breach of Art. 2 but the NHS Trust argued that no further damages were necessary as her parents had already settled a negligence claim for £7,500. The Supreme Court concluded that this was not adequate redress in respect of their personal losses bearing in mind the importance of compensation for non-pecuniary damage flowing from a breach of Art. 2.[100] It found that the family ties here were strong and that the parents had expressed anxiety to the hospital authorities about the dangers of home leave. It observed the fact that the risk which they authorities were warned about eventuated, 'must have made the death all the more distressing for them.'[101] It concluded that this was a bad case of a breach of Art. 2 which merited an award well above the lower range of awards. £5,000 was awarded to each parent.[102]

17.7.2 Article 3 – Freedom from Torture and Inhuman or Degrading Treatment or Punishment

In its judgment in *B*[103] the Administrative Court held that the decision by the Crown Prosecution Service to discontinue a prosecution for a serious assault was incompatible with Art. 3 of the ECHR. It held that this breach of the positive obligation under Art. 3 increased the victim's sense of vulnerability and of being beyond the

[97] *Savage v South Essex Partnership NHS Foundation Trust* [2010] EWHC 865 (QB).

[98] At [97].

[99] *Rabone v Pennine Care NHS Foundation Trust* [2012] UKSC 2, [2012] 2 AC 72.

[100] Per Lord Dyson at [60].

[101] At [87].

[102] At [89].

[103] *R. (B) v Director of Public Prosecutions* [2009] EWHC 106 (Admin), [2009] 1 WLR 2072.

protection of the law. It concluded that damages should be awarded to compensate the victim for being deprived of the opportunity of proceedings running their proper course and the damage to his self-respect. £8,000 was awarded in line with the customary 'modest' awards of the ECtHR in this area.[104] In the case of *OOO*[105] it was held that police had failed in their duty under Art. 3 to investigate credible allegations that individuals were being held in slavery or servitude. The Divisional Court awarded £5,000 to each of the claimants.

17.7.3 Article 5 – Right to Liberty

Detailed consideration was given by the Supreme Court to the award of damages for a violation of Art. 5(4) in its judgment in *Faulkner.*[106] The claim concerned prisoners who had served their tariff period, but had not been released as the Parole Board had not given its approval for release within a reasonable period. The Court held that where it was established, on the balance of probabilities, that a violation of Art. 5(4) had resulted from the detention of a prisoner beyond the date when he would otherwise have been released, damages should ordinarily be awarded as compensation for the resultant detention. The amount to be awarded was held to be a matter of judgment, reflecting the facts of the individual case and taking into account the guidance of the ECtHR and UK courts in comparable cases. Pecuniary losses caused by the prolongation of detention were to be compensated in full and it was held to be not generally appropriate to take into account the fact that the claimant was recalled to prison following release. It was decided that damages were not to be awarded for merely the loss of chance of earlier release or adjusted according to the degree of probability of release had the violation of Art. 5(4) not occurred. Where it was not established that an earlier hearing would have resulted in an earlier release, there was nevertheless a strong presumption that delay in violation of Art. 5(4) caused the prisoner to suffer feelings of frustration and anxiety. Where such feelings were presumed or shown to have been suffered, an award was to be made but, it was held, on a modest scale. It was held that no award was to be made where the delay was such that any resultant frustration and anxiety were insufficiently severe to warrant such an award, unlikely where the delay was 3 months or more. In the claims under consideration, £6,500 was awarded for a delay of 10 months and £300 for a delay of 3 months.[107]

---

[104] [70]–[71]. See also *R. (Waxman) v Crown Prosecution Service* [2012] EWHC 133 (Admin) where damages of £3,500 were awarded against the Crown Prosecution Service for a breach of Art. 8 resulting from its failure to pursue a prosecution against a man harassing her.

[105] *OOO v Commissioner of Police of the Metropolis* [2011] EWHC 1246 (QB).

[106] *R. (Faulkner) v Secretary of State for Justice* [2013] UKSC 23, [2013] 2 WLR 1157 at [13].

[107] See also *R. (Richards) v Secretary of State for the Home Department* [2004] EWHC (Admin) 93 where it was held that it was not necessary to award damages to a prisoner for a lack of independence

17.7.4 Article 6 – Fair Trial

No damages have yet been awarded by a UK court, in a reported case, for a breach of Art. 6. In *Mills*[108] the Privy Council determined that the remedy for a breach of the Art. 6 reasonable time guarantee post-conviction could include: an order to discontinue the prosecution; quashing of the conviction; reduction of the sentence; monetary compensation; or a declaration. In the present case it was determined that a 9 month reduction in the sentence was a just disposal in the spirit of Art. 6(1). Where a breach of the Art. 6 guarantee occurs prior to a conviction, it has been held that it is not appropriate to stay or dismiss the criminal proceedings unless there can no longer be a fair hearing or it would otherwise be unfair to try the defendant. It was held that the 'public interest in the final determination of criminal charges requires that such a charge should not be stayed or dismissed if any lesser remedy will be just and proportionate in all the circumstances.'[109]

In its judgment in *Greenfield*[110] the House of Lords considered a claim for an award of damages where there had been a breach of the guarantee of independence and impartiality.[111] It held that pecuniary damages would only be awarded in such instances where there was a causal connection between the violation found and the loss for which the applicant claimed to be compensated. With respect to non-pecuniary damages, it held that it would only award compensation for anxiety and frustration attributable to the Art. 6 violation, but noted that the ordinary practice of the ECtHR was to not make an award.[112] In the present case, there had been a denial of independence and impartiality and legal representation by the deputy controller of a private prison when determining whether the prisoner had committed a drugs offence. The House of Lords concluded that this was pre-eminently a case in which the finding in the claimant's favour afforded just satisfaction and an award of damages was not necessary. The claim for loss of opportunity to achieve a different result if he had been legally represented was also rejected. The House of Lords found that the adjudication was conducted with exemplary conscientiousness, patience and regard for the appellant's interests. The claim for damages for anxiety and frustration was also rejected.[113]

---

and impartiality, contrary to Art. 5(4) in release arrangements as there was no causal link between the breach of his Convention rights and his detention.

[108] *Mills v HM Advocate* [2002] UKPC D2, [2004] 1 AC 441.

[109] *Attorney General's Reference No.2 of 2001* [2003] UKHL 68, [2004] 2 AC 72 at [24] per Lord Bingham.

[110] *R v Secretary of State for the Home Department, ex p Greenfield* [2005] UKHL 14, [2005] 1 WLR 673.

[111] The claimant had also been denied legal representation in breach of Art. 6(3)(c).

[112] *Greenfield*, op cit, [11]–[17].

[113] *Greenfield*, ibid, at [26]–[29].

17.7.5 Article 8 – Right to Respect for Private Life, Family Life, Home and Correspondence

In an early judgment, the Court of Appeal held that where a breach of Art. 8 arose from maladministration, the scale of such damages should be modest. It observed as follows:

> The cost of supporting those in need falls on society as a whole. Resources are limited and payments of substantial damages will deplete the resources available for other needs of the public including primary care. If the impression is created that asylum seekers whether genuine or not are profiting from their status, this could bring the Human Rights Act into disrepute.[114]

But despite these early observations, some claimants have succeeded in receiving an award of damages for a violation of Art. 8. For example, in its judgment in *Bernard*[115] the Administrative Court found serious violations of the claimants' private and family lives noting that the claimants and their family had to live in 'deplorable conditions, wholly inimical to any normal family life, and to the physical and psychological integrity of the second claimant for a considerable period of time.' The public authority had not taken all necessary steps, reasonably promptly, once the problem was drawn to its attention. There had been no acknowledgment that it was in error, no explanation, no apology and nothing to indicate that procedures had been improved thereby preventing the same mistake from occurring in the future. The threat to evict the claimants, whilst it had been withdrawn, was also taken into account in the assessment of damages.[116] It found the first claimant suffered back problems which were aggravated but this caused him discomfort, distress and inconvenience rather than injury. The second claimant suffered discomfort, distress and frustration. In total, £10,000 was awarded comprising £2,000 to the first claimant and £8,000 to the second claimant.

Where the violation of Art. 8 is considered by the court to be less serious, smaller awards are made. For example, in its judgment in *W*[117] the Divisional Court awarded £1,000 for the breach of Art. 8 resulting from the disclosure of private information by a local authority and £500 was awarded against police for administering a caution to the claimant even though he had made no admission of guilt by the Administrative Court in its judgment in *Mohammed.*[118] No damages were awarded by the Court of Appeal in its judgment in *Re P*[119] although it had held that the local authority had breached a young woman's right to respect for family life by abandoning a care plan for her rehabilitation with her only child without giving her an opportunity to participate in the decision-making process.

---

[114] *Anufrijeva*, op cit, at [75]. It also held that similar considerations applied to the processing of asylum claims and the procedure for admitting the relatives of a refugee.

[115] *R. (Bernard) v London Borough of Enfield* [2002] EWHC (Admin) 2282.

[116] *Bernard*, ibid, at [34]–[41].

[117] *W v Westminster City Council* [2005] EWHC (QB) 102.

[118] *R. (Mohammed) v Chief Constable of West Midlands* [2010] EWHC 1228 (Admin).

[119] *Re P* [2007] EWCA Civ 2, [2007] 1 FLR 1957.

By contrast, where the breach of private life is perpetrated by a private sector respondent, the damages awarded have been far greater. This is because the claim is not really a claim under the HRA but a tort claim which is a modified version of the tort of breach of confidence which was created by courts as a result of obligations imposed upon them by the HRA. The level of damages awarded in this type of claim illustrates two things: first, courts are not as concerned with ensuring damages are modest where the respondent is the private sector; and second, where the tort scale of damages, rather than the ECtHR scale, is utilised, the damages awarded can be much greater. A recent example is the judgment of the Divisional Court in *Mosley*.[120] The Court had found a serious breach of the claimant's right to respect for private life in the actions of a newspaper. It observed as follows:

> . . an infringement of privacy cannot ever be effectively compensated by a monetary award. Judges cannot achieve what is, in the nature of things, impossible. That unpalatable fact cannot be mitigated by simply adding a few noughts to the number first thought of. Accordingly, it seems to me that the only realistic course is to select a figure which marks the fact that an unlawful intrusion has taken place while affording some degree of *solatium* to the injured party. That is all that can be done in circumstances where the traditional object of *restitutio* is not available. At the same time, the figure selected should not be such that it could be interpreted as minimising the scale of the wrong done or the damage it has caused.[121]

It concluded that £60,000 was an adequate financial remedy for the purpose of acknowledging the infringement and compensating, to some extent, 'for the injury to feelings, the embarrassment and distress caused.'[122]

17.7.6 Article 14 – Freedom from Discrimination in the Enjoyment of Convention Rights

In a reported case, damages have not yet been awarded for a violation of Art. 14. In its judgment in *Wilkinson*[123] the House of Lords held that putting the applicant in the position he or she would have been in had there not been a violation of Art. 14 might not result in an award of damages. Here the violation of Art. 14 found was that widow's allowance had not been extended to men (widowers). In the view of the House of Lords, if Parliament had paid proper regard to Art. 14 it would have abolished the allowance for widows. Widowers would therefore have not received the allowance either and no damages were therefore necessary to put widowers in the position in which they would have been had there not been a breach of Art. 14. It concluded here that its finding of violation of Art. 14 was sufficient just satisfaction.[124]

---

[120] *Mosley v News Group Newspapers* [2008] EWHC 1777 (QB).

[121] At [231].

[122] At [235].

[123] *R. (Wilkinson) v Inland Revenue Commissioners* [2005] UKHL 30, [2005] 1 WLR 1718.

[124] [27]–[28] per Lord Hoffmann.

17.8 Reform

17.8.1 Adoption of a Tort Model

In the UK there is very little academic discussion of the remedy available in damages under the HRA for the violation of Convention rights. Those who have commented have almost all argued that the present framework, a unique cause of action created by the HRA, should be replaced by a tort model for the award of damages.[125] It is not clear how this would be preferable to the HRA system for the award of damages. As noted in the opening chapter by Bagińska, tort law was not designed in order to resolve claims for damages involving breaches of human rights. A tort approach can result in a higher level of award where the respondent is the private sector such as in the *Mosley* judgment. But it is not clear that adoption of a tort approach would result in a higher level of award where the respondent is the public sector.[126] As Fairgrieve has noted, the ECtHR does not seem on the whole to take a 'more generous view of compensatable moral damage than the English courts.'[127]

In present times of austerity, what would be more likely to result in a higher level of award would be if the UK courts were to follow more closely developments in the ECtHR as discussed in the following paragraphs.

17.8.2 Keeping Up with the European Court of Human Rights

In many instances UK courts are now out of step with the approach of the ECtHR. A survey of judgments of the Grand Chamber over the last 5 years reveals that awards are generally higher than they have been in the past, and particularly that the ECtHR is more willing to make an award for non-pecuniary damage which it might not have made previously. Some commentators have noted that the ECtHR has begun to throw off former constraints and to embark on a more 'expansive, radical agenda' in its provision of redress to successful applicants.[128]

The best illustration of the difference in approach between UK courts and the ECtHR would be where a violation has been found at both levels, but a difference in remedies has resulted. Given 'just satisfaction' may have already been achieved at the national level, such examples are rare. However, it is possible to find some comparable cases. For example, in *Al-Skeini v UK*[129] the Grand Chamber determined that a non-pecuniary award was necessary to compensate the applicants for distress

[125] See, for example, Varuhas (2009) 750; and *Damages under the Human Rights Act 1998*, Law Com No. 266/ Scot Law Com No.180 (2000).

[126] Steele (2008) 614.

[127] Fairgrieve (2001) 706–709.

[128] Leach (2005) 148. See also Loucaides (2008) 182.

[129] 7.7.2011.

caused by the lack of a fully independent investigation into the deaths of their relatives. €17,000 was awarded to each applicant. Whilst at the national level UK courts have found numerous breaches of the Art. 2 ECHR duty to investigate but a remedy in damages for this type of breach has not yet been awarded.[130]

By contrast to the approach of UK courts, in recent years the Grand Chamber of the ECtHR has made a number of awards for the violation of Art. 6. For example, in *Svinarenko v Russia*[131] €10,000 was awarded to each of the applicants for the violation of Art. 3 resultant from being held in a metal cage in court and the violation of Art. 6 caused by the length of the proceedings. In *Taxquet v Belgium*[132] an award of €4,000 in non-pecuniary damages was made to a serving prisoner for a violation of Art. 6 in that he was given no reasons for the decision and had no right of appeal to a body with full jurisdiction.[133]

The ECtHR is also now more willing to make awards where the non-pecuniary damage is just distress and frustration. For example, in *Vallianatos v Greece*[134] a violation of Art. 14 with Art. 8 was found as civil unions were only possible for heterosexual couples. The Grand Chamber determined that a finding of violation was not sufficient redress for the non-pecuniary damage sustained and awarded each applicant €5,000.[135] In *Hermann v Germany* €5,000 was awarded to an applicant as he had been obliged, in breach of Art. 1 Protocol 1, to tolerate the exercise of hunting rights on his property.[136] And in *Oršuš v Croatia*[137] the Grand Chamber held that non pecuniary damage would be sustained as a result of frustration caused by indirect discrimination and a finding of violation would not be sufficient redress. €4,500 was awarded to each applicant.

The ECtHR has also been making awards for the distress experienced by non-nationals deported where there is a real risk of Art. 3 ill treatment although often this is combined with a violation of Art. 13 as the applicant has had no effective remedy to contest the deportation in national courts. For example, in *MSS v Belgium*

---

[130] See, e.g., *R. v Secretary of State for the Home Department, ex p Amin* [2003] UKHL 51, [2004] 1 AC 653.

[131] 17.7.2014.

[132] 16.11.2010.

[133] See also *McFarlane v Ireland,* 10.9.2010, where €5,500 was awarded to a released prisoner for violation of the Art.6 reasonable time guarantee and Art. 13; and *Cudak v Lithuania,* 23.3.2010, where €10,000 was awarded for pecuniary and non-pecuniary damage sustained from breach of the Art. 6 right of access to court.

[134] 7 November 2013.

[135] See also *X v Austria,* 19.2.2013 where a violation of Art. 14 with Art. 8 was found as the adoption of one partner's child by the other partner was prohibited where it was a same sex couple. A joint award of €10,000 was made to all three applicants. In *Konstantin Markin v Russia,* 22.3.2012 an award of €3,000 non pecuniary damages was made to the applicant who had been refused parental leave as he was male.

[136] In *Catan v Moldova and Russia,* 19.10.2012, €6,000 was awarded to each of the applicants for the breach of Art. 2 Protocol No.1 resulting from the closure of Moldovan language schools.

[137] 16.3.2010.

and Greece[138] the Grand Chamber held that Belgium had violated Articles 3 and 13 in sending the applicants back to Greece causing distress for which a finding of violation could not constitute just satisfaction. €24,900 in non-pecuniary damages were awarded.[139]

17.8.3 Reform of the HRA Generally

Finally, it is important to note that the position of the HRA in UK law remains precarious. The Conservative Party, one of the political parties forming the present coalition government, published a consultation paper in October 2014 undertaking, should it form a government following the next General Election in May 2015, to repeal the HRA and break the link between British courts and the European Court of Human Rights. Plans are also set out to replace the HRA with a "British Bill of Rights" but few details are given, with no information at all concerning planned remedies for the violation of human rights. Given the desire to limit the influence of the ECtHR and the ECHR in national law, it is likely that a new British Bill of Rights would not include a remedies provision modelled on Art. 41 of the ECHR or encourage courts to follow the ECtHR's lead in these matters. However, the concern that public authorities should not be unduly pressured by large damages awards would remain at and guidelines on such awards would most likely continue to exist.

17.9 Conclusion

Despite a complex array of barriers and principles set out in the HRA and jurisprudence of the ECtHR, what is really lacking in the UK is a discussion of why and to what extent damages should be afforded for a violation of human rights law. In common with many other systems of reparation for the violation of human rights, in the UK 'jurisprudence and doctrine almost completely fail to discuss the theoretical foundation of or rationale for reparations.'[140] A good starting point, not yet mentioned in UK jurisprudence, would be the *Guidelines on The Right to a Remedy and Reparations* adopted by the UN General Assembly on 16 December 2005.[141] These are detailed but at clause 20 examples of 'economically assessable damage' are set out including physical or mental harm, lost opportunities, material damages, moral

[138] 21.1.2011.

[139] See also *Hirsi Jama v Italy,* 23.2.2012 where non pecuniary damages of €15,000 each were awarded for violations of Arts 3 and 13 and also Art. 4 of Protocol 4.

[140] Shelton (2002) at 838.

[141] http://www.ohchr.org/EN/ProfessionalInterest/Pages/RemedyAndReparation.aspx last accessed 1 Dec. 2014.

damage and costs required for legal or expert assistance. The following extract from the Preamble, adjusted to the national context, is of particular relevance:

> Recognizing that in honouring the victims' right to benefit from remedies and reparation, the international community keeps faith with the plight of victims, survivors and future human generations and reaffirms the international legal principles of accountability, justice and the rule of law.

References

Clayton, Richard. 2005. Damage limitation: The courts and the Human Rights Act damages. *Public Law* 3: 429–439.

Fairgrieve, Duncan. 2001. The Human Rights Act 1998, damages and tort law, Public Law: 695.

Leach, Philip. 2005. Beyond the bug river – A new dawn for redress before the European court of Human Rights. *European Human Rights Law Review* 2: 148–164.

Loucaides, Louikis G. 2008. Reparation for violations of human rights under the European convention and restitution in integrum. *European Human Rights Law Review* 2: 182–192.

Home Office Rights Brought Home: The Human Rights Bill (Cm 3782) (London. TSO, 1997)

Shelton, Dinah. 2002. Righting wrongs: Reparations in the articles on state responsibility. *American Journal of International Law* 96: 833–856.

Steele, Jenny. 2008. Damages in tort and under the Human Rights Act: Remedial or functional separation. *Cambridge Law Journal* 67(3): 606–634.

Tabori, Tom. 2013. Growth industry: Article 1 of the first protocol to the ECHR. *Judicial Review* 18(2): 194.

The Law Commission (Law Com 266) and The Scottish Law Commission (Scot Law Com No. 180). 2000. *Damages under the Human Rights Act 1998.*

Varuhas, Jason. 2009. A tort-based approach to damages under the Human Rights Act 1998. *Modern Law Review* 72(5): 750–782.

Chapter 18
Damages Remedies for Infringements of Human Rights Under U.S. Law

Jacques deLisle

18.1 Human Rights Cases with a Foreign/Transnational Element[1]

18.1.1 The Foreign Sovereign Immunities Act

In cases with a transnational element, human rights violations that can yield awards of money damages under U.S. law are often the product of acts of foreign states or acts attributable to foreign states. The central role of state action in international human rights law generally is more pronounced in these types of cases, which primarily involve civil and political rights or *jus cogens*. The Foreign Sovereign Immunities Act (FSIA) of 1976 opens the door for plaintiffs seeking civil damages remedies for foreign state and foreign state-linked human rights violations, providing the "sole basis for obtaining jurisdiction over a foreign state."[2] The FSIA codified the "restrictive theory" of sovereign immunity, rejecting the long-fading traditional theory of "absolute" sovereign immunity. Institutionally, the FSIA also moved determination of immunity in particular cases from discretionary policy choices by the executive branch to a rule-governed statutory framework interpreted and applied by the courts.

Although they broadly prohibit suits against foreign states and their organs, political subdivisions, and "agencies and instrumentalities" (including state-owned

---

[1] This chapter is an updated version of an article that was previously published in the American Journal of Comparative Law 2014, vol. 62, 457–490; DOI: http://dx.doi.org/10.5131/AJCL.2013.0033.

[2] 28 U.S.C. §§ 1330, 1332(a), 1391(f) and 1601-1611; Argentine Republic v. Amerada Hess, 488 U.S. 428 (1989).

J. deLisle (✉)
Stephen A. Cozen Professor of Law and Professor of Political Science,
University of Pennsylvania, Philadelphia, PA, USA
e-mail: jdelisle@law.upenn.edu

E. Bagińska (ed.), *Damages for Violations of Human Rights*,
Ius Comparatum - Global Studies in Comparative Law 9,
DOI 10.1007/978-3-319-18950-5_18

companies), the FSIA and judicial interpretations of it have created exceptions to immunity for some state-linked defendants for some actions. Those defendants face liability generally "in the same manner" as "a private individual under like circumstances." Compensatory damage awards are available against those foreign states themselves and punitive as well as compensatory damage awards are available against their agencies and instrumentalities.

Sovereign immunity does not extend to individuals (although heads of state and some lesser officials may retain immunity under other legal principles, as discussed below). Some U.S. courts had interpreted the FSIA to prohibit suits against individuals alleged to have acted within the scope of their power as officials—particularly high-level officials—of foreign states. In some cases, these suits have been in substance suits against the state and would require enforcement against the state, and the litigation tactic of naming a natural person as a defendant has been rejected as insufficient to evade the immunity that the FSIA confers on states. Beyond such cases, some courts had found FSIA immunity available to foreign officials, at least when acting within their scope of office. The Supreme Court rejected this approach in *Samantar v. Yousuf*, holding that individuals cannot claim immunity under the FSIA (although they may be immune under common law immunity doctrine, as is discussed below).[3] Sovereign immunity does not cover enterprises that are only indirectly owned by the state.[4] For state and state-linked defendants that generally have immunity under the FSIA, there are "type of activity"-based exceptions, four of which are relevant, or potentially relevant, to cases involving human right violations.

First, the Antiterrorism and Effective Death Penalty Act of 1996 (AEDPA) amended the FSIA to create an exception to immunity for (and a later amendment explicitly provided for a cause of action for civil damages claims against) the small handful of states (currently Iran, Sudan and Syria and previously Cuba, Iraq, Libya, North Korea and South Yemen) that the U.S. has officially designated as state sponsors of terrorism.[5] This exception applies to civil claims seeking money damages for "personal injury or death that was caused by an act of torture, extrajudicial killing [both as defined in the Torture Victims Protection Act, discussed below], aircraft sabotage, hostage taking," or acts providing material support for such activities, when committed by someone acting within the scope of his or her role as a state's "official, employee or agent."[6] Foreign states are designated as state sponsors of terrorism by the Secretary of State pursuant to authority, and according to criteria, set forth in other laws, including ones governing foreign trade, aid, and arms sales.[7]

---

[3] Samantar v. Yousuf, 560 U.S. 305(2010).

[4] Dole Food Co. v. Patrickson, 538 U.S. 468 (2003).

[5] Examples of cases brought under this provision include Alejandre v. Republic of Cuba, 996 F. Supp. 1239 (S.D. Fla. 1997); Roeder v. Islamic Republic of Iran, 333 F.23d 228 (D.C. Cir. 2003).

[6] 28 U.S.C. § 1605A(a)(1),(a)(2)(A)(i); (h)(7).

[7] 28 U.S.C. § 1605A(h)(6) (referring to Export Administration Act, Foreign Assistance Act and Arms Export Control Act).

Plaintiffs invoking this "terrorism exception" must be: U.S. nationals; members of the U.S. armed forces; employees of the U.S. government or of U.S. government contractors acting within the scope of their employment; or the legal representatives of someone falling within any of the first three categories.[8] If the relevant acts occurred in the defendant state's territory, the plaintiff must exhaust any remedy available through non-U.S. arbitration.[9] Some courts have construed the FSIA's "terrorism exception" as insufficient to create a cause of action. Where that has occurred, plaintiffs have had to conjoin this FSIA provision with another source of law that creates a right of action supporting recovery for the relevant harms.

Second, foreign states (and their agencies and instrumentalities) are not immune from some suits for money damages for "personal injury or death" caused by the "tortious act or omission of [a] foreign state or any official or employee of [a] foreign state while acting within the scope of his office or employment."[10] Where this exception applies, the foreign sovereign defendant faces liability under U.S. tort law generally, which permits awards of damages for a range of behaviors that violate human rights and lead to physical injury or death (as is discussed below). There are no nationality or other status requirements for plaintiffs.

The "tort exception" to immunity under the FSIA, however, includes additional conditions that limit its utility for victims of human rights abuses. It is limited to harms "occurring in the United States"—a restriction that excludes the vast majority of torts arising from human rights violations committed by or with the authority of a foreign state, given that such violations typically occur in the state's own territory. The "tort exception" also does not extend to several types of torts usually not associated with physical harm (malicious prosecution, abuse of process, defamation or interference with contracts) or to "any claim based upon the exercise or performance of a discretionary function regardless of whether the discretion be abused." This "discretionary function exception" is generally understood as an effort to make foreign sovereigns liable for ordinary torts (such as automobile accidents and ministerial acts) but to insulate them from liability for policy choices and their consequences. As interpreted, it broadly tracks a similar exception in the Federal Tort Claims Act (discussed below and concerning U.S. government immunity). This provision can significantly limit remedies for foreign state-linked human rights violations.

Still, some plaintiffs have been able to bring damages claims based on human rights-violating torts occurring in the United States and attributable to foreign sovereigns. Principal examples include cases in which a foreign state, its leaders or officials have directed, set in motion, or undertaken killings of fellow nationals whom they considered political enemies or enemies of the state and who were present in the United States. In such cases, the territorial requirement of the torts exception is easily satisfied. In terms of the "discretionary function" exception, some U.S. courts have concluded that such serious human rights violations are not within the

[8] 28 U.S.C. § 1605A(a)(2)(A)(ii), (c).

[9] 28 U.S.C. § 1605A(a)(2)(A)(iii).

[10] 28 U.S.C. § 1605(a)(5).

scope of the policy choices that a state has discretion to make and thus are not within the scope of FSIA-granted immunity.[11]

Third, a foreign state (or its agency or instrumentality) is not immune from suits based upon: "a commercial activity" that the defendant has "carried on in the United States" (provided that the activity includes "substantial contact with the United States"); "an act performed in the United States in connection with a commercial activity elsewhere"; or "an act outside the territory of the United States in connection with" the defendant's "commercial activity elsewhere and that act causes a direct effect in the United States." Although suits relying on this "commercial activity" exception are generally not promising paths to civil damages remedies in human rights cases, the exception could provide relief in limited circumstances. The impediments to success in such cases have been that: the commercial activity that occurs, or has an effect, in the United States is not sufficiently connected to the defendant's human rights-violating activity; or a commercial activity that might be sufficiently connected to human rights violations to does not meet the territorial requirements (of occurrence in or impact on United States territory) even though those territorial requirements are less demanding than under the torts exception; or the acts in question have not been sufficiently commercial in character.[12]

Fourth, a foreign sovereign can waive immunity, explicitly or by implication.[13] Explicit waiver is vanishingly rare and especially unlikely when it could expose a foreign state to a judgment that the state is responsible for human rights violations. Attempts to claim implied waiver in human rights-related cases generally have failed.[14] Intentional waiver is least implausible in the context of human rights violations followed by discontinuous regime change, where the new government might seek to signal a clear break with the past and might welcome, or at least tolerate, transnational condemnation of its predecessor's abuses—a pattern that seemingly has characterized some relatively successful Alien Tort Statute cases (discussed below). Courts have rejected the argument that commission of *jus cogens* or other severe human rights violations constitute implicit waivers of immunity.

Plaintiffs who avoid the barrier of FSIA immunity still must (except in suits under the terrorism exception) articulate a statutory or common law cause of action

[11] Liu v. Republic of China, 892 F.2d 1419 (9th Cir. 1989); Letelier v. Republic of Chile, 488 F. Supp. 665 (D.D.C. 1980); but cf. In re Terrorist Attacks on September 11, 2001, 538 F.3d 71 (2d Cir. 2008) (torts exception not applicable to claim based on conduct addressed by terrorism exception and alleging defendants' donations to Islamic charities that funneled funds to terrorist attackers).

[12] 28 USC §§ 1605(1)(3), 1603(e). See, e.g., Saudi Arabia v. Nelson, 507 U.S. 349 (1993) (commercial activity of recruiting plaintiff occurred in U.S.; torture in retaliation for plaintiff complaints about employer's practices occurred in Saudi Arabia); Cicippio v. Islamic Republic of Iran, 30 F.3d 164 (D.C. Cir. 1994) (hostage taking for profit is not a commercial activity).

[13] 28 U.S.C. § 1605(a)(1).

[14] A rare example of (largely unintended) waiver in a case involving human rights abuses—including torture and taking of property—is Siderman v. Republic of Argentina, 965 F.2d 699 (9th Cir. 1992) (defendant's appearance in related state court claim waived immunity).

that would provide for liability of an ordinary, non-immune defendant—something that the FSIA itself generally has been held not to do.

18.1.2 Alien Tort Statute

The Alien Tort Statute (ATS)—also known as the Alien Tort Claims Act—is perhaps the most distinctive U.S. law providing damages remedies for human rights abuses.[15] It also has been one of the very few aspects of relevant U.S. law that has looked explicitly to international human rights legal norms. Adopted as part of the First Judiciary Act in 1789, the ATS provides that "[t]he [federal] district courts shall have original jurisdiction of any civil action by an alien for a tort only, committed in violation of the law of nations or a treaty of the United States."[16]

For much of the two centuries that followed, the provision lay largely dormant. In 1980, in *Filartiga v. Pena-Irala*, a court awarded damages for the torture (resulting in death) of a foreign national, outside the United States (in this case, in the victim's home country) by a foreign defendant acting under color of state authority (in this case, a city police chief of the state of which both victim and defendant were nationals).[17] In the court's analysis, certain international human rights norms (in this case, the prohibition against torture under color of official authority) were sufficiently "universally accepted norms of the international law of human rights" that they came within the scope of evolving customary international law that was received into U.S. law (as federal common law) and formed a basis for relief under the ATS. Under *Filartiga* and cases that followed it, where such norms are violated, a plaintiff may obtain money damages under the ATS.

Post-*Filartiga* cases added to the list of covered rights recognized by some (but not all) courts: summary execution, enforced disappearance, (prolonged) arbitrary detention, slavery/forced labor, forced relocation/exile, genocide, war crimes and crimes against humanity (and some of the violent and discriminatory means—including systematic rape and killing—used in the context of genocide, war crimes and crimes against humanity), and (less clearly) non-torture forms of cruel, inhuman and degrading treatment.[18]Claims invoking other human rights, even where

[15] The ATS has produced a vast and contentious body of scholarly literature. Recent examples include a large, critical body of work by Curtis A. Bradley and Jack L. Goldsmith (some of which is cited below), Davis (2008), deLisle (2003); Fletcher (2008); Hufbauer and Mitrokostas (2003). For overviews of the doctrinal issues addressed here, see Stephens et al. (2008) and Bradley (2013) (especially chs. 7–8).

[16] 28 USC § 1350.

[17] Filartiga v. Pena-Irala, 630 F.2d 876 (2d Cir. 1980).

[18] See, e.g. Hilao v. Estate of Marcos, 103 F.3d 789 (9th Cir. 1996); Forti v. Suarez-Mason, 672 F. Supp. 1531 (N.D. Cal. 1987); Kadic v. Karadzic, 70 F.3d 232 (2d Cir. 1995); Doe v. Unocal, 963 F.Supp. 880 (C.D.Cal.1997) *aff'd in part and rev'd in part* 395 F.3d 932 (9th Cir. 2002); Sexual Minorities Uganda v. Lively, 960 F.Supp.2d 304 (D. Mass. 2013).

systematically or grossly violated, have been rejected or, at most, won sporadic acceptance by lower courts.

Availability of punitive damages has varied in ATS cases and depends in part on courts' resolution of choice of law questions. Personal jurisdiction over defendants is required, but that can be achieved under U.S. law through so-called "tag jurisdiction" (serving a defendant with process when the defendant is present, even briefly, in the United States) or through satisfying the relatively low threshold of "minimum contacts" with the forum required under U.S. constitutional and statutory law (and often easily met in suits against multinational companies).

In 2013, the United States Supreme Court, in *Kiobel* v. *Royal Dutch Petroleum*, took a significant step (following its earlier decision in *Sosa v. Alvarez-Machain*) to limit the reach of the ATS and its expansion during the more than three decades after *Filartiga*.[19] The Court unanimously rejected the ATS claim of foreign plaintiffs concerning human rights violations (in this case, torture, extrajudicial killing, crimes against humanity and other human rights violations) committed in the plaintiffs' home country by a foreign defendant (in this case, a multinational company not based in the U.S.) that acted in conjunction with the country's government (in this case, on plaintiffs' account, by aiding and abetting the state's military in acts against those protesting defendant's oil extraction project). The opinion of the Court (joined by five of the nine justices) held that the general presumption against the extraterritorial reach of U.S. statutes applied to the ATS (even though the ATS is a jurisdictional law—rather than a substantive, regulatory law—and even though it explicitly addresses international matters, specifically alien plaintiffs and acts in violation of the "law of nations," long understood to mean "international law"). For the ATS to provide relief, the Court held that the case must "touch and concern the territory of the United States" with "sufficient force to displace the presumption against extraterritorial application," and that "mere corporate presence" of the defendant in the United States does not sufficiently "touch and concern" U.S. territory.

Pending further judicial decisions or legislation, the contours of the ATS after *Kiobel* remain uncertain in several respects. First, so-called "F-cubed" cases—that is, cases that have foreign plaintiffs (as all ATS claims must), arise from foreign activities, and are brought against foreign defendants—are eliminated, or nearly so. The change wrought by *Kiobel* rejects aspects of *Filartiga* and many cases that followed. *Kiobel* did not specifically conclude that no F-cubed case could sufficiently "touch and concern" the territory of the United States, however. A concurrence by one member of the majority (Justice Kennedy) stressed that the Court's decision was "careful to leave open a number of significant questions regarding the reach and interpretation" of the ATS. A concurrence joined by four justices would preserve ATS jurisdiction where a defendant's conduct (perhaps wherever it occurred) "substantially and adversely affects an important American national interest" which

[19] 133 S.Ct. 1659 (2013); Wuerth (2013); see also the symposium issue of the *Maryland Journal of International Law* in volume 28 (2013). For sharply contrasting assessments, see Colangelo (2013) 1329 and Anderson (2013) 149. *Kiobel* spawned a lively discussion among commentators in online postings such as SCOTUSblog.

might include preventing the U.S. from becoming a "safe harbor" for some types of human rights violators. But few if any F-cubed cases are likely to meet the majority's exacting standard, and at least two members of the Court would explicitly prohibit F-cubed cases entirely.[20]

Second, in terms of location of the relevant activity, one type of so-called "F-squared" claim (foreign plaintiff and foreign defendant) could still be viable if sufficient activity occurs in the United States. Seven justices did not join a two-justice concurrence (by Justice Alito) that would have excluded cases in which the "domestic conduct" in the U.S. is not itself "sufficient to violate" the especially well-entrenched and core international human rights legal norms that are within the ATS's reach. Although the Court's opinion is clear that "mere [] presence" of a corporate defendant in the U.S. will not do, the majority and other concurrences do not adopt—and a four-justice concurrence (by Justice Breyer) rejects—the narrow reading urged by Alito. Lower courts interpreting Kiobel generally have held that activity—including decision-making activity that does not include the direct infliction of harm on plaintiffs—can be sufficient, usually for "aiding and abetting" claims. But the courts have set a high bar. Courts have found that conduct meeting the standard includes: approval, encouragement, and cover-up of torture abroad (at a U.S. government contractor-run detention facility in Iraq) by senior corporate managers in the U.S.; conspiring and planning in the U.S. to orchestrate foreign state and private campaigns abroad (in Uganda) to perpetrate "crimes against humanity" through deprivation of life, liberty, property, and rights of free expression on the basis of sexual orientation or gender identity.[21] Other courts have found insufficient conduct in the U.S. that was "mere consent" to support a terrorist group with which defendant collaborated abroad, or that did not show a "purpose" of promoting relevant human rights violations abroad.[22]

Third, in terms of the nationality of the defendant, the other type of F-squared claim (foreign plaintiff and foreign activity) would seem to present a stronger case because of the U.S.'s "national interest" in regulating the behavior (including behavior abroad) of U.S. nationals (whether individual, corporate or governmental) that violates at least certain core human rights. Such claims would appear to be subject to *Kiobel*'s presumption against extraterritorial reach of the ATS and the Court's high bar to overcoming that presumption. Lower courts generally have held that a defendant's U.S. nationality is a relevant factor, but is not necessary (or sufficient) to meet Kiobel's test.

---

[20] See Simon v. Republic of Hungary, 37 F.Supp.3d 381, 441-444 (D.D.C. 2014) (U.S. interest in preventing genocide and mass expropriation did not provide basis for ATS jurisdiction where acts were committed long ago—during World War II—and occurred entirely outside the U.S.—in Hungary).

[21] See Al Shimari v. CACI, 758 F.3d 516 (4th Cir. 2014); Sexual Minorities Uganda v. Lively, 960 F.Supp.2d 304 (D. Mass, 2013).

[22] See Mastafa v. Chevron Corp., 770 F.3d 170 (2d Cir. 2014); Doe v. Drummond Co., 782 F.3d 576 (11th Cir. 2015).

Fourth, in terms of the defendants subject to ATS claims, it appears that the ATS remains relatively unaffected, at least in principle. *Filartiga* and many other ATS cases involved defendants who clearly: were foreign state agents or acting with, or under color of, foreign state authority to harm plaintiffs directly, or were commanding officers or state supervisory officials who knew or should have known, and failed to stop or punish, abuses committed by subordinates. Some later ATS cases permitted suits against other types of actors, including: the political leader of an entity that lacked status as a state under international law (specifically, the leader of a Bosnian Serb entity who was sufficiently complicit with the government of the since-defunct Yugoslav state to meet state action requirements for liability for torture, executions and other abuses committed in pursuit of "ethnic cleansing," and who could be held liable even in the absence of state action for genocide, war crimes or crimes against humanity)[23]; and, more often, corporations that aided and abetted state violations of human rights (the claim in *Kiobel*), or that were so deeply entangled with the state that corporate acts constituted state action, or that engaged in one of the few types of human rights violations for which state action was not required (a principle embraced in *Kadic*)[24]; and, after 9/11, U.S. government officials involved in detention and abuses of detainees in the context of the "war on terror."[25] Like some but not all of the courts that had addressed the issue, the lower court in *Kiobel* had held that ATS claims could not be brought against private actors such as multinational corporations. The Supreme Court did not accept, or address, that conclusion. Since Kiobel, courts have generally been willing to accept suits against corporations where other requirements for ATS jurisdiction are met.

Fifth, the range of violations of human rights that fall within the scope of the ATS remains uncertain and relatively limited—and possibly is significantly more limited (and clearly is less likely to expand) than before *Kiobel* and the earlier Supreme Court ATS-related decision in *Sosa v. Alvarez-Machain*.[26]*Filartiga* addressed broadly the reception of clearly accepted norms of international human rights law into U.S. federal common law as a basis for recovery under the ATS. While *Filartiga* and some cases that followed involved violations of core international human rights—and often *jus cogens*—such as torture (at issue in *Filartiga* itself) or genocide, war crimes and crimes against humanity (at issue in *Kadic*), other cases cast the net more broadly. In *Sosa*, however, the Court characterized the ATS as confined to a "very limited" range of customary international legal norms that are "definable, universal and obligatory" and are "of an international character accepted by the civi-

[23] Kadic v. Karadzic, 70 F.3d 232 (2d Cir. 1995).

[24] See, for example, Doe v. Unocal, 963 F.Supp. 880 (C.D.Cal.1997); South African Apartheid Litigation, 617 F. Supp. 2d 228 (S.D.N.Y. 2009); Sarei v. Rio Tinto, 456 F.3d 1069 (9th Cir. 2006); Wiwa v. Royal Dutch Petroleum, 226 F.3d 88 (2d Cir. 2000). For contrasting scholarly analyses, see Bradley (2010) and Chomsky (2010).

[25] See, e.g., Rasul v. Bush, 542 U.S. 466 (2004), Ku (2005) 205.

[26] 542 U.S. 692 (2004).

lized world and defined with a specificity comparable to the features of the 18th-century paradigms" (such as the prohibition of piracy) in existence when Congress enacted the ATS.[27] The Court broadly warned against expansive recognition of ATS claims, urging "judicial caution" and "vigilant door keeping," in part lest the courts infringe on the executive branch's foreign affairs powers or make decisions that could have adverse "implications for the foreign relations of the United States."

As this reflects, significant limitations to the ATS's scope in providing damages remedies for human rights abuses predate *Kiobel*. Pure "F-cubed" cases had long been on shaky ground. They were often understood as resting on an interpretation of the ATS that saw it as an exercise of universal jurisdiction—a relatively weak basis for prescriptive jurisdiction in international law, one that has not won official or judicial favor in the United States, and one that, if accepted at all, is likely limited to addressing a very narrow range of *jus cogens* or other "core" rights. From immediately after *Filartiga*, expanded use of the ATS was controversial and contested, with some critics—and judges—arguing that the ATS should be construed narrowly.[28] After *Sosa*, it was no longer possible to claim that the ATS created a cause of action, rather than served as a jurisdictional statute opening federal courts to causes of action rooted in other sources (whether federal common law—including that drawn from the "law of nations," or federal statute, or treaty). Since long before *Sosa* and *Kiobel*, most ATS claims have been dismissed, and the relatively few successful ATS actions have largely been limited to those against agents of small states disfavored by U.S. foreign policy, or against those who had acted on behalf of defunct regimes. ATS suits against corporate defendants received considerable support from scholars and activists and grew sharply as a share of ATS cases, but such claims have had only limited success since plaintiffs began to bring them in the 1990s. Victory has been still more elusive for plaintiffs bringing suits against U.S. officials and agents of the U.S. government, most of which have arisen from abuses committed in the post-9/11 "war on terror." As discussed below, several defenses (including doctrines of immunity) have been among the daunting obstacles for ATS plaintiffs. The Supreme Court ruled nearly a quarter century ago that the ATS provides no basis for a claim against foreign sovereign state defendants, which could be brought only under the FSIA (discussed above).

---

[27] Although acknowledging that prolonged arbitrary detention might be a covered right, the one-day legally unauthorized deprivation of liberty alleged by plaintiff did not violate such a right.

[28] See, for example Bradley and Goldsmith (1997); Tel-Oren v. Libyan Arab Republic, 726 F.2d 774, 798–823 (D.C. Cir. 1984) (Bork, J. concurring). Among the arguments to restrict the ATS were: the ATS did not provide a cause of action but was only a jurisdictional statute that opened courts to some claims for which the plaintiff could articulate an independent cause of action (a position adopted in *Sosa*); there was no federal common law claim based on violation of customary international law of human rights; covered human rights were limited to those generally recognized in 1789, when the ATS was enacted; and creation of remedies for the human rights violations asserted by ATS plaintiffs was a matter for Congress, not the courts. See also Young (2015).

18.1.3 The Torture Victims Protection Act

The Torture Victims Protection Act (TVPA) of 1991 provides that an "individual who, under actual or apparent authority, or color of law, of any foreign nation [] subjects an individual to torture… or extrajudicial killing shall, in a civil action, be liable for damages" to the victim (in cases of torture) or the victim's legal representative or "any person who may be a claimant in an action for wrongful death" (in cases of extrajudicial killing).[29] Plaintiffs in a wrongful death action vary somewhat, with different states having different laws. But they generally include surviving spouses, children and, less commonly, others with close familial or quasi-familial relationships with the victim. In cases involving foreign plaintiffs, some courts have looked to foreign law on this issue.

The TVPA is unusual in U.S. law in specifically looking to international human rights law. Its declared purpose is "[t]or carry out obligations of the United States under the United NationsCharter and other international agreements [such as the Convention Against Torture and Other Cruel, Inhuman or Degrading Treatment or Punishment] pertaining to the protection of human rights."

Unlike the ATS, the TVPA allows actions by U.S., as well as foreign, plaintiffs. There seems to be little prospect of a *Kiobel*-like judicial construction of the TVPA as not applying extraterritorially. In a restriction that seems to assume applicability to human rights violations occurring outside the United States, the TVPA requires plaintiffs to exhaust any "adequate and available remedies in the place in which the conduct giving rise to the claim occurred."[30]

In terms of the scope of defendants, the TVPA's "color of [foreign state] law" provision will rarely allow suit against U.S. (or other non-local-country) defendants. It also is generally interpreted similarly to the "color of law" provision in Section 1983 of the Civil Rights Act (discussed below). In 2012, the United States Supreme Court, in *Mohammed v. Palestinian Authority*, limited the range of TVPA defendants, holding that the statute's use of "individual"—rather than the broader "person"—means that the TVPA permits only suits against natural persons, not organizational entities.[31] The unanimous decision closes off definitively some uses that plaintiffs sometimes had made of the TVPA to sue multinational corporations or foreign states.[32] In suits against corporations, the TVPA had been used to supplement, or substitute for, the controversial ATS as a basis for a cause of action. In suits against foreign state entities, plaintiffs had invoked the TVPA in conjunction with the FSIA's "terrorism exception" to sovereign immunity, which some courts found had not (before later, clarifying amendments) created a cause of action.

[29] 28 USC § 1350 note.

[30] 28 USC § 1350 note § 2(b). See Doe v. Drummond, 782 F.3d 576 (TVPA applies extraterritorially in post-Kiobel case).

[31] 132 S. Ct. 1702 (2012).

[32] See, e.g., Baloco ex rel. Tapia v. Drummond Co., 640 F.3d 1338 (11th Cir. 2011); Bauman v. Daimler Chrysler, 579 F.3d 1088 (9th Cir. 2009); Daliberti v. Iraq, 146 F. Supp. 2d 19 (D.D.C. 2001); Alejandre v. Republic of Cuba, 996 F. Supp. 1239 (S.D. Fla. 1997).

The Anti-Terrorism Act (ATA), adopted in 1994, offers another, broadly similar, potential avenue to civil damages for human rights violations in cases with a transnational or foreign dimension. The ATA includes authorization of treble damages awards for a U.S. national "injured in his or her person, property, or business by reason of an act of international terrorism," which is defined as a violent criminal act that appears to be intended to intimidate or coerce a civilian population or influence a government policy.[33] Thus far, the ATA has not been a very fruitful source of successful litigation, in part because of difficulties in obtaining personal jurisdiction over defendants.

18.1.4 Additional Limitations to Damages Relief against Foreign State and State-Linked Actors

Other aspects of U.S. law further limit the access of those suffering human rights violations to civil damages remedies in cases where the defendant is a foreign state or state-linked actor. First, official immunity often is a formidable barrier. Status-based official immunity shields some individual defendants (although not foreign states and their agencies or instrumentalities). Foreign heads of state generally enjoy this immunity, which is generally regarded as a vestige of the absolute theory of sovereign immunity or as a principle related to still-vibrant doctrines of diplomatic immunity (which also accords status-based immunity to diplomats). Some—but by no means all—U.S. courts have extended this type of official immunity more broadly, for example to heads of government, cabinet ministers, ex-presidents and even presidents' close family members.[34]

Other foreign officials lack this robust status-based immunity but still can avoid liability under doctrines of conduct-based immunity. In denying FSIA immunity to individual defendants, the Supreme Court in *Samantar* explicitly left open (but did little to clarify) the possibility that foreign official defendants might be shielded by common law doctrines of official immunity and perhaps even common law doctrines of foreign sovereign immunity (which the FSIA has displaced for foreign state defendants but which the Court indicated might still have vitality for individual official defendants, presumably where their challenged actions arguably occurred within their scope of office). Among the uncertainties sown by *Samantar* has been the question of the extent to which the common law of foreign official immunity does, will, or should, track the doctrine of official immunity that has developed in U.S. domestic civil rights law, especially Section 1983 (discussed below).[35] Under a

---

[33] 18 U.S.C. §§ 2331–2338.

[34] For a recent overview of these patterns, see Dellapenna (2011) 570–582.

[35] Much, but not all, of the scholarly commentary has argued against common law foreign official immunity being as broad as the "qualified immunity" doctrine in domestic law and especially under Section 1983. For views at both ends of the spectrum, see Stephens (2011) 2669 (against broad official immunity for foreign officials) and Bradley and Goldsmith (2010) 137 (immunity broader for foreign than domestic officers). See also Bradley and Helfer (2011); Rutledge (2011).

Section 1983-like (or even a somewhat more "pro-defendant") common law standard, immunity would not have insulated foreign officials in the many pre-*Samantar* cases (and *Samantar* itself) that went forward alleging significant abuses of core human rights by officials acting under color of home state law.

As the foregoing reflects, the contours of official immunity remain vague and unsettled in the context of suits involving human rights claims against foreign defendants. U.S. courts generally defer to views expressed by the executive branch on cases in which the government (ordinarily through the Department of State) expresses support for, or opposition to, official immunity for a foreign official. The executive branch had indicated that it did not support immunity in *Samantar*, and U.S. administrations often have taken similar positions in many—but not all—cases alleging serious human rights violations by foreign officials. After *Samantar*, the government has continued to express views for and against conduct-based immunity for foreign officials in human rights-related cases, and courts have continued usually to defer to those views.

Second, the Act of State doctrine can pose a challenge to some plaintiffs who seek damages for transnational human rights violations in U.S. courts. Rooted in notions of sovereign equality internationally and constitutional separation of powers domestically, this judicially created doctrine provides that U.S. courts ordinarily will not sit in judgment of sovereign acts of another state taken in that state's own territory, even if the acts violate international law. Although the doctrine has in a relatively small number of cases blocked litigation asserting human rights violations, its effect has been limited. This is to be expected, given: judicial determinations that many human rights violations are not acts of state (in part because they violate the host state's law); the Supreme Court's determination that the doctrine is least appropriately applied where there is a high level of consensus on relevant international legal standards, where adjudicating the case is not likely to have a significant impact on U.S. foreign policy, or (in a lower court's interpretation) where the foreign government was not acting in the public interest; and the norm and practice (embodied in the so-called "Bernstein exception") that the doctrine is not to be applied where the U.S. executive expresses lack of support for its application. The doctrine still can have an impact even where it does not fully insulate foreign state human rights-violating activity from scrutiny in U.S. civil litigation. For example, in a case seeking damages for what plaintiff claimed was the politically motivated killing of her dissident journalist husband, the defendant sought to invoke the Act of State doctrine to induce the U.S. court to defer to the legal conclusion (lack of state liability) and not just accept the factual findings (which could support a finding of state liability under U.S. law) of the foreign sovereign's courts that adjudicated cases arising from the same incident.[36]

Third, plaintiffs in transnational human rights cases face a cluster of obstacles rooted in concerns about the risks of court encroachment on, or undermining of, the political branches'—and especially the executive's—conduct of foreign affairs. Courts sometimes apply the political question doctrine—albeit rarely in transnational

[36] Liu v. Republic of China, 892 F.2d 1419 (9th Cir. 1989).

human rights cases but somewhat more often when the defendant is a U.S. government official. [37] Under this judicially created doctrine, courts are not to adjudicate a case if it involves: "a textually demonstrable commitment of the issue to a coordinate political department"; "a lack of judicially discoverable and manageable standards"; the need for a "policy determination" exercising "nonjudicial discretion"; a judicial decision that would show a lack of the "respect due" other branches; an "unusual need" for adherence to an already-made political decision; or the potential "embarrassment" of disparate pronouncements from different branches of the government.[38] More commonly, related concerns motivate judicial development of other doctrines that impede plaintiffs seeking damages for transnational human rights violations. In *Sosa* and *Kiobel*, for example, concerns about the impact on U.S. foreign policy, the constitutional allocation of roles in foreign affairs, and other political question-like worries appeared to shape the Court's adoption of a narrow view of what human rights are cognizable as ATS claims and to apply the presumption against the extraterritorial effect of U.S. statutes to the ATS.

For the same and similar reasons, U.S. courts often defer to executive branch views in particular cases and on particular issues where the executive argues (though formal statements of interest, amicus briefs and other mechanisms) that cases should not go forward—most often because of what the executive claims will be their effect on the foreign relations interests of the United States, for example by potentially upsetting U.S. relations with particular countries, or undermining U.S. foreign economic policy. As the foregoing account suggests, these types of limits to judicial remedies for international human rights violations are formidable in part because they have deep roots and strong foundations in principles of separation of powers that loom large in U.S. constitutional law and jurisprudence more generally and in foreign affairs-related cases especially. But judicial deference to executive views is not unlimited in foreign-related cases, including those seeking damages for human rights violations. Courts sometimes reject executive-branch calls to dismiss cases (including human rights cases) because of asserted foreign policy interests, and courts are less deferential to the executive on questions of interpreting international law than they are on other foreign affairs-related issues.[39]

---

[37] See, e.g., Schneider v. Kissinger, 310 F. Supp. 2d 251 (D.D.C. 2004) (dismissal, partly on political question grounds of claim against senior U.S. official for ordering foreign official's murder); Saldana v. Occidental Petroleum Corp., 774 F.3d 544 (9th Cir. 2014) (political question doctrine bars ATS claim that was "inextricably tied" to political question of U.S. decision to support paramilitary group that harmed plaintiffs); Du v. Cisco Systems, 2 F.Supp.3d 717 (D. Md. 2014) (political question doctrine bars consideration of claims concerning China's use of defendant's exported technology to effect political persecution/human rights violations because of complex U.S. government regulatory scheme governing export of multiple use technology to China). For an inventory of doctrinal bases for dismissals of cases in this general category, see Davis (2008) 92–95.

[38] Baker v. Carr, 369 U.S. 186, 217 (1962).

[39] See, e.g., Doe v. Liu Qi, 349 F. Supp. 2d 1258 (N.D. Cal. 2004); see also Bradley (2001) 457, deLisle (2003), Stephens (2004) 182 (contrasting views of human rights civil litigation's potential to affect adversely U.S. foreign policy interests); and Bradley (2000) 649 (arguing for deference to executive, including interpretations of international law).

Other doctrines that can vex plaintiffs in transnational civil litigation in U.S. courts have had relatively little impact in human rights cases. *Forum non conveniens* motions face relatively bleak prospects where they would lead to sending a plaintiff seeking redress for human rights violations back to the courts of the state where, or by which, the violations were committed.[40] Although some courts have indicated that plaintiffs may be required to exhaust available and adequate foreign forum remedies, plaintiffs in transnational human rights cases can often show that such remedies are unavailable or futile. Statute of limitations problems have been eased by relatively generous equitable tolling doctrines or the inclusion of long statutes of limitations in some human rights-focused statutes.

In suits against U.S. government defendants (especially arising from the post-9/11 war on terror), plaintiffs have faced often-daunting barriers, including: the political question doctrine (discussed above), sovereign immunity (discussed below), specific statutory immunity (in the case of claims brought by possible "enemy combatants"),[41] official immunity (discussed below), and protection of state secrets (which can bring dismissal of cases where the court finds adjudicating the case would entail disclosure).

A final difficulty for plaintiffs is that judgments are often impossible to collect against foreign defendants, given the immunity of most property owned by foreign sovereigns from execution of judgments, courts' deference to executive branch judgments that enforcement would interfere with foreign policy or treaty obligations, and the lack of resources or reachable resources held by individual and other non-sovereign defendants. These difficulties are part of what has made multinational corporations an increasingly common target of transnational human rights litigation. For some plaintiffs, slim chances for financial reward are not a major concern because their principal aims are formal vindication or public awareness.

18.2 Domestic Law: Damages for Human Rights Violations Without an International Element

18.2.1 U.S. Domestic Law and International Human Rights Obligations

As the foregoing overview of U.S. law concerning transnational cases reflects, U.S. law can (or at least has and could) provide civil damages remedies to address violations of human rights committed abroad or against non-nationals. Human rights law

[40]A rare contrary case involved claimed environmental harms, Aguinda v. Texaco, 303 F.3d 470 (2d Cir. 2002).

[41]The Military Commissions Act of 2006 prohibits civil claims against U.S. defendants by non-citizen plaintiffs who were determined to be, or were in the process of being considered for determination as, "enemy combatants"—later changed to "unprivileged enemy belligerents"—and who were challenging their detention, treatment or conditions of confinement. 10 USC 948a-950w.

is, however, an anomaly in international law in that it primarily concerns obligations that a state owes to its own citizens (or others in its territory), principally to protect them from abuse by the state's organs, officials and nationals. Much of the U.S. law providing damages remedies for acts that infringe international human rights focuses on such "domestic" violations.[42] U.S. law does this in several ways.

Human rights treaties provide a source of international legal obligation to protect human rights in the United States.[43] But in acceding to human rights treaties, the U.S. declares—or, still more broadly, courts interpret (sometimes at the urging of the executive)—such treaties as non-self-executing and thus dependent on domestic lawmaking to make treaty-based rights and duties enforceable through private civil actions.[44] Any treaty-based rights that enter fully into U.S. law are vulnerable to being overridden by subsequent inconsistent congressional legislation (under the so-called "last in time" rule). On rare occasion, U.S. legislation states that it is adopted to implement international human rights treaty obligations. The more common U.S. approach is to assert that existing domestic law is sufficient to satisfy the U.S.'s human rights treaty obligations. In many cases, the U.S. also adopts reservations, understandings or declarations (RUDs) stating that the U.S. limits or interprets its obligations under a treaty as consistent with U.S. law, including especially constitutional law. The constitutional law invoked in these RUDs principally concerns freedoms of speech, association and conscience (First Amendment rights), federalism, and capital punishment (including for juveniles).[45] This is the approach that was taken, for example, when the U.S. ratified the International Covenant of Civil and Political Rights (ICCPR), the Convention against Torture and Other Cruel, Inhuman or Degrading Treatment or Punishment (CAT), and the Convention on the Elimination of All Forms of Racial Discrimination (CERD), among others. (The U.S. has not acceded to the International Covenant of Economic, Social and Cultural Rights and therefore has no treaty-based obligations to implement its requirements.)

Customary international human rights law is part of the body of customary international law that U.S. courts, in principle, can look to as part of the common law to be applied in adjudicating damages-seeking suits, including those arising from

---

[42] To the extent that other requirements can be met—including but not limited to personal jurisdiction—these laws are available to address cases with a transnational element as well. As noted above and discussed below, some transnational human rights cases involve claims against U.S. government defendants, sometimes by U.S. citizen plaintiffs, particularly in cases arising from the "war on terror."

[43] As noted above, treaties also provide a basis—albeit an almost entirely idle one—for ATS claims.

[44] See, e.g., UN Human Rights Council, Report of the Working Group on the Universal Periodic Review, United States of America, UN Doc. A/HRC/16/11 (Jan. 4, 2011); UN Human Rights Council, Report of the Working Group on the Universal Periodic Review, United States of America, Addendum, UN Doc. A/HRC/16/11/Add.1 (Mar. 8, 2011). For a review of human rights related RUDs, see Jowanna (2010, pp. 35–41).

[45] The Supreme Court has since held unconstitutional capital punishment for crimes committed when the defendant was a minor. Roper v. Simmons, 543 U.S. 551 (2005).

actions that violate human rights.[46] As with treaty-based law, so too with the customary law of human rights: U.S. courts do not look explicitly to international human rights norms in cases that lack a clear foreign or transnational dimension.

As this all suggests and reflects, the principal laws providing damages remedies for human rights violations committed against U.S. nationals (and some non-nationals) in the United States (and primarily by U.S. defendants) are domestic laws that are characterized by little connection to international human rights law or explicit reference to human rights in any form.

18.2.2 Section 1983 Actions

Enacted on the basis of the post-Civil War constitutional amendments and as part of the Reconstruction Civil Rights Acts (of 1866, 1870, and 1871), 42 U.S.C. § 1983 provides for a remedy (including damages) against any "person who, under color of any" law, "custom, or usage" of any U.S. state "subjects, or causes to be subjected, any citizen of the United States" or any "other person within the jurisdiction thereof to the deprivation of any rights, privileges, or immunities secured by the Constitution and laws."[47] Relatively fallow for most of the near-century preceding the Civil Rights movement of the 1960s, Section 1983 has become a principal mechanism for obtaining damages awards in cases involving violations of human rights, primarily civil and political rights.[48] As the text of the law indicates, plaintiffs can be U.S. citizens or non-citizens present in the United States when the violation occurs (although non-citizens, even when in the U.S., do not enjoy some constitutional and federal law rights—and, in turn, protection of those rights through Section 1983 litigation—that citizens do). Exhaustion of state law remedies is not a prerequisite to a Section 1983 claim.

Although the text appears to leave open the possibility that provisions in a self-executing human rights treaty are "laws" of the United States for purposes of Section 1983 (and some limited, oblique and inconsistent authority supports this reading[49]), Section 1983's focus in providing damages for human rights violations lies elsewhere, in offering redress for violations of U.S. constitutional rights and other federal rights embodied in domestic-oriented laws. Several of the federal, pri-

---

[46] This principle was established early in U.S. law, in *The Paquette Habana*, 175 U.S. 677 (1900).

[47] 42 U.S.C. § 1983. On Section 1983 generally, see Schwartz and Urbonya (2008); Lewis and Norman (2004) 45–273, 279–294.

[48] A seminal case was Monroe v. Pape (1961), in which the Supreme Court established that relief was available under Section 1983 where the acts of state actors, broadly defined—including, city police officers who improperly entered and ransacked plaintiff's home and took him into custody—have violated constitutional (or other federal law) rights, which can include human rights. Monroe held that a claim existed even when the state actors' acts violated state law as well.

[49] Jogi v. Voges, 480 F.3d 822 (7th Cir. 2007) (Section 1983—as well as ATS—remedy for violation of rights conferred *pursuant* to the Vienna Convention on Consular Relations); Vazquez (1992) 1082.

marily constitutional rights that have been common foci of Section 1983 claims overlap key internationally recognized human rights.

Cases involving these rights fall into a few categories: violations of constitutional procedural due process when state action deprives the victim of life, liberty or property interests; violations of constitutional substantive due process, which provides protection of fundamental individual constitutional rights (including many enumerated in the Bill of Rights, and other rights discerned by the courts, such as privacy-based rights to family autonomy, reproductive/procreative freedom and freedom from unconscionable assaults on bodily integrity); violations of specific provisions of the Bill of Rights, many of which are incorporated, and thus made applicable to the states (including local government entities) by the Fourteenth Amendment (which, along with the slavery-abolishing Thirteenth Amendment, forms the principal constitutional basis for the Civil Rights Acts, including Section 1983); and violations of rights to equal protection of the laws, principally discrimination on the basis of classifications such as race, citizenship, and gender. The standard of "culpability" of the defendant that is required for an actionable violation differs somewhat across the relevant constitutional rights, and the requirements for a Section 1983 claim vary in tandem, generally tracking the constitutional law defining the contours of the specific type of right.

Common types of behavior by state actors that have been targets of cognizable Section 1983 claims and that overlap with violations of human rights include unconstitutional or other federal rights-violating: arrests, searches and seizures; conditions of confinement in prisons or jails; excessive use of force by police or penal system officers; retaliation against government employees or retaliatory prosecution of plaintiffs for exercises of freedom of speech or political affiliation (or complaints about rights violations); denial of a fair trial/wrongful conviction;[50] and some forms of race-based and gender-based discrimination by state actors.

There are significant limits to section 1983's reach in providing damages remedies for human rights violations. First, most fundamentally and as the foregoing partial inventory suggests, some international human rights norms are not U.S. constitutional rights or federal law rights and thus are not bases for a Section 1983 claim. This is especially the case with social and economic human rights, but it is also true for some civil and political human rights (including, most notoriously, those imposing limitations on capital punishment) and some human rights that impose affirmative duties of action on states.[51]

Second, the range of covered rights under Section 1983 has been rendered narrower than the statutory text might suggest. This has occurred largely by judicial construction, especially with regard to non-constitutional federal rights, and with

---

[50] The Supreme Court has limited relief in this area by barring Section 1983 claims that would have the effect of invalidating a not-otherwise-invalidated state court conviction. See Heck v. Humphrey, 512 U.S. 477 (1994).

[51] Here, "states" means states in the international law sense, not the Section 1983 sense of states in the United States.

escalating restrictions on Section 1983 remedies in recent years.[52] Federal laws are not automatically construed to confer the legal rights required for potential protection through Section 1983 actions. A plaintiff must show that, in the asserted rights-creating federal law: the plaintiff was an intended beneficiary of the law; the asserted right is not so vague or amorphous as to be unsuitable for judicial enforcement; and the law clearly imposes a binding legal obligation on the defendant.[53] Where these requirements are met, relief under Section 1983 still will not be available if the court finds that Congress intended to foreclose such a remedy—a finding that is likely whenever the statute provides a private remedy that is less expansive than Section 1983. Moreover, with respect to some rights, where a defendant can show that it would have reached the "same decision"—for example, where plaintiff would have been fired even if retaliation for plaintiff's exercise of First Amendment free speech rights, or discrimination that violated plaintiff's Equal Protection clause rights, had not been among the defendant's motives—the defendant will not be liable.

A diverse set of doctrines limits plaintiffs' ability to bring Section 1983 actions in federal courts (where Section 1983 claims often are brought and access to which—as an alternative to distrusted state courts—was a key concern motivating Section 1983's creation). The Supreme Court recently has tightened pleading standards in terms that extend to Section 1983 claims in federal court. In *Ashcroft v. Iqbal* (a *Bivens* action, discussed below), the Court held that a federal court, in deciding whether to dismiss a complaint for failure to state a claim on which relief may be granted, should not credit merely conclusory allegations by the plaintiff and must apply "its judicial experience and common sense" in determining whether the plaintiff's complaint states a "plausible claim for relief."[54]

Other judicially created doctrines impose additional barriers to Section 1983 damages suits in federal court. For example, federal courts may abstain from adjudicating a case where going forward would interfere with an ongoing state prosecution.[55] For another example, federal courts do not hear Section 1983 claims where granting relief would have the effect of invalidating an existing state court criminal conviction that has not otherwise been invalidated.[56]

Such restrictions on Section 1983 claims in federal courts do not bar Section 1983 actions in state courts. But (as noted above) suits in state court against the state, its officials and those acting with its authority can be relatively unappealing for plaintiffs, and (as discussed below) other laws can block Section 1983 suits in

---

[52] See Bodensteiner (2010) 29; also the symposium issue on *Enforcing Constitutional Rights in the Twenty-First Century: Section 1983 Thirty Years After Owen v. Independence*, in University of Missouri, Kansas City Law Review, volume 78 (2010); Rudovsky (2005) 1199.

[53] Blessing v. Freestone 520 U.S. 319 (1997).

[54] Ashcroft v. Iqbal, 556 U.S. 662 (2009); Wasserman (2010). Assessments of the impact of the heightened pleading standard are ongoing and uncertain. See Malveaux (2012–2013).

[55] See generally Deakins v. Monaghan, 484 U.S. 193 (1988) (possibility of Younger v. Harris-like abstention in Section 1983 action for damages only). On abstention in Section 1983 cases generally, see, Schwartz and Urbonya (2008) 177-189, Lewis and Norman (2004) 419–431.

[56] See Heck v. Humphrey, 512 U.S. 477 (1994). Courts divide over whether this limitation applies in all cases or only those in which habeas corpus relief is available.

state courts. If a plaintiff does bring a Section 1983 claim in state court, the defendant can remove the case to federal court.

Third, the range of defendants is limited, and in some respects more limited than the statutory language of Section 1983 and the civil rights statutes might suggest and case law once allowed. In the many Section 1983 claims that assert violations of constitutional rights, the claim rests on the Fourteenth Amendment and thus requires that the acts for which the plaintiff seeks recovery meet a state action requirement—that is, that the acts constituting rights violations be legally attributable to the government or those acting in concert with government actors. Suits against federal government entities and officials are not authorized by Section 1983[57] (although they sometimes can be brought on other bases, including *Bivens* actions or the Federal Tort Claims Act, discussed below). Suits in federal court for damages against state governments themselves are barred by the Eleventh Amendment, absent state consent to suit or clear and express indication of Congress's intent to abrogate immunity (which the courts have not found in Section 1983), and because neither the state nor officials, when sued in their official capacities, are "persons" under Section 1983.[58] Suits against state officers in their official capacities cannot be for money damages because such damages would come from the state treasury, and this, in the Supreme Court's analysis, makes such suits indistinguishable from suits against the state itself.[59] State immunity doctrines and defenses under state law (discussed below) can create additional barriers for plaintiffs seeking damages remedies in state courts for human rights violations.

Damages remedies are available under Section 1983 against local government entities. But these defendants are not liable for discrete violations of relevant rights, nor are they vicariously liable—on the basis of *respondeat superior* or similar theories—for rights violations committed by their employees or agents. Local government entities are liable only where the plaintiff can show that the violation of a relevant constitutional or other federal law right followed from: an official "policy"; a decision (including ratification or delegation of authority) by a policymaker with final authority; a "custom" or "practice" of pervasive rights violations of which policymaking officials had actual or constructive knowledge; or "deliberate indifference" toward recurring rights violations as manifested, typically, in failure to screen (in hiring), train, supervise or to take corrective action.[60] Based as they are on claims

[57] This limitation usually applies because federal officials ordinarily act under color of federal law, not state law, although a federal officer who conspires with a state officer might be found to have acted under color of state law and thus be subject to a Section 1983 claim. See Arar v. Ashcroft, 585 F.3d 559, 568 (2d Cir. 2009).

[58] See Will v. Michigan Dept of State Police, 491 U.S. 58 (1989). As discussed below, bars on official capacity suits do not bar suits against officials in their "personal capacities" for acts committed under "color of law," including acts made possible by their powers of office.

[59] See Ford Motor Co. v. Department of Treasury of the State of Indiana, 323 U.S. 459 (1945) (overruled on other grounds).

[60] Key cases include Monell v. Department of Social Services, 436 U.S. 658 (1978); City of Canton v. Harris, 489 U.S. 378 (1989) Board of County Commissioners of Bryan County, Okla. v. Brown, 520 U.S. 397 (1997).

about decisions by those who do not directly harm plaintiffs and claims about failures to act, suits against municipalities and similar entities can founder on plaintiffs' difficulties in proving causation (generally under ordinary tort law standards). Only compensatory, not punitive, damages are available against local government entities. Suits against local officials in their official capacity face limitations that track those applicable to suits against local government entities.

Given these restrictions on defendants amenable to Section 1983 damages suits, it is not surprising that much Section 1983 litigation—especially that which addresses acts that constitute human rights violations—targets officials in their individual capacities. Section 1983 actions of this type can proceed against officials who act "under color of state law," broadly defined. This includes unlawful acts that were made possible by the defendant's powers of office even though they may have violated the relevant government entity's policies and rules and occurred outside the ordinary scope of the defendant's duties.

Supervisory officials may be held liable in these types of suits, but only on standards that have generally tracked the rules for municipal liability (including a rejection of *respondeat superior* or other vicarious liability and a requirement that the supervisor have actual or constructive knowledge of pervasive or recurring abuses of rights by subordinates and have responded in so inadequate a way as to show deliberate indifference or tacit authorization). The Supreme Court's somewhat opaque but clearly critical view of supervisory liability in *Iqbal* (discussed below) has created disagreement among courts and scholars about whether its restrictive language and possibly seriously narrowing effect on supervisory liability does or should extend to Section 1983 (where, unlike the *Bivens* claim in *Iqbal*, the cause of action has a basis in an act of Congress—and one that includes specific language concerning the scope of liability).[61]

In addition to compensatory damages for economic, physical and psychological harms[62] (and in some cases defamation-caused harm to reputation), punitive damages are available in Section 1983 personal capacity suits if the defendant had malicious or evil intent, or showed reckless or callous indifference to the plaintiff's federally protected rights. In personal capacity suits against individual defendants, the damages award is formally against the defendant's own assets but, in practice, the government entity often bears the burden of the award through indemnification or insurance.

Official immunity can pose formidable barriers to Section 1983 plaintiffs. Legislators, prosecutors and judges—and other officials exercising similar authority—enjoy absolute immunity for actions taken within the scope of their legislative, prosecutorial or judicial functions. Such officials when acting outside those functions

---

[61] See Levinson (2012) 273; Pfander (2010) 1387. Some courts have held specifically that Iqbal does apply; others have held that it does not. See Dodds v. Richardson, 614 F.3d 1185 (10th Cir. 2010). A recent Supreme Court case uses pre-Iqbal analysis, and does not mention Iqbal, in a supervisory liability case brought under Section 1983. Connick v. Thompson, 131 S.Ct. 1350 (2011).

[62] Under the Prison Litigation Reform Act, prisoners may not bring Section 1983 claims for mental or emotional injuries suffered in custody without a prior showing of physical harm. 42 U.S.C. § 1997e(e).

and other officials enjoy lesser, "qualified immunity" in damages suits. Qualified immunity applies unless the official knew, or unless it would have been clear to a reasonable official under the circumstances, that his or her relevant conduct violated a clearly established legal right (one of which a reasonable person in the official's position would be aware).[63] This test is often an insurmountable hurdle for plaintiffs[64] although it is, of course, less relevant in cases asserting the most obvious and egregious human rights violations. This official immunity does not apply in suits against municipalities.

The "color of state law" provision in Section 1983 allows suits against some private actors (notwithstanding the constitutional "state action" requirement discussed above). Courts have characterized the requisite degree of connection between private actors or actions and the state or its laws in various ways: the existence of a symbiotic relationship between private actor and the state; pervasive entwinement of the private actor with the state; joint participation akin to a private actor's conspiracy with, or aiding and abetting of, state officials; the private actor's exercise or performance of a distinctively public function (such as one that was traditionally the exclusive role of the state); or the private actor's acting sufficiently at the encouragement or direction of the state that its acts can be said to reflect the state's choices. In such cases, official immunity generally has not been available.[65]

A final difficulty for Section 1983 (and, as discussed below, *Bivens*) plaintiffs is that in some cases, including some involving rights that overlap with international human rights, plaintiffs may not be able to prove significant, measurable harm. Courts sometimes insulate plaintiffs from the peril of losing despite showing a relevant rights violation by awarding nominal damages. In some cases, plaintiffs can show conventional compensable harms, but only on a modest scale. This, of course, limits compensatory damages awards[66] and, under recent Supreme Court jurisprudence (which, outside of human rights contexts, has struck down punitive damage awards that exceed single-digit multiples of compensatory awards), low compensatory awards might be found to preclude some especially large punitive damages awards where punitive damages are permissible under Section 1983. Courts sometimes have found the "reprehensibility" of acts grounding some successful Section 1983 claims sufficient to sustain high punitive awards in cases with low compensatory awards.[67]

---

[63] Harlow v. Fitzgerald, 457 U.S. 800 (1982); see also Taylor v. Barkes, 135 S.Ct. 2042 (2015) (post-Iqbal decision applying same qualified immunity standard in supervisory liability § 1983 case); Wells (2012). Unlike under earlier common law qualified official immunity, subjective good faith is not the standard.

[64] See Blum (2015).

[65] Although the issue has not been definitively resolved, private defendants, who do not enjoy the qualified immunity available to official defendants, might be able to claim "good faith" immunity, but such claims would be hard to sustain in many cases involving human rights violations.

[66] It does not preclude significant attorneys' fees, which are available under Section 1983 and several other civil rights statutes discussed below, but not in Bivens actions. Such fees can dwarf compensatory damages awards.

[67] See generally, Wells (2012); Roberts (2006); Anthony DiSarro (2012).

18.2.3 Constitutional Torts/Bivens Actions

Named after the seminal 1971 case of *Bivens v. Six Unknown Named Agents of the Federal Bureau of Narcotics*, *Bivens* actions are based on a judicially implied right of action for violations of constitutional rights by federal officials or employees. Broadly parallel to Section 1983 litigation against state and local government officials or employees in their personal capacities (discussed above), *Bivens* suits permit damages awards for violations of a range of constitutional rights that overlap with human rights, principally civil and political rights. As with section 1983 claims, *Bivens* plaintiffs need not be U.S. citizens, but suits by non-citizens are limited by broader constitutional principles that do not extend the full range of human rights-relevant constitutional rights to non-citizens. Punitive damages are available, largely on the same terms as in Section 1983 suits against state actors in their individual capacities.

Constitutional rights that have been foci of *Bivens* suits and that can overlap with human rights include many of the constitutional rights that have been at issue in Section 1983 actions. These rights include: freedom from unreasonable and warrantless searches, seizures and arrests; freedom from cruel and unusual punishment, primarily in the form of impermissible conditions of confinement or treatment in custody (in federal facilities); equal protection of the laws and thus freedom from discrimination, particularly on the basis of race or gender; and (to a less certain extent) freedom from religious, national origin, or political viewpoint-based discrimination.

There are significant limits to *Bivens* actions as sources of damages remedies for human rights violations. First, as is the case with Section 1983 actions, many international human rights lie outside the scope of the U.S. constitutional rights that fall within the potential reach of a *Bivens* suit. Second, as with Section 1983, judicial constructions have limited the ambit of *Bivens* constitutional tort suits. Not all potentially human rights-related federal constitutional rights have been the objects of successful *Bivens* suits. After substantial growth in *Bivens* suits' reach during the first decade, the courts—and especially the Supreme Court—have rejected efforts to expand *Bivens* actions' scope during the last twenty years. Although the comparison is complicated, *Bivens* remedies are generally seen as narrower than analogous forms of redress that enjoy congressional authorization under Section 1983.[68] *Iqbal* (discussed above), which is widely regarded as calling for tighter scrutiny—and thus more frequent dismissal—of plaintiff's claims at the pleading stage, was a *Bivens* suit (involving alleged discriminatory detention—on the basis of religion or national origin—and in-custody abuse of a Pakistani-American Muslim in the aftermath of the 9/11 terrorist attacks).

Before *Iqbal*, the Supreme Court had foreclosed *Bivens* actions where: Congress had provided an alternative remedy that supplanted a *Bivens* action; or other

---

[68] For an overview of these issues, see Pfander and Baltmanis (2009), Reinert and Mulligam (2013).

"special factors" counseled hesitation in implying a cause of action.[69] Relying primarily on the "special factors" prong, courts have rebuffed several categories of *Bivens* suits that could address human rights violations, including claims of improper state takings of property, politically retaliatory firing, and conditions in privately operated federal prisons (in purely domestic contexts), and conditions of—and reasons for—confinement (in the context of the war on terror).[70] As this last point suggests, human rights-related *Bivens* actions have fared especially poorly when they have arisen from the post-9/11 war on terror; the courts have rejected even claims asserting torture by, or as a consequence of unlawful acts by, U.S. government officials, including against U.S. citizen victims.[71]

"Special factors" counseling hesitation upon which the courts have relied include perceived risks that allowing a *Bivens* action would: undermine law enforcement officers in the zealous performance of their duties; prove unnecessary given the existence of federal or state law remedies that could address the same behavior; entangle the court in cases with no workable cause of action; or—especially in the war on terror-related cases—interfere with foreign affairs, national security policy, military decision-making, or the need to protect state secrets. The reasoning behind these judicial rejections of *Bivens* claims resonate with those underlying judicially recognized defenses in transnational human rights claims, including: political question-like concerns about each branch's proper constitutional roles and institutional competence; and foreign affairs power-linked deference to the political branches and especially the executive in matters affecting national security and international relations more generally—all the more so in the post-9/11 era.[72]

Third, the range of *Bivens* defendants is limited. Suits must be against individuals who act as officials or agents of the federal government, and not federal government entities themselves. Federal supervisory and high-ranking officials may be less subject to *Bivens* actions than are their state counterparts to Section 1983 suits. Although some critics have sought, perhaps wishfully, to dismiss it as dicta or as not clearly altering preexisting law, the Supreme Court's approach to supervisory liability in *Iqbal* indicated that supervisory officials (in this case top-level federal officials, specifically the Attorney General and the Director of the Federal Bureau of Investigation) could not be held liable (in this case in a *Bivens* action) based on principles of *respondeat superior* liability or even "knowledge and acquiescence in their subordinates'" rights-violating behavior. To be liable, such a supervisory official must himself or herself have violated plaintiff's Bivens-covered constitutional

[69] Carlson v. Green, 446 U.S. 14 (1980); see also Bush v. Lucas, 462 U.S. 367 (1983) (denying *Bivens* remedy given availability of alternative remedies for federal employee claiming retaliatory demotion).

[70] See, e.g., Wilkie v. Robbins, 551 U.S. 537 (2007); Bush v. Lucas, 462 U.S. 367 (1983); Minneci v. Pollard, 132 S.Ct. 617 (2012); cf. Davis v. Passman, 442 U.S. 228 (1979).

[71] See, for example, Arar v. Ashcroft, 585 F.3d 559 (2d Cir. 2009); Vance v. Rumsfeld, 653 F.3d 591 (7th Cir. 2012).

[72] On these issues, especially post-9/11, see Pfander and Baltmanis (2009); Brown (2009); Vladeck (2006) 4–5.

rights. In the context of the rights at issue in *Iqbal*, this required "intent," in a sense stronger than "volition" or "awareness of consequences" and amounting to the "decision-maker's undertaking a course of action 'because of'" the constitutionally prohibited discriminatory motivation (in this case, detention on the basis of religion or national origin). *Bivens* actions' potential as a means that alleged or possible "enemy combatant" detainees in the war on terror might have used was undermined by the Military Commissions Act's ban (discussed above) on such plaintiffs bringing detention-related civil actions against U.S. defendants.

Fourth, official immunity can bar *Bivens* suits, very much as it does Section 1983 claims against individual defendants. Qualified immunity can be an effective bar in some human rights-related cases—as occurred when a court held that there was no violation of a clearly established constitutional right when a border patrol agent used deadly force against an illegal immigrant from Mexico who had no prior contact with the United States.[73] In recent *Bivens* suits arising from the "war on terror," the courts also have deferred to executive branch views on immunity, extending a longstanding practice in foreign affairs-related cases to the foreign relations-related (or, perhaps more narrowly, terrorism-related) subset of *Bivens* cases.

18.2.4 Other Civil Rights and Related Laws

Although Section 1983 and *Bivens* actions are the most prominent federal law providing damages remedies for acts that violate human rights, some other federal laws do so as well.[74] Primarily, these laws prohibit discrimination, principally on the basis of race, national origin or, somewhat less commonly, gender. Section 1981—also part of the post-Civil War Civil Rights Acts—prohibits racially discriminatory denials of the right to make and enforce contracts (although damages claims against government actors can be brought only under Section 1983), as section 1982 does for rights to acquire, hold or dispose of property. Section 1985 provides civil remedies for racially and, to a limited extent, other discriminatorily motivated conspiracies to deprive victims of equal protection of the laws, including equal enjoyment of constitutional rights. In suits against state actors, the contours of the remedies provided under these laws are similar to those of section 1983.

Titles VI and VII of the 1964 Civil Rights Act and Title IX (adopted in a 1972 amendment to education laws)—and especially the latter two—have been significant sources of law offering damages remedies in cases of discrimination that can overlap with denials of human rights.[75] Title VI prohibits discrimination on the basis of race and national origin in any federally funded program (although it generally does not reach employment-related claims). Title VII prohibits discrimination on

[73] Hernandez v. U.S. 785 F.3d 117 (5th Cir. 2015) (Bivens action).

[74] 42 U.S.C. §§ 1981–1985. See generally, Days (2005), Lewis and Norman (2004) 1–36, 310–338.

[75] 42 U.S.C §§ 2000d-2000d-7, 2000e-2000e-17; 20 U.S.C. 20 U.S.C. §§ 1681–1688.

the basis of race, sex, religion or national origin in employment, including by private employers with more than a small number of employees. Title IX bars gender-based discrimination in federally funded educational programs. Other federal laws address related and overlapping issues, including the Equal Pay Act (EPA—gender discrimination in pay by employers or in employment affecting interstate commerce), the Age Discrimination in Employment Act (ADEA—discrimination against those over age 40 by employers with more than a small number of employees) and the Americans with Disabilities Act (ADA—discrimination against those with disabilities).[76]

These anti-discrimination laws provide—by explicit text or judicial interpretation—private rights of action that include claims for money damages. The form, scope and amount of damages vary across the laws. Punitive damages, for example, are restricted to a subset of cases of "intentional" discrimination under Title VII and Title IX,[77] are not available under Title VI, and are capped under Title VII, the ADEA and the EPA. Remedies for lost back pay and future pay are handled differently under employment-related laws. Unlike Section 1983, Titles VI, VII and IX abrogate state immunity from suit in federal court.

Although the Religious Freedom Restoration Act (RFRA) provides for claims against the U.S. government for actions that "substantially burden" a plaintiff's "exercise of religion" unless the government's action is "in furtherance of a compelling governmental interest" and employs the "least restrictive means available" (the standards imposed by the "strict scrutiny" test applied in constitutional law to government actions that burden fundamental rights), federal courts in recent years have increasingly construed it as not waiving the government's sovereign immunity from suits for money damages.[78]

Other federal statutes sometimes provide a right to damages remedies for acts that can include human rights violations. As noted above, Congress's explicit provision of an alternative remedial scheme in a substantive statute is a basis for courts to reject *Bivens* actions (and the existence of alternative remedies also has been a "special factor" weighing against allowing a *Bivens* action). Still, among the many federal laws that address behavior that can infringe human rights, few have been or will be held to provide an independent basis for a civil suit for damages. In the absence of clear affirmative evidence of legislative intent to authorize a private right of action (or in the presence of congressional creation of an alternative remedial frame-

---

[76] 29 U.S.C. §§ 206(d), 216(b), 621–634; 42 U.S.C. §§ 12101–12117.

[77] Under Title VII, courts have held that intentional discrimination is a necessary but not sufficient condition for punitive damages. Damages under Title VII are also limited where the defendant can show that the "same decision" would have been reached absent impermissible discrimination against plaintiff. Under Title IX, intentional, willful, or deliberate discrimination is required for compensatory damages. Some lower courts have disallowed punitive damages in Title IX claims generally.

[78] 42 U.S.C. §§ 2000bb-2000bb-4. The Supreme Court similarly has found that sovereign immunity survives and damages in suits against state defendants are therefore unavailable in prisoner religious liberty cases brought under the Religious Land Use and Institutionalized Persons Act. See Sossamon v. Texas, 131 S.Ct. 1651 (2011).

work), courts will not construe such laws to provide the relief plaintiffs seek. The Supreme Court has created a strong presumption against implying a private right of action in a regulatory statute.[79] Further, the Court sometimes rejects efforts by Congress to create damages remedies for acts that may violate human rights. For example, until the provision was struck down as beyond Congress's constitutional powers to legislate, the Violence against Women Act briefly provided a damages remedy (both compensatory and punitive) for women who were injured by "a crime of violence motivated by gender."

In the U.S.'s federal structure, individual states have their own elaborate constitutions, constitutional rights provisions and, sometimes, civil rights statutes. In some cases, these are more protective than the federal law that is the focus of the foregoing discussion. And those who seek to expand judicial protections (including damages remedies) for rights (including those overlapping with human rights) have turned—or advocated a turn—to greater reliance on state law (especially state constitutional law), particularly in the wake of the legal developments described above that have limited federal remedies. There is, however, considerable variety in relevant state law, and there are limits akin to those found in federal law (including immunity doctrines, which have their origins in common law) that impede otherwise viable state law claims.[80] Although they are limited (and in many respects have become increasingly limited), federal law remedies such as the Civil Rights Act, federal constitutional tort suits, and so on, still loom larger than individual states' laws among the U.S. laws that are most immediately connected with protection of human rights and awarding of damages for violations.

Another factor limiting constitutional and civil rights-based damages awards' role in addressing human rights violations may stem from the view—particularly in an era of widespread criticism of court "activism"—that private damages remedies are a second-best alternative to legislative remedies or state enforcement actions or injunctions. To some critics, damages remedies also suggest an unsavory commodification of inalienable rights.[81]

18.2.5 Common Law Torts and the Federal Tort Claims Act

Common law tort actions are another means for obtaining damages awards for some acts that violate human rights.[82] The United States has waived sovereign immunity for many torts, generally through the Federal Tort Claims Act (FTCA) and more

---

[79] Alexander v. Sandoval, 532 U.S. 275 (2001).

[80] Shapiro (1994); Gildin (2011); Vazquez and Vladeck (2013); Preis (2008).

[81] Reinert (2010); Roberts (2006) 2010.

[82] The FSIA's tort exception, discussed above, opens the door to common law tort suits against foreign sovereigns. As also discussed above, common law torts sometimes provide the requisite cause of action in ATS and other transnational human rights cases.

narrowly in a small number of specific statutes.[83] The FTCA generally subjects the federal government (including its component agencies and organs) to claims for money damages for harms due to its employees' acts in many circumstances in which a private defendant would be liable for injury to property or person under the common law of the relevant state. Under the Westfall Act, suits against federal officials for actions taken within their scope of employment—but not for some acts in violation of the constitution or federal statutes—are treated as FTCA claims against the government (and thereby are subject to the government's expansive defenses, including sovereign immunity).[84]

There are, however, significant limits to the FTCA's waiver of immunity and thus its utility for plaintiffs seeking damages for harms that stem from acts violating their human rights.[85] The FTCA does not waive immunity for: intentional torts relevant to human rights violations—including assault, battery, false imprisonment, false arrest, malicious prosecution, abuse of process and defamation (but not intentional infliction of emotional distress or invasion of privacy)—unless committed by an investigative or law-enforcement official (a caveat that can be significant for human rights cases); injuries occurring outside the United States (even if some relevant tortious acts and underlying decisions occurred in the U.S.); or injuries occurring in combat activities. Punitive damages are not allowed. Suits for negligent supervision of tort-committing employees are sometimes allowed. The FTCA also imposes a relatively strict exhaustion of administrative remedies requirement: victims must first seek redress from the relevant federal government agency before proceeding to court. And courts have barred FTCA claims when they find that other, more specific statutes provide their own remedial schemes.

Like the FSIA's tort exception (discussed above), the FTCA's waiver of the U.S.'s immunity adopts a "discretionary function" exception that, in the FTCA context, often means defeat for plaintiffs. The exception (in effect) "reconfers" immunity where the tort claim is, in the words of a leading Supreme Court opinion, "based upon [a federal agency's or employee's] exercise or performance or failure to exercise or perform a discretionary function…, whether or not [that] discretion [is] abused."[86] Subsequent Supreme Court decisions have made clear that discretionary functions include conduct that involves—in a broad sense—a mandate in the relevant law for a state actor (regardless of his or her status or office) to exercise social, economic or political policy-based choice. Where the court finds that such room for choice existed, the court adopts a "strong presumption" that defendant made the choice based on the permissible policy considerations (and the discretionary

[83] 28 U.S.C. § 2680.

[84] The legislative history of the Westfall Act indicated an intention not to shield federal employee defendants from liability for "egregious torts" by substituting the U.S. as a defendant. Stephens et al. (2008) 291. As this suggests, *Bivens* actions can be available for some acts not covered by the Westfall Act that violate human rights.

[85] Fuller (2011); Niles (2002); Skinner (2012–2013); Nelson (2009).

[86] Dalehite v. United States, 365 U.S. 15 (1953).

function exception therefore applies), lest courts unduly second-guess political branches' policy decisions.[87]

As addressed above, federal and state laws governing suits against foreign or domestic state entities and actors sometimes open the door (albeit often only a crack) to common law tort suits seeking money damages for harms that can include harms stemming from violations of human rights. And suits against non-state actors for acts that violate human rights (particularly, violations that do not require conventional state action) sometimes can be—and sometimes only can be—brought as ordinary tort claims. Many forms of human rights abuse constitute battery (the intentional infliction of a harmful or offensive touching) or assault (whether attempted battery known to the plaintiff or a threat that seeks to put, and succeeds in putting, the plaintiff in apprehension of an imminent battery). Some human rights violations can ground tort suits that claim intentional infliction of emotional distress or false imprisonment. Some plaintiffs have sought to bring claims for human rights abuses in the employment context (including forced labor) within the reach of statutory unfair business practices law.[88] Defamation actions could reach some forms of communication, such as those that incite or contribute to human rights violations, particularly those targeting racial and other groups. Where human rights violations lead to the victim's demise, surviving relatives sometimes can bring wrongful death actions for their losses due to the victim's death. When not barred by various doctrines applicable to state entities or actors (discussed above), employers and other institutions potentially can be held vicariously liable for human rights-violating acts of their employees (although tort doctrines limiting employers' responsibility for employees' acts unrelated to employment can be a significant obstacle in cases of serious human rights violations), or for their own negligence (or worse) in failing to prevent their employees' acts.

18.3 Patterns in Addressing Human Rights Through DamagesRemedies in U.S. Law

U.S. law has been strikingly expansive in holding out the prospect of civil damages for human rights violations that include foreign actions, perpetrators or victims. While other countries' laws and international institutions sometimes have sought to reach human rights-violating behavior through criminal sanctions and other public

[87] Berkowitz v. United States, 486 531 (1988); United States v. Gaubert, 488 U.S. 391 (1991). Although this exception is generally ample and although the FTCA has not generated cases closely analogous to the FSIA cases permitting recovery in cases of politically motivated extrajudicial killings (discussed above), the FTCA's discretionary function exception would have relatively little purchase in cases of the most severe and flagrant human rights abuses, but other FTCA exceptions (including the intentional torts exception) would have to be overcome as well.

[88] For examples from cases involving human rights abuses committed largely abroad, see Stephens et al. (2008) 125–126.

enforcement measures, the laws and courts of the United States have been unusual in offering private law damages (albeit on relatively rare occasion), through such mechanisms as the Alien Tort Statute, the Torture Victims Protection Act, and the Foreign Sovereign Immunities Act (in conjunction with U.S. law's relatively broad rules on personal jurisdiction over defendants and tort liability).

U.S. law also offers a variety of means to obtain civil damages for purely domestic human rights violations. Although U.S. law provides mechanisms for receiving customary international law, including international human rights law, into U.S. law and although the U.S. has joined several major international human rights treaties, international legal norms and rules have had no significant or direct impact on U.S. law concerning damages remedies for purely domestic human rights violations. Such law comes from domestic sources—the federal constitution, federal statutes, state constitutions and statutes, judicial glosses thereon, and the common law of torts—that sometimes track or parallel, but do not engage or explicitly draw from, international human rights and related international law.

Both at home and abroad, U.S. law's offer of damages remedies has been much more robust for violations of civil and political human rights than for violations of economic, social or cultural human rights. This is hardly surprising, given the particular liberal political traditions that have shaped the U.S. constitution and other laws and, relatedly, the U.S.'s international practice of endorsing and promoting civil and political human rights much more than economic, social and cultural ones.

During the last ten to twenty or more years, the availability of damages remedies under U.S. law for human rights violations—both transnational and purely domestic—has been under pressure and, in some respects, in decline. This has occurred largely through judicial action, especially through statutory interpretation, the articulation of statutory and constitutional interpretive norms and the exercise of powers of constitutional judicial review—especially by the U.S. Supreme Court. These court-centered developments have not occurred in a political vacuum. Amid sharp and deepening political polarization in the United States, clashing ideologies and policy agendas have been part of the story. Liberal preferences for expansive remedies through litigation have faced successful conservative opposition. That opposition has been coupled with a campaign for "tort reform" that portrays damages awards as excessive and out of control and, especially during the George W. Bush administration, consistent expression by the executive branch of foreign affairs and national security-based opposition to litigation seeking damages for human rights violations occurring abroad. Conservative conceptions of the role of courts have been a major factor as well, particularly in the long-rising reluctance to imply private rights of action in statutes and regulations, a notable willingness to strike down human rights-resonant rights-protecting and remedy-providing legislation as beyond Congress's constitutional powers, and a strong tendency—in human rights-related contexts and especially in foreign affairs-related human rights contexts—of judges to defer to the government's views (which have not always been consistent over time) or interests (whether expressed by the executive or inferred by the courts).

In the post-9/11 period especially (and under both Republican and Democratic presidents), the long-running tension in U.S. foreign policy between an ameliorative or "values-based" strain that seeks to foster respect and protection for human rights, on one hand, and a more "realist" perspective that focuses on protecting traditional, narrowly defined, security-based national interests, on the other hand, has shifted notably in favor of the latter. This swing has created a less hospitable environment for legal rules and agendas that stress protection of individual rights (including human rights and especially human rights abroad), especially when solicitude for rights might come at a cost in terms of effective law enforcement, anti-terrorism efforts and so on.

As in the law of other countries, in U.S. law damages remedies are only part of a larger, complex picture of human rights-related law. They coexist with many other law-based means, including criminal prosecution, administrative enforcement, court-issued injunctions, grants of asylum to refugees, and legally mandated denials of various privileges to—or imposition of sanctions on—foreign and domestic individuals and entities that commit abuses or infringements of human rights.

References

Anderson, Kenneth. 2013. Kiobel v. Royal Dutch Petroleum: The Alien Tort Statute's jurisdictional universalism in retreat. *Cato Supreme Court Review* 149–185.

Blum, Karen A. 2015. Section 1983 Litigation: The maze, the mud and the madness, *William and Mary Law Review* 23: 913–964.

Bodensteiner, Ivan E. 2010. Congress needs to repair the court's damage to § 1983. *Texas Journal of Civil Liberties and Civil Rights* 16: 29–76.

Bradley, Curtis A. 2000. Chevron deference and foreign affairs. *Virginia Law Review* 86: 649–726.

Bradley, Curtis A. 2001. The costs of international human rights litigation. *Chicago Journal of International Law* 2: 457–474.

Bradley, Curtis A. 2010. State action and corporate human rights liability. *Notre Dame Law Review* 85: 1823–1838.

Bradley, Curtis A. 2013. *International law in the U.S. legal system.* Oxford: Oxford University Press.

Bradley, Curtis A., and Jack L. Goldsmith. 1997. Customary international law as federal common law: A critique of the modern position. *Harvard Law Review* 110: 815–876.

Bradley, Curtis A., and Jack L. Goldsmith. 2010. Foreign Sovereign immunity and domestic officer suits. *Green Bag* 13: 137–151.

Bradley, Curtis A., and Laurence Helfer. 2011. International law and the U.S. common law of foreign officer immunity. *Supreme Court Review* 213–278.

Brown, George D. 2009. Counter-Counter-Terrorism via Lawsuit—The Bivens impasse. *Southern California Law Review* 82: 841–912.

Chomsky, Judith. 2010. Will the real ATS please stand up? *Suffolk Transnational Law Review* 33: 461–474.

Colangelo, Anthony J. 2013. The Alien Tort Statute and the law of nations in Kiobel and beyond. *Georgetown Journal of International Law* 44: 1329–1346.

Davis, Jeffrey. 2008. *Justice across borders: The struggle for human rights in U.S. courts.* Cambridge: Cambridge University Press.

Days, Drew S. III. 2005. Feedback loop: The Civil Rights Act of 1964 and its progeny. *St. Louis University Law Journal* 49: 981–1005.

deLisle, Jacques. 2003. Human rights, civil wrongs and international politics: A 'Sinical' look at the use of U.S. litigation to address abuses abroad. *DePaul Law Review* 52: 473–561.

Dellapenna, Joseph W. 2011. Interpreting the foreign Sovereign Immunities Act. *Lewis and Clark Law Review* 15: 555–588.
DiSarro, Anthony. 2012. When a jury can't say no: Presumed damages for constitutional torts. *Rutgers University Law Review* 64(2): 333–380.
Enforcing Constitutional Rights in the Twenty-First Century: Section 1983 Thirty Years After Owen v. Independence. 2010. *UMKC Law Review* 78: 869–1013.
Fletcher, George P. 2008. *Tort liability for human rights abuses*. London: Hart Publishing.
Fuller, David W. 2011. Intentional torts and other exceptions to the federal tort claims act. *University of St. Thomas Law Journal* 8: 375–397.
Gildin, Gary S. 2011. Redressing Deprivations of rights secured by state constitutions outside the shadow of the supreme court's constitutional remedies jurisprudence. *Penn State Law Review* 115: 877–921.
Hufbauer, Gary Clyde, and Nicholas K. Mitrokostas. 2003. *Awakening the monster: The Alien Tort Statute of 1789*. Washington, DC: Institute for International Economics.
Jowanna, Matthew J. 2010. 42 U.S.C. § 1983: A legal vehicle with no international human rights treaty passengers? *University of New Hampshire Law Review* 9:31–66.
Ku, Julian G. 2005. The third wave: The Alien Tort Statute and the war on terrorism. *Emory International Law Review* 19: 205–227.
Levinson, Rosalie B. 2012. Who will supervise the supervisors?Establishing liability for failure to train, supervise, or discipline subordinates in a post Iqbal/Connick world. *Harvard Civil Rights Civil Liberties Law Review* 47: 273–311.
Lewis Jr., Harold S., and Elizabeth J. Norman. 2004. *Civil rights law and practice*, 2nd ed. St. Paul: Thomson-West.
Malveaux, Suzette M. 2012–2013. The jury (or more accurately the judge) is still out for civil rights and employment cases post-Iqbal. *New York Law School Law Review* 57: 719-746.
Nelson, Stephen L. 2009. The King's wrongs and the Federal District Courts: Understanding the discretionary function exception to the Federal Tort Claims Act. *South Texas Law Review* 51: 259.
Niles, Mark C. 2002. "Nothing but Mischief": The Federal Tort Claims Act and the scope of discretionary immunity. *Administrative Law Review* 54: 1275–1353.
Pfander, James E. 2010. Iqbal, Bivens and the role of judge-made law in constitutional litigation. *Penn State Law Review* 114: 1387–1417.
Pfander, James E., and David Baltmanis. 2009. Rethinking Bivens: Legitimacy and constitutional adjudication. *Georgetown Law Journal* 98: 117–151.
Preis, John F. 2008. Alternative state remedies in constitutional torts. *Connecticut Law Review* 40: 723–767.
Reinert, Alex. 2010. Procedural barriers to civil rights litigation and the illusory promise of equity. *UMKC Law Review* 78: 931–948.
Reinert, Alexander A., and Lumen N. Mulligan. 2013. Asking the first question: Re- framing Bivens after Minneci. *Washington University Law Review* 90: 1473–1513.
Roberts, Caprice L. 2006. Ratios, (Ir)rationality and civil rights punitive awards. *Akron Law Review* 39: 1019–1052.
Rudovsky, David. 2005. Running in place: The paradox of expanding rights and restricted remedies. *University of Illinois Law Review* 1199–1256.
Rutledge, Peter B. 2011. Samantar, official immunity and federal common law. *Lewis and Clark Law Review* 15: 589–608.
Schwartz, Martin A., and Kathryn R. Urbonya. 2008. *Section 1983 litigation*, 2nd ed. Federal Judicial Center.
Shapiro, Stephen J. 1994. Suits against state officials for damages for violations of constitutional rights. *University of Baltimore Law Review* 23: 423–460.
Skinner, Gwynne L. 2012–2013. Roadblocks to remedies: Recently developed barriers to relief for aliens injured by U.S. officials, contrary to the founders' intent. *University of Richmond Law Review*: 555–629.
Stephens, Beth. 2004. Upsetting checks and balances: The Bush administration's efforts to limit human rights litigation. *Harvard Human Rights Journal* 17: 169–182.

Stephens, Beth. 2011. The modern common law of foreign official immunity. *Fordham Law Review* 79: 2669–2719.
Stephens, Beth, et al. 2008. *International human rights litigation in U.S. courts*, 2nd ed. Leiden: Martinus Nijihoff Publishers.
UN Human Rights Council, Report of the Working Group on the Universal Periodic Review, United States of America, UN Doc. A/HRC/16/11 (Jan. 4, 2011).
UN Human Rights Council, Report of the Working Group on the Universal Periodic Review, United States of America, Addendum, UN Doc. A/ HRC/16/11/Add.1 (Mar. 8, 2011).
Vazquez, Carlos M. 1992. Treaty- based rights and remedies of individuals. *Columbia Law Review* 92: 1082–1163.
Vazquez, Carlos M., and Stephen I. Vladeck. 2013. State law, the Westfall Act and the nature of the Bivens question. *University of Pennsylvania Law Review* 161: 509–583.
Vladeck, Stephen I. 2006. Rights without remedies: The new- found national security exception to Bivens. *ABA National Security Law Report* 28(2): 4–5.
Wasserman, Howard W. 2010. Iqbal, procedural mismatches and civil rights litigation. *Lewis and Clark Law Review* 14: 157–183.
Wells, Michael L. 2012. Civil recourse, damages-as-redress and constitutional torts. *Georgia Law Review* 46: 1003–1057.
Wuerth, Ingrid. 2013. Kiobel v. Royal Dutch Petroleum Co.: The supreme court and the Alien Tort Statute. *American Journal of International Law* 107: 601–621.
Young, Ernest A. 2015. Universal jurisdiction, the Alien Tort Statute, and transnational public-law litigation after Kiobel. *Duke Law Journal* 64: 1023–1127.

Chapter 19
Action for Damages in the Case of Infringement of Fundamental Rights by the European Union

Nina Półtorak

19.1 Preliminary Remarks

The actions for damages in the legal system of the European Union are peculiar. This is obviously because the EU is not a state but an international organisation. Consequently, it had to apply specific solutions taking into account its nature as an international organisation and its autonomous institutional and legal system. At the same time, the EU system of non-contractual liability reflects the systems of the states. It is based on the principles of international law regarding the responsibility of the states.[1] More importantly, the non-contractual liability of the Union has been directly linked with the principles of the national law of the Member States in the provisions of the treaties establishing the European Communities and then the European Union. Article 340 of the Treaty on the Functioning of the European Union (TFEU) provides that the Union shall, in accordance with the general principles common to the laws of the Member States, make good any damage caused by its institutions or by its servants in the performance of their duties.

The European Union respects the fundamental rights. This was first confirmed by the Court of Justice of the European Union (CJEU) in its case law,[2] and then adopted by EU Treaties. Now the provisions of the Treaty on European Union (TEU) provide that the Union is founded on the values of respect for human rights (Article 2 TEU); the fundamental rights (as guaranteed by the European Convention for the Protection of Human Rights and Fundamental Freedoms [ECHR] and as

[1] As stated by the Permanent Court of International Justice in judgment of 26.7.1927: "It is a principle of international law that the breach of an engagement involves an obligation to make reparation in an adequate form." Chorzów Factory case (1927) PCIJ ser. A, No 9, p. 21.

[2] 36/75, Rutili, [1975] ECR 1219; 44/79, Hauer, [1979] ECR 3727.

N. Półtorak (✉)
Professor at Jagiellonian University, Kraków, Poland
e-mail: nina.poltorak@uj.edu.pl

E. Bagińska (ed.), *Damages for Violations of Human Rights*,
Ius Comparatum - Global Studies in Comparative Law 9,
DOI 10.1007/978-3-319-18950-5_19

they result from the constitutional traditions common to the Member States) constitute general principles of the Union's law, and the Union shall accede to the ECHR (Art. 6 TEU). The Union also has its own act on human rights – the Charter of Fundamental Rights, which, since the Treaty of Lisbon, has the same legal value as the Treaties. In relation to the EU legal system, it is justified to refer to fundamental rights rather than human rights, since this broader category (fundamental rights) has a long tradition in EU case law and legislation. Presently, the Treaty on European Union uses the term fundamental rights,[3] and the phrase of fundamental rights appears in the EU bill of rights – Charter of Fundamental Rights. This category includes the traditional human rights, together with political and social rights, but also rights and freedoms characteristic for the EU legal system, such as the freedoms of the internal market.

There can be no doubt that the EU recognises its responsibility for human rights violations. Moreover, the EU liability in damages has been classified by the Charter of Fundamental Rights as a fundamental right of the EU system. This study aims to analyse the issue of EU liability for breach of fundamental rights, its evolution in the case law and the EU legislation. It does not have the ambition to be comprehensive, but aims at pointing out a few important points in the development of the action for damages in relation to fundamental rights.

19.2 Right to Compensation as a Fundamental Right of the EU

The regulation of the EU treaties regarding the non-contractual liability of the European Union is modest. Basically, it is based on Art. 340(2) and (3) TFEU supplemented with Art. 268 granting the exclusive jurisdictional competence of the CJEU in the field of non-contractual liability of the EU. The provision of Art. 340 has existed in the founding treaties since the beginning (Art. 215 TEEC, then Art. 288 TEC) and has not been subject to significant changes. As the CJEU stated, "The principle of the non-contractual liability of the Community expressly laid down in Article 215 of the Treaty [now Art. 340] is simply an expression of the general principle familiar to the legal systems of the Member States that an unlawful act or omission gives rise to an obligation to make good the damage caused."[4] However, the interpretation of this provision was subject to evolution, in particular with regard to the conditions of liability. It is important that this provision was, in the jurisprudence of the CJEU, one of the normative bases for the formulation of the principle of liability of Member States for breaches of EU law.

[3] Art. 6 (3) TEU: "Fundamental rights, as guaranteed by the European Convention for the Protection of Human Rights and Fundamental Freedoms and as they result from the constitutional traditions common to the Member States, shall constitute general principles of the Union's law".

[4] C-46/93 and C-48/93, Brasserie du Pêcheur vs. Germany and The Queen vs. Secretary of State for Transport ex parte Factortame Ltd and others, [1996] ECR I-102, para. 29.

The regulation of EU liability was also introduced in Art. 41(3) of the Charter of Fundamental Rights of the EU (CFR), which states that "Every person has the right to have the Union make good any damage caused by its institutions or by its servants in the performance of their duties, in accordance with the general principles common to the laws of the Member States."

The wording of Art. 340 TFEU and Art. 41(3) CFR is not identical. Art. 340 underlines the obligation of the EU to make good any damage caused by its institutions or by its servants, while Art. 41(3) of the Charter emphasises the rights of individuals to damages ("every person has the right to have the Union make good any damage"). This change of emphasis is consistent with the aims and objectives of the Charter as an act that collects the rights of individuals and makes them more visible. However, Art. 41(3) as well as other provisions of the Charter shall not extend in any way the competences of the Union as defined in the Treaties (Art. 6(1) TEU) and does not alter the understanding of the right for damages as regulated in Art. 340 TFEU (Art. 52(2) CFR).[5] Thus, it may be stated that the principle of compensation for damage caused by the Union has the rank of a fundamental right, which is implemented within the limits set by the Treaties (Art. 52(2) CFR).

It should be emphasised that the right recognised in Art. 41(3) CFR has not been confined to the damage caused only in violation of the rights guaranteed in the Charter. Thus, it is not seen as the sanction for violation of fundamental rights such as in the classic international agreements relating to such rights (in particular Art. 41 of the ECHR). It is not a provision to ensure compensation in case of violations of fundamental rights (but of course also covers such violations). It is a rule, which recognises the obligation to compensate the damages caused by any actions of the EU institutions as one of the fundamental rights and principles of the EU legal order. This is also emphasised by placing this regulation in the article of CFR titled "Right to good administration".

It is worth noting that the principle of the liability in damages of the Member States of the EU has not been included in the provisions of the CFR, although it is also the general principle of the EU system since the milestone ruling of the CJEU in the *Francovich* case.[6] There may be several reasons for this. The most obvious is the lack of the political will of the Member States to codify this principle directly in the primary law of the EU. Second, that the CFR is, as a rule, addressed to the institutions of the EU, and it applies to the Member States only when they are implementing Union law (Art. 51(1) CFR). Third, the CFR may not extend the field

[5]As stated in the Explanations to Art. 52(2): "It clarifies that such rights remain subject to the conditions and limits applicable to the Union law on which they are based, and for which provision is made in the Treaties. The Charter does not alter the system of rights conferred by the EC Treaty and taken over by the Treaties.", O.J. 2007 C 303, p. 2.

[6]C-6/90 and C-9/90, Andrea Francovich and Danila Bonifaci and others vs. Italy, [1991] ECR I-5357; see, e.g., the opinion of the Advocate General Mengozzi in C-279/09, Deutsche Energiehandels- und Beratungsgesellschaft mbH vs. Bundesrepublik Deutschland, ECLI:EU:C:2010:489 para. 46, "the right to reparation of persons harmed by an infringement of EU law is a fundamental principle of the Union based on the rule of law established by the treaties and a specific variation on the principle of effective judicial protection".

of application of Union law beyond the powers of the Union or establish any new power or task for the Union, or modify powers and tasks as defined in the Treaties (Art. 51(2) CFR). The action for damages against the Member States is still a case-law rule, it is not codified in the Treaties; thus, introducing it into the CFR without the respective amendments of the Treaties might be seen as the modification of powers "as defined in the Treaties".

19.3 Conditions of EU Non-contractual Liability

Article 340(2) TFEU does not specify the conditions of responsibility of the EU, referring in this regard only to the "general principles common to the laws of the Member States". This formulation in practice gave to the CJEU, as the authority competent to decide on complaints for damages, the ability to formulate the conditions for non-contractual liability of the Union. At the same time, the vagueness of the provision and the diversity of the rules on liability in the legal systems of the Member States allowed for wide discretion of the CJEU in determining both the substantive and procedural rules of redress. The CJEU case law indicates that the conditions and principles of responsibility, which the CJEU formulated on the basis of general principles common to the Member States, result from both public and private law.[7] This reference is understood as indicating the whole of the legal systems of the Member States relating to the issue of liability. It is at the same time a reference to principles rather than specific legislation.

One of the means to establish principles common to the laws of the Member States may be a comparative indication of rules actually identical to the laws of all States in terms of liability. Given the diversity of the Member States' legal systems, it could lead only to determining the fundamental principles, and not the precise conditions that could be the basis for the liability. As stated by Advocate General Maduro "Such a mathematical logic of the lowest common denominator would lead to the establishment of a regime for Community liability in which the victims of damage attributable to the institutions would have only a very slim chance of obtaining compensation".[8] It would also require updating these rules with the accession of each new Member State.

[7] See, e.g. Edward (1988) 121; Edward Robinson (1997) 339 et seq.

[8] Opinion in case C-120/06 P and C-121/06 P, Fabbrica italiana accumulatori motocarri Montecchio SpA (FIAMM) and others, para.55. He also stated: "Although the Court of Justice must certainly be guided by the most characteristic provisions of the systems of domestic law, it must above all ensure that it adopts a solution appropriate to the needs and specific features of the Community legal system. In other words, the Court has the task of drawing on the legal traditions of the Member States in order to find an answer to similar legal questions arising under Community law that both respects those traditions and is appropriate to the context of the Community legal order. From that point of view, even a solution adopted by a minority may be preferred if it best meets the requirements of the Community system."

Another method for determining the principles common to the laws of the Member States is to treat them as a source of inspiration. As shown by the case law, the CJEU is using the latter method, i.e. it does not examine in detail the legal systems of the Member States to formulate the conditions and principles of the EU's liability, but rather looks at these systems' general common features. The CJEU then uses the axiological method, comparing these common general elements with the objectives of the founding treaties, as well as the specific tasks and competences of the EU. However, the CJEU does not reject the comparative method entirely, and it uses it also to justify that the given condition is not common to the legal systems of the Member States (e.g. in relation to the liability for the lawful acts[9]).

The model described above applies also to the liability for a breach of fundamental rights. The CJEU does not examine the legal systems of the Member States in order to identify whether there are some common rules on liability for violation of human rights. Without a doubt, however, the CJEU recognises the responsibility of the EU for such violations.

Until recently, CJEU case law has indicated that there are two regimes of liability of the EU: for administrative actions and for legislative acts. The premises of liability for administrative action were the occurrence of the damage, infringement and a causal link between the wrongful act and the damage. The administrative actions were considered to be the actions of the EU institutions in individual cases.[10] Thus, the main criterion for distinction between legislative and administrative acts is the individual or general addressee. However, the legislative nature of a measure should not be called into question by the fact that it is possible to determine or identify the persons to whom it applies, as long as it applies to them by virtue of an objective legal or factual situation.[11] The conditions of the liability for the EU legislative acts have been formulated for the first time in the CJEU judgment of 1971 in the *Schöppenstedt* case. The CJEU has held that, in respect to the legislative action, the EC can incur non-contractual liability only if a sufficiently flagrant violation of a superior rule of law for the protection of the individual has occurred.[12] Those conditions were more difficult to meet than the condition of responsibility for the non-legislative actions of the EU. According to the CJEU, it was justified by the rules common to the legal systems of the Member States, providing that the public

---

[9] C-120/06 P and C-121/06 P, Fabbrica italiana accumulatori motocarri Montecchio SpA (FIAMM), ECLI:EU:C:2008:476 para.175: "(...) while comparative examination of the Member States' legal systems enabled the Court to make at a very early stage the finding (...) concerning convergence of those legal systems in the establishment of a principle of liability in the case of unlawful action or an unlawful omission of the authority, including of a legislative nature, that is in no way the position as regards the possible existence of a principle of liability in the case of a lawful act or omission of the public authorities, in particular where it is of a legislative nature."

[10] See van der Woude (1997) 126.

[11] T-390/94, Aloys Schröder, Jan and Karl-Julius Thamann vs. Commission, ECLI:EU:T:1997:51, para. 57.

[12] 5/71, Aktien-Zuckerfabrik Schöppenstedt vs. Council of the European Communities, ECLI:EU:C:1971:116 para. 11; C-104/89 and C-37/90, J. M. Mulder and others vs. Council and Commission, [2000] ECR I-203, para 12–13.

authorities can only exceptionally and in special circumstances incur liability for legislative measures that are the result of choices of economic policy, and that the legislature "cannot always be hindered in making its decisions by the prospect of applications for damages whenever it has occasion to adopt legislative measures in the public interest which may adversely affect the interests of individuals".[13] In practice, the successful damages claims relating to the EU legislative acts were only exceptional.

From the point of view of the subject of this work, it is important that, according to the *Schöppenstedt* formula, the condition of the liability was not only the violation of the law of a specific degree, but also a violation of specific legal standards – a superior rule of law for the protection of the individual. For a superior rule of law the CJEU recognised primarily the provisions of the founding treaties, as well as general principles of law developed by the CJEU, such as the principle of equality, the protection of legitimate expectations, and the protection of the acquired rights.[14] In accordance with this early case-law of the CJEU the infringed norm should not only be superior but should also protect the individuals. This phrase was interpreted in light of the German *Schutznorm* doctrine meaning that granting damages is only possible if there was a breach of the rule of law protecting the given individual or defined group of individuals. In terms of Art. 288(2) TEC (now Art. 340(2) TFEU), this concept was also linked to the injury, which should apply to a restricted circle of recipients, on which the EU norm imposed special burdens.[15]

Certainly, the principles of protection of human rights constitute the superior rules of law. When the CJEU formulated the *Schöppenstedt* conditions, there was no act codifying fundamental rights in EU law. These rights were only identified by the CJEU and derived from the provisions of the founding treaties, the ECHR and the constitutional traditions of the Member States. For a long time these rights have had the status of general unwritten rules of EU law originating from the case law.[16]

Since the judgment of 2000 in the case *Bergaderm vs. Commission*, the *Schöppenstedt* formula has been modified.[17] This modification was related to, or even caused by, the development of the rules of liability of the Member States. Already in one of the first rulings on the liability of the Member States for the infringement of the EU law – in the case *Brasserie du Pêcheur* of 1996 – the CJEU stated that the protection of the rights that individuals derive from EU law cannot vary depending on whether a national or an EU authority is responsible for the damage, and therefore the conditions of the States and EU liability for damage

[13] 83 and 94/76 and 4, 15 and 40/77, Bayerische Vermehrungsbetriebe and others vs. Council and the Commission, [1978] ECR 1209, para. 5.

[14] E.g. C-104/89 and C-37/90, Mulder, para. 15. See also Arnull (1997) 138; Heukles and McDonnell (1997) 5.

[15] 83 and 94/76, 4, 15 and 40/77, Bayerische Vermehrungsbetriebe, para. 7; opinion of Advocate General Van Gerven in C-104/89 and C-37/90 Mulder v. Council and Commission, para. 29 et seq.

[16] Tridimas (2009) 298.

[17] C-352/98 P, Laboratoires pharmaceutiques Bergaderm SA and others vs. Commission, [2000] ECR I-5291.

cannot, in the absence of particular justification, be different.[18] This presumption led to the unification of the conditions of liability of the Member States and the European Union in the subsequent case law of the CJEU. Regarding the liability of the Member States, the CJEU did not make any distinction between the conditions of liability for the administrative and legislative acts, but formulated uniform conditions for such liability, i.e.: the rule of law infringed must be intended to confer rights on individuals; the breach must be sufficiently serious; and there must be a direct causal link between the breach and the damage.[19] Since the *Bergaderm* judgment, those conditions have been uniformly applied as the premises of EU liability regardless of the nature of the action that caused the damage.

The character of the rule infringed is still important within the modified conditions for EU liability. However, it is understood differently than in the *Schöppenstedt* formula. The rule does not have to be a superior rule of law, but it should confer rights on individuals. As regards the liability of the Member States, the CJEU rejected the understanding of this condition in accordance with the German *Schutznorm* doctrine because it would in practice make it impossible or extremely difficult to obtain effective reparation for loss or damage resulting from a breach of EU law by the legislature.[20] In its recent case law, the CJEU explains also that the existence of a right conferred on individuals by a rule of law does not relate to the actual nature of the harm alleged but instead constitutes a condition for a finding of a sufficiently serious breach of such a rule.[21]

The element crucial for the assessment of the condition of sufficient seriousness of the breach is the discretion available to the institution. The decisive test for finding that a breach of EU law is sufficiently serious is whether the EU institution manifestly and gravely disregarded the limits on its discretion.[22] When the degree of the discretion is limited or non-existent, any breach of the law should be considered sufficiently serious for the responsibility of the EU.[23] At the same time, when deciding on the seriousness of the breach, the CJEU takes into account not only the margin of discretion available to EU institution, but also *inter alia* the complexity of the situations to be regulated and difficulties in the application or interpretation of the

[18] C-46/93 and C-48/93, Brasserie du Pêcheur, para. 42

[19] C-46/93 and C-48/93, Brasserie du Pêcheur, para. 51; in respect of the liability of the EU see, e.g., C-198/03 P, Commission vs. CEVA Santé Animale SA and Pfizer Enterprises Sàrl, [2005] ECR I-6357, para. 63.

[20] C-46/93 and C-48/93, Brasserie du Pêcheur, para.s 69–72.

[21] C-611/12 P, Jean-François Giordano vs. Commission, ECLI:EU:C:2014:2282, para.40.

[22] 238/78 Ireks-Arkady vs. Council, para. 9; C-312/00 P, Commission vs. Camar and others, [2002] ECR I-11355, para. 54 and 55; C-198/03 P, Commission v. CEVA, para. 64; see more, e.g. Harlow, (1996) 80 et seq.

[23] As the CJEU states: "Where that institution has only a considerably reduced, or even no, discretion, the mere infringement of Community law may be sufficient to establish the existence of a sufficiently serious breach (…). The determining factor in deciding whether there has been such an infringement is therefore the discretion available to the institution concerned (…)", C-198/03 P, Commission vs. CEVA, para. 65–66; C-352/98 P, Bergaderm vs. Commission, para. 44; C-312/00 P, Commission vs. Camar, para. 54.

given provisions.[24] Thus, not only the scope of the discretion is important for the fulfilment of the conditions of the sufficiently serious breach. The assessment should also take into account other circumstances specific for the given action (both legislative and administrative). The General Court expressly states that the condition of sufficiently serious breach is to avoid a situation in which the risk of incurring liability hinders the ability of the EU institutions to exercise their powers in the general interest; however, on the other hand, the individuals should not bear "the consequences of flagrant and inexcusable misconduct" of these institutions.[25]

19.4 Violation of Fundamental Rights and Action for Damages

Prior to the entry into force of the CFR, the individuals have already claimed damages for alleged infringement of the rights, which should be regarded as fundamental. Most frequently they were procedural rights related to the administrative proceedings conducted by the EU institutions (e.g. the principle of equal treatment of the parties; right of defence or impartiality of the administrative organ).[26]

Currently, the action for damages can also be a consequence of the infringement of the provisions of the CFR. For example, there are several cases pending before the General Court claiming the damages for violation of Art. 47 CFR (right to fair trial) by the delayed proceedings before the General Court. The CJEU in *Kendrion* judgment allowed for such claims stating that the sanction for a breach by CJEU of its obligation to adjudicate on the cases within a reasonable time must be an action for damages.

In other case, the complainant claimed damages for harm suffered on account of EU regulation allegedly infringing the right to pursue and carry out an occupation (Art. 15 CFR) and the right to property (Art. 17 CFR). Considering the case, the CJEU examined whether such a breach occurred in light of Art. 52(1) of the CFR, stating the conditions for limitation of the rights and freedoms recognised by the CFR. It held that the above freedoms and rights do not constitute an absolute prerogative, but may be subject to limitations under the conditions specified in the

[24] C-352/98 P, Bergaderm vs. Commission, para. 40, C-312/00 P, Commission v. Camar, para. 52; C-472/00 P, Commission vs. Fresh Marine Company A/S, [2003] ECR I-7541, para. 24, C-198/03 P, Commission vs. Ceva, para. 64). The General Court is even more specific, stating that what should be considered is "the complexity of the situation to be regulated, the difficulties in the application or interpretation of the legislation, the clarity and precision of the rule infringed, and whether the error of law made was inexcusable or intentional (…)", T-429/05, Artegodan GmbH vs. Commission, [2010] ECR II-491, para. 62.

[25] T-429/05, Artegodan GmbH vs. Commission, para. 55.

[26] T-160/03, AFCon Management Consultants and others vs. Commission, [2005] ECR II-981; T-196/99, Area Cova and others vs. Commission, [2001] ECR II-3597; T-351/03, Schneider Electric SA vs. Commission, ECR [2007] II-2237. See also examples provided for by Ward (2012) 596–597.

CFR.[27] This decision indicates the jurisdictional pattern that should be used by the CJEU in other cases regarding the provisions of the CFR. It is assumed to examine whether the restriction of a fundamental right was acceptable in light of the EU standard. This view is consistent with other rulings of the CJEU referring to damages for lawful acts (which will be analysed below).

It is doubtful whether violation of every rights and freedoms guaranteed by the CFR will cause liability of the EU. As indicated above, the condition of the claim for damages as defined by the CJEU is still that the infringed norm conferred rights on individuals. Not all norms of CFR can be considered as conferring such rights. In particular, it is doubtful in respect to the norms of the CFR that are considered as principles. According to Art. 52(5) of the CFR, the provisions of Charter, which contain principles, may be implemented by legislative and executive acts taken by institutions, bodies, offices and agencies of the Union, and by acts of Member States when they are implementing Union law, in the exercise of their respective powers. They shall be judicially cognisable only in the interpretation of such acts and in the ruling on their legality. As the Explanations to the CFR provide, the principles "do not, however, give rise to direct claims for positive action by the Union's institutions or Member States' authorities".[28] The Explanations lists the following provisions of the CFR as the principles: Art. 26 – the rights of the elderly; Art. 26 – integration of persons with disabilities and Art. 37 – environmental protection. This is, however, not an exhaustive list, the provisions of the CFR may constitute partly the principles and partly the rights.

It is worth noting the special nature of the right to good administration. There may be no doubt that the right to good administration grants specific subjective rights to individuals (and in case of infringement of those rights, the claim for damages arises); however, it is not clear if the right to good administration as such is a subjective right.[29] The elements of the right to good administration specifically listed in Art. 41(1) CFR, i.e. the right to be heard; the right to have access to files and the obligation of the administration to give its reasons for decisions, should be considered as the rights in the meaning of art. 52(5) CFR; however, if we accept the idea that there are other elements of the right to good administration that are not listed there, their character is not clear. The General Court in particular held that the principle of good administration is associated also with other rules – of the presumption of innocence and confidentiality, which confer rights on individuals.[30] In another case, the General Court awarded damages for breach of intellectual

[27] C-611/12 P, Giordano vs. Commission, para. 49.

[28] Explanations to Art. 52(5) CFR, O.J. 2007 C 303 p. 2.

[29] See, e.g., Hofmann and Mihaescu (2013) 95

[30] T-48/05, Yves Franchet and Daniel Byk vs. Commission, ECLI:EU:T:2008:257, para. 218: "(...) the principle of the presumption of innocence confers rights on individuals. It should be observed that the obligation to maintain confidentiality also confers rights on individuals who are affected by an OLAF investigation in so far as they are entitled to expect that the investigations concerning them will be conducted in a manner that respects their fundamental rights. In the same way, the applicants are entitled to rely in the present case on the principle of sound administration in that it entails the right to have their cases dealt with in such a way that confidentiality is maintained."

property rights by the Commission, invoking inter alia the legitimate interests of confidentiality and of professional and business secrecy as the components of the right to good administration.[31]

On the other hand, the General Court stated that the principle of sound administration does not, in itself, confer rights upon individuals except where it constitutes the expression of specific rights, such as the right to have affairs handled impartially, fairly and within a reasonable time, the right to be heard, the right to have access to files, or the obligation to give reasons for decisions.[32] This is interesting in view of the earlier case law of the CJEU, which held that not all constitutional principles of the EU legal order are intended to confer rights on individuals; this refers, e.g., to the rules on the division of powers between the Union institutions, since their purpose is not to protect the rights of individuals, but to maintain a balance between the different EU authorities;[33] and the Treaty provision (now Art. 296 TFEU) obliging the EU institutions to state the reasons for the legal acts.[34] The above-mentioned ruling of the General Court indicates, however, that obligation to give reasons for decisions as part of the Charter's right to good administration shall be treated as granting rights to individuals (and consequently its violation may result in the non-contractual liability of the EU institution).

19.5 Liability for Lawful Actions

In its early case law, the CJEU suggested the acceptance of the rule of liability in damages for lawful actions.[35] This view was formulated in the judgment of the General Court of 1998 in relation to the responsibility for legislative acts. In this judgment, the General Court held that the Community's liability in respect of lawful acts can be incurred if the alleged damage was not foreseeable or could not be avoided by a diligent economic operator.[36] However, in later judgments the CJEU stated that such a principle cannot be deduced from the case law.[37] The CJEU justified this position, invoking the principles common to the laws of the Member States

[31] T-19/07, Systran SA and Systran Luxembourg SA vs. Commission, ECLI:EU:T:2010:526. This judgment was subsequently annulled by the Court of Justice, which held that General Court was wrong in its a view that the dispute in question was of a non-contractual nature; C-103/11 P, Commission vs. Systran SA and Systran Luxembourg SA, ECLI:EU:C:2013:245.

[32] T-193/04, Hans-Martin Tillack vs. Commission, ECLI:EU:T:2006:292, para. 127; T-187/11, Mohamed Trabelsi and others, ECLI:EU:T:2013:273.

[33] C-282/90, Industrie- en Handelsonderneming Vreugdenhil BV vs. Commission, [1992] ECR I-1937; T-429/05, Artegodan vs. Commission.

[34] 106/81, Julius Kind KG vs. European Economic Community, [1982] ECR 2885.

[35] 59/83, Biovilac NV vs. European Economic Community, [1984] ECR 4057; see. more Bronkhorst, (1997) 153.

[36] T-184/95, Dorsch Consult v. Council and Commission, [1998] ECR II-667, para. 35.

[37] C-120/06 P and C-121/06 P, FIAMM, para. 168. See more, e.g. Gutman (2011) 740.

and teleological interpretation of Art. 288(2) TEC (now Art. 340 TFEU).[38] This statement was in opposition to the opinion of Advocate General Maduro, who supported the view that liability for the lawful acts should be accepted in the EU law. He argued that the idea of such liability "may be based both on the idea of a 'rupture' in the equality of citizens in shouldering public burdens and on the protection that must be given to the fundamental right to property."[39]

The CJEU has not approved this view[40]; however, at the same time, it accepted the liability of the EU for damages arising from the EU normative act restricting fundamental rights thereby causing the particular damage to the very essence of those rights. It held that: "It follows that a Community legislative measure whose application leads to restrictions of the right to property and the freedom to pursue a trade or profession, that impair the very substance of those rights in a disproportionate and intolerable manner, perhaps precisely because no provision has been made for compensation calculated to avoid or remedy that impairment, could give rise to non-contractual liability on the part of the Community."[41] It seems that the CJEU referred to such restrictions of the fundamental rights that may not be accepted by the EU standard – affect the substance of the rights, disproportionately interfere and excessively affect the interests of the individual. This EU standard is now regulated by Art. 52(1) CFR, which allows only such limitation on the exercise of the rights and freedoms recognised by the CFR, which are provided for by law and respect the essence of those rights and freedoms and the principle of proportionality, meaning that limitations may be made only if they are necessary and genuinely meet the objectives of general interest recognised by the Union or the need to protect the rights and freedoms of others. In fact, the above statement of the CJEU should not be seen as allowing the liability for the lawful actions that, however, interfere with the fundamental rights, but rather as referring to the liability for the disproportionate limitations (without adequate guarantees) of the fundamental rights which infringe the EU standard specified in Art. 52(1) CFR.

19.6 Limitations of the Liability

Before the Treaty of Lisbon, one of the significant limitations of the claim for damages in EU law was the specific character of the former second and third pillar of the EU. The CJEU refused to interpret the provisions of the third pillar (police and

---

[38] C 120/06 P and C-121/06 P, FIAMM, para. 168–176.

[39] Opinion in C-120/06 P and C-121/06 P, FIAMM, para. 74.

[40] CJEU confirmed this position in further judgments, e.g. C-12/13 P and C-13/13 P, Gérard Buono and others vs. Commission, ECLI:EU:C:2014:2284, para. 43: "It is undisputed that, as EU law currently stands, a comparative examination of the Member States' legal systems does not permit the affirmation of a regime providing for non-contractual liability of the European Union for the lawful pursuit by it of its activities falling within the legislative sphere".

[41] C-120/06 P and C-121/06 P, FIAMM, para. 184.

judicial cooperation in criminal matters) as providing for the claim for damages.[42] This statement was not quite compliant with a Council declaration annexed to the minutes at the time of the adoption of Common Position 2001/931 and Regulation No 2580/2001 in which the Council recalled that in case of any error in the Common Position on the application of specific measures to combat terrorism, the injured party shall have the right to seek judicial redress. The CJEU decided that such Council declaration is insufficient to create a legal remedy not provided for by the Treaty. It is interesting to note that the view of the Council has been shared by the European Court of Human Rights (ECtHR). Before applying to the CJEU, the parties injured by the Common Position brought an action to the ECtHR against 15 States as Members of the Council adopting the Common Position. They claimed a violation of several provisions of the Convention, including freedom of expression, freedom of association, the right to appeal and effective remedy. The ECtHR dismissed the action as inadmissible, stating that the applicants did not have the status of victims of violations of the Convention, since they are not directly affected by the Common Position "and even if they were affected, they could always apply to the Court of Justice of the European Communities".[43] However, as mentioned above, the CJEU did not allow for such an application in the form of the claim for damages; it allowed only the national courts to refer a question to the CJEU for a preliminary ruling on a common position. The lack of the procedure allowing claims for damages from the EU in the field of cooperation in criminal matters was problematic from the point of view of both the EU and ECHR principles. Since the Treaty of Lisbon, however, the scope of application of Art. 340 TFEU covers also the area of freedom, security and justice, including the matters governed by the former third pillar of the EU. The only policy, as a rule, still not subject to the damages claims is the common foreign and security policy (former second pillar of the EU). This policy is specific, distinct from other policies, more intergovernmental than common, in which the Member States rather than the EU could be responsible towards the individuals.

Other restrictions of the claim for damages concern the infringements of international law by the EU. As stated by the CJEU, non-compliance of the EU with certain WTO regulations does not constitute grounds for liability of the Union.[44] Therefore, it seems that even if a violation of WTO regulations results in the breach of fundamental rights (e.g. the right of ownership), there would be no claim for damages according the EU law.

---

[42] Case C-355/04 P, Segi, AraitZubimendi Izaga and Aritza Galarraga vs. Council, [2007] ECR I-1657, para. 44–48; C-354/04 P, Gestoras Pro Amnistía, Juan Mari Olano Olano and Julen Zelarain Errasti vs. Council, [2007] ECR I-1579; see also view of Advocat General Kokott in 2/13, ECLI:EU:C:2014:2475, para. 94–95.

[43] Decision of 23.5.2002, no 6422/02 and 9916/02, Segi and Others & Gestoras Pro-Amnistia And Others vs. 15 States of The European Union, http://hudoc.echr.coe.int. Accesed 4 March 2015.

[44] T-383/00, Beamglow Ltd vs. European Parliament, Council of the European Union and Commission of the European Communities, [2005] ECR II-5459, para. 127; C-120/06 P and C-121/06 P, FIAMM, para. 128–131.

A quite different problem can be seen in respect to the infringement of the rights guaranteed by the ECHR. Of course, as long as the EU is not a party to the ECHR, it is not subject to the jurisdiction of the ECtHR. However, all Member States, being the parties to the ECHR, can be responsible for the actions of the EU. Member States' liability for infringing the ECHR is not excluded by the fact that the disputed action resulted from the State's obligations towards the EU.[45] At the same time, the ECtHR applies the *Bosphorus* principle, according to which the EU law provides an equivalent protection to that guaranteed by the Convention, and therefore the ECtHR presumes that a State has acted in compliance with the ECHR, where it had no discretion in implementing the EU law. Such a presumption can obviously be rebutted if, in the circumstances of a particular case, it is found that the protection of ECHR rights was manifestly deficient.[46] It was not found as such by the ECtHR in the *Biret* case, in which the applicant first failed in the action for damages before the General Court relating to the infringement of the WTO regulations and then applied to the ECtHR claiming that violation of the right to court and property right as guaranteed by the ECHR.[47]

19.7 Conclusions

The EU law recognises damages claims in the case of the violation of fundamental rights by EU institutions. For a long time, only the infringement of the superior (fundamental) norm protecting rights of individuals could give rise to liability of the EU for legislative acts. Currently, such a condition is not expressly required; however, in practice, the character of the norm is taken into account when considering the fulfilment of the conditions for the liability. EU law not only accepts the liability for the infringements of human rights, but the right to make good any damage caused by the EU is recognised as a fundamental right.

The special status of the non-contractual liability of the EU does not mean that this right is often used. Taking into account both the number of damages claims against the EU and their success rate, the liability in damages of the EU can hardly be treated as an effective remedy protecting individuals.[48] However, there is the positive trend in the case law of the CJEU showing that in more claims the damages are awarded.[49] This is certainly the consequence of alleviation of the conditions of EU liability in the *Bargaderm* judgment, but this may also be seen as a result of

[45] Judgment of 18.2.1999, 24833/94, Matthews vs. UK; Judgment of 30.6.2005, 45036/98, Bosphorus vs. Ireland, para. 155.

[46] 45036/98, Bosphorus vs. Ireland, para. 155.

[47] Decision of 9.12.2008, 13762/04, Societe Etablissements Biret vs. 15 EU Member States.

[48] Annually, there is only an average of 16 claims for damages, and the success rate is currently about 8 % (based on Kawczyńska 2014, 279).

[49] Before 2000 (the Bergaderm judgment), only in 20 claims were the damages awarded; in the 14 years after Bagarderm, 19 claims have been successful, see. Kawczyńska (2014) 279.

strengthening the importance of the damages claims by giving them the status of the fundamental right of individuals by the Charter of Fundamental Rights. The Charter itself – being a binding act with the same legal value as the Treaties and collecting the fundamental rights respected by the EU – makes it easier for the claimants to invoke the infringement of the given right or freedom as the basis of the claim. It also provides for the clear pattern of evaluation if the given limitation of the right or freedom could be justified (Art. 52(1) CFR).

It should be emphasised that the accession of the EU to the ECHR would be of considerable importance for EU non-contractual liability in cases of infringement of human rights. Firstly, the ECtHR would be entitled to examine whether the regime of liability provided for in EU law, and its practical application, meets the ECHR standards (primarily as part of the right to court and the protection of ownership). Secondly, the ECtHR would be able to afford just satisfaction to the injured party if it finds that there has been a violation of the Convention by the EU (in any policy, including the common foreign and security policy). The ECtHR would also be entitled to assess the compliance of the rulings of the CJEU with the Convention. Last but not least, the *Boshprus* test would likely to be rejected after the accession, and joint liability of the EU and the Member States should be reconsidered.[50] However, in view of the opinion of December 2014, in which the CJEU declared that the accession agreement is not compatible with the EU Treaties, the accession cannot be expected in the near future.[51]

References

Arnull, Anthony. 1997. Liability for Legislative Acts under Article 215(2) EC. 138. In *The action for damages in community law*, ed. Ton Heukles and Alison Mc. Donnell, 129–152. The Hague: Kluwer Law International.

Bronkhorst, H.J. 1997. The valid legislative act as a cause of liability of the communities. In *The action for damages in community law*, ed. Ton Heukles and Alison Mc. Donnell, 153–166. The Hague: Kluwer Law International.

Edward, David. 1988. Is there a place for private law principles in community law? In *Non-contractual liability of the European communities*, ed. Henry G. Schermers, Heukles Ton, and Mead Philip, 121–124. The Hague: Martinus Nijihoff Publishers.

Edward, David, and William Robinson. 1997. Is there a place principles for private law in community law? In *The action for damages in community law*, ed. Ton Heukles and Alison Mc. Donnell, 339–349. The Hague: Kluwer.

Groussot, Xavier, Tobias Lock, and Laurent Pech. 2011. EU accession to the European convention on human rights: A legal assessment of the draft accession agreement of 14th October 2011. *Fondation Robert Schuman, "Policy Paper – European Issues"*, no. 218.

Gutman, Kathleen. 2011. The evolution of the action for damages against the European Union and its place in the system of judicial protection. *Common Market Law Review* 48(3): 695–750.

Harlow, Carol. 1996. State liability: Problem without solution. *National Journal of Constitutional Law* 6: 67.

[50] See e.g. Groussot et al. (2011).

[51] Opinion 2/13 (Full Court), ECLI:EU:C:2014:2475

Heukles, Ton, and Mc. Donnell Alison. 1997. The action for damages in a community law perspective: Introduction. In *The action for damages in community law*, ed. Ton Heukles and Alison Mc. Donnell, 5–10. The Hague: Kluwer Law International.

Hofmann, Herwig C.H., and Bucura C. Mihaescu. 2013. The relation between the Charter's fundamental rights and the unwritten general principles of EU law: Good administration as the test case. *European Constitutional Law Review* 9(1): 73–101.

Kawczyńska, Monika. 2014. *Pozaumowna odpowiedzialność odszkodowawcza Unii Europejskiej* (not published doctoral thesis), Kraków.

Tridimas, Takis. 2009. *The general principles of EU law*. Oxford: Oxford University Press.

van der Woude, Marc H. 1997. Liability for Administrative acts under Article 215 (2) EC. In *The action for damages in community law*, ed. Ton Heukles and Alison Mc. Donnell, 109–128. The Hague: Kluwer Law International.

Ward, Angela. 2012. Damages under the EU charter of fundamental rights. *ERA Forum* 12(4): 589–611.

Chapter 20
Damages for Violations of Human Rights: A Comparative Analysis

Ewa Bagińska

20.1 Constitutionalisation of the Right to Damages for Violation of Human Rights

20.1.1 Forms and Scope of Constitutionalisation of the Right to Damages for Violations of Human Rights

'Constitutionalisation' is understood here in its strict (formal) sense, i.e. as the process of elevating the right to damages in cases of infringement of human rights to the normative level of constitutional rules and principles. The constitutionalisation first results in prevalence of the constitutionally protected right over a right protected by ordinary legislation in cases of their conflict, and secondly, it may result in the creation of a special cause of action on the constitutional level, independent of ordinary law causes of action for such a claim. In consequence, a court will be able to apply the constitutional cause of action where there are no legal bases in ordinary law, whether statutory or case law, depending on the system, on which a claim for compensation could be based. In this way human rights receive effective and direct protection in domestic courts by operation of domestic legal rules.

This is an abridged, revised and updated version of the general report presented to the 19th International Congress of Comparative Law. The unabridged version will be published in the general reports volume (General Reports to the 19th Congress of Comparative Law. Springer Verlag). The list of reports initially prepared for the Congress, but not revised for publication in this book include the following: Argentina (Hortensia D.T. Gutierrez Posse), Brazil (Antonio Celso Calves Pereira), Canada (Jane Glenn) and Romania (Corneliu-Liviu Popescu). The reports are on file with the Author; detailed citations to country reports are omitted.

E. Bagińska (✉)
Department of Civil Law, Gdańsk University, Gdańsk, Poland
e-mail: baginska@prawo.ug.edu.pl

E. Bagińska (ed.), *Damages for Violations of Human Rights*,
Ius Comparatum - Global Studies in Comparative Law 9,
DOI 10.1007/978-3-319-18950-5_20

'Constitutionalisation' is also just one of the methods of conceptualisation of the effect that human rights may have in the private sphere. The other theories are the Germanic *mittelbare* and *unmittelbare Drittwirkung* or its equivalent – horizontal direct and indirect effect, among other examples.[1] Modern constitutions, and hence also the rights enshrined therein, enjoy direct applicability (direct enforcement, direct effect), although the extent of such a direct applicability may of course differ. While the vertical effect (State – citizen) is commonly accepted nowadays, the horizontal effect of rights and its scope (direct or indirect) is an evolving phenomenon.[2] In particular, the true effect of human rights in a given system will depend, among other factors, on the ability of an aggrieved person to file a constitutional complaint regarding legislation that violates fundamental rights (an action that is generally limited to constitutional rights).

It should also be indicated that from the perspective of international law, if domestic law were simply to be interpreted in conformity with international and regional human rights law we would not speak of constitutionalisation, but rather refer to it as 'indirect effect of human rights', unless such rights were incorporated in the constitutional act.

In many countries under review, the enforcement of human rights is first of all a matter of introducing a constitutional guarantee of the right to redress in cases of violations of such rights. Such a guarantee has been provided on the constitutional level in many jurisdictions. A 'constitutional level' is understood here to mean a domestic constitutional act (or acts), such as the Constitution or basic laws as well as any national rules of the constitutional ranking.

The process of creating domestic guarantees to the values enshrined in the umbrella notion of human rights began in the aftermath of the Second World War. These guarantees have been increasingly intensified over time, and we can now observe a greater emphasis on monetary protection of the victim of human rights abuses.

As the foregoing review of national solutions reflects, the constitutional guarantee can be designed as follows:

(a) a general right to compensation for violation of every constitutionally protected right, or
(b) a right implicit in the constitutional right to claim damages for unlawful conduct of public authorities, or
(c) a specific right to compensation in cases of violations of specific human (constitutional) rights.

Not surprisingly, it is hard to find a system with a general right to compensation for violation of constitutionally protected rights committed by any person, Estonia and Slovenia being notable examples[3].

---

[1] See Oliver and Fedtke (2007) 3, 499 ff, See in general Fairgrieve et al. (2002).

[2] See a separate general report to the 19th Congress of Comparative Law by Verica Trstenjak, 'The influence of human rights and basic rights in private law'.

[3] § 25 of the Estonian Constitution (1992), the Slovenian Constitution 1991 – Bill of Rights, § 15.

The mixture of solutions (b) and (c) appears to have been adopted most frequently. In fact, in each country we will find specific rights to compensation in cases of violations of specific human (constitutional) rights (see infra at 20.8).

Having been influenced by international and regional human rights systems, democratic constitutions provide for an effective remedy for the victims of breaches of human rights by the State. Since the obligation to compensate for damages incurred by individuals is regarded as a fundamental duty of a democratic State (as well as of EU law), many countries have introduced a right to claim damages for wrongs committed by public authorities.

The entitlement to damages has been designed either as a standalone cause of action or in combination with tort or administrative law.[4] Although it is evident that general provisions of State liability will also apply to breaches of human rights, the concept according to which a concrete, subjective right must have been violated in order to demand compensation has limited the operation of the constitutional safeguards. By way of example, the German Constitution (Basic Law) stipulates that everyone who is violated in his/her rights by acts or omissions of the German public authority has the right to a judicial remedy (art. 19 § 4) and the principle of liability of the State for tortious acts of its agents (art. 34). However, in light of the German courts case law the right to effective remedy can be claimed only in connection with a subjective right conferred on the individual in the Basic Law, statutory law or international human rights law. The same solution exists in Portugal.

In Italy, the constitutional regime for claims based on violations of human rights enshrined in the Constitution is primarily grounded in the criminal and administrative law. For these cases, the legal basis for compensation is to be found in the Constitution and in the general liability clause in the Civil Code.

The constitutionalisation of the right to compensation for violations of human rights is of particular significance in post-socialist democracies[5] as well as in countries that are still undergoing a democratisation process (e.g. Brazil). In Slovenia, the right to be compensated for damage caused by unlawful actions by public authorities, which exists in addition to the general right to redress mentioned above, has been considered to be a human right in itself. Similarly in Poland, art. 77 § 1 of the Polish Constitution is construed as providing a subjective right to compensation that reflects the rule of law. In consequence, this right is subject to special constitutional protection and can be the basis of a constitutional complaint to the Constitutional Court.

In the United States the entitlement to damages remedy based on the violation of constitutional rights escapes easy categorisation, but it can also be seen as a form of 'constitutionalisation'. 'Constitutional torts' is a common name given to the so-called Section 1983 suits and Bivens actions, which are court-shaped mechanisms for obtaining damage awards in cases involving violations of U.S. constitutional rights and other federal rights embodied in domestic laws that overlap with civil and political human rights. A Section 1983 claim can be brought against two

[4] The Czech Republic, Poland, Slovenia, Estonia, Croatia, Turkey Brazil and Portugal.

[5] Poland, the Czech Republic, Slovenia, Estonia.

types of defendants: local government entities and officials in their individual capacities. The Bivens doctrine[6] has extended this cause of action to cover federal officials as defendants. An explicit relief provided by the legislator justifies a rejection of a Bivens claim.

In Canada, the Charter of Rights and Freedoms (1982), which forms part of the Constitution, enforces civil and political rights against government entities. The damages remedy is available as long as the court (of a general jurisdiction) considers it 'appropriate and just in the circumstances'. There also exists a quasi-constitutional regime in the Canadian Provinces – the Human Rights Codes – to remedy discrimination issues in each level of jurisdiction. Under the codes the human rights tribunals may order the violator to pay monetary compensation to the victim. Interestingly, the codes have effect also between private parties, but it is not possible to establish civil liability without calling in aid common law principles relating to intentional invasions of legally protected interests.[7]

Apart from the above-mentioned differences, the right to compensation for human rights abuses can vary in the scope of coverage. In general, it can be limited to certain rights or to certain violations.

Principally, most political and civil rights are both directly applicable and protected by damages remedies, while social, economic and cultural rights are considered as not directly applicable without further statutory contents, and in general a claim for compensation may not be raised in cases of infringement.[8] Consequently, damages remedies are more broadly admitted for violations of civil and political human rights than for violations of economic, social or cultural human rights. An 'All-rights-are-equal' approach in the context of compensation claims rarely exists. It is to be found mainly in jurisdictions where reparable damage is not curbed by the concept of protected rights, because the focal point and the primary element triggering liability is the existence of damage (i.e. in the French legal tradition). In contrast, in Brazil the constitutional right to damages is only guaranteed in respect of inviolable rights, i.e. personality rights, privacy, private life, honour and image of persons; all those rights rooted in dignity and respect for every human being.[9]

Another distinction of the protection of rights can be observed with respect to 'constitutional' as opposed to 'human' rights. For example, in Italy the regime applicable to violations of *constitutional* rights differs from the rules on State liability, which primarily concern *human* rights violations.

Finally, the Estonian legislator introduced a rather unique distinction in the treatment of particular types of human rights, depending on whether a person demands redress of pecuniary or non-pecuniary loss. A claim for pecuniary damages is valid regardless of which individual right has been violated. Compensation of non-pecuniary damage, on the other hand, is available only for certain fundamental rights enumerated in the State Liability Act, such as wrongful degradation of

[6] *Bivens vs. Six Unknown Named Agents of Federal Bureau of Narcotics*, 403 U.S. 388.

[7] *Seneca College vs. Bhadauria* [1981] 2 SCR.

[8] Explicitly in Germany, Portugal, Italy and the U.S.

[9] Art. 5 of the Brazilian Constitution of 1988.

dignity, damage to health, deprivation of liberty, violation of the inviolability of home or private life or the confidentiality of messages or defamation of honour or good name of the person.

As the foregoing reflects, in relation to some countries we can speak of an internal hierarchy of rights from the perspective of entitlement to damages.

20.1.2 International Human Rights and Constitutional Human Rights – Threshold of Protection by Damages Remedy

Although an unlawful conduct of public authorities frequently consists of a violation of internationally protected human rights, the national treatment of such cases does not always mirror the treatment of infringement of constitutional, i.e. domestically entrenched, rights. The distinction in protection of rights can be ascribed, first and foremost, to the dualist or monist model of reception/incorporation of international law into domestic systems and, secondly, to the autonomous development of human rights in national constitutions. One has to bear in mind that the mentioned divide between monist and dualist countries is significantly blurred and that many systems take a hybrid approach.

The country reports demonstrate that there are divergent tendencies in monist and dualist legal systems as regards the legal status of unincorporated international conventions that can give rise to rights enforceable in national courts. The influence of the dualist model on human rights protection is particularly noticeable in the American and Canadian systems (other countries traditionally classified as dualist include Germany, Norway, the U.K. and Ireland).[10] In the United States and Canada there is a clear distinction of treatment of international human rights and other civil rights protected by the federal and state constitutions. In acceding to human rights treaties, the U.S. declares such treaties as non-self-executing and thus dependent on domestic law making to make treaty-based rights and duties enforceable through private civil actions. According to court practice subsequent inconsistent congressional legislation may override any treaty-based rights. Much of the U.S. law providing damages remedies for acts that infringe international human rights focuses on domestic violations. When constitutional rights overlap with international human rights (e.g. freedom from unreasonable and warrantless searches, seizures and arrests; freedom from cruel and unusual punishment; equal protection of the laws) the federal Civil Rights Act (Section 1983) as well as federal constitutional torts (*Bivens*) doctrine will apply (see *infra*). Many international human rights, however, lie outside the scope of U.S. constitutional rights or federal law rights and thus are not bases for the types of claims mentioned above (human rights that impose affirmative duties of action on States, limitations on capital punishment, social and

[10] It is also present in Germany and Norway.

economic human rights). Moreover, American courts do not refer to international human rights norms in cases where no foreign or transnational element is present. The Alien Tort Statute, referring explicitly to international human rights legal norms, is the most distinctive federal U.S. law providing damage remedies for international human rights abuses.

The situation in Israel is also worthy of a mention. International treaties and conventions, although ratified by the government, are not directly enforceable in Israeli law (but only indirectly – through favourable interpretation) until they are either formally imported by parliamentary legislation or recognised as customary international law. As no implementing legislation has been passed, only human rights that enjoy the status of customary international law form part of Israeli domestic law. No awards, however, have been adjudicated solely on the basis of customary international law. The available avenue for the victim is thus a tort law cause of action, predominantly through the tort of negligence, or special legislation.

In general, in the jurisdictions under review the courts appear to take a monist approach as regards the enforcement of international human rights. In so-called 'monist' States the international norms protecting human rights have direct application (e.g. in Argentina,[11] Italy, France, Greece, the Netherlands, and many Central and Eastern European countries such as Poland, Croatia and the Czech Republic – since 2001[12]). In particular, in Council of Europe countries the victims can invoke the rights guaranteed by respective conventions before national authorities. This means that the domestic courts directly enforce the right to compensation for the infringement of human rights, if such a right is provided for in the treaty that is binding upon forum State. However, this does not necessarily mean that a domestic court would apply international human rights norms as the sole basis for adjudicating compensation or monetary satisfaction. It can be observed that in post-socialist countries the courts have been rather reluctant to directly apply international or regional human rights norms, although the trend is changing in favour of more effective protection.

A further point to note is that the time of the creation of the national constitution is an influential factor. In some countries, such as the U.S. or France, where civil rights (*libertes civils*) became the cornerstone of the legal order quite early on, international human rights obligations have played a limited role in domestic practice. The German legal system occupies a specific place for historical reasons, but also there the post-war period was the time of a rapid development of the human rights rhetoric. In other countries, however, in particular in the post-socialist zone, where domestic human rights rules are mainly derivative of international human rights, international influences illuminate the judicial responses to the problem of

[11] In Argentina the Inter-American Convention and its interpretation by the Inter-American Court are part of domestic law in the field of human rights, and the reparation of damages caused by the violation of rights enshrined in the Convention is legally binding.

[12] After the 2001 amendments to the Constitution – see the Czech report (Chapter 3).

developing a compensatory claim. The judiciary acts alongside of the legislator in order to fulfil the country's obligations at international law.[13]

Notwithstanding the intricacies of the problem of direct horizontal effect of international (regional) human rights, it is undoubted that the obligations of States under international treaties and customary international law implicate the duty to follow the jurisprudence of international courts and tribunals to whose jurisdictions the States have submitted. Accordingly, in the Council of Europe countries the ECtHR jurisprudence has become the most influential intervening factor in the development of domestic remedies in the European legal systems.[14] By contrast, neither Canada nor the United States has accepted the jurisdiction of the Inter-American Court of Human Rights, and no relevant international jurisdiction was accepted by Israel, either. Consequently, the impact of international human rights common law in these countries is very limited.

20.1.3 The Implications of Constitutionalisation of the Right to Damages

The constitutional character of the right to damages implicates its direct application as well as enhanced protection of human rights. A question that has arisen in many countries is whether the direct applicability (direct enforceability) concept should be understood as granting a court the competence to apply the constitutional norm and not to apply 'ordinary law' rules. To put it differently, the question essentially asks whether the court is generally permitted to ignore the rules of civil liability, or other special rules on public liability, when such rules appear to be in conflict with the constitutional right to damages, or to directly apply the constitutional norm when no legal basis for claiming compensation in civil law is admissible. The answer appears to be in the negative in most systems, but of course courts must anyway give effect to relevant international human rights through favourable interpretation of national law.

A rights-based approach, specific to the Germanic tradition, rephrases the above question in the following way: should constitutional fundamental rights be regarded as containing a subjective claim against a government to restore the legal situation and to compensate for harm sustained when infringed? This question is subject to theoretical discussions in a number of civil law countries and also in Israel. The German Constitutional Court has denied the existence of a general obligation to compensate an individual for violations of fundamental (human) rights in the German legal system. In other words, the German Constitution (Basic Law) does not create a separate cause of action for damages in every case of violations of human rights. From the constitutional perspective the right to a judicial remedy (art.

---

[13] See Shelton (2011) 4–5.

[14] For an illuminating comparative analysis of this influence see Gerards and Fleuren (2014a) 335 ff.

19 § 4) can be claimed only in connection with a subjective right conferred on the individual in the Basic Law, statutory law or the international human rights law. The German Constitutional Court has also held that the non-existence of an individual title in international law is no bar to a possible title based on German law tortious liability (art. 839 of the German Civil Code). The solution, according to which another fundamental right or other individual right must have been violated first in order to claim for compensation for damage, is also present in Portugal.

One also should not overlook the national restrictions on redressing non-pecuniary harm, which play an important role in this context. In particular, claiming compensation for non-pecuniary damage caused by a violation of human rights can be dependent on whether the violation can be considered an infringement of a personality right. The Polish Supreme Court has responded in the negative to the question of whether this condition should be disposed of through pro-constitutional (art. 77) construction of the Civil Code.[15]

In the systems that lack an explicit constitutional formulation of the right to compensation in the case of violations of human rights, such a right is regarded to be rooted in the rule of law, the principle of equality and the protection of human dignity. Hence, it can also be considered as being a constitutionally guaranteed right (e.g. in Italy, Greece, France, Ireland, the U.S. and Israel). The Dutch expert argues strongly in favour of explicit constitutionalisation of the right to damages in her country; moreover, such a right should cover both State and non-State actors.

The reference to the rule of law and the rule of legality implies that the right to damages aims to remedy the consequences of an action or inaction of public authorities, their agents and functionaries, but not the conduct of private persons. Moreover, those jurisdictions that underline the public authority liability approach refuse to accept a full (direct) horizontal effect of human rights (see the chapters on the Czech Republic, Slovenia, Poland, Norway, Italy – except when there is a gap in legislation, the U.K., the U.S. and Canada).

20.2 The Creation of a New General Cause of Action for Remedying Human Rights Violations (By Legislators Or By Courts)

In a few jurisdictions (the U.K., Ireland or Canada) legislators have enacted special acts on human rights protection, where a separate regime of liability for human rights violations has been laid down.

In the U.K., under the of the Human Rights Act of 1998, a claim for a breach of a Convention right is a claim against a public authority, the latter notion having been interpreted by case-law. Section 8(1) (HRA) provides that the court may grant such relief or remedy, or make such order, within its powers as it considers just and

[15] Polish Supreme Court, judgment of 6.5.2010, II CSK 640/09, OSNZD A/2011, item 4.

appropriate. 'Just and appropriate' in Convention terms really means 'effective, just and proportionate'. 'Just' implies that it must be fair to all who are affected by it, including persons other than the person whose right was violated. Secondly, the remedy must be appropriate, i.e. it must effectively address the grievance brought about by the violation. The English courts have a broad discretion in choosing the remedy appropriate in each case, a grant of compensatory damages being one such remedy often considered to be of secondary importance, after the declaratory judgment. The courts must take into account the principles applied by the ECtHR under art. 41 of the ECHR.[16]

In Ireland, the courts have created a unique solution of enforcing constitutional rights against any party, both public and private. The issue of remedies for infringement of human rights, which are set out in the Constitution, is not addressed in the Constitution act, and therefore the courts have quite a lot of discretion in deciding the appropriate remedy, including damages, for infringements. Under the general principle of the supremacy of the Constitution over common law, the courts allowed litigants to challenge existing principles of common law on the grounds that they do not adequately protect or vindicate relevant constitutional rights. This has led to the creation of the concept of a 'constitutional tort', i.e. a cause of action, on the basis of which damages can be awarded for tortious actions that have infringed human rights. The Irish concept is different from the U.S. concept of a constitutional tort. The former is not curbed by the 'State action' doctrine, but aims primarily at granting direct horizontal effect to constitutional rights. Hence, a constitutional tort can be committed by anyone: private individuals, corporations and by the State. Unfortunately, the exact parameters of application of this constitutional tort cause of action are unclear and uncertain.[17] If a constitutional right is also protected by means of legislation or may be enforced effectively and adequately within the parameters of an existing tort, then the trial court cannot exclusively rely upon the Constitution. Damages are calculated in accordance with common law principles.[18]

By contrast, the Canadian Supreme Court has rejected the idea of the creation of a new tort (more specifically 'a tort of intentional discrimination'). Firstly, because the Human Rights Codes foreclosed any civil action based directly upon a breach thereof, and, secondly, they also excluded any common law action based on an invocation of public policy expressed in the Codes. The claimants must then use the Code procedures laid out for vindication of that public policy.[19]

In Israel, with its mixed legal system, the avenue for the victim is a tort law cause of action, predominantly through the tort of negligence, or special legislation. The

---

[16] See the report for the U.K., at 7.1, citing the judgment *R vs. Secretary of State for the Home Department, ex p Greenfield* [2005] UKHL 14, [2005] 1 WLR 673.

[17] O'Cinneide (2007, 215) comments that "[t]he existence of the constitutional tort is widely seen as an essential safety net to protect fundamental rights from violations instigated by non-state bodies, if legislation and other forms of legal regulation do not do the job.".

[18] See O'Cinneide (2007) 215, 243 ff.

[19] *Seneca College vs. Bhadauria* [1981] 2 SCR, *Honda Canada Inc. vs. Keays* [2008] 2 SCR 362– both cases concerned the Ontario Human Rights Code.

Israeli Basic Laws are not regarded as constituting a new source of tort liability, neither through constitutional claims nor though the tort of breach of statutory duty. This notwithstanding, compensation can be sought through various causes of action (mainly in tort), and the Israeli courts are considered plaintiff-friendly. The admissibility of a right to compensation in every case of human rights violations, with no additional duty to prove the elements of a tortious cause of action, has recently been considered by the Israeli Supreme Court. The Court held that in principle the right to property should be fully protected; in certain limited circumstances in which it is unreasonable to deny compensation, a no-fault tort cause of action might arise. This decision is regarded as recognition of a very limited concept of a 'constitutional tort'. As the foregoing reflects, the majority of investigated legal systems, lack either a special human rights legislative enactment which would grant a direct claim for compensation on the statutory level or explicit constitutional safeguards of the right to have the damage redressed. The country reports also demonstrated that all systems are in the natural, constant process of shaping the relations between the human rights norms (whether constitutional or international) and the rules on tort law or administrative liability.

20.3 The Interplay Between International Pecuniary Remedies and Domestic Causes of Action

We now turn to the problem of the interplay between domestic claims for compensation and the monetary compensation in the form of 'just satisfaction' that is directly available to the victim under international human rights treaties and which may or may not by awarded as financial compensation by a competent tribunal.[20] The range of jurisdictions under review in this comparative exercise has limited these remarks to the European human rights system.

Before moving on to specific national responses, it should be recalled that the ECtHR, being an international tribunal, recognises that States have a 'margin of appreciation' as concerns their obligations under the Convention, as well as the fact that many decisions of the Court are contextual (justified *in concreto*). In general, the European States under survey follow the jurisprudence of the ECtHR, respecting so-called *res interpretata* of the Court's judgments, albeit there have been some clashes reported between constitutional courts and the Strasbourg Court.[21] In particular, the German Constitutional Court has allowed departure from rulings by international courts in regard to human rights when these decisions do not conform

[20] See Art. 41 of the ECHR, Art. 63 §1 American Convention on Human Rights, art. 27 §1 of the Protocol to the African Charter on Human and Peoples' Rights on the Establishment of an African Court on Human and Peoples' Rights (1998/2004).

[21] See in more detail Gerards and Fleuren (2014a, b) 357 ff

to the constant jurisprudence of domestic courts. For example, this concerns the balancing of privacy rights and the freedom of the press and post-sentence preventive detention in Germany.

In most European states art. 41 of the ECHR is not construed as a standalone cause of action in a domestic court. The issue was directly resolved by the legislator in Estonia: a complementary basis for compensatory claims has been set forth in the State Liability Act for the breaches of the ECHR. It is an independent domestic cause of action. Some other systems accept the interpretation that the ECHR adds new compensatory claims and modifies existing ones, e.g. in Germany.

In Italy, the legal basis for State liability for breaches of the ECHR was initially found in the general clause on liability for faulty conduct (art. 2043 of the Civil Code) and art. 5 § 5 of the ECHR. In 1992 the Supreme Court held that the ECHR could not be construed as a self-executing source of law under domestic law, but in 2005 it reversed its case-law and declared that the violation of the rights enshrined in the Convention has immediate relevance within the domestic legal order.[22] We encounter the same approach in Croatia, where provisions of the ECHR, insofar as they mention damages for violation of human rights, are considered as an explicit legal basis for damages in such cases.

In France, international/regional human rights have not been incorporated into the Constitutional documents because the Declaration of the Rights of Man of 26 August 1789 had pre-dated any international and regional human rights treaties. However, the French courts have developed a stable practice of application of the ECHR not only in cases against public authorities within administrative jurisdiction (*responsabilité administrative*), but also in civil suits against private parties and in cases that entail a flagrant irregularity by the administration infringing a fundamental freedom or a property right (*voie de fait*), also decided by civil courts. In addition, criminal courts apply the ECHR when awarding compensation for crimes in adhesion claims.

According to the Greek reporter, the entitlement to just satisfaction under art. 41 is a quasi-'secondary right' recognised by public international law (the ECHR) as a personal claim of the victim against the State. Based on the same logic, the right to just satisfaction should be granted the same character under Greek domestic law; hence it is not an enforceable claim. However, the debate whether the right to just satisfaction awarded by the ECtHR is a subjective entitlement under national Greek law or a right under public international law is not definitively settled.

Although Norway adopted the Human Rights Act in 1999, the said act does not stipulate any right to damages. It is disputed whether human rights infringements may give rise to a liability *sui generis*, possibly based on Art. 13 or 41 of the ECHR in conjunction with Art. 2 of the Human Rights Act (which gives full effect to the international instruments). A claimant must hence base her claim on tort law.

In the U.K., a victim of a breach of Convention rights contained in primary legislation does not have a claim under the HRA; he/she may either receive an *ex gratia*

[22] See decision Corte di Cassazione no. 28507 of 23.12.2005.

payment from the State or bring proceedings in the ECtHR and seek just satisfaction under art. 41 of the ECHR.

By means of the Irish ECHR Act of 2003 the ECHR became part of Irish law at the sub-constitutional level. Consequently, Irish courts are obliged to interpret Irish laws in a way that gives effect to Ireland's obligations under the ECHR. Under the Irish ECHR Act, any person who has suffered injury, loss or damage due to a breach of the Act may, if no other remedy in damages is available, institute High Court proceedings; the High Court may then award damages if it deems it to be the appropriate remedy for the breach (sec. 3 ECHR Act 2003).

Generally, it can be concluded that except for the U.K. the European claimants are normally not prevented from seeking further compensation (in order to obtain full damages) in domestic courts after they have been awarded just satisfaction by an international tribunal (ECtHR), provided that the time limit for filing a claim for compensation has not passed (see chapters on Portugal, Poland, Estonia, Greece and the Czech Republic). This may also be the case when the ECtHR finds the State to have breached the Convention, but dismisses the damage claims due to uncertainty as to the losses suffered.[23] In fact, a relatively low level of damages awarded by the ECtHR encourages applicants from some countries to seek full damages in domestic courts. As the Czech reporter explains, financial compensation under the Czech State liability law is considered an internal legal remedy that ensures compliance with the respective obligations under human rights treaties while compensation under Art. 41 of the ECHR is seen as an independent cause of action, which is contingent upon the declaratory decision on violation of human rights by the ECtHR.

Naturally, most jurisdictions follow the bedrock principle of *compensatio lucri cum damno* as long as monies from different sources aim to compensate the same prejudice. As regards the sums awarded in order to compensate non-pecuniary damage, it is submitted that it may be correct to take such sums into account when assessing whether and to what extent the claimant should be awarded further compensation for non-pecuniary harm.

Unlike in the majority of analysed jurisdictions, U.K. courts have construed the purpose of the HRA quite restrictively. Consequently, domestic law (HRA) is 'not to give victims better remedies at home than they could recover in Strasbourg, but to give them the same remedies without the delay and expense of resorting to Strasbourg'. Merris Amos has rightly pointed out that the ECtHR does not undertake fact-finding in as detailed a manner as a common court on the question of damages. Also, the awards of just satisfaction are not based on the principle of full compensation, and lastly, they have the relative value of money in the contracting States. Despite these differences between an international court and domestic court, a U.K. court would probably not allow further compensation.[24]

[23] This example comes from the Norwegian report; the domestic cases in the aftermath of *Lindheim et al. vs. Norway* (12.6.2012 – breach of art. 1 of prot. 1 to the ECHR by the regulation on ground lease contracts) are pending.

[24] See Amos in Chap. 17, at 17.6.

As the foregoing reflects, compensation for economic losses awarded under art. 41 of the ECHR must be accounted for in eventual compensation for economic losses founded upon another (domestic) legal basis. Second, compensation for non-pecuniary loss may be reduced or excluded if the sum already awarded was considered sufficient to compensate the loss suffered. Third, when the conditions for just satisfaction under art. 41 of the ECHR differ from those under relevant national law, the claimant may usually seek compensation in the domestic system.

20.4 Overview of the Scope and Way of Application of General Rules of Liability (Tort) Law

In principle, the private law elements of a cause of action based on an infringement of a human right will find application without essential modifications. Almost all the jurisdictions surveyed agree that the specific type of damaging event (i.e. violation of human rights) will not change the applicability of general institutes of liability law, such as damage, causation, contributory conduct or burden of proof, unless they have been modified by the rules on State liability. Naturally, this does not mean that the *method* of application is unchanged. The interpretation of all elements of liability by a court will no doubt be influenced by considerations of human rights law. In Europe, the ECHR through its horizontal effect has impacted the contents and balancing in a concrete case of general values and interests (dignity, autonomy, equal treatment) promoted by tort law. Where a tort implies a human rights infringement, a clear influence of the Convention values is seen in all systems, and reflected in particular in the enhanced compensability of non-pecuniary damage, alleviation of burden of proof of harm and the more lenient standard of proof of causation. Still, the traditional concepts of causation are applied as controlling mechanisms. Causation plays a role in identifying the victims who suffered from the breach of rights as well as limits the extent of damaging consequences to be compensated by the defendant.

In the U.K., the range of applicable tort law rules is not entirely clear, as it depends on the response to the question of whether a cause of action under the HRA is an action in tort.[25] The dominant position is that the victim has no automatic right (claim) to damages, which would be correlated with the defendant's obligation to pay. It is rather a competence of the court to award damages if no other relief or remedy could be granted in order to appropriately and justly sanction the violation. Even a finding of violation, without a grant of just satisfaction, will be an important remedy and vindication of the right of the claimant. The HRA is not considered by the U.K. courts to be a tort statute, because its objects are different and broader, although arguments in favour of a tort-based approach are also presented in the legal writings. If a given human right violation can be linked to a common law tort

[25] See e.g. Rogers (2003) 35, 38.

(e.g. false imprisonment, nuisance, misfeasance in public office) or to a breach of EU law, damages can be awarded for a private law wrong or breach of EU law. Such a situation will be treated as an alternative route, and hence no further compensation would be required under Section 8(3) (a) of the HRA. Of course, a right to protection of private life and freedom of speech may also be breached by private parties. The cause of action is then the tort of breach of confidence as modified by Art. 8 and Art. 10 of the HRA (the award has to be proportionate).

Given that infringements of human rights are dealt with under the general rules of tort law, which evidently vary between the jurisdictions, the comparative overview discloses some diversity of techniques and methods of interpretation and application of the rules to private and public defendants (noted in particular in the reports for France, Israel and Norway).

For some jurisdictions, in particular in French legal culture, the distinction linked to the category of defendants is irrelevant as all persons are put on an equal footing. Such an approach can result in either (a) the same rules of liability in damages being applied to all defendants, or (b) different bases of liability applicable by the person's status:

(a) in the first group of systems, all claims for compensation for violations of human rights will be adjudicated under the same private law rules (e.g. under the tort of negligence or breach of statutory duty);
(b) in the second group, a claim against a public body will be examined under the relevant national rules of public liability, whereas a claim against a private corporation/person will be decided in the regime of private law, unless the fact of exercising public authority/functions permits the application of the public liability regime. Hence, the foundation of liability (strict or fault) as well as the scope of liability can vary even if the victim has suffered the same type of harm.

If State liability law belongs to the realm of public law, one important implication is the possible hierarchy and interdependence of remedies. Moreover, different courts may have jurisdiction over matters belonging to the two categories of cases.

A rather unique position is occupied by Ireland. In situations where private law remedies are not clearly applicable, 'constitutional rights' have been treated as binding private individuals, thereby providing a safety net to protect fundamental rights from infringements by private bodies.

20.5 Claims for Damages Against Private Parties

The admissibility of claims against private parties is of course linked with the mentioned concept of horizontal effect of human rights. It should be recalled that in most States the primary function of fundamental rights still remains to shape the relations of individuals vis-á-vis the State and any organ or person emanating the State. The direct horizontal effect of human rights has been explicitly admitted in most European countries (apart from those already mentioned – also in Germany,

Greece, Romania Portugal, Italy and Estonia), while in the U.S. and Canada it is almost non-existent as the doctrine of 'State action' plays a primary role in the admission of a compensation claim.[26] Under this doctrine the fact that the human (constitutional) right was directly violated by a private person would mean that the victim could not raise a constitutional claim to protect that right. The recent court practice in the U.S. seems to reinstate the limitations of liability brought about by this doctrine. This notwithstanding, in the U.S. some human rights violations can ground tort claims for intentional infliction of emotional distress, false imprisonment, abuses in the employment context, including forced labour, and within the reach of statutory unfair business practices law. In Canada, the situation is more complex. On the one hand, the federal Charter of Rights and Freedoms does not apply to 'private litigation completely divorced from any connection with the government'.[27] On the other hand, the Human Rights Codes in the Provinces are regarded as applicable horizontally; such an application is implicit both in the fact that the substantive rights are formulated in an open manner and in the provision of a general complaint in the event of infringement, which also belongs to 'anyone'.

Many jurisdictions may be placed somewhere in between direct and indirect effect, in particular as regards direct application of certain rights that were never regarded as being exclusively against the State. In most countries, the link to tort law and its inherent restrictions is clearly visible in the area of personality (or personal) rights (personal liberty, right to health, reputation, image, right to privacy, to name a few). Those rights are traditionally protected by tort law, but are not automatically equated with human rights (cf. Poland, Croatia). The scope of protection of personality rights is shaped by courts, which in principle ensure the compatibility of domestic rules with the standards of protection developed by the regional human rights tribunals. The process is hence dynamic.[28] It should be stressed that as regards relations between private persons, the courts have either created new claims (types of torts – e.g. constitutional torts) or expanded the application of the general clause of liability. Hence, the horizontal effect is stronger in those systems where the judiciary is intrinsically active and where the tort law is founded on general clauses or a general duty of care (France, Ireland, Italy, Israel, the Netherlands). This judicial activism is conceptualised in France as 'conventionalisation' of private law. The trend has attracted doctrinal criticism, mainly due to the fear of judge-made norms, and especially the risk of uncontrolled expansion of liability, and of overly deep interference of the Convention logic with private law logic. Xavier Philippe refers to 'invasion of human rights in private law relations', although the invasion is generally restricted to relations unequal by nature, e.g. natural person-legal person, cases of subordination or hierarchy.

[26] The Canadian courts tend to refer to U.S. case law when interpreting the Charter of Rights and Freedoms – see Barendt (2007) 398.

[27] Under the Supreme Court ruling in *Dolphin Delivery* (*Retail, Wholesale and Department Store Union [RWDSU], Local 580 vs. Dolphin Delivery Ltd* [1986] 2 SCR 573.

[28] See e.g. the legislative changes brought by the new Czech Civil Code – Chap. 3 at 3.1.2.

When a claim for pecuniary redress is directed at a private person on account of violation of human rights in private relations, it is placed either in the realm of tort law or in contract law. As a principle, the violation of individual rights by private parties falls within the realm of tort law, unless the violation has occurred within a contractual relation, such as an employment relation. In order for the claim to succeed, all necessary elements of a relevant tort (tort of negligence, breach of confidence, invasion of privacy, a general clause of liability for tort, etc.) must be proven.

In most countries fault (negligence) remains a prerequisite of the liability for human rights' infringements, with a range of exceptions provided for the protection of personality rights, where simple wrongfulness of the defendant's conduct might be sufficient. No reporter appears to suggest that a claim will arise automatically when a 'pure' violation of the right to privacy or freedom of expression has occurred, without consideration of other elements of the claim stemming from relevant private law rules. Nevertheless, this approach can be modified in respect of discriminatory conduct. Many legislators have created separate statutory grounds for a compensatory claim.[29] In a few systems no proof of harm is necessary in order to effectuate protection (e.g. Israel, Ireland, the U.S. – see Sect. 20.9.2).

20.6 Additional Prerequisites of the Claim for Damages

In order to explain the vague contours of the cause of action for damages one has to consider additional requirements of liability that can stem either from the logic of a given national liability system or from explicit norms of the human rights protection regime.

Under the American 'constitutional torts' doctrine, claims made under Section 1983 have to meet certain conditions. As regards claims brought against local entities the plaintiff must prove that the violation of rights (constitutional rights and other federal rights) followed from the following: an official 'policy', a 'custom' or 'practice' of pervasive rights violations of which policymaking officials had actual or constructive knowledge; or 'deliberate indifference' toward recurring rights violation.

Moreover, an American court will first apply any federal or state law remedies, such as the Federal Tort Claims Act, state tort claims acts, specific anti-discrimination laws, among other examples, before it can address the same behaviour as falling under the so-called 'constitutional tort'.

The overview of European jurisdictions discloses a great variety of approaches.

First, in the Germanic legal family, the alleged violation must concern a duty not only owed to the State, but also to the citizen (*drittbezogene Amtspflicht*). In the case of human rights violations this precondition is generally met.

[29] For example, since 2006 the Ontario Human Rights Code, s 46.1 authorises a court that, in an ordinary civil proceeding (e.g. for wrongful dismissal under the general private law contract rules), finds that one of the parties has infringed a Code right (e.g. discriminatory dismissal) of the other, to make a remedial order for payment of monetary and/or non-monetary compensation; however, this provision 'does not permit a person to commence an action based solely on an infringement of a right under Part I' of the Code.

Secondly, a claim for damages may depend on first using another, non-compensatory remedy or on the exhaustion of all available non-compensatory remedial means. According to the German approach, compensation is the *ultima ratio* of the constitutional State, hence the individual is not free in the choice of remedies. An important implication of this is that a person may not claim damages if he/she was able to prevent harm by challenging an act of State violating his/her rights. For example, if the right to trial in due time was breached, compensation may only be awarded if, prior to filing a compensatory claim, a party to the dispute has complained about the length of the proceedings to the court of proceedings. The German approach is shared i.a. in the U.K., the Netherlands and the Czech Republic.

Nevertheless, in most European jurisdictions there is no requirement to exhaust other remedies before claiming compensation. This notwithstanding, traditional models of State liability admit a civil action for damages against the State only after an earlier or simultaneous complaint against the administrative or judicial act that caused the damage has been filed. Annulment or a similar action purporting to cancel that act or to established its illegality is the prerequisite of a claim for damages in Poland, the Czech Republic and Estonia.

In other jurisdictions an action for damages is independent or can be joined with other legal remedies (e.g. Greece, Portugal). In the systems whose focal point is on the infliction of damage (the French tradition), the claim for damages can be brought regardless of other remedial means.

If a claim for compensation is governed by public law (e.g. in Estonia and Turkey), it is almost always not a primary, but a secondary remedy. Exceptions concern unlawful expropriations, where the legislator balances public and private interests and the choice between restoration or compensation is not always obvious (e.g. in Germany and Israel).

Interestingly, in Slovenia and Croatia, a friendly settlement procedure with the State Attorney or a public prosecutor must be undertaken before the claim can be litigated.

20.7 The Purpose and Functions of the Damages Remedies in Cases of Infringement of Human Rights

From the public law and the international law perspectives, the response of any legal system to the violation must be proportionate and just, and these two criteria appear in constitutional rules or human rights legislation.

From the perspective of tort law three goals of damages can be identified:

- compensation (reparation),
- deterrence (prevention),
- punishment (repression).

There is a general agreement that the main purpose of the claim for compensation of the infringement of human rights is to compensate those who have fallen victim to abuses. The victim must be put to the position she/he would have been in had the event causing the damage not occurred. Country reports have shown that the general principle of full compensation applies except in some specific cases expressly foreseen in the law. These exceptions include inter alia liability arising from State political and legislative power and compensation for sacrifice in the name of the public interest. In a few countries, such as the U.K. and Canada, the legislator has used the concept of 'just satisfaction', which is distinct from the concept of damage. The former is about equitable indemnity rather than reparation of the proven damage. Interestingly, the House of Lords held that 'the general principle applied to affording just satisfaction was to put the applicant as far as possible in the position in which he/she would have been if the State had complied with its obligations under the HRA'.[30] This interpretation brings most cases on the same level of financial compensation, be it just satisfaction or classical damages.

Furthermore, the compensatory function resting on the bedrock principle of full compensation is supplemented by the deterrent function. Repression is less frequently emphasised. In some countries, promoting social solidarity and repression are seen as subsidiary functions of compensation in human rights cases. More specifically, the deterrent function as well as repression is often ascribed to the award of non-pecuniary loss damages.[31] In a similar context the Dutch Supreme Court has attributed the function of 'rights vindication' to the law of damages. The idea is that a right to damages for non-pecuniary loss can arise from a severe violation of fundamental rights or of other standard of conduct, which resulted in harmful consequences.

Recognition of the violation plays a limited role. The Norwegian reporter, among others, observes that modest sums are in fact awarded in the result of lengthy and costly proceedings; he thus concludes that to the victims the damages remedy is a tool to obtain an authoritative decision holding that the actor wrongfully infringed upon their rights.

As regards State liability for breaches of human rights, two more ideas should briefly be mentioned. In the Germanic legal tradition the rationale behind the entitlement to pecuniary compensation lies in the idea of 'sacrificial encroachment' because the aggrieved person has to bear a 'special burden' for the interest of the public (the whole society). 'Sacrificial encroachment' justifies property-related claims as well as compensation for personal harm of a person criminally prosecuted, lawfully detained or arrested and then acquitted.[32] By the same token, in the French legal tradition, the principle of *égalité devant les charges publiques* says that compensation should be provided for those who have suffered a disproportionately large burden or loss caused by activities pursued in the common good. In this way the overly onerous burden is shared by means of taxation between all members of society who benefit from the activities.

---

[30] See *R (on the application of Wilkinson) vs. Inland Revenue Commissioners* [2005] UKHL 30, [2005] 1 WLR 1718.

[31] See the Supreme Court in Estonia: judgment of 26.6.2013, 3-2-1-18-13.

[32] In Germany and Portugal, as well as in other countries, special entitlements to compensatory remedies supersede other titles based on sacrificial encroachment.

20.8 State Liability for Infringements of Human Rights in More Detail

20.8.1 Specific Categories of Rights Protected By Damages Remedy Through Explicit Rules

Following the internationally recognised standards, explicit claims for financial compensation are widely provided for:

- specific cases of the violation of personal freedom, namely unjust or unlawful detention and arrest,
- property-related infringements,
- the delay of justice (a violation of a right to process in reasonable time) – see Sect. 20.8.2.3,
- discriminatory conduct.

Other examples of specific entitlements include i.a. laws on data protection that seek to protect privacy rights and other rights relating to the general right of personality, and protection of individuals against terrorism (in the U.S., Greece and Turkey).

The right to personal freedom has always enjoyed enhanced protection in international and national laws. In all reported jurisdictions explicit provisions give effect to the right to compensation for violations of the right to liberty in cases of deprivation of freedom through arrest or detention when the victims have been subsequently acquitted or sentenced to a different penalty. In many instances also secondary victims, such as family members and persons entitled to maintenance from the person deprived of freedom, have claims of their own.

In cases of unlawful detention the claim derives directly from international or regional human rights acts (see art. 5 § 5 of the ECHR). This entitlement is very specific and provides for strict State liability. By contrast, degrading conditions of detention are subject to art. 3 of the ECHR protection and according to the German and Polish courts a claim for compensatory damages must meet the requirements of an action in tort. The domestic rules governing the said claims are typically found in the provisions on criminal procedure or in separate legislation, which implement both constitutionally and internationally set standards.

The property-related cases account for a vast number of State liability cases in many countries, including Germany, Israel and post-socialist States. Furthermore, legislation that provides for expropriation is not immune to liability if unconstitutionality, due to lack of proportionality or other illegality, could be established.

A common feature of all mentioned cases is, firstly, that the violator is a State entity. Secondly, the claims embedded in the special provisions are not necessarily subject to the rules of civil law; hence, the scope of redress is not identical to the compensation paid under civil law. The national reports provide a great deal of details on caps, limitations, flat rates, adequate instead of full compensation, shorter prescription periods and different procedures of seeking damages.

Prohibition of discrimination is usually guaranteed by an independent entitlement to compensation. This is a common solution in EU countries, derived from the anti-discrimination directives (see also infra at 20.9.3).[33] In the U.S. and Canada anti-discrimination laws provide – by explicit text or judicial interpretation – private rights of action that include claims for money damages.

20.8.2 Illegal Conduct of Public Authority

20.8.2.1 Fault-Unlawfulness-Mere Infringement

For many systems human rights violations are traditionally regarded as a subcategory of illegal conduct of public authority. Hence, the claims stemming from such violations, if brought against public organs or persons, are accommodated within the existing system of public authority liability. Accordingly, the applicable regime can have, depending on the country, a vertical structure that may or may not begin at the constitutional level and be further developed by statutory substantive rules and procedural measures. It should be added that commercial activities of the public administration are not per se exempt from the risk of being in violation of human rights (e.g. in employment, marketing of consumer products).

Given the national constitutional rules, a public organ's breach of human rights is frequently subject to the same rules as breaches of other rights. However, the involvement of human rights is crucial for the establishment or/and interpretation of fault or unlawfulness by a court.

The traditional principle of liability is fault. However, many jurisdictions have followed the French idea of *faute de service* that comes close to the understanding of wrongfulness. *Faute de service* is necessary and sufficient to hold the authorities liable for administrative risk. Despite the language, public liability is generally objective in the systems that derive the cause of action for any conduct, including human rights abuses, from the general clause of liability for fault (e.g. in Italy and the Netherlands).

In many other countries public liability is strict (put differently, it is objective), founded openly on the element of unlawfulness (i.a. in Poland, the Czech Republic, Slovenia, Croatia, Estonia, Portugal and Greece[34]) or partially strict and partially

[33] Council Directive 2000/43/EC of 29 June 2000 implementing the principle of equal treatment between persons irrespective of racial or ethnic origin ('Racial Equality Directive') and of Council Directive 2000/78/EC of 27 November 2000 establishing a general framework for equal treatment in employment and occupation ('Employment Equality Directive').

[34] Greece: art. 105 of the civil code expressly States that 'The State shall be under a duty to make good any damage caused by the unlawful acts or omissions of its organs in the exercise of public authority, except where the unlawful act or omission is in breach of an existing provision that is intended to serve the public interest.'

based on objective fault – depending on the nature of the violated right (Norway, Turkey). Under the U.K. HRA there must be a finding of unlawfulness or 'prospective unlawfulness' based on breach or prospective breach by a public authority of a Convention right. In addition, bad faith is a precondition of an award of damages if the victim alleges the violation of human rights by a judicial act.

Furthermore, in countries where the notion of subjective right is the centre of liability law unlawfulness of the conduct and unlawfulness of the result is required. Unlawfulness of the result relates to the offence of subjective rights or infringement of legally protected interests (Germany, Italy and Portugal; in the Netherlands this idea is referred to as the requirement of relativity).

In the remaining jurisdictions under survey public liability is based on fault in its classic sense (the U.S., Canada, Romania and Israel). Interestingly, in Estonia, only compensation for non-pecuniary damage is conditional upon the existence of fault. The exception is when such compensation is awarded on the basis of a decision of the ECtHR declaring violation of the ECHR or any of its protocols.

On balance, we can conclude that the sole requirement of unlawfulness is a general trend or at least a solution under consideration (e.g. in Israel and Norway). Various legal devices have been adopted by courts to reach the objectivisation of fault and, in consequence, of liability.

However, it is unclear whether mere infringement suffices for a court to acknowledge unlawfulness of that infringement. It appears that it does not. The countries may be grouped in various ways. In the systems where a subjective right is at the centre of the liability logic, the violation of such a right, i.e. also of a human right – as a right for a person – can suffice to trigger liability for moral harm. Of course, many of the human rights violations demonstrate an inherent element of fault, as they involve deliberate or negligent wrongdoing, such as in cases of intentional deprivation of liberty, torture or deprivation of property.

Finally, it can be noted that combined illegality of conduct of public authorities and the fault of a functionary/personnel member in the form of intent, malice or gross negligence will in most jurisdictions trigger personal liability of the latter.[35] Personal liability may be realised either through direct liability of both the public organ and a physical person acting in the capacity of a functionary (the liability will hence be joint and several)[36] or – a majority view – through recourse actions, while the public authority answers primarily and directly in a lawsuit instituted by the injured party.[37]

[35] Except for Israel, where the Civil Wrongs Ordinance in its current version grants immunity to civil servants, including State organs for acts performed in the course of governmental duty and in a public capacity.

[36] Germany, Italy, Portugal.

[37] Greece, Turkey, Brazil, Poland.

20.8.2.2 Can the Legislator Be Held Liable in Damages for Violations of Human Rights?

A right to claim damages is uncontroversial when the infringements are authored by an institution or person who can be regarded as emanation of the State's executive power, charged with executive acts, omissions or misconduct. The other two branches of government – legislature and judiciary – tend to implicate modifications to the contents of the right to compensation if the damage is alleged to arise from the performance of the legislative or judiciary power in breach of human rights.

The problem of liability for legislative acts is connected with the concept of the control of constitutionality of laws, on the one hand, and the admissibility or non-admissibility of a claim against the legislative organs or executive organs that legislate (*pouvoir réglementaire*), on the other hand. The admissibility of the liability in damages for violations that stem from legislative acts is first of all dependent on the choice of the constitutional control model in a given country. In several democratic systems the concrete control of the constitutionality of laws is embedded in the legal culture (e.g. in Greece, Poland, Turkey, Portugal, the Czech Republic and Slovenia), yet in other systems there is no direct right of appeal to a constitutional court (e.g. in France and Italy). In a few countries the possibility of lodging a constitutional complaint is linked with the option to claim compensation for damage in the same procedure, although this competence is neither characteristic nor confined to cases of legislative wrongs (Slovenia and Croatia).

Legislative unlawfulness or wrongfulness, if accepted as a source of civil liability, typically requires the determination of the unconstitutionality of a defective act or of unlawful legislative omission. In Greece, liability can be acknowledged when a parliamentary enactment contravenes higher sources of the Greek legal order and does *in concreto* cause a violation of a protected human right of concrete person(s). The State can also incur civil liability for human rights violations in the exercise of delegated normative competence of the executive, if the State organ authorised to issue the normative act is bound by the authorising provision to adopt the act it omitted. In Slovenia, only the most severe infringements of constitutional provisions or of basic civilised standards by a legislative act can trigger State liability. In effect, the courts have to distinguish different violations of different constitutionally protected human rights assessing their severity, although the constitution makes no such distinction.[38]

The nature and scope of compensation substantially differs. It either resembles *ex gratia* payment or relates to the scope of real loss. In Portugal, the 2007 Act on public authorities liability authorises a court to award compensation on the basis of equity, when a very large number of victims and relevant public interest justify it. This is an exceptional solution regarding the scope of compensation in the field of public liability.

This liability is not accepted in common law jurisdictions. In the U.K. a court cannot overturn legislation that is contrary to Convention rights, but it should choose

[38] Slovenia.

an interpretation compatible with the Convention. A High Court (and court of that level) or a higher-level court can make a declaration of incompatibility of the questioned legislation with the Convention rights, shifting the problem to the Parliament.[39] Interestingly, in Ireland damages could be recovered where constitutional rights have been infringed as a result of an invalid legislative act once the damage is proven to have ensued directly from the effects of the invalidity without intervening events.

State liability for legislative wrongs is alien to the Germanic legal tradition. Since the legislator is not understood to be obliged towards specific individuals but towards the common good (i.e. there is no *drittbezogene Amtspflicht*), violations of individual rights by laws and statutes do not give rise to compensation under § 839 BGB. The 'expropriating encroachment' action has practically been reduced to cover unforeseeable effects of statutory law or its application while foreseeable effects of legislation must be compensated by the legislator according to the doctrine of the determination of content and limits to property subject to compensation (*ausgleichspflichtige Inhaltsbestimmung*).

In all EU countries, when laws or regulations or court decisions infringe individual rights conferred by EU law (such as the Charter rights), the duty to compensate is rooted directly in EU law. This has in many countries added yet another cause of action to the system. With respect to the non-contractual liability of the EU only the infringement of the superior (fundamental) norm protecting rights of individuals could initially give rise to liability for legislative acts. Presently, however, the character of the norm is taken into account as part of the analysis of the conditions of the liability, but not expressly required. The CJEU has rejected the interpretation in accordance with the German *Schutznorm* doctrine because it would in practice make it impossible or extremely difficult to obtain effective reparation for loss or damage resulting from a breach of EU law by the legislature. In its recent case law, the CJEU also explains that the existence of a right conferred on individuals by a rule of law does not relate to the actual nature of the harm alleged but instead constitutes a condition for a finding of a sufficiently serious breach of such a rule.[40]

20.8.2.3 Compensation Claims Stemming from the Acts and Omissions of the Judiciary

Turning to the liability of the judiciary, we should distinguish between violation of the right to due process and other cases of miscarriage of justice.

National positions differ widely as regards liability for judicial errors. In the majority of jurisdictions judicial errors that make a judgment unlawful are not sources of compensatory claims,[41] even if they violate fundamental rights. The liability may arise in a few systems (Poland and Portugal), provided that the judgment has earlier been annulled or declared unlawful in proper proceedings. In a few countries

---

[39] HRA, s. 3(1) and s.4

[40] C-611/12 P, Jean-François Giordano vs. Commission, para.40.

[41] The U.S., the U.K. and Germany.

(the U.K. and Greece) the judges may be held liable in their personal capacity, which is more in theory than practice. The liability, if admitted, is restricted to the cases of 'manifest error' of the court, thus excluding any liability for erroneous application or interpretation of the law. However, even long-standing negative approaches to the liability of State for unlawful judgments are slowly changing in view of the constitutional guarantees (e.g. in Greece).

By contrast, excessive delays in the judicial proceedings normally give rise to some kind of pecuniary indemnity. The delay of justice appears from the reports as the most common systemic problem of the judicial systems in Europe and also in Brazil (where, however, no pecuniary compensation is available). Domestic damages remedies are introduced in the Council of Europe countries in realisation of art. 6 of the ECHR. Not infrequently, however, 'effective measures' against excessively lengthy court proceedings had been preceded by the ECtHR pilot judgment or a judgment that imposed a deadline to introduce such measures, as was the case with the Czech Republic, Poland, Germany, Greece, Italy, Slovenia and Turkey. As the reports reflect, most often a new title to pecuniary remedy is introduced by a legislator, and rarely by the supreme judicial bodies (as in the Netherlands and Greece). Those entitlements may deviate from damages in the classic civil law sense. For example, German law provides for 'reasonable' compensation and a lump sum for the immaterial disadvantages, the Italian Pinto Law provides for 'indemnity' rather than 'restoration' (compensation), and in Poland it is called 'an appropriate sum'. Typically, a differently named claim authorises the legislator to allow for partial indemnification instead of full compensation for the loss suffered (see Sect. 20.9.4). These two features – a new 'name' and the finite scope of the remedy – allow an observation that the remedy is closer to a public cause of action than a private one. In the cases of judicial wrongs that reflect a structural problem, national legislators purport to prevent further abuses of fundamental rights rather than concentrate on compensating for the losses suffered.

20.9 Reparable Harm and Scope of Damages

20.9.1 General Remarks

In general, compensation may be awarded when there is a legally recognised form of damage. As regards human rights infringements, the requirement of legally relevant damage generally does not create much debate.

The existence of a violation will usually not suffice. Although we would be able to find a number of judgments in which a pure violation, at least as regards infringements of some human rights, was considered as giving a *per se* right to damages,[42] in most cases an economically assessable damage that is proven by the claimant will

[42] E.g. in Norway.

be redressed. Private law rules govern both reparable damage and the causal link between the damage and the damaging event.

In the French legal tradition a claimant must prove concrete, actual and direct damage arising from the defendant's conduct. In other systems the reports refer to pecuniary loss and non-pecuniary losses.

In all jurisdictions in which tort law is applied to the claim material damage typically encompasses positive loss (the decrease of assets, expenditures, etc. – *damnum emergens*) as well as lost profits (*lucrum cessans*). All elements must be causally linked to the unlawful/faulty act or omission of the actor. Reparable material damage may also include costs and expenses, loss of earnings (including loss of earning potential), loss of chance and lost opportunities (including employment, education and social benefits).[43]

When personal injury is the consequence of the human rights violations, all claims available under the general rules are also available in the discussed scenario.

In principle, except for France, the reparation of non-pecuniary harm has to be explicitly provided for by the law. The combination of this rule and the State (public) actor as a defendant can be detrimental to the victim in the sense that the scope of coverage of non-pecuniary losses is subject to double control. In cases of human rights abuses non-pecuniary damage includes distress and anxiety, loss of reputation, humiliation, insult, indignation, bouts of depression, enduring psychological harm, feelings of helplessness and frustration. In many countries any physical or emotional distress that was brought upon the person needs to be related to the fault-based violation of the person's subjective right (or personal right).[44]

The burden of proof of harm may be alleviated with a view of granting effective protection to the injured person. For certain violations of law, the existence of harm is presumed (e.g. deprivation of liberty). For example, the Czech Civil Code presupposes the existence of harm in cases of violations of 'natural' rights.

20.9.2 Exceptional Instances Where No Proof of Harm Is Necessary

There are several instances in which compensation without proof of harm has been admitted in various jurisdictions.

In Israel, a violation of the right to equality in public services may give rise to an action in tort, and can lead to liability of up to approx. €10,400 without proof of harm.

Under the U.K. section (8) HRA may justify a monetary remedy for an intentional invasion of privacy by a public authority, even if no damage is suffered other than distress, for which damages are not ordinarily recoverable.

---

[43] Damages for violations of human rights are treated as damages for torts; hence tax rules apply equally to all categories (in most countries they are tax exempt).

[44] E.g. as Estonia or Poland.

The U.S. reporter points out that in the U.S. plaintiffs in constitutional torts actions, including some involving rights that overlap with international human rights, may not be able to prove measurable harm. In such cases courts sometimes awarded nominal damages.

In Irish law, in a case where the plaintiff has established a wrong but has not suffered any harm, nominal damages can be awarded.

In Estonia, a person who has been unjustly deprived of his or her liberty or has been injured as a result of the use of force does not need to prove the occurrence of the damage or the extent of the damage. The Estonian Compensation for Damage Caused by State to Person by Unjust Deprivation of Liberty Act draws on the assumption that the restriction of the fundamental right of liberty causes non-pecuniary damage and results in a loss of profit in any case.

20.9.3 Scope of Damages and the Levels of Discretion in Adjudicating Damages

In almost all jurisdictions under survey, damages for infringement of human rights are calculated in accordance with general rules. This holds true even if a claim is directly and solely based on the constitutional norm (as, e.g., in Ireland). Commonly recognised principles, such as individual calculation and consideration of concrete circumstances, are taken into account.

The damages due in cases of patrimonial loss should be full, i.e. they should repair all losses sustained. In a number of cases the principle of encroachment/*sonderopfer* only obliges the State to pay an appropriate compensation, not full damages.

The discretion of the courts is greater as far as damages for non-pecuniary loss are concerned. A variety of factors are taken into account by the courts in awarding damages, including the gravity of the violation and severity of the injury. In personal injury cases breach of Convention rights may justify a rise in a particular level of compensation.[45]

On the other hand, if the award of money is to provide just satisfaction – and not to repair the damage – the court's discretion is broad: both as to 'award-no award' and with respect to the extent of the award. This model of adjudication has been adopted in the U.K., where there is no 'right' to monetary compensation under the U.K. HRA. In this regard it may be important for a U.K. court to take into account the question of fault as it can make a difference to the award of damages if the breach was intentional, negligent or innocent. In general, awards under the HRA are seen as equitable, they are not precisely calculated, but are judged to be fair in each individual case. The British courts' practice is unclear as to whether a victim would receive a higher or similar level of compensation under the HRA than under tort law. According to the House of Lords, in awarding damages under the HRA courts

[45] E.g. in the Netherlands and Norway.

should not follow the domestic scale, but that of the ECtHR. The Italian Court of Cassation which has held that 'domestic judges retain an autonomous margin of appreciation, which allows them to reasonably distance themselves from ECtHR case-law'.[46] By contrast, in the Irish common law damages for infringement of constitutional rights are generally assessed on the same basis as damages in tort, not on any higher basis, but the discussion about lower damages if a breach of human rights is involved would probably be seen as paying little respect to the intrinsic value of constitutional rights.

The courts in the European Union appear to have a tendency to apply the lower scale of sanctions provided for by law and in terms of the level and amount of compensation awarded in discrimination cases. This is critically assessed by the human rights bodies[47] and the EU organs. The EU Commission considers it incorrect to maintain an upper limit for compensation in cases of discrimination as far as the laws implementing anti-discrimination directives are concerned.[48] It should be recalled that Directive 2000/43/EC precludes national law under which sanctions are purely symbolic and that under certain conditions it would be in breach of the Directive if it is only possible to give a warning in a case of discrimination.

Interestingly, in Canada the awards of damages for material losses in discrimination cases can be large because the aim is to put the complainant back into the position they otherwise would be if it were not for the discriminatory activity; awards for non-material losses are less generous.

20.9.4 Limitations and Caps on Damages

According to most European reports special rules on damages for deprivation of freedom through arrest or detention introduce limitations on both pecuniary and moral harm. In some systems a lump sum or a rate per day, per month or per year is allowed (in particular in Germany, Greece, Estonia).

Other limitations apply to the length of proceedings breaches. For example, in Slovenia, the lower limit is €300 and the upper limit at €5,000, in Poland, it is accordingly €500 and €5,000, and in Italy €500 and €1,500. In Germany, a sum of €1,200 per year of delay is awarded, subject to adjustment by the court, and in the Netherlands €500 per 6 months of delay. A special scheme to this effect has recently been established in Turkey and in Greece. Typically, an aggrieved party can also file a separate lawsuit to claim monetary compensation for material damage caused by delay in judgment.

---

[46] See Court of Cassation, decision no. 10894 of 11.5.2006 and the Italian Chapter.

[47] E.g. in the Netherlands.

[48] See Joint Report of the Commission of 17.1.2014 on the application of Council Directive 2000/43/EC of 29 June 2000 implementing the principle of equal treatment between persons irrespective of racial or ethnic origin ('Racial Equality Directive') and of Council Directive 2000/78/EC of 27 November 2000 establishing a general framework for equal treatment in employment and occupation ('Employment Equality Directive'). COM(2014) 2 final, at 3.5.

The foregoing sums demonstrate that the level of this type of compensation is very similar in Europe, which is not surprising in view of the fact that in many countries such pecuniary remedies were introduced in order to enforce the ECtHR jurisprudence regarding the right to a hearing within a reasonable time. This also suggests that the flat rate payments aim to remedy the frustration and distress caused by the delay of justice, not the proven harm, and that their nature is more public than private.

Finally, limitations on damages are inherent in the compensatory schemes. Providing for fast and efficient settlement of claims, the schemes are generally considered an effective domestic remedy under the international or regional human rights law. However, they are assessed critically at home, if the thresholds or caps are set too low, thereby hindering the compensatory aim of State liability.

20.9.5 Punitive Or Exemplary Damages

In common with 'normal' liability cases, no punitive damages can be awarded in human rights cases in most continental legal systems. Notable exceptions are the common law jurisdictions, where punitive (exemplary) damages are permissible, provided that the general law on damages is applicable to claims based on human rights abuses. Ireland is one example. Beyond the Irish Defamation Act 2009, exemplary damages may be awarded when the severity of the wrongful conduct requires certain deterrence, provided that a conscious and wilful disregard of the plaintiff's constitutional rights could be proven.

In the U.S., punitive damages are available in many instances of human rights infringements, and in particular in cases of intentional discrimination, cases based on the Anti-Terrorism Act and on Section 1983, if the defendant had malicious or evil intent, or showed reckless or callous indifference to the plaintiff's federally protected rights.

20.10 Legal Standing and Selective Procedural Issues

20.10.1 Plaintiffs and Defendants

In Council of Europe countries, virtually all persons present in the country may seek protection of human rights. The national systems may very as far as the protection of constitutional rights is concerned. In most countries political rights are usually confined to citizens as opposed to be vested with 'anyone' or 'a person'.

The defendant category includes State organs, municipalities and persons acting as an emanation of the State (see in the U.S. and Canada the 'State action doctrine'), which may include *de facto* State organs whose existence is based on violence or an illegal act (Greece).

Few interesting points can be made here in respect of foreign State defendants.

In general, European civil law countries follow the principle of sovereign equality of States and the principle of *par in parem non habet imperium*, which prevent national courts from accepting any claim relating to a foreign act of State unless the State in question waives its right to immunity. In particular, this immunity is embedded in art. 11 of the European Convention on State Immunity (1972). Interestingly, a number of lawsuits brought by Italian and Greek citizens against the German government or a Germany-based corporation for historical injuries suffered in the Second World War period has led to a number of domestic awards in Italy and Greece. The cases, in which the immunity of the German State was considered waived by the courts, reached the phase of execution, which was successful in Italy and unsuccessful in Greece and Germany. The ICJ in *Germany vs. Italy* ruled in favour of Germany, stating that any possibility to bypass State immunity in cases of gross violations of human rights and international humanitarian law is excluded.[49] Only special agreements might provide otherwise.

It should be noted that the laws and courts of the United States have been unusual in offering private law damages through the Alien Tort Statute, the Torture Victims Protection Act, and the Foreign Sovereign Immunities Act, which are interpreted in conjunction with U.S. law's relatively broad rules on personal jurisdiction and tort liability. The U.S. is the unique system where explicit jurisdictional bases make it possible (subject to certain conditions established by the U.S. Supreme Court) to adjudicate a case in a federal U.S. court and obtain damages when the alleged violations of human rights were committed abroad or against non-nationals and by a foreign State (exceptions to immunities granted by The Foreign Sovereign Immunities Act, however, limited to harms 'occurring in the U.S.').

The question of whether non-State actors, or else, individuals, are covered by the available causes of action for damages depends on the acceptance of the claim against private parties, which has been dealt with in Sect. 20.5 of this chapter.

In many European systems and in Israel direct perpetrators (functionaries, public gents) may be held personally liable for human rights abuses and be sued for damages directly. In some countries the public organ has legal standing in a suit, but the legislators reserve the right of recourse to the official responsible for the violation at a later stage. In almost all countries compensatory claims directly against judges are inadmissible, unless it is a bad faith or ultra vires situation.

Specifically in the U.S., under Section 1983 suits are brought against individuals who act as officials or agents of the federal or state government. Official immunity can, however, bar those suits. In practice, the government entity often bears the burden of the award against official personal assets through indemnification or insurance. Furthermore, the Torture Victims Protection Act of 1991 provides for civil liability of natural persons for torture or extrajudicial killing; however, a plaintiff must first exhaust any 'adequate and available remedies in the place in which the conduct giving rise to the claim occurred'.[50] In the U.S., legislators, prosecutors and

[49] ICJ, judgment of 3.2. 2012, *Germany vs. Italy*.

[50] *Mohammed vs. Palestinian Authority*, 132 S. Ct. 1702 (2012).

judges – and other officials exercising similar authority – enjoy absolute immunity for actions taken within the scope of their functions, and 'qualified immunity' when acting outside those functions. Qualified immunity applies unless the defendant official knew or reasonably should have known that his or her conduct violated a clearly established legal right of which a reasonable person in the official's position would be aware.

20.10.2 *Jurisdictional Issues*

In general, civil law claims for compensation are within competence of ordinary civil courts. When infringements of human rights amount to a crime – i.e. when a right to life or health or dignity or other personal rights are infringed – most European jurisdictions permit the victim to attach their compensatory claim against the perpetrator to the criminal proceedings (adhesive procedure). In addition, special provisions regarding compensation for victims of violence are widely introduced. This means that the victims' harm is at the centre of attention, because they may obtain redress for serious harm to their health and their economic situation resulting from the crime from the State, while the latter is charged with the right of recourse against the perpetrator.

If a claim is directed against a public defendant, jurisdiction and applicable procedural laws primarily depend on a model of public authority liability in the given legal systems.

In some of the civil law countries civil courts have jurisdiction over all compensatory claims, and in others administrative courts have been competent for adjudicating claims for damages for human rights abuses attributed to the State (the French model). In a number of countries the jurisdiction is shared between administrative and civil courts. The dualism can appear in a different dimension. In Portugal for example, administrative courts have general competence over actions for damages, but by way of exception the competence is given to common courts as regards liability arising out of judicial error of civil and criminal courts. In the German model, an action addressing the violation as such is brought before administrative courts, whilst a claim for compensation belongs to the jurisdiction of civil courts.

In the 'just satisfaction' approach, the jurisdiction belongs to a common court. For example, in the U.K., the court must have the power to award damages under Section 8(2) of the HRA, which means that damages may be awarded only by court civil proceedings. If the victim brings judicial review proceedings against a public authority purely on Convention grounds, he/she may also claim damages. A similar model has been adopted in Ireland and in Canada.

A rare solution is to bring claims arising from violations of human rights within the competence of constitutional courts. It is the case in Romania, Turkey and Croatia – with respect to infringements of rights by the judiciary, except for claims relating to excessive length of court proceedings, which are dealt within the regular judiciary system.

A further point to note is that although class actions seem to be permitted on general grounds, they are not popular in the context of human rights violations, except for in Israel, where in certain cases (anti-discrimination law, the protection of minimum wages law, and consumer protection) a class action may be brought against non-State defendants.[51]

Finally, a popular method to deal with mass cases is to establish an ad hoc compensatory scheme, as the ECtHR appears to suggest.[52]

20.11 Special Indemnity Regimes

20.11.1 Indemnity for Historical Injustices

According to the view that prevails in public international law, compensation for historical injustices involving violations of human rights stemming from international conflicts should be regulated at inter-State level. This approach is still represented by most countries under review. Historical injustices are increasingly met with apologetic statements by governments (e.g. in France), in particular when personal injuries and rights of personalities form the subject matter of mass claims. The most frequently used method of remedying personal harm is the rehabilitation of political prisoners and annulment of criminal sentences and of administrative decisions (e.g. in Poland and the Czech Republic).

We can observe that financial compensation for historical violations of personal rights and freedoms is not a true compensation at all, but a type of social allowance or benefit due to deprivation of freedom and a loss of working capacity (see examples below). The reparations for historical injustices almost always have an equitable nature and do not follow the principle of full compensation.

As regards historical injustices, the individualistic approach of tort law is not useful. Moreover, under the commonly accepted rules of inter-temporal law, the law of the period must be applied to any tort action. Hence, under private law rules private claims for damages have long been prescribed before they are filed in national courts. Therefore, historical injustices are most often subject to special compensatory schemes, which are created in result of a political compromise and of balancing budgetary concerns and societal expectations. The idea of social State prevails over the idea of corrective justice.

Many special schemes were reported as regards indemnities paid by respective States to the victims of the Second World War and other post-war conflicts (in Germany, France, Italy, Slovenia, Brazil).

Despite the existence of special entitlements, and because of their many drawbacks and limitations, many post-WW II victims have brought individual claims for

[51] Eg. in Israel.

[52] This is the policy in Slovenia and Turkey, in particular.

compensations based on civil law and international human rights regulations.[53] Despite the lapse of prescription periods some claimants were successful in trial courts. We should take note of the claims filed by former forced labourers and war crimes victims, who were not embraced by reparation treaties or inter-State agreements. Lacking any legislative entitlements, their claims were dismissed by German courts with the support of the Federal Constitutional Court. The victims then sought redress in other jurisdictions, such as the United States (on the basis of the Alien Tort Claims Act), Italy and Greece. In the reaction to the suits in the U.S. a special fund was established,[54] financed partly by the German government and partly by the German companies who used slave labour. In Italy and Greece, on the other hand, domestic courts, including the highest courts, adjudicated compensation and then subjected them to enforcement procedures against the German State's assets in the given country. In particular, the Italian Supreme Court held that "in cases involving serious breaches of human rights, the State cannot claim immunity from jurisdiction in order to avoid paying compensation to victims." Ultimately, the efforts made by Italian courts to assert the right to obtain redress for gross and systematic violations of human rights were frustrated by the ICJ's judgment in *Germany vs. Italy*, reinstating the principle of State immunity.

As far as property rights protection is concerned (war-time and post-war expropriations, nationalisation) among the traditional private law remedies, claims for the restitution of property and other resources seem to find support in most countries, in particular in post-socialist States, while in other countries damages awards are preferred to any restitution demands (e.g. in the former Eastern German Republic and Israel).

In the post-socialist countries, claims related to property unlawfully expropriated by the socialist authorities have most often been addressed by special (reprivatisation) laws (e.g. in Estonia and the Czech Republic). By contrast, in Norway historical injustices and systemic violations are handled through *ex gratia* payments from the State, which by their nature do not involve the question of prescription.

20.11.2 Gross and Systematic Violations

As regards domestic compensation systems, two common themes that can be drawn from the reports are the following:

1. pecuniary compensation is narrow in scope and most often aimed at the restoration of property rights, if possible,
2. only limited financial awards are envisaged to redress personal injuries and deaths.

---

[53] See Shelton, Dinah (2006) 430 ff.

[54] Foundation "Remembrance, Responsibility and Future" (*Erinnerung, Verantwortung und Zukunft*, EVZ).

As regards personal injuries, compensatory schemes are put in place in order to limit the financial burden on the State that pays for an unknown number of consequences of violations authored or ascribed to the previous political regime. Such schemes were developed in countries in political transitions to democracy, i.a. in Central and Eastern Europe. In a few States the schemes were prompted by the decisions (recently by pilot judgments) of the ECHR. Under a typical compensatory scheme the State may not invoke defences related to the conduct of the responsible officials, hence the liability is strict.

An interesting example of a compensatory scheme involving claims that can be described as based on mass violations is the *ad hoc* Slovenian compensatory scheme set up by the Act on Restitution of Damage for Persons Who Were Erased from the Register of Permanent Population (2013).[55] Under this scheme an administrative authority awards €50 per month of being erased. An alternative judicial avenue is through civil litigation, and the courts must apply the same cap on damages, and private law of obligations by analogy, except for the rules on time limits.

20.12 Comparative Conclusions

As the foregoing analysis reflects, liability in damages for violations of human rights is governed by a plethora of rules scattered between the directly enforceable constitutional norms, directly or indirectly applicable regional Convention rights, public authority liability regimes and tort law.

The question that has not found a clear response in many systems is whether a right to effective remedy or a right to just satisfaction form a separate claim under domestic law, or whether this is foremost a standard against which the domestic liability rules should be tested. The first option prevails not only in the systems which themselves have introduced the right to just satisfaction (the U.K. and Canada), but also in the states that have opened, either via the constitutional rule or around the constitution and via the Convention (France and Italy), to claims for compensation in both public and private spheres. Other countries appear to prefer to leave the matter of the legal basis for compensation in human rights cases in the hands of the courts. This approach is safer from the perspective of the coherence of the legal system because in most states human rights law and the principles of direct or indirect horizontal effect have not impacted the main institutes of civil law and have not changed the core prerequisites of liability established for different types of torts.

The survey has demonstrated that tort law and its methods and techniques offer broad protection of human rights, although the rules on tort liability were not originally designed, whether by legislators or by courts, to resolve claims for damages involving breaches of human rights; they have had little connection to international

[55] In 1992 the newly established Slovenian authorities erased approximately 25,000 non-citizens without any notification and without being heard– see Chap. 15.

human rights law, and until recently also to constitutional law. Moreover, where a conflict arises in a private relation, several values may be involved, and no predetermined hierarchy of interests may be assumed in private law. On the other hand, factors that influence the scope of liability, such as the definition of wrongfulness/fault, attribution, causation etc. can be seen either as barriers or as necessary limits to the liability.

Nevertheless, the role of tort law has changed over time and under the influence of international and regional standards of human rights protection. All reports have demonstrated that in response to the societal needs and expectations the courts have been developing a new function and purpose of the general liability rules. Some especially elevated rights, such as the right to liberty, freedom of speech, right to privacy or equality, have had a significant impact on tort law litigation. As noticed by Jessy Emaus, the advantage of fundamental rights over other open norms in private law is that the former convey information regarding the interests that they aim to protect. The judicial balancing of fundamental rights is made on a case-by-case basis.

However, what appears to be a correct balance of rights in one country is not necessarily correct for another one; there is no single proper solution for all legal cultures and for all societies – certainly not for Europe, where quality of public service, legal cultures and societal expectations vary. Notwithstanding this clear trend of openness of tort law, its limitations are still applied by courts and consequently the treatment of private and public defendants sometimes differs.

Naturally, certain infringements will only trigger liability of public authorities, because certain human rights may only abide State institutions (e.g. the right to fair trial within reasonable time/due process, the right to compensation for unlawful detention or arrest, and the right to be adequately compensated for expropriation). One of the greatest impacts of the ECHR on the national systems is the adequacy of compensation for the breaches of Convention rights by public authorities. The focus of the Convention on some special categories of rights (art. 5, art. 6) forced the national legislators to amend their legislation at least in these fields under the pain of being declared guilty of breaching art. 13 of the ECHR. This process resulted in the significant enhancement of protection of victims of judicial errors, primarily in criminal justice and judicial delays. It should be noted that systematic violations of this kind are preferably dealt with through special compensatory routes rather than through ordinary courts and litigation based on general tort law rules. A clear convergence of European governments' legal policies in these fields, brought about by the case law and policy of the ECtHR, can be observed. The general measures, however, are convenient for the government and for the ECtHR, but not necessarily for individuals. It is therefore important not to completely compromise individual interests and allow further claims to be submitted outside a compensatory mechanism by those who suffered exceptional loss or harm. It is clear that the underlying policy consideration of many of the European legislators was to minimise the number of violation judgments and awards of just satisfaction under art. 41 of the ECHR.

When infringements of rights occur in relations between private persons, a claim for compensation has in some jurisdictions given rise to the creation of a new claim (new basis of liability), that can be conceptualised as 'a constitutional tort' (Ireland), although the same name also relates to the direct liability for breaches of constitutional rights by public defendants in the U.S. and in Israel. There are also purely doctrinal concepts created, which are not yet supported by the judiciary. One example is a 'breach of a fundamental right' (the Netherlands). The Dutch proposal is based on several telling arguments in favour of the new claim, separate from the general claim for compensation for unlawful act, and applicable to all defendants. While the concept of a 'breach of a fundamental right' may appear as attractive in a system where neither the constitution nor the statutory rules provide for an explicit or coherent basis for public authority liability, its contours are vague, as is the case with any new, generalised cause of action, and, moreover, controlled by the home jurisdiction rules.

As the foregoing reflects, the sense and utility of creating a new type of tort to deal with new sources of harm may be put into question, although it may *prima facie* seem an attractive solution. Needless to say, any new concept is confined to its own jurisdiction. Therefore, it is perhaps worth exploring an approach (present in many surveyed systems, in particular in France, Italy and Portugal) that is based on innovative, constitution-compliant and/or Convention-compliant interpretations of liability rules contained in the civil codes while surpassing the restrictions inherent in those rules, such as the limited availability of non-pecuniary loss damages or fault as a prerequisite of non-pecuniary damages. It is almost a truism that the liability norms should and are interpreted and applied in a human-rights-compliant manner.

A major concern for the creation of constitutional torts as well as the 'conventionalisation' of private law is the expansion of liability through broadening the contents of rights that have already been protected by tort law based on a careful balance of individual and public interests. To put this argument to an extreme, it may lead to the creation of alternative tort systems in some contexts. Such a result would be undesirable. Therefore, the legislators tend to introduce various instruments to control the expansion of the liability. The principle of subsidiarity of the damages remedy and friendly settlements as pre-conditions of filing a suit are concepts alien to tort law, but they play some controlling function. Other methods include restricting compensation for breaches of second and third generation human rights, setting caps on the amount of damages and establishing financial compensation schemes. Budgetary constraints and the 'floodgate' argument also support the controlling mechanisms, which is especially seen in the U.K. Also American courts, appearing to be swayed by considerations of policy in recent decades, try to strike the right balance between individual interests and public interests. They have shown some reluctance to imply private rights of action in statutes and regulations. Through judicial review, as noted by Jacques deLisle, the courts 'strike down human rights-resonant, rights-protecting and remedy-providing legislation as beyond Congress's constitutional powers'.

A final point to make is that the contributions collected in this volume reflect a growing role of special statutory mechanisms that escape easy classification and thus belong to the grey area between public and private law. When systematic violations embrace civil and political rights, the creation of a scheme that allows for expeditious and less expensive handling of claims is clearly preferred to tort law liability. However, the way in which the government has set up a compensation regime for human rights abuses proves to be in some countries one of the most controversial aspects of the damages regime for breaches of human rights.

References

Barendt, Eric. 2007. The United States and Canada: State action, constitutional rights and private actors. In *Human rights and the private sphere. A comparative study*, ed. Dawn Oliver and Jőrg Fedtke, 399–426. London: Routledge Cavendish.

Fairgrieve, Duncan, Mads Andenas, and John Bell (eds.). 2002. *Tort liability of public authorities in comparative perspective*. London: BICL.

Gerards, Janneke, and Joseph Fleuren. 2014a. Comparative analysis. In *Implementation of the European convention on human rights and of the judgments of the ECtHR in national case-law. A comparative analysis*, ed. Janneke Gerards and Joseph Fleuren, 335 ff. Cambridge/Antwerp/Portland: Intersentia.

Gerards, Janneke, and Joseph Fleuren. 2014b. *Implementation of the European Convention on Human Rights and of the judgments of the ECtHR in national case-law. A comparative analysis*, ed. Janneke Gerards and Joseph Fleuren. Cambridge/Antwerp/Portland: Intersentia.

O'Cinneide, Colm. 2007. Irish constitutional law and direct horizontal effect – A successful experiment? In *Human rights and the private sphere. A comparative study*, ed. D. Oliver and J. Fedtke, 213–243. London: Routledge Cavendish.

Oliver, Dawn, and Jőrg Fedtke (eds.). 2007. *Human rights and the private sphere – A comparative analysis*. London: Routledge Cavendish.

Rogers, Horton W.V. 2003. Tort law and human rights: A new experience. In *European Tort Law 2002*, ed. H. Koziol and B. Steininger. Wien/New York: Springer.

Shelton, Dinah. 2006. *Remedies in international human rights law*, 2nd ed. Oxford: Oxford University Press.

Shelton, Dinah. 2011. *International law and domestic legal systems. Incorporation, transformation and Persuasion*. Oxford: OUP.

Appendix: Questionnaire for National Reports

A. Liability Regime: In General

1. Please, describe the main features of the general law of public authority liability insofar as it concerns the liability for violations of HRs in your jurisdiction.
2. Does liability/responsibility for violations of HRs fall under public law or private law (the law of tort or civil responsibility)? Is compensation (also/only) available under other branches of the law (e.g. criminal law)?
3. Is there an explicit legal basis for claiming damages for violations of human rights?
4. Does a claim for financial compensation arising from infringement of HRs involve the application of general principles or special rules?
5. What is the purpose (idea) of the damages in cases of infringement of HRs?
6. What is the correlation between different remedies for violations of HRs in your jurisdiction? Does one remedy exclude the other (or must be preceded by the other)?
7. What doctrines are used to support a claim for financial compensation (subjective public right, protected interests/protective purpose of the rule doctrines, etc.)?

B. Scope of Liability Regime

1. What types of rights that have been infringed are covered by explicit/implicit liability rules? Is there any distinction in treatment of claims stemming from violations of international norms/duties (also referred to as "State responsibility") and violations of domestic (e.g. constitutional) norms?
2. Is compensation for historical injustices available under the same rules?

E. Bagińska (ed.), *Damages for Violations of Human Rights*,
Ius Comparatum - Global Studies in Comparative Law 9,
DOI 10.1007/978-3-319-18950-5

3. Are gross and systematic violations covered?
4. What is the scope of any applicable special compensatory schemes (if any)?

C. Liability Regime[1] in Detail

1. **The foundation of claims for damages (grounds and premises of liability):**
   - What is considered as the principle (basis) of liability for infringement of HRs: fault, strict liability (risk) or equity (or other)? Indicate the approach of case law and/or legal scholarship in a jurisdiction where no special legislative solutions exist. Please, indicate the correlation of concepts used, such as e.g. 'infringement', 'fault', 'illegality', 'wrongfulness' (where appropriate);
   - Are the same principles, whether tort law rules or public law, applied to compensatory and non-compensatory remedies for violations of human rights?
   - Is harm (loss) to property or person considered as a prerequisite of a claim for damages, or is "pure violation" considered sufficient to claim compensation?
   - What is the burden of proof concerning damage/harm?
   - What doctrine of causation is applied?
2. **What is the nature of harm (damage/injury):**
   - Reparable non-material (moral) harm;
   - Reparable material damage: real loss, lost profits (lucrum cessans), loss of chance (opportunities), costs and expenses, etc.
3. **Scope of damages (compensation):**
   - Do general or special rules apply to the scope (extent) of damages?
   - Please, specify elements of pecuniary damages for the following instances: personal injury, including death, loss or damage to property, deprivation of liberty, procedural infringements;
   - How is compensation for non-pecuniary harm calculated?
   - Taxation of damages and interest;
   - Are damages discretionary (equitable awards)? if yes, what are the levels of discretion (award-no award, calculation)?
   - Is there a limitation/cap on damages?
   - Is accumulation of claims (damages) permitted in cases of multiple violations?

[1] 'State responsibility' where appropriate.

- Do pecuniary claims survive the death of a direct victim if she dies during the proceedings? What is the standing of successors of the victim before the commencement of the proceedings? Can the heirs/family/next of kin/other beneficiary have claims *sui generis* (in its own right)?

4. **Are punitive or exemplary damages allowed?**
5. **Defences:**
   - Is contributory conduct (negligence, fault) taken into account? What is its role?
   - Is the claimant obliged to exhaust all available procedures before claiming financial compensation?
   - What are the exclusions (including immunities) of liability?
6. **Who to sue and who may sue**:
   - Who incurs liability in damages for infringement of HRs? Does the liability in damages embrace non-state actors (private entities performing public functions, multinational corporations)?
   - Does the liability also fall on the individuals (public official, agent)?
   - Are aliens entitled to claim compensation?
7. **Courts/competent bodies and procedures**
   - What, if anything, is distinctive about the procedures applied by courts or other competent bodies?
   - Do any special time limits apply?
   - Are group claims available?

D. The Interplay Between Principles of National and International Human Rights Law (Concerning Financial Compensation)

- Describe the correlation between monetary remedies (financial compensation) available to victims of violations of HRs under international law (such as e.g. under the European Convention system, Inter-American system, international criminal tribunals and other) and under domestic law.
- What is the influence of compensation granted by an international tribunal (body) on the claim brought under relevant domestic regime? In particular, is the claimant who has already been awarded compensation by an international tribunal/organization/body (such as e.g. "just satisfaction" under art 41 ECHR) entitled to seek further compensation in the domestic system? Is compensation awarded by

a national court (other competent body) in any way influenced (reduced, excluded) by the sums already awarded?
- What are policy considerations that have exerted the greatest influence on the development of your legal system in the discussed area?

E. Other Matters and Evaluation of the Existing Law

Please, provide any other remarks; personal evaluation of the system; calls for reforms or reforms under way.

Index

E. Bagińska (ed.), *Damages for Violations of Human Rights*,
Ius Comparatum - Global Studies in Comparative Law 9,
DOI 10.1007/978-3-319-18950-5

Printed by Printforce, the Netherlands